second Canadian edition

Macroeconomics

second Canadian edition

Macroeconomics

RUDIGER DORNBUSCH
Massachusetts Institute of Technology

STANLEY FISCHER
Massachusetts Institute of Technology

GORDON R · SPARKS
Queen's University

McGraw-Hill Ryerson Limited

Toronto Montreal New York Auckland Bogotá Cairo Guatemala Hamburg
Lisbon London Madrid Mexico New Delhi Panama Paris
San Juan São Paulo Singapore Sydney Tokyo

Macroeconomics, *second Canadian edition*

ISBN 0-07-548903-1

3 4 5 6 7 8 9 0 JD 4 3 2 1 0 9 8 7

Printed and bound in Canada by John Deyell Company

Canadian Cataloguing in Publication Data

Dornbusch, Rudiger.
  Macroeconomics

Includes bibliographical references and index.
ISBN 0-07-548903-1

1. Macroeconomics.   I. Fischer, Stanley.   II. Sparks, Gordon R.   III. Title.

HB172.5.D618 1985   339   C85-098762-8

Table of Contents

To
Sandra, Leslie and Ian

Preface

This second Canadian edition presents a complete rewriting of our book. We have remained faithful to our basic approach — presenting the relevant theory and at the same time showing both its empirical relevance and policy applications. We have, of course, stayed with our general eclectic outlook on macroeconomics. But in the details of presentation and development, and in the weight given to various topics, much has changed to meet the changing emphasis of macroeconomic issues and theory over the last few years. More than before, the book focusses on *current* policy issues, ranging from budget deficits and the public debt to the tradeoff between inflation and unemployment. On the theory side we give more room to the discussion of the challenge rational expectations poses for traditional macroeconomics, and to a mainstream synthesis of the ideas of the 1970s as they apply to the policy issues of the 1980s.

Although few paragraphs remain unchanged from the two earlier editions, the book remains recognizably the same in that it develops, and teaches students to use, a broad-based, critical, and useful macroeconomics. Our overriding objective is still to explain how modern macroeconomics is used in understanding important economic issues, and to help the reader analyze macroeconomic problems for herself or himself. The book provides full coverage of basic macroeconomics, such as national income accounting, aggregate demand, and the *IS-LM* analysis. It goes beyond the standard coverage in presenting also the theory of aggregate supply, the interesting and vitally important topics of inflation and unemployment, and a detailed treatment of open-economy macroeconomics. No important topic has been omitted because it is too difficult, but we have taken great pains to make nothing more difficult than it need be.

THIS EDITION

There are major innovations in the organization of chapters and in the material covered. Most visibly, boxes with topical material, either conceptual or applied, have been added to broaden the coverage and develop some points without detracting from the flow of the main topic. The content of the boxes ranges from post-Keynesian economics to the use of econometric models, to descriptions of the chief financial instruments in the assets markets. We have also added legends to the diagrams to make them a more self-contained tool for review and summary.

We have gone beyond revision and updating to recast our treatment altogether in three areas. We have made substantial changes to aggregate demand and supply to simplify the analysis and make it more accessible than before. We thus make it possible to draw on the inflation-unemployment analysis throughout the remainder of the book. This is a major change and advantage because it opens up the really interesting issues in stabilization policy for treatment in this course. We have achieved that simplification by no longer attempting to trace out the dynamics of a formal model, but rather using short-run and long-run Phillips curves as the basic tools.

The material on open-economy macroeconomics has been reorganized and rewritten to provide a better integration with the rest of the book. The analysis based on extensions of the *IS-LM* model to an economy with foreign trade and capital flows is covered in two chapters following the discussion of the *IS-LM* model for a closed economy. The discussion of inflation in an open economy is postponed to a later chapter following aggregate supply and demand. Users who prefer the order of presentation in the previous edition can skip Chapters 5 and 6 and take up this material along with Chapter 18 after aggregate supply and demand have been covered.

Our third major rewriting effort has been in the policy chapters dealing with the inflation-unemployment tradeoff, the budget, and the development of macroeconomic policy and ideas. That block of chapters has been entirely recast to focus on the policy concerns of the 1980s, and also to understand the issues in the broader context of alternative approaches — Keynesian economics, monetarism, rational expectations, and supply-side economics. The discussion serves to show how mainstream macroeconomics has evolved substantially over the last 10 years — and how it has been enriched by the challenges. We include this material because one of the most useful things a student can get from a course in macroeconomics is the ability to sort out the competing claims for alternative approaches made in the media.

Beyond these three specific areas, we have completely updated the material and references. We have also used the opportunity of this revision to follow up on the suggestions received from many readers and users.

With regard to the organization of the book, some users have suggested that we move directly from the *IS-LM* model to the aggregate supply chapters. We see some advantages in doing that, particularly because the student gets quickly to the central issues of inflation and unemployment. However, we prefer to pause for consolidation and extension, after the basic *IS-LM* model has been introduced. That is why we follow it with a discussion of the components of aggregate demand, the role of financial markets, and the details of policy making. These chapters deepen understanding of the *IS-LM* framework, but those who prefer to move ahead directly to aggregate supply can do so. Consideration of Chapters 7 through 12 can easily be postponed.

An *Instructor's Manual*, prepared by Patricia Pando and Gordon Sparks, is available to accompany this edition. It is an updated, expanded and improved version of the manual that accompanied the previous edition.

Acknowledgments

The debts incurred by authors are among the nicest there are, and we are fortunate to have acquired many in a short time. We have been delighted with the success of the first Canadian edition and are grateful to the many readers who have given us suggestions for improving the text. Since we have been unable to accept all their suggestions, none of them should be held responsible for the deficiencies — we hope they are few — contained in this edition.

We would also like to thank Charlotte David and Sandra Sparks, who assisted in the preparation of the manuscript for the present edition.

TO THE STUDENT

Macroeconomics is not cut and dried. There are disputes over basic issues, for instance over whether the government should try actively to fight unemployment. That makes macroeconomics unsatisfying if you are looking for clear-cut definite answers to all the economy's problems, but it should also make it more interesting because you have to think hard and critically about the material being presented.

Despite the disagreements, there is a substantial basic core of macroeconomics that we present in this book, and that will continue to be useful in understanding the behaviour of the economy. We have not hesitated to say where we think theories are incomplete, or where the evidence on a question is not yet decisive. We have not hesitated, either, to describe the many areas in which macroeconomic theory does a good job of explaining the real world.

Because we have not shied away from important topics even if they are difficult, parts of the book require careful reading. There is no mathematics except simple algebra. Some of the analysis, however, involves sustained reasoning. Careful reading should therefore pay off in enhanced understanding. Chapter 1 gives you suggestions on how to learn from this book. The single most important suggestion is that you learn actively. Some of the chapters (such as Chapter 11) are suitable for bedtime reading, but most are not. Use pencil and paper to be sure you are following the argument. See if you can find reasons to disagree with arguments we make. Work the problem sets! Be sure you understand the points contained in the summaries to each chapter. Follow the economic news in the press, and see how that relates to what you are learning. Try to follow the logic of a budget or other economic matter brought before Parliament.

A *Study Guide* prepared and updated by Gordon Sparks and Richard Startz is available to accompany this edition. It contains a wide range of questions, starting from the very easy and progressing in each chapter to material that will challenge the more advanced student. It is a great help in studying, particularly since active learning is so important.

Rudiger Dornbusch
Stanley Fischer
Gordon Sparks

Statistics Canada Data Sources

General Economic Data
11-003 Canadian Statistical Review (monthly)
11-206 Annual Supplement to Section I, Canadian Statistical Review
11-505 Canadian Statistical Review — Historical Summary 1970

National Accounts
13-201 System of National Accounts — National Income and Expenditure
Accounts (annual)
13-531 System of National Accounts — National Income and Expenditure
Accounts, Volume I, The Annual Estimates 1926-1974
13-533 Volume II, The Quarterly Estimates 1947-1974
13-549 Volume III, A Guide to the National Income and Expenditure Accounts
— Definitions — Concepts — Sources — Methods

Prices
62-010 Consumer Prices and Price Indexes (monthly)

Labour Force
71-001 The Labour Force (monthly)
71-201 Historical Labour Force Statistics (annual)

Other Sources
Bank of Canada Review (monthly)
Department of Finance, *Economic Review* (annual, published in April)

Macroeconomics

Determination of
National Income

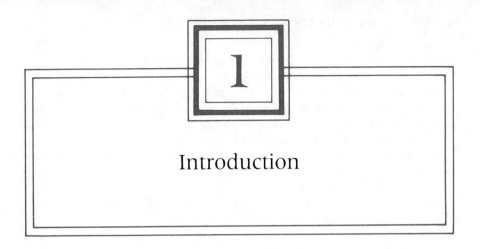

Introduction

Macroeconomics is concerned with the behaviour of the economy as a whole — booms and recessions, the economy's total output of goods and services and the growth of output, the rates of inflation and unemployment, the balance of payments, and exchange rates. To study the overall performance of the economy, macroeconomics focusses on the economic policies and policy variables that affect that performance such as monetary and fiscal policies, the money stock and interest rates, the public debt, and the federal government budget. In brief, macroeconomics deals with the major economic issues and problems of the day.

Macroeconomics is interesting because it deals with important issues. But it is fascinating and challenging too, because it reduces complicated details of the economy to manageable essentials. *Those essentials lie in the interactions among the goods, labour, and assets markets of the economy.*

In dealing with the essentials, we have to disregard details of the behaviour of individual economic units, such as households and firms, or the determination of prices in particular markets, or the effects of monopoly on individual markets. These are the subject matter of microeconomics. In macroeconomics we deal with the market for goods as a whole, treating all the markets for different goods, such as the markets for agricultural products and for medical services, as a single market. Similarly, we deal with the labour market as a whole, abstracting from differences between the markets for, say, migrant labour and doctors. We deal with the assets markets as a whole, abstracting from the differences between the markets for provincial bonds and Rembrandt paintings. The cost of the abstraction is that omitted details sometimes matter. The benefit of the abstraction is increased understanding of the vital interactions among the goods, labour, and assets markets.

Despite the contrast between macroeconomics and microeconomics, there is no basic conflict between them. After all, the economy in the

3

aggregate is nothing but the sum of its submarkets. The difference between microeconomics and macroeconomics is therefore primarily one of emphasis and exposition. In studying price determination in a single industry, it is convenient for microeconomists to assume that prices in other industries are given. In macroeconomics, where we study the price level, it is for the most part sensible to ignore changes in relative prices of goods among different industries. In microeconomics, it is convenient to assume the total income of all consumers is given and to ask how consumers divide their spending out of that income among different goods. In macroeconomics, by contrast, the aggregate level of income or spending is among the key variables to be studied.

The great macroeconomists, including Keynes, and modern American leaders in the field, such as Milton Friedman of the University of Chicago, Franco Modigliani of MIT, and James Tobin of Yale, have all had a keen interest in the applications of macrotheory to problems of policy making. Indeed, developments in macrotheory are closely related to the economic problems of the day. Keynesian economics developed during the great depression of the 1930s and showed the way out of such depressions. Monetarism developed during the 1960s, promising a way of solving the inflation problem. *Supply-side economics* became the fad of the early 1980s, promising an easy way out of the economic mess of the time, by cutting taxes. But supply-side economics overpromised, and there was no easy way out.

Because macroeconomics is closely related to the economic problems of the day, it does not yield its greatest rewards to those whose primary interest is theoretical. The need for compromise between the comprehensiveness of the theory and its manageability inevitably makes macrotheory a little untidy at the edges. And the emphasis in macroeconomics is on the manageability of the theory and on its applications. To demonstrate that emphasis, this book uses the theories we present to illuminate recent economic events from the 1950s to the 1980s. We also refer continually to real world events to elucidate the meaning and the relevance of the theoretical material.

Schools of Thought

There have for long been two intellectual traditions in macroeconomics. One school of thought believes that markets work best if left to themselves; another believes that government intervention can significantly improve the operation of the economy. In the 1960s the debate on these questions involved *monetarists*, led by Milton Friedman, on one side and *Keynesians*, including Franco Modigliani and James Tobin, on the other side. In the 1970s the debate on much the same issues brought to the fore a new group — the *new classical macroeconomists* — including among the leaders Robert

Lucas of the University of Chicago and Thomas Sargent of the University of Minnesota.

The new classical macroeconomics shares many policy views with Friedman. It sees the world as one where individuals act rationally in their self-interest in markets that adjust rapidly to changing conditions. The government, it is claimed, is likely only to make things worse by intervening. That model is a challenge to traditional macroeconomics, which sees a role for useful government action in an economy which is viewed as adjusting sluggishly, with rigidities, poor information, and social customs impeding the rapid clearing of markets.

Macroeconomics is often presented as the battleground between implacably opposed schools of thought. There is no denying that there are conflicts of opinion and even theory between different camps. But it is also the case that there are significant areas of agreement and that the different groups, through discussion and research, continually evolve new areas of consensus and a sharper idea of where precisely the differences lie. In this book we do not emphasize the debate, preferring to discuss substantive matters while indicating alternative views of an issue whenever relevant.

In Section 1-1 we present an overview of the key concepts with which macroeconomics deals. Section 1-2 examines relationships among the key macroeconomic variables, while Section 1-3 discusses stabilization policy. Section 1-4 presents a diagrammatic introduction to aggregate demand and supply and their interaction; it gives a very general perspective on the fundamentals of macroeconomics and the organization of this book. Then, in Section 1-5, we outline the approach of the book to the study of macroeconomics and macropolicy making, and present a preview of the order in which topics are dealt with. Section 1-6 contains brief remarks on how to use the book.

1-1 KEY CONCEPTS
Gross National Product

Gross national product (GNP) is the value of all goods and services produced in the economy in a given time period (quarter or year). GNP is the basic measure of economic activity.

Figure 1-1 shows two measures of GNP — *nominal*, or *current dollar*, GNP and *real*, or *constant dollar*, GNP.[1] Nominal GNP measures the value of output at the prices prevailing in the period the output is produced, while real GNP measures the output produced in any one period at the prices of some base year. At present, 1971 serves as a base year for real income measurement.

Figure 1-1 shows that nominal GNP was equal to $388.7 billion in 1983 and $123.6 billion 1973. Thus nominal GNP grew at an average rate of 12.1 percent during that period. On the other hand, real GNP was $134.0 billion in 1983 and $107.8 in 1973,[2] implying an average annual growth rate of real GNP of only 2.2 percent over the period.

Note: Real GNP is calculated using 1971 prices.
The scale is logarithmic. The logarithmic scale is explained in footnote 1.

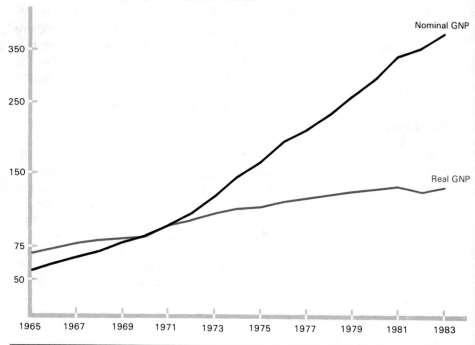

FIGURE 1-1   REAL AND NOMINAL GNP, 1965–1983
(*Source*: Statistics Canada, 13-201, 11-003)

Inflation and Nominal GNP

Figure 1-1 shows that nominal GNP has risen much more rapidly than real GNP. The difference between the growth rates of real and nominal GNP occurs because the prices of goods have been rising, or there has been *inflation*. The inflation rate is the percentage rate of increase of the level of prices during a given period.

Real GNP grew at an average rate of 2.2 percent over the 10 years from 1973–1983, while nominal GNP grew at an average annual rate of

12.1 percent per year. Because real GNP is calculated holding the prices of goods constant, the difference is entirely due to inflation, or rising prices. Over the 10-year period, prices were on average rising at 9.9 percent per year. In other words, the average rate of inflation over that period was 9.9 percent per year.

With 1971 as the base year for the prices at which output is valued, we observe in Figure 1-1 two implications of the distinction between nominal and real GNP. First, in 1971 the two are equal because, in the base year, current and constant dollars are the same dollars. Second, with inflation, nominal GNP rises faster than real GNP, and therefore, after 1971, nominal GNP exceeds real GNP. The converse is of course true before 1971.

Growth and Real GNP

We turn next to the reasons for the growth of real GNP. The *growth rate* of the economy is the rate at which real GNP is increasing. Anytime we refer to growth or the growth rate without any other qualifying word, we mean the growth rate of GNP. On average, most economies grow by a few percent per year over long periods. For instance, Canadian real GNP grew at an average rate of 3.7 percent per year from 1965 to 1983. But this growth has certainly not been smooth as Figure 1-1 confirms.

What causes GNP to grow? The first reason real GNP changes is that the available amount of resources in the economy changes. The resources are conveniently split into capital and labour. The labour force, consisting of people either working or looking for work, grows over time and thus provides one source of increased production. The capital stock including buildings and machines, likewise has been rising over time, thereby making increased output possible. Increases in the availability of factors of production — the labour and capital used in the production of goods and services — thus account for part of the increase in real GNP.

The second reason for real GNP to change is that the efficiency with which factors of production work may change.[3] Over time, the same factors of production can produce more output. These increases in the efficiency of production result from changes in knowledge, including learning by doing, as people learn through experience to perform familiar tasks better.

Employment and Unemployment

The third source of change in real GNP is a change in the employment of the given resources available for production. Not all the capital and labour available to the economy are actually used at all times.

The *unemployment rate* is the fraction of the labour force that cannot find jobs. For example, in 1982, a reduction in the employment of labour, or a rise in unemployment, shows up in Figure 1-1 as a fall in real GNP. Indeed, in that year unemployment rose to 12.8 percent, the highest unemployment rate in the post-World War II period. More than one person out of every eight who wanted to work could not find a job. Such unemployment levels had not been experienced since the great depression of the 1930s.

Inflation, Growth, and Unemployment: The Record

Macroeconomic performance is judged by the three broad measures we have introduced: the *inflation* rate, the *growth* rate of output, and the rate of *unemployment*. News of these three variables makes the headlines, because they affect our daily lives.

When the inflation rate is high, the prices of goods people buy are rising. Partly for this reason, inflation is unpopular, even if people's incomes rise along with the prices. Inflation is also unpopular because it is often associated with other disturbances to the economy, such as the oil price increases of the 1970s, that would make people worse off even if there were no inflation.

When the growth rate is high, the production of goods and services is rising, making possible an increased standard of living. Along with the high growth rate typically goes lower unemployment, and more jobs. High growth is a target and hope of most societies.

High unemployment rates are a major social problem. Jobs are difficult to find. The unemployed suffer a loss in their standard of living, personal distress, and sometimes a lifetime deterioration in their career opportunities. When unemployment reaches 11 percent, and even well short of that, it becomes the number one social and political issue.

Table 1-1 confirms that the recent years have not been happy ones economically. Inflation has risen in every 10-year period shown in the table, from 1.2 percent per year to 9.6 percent per year. In 1983 inflation did show a rapid decline, but that decline was associated with a large increase in unemployment.

TABLE 1-1   MACROECONOMIC PERFORMANCE

Period	Inflation % p.a.	Growth % p.a.	Unemployment rate, % of the labour force
1952–1962	1.2	4.3	5.5
1962–1972	3.3	5.5	4.4
1972–1982	9.6	2.5	6.6
1982–1983	5.8	3.0	11.5

Source: Dept. of Finance, *Economic Review*. *Note*: Unemployment rate is average of rates for years shown. Inflation rate is for CPI, year over year.

The growth performance over the last 30 years has been very uneven: high growth in the 1962–1972 period, less in the 1950s, and much less in the most recent decade. And, of course, recent unemployment has been the worst of the post-World War II period.

As we develop macroeconomics in this book, we are looking for answers to the questions that recent macroeconomic performance raises: Why has the inflation rate increased? Why has growth slowed? Why is unemployment so high? And, of course, is there anything that can be done to improve the situation?

The Business Cycle and the Output Gap

Inflation, growth, and unemployment are related through the *business cycle*. The business cycle is the more or less regular pattern of expansion (recovery) and contraction (recession) in economic activity around the path of trend growth. At a cyclical *peak*, economic activity is high relative

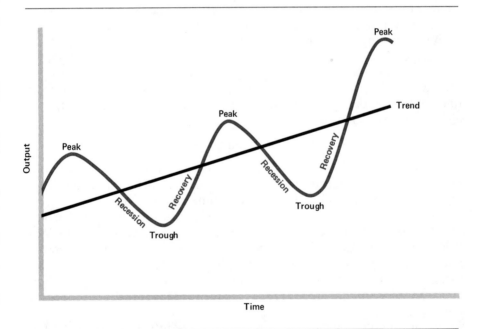

FIGURE 1-2   THE BUSINESS CYCLE. Output or GNP does not grow smoothly at its trend rate. Rather, it fluctuates irregularly around trend, showing business cycle patterns from trough, through recovery, to peak, and then from peak, through recession, back to the trough. Business cycle output movements are not regular in timing or in size.

to trend, and at a cyclical *trough*, the low point in economic activity is reached. Inflation, growth, and unemployment all have clear cyclical patterns as we will show below. For the moment we concentrate on measuring the behaviour of output or real GNP relative to trend over the business cycle.

Figure 1-2 shows as the straight line the trend path of real GNP. Over time real GNP will grow for two reasons, as we already noted. First, more resources become available: the size of the population increases; firms acquire machinery or build plants; land is improved for cultivation. This increased availability of resources allows the economy to produce more goods and services every year. Second, given resources are used with increased efficiency. New technology, learning by doing, acquisition of skills, new kinds of products (computers, fertilizers as examples) may dramatically increase the amount of goods that can be produced.

But output does not grow smoothly. Rather, it fluctuates around trend, in the business cycle. During an *expansion* (or *recovery*) the *employment* of factors of production increases, and that is a source of increased production. Output can rise above trend because people work overtime, and machinery is used for several shifts. Conversely, during a *recession* unemployment develops and less output is produced than can in fact be produced with the existing resources and technology. The wavy line in Figure 1-2 shows these cyclical departures of output from trend. Deviations of output from trend are referred to as the *output gap*. The output gap measures the gap between actual output and the output the economy could produce at full employment given the existing resources. Full-employment output is also called *potential output*.

$$\text{Output gap} \equiv \text{potential output} - \text{actual output} \qquad (1)$$

The output gap allows us to measure the cyclical deviations of output from potential output or trend output (we use these terms interchangeably). Figure 1-3 shows actual and potential output for Canada.

The figure shows that the output gap grows during a recession, such as in 1982. More resources become unemployed, and actual output falls below potential. Conversely, during an expansion, most strikingly in the long expansion of the 1960s, the gap declines and ultimately even becomes negative. A negative gap means that there is overemployment, overtime of workers, and more than the usual rate of utilization of machinery.

Establishing the level of potential output is a difficult problem. In the 1960s it was believed that full employment corresponds to a measured rate of unemployment of 4 to 4.5 percent of the labour force. Changes in the composition of the labour force toward younger workers and female workers who change jobs more frequently have raised the estimate of the full employment rate of unemployment to a range above 6 percent in the

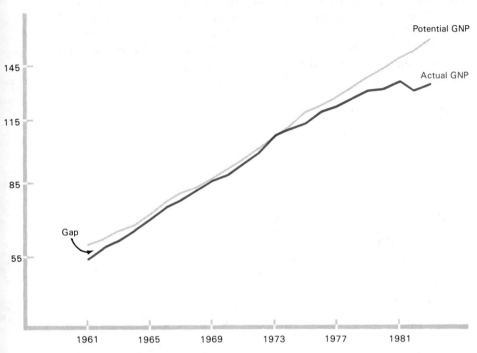

Note: The scale is logarithmic. Actual and potential GNP are in 1971 dollars.

FIGURE 1-3   ACTUAL AND POTENTIAL OUTPUT, 1961–1983. Potential output is the full employment level of output. It grows like trend output in Figure 1-2. Actual GNP fluctuates around potential, falling below during recession, and rising back toward the potential level during recoveries. (*Source*: E. A. Carmichael, *Reassessing Canada's Potential Economic Growth*, The Conference Board in Canada, 1979)

1970s. This is a benchmark for calculating what potential output or full employment output is, but it is only a benchmark, not a rigid, undebatable rule. Even so, the GNP gap provides an important indicator of how the economy is performing and in which direction policies should try to move the level of activity.

Seasonal Variation

Figure 1-4 shows the actual monthly unemployment rate from October 1982 to December 1983 together with the *seasonally adjusted* rate, as calculated by Statistics Canada. The seasonally adjusted series is corrected for the typical seasonal pattern observed in the past and is a measure of the underlying cyclical movement. For example, from October 1982 to March 1983, the unadjusted rate rose from 11.7 to 14 percent but this was somewhat below the increase typically experienced in the winter months. Thus when seasonal factors are removed, the seasonally adjusted rate shows a decline from 12.8 to 12.5 percent.

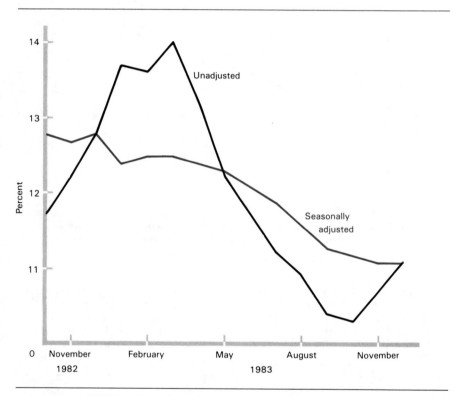

FIGURE 1-4   ACTUAL AND SEASONALLY ADJUSTED UNEMPLOYMENT RATE (*Source*: Statistics Canada, 11-003)

Balance of Payments

The balance of payments is the record of transactions of the economy with the rest of the world. It includes borrowing and lending and exchange of assets between countries as well as imports and exports of goods and services. Trade in goods is recorded in the merchandise trade balance. Figure 1-5 shows Canada's trade balance for 1965 through 1983. There have been wide swings, but exports exceeded imports in every year except 1975.

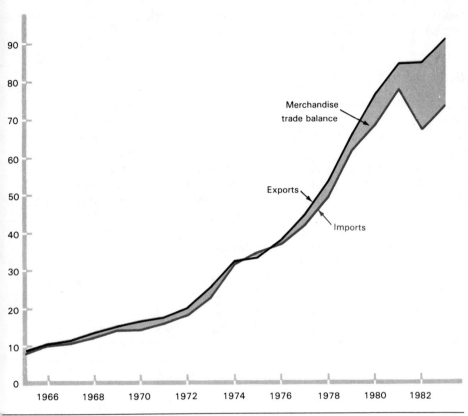

FIGURE 1-5   MERCHANDISE TRADE BALANCE, 1965–1983
(*Source: Bank of Canada Review*)

Under a fixed exchange rate, the external value of a country's currency is pegged within narrow bounds around a preannounced value. This system was followed by Canada from 1962 to 1970 when the Canadian dollar was fixed at 92.5 U.S. cents. If a country allows the value of its currency to be determined by market forces, it is said to have a flexible or floating exchange rate. This practice was followed by Canada in the 1950s and from 1970 to the present and the value of our dollar has fluctuated between a high of about 105 U.S. cents and recent lows near 75 U.S. cents.

1-2   RELATIONSHIPS AMONG MACROECONOMIC VARIABLES

The preliminary look at the data presented above, and our discussion of the business cycle, correctly suggests that we should expect to find simple relationships among the major macroeconomic variables: growth, unemployment, and inflation. There are indeed such relationships, as we now document.

Growth and Unemployment

We have already noted that changes in the employment of factors of production provide one of the sources of growth in real GNP. We would then expect high GNP growth to be accompanied by declining unemployment. That is indeed the case, as we observe from Figure 1-6. On the vertical axis, Figure 1-6 shows the growth rate of output in a particular year and on the horizontal axis the change in the unemployment rate in that year. For example, in both 1964 and 1965, the growth rate of output was 6.7 percent and the reduction in the unemployment rate was 0.8 percentage points. Thus we plot the points labelled 64-65 in the upper left-hand region. That region corresponds to a period of expansion and falling unemployment rates.

By contrast, in the lower right-hand region, such as the points labelled 1975 and 1982, are periods of recession — low growth and rising unemployment rates. Note that even when there is some growth, such as in 1981, unemployment rates may be rising. It takes growth rates above about 3 percent to cause unemployment rates to come down.

Okun's Law

A relationship between real growth and changes in the unemployment rate is known as *Okun's law*, named after its discoverer, the late Arthur Okun of the Brookings Institution, former chairperson of the U.S. Council of Economic Advisers. Okun's law says that for every 2½ percentage points of growth in real GNP above the trend rate that is sustained for a year, the unemployment rate declines by 1 percentage point. This 2½-to-1 relationship, the status of which is somewhat exaggerated by calling it a law rather than an empirical regularity, provides a rule of thumb for assessing the implications of real growth for unemployment.[4] While the rule is only approximate and will not work very precisely from year to year, it still gives a sensible translation from growth to unemployment.

The relation is a useful guide to policy because it allows us to ask how a particular growth target will affect the unemployment rate over time. Suppose we were in a deep recession with 9 percent unemployment. How many years would it take us to return to, say, 6 percent unemployment? The answer depends, of course, on how fast the economy grows in the recovery. Assume the growth rate of potential output is 3 percent per year. One possible path to return to 6 percent unemployment is for output to

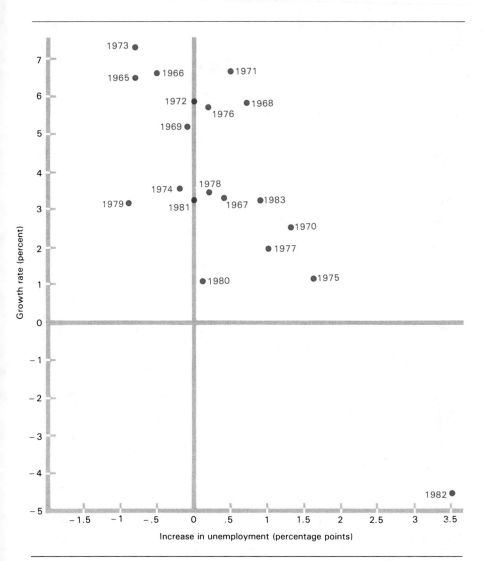

FIGURE 1-6 GROWTH AND THE CHANGE IN THE UNEMPLOYMENT RATE,
1965–1983. High rates of growth cause the unemployment rate to fall, and low or
negative rates of growth are accompanied by increases in the unemployment rate.
The relationship shown by the scatter of the points in this figure is summarized
by *Okun's law*, linking the growth rate to the change in the unemployment rate.

grow at 5½ percent per year for 3 years. On this path, each year we are
growing 2½ percent above trend, and thus each year we take 1 percentage point off the unemployment rate. An alternative recovery strategy is
front-loaded: growth is high at the beginning and then slows down. Such

a path might be one of growth rates in successive years equal to 6½, 5½, and 4½ percent, also allowing a return to 6 percent unemployment in 3 years.

Inflation and the Cycle

Inflation is the rate of increase of prices. Expansionary aggregate demand policies tend to produce inflation, unless they occur when the economy is at high levels of unemployment. Protracted periods of low aggregate demand tend to reduce the inflation rate. Figure 1-7 shows one measure of inflation for the Canadian economy for the period since 1960. The inflation measure in the figure is the rate of change of the *consumer price index*, the cost of a given basket of goods, representing the purchases of a typical urban consumer.[5]

The rate of inflation shown in Figure 1-7 fluctuates considerably. Just as we could tell much about the recent history of the economy from looking at Figure 1-3's picture of the course of actual and potential GNP, we can likewise see much of recent economic history in Figure 1-7. In particular, there is the long period of steady inflation from 1957 through 1964 when the inflation rate hovered around the 2 percent level. Then there is a slow climb in the inflation rate from 1965 to 1969, followed by a brief pause in 1970. Finally there are the inflationary bursts from 1971 through 1974 and 1977 to 1980 as the inflation rate rose to 12 percent and above. In 1982–83 inflation was again down, under the impact of a deep recession.

Figure 1-7 shows the *rate of increase* of prices. We can also look at the *level* of prices. All the inflation of the 1960s and 1970s adds up to a large increase in the price level. In the period from 1960 to 1983 the price level more than tripled. A product that cost $1 in 1960 cost $3.74 by 1983. Much of that increase in prices took place since the early 1970s.

Inflation, like unemployment, is a major macroeconomic problem. However, the costs of inflation are much less obvious than those of unemployment. In the case of unemployment, it is clear that potential output is going to waste, and therefore it is clear why the reduction of unemployment is desirable. In the case of inflation, there is no obvious loss of output. As we noted above, consumers in part dislike inflation because it is often associated with disturbances, such as the oil price shocks, that reduce their real incomes. It is also argued that inflation upsets familiar price relationships and reduces the efficiency of the price system. Whatever the reasons, policy makers have been willing to increase unemployment in an effort to reduce inflation — that is, to trade off some unemployment for less inflation.

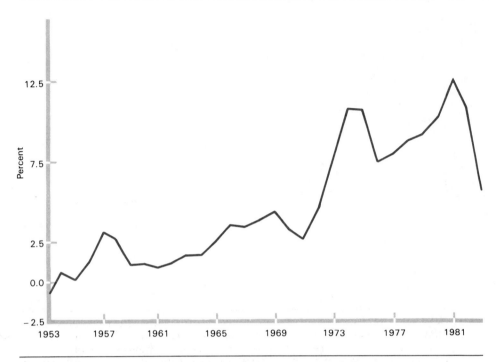

FIGURE 1-7 THE RATE OF INFLATION OF CONSUMER PRICES
(*Source*: Department of Finance, *Economic Review*)

Inflation-Unemployment Tradeoffs

The *Phillips curve* describes a relationship between inflation and unemployment: the higher the rate of unemployment, the lower the rate of inflation. The Phillips curve is an empirical relationship that relates the behaviour of wage and price inflation to the rate of unemployment. It was made famous in the 1950s in Great Britain and has since become a cornerstone of macroeconomic discussion. Figure 1-8 presents a typical downward-sloping Phillips curve showing that high rates of unemployment are accompanied by low rates of inflation and vice versa. The curve suggests that less unemployment can always be attained by incurring more inflation and that the inflation rate can always be reduced by incurring the costs of more unemployment. In other words, the curve suggests there is a tradeoff between inflation and unemployment.

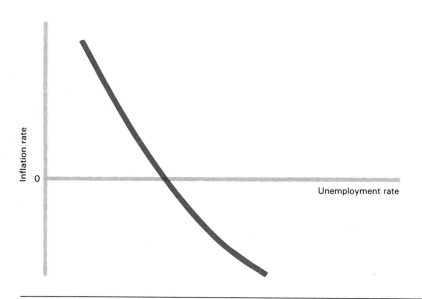

FIGURE 1-8   A PHILLIPS CURVE. The Phillips curve suggests a tradeoff between inflation and unemployment: less unemployment can always be obtained by incurring more inflation — or inflation can be reduced by allowing more unemployment. Recent events, particularly the combination of high inflation *and* high unemployment in years such as 1975 and 1981, have led to skepticism about the Phillips curve. It nonetheless remains useful, as we shall show later.

Figure 1-9 shows that the Phillips curve broadly describes Canadian experience in the period 1956–1966. However, we can see also that economic events of the last decade, particularly the combination of high inflation *and* high unemployment are not consistent with the curve traced out in the earlier years.

Nonetheless, there remains a tradeoff between inflation and unemployment which is more sophisticated than a glance at Figure 1-8 would suggest, and which will enable us to make sense of Figure 1-9. In the short run of, say, 2 years, there is a relation between inflation and unemployment of the type shown in Figure 1-8. The *short-run Phillips curve*, however, does not remain stable. It shifts as expectations of inflation change. In the long run, there is no tradeoff worth speaking about between inflation and unemployment. In the long run, the unemployment rate is basically independent of the long-run inflation rate.

The short- and long-run tradeoffs between inflation and unemploy-

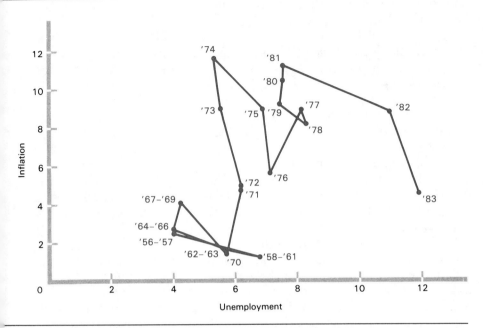

FIGURE 1-9   INFLATION AND UNEMPLOYMENT
(*Source*: Statistics Canada, 11-003, 11-206, 11-505, 71-201)

ment are obviously a major concern of policy making and are the basic determinants of the potential success of stabilization policies.

1-3   MACROECONOMIC POLICY

Policy makers have at their command two broad classes of policies with which to affect the economy. *Monetary policy* is controlled by the Bank of Canada. The instruments of monetary policy are changes in the stock of money, changes in the interest rate — the bank rate — at which the Bank of Canada lends money to banks, and some controls over the banking system. *Fiscal policy* is under the control of Parliament, and usually is initiated by the government of the day. The instruments of fiscal policy are tax rates and government spending.

One of the central facts of policy is that the effects of monetary and fiscal policy on the economy are not fully predictable, neither in their *timing* nor in the *extent* to which they affect demand or supply. These two uncertainties are at the heart of the problem of stabilization policy. *Stabilization policies* are monetary and fiscal policies designed to moderate the fluctuations of the economy; in particular, fluctuations in the rates of growth, inflation, and unemployment.

Figure 1-9, which showed the recent fluctuations of the rates of inflation and unemployment, suggests strongly that stabilization policy has not been fully successful in keeping them within narrow bounds. The failures of stabilization policy are due mostly to uncertainty about the way it works.

However, questions of political economy are also involved in the way stabilization policy has been operated. The speed at which to proceed in trying to eliminate unemployment, at the risk of increasing inflation, is a matter of judgment about both the economy and the costs of mistakes. Those who regard the costs of unemployment as high, relative to the costs of inflation, will run greater risks of inflation to reduce unemployment than will those who regard the costs of inflation as primary and unemployment as a relatively minor misfortune.

Political economy affects stabilization policy in more ways than through the costs which policy makers of different political persuasions attach to inflation and unemployment, and the risks they are willing to undertake in trying to improve the economic situation. There is also the so-called *political business cycle*, which is based on the observation that election results are affected by economic conditions. When the economic situation is improving and the unemployment rate is falling, there is an environment favourable to the government. There is thus the incentive to policy makers running for reelection, or who wish to affect the election results, to use stabilization policy to produce booming economic conditions before elections.

Stabilization policy is also known as *countercyclical policy*, that is, policy to moderate the trade cycle or business cycle. Figure 1-3 shows that cycles in the past 20 years have been far from regular. The behaviour, and even the existence, of the trade cycle is substantially affected by the conduct of stabilization policy. Successful stabilization policy smooths out the cycle, while unsuccessful stabilization policy may worsen the fluctuations of the economy. Indeed, one of the tenets of monetarism is that the major fluctuations of the economy are a result of government actions rather than the inherent instability of the economy's private sector.

Monetarists and Activists

We noted above that there is some controversy over the existence of the tradeoff between inflation and unemployment. That controversy arose around 1967–1968 in the context of the debate in macroeconomics between monetarists and nonmonetarists, or fiscalists. We have already identified some of the major participants in the debate as Milton Friedman on the monetarist side and Franco Modigliani and James Tobin on the nonmonetarist side. Among Canadian economists, prominent exponents of monetarism include Tom Courchene and David Laidler (University of Western Ontario) and their views have been vigorously challenged by Clarence Barber (University of Manitoba). However, macroeconomists cannot be neatly classified into one camp or the other. Instead, there is a spectrum of views. There are monetarists who make Friedman look like a fiscalist or Keynesian, and Keynesians who make Modigliani look like a monetarist. Not only that; there is no compelling unity in the views that are identified with monetarism, and the balanced economist is likely to accept some monetarist arguments and reject others. Nor is the debate one in which there is no progress. For example, both theory and empirical evidence have been brought to bear on the issue of the inflation-unemployment tradeoff, and it is no longer central to the monetarist-fiscalist debate.

Another major point of contention is the relation between *money* and *inflation*. *Monetarists* tend to argue that the quantity of money is the prime determinant of the level of prices and economic activity, and that excessive monetary growth is responsible for inflation and unstable monetary growth for economic fluctuations. Since they contend that variability in the growth rate of money accounts for variability of real growth, they are naturally led to argue for a monetary policy of low and constant growth in the money supply — a monetary growth rule. *Activists*, by contrast, point out that there is no close relationship between monetary growth and inflation in the short run and that monetary growth is only one of the factors affecting aggregate demand. Activists maintain that policy makers are, or at least can be, sufficiently careful and skillful to be able to use monetary and fiscal policy to control the economy effectively.

The skill and care of the policy makers are important because monetarists raise the issue of whether aggregate demand policies might not worsen the performance of the economy. Monetarists point to episodes, such as the overexpansionary policies followed by the Bank of Canada in 1971, to argue that policy makers cannot and do not exercise sufficient caution to justify using activist policy. Here the activists are optimists, suggesting that we can learn from our past mistakes.

A further issue that divides the two camps concerns the proper role of government in the economy. This is not really an issue that can be analysed using macroeconomic theory, but it is difficult to follow some of the debate without being aware that the issue exists. Monetarists and the new classical macroeconomists tend to be conservatives who favour small government and abhor budget deficits and a large public debt. They favour tax cuts during recessions and cuts in public spending during booms, with the net effect of winding up with a smaller share of government in the economy. Activists, by contrast, tend to favour an active role for government and are therefore quite willing to use increased government spending and transfers as tools of stabilization policy. Differences between monetarists and activists must, therefore, be seen in a much broader perspective than their particular disagreements about the exact role of money in the short run.

1-4   AGGREGATE DEMAND AND SUPPLY

We have sketched the major issues and variables we shall be discussing and using in the book.

The key overall concepts in analysing output, inflation and growth, and the role of policy are *aggregate demand* and *aggregate supply*. In this section we provide a brief preview of those concepts and of their interaction, with the aims of showing where we are heading and of keeping the material of Chapters 3 through 12 in perspective.

The level of output and the price level are determined by the interaction of aggregate demand and aggregate supply. Under some conditions, employment depends only on total spending, or aggregate demand. At other times, supply limitations are an important part of the policy problem and have to receive major attention. From the 1930s to the late 1960s, macroeconomics was very much demand-oriented.

But in recent years the emphasis has shifted, and aggregate supply and *supply-side economics* have gained in importance. This shift of emphasis and interest was no doubt fostered by the slow growth and high inflation experienced by the industrialized countries in the 1970s.

What are the relationships among aggregate demand and aggregate supply, output or employment, and prices? Aggregate demand is the relationship between spending on goods and services and the level of prices. If output limitations are not present, increased spending or an increase in aggregate demand will raise output and employment with little effect on prices. In such conditions, for example, during the great depression of the thirties, it would certainly be appropriate to use expansionary aggregate demand policies to increase output.

However if the economy is close to full employment, increased aggregate demand will be reflected primarily in higher prices or inflation. The aggregate supply side of the economy has then to be introduced. The aggregate supply curve specifies the relationship between the amount of output firms produce and the price level. The supply side not only enters the picture in telling us how successful demand expansions will be in raising output and employment, but also has a role of its own. Supply disturbances, or *supply shocks*, can reduce output and raise prices, as was the case when increases in the price of oil reduced the productive capacity of the economy. Conversely, policies that increase productivity, and thus the level of aggregate supply at a given price level, can help reduce inflationary pressures.

Graphical Analysis

Figure 1-10 shows aggregate demand and supply curves. The vertical axis P is the price level, and the horizontal axis Y is the level of real output or income. Although the curves look like the ordinary supply and demand curves of microeconomics, a full understanding of them will not be reached until Chapter 14.

Aggregate demand is the total demand for goods and services in the economy. It depends on the aggregate price level, as shown in Figure 1-10. It can be shifted through monetary and fiscal policy. The aggregate supply

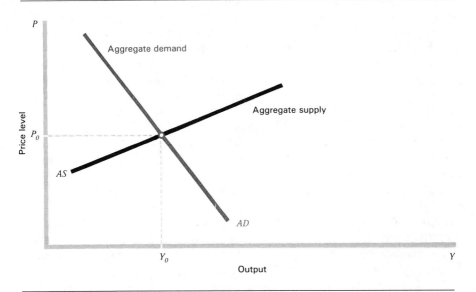

FIGURE 1-10   AGGREGATE DEMAND AND SUPPLY. The basic tools for analyzing output, inflation, and growth are the aggregate supply and demand curves. Shifts in either aggregate supply or demand will cause the level of output to change — thus affecting growth — and will also change the price level — thus affecting inflation. Through Okun's law, changes in output are linked to changes in the unemployment rate. For the first 12 chapters, we concentrate on aggregate demand. Then in the later chapters we introduce the aggregate supply curve, thereby completing the analysis.

curve shows the price level associated with each level of output. It can, to some extent, be shifted by fiscal policy.

Aggregate supply and demand interact to determine the price level and output level. In Figure 1-10, P_o is the equilibrium price level and Y_o the equilibrium level of output. If the AD curve in the figure shifts up to the right, then the extent to which output and prices, respectively, are changed depends on the steepness of the aggregate supply curve.[6] If the AS curve is very steep, then a given increase in aggregate demand mainly causes prices to rise and has very little effect on the level of output. If the AS curve is flat, a given change in aggregate demand will be translated mainly into an increase in output and very little into an increase in the price level.

One of the crucial points about macroeconomic adjustment is that the aggregate supply curve is not a straight line. Figure 1-11 shows that at low levels of output, below potential output Y, the aggregate supply curve is quite flat. When output is below potential, there is very little tendency for prices of goods and factors (wages) to fall. Conversely, for output above potential, the aggregate supply curve is steep and prices tend to rise continuously. The effects of changes in aggregate demand on output and prices therefore depend on the level of output relative to potential.

All these observations are by way of a very important warning. In Chapters 3 through 12 we focus on aggregate demand as the determinant of the level of output. We shall assume that prices are given and constant, and that output is determined by the level of demand — that there are no supply limitations. We are thus talking about the very flat part of the aggregate supply curve, at levels of output below potential.

The suggestion that output rises to meet the level of demand without a rise in prices leads to a very activist conception of policy. Under these circumstances, without any obvious tradeoffs, policy makers would favour very expansionary policies to raise demand and thereby cause the economy to move to a high level of employment and output. There are circumstances where such a policy view is altogether correct. The early 1960s are a case in point. Figure 1-3 shows that in those years output was substantially below potential. There were unused resources, and the problem was a deficiency of demand. By contrast, in the late 1960s and the early 1970s the economy was operating at full employment. There was no significant GNP gap. An attempt to expand output or real GNP further would run into supply limitations and force up prices rather than the production of goods. In these circumstances, a model that assumes that output is demand-determined and that increased demand raises output and *not* prices is simply inappropriate.

Should we think that the model with fixed prices and demand-determined output is very restricted and perhaps artificial? The answer is no.

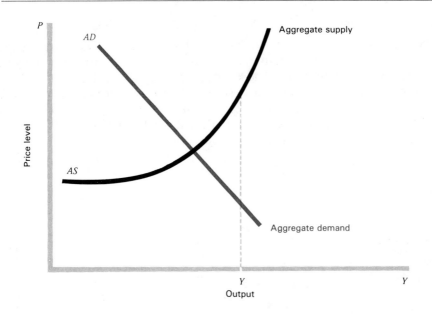

FIGURE 1-11   AGGREGATE DEMAND AND NONLINEAR AGGREGATE SUPPLY. A key fact about the aggregate supply curve is that it is not linear. At low levels of output, prices do not change much on the aggregate supply schedule, implying that more output will be supplied without much increase in prices. But as the economy gets close to full employment or potential output, further increases in output will be accompanied by increased prices.

There are two reasons for this. First, the circumstances under which the model is appropriate — those of high unemployment — are neither unknown nor unimportant. Unemployment and downward price rigidity are continuing features of the Canadian economy. Second, even when we come to study the interactions of aggregate supply and demand in Chapter 13 and later, we need to know how given policy actions *shift* the aggregate demand curve at a given level of prices. Thus all the material of Chapters 3 through 12 on aggregate demand plays a vital part in the understanding of the effects of monetary and fiscal policy on the price level as well as output in circumstances where the aggregate supply curve is upward-sloping.

What, then, is the warning of this section? It is simply that the very activist spirit of macroeconomic policy under conditions of unemployment must not cause us to overlook the existence of supply limitations and price adjustment when the economy is near full employment.

1-5   OUTLINE AND PREVIEW OF THE TEXT

We have sketched the major issues we shall discuss in the book. We can now outline our approach to macroeconomics and the order in which the material will be presented. The key overall concepts, as already noted, are aggregate demand and aggregate supply. Aggregate demand is influenced by monetary policy, primarily via interest rates and expectations, and by fiscal policy. Aggregate supply is affected by fiscal policy and also by disturbances such as changes in the supply of oil.

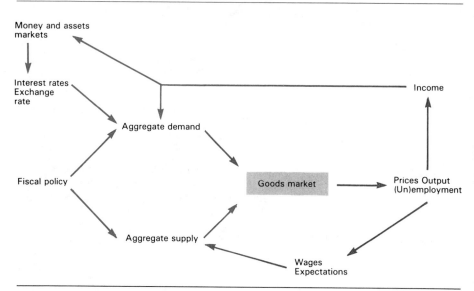

FIGURE 1-12   BASIC APPROACH TO MACROECONOMICS. Aggregate demand and aggregate supply are the key elements in determining prices and output. Aggregate supply is affected by fiscal policy and by wage behaviour and expectations. Aggregate demand is affected by fiscal policy and by monetary policy. There are also feedbacks through the money market—a high level of income increases the demand for money, which raises interest rates and reduces aggregate demand. This figure is a road map for the rest of the book. It will be helpful to return to it later, to see where the material being covered in later chapters fits in to the overall approach to the economy outlined here.

Figure 1-12 presents a schematic view of the approach of the book to macroeconomics. Being schematic, the diagram is not comprehensive, but it does show the most important relationships we shall examine.

The coverage by chapters starts in Chapter 2 with national income accounting, emphasizing data and relationships that are used repeatedly later in the book. Chapters 3 and 4 are concerned with aggregate demand in a closed economy without external economic relationships, and Chapters 5 and 6 extend the analysis to an open economy with trade and international capital flows. Chapters 13 to 15 deal with aggregate supply and the interactions between aggregate supply and demand. Chapters 7 through 12 present material which clarifies and deepens understanding of aggregate demand and of the ways in which monetary and fiscal policies affect the economy. Chapters 16 to 19 perform a similar service for aggregate supply and the interactions of aggregate supply and demand.

1-6 PREREQUISITES AND RECIPES

A few words on how to use this book are helpful in concluding this introductory chapter. First, we note that there is no mathematical prerequisite beyond high school algebra. We do use equations whenever they appear helpful, but they are not an indispensable part of the exposition. Nevertheless, they can and should be mastered by any serious student of macroeconomics.

The technically harder chapters or sections are marked by an asterisk (*). They can be skipped or dipped into. Either we present them as supplementary material, or we provide sufficient nontechnical coverage to help the reader get on without them later in the book. The reason we do present more advanced material or treatment is to afford a complete and up-to-date coverage of the main ideas and techniques in macroeconomics. Even though you may not be able to grasp every point of a section marked by an asterisk on first reading — and should not even try to — these sections should certainly be read to get the main message and an intuitive appreciation of the issues that are raised.

The main problem you will encounter comes from the interaction of several markets and many variables. As Figure 1-12 already suggests, the direct and feedback effects in the economy constitute a quite formidable system. How can you be certain to progress efficiently and with some ease? The most important thing is to ask questions. Ask yourself, as you follow the argument: Why is it that this or that variable should affect, say, aggregate demand? What would happen if it did not? What is the critical link?

There is no substitute for an active form of learning. Reading sticks at best for 7 weeks. Are there simple rules for active study? The best way to study is to use pencil and paper and work the argument by drawing diagrams, experimenting with flowcharts, writing out the logic of an argument, working out the problems at the end of each chapter, and underlining key ideas. The *Study Guide*, by Gordon Sparks and Richard Startz, contains much useful material and problems that will help in your studies. Another valuable exercise is to take issue with an argument or position, or to spell out the defence for a particular view on policy questions. Beyond that, if you get stuck, read on for half a page. If you are still stuck, go back five pages.

You should also learn to use the Index. Several concepts are discussed at different levels in different chapters. If you come across an unfamiliar term or concept, check the Index to see whether and where it was defined and discussed earlier in the book.

As a final word, this chapter is designed for reference purposes. You should return to it whenever you want to check where a particular problem fits or where a particular subject matter is relevant. The best way to see the forest is from Chapter 1.

KEY TERMS

Monetarists

Keynesians

New classical macroeconomists

GNP, nominal and real

Inflation

Growth

Unemployment

Business cycle

Trend or potential output

Peak

Trough

Recovery or expansion

Recession

Output gap

Okun's law

Phillips curve

Monetary policy

Fiscal policy

Stabilization policies

Activists

Aggregate demand and supply

CHAPTER 1: FOOTNOTES

[1]Notice that the scale for GNP in Chart 1-1 is not linear. For example, the distance from 60 to 65 is bigger than the distance from 145 to 150. The scale is logarithmic, which means that equal ratios are represented by equal distances. For instance, the distance from 60 to 120 is the same as the distance from 75 to 150, since GNP doubles in both cases. On a logarithmic scale, a variable growing at a constant rate (e.g., 4 percent per annum) is represented by a straight line.

[2]Why are real and nominal GNP the same in 1971? This is because we use 1971 prices to calculate real GNP.

[3]These efficiency improvements are often called productivity increases.

[4]The analysis of Canada's medium-term prospects shown in the Economic Council of Canada's Sixteenth Annual Review (1979) suggests a ratio of about 2 to 1.

[5]By contrast, the measure of inflation obtained in Figure 1-1 by comparing nominal and real GNE is the rate of change of the GNE deflator. The consumer price index (CPI) is most frequently used to measure inflation, and the GNE deflator is next most popular. Chapter 2 presents more details on the different price indexes.

[6]Experiment with graphs like Figure 1-10 to be sure you understand this fact.

National Income Accounting

Macroeconomics is ultimately concerned with the determination of the economy's total output, the price level, the level of employment, interest rates, exchange rates, and other variables discussed in Chapter 1. A necessary step in understanding how these variables are determined is *national income accounting*.

The national income accounts give us regular estimates of GNP, the basic measure of the performance of the economy in producing goods and services. The first part of the chapter discusses the measurement and meaning of GNP, and the second part describes the relationships between three key macroeconomic variables: output, income, and spending. These relationships are summarized in the circular flow diagram, Figure 2-1.

Figure 2-1 illustrates the interactions of firms and households in the economy. Output is produced by firms. The value of the output produced is the gross national product. GNP includes the value of goods produced, such as automobiles and eggs, along with the value of services, such as haircuts and medical services.

Firms produce the output by employing factors of production — land, labour, and capital — and paying for their use. The payments made by the firms are the *incomes* earned in the economy. The flow of income is shown in the lower bottom loop of the circular flow diagram. Thus the value of output is equal to the value of incomes received in the economy.

The goods produced by the firms are sold to households (and to other firms). Total *spending* is called gross national expenditure (GNE) and is also equal to the value of output. The flow of spending is also shown in Figure 2-1.

Looking at the relationships summarized in Figure 2-1, we see that *the value of total output is equal to total income earned in the economy (GNP), and is also equal to total spending (GNE)*. That is the main lesson of this chapter, and the single most important point to remember about national income accounting. There is, however, considerable complexity in the actual national income accounts in relating GNP to incomes and to spending. Those complexities arise in large part from the role of the government and from the presence of foreign trade, and we shall have to explain some of them.

We start in Section 2-1 by examining GNP and its measurement, and then move in Sections 2-2 and 2-3 to the relationships among output, income, and spending summarized in the circular flow diagram. Section 2-4 returns to the distinction between real and nominal GNP, a distinction which is necessary because of inflation. Section 2-5 compares alternative measures of inflation.

Section 2-7 paves the way for the economic analysis of the determination of the level of output that begins in Chapter 3, by systematically setting out the national income relationships studied in this chapter.

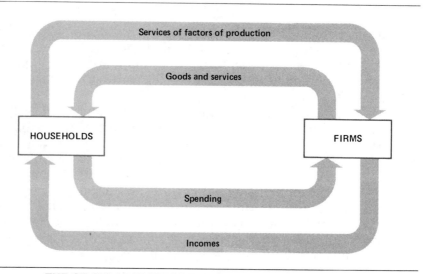

FIGURE 2-1   THE CIRCULAR FLOW OF INCOME AND SPENDING. Production is carried out by firms, whose total output is equal to GNP. The output is produced using the services of factors of production, mostly labour, owned by households and paid for by the firms. The payments for the use of factors of production generate the households' income. Household spending out of those incomes, in turn, generates the demand for the goods produced by the firms. Spending on goods is, in the simple case shown here where there is no government and no foreign trade, equal to GNP, and also equal to the income of households. The diagram shows the key relation: output is equal to income is equal to spending.

2-1   GROSS NATIONAL PRODUCT AND NET NATIONAL PRODUCT

GNP is the value of all final goods and services produced by domestically owned factors of production within a given period. It includes the value of such goods produced as houses and whiskey, and the value of services, such as brokers' services and economists' lectures. The output of each of these is valued at its market price, and the values are added together to give GNP.

TABLE 2-1   CALCULATING GNP IN A SIMPLE ECONOMY

	Output	Price per unit	Value of output	GNP
Bananas	20	$0.30	$ 6.00	
Oranges	60	$0.25	$15.00	
				$21.00

Table 2-1 shows the calculation of GNP in a simple economy that produces only bananas and oranges. Twenty bananas and sixty oranges are produced. The bananas are valued at $0.30 each and the oranges at $0.25 each. GNP is equal to $21, the total value of output.

GNP in Canada in 1983 was $388.7 billion. Dividing by population, equal to 24.883 million in 1983, we obtain GNP per person or per capita, which was $15,621. We can also calculate output per person employed. In 1982 there were on average 10.644 million people employed. Thus GNP per person employed or output per person employed was $36,212.

GNP has increased rapidly in the last 18 years, as Figure 1-1 shows. GNP has grown on average at a rate of 11.4 percent per year since 1965. In that year GNP was only $55.4 billion, one seventh of its value in 1983. Recall that much of the increase is a result of inflation.

A number of subtleties in the calculation of GNP should be kept in mind.

Final Goods and Value Added

GNP is the value of *final* goods and services produced. The insistence on final goods and services is simply to make sure that we do not double-count. For example, we would not want to include the full price of an automobile in GNP and then also include the value of the tires that were sold to the automobile producer as part of the GNP. The components of the car, sold to the manufacturers, are called *intermediate* goods, and their value is not included in GNP. Similarly, the wheat that goes into bread is an intermediate good, and we do not count the value of the wheat sold to the miller and the value of the flour sold to the baker, as well as the value of the bread, as part of GNP.

In practice, double counting is avoided by working with *value added*. At each stage of the manufacture of a good, only the value added to the good at that stage of manufacture is counted as part of GNP. The value of the wheat produced by the farmer is counted as part of GNP. Then the value of the flour sold by the miller minus the cost of the wheat is the miller's value added. If we follow this process along, we will see that the sum of value added at each stage of processing will be equal to the final value of the bread sold.[1]

Current Output

GNP consists of the value of output *currently produced*. It thus excludes transactions in existing commodities such as old masters or existing houses. We count the construction of new houses as part of GNP, but we do not add trade in existing houses. We do, however, count the value of realtor's fees in the sale of existing houses as part of GNP. The realtor provides a current service in bringing buyer and seller together, and that is appropriately part of current output.

Market Prices

GNP values goods at *market prices*. The market price of many goods includes indirect taxes such as the sales tax and excise taxes, and thus the market price of goods is not the same as the price the seller of the good receives. The price net of indirect taxes is the *factor cost*, which is the amount received by the factors of production that manufactured the good. GNP is valued at market prices and not at factor cost. This point becomes important when we relate GNP to the incomes received by the factors of production.

Valuation at market prices is a principle that is not uniformly applied, because there are some components of GNP that are difficult to value. There is no very good way of valuing the services of housepersons, or a self-administered haircut, or, for that matter, the services of the police force or the government bureaucracy. Some of these activities are simply omitted from currently measured GNP, as, for instance, housepersons' services. Government services are valued at cost, so that the wages of government employees are taken to represent their contribution to GNP. There is no unifying principle in the treatment of these awkward cases, but rather a host of conventions is used.

GNP and Gross Domestic Product

Statistics Canada provides an alternative measure of output called *gross domestic product, or GDP*. GDP is the value of current output produced within Canada using both Canadian and nonresident factors of production. Interest and dividends paid by Canadian companies to nonresidents are part of Canadian GDP but not GNP. Since income paid to nonresidents typically exceeds income earned by Canadians from foreign sources, GDP exceeds GNP. In 1983 this difference amounted to about three-and-a-half percent of GNP.[2]

Net National Product

Net national product (NNP), as distinct from GNP, deducts from GNP the *depreciation* of the existing capital stock over the course of the period. The production of GNP causes wear and tear on the existing capital stock; for example, machines wear out as they are used. If resources were not used to maintain or replace the existing capital, GNP could not be kept at the current level. Accordingly, we use NNP as a better measure of the rate of economic activity that could be maintained over long periods, given the existing capital stock and labour force.

Depreciation is a measure of the part of GNP that has to be set aside to maintain the productive capacity of the economy, and we deduct that from GNP to obtain NNP. In 1983 depreciation was $47 billion, or about 12 percent of GNP. The GNP is the more commonly used measure of output because of the difficulties in measuring depreciation accurately.

2-2   GNP AND INCOME

We now consider the relation between the value of output or GNP and the incomes that are generated in the production process. In this section we show that *income is equal to the value of output* because the receipts from the sale of output must accrue to someone as income. The purchaser of bread is indirectly paying the farmer, the miller, the baker, and the supermarket operator for the labour and capital used in production and is also contributing to their profits.

GNP and National Income

Our statement above equating the value of output and income is correct with two qualifications:

1 The first correction arises from depreciation. As already noted, part of GNP has to be set aside to maintain the productive capacity of the economy. Depreciation should not be counted as part of income, since it is a cost of production. As a rule, depreciation amounts to about 10 percent of GNP. Depreciation is usually referred to in the national income accounts as *capital consumption allowances*. After subtracting depreciation from GNP, we have NNP.

2 The second adjustment arises from indirect taxes, in particular, sales and excise taxes, that introduce a discrepancy between market price and prices received by producers. GNP is valued at market price, but the income accruing to producers does not include the sales and excise taxes that are part of market price, and thus falls short of GNP. Indirect taxes, along with some other items of the same nature, account for about 10 percent of GNP.

With these two deductions we can derive *national income* from GNP, as shown in Table 2-2, which gives the dollar figures for 1983. National income gives us the value of output at *factor cost* rather than market prices, which is GNP. It tells us what factors of production actually receive as income before direct taxes and transfers.

TABLE 2-2   GNP AND NATIONAL INCOME, 1983
(billions of dollars)

Gross national product (GNP)		$388.7
Less:		
Capital consumption allowances	$47.0	
Equals:		
Net national product (NNP)		341.7
Less:		
Indirect taxes less subsidies	42.4	
Residual error of estimate	−0.5	
Equals:		
National income		299.8

Source: Statistics Canada, 11-003.

Factor Shares in National Income

We next ask how national income is split among different types of incomes, as shown in Table 2-3.

The most striking fact of Table 2-3 is the very large share of wages and salaries in national income. This accounts for over 70 percent. Dividends paid to nonresidents are deducted from corporation profits because national income is defined to include earnings of Canadian residents only.[3] The inventory valuation adjustment is made in order to exclude capital

TABLE 2-3   NATIONAL INCOME AND ITS DISTRIBUTION, 1983
(billions of dollars)

National income		$299.8	100.0%
Wages, salaries and other labour income		222.2	74.1
Corporate profits	$32.3		
Less dividends paid to nonresidents	2.9		
Plus inventory valuation adjustment	−2.5	26.9	9.0
Interest and misc. investment income		30.4	10.1
Net income of unincorporated business			
Farm	3.9		
Nonfarm, including rent	16.4	20.3	6.8

Source: Statistics Canada, 11-003.

gains or losses on inventories that appear as part of profits measured under business accounting procedures but are not related to current production. Rental income includes not only rents received by landlords but also the *imputed* income of owner-occupied housing.[4]

The division of national income into various classes is not too important for our macroeconomic purposes. It reflects, in part, such questions as whether corporations are financed by debt or equity, whether a business is or is not incorporated, and whether the housing stock is owned by persons or corporations — which, in turn, are owned by persons.[5]

National Income and Personal Income

A considerably more important question from the macroeconomic viewpoint is how much the personal sector — households and unincorporated businesses — actually receives as income, inclusive of transfers. This quantity is measured by *personal income. Transfers* are those payments that do *not* arise out of current productive activity. Thus, welfare payments and unemployment benefits are examples of transfer payments. The level of personal income is important because it is a prime determinant of household consumption and saving behaviour.

To go from national income to personal income, we have to remove the part of national income that accrues to the corporate sector and add back dividends paid out to Canadian residents. As shown in Table 2-4, we also add transfers from government which include such payments as unemployment insurance benefits, family allowances and old age pensions. Interest on government debt is also treated like a transfer payment. It is part of personal income, but is excluded from national income because much of the debt has been incurred to finance past government expenditure which does not contribute to current production of goods and services.

Although we have derived personal income in Table 2-4 by starting

---

TABLE 2-4   NATIONAL INCOME AND PERSONAL INCOME, 1983
(billions of dollars)

National income		$299.8
Less:		
Corporation profits	$26.9	
Other adjustments	.3	
Plus:		
Dividends and interest on government debt	9.9	
Transfers from government	50.9	
Other transfers	1.2	
Equals:		
Personal income		334.7

Source: Statistics Canada, 11-003.

with national income and making adjustments, we should recognize that it is also possible to build up to an estimate of personal income by looking at its components in a way similar to that shown in Table 2-3. In particular, personal income consists of labour income, plus income of unincorporated business, plus interest and dividends, plus transfers.

Personal Disposable Income and Its Allocation

Not all personal income is available for spending by households. The amount available for spending, *personal disposable income*, deducts from personal income the personal tax payments and other transfers to government made by the household sector. The other transfers include such items as licence fees and traffic tickets.

Personal disposable income is then available for personal consumption expenditure, other transfers, and saving. By far the largest outlay is for personal consumption, as shown in Table 2-5.

TABLE 2-5   DISPOSITIONS OF PERSONAL INCOME, 1983
(billions of dollars)

Personal income		$334.7
Less:		
Personal taxes	$63.1	
Other transfers to government	3.3	
Equals:		
Personal disposable income		268.4
Less:		
Personal consumption expenditure	229.0	
Other transfers	4.8	
Equals:		
Personal saving		34.6

Source: Statistics Canada, 11-003.

In summary, this section has shown the relation between GNP, which is a measure of productive activity in the economy, and income receipts that accrue to the household sector. The main steps in the long chain we have followed arise from taxes, transfers between sectors, depreciation, and corporation profits.

These intermediate steps remind us that there is an important difference between GNP as the value of output at market prices and the spendable receipts of the household sector. We could have a positive personal disposable income even if GNP were zero, provided there was someone to make the necessary transfer payments. Likewise, GNP could be large and disposable income small if the government sector took in a lot of taxes. The larger taxes are relative to government transfers, the smaller is disposable income relative to GNP.

Summary

We summarize here in a few identities (and in the accompanying Figure 2-2) the relationships reviewed in each table:

GNP–capital consumption allowances $\equiv$ NNP (Table 2-2)   (1)
NNP–indirect taxes $\equiv$ national income   (2)
National income $\equiv$ labour income + corporation profits + interest + net income of unincorporated business (Table 2-3)   (3)
National income–corporation profits + dividends and interest on government debt + transfers $\equiv$ personal income   (4)
Personal income–personal taxes and other transfers to government $\equiv$ personal disposable income (Table 2-5)   (5)
Personal disposable income $\equiv$ personal consumption expenditure and other transfers + personal saving (Table 2-5)   (6)

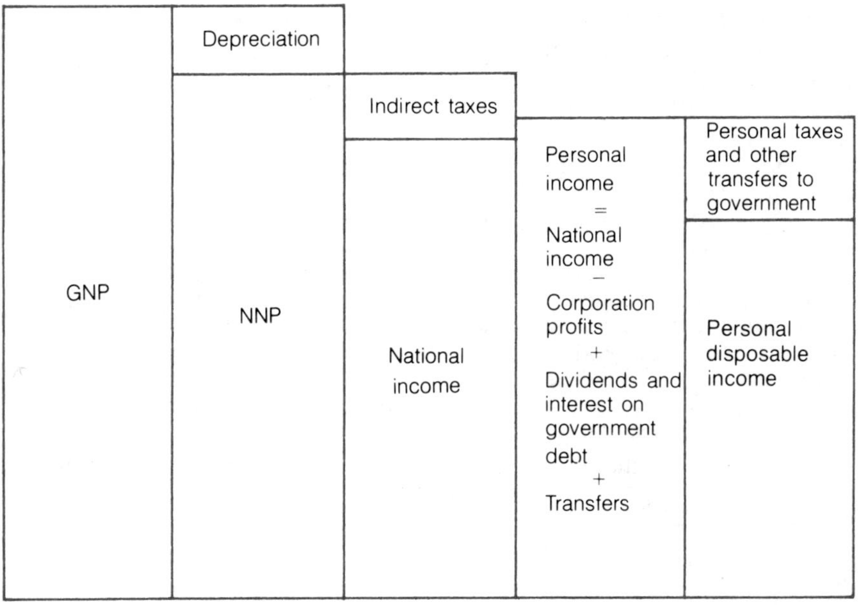

GNP				
	Depreciation			
	NNP	Indirect taxes		
		National income	Personal income = National income − Corporation profits + Dividends and interest on government debt + Transfers	Personal taxes and other transfers to government
				Personal disposable income

FIGURE 2-2   THE RELATION BETWEEN GNP AND PERSONAL DISPOSABLE INCOME

2-3   GROSS NATIONAL EXPENDITURE AND ITS COMPONENTS

In the previous section, we started with GNP and asked how much of the value of goods and services produced actually gets into the hands of households. In this section we present a different perspective on GNP by asking who buys the output, rather than who receives the income. More technically, we look at the demand for output and speak of the components of *gross national expenditure (GNE)*. Total demand is made up of four components: (1) consumption spending by households; (2) investment spending by businesses; (3) government (federal, provincial and municipal) expenditure on goods and services; and (4) net foreign demand. We shall now look more closely at each of these components.

Consumption

Table 2-6 presents a breakdown of gross national expenditure in 1983 by components of demand. The table illustrates that the chief component of demand is consumption spending by the personal sector. This includes anything from food to golf lessons but involves also, as we shall see in discussing investment, consumer spending on durable goods such as automobiles, spending which might be regarded as investment rather than consumption.

TABLE 2-6   COMPONENTS OF GROSS NATIONAL EXPENDITURE, 1983 (billions of dollars)

Personal consumption expenditure		$229.0	58.9%
Gross business investment		63.8	16.4
Government exp. on goods and services		94.6	24.3
Net exports of goods and services			
Exports	$108.2		
Less imports	107.5	.7	.2
Residual error of estimate		.5	.2
Gross national expenditure (GNE)		$388.7	100.0%

Source: Statistics Canada, 11-003.

Government

Next in importance we have government expenditure on goods and services. Here we have such items as national defence expenditures, road paving by provincial and municipal governments, and salaries of govern-

ment employees. It is important to note here that the government component of GNE is expenditure on *goods and services* and excludes transfer
payments. For all levels of government in 1983 the transfer component of
spending amounted to about $50 billion, so that total budgetary spending
was about $144 billion.

Investment

Gross business investment is an item that requires some definitions. First,
throughout this book, we will mean by investment additions to the physical stock of capital. As we use the term, investment does *not* include
buying a bond or purchasing stock in General Motors. In practice, investment includes expenditure on machinery and equipment, nonresidential
construction, residential construction, and additions to business inventories of goods. The classification of spending as consumption or investment
remains to a significant extent a matter of convention. From the economic
point of view, there is little difference between a household building up an
inventory of peanut butter and a grocery store doing the same. Nevertheless,
in the national income accounts, the individual's purchase is treated as a
personal consumption expenditure, whereas the store's purchase is treated
as investment in the form of inventory investment. Although these border-
line cases clearly exist, we can retain as a simple rule of thumb that investment is associated with the business sector's adding to the physical
stock of capital, including inventories.

Similar issues arise in the treatment of household sector expenditures.
For instance, how should we treat purchases of automobiles by households?
Since automobiles usually last for several years, it would seem sensible to
classify household purchases of automobiles as investment. We would
then treat the *use* of automobiles as providing consumption services. (We
could think of imputing a rental income to owner-occupied automobiles.)
However, the convention is to treat all household expenditures as consumption spending. This is not quite so bad as it might seem, since the
accounts do separate out households' purchases of durable goods like cars
and refrigerators from their other purchases. There is thus information in
the accounts on those parts of household spending that, with considerable
justification, could be categorized as investment spending. When consumer
spending decisions are studied in detail, expenditures on consumer durables are usually treated separately.

The convention that is adopted with respect to the household sector's
purchases of houses also deserves comment. The accounts treat the building of a house as investment by the business sector. When the house is sold
to a private individual, the transaction is treated as the transfer of an asset,
and not then an act of investment. Even if a house is custom-built by the
owner, the accounts treat the builder who is employed by the owner as

undertaking the act of investment in building the house. The investment is thus attributed to the business sector.

In passing, we note that in Table 2-6, investment is defined as "gross." It is gross in the sense that depreciation is not deducted. Net investment is gross investment minus depreciation. Thus NNP is equal to net investment plus the other categories of spending in Table 2-6.

Net Exports

The item net exports appears in Table 2-6 to show the effects of foreign trade on the demand for domestic output. Exports are added in as they represent demand by foreigners for our goods. Imports are subtracted out since they represent the part of domestic spending that is not for domestically produced goods. The practice in the national accounts is to include under consumption, investment and government expenditure all spending by Canadian residents both on domestically produced and foreign goods. To obtain total spending on domestically produced goods (GNE), imports are subtracted out.

The point can be illustrated with an example. Assume that instead of having spent $229 billion, the personal sector had spent $2 billion more. What would GNP have been? If we assume that government and investment spending had been the same as in Table 2-6, we might be tempted to say that GNP would have been $2 billion higher. That is correct if all the additional spending had fallen on our goods. The other extreme, however, is the case where all the additional spending falls on imports. In that event, consumption would be up $2 billion *and* net exports would be down $2 billion, with no net effect on GNP.

2-4   REAL AND NOMINAL GNE

Nominal GNE measures the value of output in a given period in the prices of that period or, as it is sometimes put, in *current dollars*. Thus 1985 nominal GNE measures the value of the goods produced in 1985 at the market prices that prevailed in 1985, and 1976 GNE measures the value of goods produced in 1976, at the market prices that prevailed in 1976. Nominal GNE changes from year to year for two reasons. The first is that the physical output of goods changes. The second is that market prices change. As an extreme and unrealistic example, one could imagine the economy producing exactly the same output in two years, between which all prices have doubled. Nominal GNE in the second year would be double nominal GNE in the first year, even though the physical output of the economy has not changed at all.

Real GNE measures changes in *physical* output in the economy between different time periods by valuing all goods produced in the two periods *at the same prices,* or in *constant dollars.* Real GNE is now measured in the national income accounts in the prices of 1971. That means that, in calculating real GNE, today's physical output is multiplied by the prices that prevailed in 1971 to obtain a measure of what today's output would have been worth had it been sold at the prices of 1971.

We return to the simple example of Table 2-1 to illustrate the calculation of real GNP. The hypothetical outputs and prices of bananas and oranges in 1971 and 1985 are shown in the first two columns of Table 2-7. Nominal GNP in 1971 was $9, and nominal GNP in 1985 was $21, or an increase in nominal GNP of 133 percent. However, much of the increase in nominal GNP is purely a result of the increase in prices between the 2 years and does not reflect an increase in physical output. When we calculate real GNP in 1985 by valuing 1985 output in the prices of 1971, we find real GNP equal to $11, which is an increase of 22 percent rather than 133 percent. The 22 percent increase is a better measure of the increase in physical output of the economy than the 133 percent increase.

TABLE 2-7   REAL AND NOMINAL GNE: AN ILLUSTRATION

1971 nominal GNE		1985 nominal GNE		1985 real GNE*	
15 bananas		20 bananas		20 bananas	
at $0.10	$1.50	at $0.30	$ 6.00	at $0.10	$ 2.00
50 oranges		60 oranges		60 oranges	
at $0.15	$7.50	at $0.25	$15.00	at $0.15	$ 9.00
	$9.00		$21.00		$11.00

*Measured in 1971 prices

We see from the table that the output of bananas rose by 33 percent, while the output of oranges increased by 20 percent from 1971 to 1985. We should thus expect our measure of the increase in real output to be somewhere between 20 percent and 33 percent, as it is.[6]

Figure 2-3 shows the behaviour of real and nominal GNE over the past few years. It is particularly noteworthy that nominal GNE rose continuously during the period, even while real GNE fell as it did, for example, during 1982. It would clearly be a mistake to regard the increases in nominal GNE as indicating that the performance of the economy was improving during 1982 despite the fall in physical output. Real GNP is the better measure of the performance of the economy in producing goods and services, and it is the measure we use in comparing output in different years.

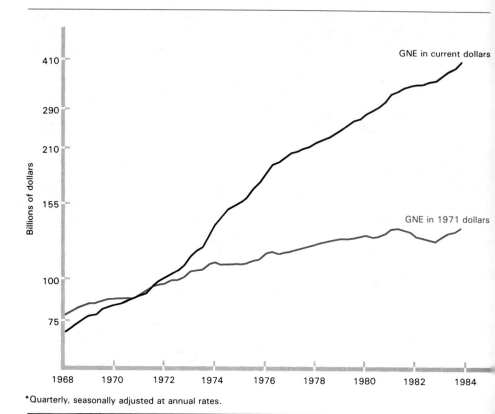

*Quarterly, seasonally adjusted at annual rates.

FIGURE 2-3   REAL AND NOMINAL GNE*
(*Source*: Statistics Canada, 11-003, 11-206)

Problems of GNP Measurement

GNP data are, in practice, used not only as a measure of how much is being produced, but also as a measure of the welfare of the residents of a country. Economists and politicians talk as if an increase in real GNP means that people are better off. But GNP data are far from perfect measures of either economic output or welfare.

Badly Measured Outputs

Most of the difficulties of measuring GNP arise because some outputs do not go through the market. We already noted that government production is valued at cost. That is because much of government output is not sold in the market, nor is anything comparable available that would make it possible to estimate the value of government output. How would we measure the value of output of safety from criminals that police expenditures are supposed to produce?

But there is also a conceptual problem with much of government output. We include in GNP the value of wages paid for the police and the defence forces. Suppose there was an improvement in public safety and police were taken out of the police force and put to work making candy — at their previous wage. GNP would not change. But the economy's output of useful goods and services certainly would seem to rise.

The problem in this case is that we generally do not deduct negative outputs, or *bads*, from GNP. We do not attempt to value the decline in public safety that requires increased police forces. Nor do we deduct from GNP the value of pollution produced by factories and cars. These are bads, but they do not show up in the GNP accounts. If we were somehow able to value the amount of public safety provided by society, then a shift of labour out of the police force resulting from an increase in public safety would indeed show up as an increase in GNP. Similarly, the improvement in the quality of the environment in the 1970s would show up as having raised output over that decade.

Other nonmarket activities, including do-it-yourself work and volunteer activities, are also excluded from GNP. The most important category here is the value of work done in the home by housepersons. Measured GNP would increase if someone stopped cleaning the house by himself and instead hired a cleaning service to do the same thing. But the output of the economy has not really risen.

Thus real GNP suffers from weaknesses even as a measure of goods and services produced in the economy.

Real GNP as a Measure of Well-being

The second use of GNP is as a *measure of economic welfare* or well-being of the residents of a country. When GNP rises, it is assumed that people are better off. Of course, it is necessary first to divide real GNP by the number of people to use GNP in this sense: it is per capita (per person) GNP that is used as a welfare measure.

The difficulties of measuring nonmarket outputs already suggest that real GNP per capita is an imperfect measure of economic well-being. In addition, real GNP has to be adjusted to include the value of leisure. If the value of output falls because people have decided they would like to work less, that is not necessarily a sign that they are worse off. Much economic progress over the last century is reflected in a falling workweek. One hundred years ago the average workweek was well above 60 hours and in manufacturing it was higher still. Now it is under 40 hours. Real GNP should be adjusted to include the value of the increased leisure people have as a result of the declining workweek, if GNP is to be used as a measure of economic welfare.

An ideal measure of welfare is not available, and thus we continue to use real GNP as the chief measure of the economy's output and, although we know its shortcomings, as a measure of how the economy is peforming in providing material well-being. The justification for doing so, in addition to the lack of choice, is that, in the short run, changes in real GNP are probably in the same direction as changes in welfare.

2-5   PRICE INDEXES

The calculation of real GNE gives us a useful measure of inflation known as the *GNE deflator*. Returning to the hypothetical example of Table 2-2, we can get a measure of inflation between 1971 and 1985 by comparing the value of 1985 GNP in 1985 prices and 1971 prices. The ratio of nominal to real GNE in 1985 is 1.91 ($= 21 \div 11$). In other words, output is 91 percent higher in 1985 when it is valued using the higher prices of 1985 than valued in the lower prices of 1971. We ascribe the 91 percent increase to price changes, or inflation, over the period 1971–1985.

The GNE deflator is the ratio of nominal GNE in a given year to real GNE, and it is a measure of inflation from the period from which the base prices for calculating real GNE are taken, to the current period. Since the GNE deflator is based on a calculation involving all the goods produced in the economy, it is a very widely based price index that is frequently used to measure inflation.

The Consumer Price Index

The *consumer price index (CPI)* measures the cost of buying a fixed bundle of goods, representative of the purchases of consumers. The GNE deflator differs in three main ways from the CPI. First, it measures the prices of a much wider group of goods than the CPI, which is based on the market basket of goods purchased by an average consumer. Second, the CPI measures the cost of a given basket of goods, which is the same from year to year. The basket of goods included in the GNE deflator, however, differs from year to year, depending on what is produced in the economy in each year. The goods valued in the deflator in a given year are the goods that are produced in the economy in that year. When wheat production is high, wheat receives a relatively large weight in the computation of the GNE deflator. By contrast, the CPI measures the cost of a fixed bundle of goods that does not vary over time.[7] Third, the CPI directly includes prices of imports, whereas the deflator includes only prices of goods *produced* in Canada. The behaviours of the two main indexes used to compute inflation, the GNE deflator and the CPI, accordingly differ from time to time. For example, at times when the price of imported oil rises rapidly, the CPI is likely to rise faster than the deflator.

Industry Selling Price Index

A third important price index is the industry selling price index. Like the CPI, this is a measure of the cost of a given basket of goods. It differs from the CPI partly in its coverage, which includes, for example, semifinished goods. It differs, too, in that it is designed to measure prices at an early stage of the distribution system. Whereas the CPI measures prices where households actually do their spending, that is at the retail level, the industry selling price index is constructed from prices at the level of the first significant commercial transaction. This difference is important because it makes the latter a relatively flexible price index and one that signals changes in the general price level, or the CPI, some time before they actually materialize.

TABLE 2-8   THREE PRICE INDEXES (1971 = 100)

	Consumer Price Index	Industry Selling Price Index	GNE Deflator
1961	75.0	82.4	72.4
1971	100.0	100.0	100.0
1981	237.0	272.3	249.1
1983	277.7	298.8	290.0
percent increase 1961–1983	270%	263%	301%

Source: Statistics Canada, 11-003, 11-505.

Table 2-8 shows the CPI, the industry selling price index, and the GNE deflator for the last 23 years. We note from the table that all three indexes have been increasing throughout the period. This is a reflection of the fact that the average price of goods has been rising, whatever basket we look at. We note, too, that the cumulative increase (price 1983/price 1961) differs across indexes. This difference occurs because the indexes represent the prices of different commodity baskets.[8]

2-6   SOME IMPORTANT IDENTITIES

In this section we formalize the discussion of the preceding sections by writing down a set of relationships which we use extensively in Chapter 3. We introduce here some notation and conventions that we follow throughout the book.

For analytical work in the following chapters, we simplify our analysis by omitting the distinction between GNP and national income. For the most part we disregard depreciation and thus the difference between GNP and NNP, as well as the difference between gross and net investment. We refer simply to investment spending. We also disregard indirect taxes and non government transfer payments. With these conventions in mind *we refer to national income and GNP interchangeably as income or output.* These simplifications have no serious consequence and are made only for expositional convenience. Finally, and only for a brief while, we omit both the government and foreign sector. Thus the assumptions we are making conform to those of the circular flow diagram, Figure 2-1.

A Simple Economy

We denote the value of output in our simple economy, which has neither a government nor foreign trade, by Y. Consumption is denoted by C and investment spending by I. The first key identity we want to establish is that between output produced and output sold. Output produced is Y, which can be written in terms of the components of demand as the sum of consumption and investment spending. (Remember, we have assumed away the government and foreign sectors.) Accordingly, we can write the identity of output sold and output produced as[9]

$$Y \equiv C + I \qquad (7)$$

Now the question is whether Equation (7) is really an identity. Is it inevitably true that all output produced is either consumed or invested? After all, do not firms sometimes make goods that they are unable to sell? The answer to each of the questions is yes. Firms do sometimes make output that they cannot sell, and that accumulates on their shelves. *However, we count the accumulation of inventories as part of investment* (as if the firms sold the goods to themselves to add to their inventories), and therefore, all output is either consumed or invested. Note that we are talking here about *actual* investment, which includes investment in inventories that firms might be very unhappy to make. Because of the way investment is defined, output produced is identically equal to output sold.

Identity (7) formalizes the basis of Table 2-6 (we all still assuming away the government and external sectors). The next step is to draw up a corresponding identity for Table 2-5 and identity (6), which examined the disposition of personal income. For that purpose, it is convenient to ignore the existence of corporations and consolidate or add together the entire private sector. Using this convention, we know that private sector income is Y, since the private sector receives as income the value of goods and services produced. Why? Because who else would get it? There is no government or external sector yet. Now the private sector receives, as disposable personal income, the whole of income Y. How will that income be allocated? Part will be spent on consumption, and part will be saved. Thus we can write

$$Y \equiv S + C \tag{8}$$

where S denotes private sector saving. Identity (8) tells us that the whole of income is allocated to either consumption or saving.

Next, identities (7) and (8) can be combined to read:

$$C + I \equiv Y \equiv C + S \tag{9}$$

The left-hand side of Equation (9) shows the components of demand, and the right-hand side shows the allocation of income. The identity emphasizes that output produced is equal to output sold. The value of output produced is equal to income received, and income received, in turn, is spent on goods or saved.

The identity in Equation (9) can be slightly reformulated to look at the relation between saving and investment. Subtracting consumption from each part of Equation (9), we have

$$I \equiv Y - C \equiv S \tag{10}$$

Identity (10) is an important result. It shows first that in this simple economy, saving is identically equal to income less consumption. This result is not new, since we have already seen it in Equation (8). The new part concerns the identity of the left and right sides: *investment is identically equal to saving*.

One can think of what lies behind this relationship in a variety of ways. In a very simple economy, the only way the individual can save is by undertaking an act of physical investment — by storing grain or building an irrigation channel. In a slightly more sophisticated economy, one could think of investors financing their investing by borrowing from individuals who save.

However, it is important to recognize that Equation (10) expresses the identity between investment and saving, and that some of the investment might well be undesired inventory investment, occurring as a result of mistakes by producers who expected to sell more than they actually did. The identity is really only a reflection of our definitions — output less consumption is investment, output is income, and income less consumption is saving. Even so, we shall find that identity (10) plays a key role in Chapter 3.

Reintroducing the Government and Foreign Trade

We can now reintroduce the government sector and the external sector. First, for the government we denote purchases of goods and services by G

and all taxes by TA. Transfers to the private sector (including interest) are denoted by TR. Net exports (exports minus imports) are denoted by NX.

We return to the identity between output produced and sold, taking account now of the additional components of demand G and NX. Accordingly, we restate the content of Table 2-6 by writing

$$Y \equiv C + I + G + NX \tag{11}$$

Once more we emphasize that in Equation (11) we use actual investment in the identity and thus do not rule out the possibility that firms might not at all be content with the investment. Still, as an accounting identity, Equation (11) will hold.

Next we turn to the derivation of the very important relation between output and disposable income. Now we have to recognize that part of income is spent on taxes, and that the private sector receives net transfers TR in addition to national income. Disposable income is thus equal to income plus transfers less taxes:

$$YD \equiv Y + TR - TA \tag{12}$$

We have written YD to denote disposable income. Disposable income, in turn, is allocated to consumption and saving, so that we can write

$$YD \equiv C + S \tag{13}$$

Combining identities (12) and (13) allows us to write consumption as the difference between income, plus transfers minus taxes, and saving:

$$C + S \equiv YD \equiv Y + TR - TA \tag{14}$$

$$\text{or} \qquad C \equiv YD - S \equiv Y + TR - TA - S \tag{14a}$$

Identity (14a) states that consumption is disposable income less savings, or alternatively, that consumption is equal to income plus transfers less taxes and saving. Now we use the right-hand side of Equation (14a) to substitute for C in identity (11). With some rearrangement we obtain

$$S - I \equiv (G + TR - TA) + NX \tag{15}$$

Saving, Investment, the Government Budget, and Trade

Identity (15) cannot be overemphasized. Its importance arises from the fact that the first set of terms on the right-hand side $(G + TR - TA)$ is the *government budget deficit*. $(G + TR)$ is equal to government[10] purchases of goods and services (G) plus government transfer payments (TR), which is total government spending. TA is the amount of taxes received by the government. The difference $(G + TR - TA)$ is the excess of government spending over its receipts, or its budget deficit. The second term on the right-hand side is the excess of exports over imports, or the *trade surplus*.

Thus identity (15) states that the excess of savings over investment $(S - I)$ of the private sector is equal to the government budget deficit plus the trade surplus. The identity correctly suggests that there are important relations among the accounts of the private sector, $S - I$, the government budget, $G + TR - TA$, and the external sector. For instance, if, for the private sector, savings is equal to investment, then the government's budget deficit (surplus) is reflected in an equal external deficit (surplus).

Table 2-9 shows the significance of Equation (15). To fix ideas, suppose that private sector saving S is equal to $30 (billion). In the first two rows we assume that exports are equal to imports, so that the trade surplus is zero. In row 1, we assume the government budget is balanced. Investment accordingly has to equal $30 billion. In the next row we assume the government budget deficit is $10 billion. *Given the level of saving* of $30 billion and a zero trade balance, it has to be true that investment is now lower by $10 billion. Rows 3 and 4 show how these relationships are affected when there is a trade surplus.

To interpret these relationships, realize that any sector that spends more than it receives in income has to borrow to pay for the excess spending. The private sector has three ways of disposing of its saving. It can make loans to the government, which thereby pays for the excess of its spending over the income it receives from taxes. Or it can lend to foreigners, who are buying more from us than we are buying from them. They therefore are earning less from us than they need to pay for the goods they buy from us, and we have to lend to cover the difference. Or it can lend to business firms which use the funds for investment.

TABLE 2-9   THE BUDGET DEFICIT, TRADE, SAVING,
AND INVESTMENT

S	I	BD (budget deficit)	NX (trade surplus)
30	30	0	0
30	20	10	0
30	25	0	5
30	15	10	5

In Table 2-9 we take saving as fixed at $30 billion. When the budget and trade are balanced, the private sector has to lend the $30 billion to firms, which invest that amount. But suppose the government runs a budget deficit of $10 billion. Then the private sector has to lend $10 billion to government to cover its excess of spending over revenue. Only $20 billion is left to lend to firms for investment. Similarly, if we export more than we import, foreigners need to borrow from us to pay for the excess of what they buy from us over what they sell to us. In rows 3 and 4 we are using $5 billion of our saving to lend to foreigners. Then only $25 billion is left to lend either to firms or to the government.

2-7   SUMMARY

1   As the circular flow diagram shows, output is equal to income (GNP) and spending (GNE).

2   GNP is the value of the output of final goods and services produced by domestically owned factors of production, measured at market prices.

3   Gross domestic product is the value of output produced within the country. It differs from GNP since it includes net payments to nonresident factors of production.

4   National income is equal to GNP minus depreciation and indirect taxes.

5   National income is equal to the incomes received in the economy, valued at factor cost.

6   Gross national expenditure is conveniently divided into consumption, investment, government expenditure on goods and services, and net exports. The division between consumption and investment in the national income accounts is somewhat arbitrary at the edges.

7   Real GNE is the value of the economy's output measured in the prices of some base year. Real GNP comparisons, based on the same set of prices for valuing output, provide a better measure of the change in the economy's physical output than nominal GNP comparisons, which also reflect inflation.

8   The GNE deflator is the ratio of nominal to real GNP. It reflects the general rise in prices from the base date by which real GNP is valued. Other frequently used price indexes are the consumer and producer price indexes.

9   The excess of the private sector's saving over investment is equal to the sum of the budget deficit and the foreign trade surplus.

10   For the remainder of the book we use a simplified model for expositional convenience. We assume away depreciation, indirect taxes,

business transfer payments, and the difference between households and corporations. For this simplified model, Figure 2-4 and Equation (16) review the *basic macroeconomic identity:*

$$C + G + I + NX \equiv Y \equiv YD + (TA - TR) \equiv C + S + (TA - TR) \quad (16)$$

The left-hand side is the demand for output by components which is identically equal to output supplied. Output supplied is equal to income. Disposable income is equal to income plus transfers less taxes. Disposable income is allocated to saving and consumption.

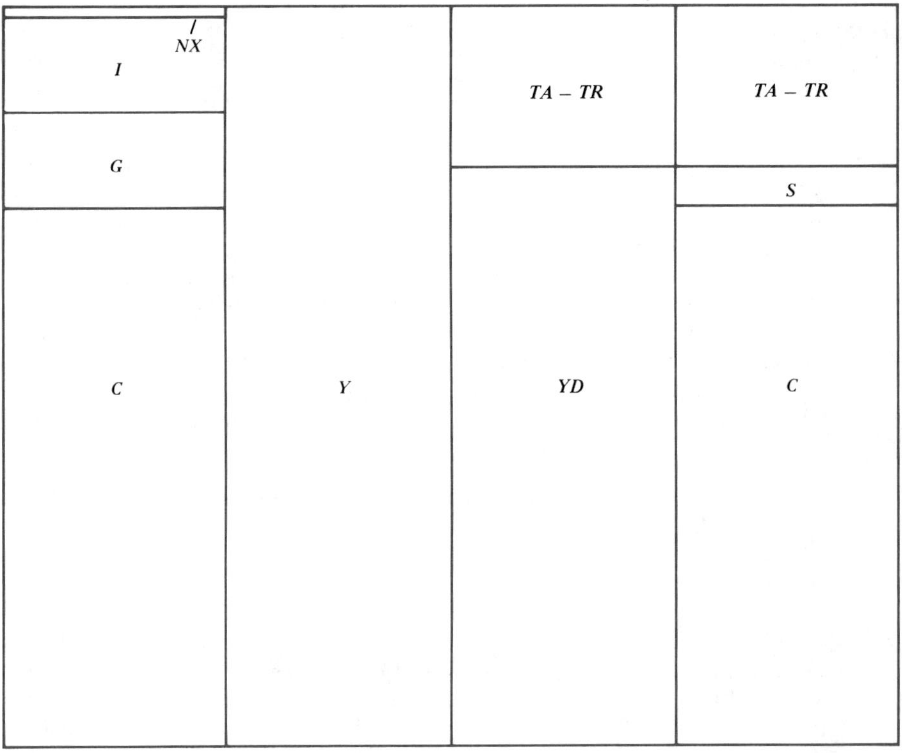

FIGURE 2-4   THE BASIC MACROECONOMIC IDENTITY.

$$C + G + I + NX \equiv Y \equiv YD + (TA - TR) \equiv C + S + (TA - TR) \quad (16)$$

The left-hand side is the demand for output by components which is identically equal to output supplied. Output supplied is equal to income. Disposable income is equal to income plus transfers less taxes. Disposable income is allocated to saving and consumption.

KEY TERMS

Gross national product (GNP)
Final goods
Value added
Market prices
Factor cost
Gross domestic product (GDP)
Net national product (NNP)
Depreciation
National income
Factor shares
Personal income
Transfers

Personal disposable income
Gross national expenditure (GNE)
Consumption
Government expenditure on goods and
   services
Investment
Net exports
Consumer durables
Real GNE
GNE deflator
Consumer price index
Government budget deficit

PROBLEMS

1 Show from national income accounting that:
   (a) An increase in taxes (while transfers remain constant) must im-
       ply a change in the trade balance, government purchases or the
       saving-investment balance.
   (b) An increase in disposable income must imply an increase in
       consumption or an increase in saving.
   (c) An increase in both consumption and saving must imply an
       increase in disposable income.

2 The following is information from the national income accounts for
   a hypothetical country:

GNP	240
Gross investment	40
Net Investment	15
Consumption	150
Government expenditure on goods and services	48
National income	190
Wages and salaries	146
Net income of unincorporated business	16
Dividends	5
Interest income	13
Government budget surplus	−15
Interest on government debt	7
Government transfer payments	25

   What is:
   (a) NNP?
   (b) Net exports?
   (c) Indirect taxes?

(d) Corporate profits?
(e) Personal income?
(f) Personal disposable income?
(g) Personal saving?

3 What would happen to GNP if the government hired unemployed workers, who had been receiving amount TR in unemployment benefits, as government employees to do nothing, and now paid them TR? Explain.

4 What is the difference in the national income accounts between:
(a) A firm's buying an auto for an executive and the firm's paying the executive additional income to buy himself a car?
(b) Your hiring your spouse (who takes care of the house) rather than just having him or her do the work without pay?
(c) Your deciding to buy a Canadian-made car rather than a German car?

5 Explain the following terms:
(a) Value added
(b) Factor cost
(c) Inventory investment
(d) GNE deflator

6 (a) In 1982 GNP was $356.6 billion and GDP was $369.8 billion. Why is there a difference?
(b) In 1982 NNP was $312.3 billion. What accounts for the difference between GNP and NNP?

7 This question deals with price index numbers. Consider a simple economy where only three items are in the CPI: food, housing, and entertainment (fun). Assume in the base period, say, 1967, the household consumed the following quantities at the then prevailing prices:

	Quantities	Prices per unit, $	Expenditure, $
Food	5	14	70
Housing	3	10	30
Fun	4	5	20
Total			120

(a) Define the consumer price index.
(b) Assume that the basket of goods that defines the CPI is as given in the table. Calculate the CPI for 1984 if the prices prevailing in 1984 are: food, $30 per unit; housing, $20 per unit; and fun, $6 per unit.
*(c) Show that the change in the CPI relative to the base year is a weighted average of the individual price changes, where the

weights are given by the base year expenditure shares of the various goods.

8 Here are some 1982 national accounts data, in billions:
   GNP = $356.6   Indirect taxes = $40.8
   NNP = $312.3   Residual error = – $.1
   (a) What are (*i*) depreciation and (*ii*) national income?
   (b) Why are indirect taxes deducted from NNP to get national income?

9 Refer to Table 2-3 to answer the following.
   (a) How would a shift by corporations from equity to debt finance affect the distribution of national income?
   (b) How would the incorporation of a business affect the table?
   (c) What difference would it make if some existing houses were owned by corporations instead of individuals?

10 Assume that GNP is $120, personal disposable income is $100, and the government budget deficit is $7. Consumption is $85 and the trade surplus is $2.
   (a) How large is saving *S*?
   (b) What is the size of investment *I*?
   (c) How large is government spending?

APPENDIX: PRICE INDEX FORMULAE

The CPI is a price index which compares the current and base year cost of a basket of goods of *fixed* composition. If we denote the base year quantities of the various goods by q_0^i and their base year prices by p_0^i, the cost of the basket in the base year is $\Sigma p_0^i q_0^i$, where the summation (Σ) is over all the goods in the basket. The cost of a basket of the *same* quantities but at today's prices is $\Sigma p_t^i q_0^i$, where p_t^i is today's price. The CPI is the ratio of today's cost to the base year cost, or

$$\text{Consumer price index} = \frac{\Sigma p_t^i q_0^i}{\Sigma p_0^i q_0^i} \times 100$$

This is a so-called *Laspeyres*, or *base-weighted*, price index.

The GNE deflator by contrast uses the weights of the *current* period to calculate the price index. Let q_t^i be the quantities of the different goods produced in the current year.

$$\text{GNE deflator} = \frac{\text{GNE measured in current prices}}{\text{GNE measured in base year prices}}$$

$$= \frac{\Sigma p_t^i q_t^i}{\Sigma p_0^i q_t^i} \times 100$$

This is known as a *Paasche*, or *current-weighted*, price index.

Comparing the two formulas we see that they differ only in that q_0^i, or the base year quantities, appears in both numerator and denominator of the CPI formula, whereas q_t^i appears in the formula for the deflator.

Problem: Calculate both Laspeyres and Paasche price indexes for the information in Table 2-7.

CHAPTER 2: FOOTNOTES

[1]How about the flour that is directly purchased by households for baking in the home? It is counted as a contribution toward GNP since it represents a final sale.

[2]Gross domestic product as published by Statistics Canada is measured at factor cost and therefore differs from GNP by the amount of indirect taxes as well.

[3]See section 2-1 above for a discussion of GNP vs. GDP which measures production within Canada using both Canadian and nonresident factors of production.

[4]GNP includes an estimate of the services homeowners receive by living in their homes. This is estimated by calculating the rent on an equivalent house. Thus the homeowner is treated as if she pays herself rent for living in her house.

[5]You might want to work out how Table 2-3 would be modified for each of the possibilities described in this sentence. Problem 9 asks for the answers.

[6]The increase in real GNE that is calculated depends on the prices that are used in the calculation. If you have a calculator, you might want to compare the increase in real GNE between 1971 and 1985 if the prices of 1985 are used to make the comparison. (Using 1985 prices, real GNE rises 23.5 percent from 1971 to 1985, compared with 22.2 percent using 1971 prices.) The ambiguities that arise in comparisons using different prices to calculate real GNE are an inevitable result of the attempt to use a single number to capture the increase in output of both bananas and oranges when those two components did not increase in the same proportion. However, the ambiguity is not a major concern when there is inflation at any substantial rate, and that is precisely when we most want to use real (rather than nominal) GNE to study the performance of the economy.

[7]Price indexes are, however, occasionally revised to change weights to reflect current expenditure patterns.

[8]The mechanics of price indexes are briefly described in the appendix to this chapter. Detailed discussion of the consumer price index can be found in Statistics Canada, 62-010.

[9]Throughout the book we distinguish identities from equations. Identities are statements that are *always* true because they are directly implied by definitions of variables or accounting relationships. They do not reflect any economic behaviour but are extremely useful in organizing our thinking. Identities, or definitions, are shown with the sign $\equiv$, and equations with the usual equality sign $=$.

[10]*Government* throughout this chapter means the federal government plus provincial and municipal governments. A breakdown by level of government can be found in Statistics Canada publications and Dept. of Finance, *Economic Review*.

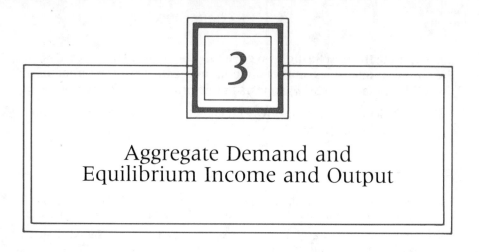

3

Aggregate Demand and
Equilibrium Income and Output

In Chapter 2 we studied the measurement of national income and output (GNP). With these fundamental concepts, we are now able to begin our study of the factors that determine the level of national income and product. Ultimately, we want to know why real GNP sometimes falls (and the rate of unemployment rises), as it did in 1982, and why at other times income rises very rapidly (and unemployment falls), as it did in 1972–1973.

We also want to know what determines the rate of inflation. Why was it so high in 1975 and 1981? Why did it rise from 1978 to 1981? We want to know whether public policies, such as changes in government spending and tax rates, or changes in the growth rate of the money supply, or changes in interest rates, can affect the level of income and the rates of inflation and unemployment. And if they can, we want to know how.

The study of those questions occupies the rest of the book. But we shall proceed slowly. We begin in this chapter with a simplified model of the economy that isolates the crucial concept of *aggregate demand*, while still omitting both some factors that affect aggregate demand and considerations of aggregate supply. In later chapters we gradually introduce those other factors. By the time we have completed Chapter 15, we shall be able to understand the behaviour of the key macroeconomic variables — the rates of unemployment and inflation and the level of GNP.

Our discussion is based on the macroeconomic identities in Equation (16) of Chapter 2 and in Figure 2-4. First, GNP is equal to total spending on goods and services, consisting of consumption C, investment I, government expenditure on goods and services G, and net exports NX. Second, GNP is also equal to income received in the economy.[1] Income, in turn, increased by transfers TR and reduced by taxes TA, is allocated to consumption C and saving S.

Thus: $$C + I + G + NX \equiv Y \equiv C + (TA - TR) + S$$

In this chapter we go beyond that *accounting identity* to begin our study of the factors that determine the level of national product or output. In particular, we focus on the interactions between the level of output and aggregate demand. The main point of the chapter is to show that *there is a single level of equilibrium output at which the aggregate (total) demand for goods and services is equal to the level of output.*

To begin with, we simplify our task by discussing a hypothetical world without a government ($G \equiv TA \equiv TR \equiv 0$) and without foreign trade ($NX \equiv 0$). In such a world, the accounting identity simplifies to

$$C + I \equiv Y \equiv C + S \tag{1}$$

where Y denotes the *real* value of output and income. Throughout this chapter a change in a macroeconomic aggregate is a change in its *real* value. For instance, when we speak of a change in consumption spending, we mean a change in real consumption spending.

The key concept of *equilibrium output* is introduced immediately, in Section 3-1. To keep the analysis as simple as possible, we assume to begin with that the demand for goods is *autonomous*—that is, independent of the level of income.[2] In fact, though, increases in income increase the demand for consumption goods. Accordingly, in Section 3-2 we extend the basic analysis by introducing the *consumption function*, which relates the demand for consumption goods to the level of income. In Sections 3-2 and 3-3 we derive explicit formulas for the equilibrium level of income.

The government sector is reintroduced in Section 3-4, which includes the first discussion of fiscal policy. The government budget is examined in Section 3-5 and foreign trade is introduced in Section 3-6.

3-1   EQUILIBRIUM OUTPUT

In this chapter and the next we assume a world where all prices are given and constant.[3] In terms of Figure 1-10, we are dealing with a situation in which the aggregate supply curve is horizontal.

If firms could supply any amount of output at the prevailing level of prices, what would determine the level of output actually produced? *Demand* must enter the picture. We would expect firms to produce at a level just sufficient to meet demand.

To develop this point, we define the concepts of *aggregate demand* and *equilibrium output*.

Aggregate Demand

Aggregate demand is the total amount of goods demanded in the economy. In general, the quantity of goods demanded, or aggregate demand, depends on the level of income in the economy and perhaps — as we shall see later — on interest rates. But for now we shall assume that the amount of goods demanded is constant, independent of the level of income.

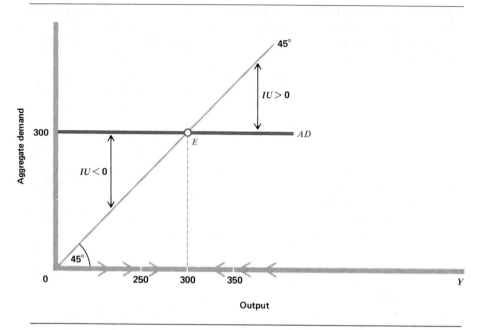

FIGURE 3-1   EQUILIBRIUM WITH CONSTANT AGGREGATE DEMAND. Aggregate demand is shown by the *AD* line, and is equal to 300. Output is at its equilibrium level when it is equal to aggregate demand, equal to 300. Thus the equilibrium is shown at point *E*. At any other output level, inventories are changing in a way that causes firms to change their production in a direction that moves output toward the equilibrium level.

Aggregate demand is shown in Figure 3-1 by the horizontal line AD. In the diagram, aggregate demand is equal to 300 (billion dollars). This means that the total amount of goods demanded in the economy is $300 billion, independent of the level of income.

But if the quantity of goods demanded is constant, independent of the level of income, what determines the actual level of income? We have to turn to the concept of equilibrium output.

Equilibrium Output

Output is at its *equilibrium* level when the quantity of output produced is equal to the quantity demanded. An equilibrium situation is one which no forces are causing to change. We now explain why output is at its equilibrium level when it is equal to aggregate demand.

In Figure 3-1 we show the level of output on the horizontal axis. The 45° line serves as a reference line in that it translates any horizontal distance into an equal vertical distance. For any given level of output *Y* on the horizontal axis, the 45° line gives the level of aggregate demand that is equal to that level of output. For instance, at point E, both output and aggregate demand are equal to 300.

Point E is the point of equilibrium output, at which the quantity of output produced is equal to the quantity demanded. To understand why this should be the equilibrium level of output, suppose that firms were producing some other amount, say, 350 units. Then output would exceed demand. Firms would be unable to sell all they produce, and would find their warehouses filling with inventories of unsold goods. They would then cut their output. This is shown by the horizontal arrow pointing left at the output level of 350 on the horizontal axis.

Similarly, if output were less than 300, say, at 250, firms would either run out of goods or be running down their inventories. They would therefore increase output, as shown by the horizontal arrow pointing to the right from the output level of 250.

Thus at point E, the equilibrium level of output, firms are selling as much as they produce, people are buying the amount they want to purchase, and there is no tendency for the level of output to change. At any other level of output, the pressure from increasing or declining inventories causes firms to change the level of output.

Equilibrium Output and the National Income Identity

We have defined equilibrium output as that level of output at which aggregate demand for goods is equal to output. To clarify that definition, we have to dispose of an unsettling issue that arises from the accounting identity in Equation (1), derived from our study of national income accounting. The identity in Equation (1) states that demand, $C + I$, is *identically* equal to supply Y, *whatever* the level of output. That seems to mean that demand equals supply at *any* level of output, so that any level of output could be the equilibrium level.

The issue is resolved by recalling that aggregate demand is the amount of goods people *want to buy*, whereas in the national income accounts investment and consumption are the amounts of the goods *actually* bought for investment or consumption, whether or not people wanted to or planned to buy them. In particular, the investment measured in Equation (1) includes *involuntary*, or *unintended* (or *undesired*), inventory changes, which occur when firms find themselves selling more or less goods than they had planned to sell. Similarly, if households cannot buy all the goods they want, the consumption measured in Equation (1) will be different from planned consumption.

We have to make a distinction between the actual aggregate demand that is measured in an accounting context and the relevant economic concept of planned (desired, intended) aggregate demand.

Actual aggregate demand $(C + I)$ is, by the accounting identity in Equation (1), equal to the level of output (Y). The output level is determined by firms. In deciding how much to produce, firms calculate how much investment, including inventory investment, they want to undertake. They also produce to meet the demand for consumption they forecast will be forthcoming from households. *Planned aggregate demand* consists of the amount of consumption that households plan to carry out plus the amount of investment planned by firms.[4]

If firms miscalculate households' consumption demands, planned aggregate demand does not equal actual aggregate demand. Suppose first that firms overestimate consumption demand. In terms of Figure 3-1, suppose that firms decide to produce 350 units of output, expecting to be able to sell that amount. However, aggregate demand is only 300. The firms thus sell 300 units of output. But they are left with 50, which they have to add to their inventories. It is as if they buy those extra 50 units of output themselves. In the national income accounts, additions to inventories count as investment. Of course, this is not *planned* or *desired* investment, but it does count as part of investment. Looking at the national income accounts for such an economy, we would see output equal to 350 and consumption plus investment equal to 350. But the equality of output and $(C + I)$ does not mean that 350 is the equilibrium level of output, because 50 units of investment were undesired additions to inventories.

When aggregate demand, the amount people *want* to buy, is not equal to output, there is unplanned inventory investment. We summarize this in Equation (2):

$$IU = Y - AD \qquad (2)$$

where *IU* is unplanned additions to inventory.

In terms of Figure 3-1, unplanned inventory investment is shown by the vertical arrows. When output exceeds 300, there is unplanned inventory investment. When output is less than 300, there are unplanned reductions in inventories.

An alternative way of seeing the link between the national income accounting relations and the economic concepts is in (2a). Here we state that actual output is equal to planned spending or aggregate demand plus involuntary inventory adjustment.

Output = Planned spending + Involuntary inventory adjustment (2a)

The *equilibrium* level of income is the level of income (or output) at which planned spending is equal to actual output, so that there is no involuntary inventory accumulation or decumulation.

Table 3-1 presents another way of looking at the equilibrium that is shown in both Figure 3-1 and Equation (2a). When income is below 300, aggregate demand exceeds output and inventories are being (involuntarily) reduced. When income exceeds 300, output exceeds aggregate demand and inventories are being (involuntarily) accumulated. Only at the output level of 300, when aggregate demand is equal to output, is there no involuntary accumulation or decumulation of inventories: output is then at the equilibrium level.

TABLE 3-1   EQUILIBRIUM, OUTPUT, AND INVOLUNTARY
             INVENTORY CHANGE

Output	Aggregate demand	Involuntary inventory changes
200	300	– 100
250	300	– 50
300	300	0
350	300	+ 50
400	300	+ 100

Equilibrium Output and Demand

We can now define equilibrium output more formally, using Equation (2). Output is at its equilibrium level when it is equal to aggregate demand, or when unplanned inventory accumulation is zero. That is, output is at its equilibrium level when

$$Y = AD \qquad\qquad (3)$$

There are three essential notions from this section:

1 Aggregate demand determines the equilibrium level of output.
2 At equilibrium, unintended changes in inventories are zero, and households consume the amount they want to consume.
3 An adjustment process for output based on unintended inventory changes will actually move output to its equilibrium level.[5]

Note, too, that the definition of equilibrium implies that actual spending on consumption and investment equals planned spending. In equilibrium, aggregate demand, which is planned spending, equals output. Since output identically equals income, we see also that *in equilibrium, planned spending equals income.*

3-2   THE CONSUMPTION FUNCTION AND AGGREGATE DEMAND

The preceding section studied the equilibrium level of output (and income) on the assumption that aggregate demand was simply a constant. In this section we extend the discussion to a more realistic specification of aggregate demand and begin to examine the economic variables that determine it.

In the simplified model we are working with, which excludes both the government and foreign trade, aggregate demand consists of the demands for consumption and investment. The demand for consumption goods is not in practice autonomous as we have so far assumed, but rather increases with income — families with higher income consume more than families with lower income, and countries where income is higher typically have higher levels of total consumption. The relationship between consumption and income is described by the *consumption function*.

The Consumption Function

We assume that consumption demand increases along with the level of income[6]:

$$C = \overline{C} + cY \qquad (4)$$
where $\qquad \overline{C} > 0 \qquad$ and $\qquad 0 < c < 1$

This consumption function is shown in Figure 3-2a. The *intercept* is $\overline{C}$, and the *slope* is c. The consumption function shows that consumption increases as income increases.

The consumption function [Equation (4)] implies that at low levels of income, consumption exceeds income, while at high levels of income, consumption falls short of income. This feature can be seen in Figure 3-2a, which includes a 45° line along which income is equal to consumption. At low levels of income, the consumption function lies above the 45° line, and consumption therefore exceeds income. As we shall see, that means that at low levels of income, the individual or household is dissaving. At high levels of income, the household saves, since consumption is less than income.

These relationships between income and consumption arise from the positive intercept $\overline{C}$ in Equation (5) and the fact that the coefficient c is less than unity. The coefficient c is sufficiently important to have a special name. The coefficient c is called the *marginal propensity to consume*. The marginal propensity to consume is the increase in consumption per unit increase in income. In our case, the marginal propensity to consume is less than 1, which implies that out of a dollar increase in income, only a fraction c is spent on consumption. For example, if c is 0.8, then when income rises by $1, consumption increases by $0.80.

Consumption and Saving

What happens to the rest, the fraction $(1 - c)$ that is not spent on consumption? If it is not spent, it must be saved. Income is either spent or saved; there are no other uses to which income can be put.

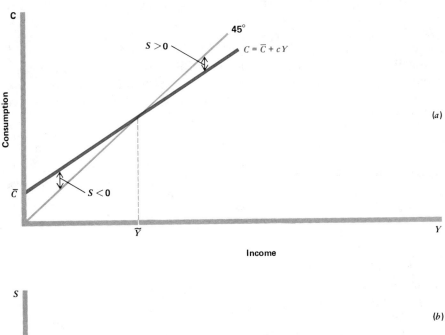

FIGURE 3-2   THE CONSUMPTION AND SAVING FUNCTIONS. (*a*) The consumption function shows consumption increasing with income. Its intercept is C, and its slope, the marginal propensity to consume, is c. At low levels of income, consumption is above the level of income, implying that people spend more than they earn. At higher levels of income, consumption is below the level of income, implying that people save part of their income. (*b*) The saving function in Figure 3-2*b* is consistent with the consumption function above it: at low income levels, saving is negative, and it is positive at higher income levels. At income level Y, saving is exactly zero.

More formally, we look at Equation (1), which says that income that is not spent on consumption is saved, or

$$S \equiv Y - C \tag{5}$$

What Equation (5) tells us is that by definition, *saving is equal to income minus consumption*. This means that we cannot postulate, in addition to the consumption function, an independent saving function and still expect consumption and saving to add up to income.

The consumption function in Equation (4), together with Equation (5), which we call the *budget constraint*, implies a saving function. The saving function is the function that relates the level of saving to the level of income. Substituting the consumption function in Equation (5) into the budget constraint in Equation (6) yields the saving function.

$$\begin{aligned} S &\equiv Y - C \\ &= Y - (\overline{C} + cY) \\ &= -\overline{C} + (1 - c)Y \end{aligned} \tag{6}$$

From Equation (6), saving is an increasing function of the level of income because the *marginal propensity to save*, $s = 1 - c$, is positive. For instance, suppose the marginal propensity to consume, c, is 0.8, meaning that 80 cents out of each extra dollar of income is consumed. Then the marginal propensity to save, s, is 0.2, meaning that the remaining 20 cents of each extra dollar of income is saved.

The saving function is the mirror image of the consumption function. At low levels of income, saving is negative, thus reflecting the fact that consumption exceeds income. An individual can have negative saving by using up his assets — his bank account or the stocks he owns — to pay for purchases in excess of his income. Conversely, at sufficiently high levels of income, saving becomes positive and thus reflects the fact that not all income is spent on consumption.

The interrelationship between the consumption and saving functions examined in Equation (6) can also be seen graphically in Figure 3-2, where the vertical distance between the consumption function and the 45° line at each level of income measures saving. Figure 3-2b shows the saving function that is derived from the consumption function in Figure 3-2a by plotting the vertical distance between income and consumption spending at each level of income. Of course, Figure 3-2b is merely a representation of Equation (6). Note that the slope of the saving function in Figure 3-2b is the marginal propensity to save, $s = 1 - c$, as defined above.

Planned Investment and Aggregate Demand

We have now specified one component of aggregate demand, consumption demand. We must also consider the determinants of investment spending, or an *investment function*. We cut short the discussion for the

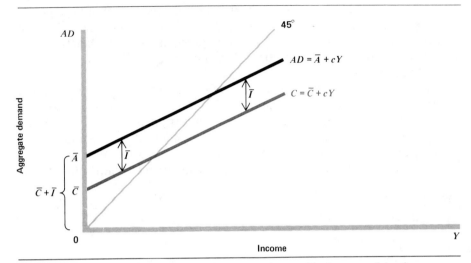

FIGURE 3-3   AGGREGATE DEMAND. Aggregate demand is the sum of the demands for consumption and investment goods. The consumption function is upward-sloping. Investment demand I is assumed constant and is added to consumption demand to obtain the level of aggregate demand at each level of income. The line AD shows how aggregate demand increases with income. Its slope is c, the marginal propensity to consume.

present by simply assuming that planned investment spending is at a constant level $\bar{I}$.[7]

Aggregate demand is the sum of consumption and investment demands:

$$\begin{aligned} AD &= C + I \\ &= \bar{C} + cY + \bar{I} \\ &= \bar{A} + cY \end{aligned} \tag{7}$$

The aggregate demand function (7) is shown in Figure 3-3. Part of aggregate demand, $\bar{A}\ [=(\bar{C} + \bar{I})]$ is independent of the level of income, or autonomous. But aggregate demand also depends on the level of income. It increases with the level of income, because consumption demand increases with income.

Equilibrium Income and Output

The next step is to use the aggregate demand function AD in Figure 3-3 and Equation (7) to determine the equilibrium level of output and income. We plot the AD schedule again in Figure 3-4.

Recall the basic point of this chapter: the equilibrium level of income is such that aggregate demand equals output (which in turn equals income). The 45° line in Figure 3-4 shows points at which output and aggregate demand are equal. The aggregate demand schedule in Figure 3-4 cuts the

45° line at E, and it is accordingly at E that aggregate demand is equal to output (equals income). Only at E, and at the corresponding equilibrium level of income and output, Y_0, does aggregate demand exactly equal output.[8] At that level of output and income, planned spending precisely matches production.

The arrows in Figure 3-4 indicate once again how we reach equilibrium. If firms expand production whenever they face unintended decreases in their inventory holdings, then they increase output at any level below Y_0, because below Y_0, aggregate demand exceeds output and inventories are declining. Conversely, for output levels above Y_0, firms find inventories piling up and therefore cut production. This process will lead us to the

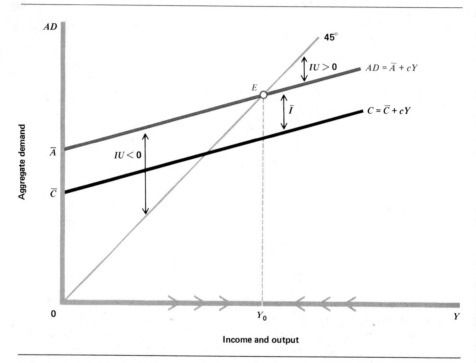

FIGURE 3-4   DETERMINATION OF EQUILIBRIUM INCOME AND OUTPUT. Output is at its equilibrium level when aggregate demand is equal to output. This occurs at point E, corresponding to the output (and income) level Y_0. At any higher level of output, aggregate demand is below the level of output, firms are unable to sell all they produce, and there is undesired accumulation of inventories. Firms therefore reduce output, as shown by the arrows. Similarly, at any level of output below Y_0, aggregate demand exceeds output, firms run short of goods to sell, and they therefore increase output. Only at the equilibrium output level Y_0 are firms producing the amount that is demanded, and there is no tendency for the level of output to change.

output level Y_0, where current production exactly matches planned aggregate spending. At output level Y_0, unintended inventory changes are equal to zero. Again, the arrows in Figure 3-4 represent the dynamic process by which the economy moves to the equilibrium level of output Y_0.[9]

The Formula for Equilibrium Output

The determination of equilibrium output in Figure 3-4 can also be described using Equation (7) and the equilibrium condition in the goods market:

$$Y = AD \tag{8}$$

This is the condition that output is equal to aggregate demand.

The level of aggregate demand AD is specified in Equation (7). Substituting for AD in Equation (8), we have the equilibrium condition as

$$Y = \overline{A} + cY \tag{9}$$

Since we have Y on both sides of the equilibrium condition in Equation (9), we can collect the terms and solve for the equilibrium level of income and output, denoted by Y_0:

$$Y - cY = \overline{A}$$

$$\text{or} \quad Y(1 - c) = \overline{A}$$

Thus the equilibrium level of income, at which aggregate demand equals output, is

$$Y_0 = \frac{1}{1 - c} \overline{A} \tag{10}$$

Figure 3-4 sheds light on the meaning of Equation (10). The position of the aggregate demand schedule is characterized by its slope c and intercept $\overline{A}$. The intercept $\overline{A}$ is the level of autonomous spending, that is, spending that is independent of the level of income. The other determinant of the equilibrium level of income is the marginal propensity to consume, c, which is the slope of the aggregate demand schedule.

Given the intercept, a steeper aggregate demand function — as would be implied by a higher marginal propensity to consume — implies a higher level of equilibrium income. Similarly, for a given marginal propensity to consume, a higher level of autonomous spending — in terms of Figure 3-4 a larger intercept — implies a higher equilibrium level of income. These results, suggested by Figure 3-4, are easily verified from Equation (10), which gives the formula for the equilibrium level of income.

Thus, the equilibrium level of output is higher, the larger the marginal propensity to consume, c, and the larger the level of autonomous spending, $\overline{A}$.

Saving and Investment

There is an alternative, useful formulation of the equilibrium condition that aggregate demand is equal to output. *In equilibrium, planned investment equals saving.* This condition applies only to an economy in which there is no government and no foreign trade.

To understand this relationship, return to Figure 3-4. The vertical distance between the aggregate demand and consumption schedules in that figure is equal to planned investment spending $\bar{I}$. Recall in addition (from Figure 3-2) that the vertical distance between the consumption schedule and the 45° line measures saving at each level of income.

We thus have two vertical distances: between the *AD* and *C* schedules in Figure 3-4 and between the 45° line and the *C* schedule in Figure 3-2a. The equilibrium level of income is one where *AD* crosses the 45° line, at *E*. Accordingly, at the equilibrium level of income — and only at that level — the two vertical distances are equal. Thus at the equilibrium level of income, saving equals (planned) investment. By contrast, above the equilibrium level of income Y_0, saving (the distance between the 45° line and the consumption schedule) exceeds investment, while below Y_0, investment exceeds saving.

Now, is the equality between saving and investment at equilibrium an essential characteristic of the equilibrium level of income, or is it a mere

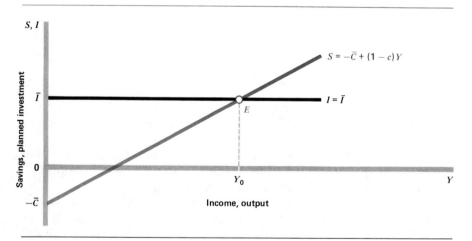

FIGURE 3-5   SAVING AND INVESTMENT. An alternative definition of the equilibrium level of output is that it occurs where saving is equal to (planned) investment. This is shown at point *E*, with corresponding output level Y_0. At higher levels of output, consumers want to save more than $\bar{I}$. They do not buy all of output, inventories accumulate, and actual investment is made equal to saving because firms undertake undesired inventory investment. They therefore cut output, and the economy moves to output level Y_0.

curiosity? It is an essential characteristic of equilibrium. We can see that by starting with the basic equilibrium condition, Equation (8), which states that in equilibrium, $Y = AD$. If we subtract consumption from both Y and AD, we realize that $Y - C$ is saving and $AD - C$ is planned investment. In symbols,

$$Y = AD$$
$$Y - C = AD - C$$
$$S = \bar{I} \tag{11}$$

Thus, the condition $S = \bar{I}$ is merely another way of stating the basic equilibrium condition.[10]

There is also a diagrammatic derivation of the equilibrium level of income that corresponds to the statement of the equilibrium condition in Equation (11) as the balance between saving and investment. In Figure 3-5, we show the saving function that was derived in Figure 3-2. We have drawn, too, planned investment spending, indicated by the horizontal line with intercept $\bar{I}$. Equilibrium income is shown at the level Y_0.

3-3   THE MULTIPLIER

In this section we develop an answer to the following question: By how much does a $1 increase in autonomous spending raise the equilibrium level of income?[11] There appears to be a simple answer. Since, in equilibrium, income equals aggregate demand, it would seem that a $1 increase in (autonomous) demand or spending should raise equilibrium income by $1. That answer is wrong. Let us now see why.

Suppose first that output increased by $1 to match the increased level of autonomous spending. This increase in output and income would in turn give rise to further *induced* spending as consumption rises because the level of income has risen. How much of the initial $1 increase in income would be spent on consumption? Out of an additional dollar of income, a fraction c is consumed. Assume then that production increases further to meet this induced expenditure, that is, that output and so income increase by $1 + c$. That will still leave us with an excess demand, because the very fact of an expansion in production and income by $1 + c$ will give rise to further induced spending. This story could clearly take a long time to tell. We seem to have arrived at an impasse where an expansion in output to meet excess demand leads to a further expansion in demand without an obvious end to the process.

It helps to lay out the various steps in this chain more carefully. We do this in Table 3-2. We start off in the first round with an increase in autonomous spending $\Delta \bar{A}$. Next we allow an expansion in production to meet exactly that increase in demand. Production accordingly expands by $\Delta \bar{A}$.

TABLE 3-2   THE MULTIPLIER

Round	Increase in demand this round	Increase in production this round	Total increase in income
1	$\Delta\overline{A}$	$\Delta\overline{A}$	$\Delta\overline{A}$
2	$c\Delta\overline{A}$	$c\Delta\overline{A}$	$(1+c)\Delta\overline{A}$
3	$c^2\Delta\overline{A}$	$c^2\Delta\overline{A}$	$(1+c+c^2)\Delta\overline{A}$
4	$c^3\Delta\overline{A}$	$c^3\Delta\overline{A}$	$(1+c+c^2+c^3)\Delta\overline{A}$
•	•	•	•
•	•	•	•
•	•	•	•
•	•	•	$\dfrac{1}{1-c}\Delta\overline{A}$
1	1.0	1.0	1.0
2	0.6	0.6	1.6
3	0.36	0.36	1.96
4	0.216	0.216	2.176
5	0.1296	0.1296	2.3056
•	•	•	•
•	•	•	•
•	•	•	•
•	•	•	2.5

This increase in production gives rise to an equal increase in income and, therefore, via the consumption function, $C = \overline{C} + cY$, gives rise in the second round to induced expenditures of size $c\,(\Delta\overline{A})$. Assume again that production expands to meet the increase in spending. The production adjustment this time is $c\,(\Delta\overline{A})$, and so is the increase in income. This gives rise to a third round of induced spending equal to the marginal propensity to consume times the increase in income $c\,(c\,\Delta\overline{A}) = c^2\,\Delta\overline{A}$. Careful inspection of the last term shows that induced expenditures in the third round are smaller than those in the second round. Since the marginal propensity to consume, c, is less than 1, the term c^2 is less than c. This can be seen also in the lower part of the table, where we assume $c = 0.6$ and show the steps corresponding to those in the upper part of the table.

If we write out the successive rounds of increased spending, starting with the initial increase in autonomous demand, we obtain

$$\begin{aligned}\Delta AD &= \Delta\overline{A} + c\,\Delta\overline{A} + c^2\,\Delta\overline{A} + c^3\,\Delta\overline{A} + \ldots \\ &= \Delta\overline{A}\,(1 + c + c^2 + c^3 + \ldots)\end{aligned} \qquad (12)$$

For a value of $c < 1$, the successive terms in the series become progressively smaller. In fact, we are dealing with a geometric series, the sum of which is calculated as

$$\Delta AD = \frac{1}{1-c}\,\Delta\overline{A} = \Delta Y_0 \qquad (13)$$

From Equation (13) therefore, the cumulative change in aggregate spending is equal to a multiple of the increase in autonomous spending. This could also have been deduced from Equation (10).[12] The multiple $1/(1 - c)$ is called the *multiplier*. The multiplier is the amount by which equilibrium output changes when autonomous aggregate demand increases by one unit. Because the multiplier exceeds unity, we know that a $1 change in autonomous spending increases equilibrium income and output by more than $1.[13] The concept of the multiplier is sufficiently important to create a new notation. Defining the multiplier as α, we have

$$\alpha \equiv \frac{1}{1 - c} \tag{14}$$

Inspection of the multiplier in Equation (14) shows that the larger the marginal propensity to consume, the larger the multiplier. With a marginal propensity to consume of 0.6 as in Table 3-2, the multiplier is 2.5; for a marginal propensity to consume of 0.8, the multiplier is 5. The reason is simply that a high marginal propensity to consume implies that a large fraction of an additional dollar income will be consumed. Accordingly, expenditures induced by an increase in autonomous spending are high, and therefore, so is the expansion in output and income that is needed to restore balance between income and demand (or spending).

Before proceeding further, we note that the relationship between the marginal propensity to consume, c, and the marginal propensity to save, s, allows us to write Equation (14) in a somewhat different form. Remembering from the budget constraint that saving plus consumption adds up to income, we realize that the fraction of an additional dollar of income consumed plus the fraction saved must add up to a dollar, or $1 \equiv s + c$. We can use the relation $s \equiv 1 - c$ and substitute in Equation (14) to obtain an equivalent formula for the multiplier in terms of the marginal propensity to save: $\alpha \equiv 1/s$.

The Multiplier in Pictures

Figure 3-6 provides a graphic interpretation of the effects of an increase in autonomous spending on the equilibrium level of income. The initial equilibrium is at point E with an income level Y_0. Consider next an increase in autonomous spending from $\overline{A}$ to $\overline{A}'$. This is represented by a parallel upward shift of the aggregate demand schedule where the shift is exactly equal to the increase in autonomous spending. The upward shift means that now, at each level of income, aggregate demand is higher by an amount $\Delta \overline{A} \equiv \overline{A}' - \overline{A}$.

At the initial level of income, Y_0, aggregate demand now exceeds income or output. Consequently, unintended inventory decumulation is taking place at a rate equal to the increase in autonomous spending, equal to the vertical distance $\Delta \overline{A}$. Firms will respond to that excess demand by expanding production, say, to income level Y'. This expansion in production gives rise to induced expenditure, increasing aggregate demand to the level A'. At the same time, it reduces the gap between aggregate demand and output to the vertical distance FG. Additional spending is induced because the marginal propensity to consume is less than 1.

Thus, a marginal propensity to consume that is positive but less than unity implies that a sufficient expansion in output will restore the balance between aggregate demand and output. In Figure 3-6 the new equilibrium is indicated by point E', and the corresponding level of income is Y'_0. The change in income required is therefore $\Delta Y_0 = Y'_0 - Y_0$.

The magnitude of the income change required to restore equilibrium depends on two factors. The larger the increase in autonomous spending, represented in Figure 3-6 by the parallel shift in the aggregate demand

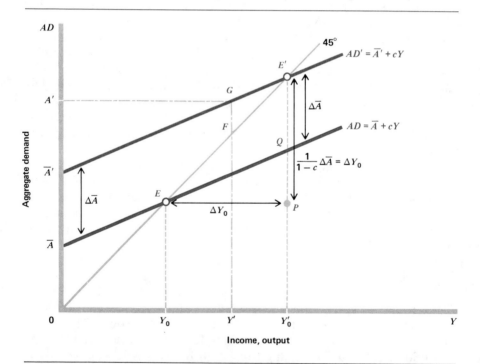

FIGURE 3-6   GRAPHICAL DERIVATION OF THE MULTIPLIER. When there is an increase in autonomous aggregate demand, the aggregate demand schedule shifts up to AD'. The equilibrium moves from E to E'. The increase in equilibrium output ($Y'_0 - Y_0$), equal to distance PE, equal to PE', exceeds the increase in autonomous demand, $E'Q$. From the diagram we see that is a result of the AD curve having a positive slope rather than being horizontal. In other words, the multiplier exceeds 1 because consumption demand increases with output—any increase in output produces further increases in demand.

schedule, the larger the income change. Furthermore, the larger the marginal propensity to consume — that is, the steeper the aggregate demand schedule — the larger the income change.

As a further check on our results, we verify from Figure 3-6 that the change in equilibrium income exceeds the change in autonomous spending. For that purpose, we use the 45° line to compare the change in income $\Delta Y_0 (= EP = PE')$ with the change in autonomous spending that is equal to the vertical distance between the new and old aggregate demand schedule (QE'). It is clear from Figure 3-6 that the change in income PE' exceeds the change in autonomous spending QE'.

Another Derivation

Finally, there is yet another way of deriving the multiplier. Remember that in equilibrium, aggregate demand equals income or output. From one equilibrium to another, it must therefore be true that the change in income ΔY_0 is equal to the change in aggregate demand ΔAD:

$$\Delta Y_0 = \Delta AD \qquad (15)$$

Next we split up the change in aggregate demand into the change in autonomous spending $\Delta \overline{A}$ and the change in expenditure induced by the consequent change in income — that is, $c \, \Delta Y_0$:

$$\Delta AD = \Delta \overline{A} + c \, \Delta Y_0 \qquad (16)$$

Combining Equations (15) and (16), we obtain the change in income as

$$\Delta Y_0 = \Delta \overline{A} + c \, \Delta Y_0 \qquad (17)$$

or, collecting terms:

$$\Delta Y_0 = \frac{1}{1-c} \Delta \overline{A} = \alpha \, \Delta \overline{A} \qquad (18)$$

Summary

There are three points to remember from this discussion:

1   An increase in autonomous spending raises the equilibrium level of income.
2   The increase in income is a multiple of the increase in autonomous spending.
3   The larger the marginal propensity to consume, the larger the multiplier, arising from the relation between consumption and income.

As a check on your understanding of the material of this section, you should develop the same analysis, and the same answers, in terms of Figure 3-5.

3-4   THE GOVERNMENT SECTOR

So far, we have ignored the role of the government sector in the determination of equilibrium income. The government affects the level of equilibrium income in two separate ways. First, government expenditure on goods and services, G, is a component of aggregate demand. Second, taxes and transfers affect the relation between output and income, Y, and the *disposable income* — income that is available for consumption or saving — that accrues to the private sector, YD. In this section, we are concerned with the way in which government purchases, taxes, and transfers affect the equilibrium level of income.

We start again from the basic national income accounting identities. The introduction of the government restores government expenditure (G) on the expenditure side of Equation (1) of this chapter, and taxes (TA) less transfers (TR) on the allocation of income side. We can, accordingly, rewrite the identity in Equation (1) as

$$C + I + G \equiv S + (TA - TR) + C \tag{1a}$$

The definition of aggregate demand has to be augmented to include government expenditure on goods and services — the purchases of military equipment and services of bureaucrats, for instance. Thus we have

$$AD \equiv C + \bar{I} + G \tag{7a}$$

Consumption will no longer depend on income, but rather on *disposable income YD*. Disposable income YD is the net income available for spending by households after paying taxes to, and receiving transfers from, the government. It thus consists of income less taxes plus transfers, $Y + TR - TA$. The consumption function is now

$$C = \bar{C} + cYD = \bar{C} + c(Y + TR - TA) \tag{4a}$$

A final step is a specifiction of *fiscal policy*. Fiscal policy is the policy of the government with regard to the level of government purchases, the level of transfers, and the tax structure. We assume that the government purchases a constant amount $\bar{G}$, that it makes a constant amount of transfers $\overline{TR}$, and that it collects a fraction t of income in the form of taxes. For example, if t equals 0.2, there is an income tax equal to 20 percent of income:

$$G = \bar{G} \qquad TR = \overline{TR} \qquad TA = tY \tag{19}$$

With this specification of fiscal policy, we can rewrite the consumption function, after substitution from Equation (19) for TR and TA in Equation (4a), as

$$C = \bar{C} + c(Y + \overline{TR} - tY)$$
$$= (\bar{C} + c\overline{TR}) + c(1 - t)Y \tag{20}$$

Note from Equation (20) that the presence of transfers raises autonomous consumption spending by the marginal propensity to consume out of disposable income c times the amount of transfers.[14] The presence of income taxes, by contrast, lowers consumption spending at each level of income. That reduction arises because households' consumption is related to *disposable* income rather than income itself, and income taxes reduce disposable income relative to the level of income.

While the marginal propensity to consume out of disposable income remains c, now the marginal propensity to consume out of income is $c(1 - t)$, where $1 - t$ is the fraction of income left after taxes. If the marginal propensity to consume, c, is 0.8 and the tax rate is 0.25, then the marginal propensity to consume out of income, $c(1 - t)$, is 0.6 [= 0.8 × (1 − .25)].

Combining (7a), (19), and (20), we have now

$$AD = (\overline{C} + c\overline{TR} + \overline{I} + \overline{G}) + c(1 - t)Y$$
$$= \overline{A} + c(1 - t)Y \tag{21}$$

The effects of the introduction of government on the aggregate demand schedule are shown in Figure 3-7. The new aggregate demand schedule, denoted AD' in the figure, starts out higher than the original schedule AD, but has a flatter slope. The intercept is larger because it now includes both

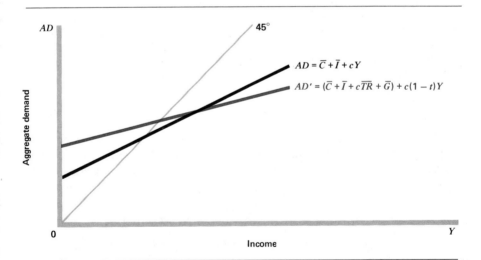

FIGURE 3-7   GOVERNMENT AND AGGREGATE DEMAND. Government affects aggregate demand through its own purchases, assumed here to be fixed at the autonomous level $\overline{G}$, through transfers $\overline{TR}$, and through taxes. Taxes are assumed to be a constant proportion, t, of income. Under these assumptions, the introduction of government shifts the intercept of the aggregate demand curve up and flattens the curve.

government spending $\overline{G}$ and the part of consumption resulting from transfer payments by the government, $c\overline{TR}$. The slope is flatter because households now have to pay part of every dollar of income in taxes, and are left
with only $(1 - t)$ of that dollar. Thus, as (21) shows, the marginal propensity to consume out of income is now $c(1 - t)$ instead of c.

Equilibrium Income

We are now set to study income determination when the government is
included. We return to the equilibrium condition for the goods market,
$Y = AD$, and using (21), write the equilibrium condition as

$$Y = \overline{A} + c(1 - t)Y$$

We can solve this equation for Y_0, the equilibrium level of income, by
collecting terms in Y:

$$Y[1 - c(1 - t)] = \overline{A}$$

$$Y_0 = \frac{1}{1 - c(1 - t)}\overline{A} \qquad (22)$$

In comparing Equation (22) with Equation (10), we see that the government sector makes a substantial difference. It raises autonomous spending by the amount of government spending, $\overline{G}$, and by the amount of
induced spending out of net transfers, $c\overline{TR}$.

Income Taxes and the Multiplier

At the same time *income taxes lower the multiplier*. As can be seen from
Equation (22), if the marginal propensity to consume is 0.8 and taxes are
zero, the multiplier is 5; with the same marginal propensity to consume
and a tax rate of 0.25, the multiplier is cut in half to $1/[1 - 0.8(0.75)] =$
2.5. Income taxes reduce the multiplier because they reduce the induced
increase of consumption out of changes in income. This can be seen in
Figure 3-7, where the inclusion of taxes flattens the aggregate demand
curve — recall from Figure 3-6 that the multiplier is larger, the steeper the
aggregate demand schedule.

Effects of a Change in Government Expenditures

We now consider the effects of changes in fiscal policy on the equilibrium
level of income. We distinguish three possible changes in fiscal variables:
changes in government purchases, changes in transfers, and income tax
changes. The simplest illustration is that of a change in government
purchases. This case is shown in Figure 3-8, where the initial level of
income is Y_0.

An increase in government purchases is a change in autonomous spending and therefore shifts the aggregate demand schedule upward by an

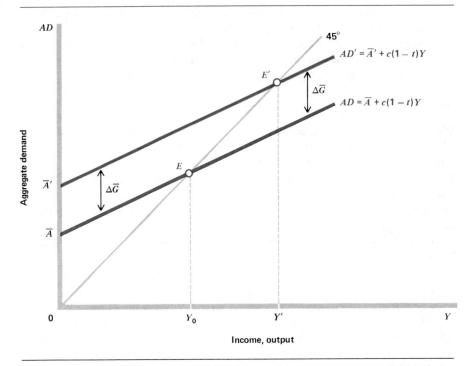

FIGURE 3-8   THE EFFECTS OF AN INCREASE IN GOVERNMENT PURCHASES.
An increase in government spending shifts the aggregate demand schedule up
from AD to AD'. Output rises from Y_0 to Y'. The multiplier is smaller now than
it was in Figure 3-6.

amount equal to the increase in government purchases. At the initial
level of output and income, the demand for goods exceeds output, and
accordingly, firms expand production until the new equilibrium at point
E' is reached. By how much does income expand? We remember that the
change in equilibrium income will equal the change in aggregate demand,
or

$$\Delta Y_0 = \Delta \overline{G} + c(1 - t)\Delta Y_0$$

where the remaining terms ($\overline{C}$, $\overline{TR}$, and $\overline{I}$) are constant by assumption.
Thus, the change in equilibrium income is

$$\Delta Y_0 = \frac{1}{1 - c(1 - t)}\Delta \overline{G} = \overline{\alpha}\Delta \overline{G} \qquad (23)$$

where we have introduced the notation $\overline{\alpha}$ to denote the multiplier in the
presence of income taxes:

$$\overline{\alpha} \equiv \frac{1}{1 - c(1 - t)} \qquad (24)$$

From Equation (23) it is apparent that a $1 increase in government purchases will lead to an increase in income in excess of a dollar. Thus, as we have already seen, with a marginal propensity to consume of $c = 0.8$ and an income tax rate of $t = 0.25$, we would have a multiplier of 2.5: a $1 increase in government spending raises equilibrium income by $2.50.

Income Taxes as Automatic Stabilizers

We have just seen that a proportional income tax reduces the multiplier. This means that if any component of autonomous demand changes, output will change by less if there is a proportional income tax than in the absence of such taxes. We say that a proportional income tax is an *automatic stabilizer*. An automatic stabilizer is any mechanism in the economy that reduces the amount by which output changes in response to a change in autonomous demand.

We shall see later that one explanation of the business cycle, the more or less regular movements of real GNP around trend, is that it is caused by shifts in investment demand. Sometimes, it is argued, investors are optimistic and investment is high — and so, therefore, is output. But sometimes they are pessimistic, and both investment and output are low.

Swings in investment demand will have a smaller effect on output when automatic stabilizers are in place. This means that in the presence of automatic stabilizers we should expect output to fluctuate less than it would without them. The income tax, which is an automatic stabilizer, is one reason that the business cycle has been less pronounced since 1945 than it was in earlier years.

The proportional income tax is not the only automatic stabilizer. Unemployment benefits enable the unemployed to continue consuming even if they do not have a job. This means that demand falls less when someone becomes unemployed than it would if there were no benefits. This too makes the multiplier smaller and output more stable. Unemployment benefits and a proportional income tax are two automatic stabilizers that keep the multiplier small, and therefore protect the economy from responding strongly to every small movement in autonomous demand.

Effects of Increased Transfer Payments

An increase in transfer payments increases autonomous demand, as can be seen from Equation (21), where autonomous demand includes a term $c\overline{TR}$. A $1 increase in transfers therefore increases autonomous demand by an amount c. For instance, if the marginal propensity to consume, c, is 0.8, a $1 increase in transfers increases autonomous demand by $0.80. The increase is less than the full $1 increase in transfers because part of the transfer — $0.20 in this case — is saved.

Given that a $1 increase in transfers increases autonomous demand by the amount c, it is clear that the multiplier for an increase in transfers is c

times the multiplier for an increase in government spending. For instance, with c equal to 0.8, and a tax rate of 0.25, the government spending multiplier is 2.5. The multiplier for transfers is 0.8 times 2.5, or 2.0.

The Effects of an Income Tax Change

The final fiscal policy question is the effects of a reduction in the income tax rate. This is illustrated in Figure 3-9 by an increase in the slope of the aggregate demand function, because that slope is equal to the marginal propensity to spend out of income, $c(1 - t)$. At the initial level of income, the aggregate demand for goods now exceeds output because the tax reduction causes increased consumption. The new higher equilibrium level of income is Y'.

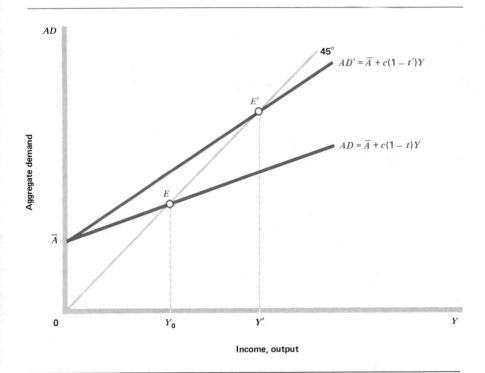

FIGURE 3-9   THE EFFECTS OF A DECREASE IN THE TAX RATE. A reduction in the income tax rate leaves the consumer with a larger proportion of every dollar of income earned. Accordingly, a larger proportion of every extra dollar of income is consumed. The aggregate demand curve swings upward, from AD to AD'. It becomes steeper, because the income tax cut, in effect, acts like an increase in the propensity to consume. The equilibrium level of income rises from Y_0 to Y'.

To calculate the change in equilibrium income, we equate the change in income to the change in aggregate demand. The change in aggregate demand has two components. The first is the change in spending at the initial level of income that arises from the tax cut. This part is equal to the marginal propensity to consume out of disposable income times the change in disposable income due to the tax cut, $cY_0 \Delta t$, where the term $Y_0 \Delta t$, is the initial level of income times the change in the tax rate. The second component of the change in aggregate demand is the induced spending due to higher income. This is now evaluated at the new tax rate t' and has the value $c(1 - t') \Delta Y_0$. We can therefore write[15]

$$\Delta Y_0 = - cY_0 \Delta t + c(1 - t') \Delta Y_0 \qquad (25)$$

$$\text{or} \qquad \Delta Y_0 = - \frac{1}{1 - c(1 - t')} cY_0 \Delta t \qquad (26)$$

Example

An exercise clarifies the effects of an income tax cut. Initially the level of income is $Y_0 = 100$, the marginal propensity to consume is $c = 0.8$, and the tax rate $t = 0.2$. Assume now a tax cut that reduces the income tax rate to only 10 percent, or $t' = 0.1$.

At the initial level of income, disposable income rises by $Y_0 \Delta t = 100(t - t') = \$10$. Out of the increase in disposable income of $\$10$, a fraction $c = 0.8$ is spent on consumption, so that aggregate demand, at the initial level of income, increases by $\$8$. This corresponds to the first term on the right-hand side of the Equation (25). The increase in aggregate demand causes an expansion in output and income. Per dollar increase in income, disposable income rises by a fraction $(1 - t')$ of the increase in income. Furthermore, of the increase in disposable income, only a fraction, c, is spent. Accordingly, induced consumption spending is equal to $c(1 - t') \Delta Y_0$, which is the second term in Equation (25).

How much does the income tax cut achieve in terms of output expansion? Substituting our numbers in Equation (26), we have

$$\Delta Y_0 = \frac{1}{1 - 0.8(1 - 0.1)}(0.8)(100)(0.2 - 0.1) = (3.57)(8)$$
$$= 28.56 \qquad (26a)$$

In our example, a cut in the tax rate, such that taxes fall by $\$10$ at the initial level of income, raises equilibrium income by $\$28.56$.

Note, however, that although taxes are initially cut by $\$10$, the government's total taxes received fall by less than $\$10$. Why? The reason is that the government receives 10 percent of the induced increase in income, or $\$2.856$, as taxes. Thus the final reduction in tax receipts by the government is not the initial $\$10$, but rather $\$7.144$.[16]

Active Fiscal Policy

Changes in government spending and taxes affect the level of income. This raises immediately the possibility that fiscal policy can be used to stabilize the economy. When the economy is in a recession, perhaps taxes should be cut or spending increased to get output to rise. And when the economy is booming, perhaps taxes should be increased or government spending cut to get back down to full employment.

Fiscal policy is in practice actively used to try to stabilize the economy, as we shall see in the next section when we examine the behaviour of the budget. But it is also true that there is some dispute over whether such fiscal policy actions really work. The disputes centre on two issues: first, whether they work fast enough to help; and second, and more complicated, whether government policy actions don't merely result in private individuals taking offsetting actions. For instance, when government spending rises, private spending might fall.

We cannot at this stage evaluate the arguments against the active use of fiscal policy. But starting in Chapter 5, we continue the discussion.

Summary

1 Government purchases and transfer payments act like increases in autonomous spending in their effects on equilibrium income.
2 Income taxes reduce disposable income relative to the level of income, and their effects on equilibrium income and output are thus the same as those resulting from a reduction in the propensity to consume.[17]

3-5 THE BUDGET

The budget — and especially the budget deficit — has become a major preoccupation of economic policy in the first half of the 1980s. Government budget deficits that sound astronomical are a prospect for the rest of the decade, and the fear is strong that the economy cannot prosper with such a threat hanging over it.

In this section we deal with the government budget, with its effects on output, and with the effects of output on the budget. We start by defining the *budget surplus*, denoted by *BS*. The budget surplus is the excess of the government's revenues, consisting of taxes, over its total expenditures, consisting of purchases of goods and services, and transfer payments.

$$BS \equiv TA - G - TR \qquad (27)$$

A negative budget surplus, an excess of expenditure over taxes, is a *budget deficit*, denoted *BD*:

$$BD \equiv -BS = G + TR - TA$$

BOX 3-1   GOVERNMENT IN THE NATIONAL INCOME ACCOUNTS

We distinguish three aspects of fiscal policy in the text. *G* is government purchases of goods and services, *TR* is government transfers, and *TA* is taxes or government receipts. We now give the data for these variables in 1983, when GNP was $388.7 billion. We also show the breakdown of the variables among federal, provincial and municipal governments.

GOVERNMENT EXPENDITURE (billions of dollars)[a]

	Goods and Services	Transfer Payments Interest on Public Debt	Other
Federal	$21.6	$17.4	$59.3
Provincial	30.1	7.4	48.5
Municipal[b]	42.9	2.9	.6
Total	$94.6	$27.7	$108.4
Percent of GNP	24.4%	7.1%	27.9%

Federal and provincial transfer payments are considerably larger than purchases of goods and services, and interest payments on the public debt are a substantial portion of transfer payments.

GOVERNMENT REVENUE (billions of dollars)[a]

	Income Taxes	Pension Contributions	Sales, Excise, and Property Taxes	Other
Federal	$44.9	$ 9.4[c]	$16.0	$ 4.7
Provincial	26.3	3.2[d]	19.5	33.0
Municipal[b]			14.9	29.1
Total	$71.2	$12.6	$50.4	$66.8
Percent of GNP	18.3%	3.3%	13.0%	17.2%

SURPLUS OR DEFICIT (−)[a]

	$ billions	Percent of GNP
Federal	−23.3	−6.0
Provincial	−4.0	−1.0
Municipal[b]	−2.5	−.6
Total	−29.8	−7.7

In 1983, the total deficit of the government sector was $29.8 billion or 7.7 percent of GNP. Most of this deficit was incurred at the federal level. It should be noted that transfers between levels of government are netted out of these figures. In 1983, the federal government transferred $17.4 billion to provinces and municipalities.

---

[a]*Source:* Statistics Canada, 11-003.
[b]Includes hospitals
[c]Canada Pension Plan
[d]Quebec Pension Plan

Of course, at the present time, government deficits are the norm, and surpluses are nowhere a prospect, but it was not always so. For example, there were surpluses in the years 1947–1953 and 1964–1974.

In the accompanying box, we describe the concepts of government budget surplus and deficit that appear in the national income accounts. For that purpose, the federal government and provincial and municipal governments are added together. Thus the government sector in the national income accounts, and in the theory we are developing here, is not just the federal government. It is all government.

However, the budget deficit on which the media and politicians focus is the federal budget deficit. Later in this section we look at the behaviour of the federal budget. For now we study the behaviour of the budget surplus in relation to income, in the simple theory of this chapter.

Substituting in Equation (27) the assumption of a proportional income tax that yields a tax revenue $TA = tY$ gives us

$$BS = tY - G - TR \tag{27a}$$

In Figure 3-10 we plot the budget surplus as a function of the level of income for given $G = \overline{G}$, $TR = \overline{TR}$, and income tax rate t. At low levels of income, the budget is in deficit (the surplus is negative) because payments $\overline{G} + \overline{TR}$ exceed income tax collection. For high levels of income, by contrast, the budget shows a surplus, since income tax collection outweighs expenditures in the form of government purchases and transfers.

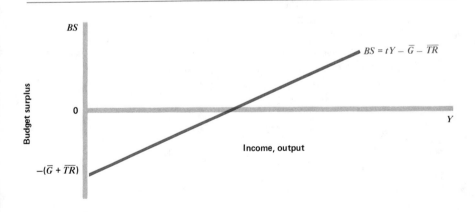

FIGURE 3-10   THE BUDGET SURPLUS. The budget surplus, or deficit, depends in part on the level of income. Given the tax rate, t, and $\overline{G}$ and $\overline{TR}$, the budget surplus will be high if income is high — because then the government takes in a lot of taxes. But if the level of income is low, there will be a budget deficit because tax receipts by the government are small.

Figure 3-10 demonstrates a significant point about budget surpluses and deficits. The point is that the budget deficit depends not only on the government's policy choices, reflected in the tax rate t, in purchases $\overline{G}$, and in transfers $\overline{TR}$, but also on anything else that shifts the level of income. For instance, suppose there is an increase in investment demand that increases the level of output. Then the budget deficit will fall, or the surplus will increase because tax revenues have risen. But the government has done nothing that changed the deficit.

We should accordingly not be surprised to see budget deficits in recessions. Those are periods when the government's tax receipts are low. And in practice, transfer payments, through unemployment benefits, also increase in recessions, even though in our model we are taking $\overline{TR}$ as autonomous.

The Effects of Government Purchases and Tax Changes on the Budget Surplus

Next we show how changes in fiscal policy affect the budget. In particular, we want to find out whether an increase in government purchases must reduce the budget surplus. At first sight, this appears obvious, because increased government purchases, from Equation (27), are reflected in a reduced surplus, or increased deficit. At further thought, however, the increased government purchases will give rise to an increase (multiplied) in income and, therefore, to increased income tax collection. This raises the interesting possibility that tax collection might increase by more than government purchases.[18]

A brief calculation shows that the first guess is right—increased government purchases reduce the budget surplus. From Equation (23) the change in income due to increased government purchases is equal to $\Delta Y_0 = \overline{\alpha}\Delta\overline{G}$. A fraction of that increase in income is collected in the form of taxes, so that tax revenue increases by $t\overline{\alpha}\Delta\overline{G}$. The change in the budget surplus, using Equation (24) to substitute for $\overline{\alpha}$ is therefore:

$$\Delta BS = \Delta TA - \Delta\overline{G}$$
$$= t\overline{\alpha}\Delta\overline{G} - \Delta\overline{G}$$
$$= \left[\frac{t}{1 - c(1 - t)} - 1 \right] \Delta\overline{G}$$
$$= -\frac{(1 - c)(1 - t)}{1 - c(1 - t)}\Delta\overline{G} \tag{28}$$

which is unambiguously negative.

We have, therefore, shown that an increase in government purchases will reduce the budget surplus, although by considerably less than the increase in purchases. For instance, for $c = 0.8$ and $t = 0.25$, a \$1 increase in government purchases will create a \$0.375 reduction in the surplus.[19]

In the same way, we can consider the effects of an increase in the tax rate on the budget surplus. We know that the increase in the tax rate will reduce the level of income. It might thus appear that an increase in the tax rate, keeping the level of government spending constant, could reduce the budget surplus. In fact, an increase in the tax rate increases the budget surplus, despite the reduction in income that it causes.[20]

A Simultaneous Change in Taxes and Purchases

Finally, we can investigate the budgetary effects of simultaneous changes in taxes and government purchases. We do this by working out an example, in Table 3-3. We assume a fiscal policy change that reduces the tax rate and government purchases. The reduction is such that at the initial equilibrium level of income, of 100, the cut in taxes is exactly equal to the cut in government purchases.

TABLE 3-3   EFFECTS OF COMBINED TAX CUT AND
             GOVERNMENT SPENDING DECREASE

Parameters: Initial tax rate, $t = 0.2$
             New tax rate, $t' = 0.1$
             Initial level of income, $Y_0 = \$100$
             Marginal propensity to consume, $c = 0.8$
             Change in government spending, $\Delta \overline{G} = -10$

Multiplier: $\bar{\alpha} = \dfrac{1}{1 - c(1 - t')} = \dfrac{1}{1 - .72} = 3.57$

Effects of tax cut: [See Equation (26)]
   Change in income $= -\bar{\alpha} c Y_0 \Delta t = -(3.57)(0.8)(100)(-0.1) = 28.56$

Effects of cut in government spending: [See Equation (23)]
   Change in income $= \bar{\alpha} \Delta \overline{G} = -35.70$

Total effect on income: $\Delta Y_0 = -35.70 + 28.56$
                                      $= -7.14$
   Therefore: $Y'_0 = 100 - 7.14 = 92.86$

Effect on tax receipts: Initial taxes $= 20$
                          Taxes in new situation $= .1 \times 92.86 = 9.29$
   Therefore: Change in taxes, $\Delta TA = -10.71$

Effects on budget surplus: $\Delta BS = \Delta TA - \Delta \overline{G}$
                                      $= -10.71 + 10.00$
                                      $= -.71$

What effect would we expect such a fiscal policy to have? A first reaction would be that since taxes are being cut the same amount as spending, there will be no effect. But the table shows that is not right. The combined effect of the two actions is actually to lower income.

Why? The reason is that part of the cut in taxes is saved, so that not all the tax cut goes to increase aggregate demand. But the entire cut in government spending reduces aggregate demand. Therefore this fiscal policy actually reduces aggregate demand, and therefore income.

Notice also from the table that the budget deficit in the end increases slightly — as a result of the fall in income — even though at the initial level of income the cuts in taxes and spending are equal.

Balanced Budget Multiplier

In the previous example, the combined tax cut and reduction of government purchases raised the budget deficit. What would happen to the level of income if government purchases and taxes changed by exactly the same amount, so that the budget surplus remained unchanged between the initial and final level of income? The answer to this question is contained in the famous *balanced budget multiplier* result. The result is that the balanced budget multiplier is exactly 1. That is, an increase in government purchases, accompanied by an equal increase in taxes, increases the level of income by exactly the amount of the increase in purchases.[21] This interesting result is derived in the Appendix at the end of this chapter.

The major points of the preceding discussion are that a balanced budget cut in government purchases lowers equilibrium income and that a dollar increase in government purchases has a stronger impact on equilibrium income than a dollar cut in taxes. A dollar cut in taxes leads only to a fraction of a dollar's increase in consumption spending, the rest being saved, while government purchases are reflected dollar for dollar in a change in aggregate demand.[22]

The Full-Employment Budget Surplus

A final topic to be treated here is the concept of the full-employment budget surplus.[23] Recall that increases in taxes add to the surplus and that increases in government expenditures reduce the surplus. Increases in taxes have been shown to reduce the level of income, and increases in government purchases and transfers to increase the level of income. It thus seems that the budget surplus is a convenient, simple measure of the overall effects of fiscal policy on the economy. For instance, when the budget is in deficit, we would say that fiscal policy is expansionary, tending to increase GNP.

However, the budget surplus by itself suffers from a serious defect as a measure of the direction of fiscal policy. The defect is that the surplus can change passively because of changes in autonomous private spending, as we have seen. Thus, if the economy moves into a recession, tax revenue automatically declines and the budget moves into a deficit (or reduced surplus). Conversely, an increase in economic activity causes the budget to move into a surplus (or reduced deficit). These changes in the budget take place automatically for a given tax structure. This implies that we cannot simply look at the budget deficit as a measure of whether government fiscal policy is expansionary or deflationary. A given fiscal policy may imply a deficit if private spending is low and a surplus if private spending is high. Accordingly, an increase in the budget deficit does not necessarily mean that the government has changed its policy in an attempt to increase the level of income.

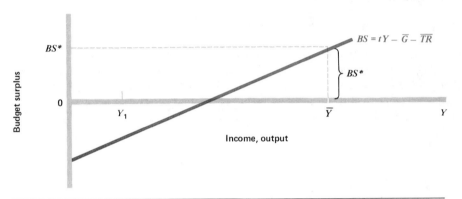

FIGURE 3-11   THE ACTUAL AND FULL-EMPLOYMENT BUDGET SURPLUSES. $\overline{Y}$ is the full-employment level of output. The full-employment budget surplus BS^* is the budget surplus that would exist if the economy were at full employment. If output is below the full-employment level, at a level such as Y_1, the budget surplus would be smaller than BS^*. Indeed, at income level Y_1 the actual budget is in deficit even though there is a full-employment surplus.

Since we frequently want to measure the way in which fiscal policy is being actively, rather than passively, used to affect the level of income, we require some measure of policy that is independent of the particular position of the business cycle — boom or recession — in which we may find ourselves. Such a measure is provided by the *full-employment budget surplus*, which we denote by BS^*. The full-employment (high-employment) budget surplus measures the budget, not at the actual level of income, but rather at the full-employment level of income or at potential output. Thus, a given fiscal policy summarized by $\overline{G}$, $\overline{TR}$, and t is assessed by the level of the surplus, or deficit, that is generated at full employment. Using $\overline{Y}$ to denote the full-employment level of income, we can write

$$BS^* = t\overline{Y} - \overline{G} - \overline{TR} \qquad (29)$$

In Figure 3-11 we show the budget surplus schedule from Figure 3-10 but add the full-employment level of income $\overline{Y}$. The full-employment budget surplus is indicated by the corresponding point on the budget surplus schedule. To see the difference between the actual and the full-employment budget, we subtract the actual budget in Equation (27a) from Equation (29) to obtain

$$BS^* - BS = t(\overline{Y} - Y) \tag{30}$$

It is apparent that the only difference arises from income tax collection.[24] Specifically, if output is below full employment, the full-employment surplus exceeds the actual surplus. Conversely, if actual output exceeds full-employment (or potential) output, the full-employment surplus is less than the actual surplus.

Budget Trends

Figure 3-12 shows the actual and cyclically adjusted surplus as a fraction of GNP for the years 1961 to 1983. In periods of rapid growth and relatively low unemployment, such as 1964–1969, the actual surplus rises above the adjusted one, while in recession years such as 1961, 1970, 1975 and 1982, the growth of tax revenues slows down and the actual surplus

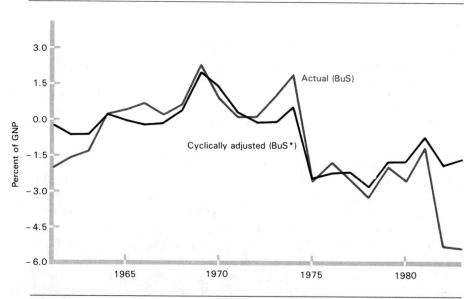

FIGURE 3-12   THE ACTUAL AND CYCLICALLY ADJUSTED BUDGET SURPLUS AS A FRACTION OF GNP
(*Source: Department of Finance, Economic Review*)

falls below the adjusted one. The emergence of large cyclically adjusted deficits in the period 1975–1978 reflects the expansionary fiscal policy adopted during that period in response to rising unemployment rates. Conversely, the very large actual deficits in 1982 and 1983 reflect the emergence of very high unemployment rates.

One final word of warning: The high-employment surplus is a better measure of the direction of active fiscal policy than the actual budget surplus, but it is not a perfect measure of the thrust of fiscal policy. The reason is that balanced budget increases in government purchases are themselves expansionary, so that an increase in government purchases matched by a tax increase that keeps the surplus constant leads to an increase in the level of income. Because fiscal policy involves the setting of a number of variables—the tax rate, transfers, and government purchases —it is difficult to describe the thrust of fiscal policy perfectly in a single number.[25] The high-employment surplus is nevertheless a useful guide to the direction of fiscal policy.

3-6   THE FOREIGN SECTOR

For a country like Canada that exports about one-quarter of its total output and spends a similar fraction of its income on imports, foreign trade plays an important role in the determination of equilibrium income. When foreign trade is taken into account, we return to the general case represented by the basic accounting identity given at the beginning of the chapter. Aggregate demand becomes:

$$AD = C + I + G + NX$$

Denoting exports by X and imports by Q, we have

$$NX = X - Q$$

As in the case of planned investment and government spending, we assume that exports are fixed at a given level (denoted by $\overline{X}$). On the other hand, since imports represent part of domestic demand, they are assumed to depend on income. Using a linear relationship we have

$$Q = \overline{Q} + mY \qquad (32)$$

where the slope m is called the *marginal propensity to import*.

To determine the equilibrium level of income, we use the equilibrium condition, $Y = A$ together with the consumption function (21) and the import function (32):

$$\begin{aligned} Y &= (\overline{C} + c\overline{TR}) + c(1 - t)Y + \overline{I} + \overline{G} + \overline{X} - \overline{Q} - mY \\ &= (\overline{C} + c\overline{TR} + \overline{I} + \overline{G} + \overline{X} - \overline{Q}) + [c(1 - t) - m]Y \\ &= \overline{A} + [c(1 - t) - m]Y \end{aligned}$$

Solving for the equilibrium level of income Y_0, we obtain:

$$Y_0 = \frac{1}{1 - c(1 - t) + m}\overline{A} \qquad (33)$$

Comparing Equation (33) with Equation (11), we see that exports add to and imports subtract from autonomous spending. In addition, imports are similar to taxes in that they reduce the increases in demand for domestic output induced by increases in income, and thereby lower the multiplier. The higher the marginal propensity to import, the lower the multiplier.

Interdependence and Repercussion Effects

When we include the foreign sector in our analysis and consider the interaction among countries, we find that income determination in the individual countries of the world economy is interdependent. An increase in income in one country (country A), by increasing country A's imports, affects demand for output abroad and leads, in turn, to a foreign expansion in imports from country A. There is thus a *repercussion effect* that we have so far ignored by assuming that export demand is autonomous.

Estimated Repercussion Effects

Table 3-4 provides estimates of the size of repercussion effects and the importance of international linkages. The table, derived from an econometric model of the OECD, shows income multipliers associated with an expansion in one country on that country itself and on other countries.[26] Consider first the case of the United States. An increase of 1 percentage point in U.S. autonomous spending would raise U.S. income by 1.47 percent.

TABLE 3-4 THE INTERNATIONAL TRANSMISSION OF
AGGREGATE DEMAND DISTURBANCES

Initiating country or group (1 percent increase in autonomous spending)	AFFECTED COUNTRY OR GROUP (PERCENTAGE CHANGE IN INCOME)				
	United States	Germany	Japan	Canada	OECD
United States	1.47	0.23	0.25	0.68	0.74
Germany	0.05	1.25	0.60	0.60	0.23
Japan	0.04	0.05	1.26	0.06	0.21
Canada	0.06	0.03	0.03	1.27	0.10
OECD	1.81	2.38	1.84	2.32	2.04

Source: OECD Occasional Paper, "The OECD International Linkage Model" January 1979.

What is the impact on selected other countries? Looking at the top row, we find that German income growth rises by about ¼ percent, and the same is true for Japan. Thus, U.S. expansion does affect these countries, although the size of the effect is not overwhelming. The comparison with Canada is of interest here. A U.S. expansion by 1.47 percent raises Canadian income growth by nearly 0.7 percent. Thus Canada appears considerably affected by U.S. expenditure disturbances. The last entry in the top row of Table 3-4 shows the impact of a U.S. expansion on industrialized countries as a group. The impact here is to increase the group's combined income by three-quarters of a percentage point.[27]

Consider for comparison a Canadian expansion. The multiplier for Canadian income growth of a 1 percent increase in Canadian autonomous spending is 1.27, about the same as the 1.47 multiplier for the United States. The impact on the rest of the world is quite minor, though. The most substantial impact is on the United States (0.06 percent induced income growth) and only 0.03 percent increased growth for Germany or Japan.

What determines the size of the multipliers and spillover effects? Three chief factors should be taken into account in interpreting the multiplier patterns revealed in Table 3-4. First, the size of the country is important. A Canadian expansion, for example, induces only a small percentage increase in U.S. income because a given dollar change in Canadian income and imports will be only a small fraction of U.S. income. By contrast, a given increase in U.S. income and imports will be a relatively large fraction of Canadian income.

The second important determinant of multiplier patterns is openness to trade. The spillover effects of an expansion in any one country on the rest of the world will be more substantial the more open the expanding economy.[28]

The third point to note is the extent to which trade patterns are reflected in the multipliers. The United States, for example, benefits relatively more from a Canadian expansion than does Germany. This reflects the fact that Canada has a high marginal propensity to import from the United States in comparison with its propensity to import from Germany.

Table 3-4 allows us to study not only the effects of an individual country's expansion and the induced spillovers but also the effect of a simultaneous joint expansion in all industrialized countries. The last row of the table provides the multipliers for this experiment. Clearly, if all countries expand together—each raising autonomous expenditure by 1 percent—the multiplier effects are much more substantial. Each country benefits not only from its own expansion and its repercussion effects through induced expansion abroad, but also from the autonomous foreign expansion. Accordingly, the multipliers are around 2 in this case, while being in the range of 1.2 to 1.5 for the case of an isolated expansion.

Interdependence, Relative Growth, and the Current Account

The effects of changes in the level of income in one country on income in another, studied in the preceding section, are transmitted through changes in the levels of imports and exports. The spillover and repercussion effects therefore also produce effects on the trade balance. A country that is growing rapidly will tend to increase its imports relatively fast. The trade balance of the rapidly growing country will therefore tend to go into deficit.

Such effects were important for Canada in the mid-1970s. Table 3-5 shows the rates of income growth in Canada and the U.S., and the Canadian balance of merchandise trade. In 1974 and 1975, the U.S. economy suffered a more severe recession than was experienced in Canada. American real GNP fell in both these years, while Canadian real GNP continued to grow although at a much slower rate than in 1973. As a result our net exports fell substantially and in 1975 there was a deficit in merchandise trade for the first time since 1960. With the resumption of growth in the United States in 1976 and 1977, our trade balance improved.

TABLE 3-5   REAL INCOME AND THE CANADIAN BALANCE OF MERCHANDISE TRADE

	1973	1974	1975	1976	1977
	Real income growth (percent per year)				
Canada	7.5	3.6	1.2	5.5	2.2
United States	5.9	-1.7	-1.3	5.9	5.3
	Merchandise trade balance (billions of dollars)				
Canada	2.7	1.7	-.5	1.4	2.7

A word of warning is needed here. The behaviour of the current account reflects more than relative income growth. Other factors, such as changes in the exchange rate, exogenous shocks such as the oil price increase, shifting trade patterns due to the emergence of new competitors and the spread of technology abroad, all affect the current account as well. Even so, Table 3-5 is highly suggestive in pointing to Canada's *relative* cyclical performance as an essential determinant of the current account.

3-7   SUMMARY

1   Output is at its equilibrium level when the aggregate demand for goods is equal to the level of output.

2   Aggregate demand consists of planned spending by households on consumption, firms on investment goods, and government on its expenditure on goods and services.

3   When output is at its equilibrium level, there are no unintended changes in inventories and all economic units are making precisely the purchases they had planned to. An adjustment process for the level of output based on the accumulation or decumulation of inventories leads the economy to the equilibrium output level.

4   The level of aggregate demand is itself affected by the level of output (equal to the level of income) because consumption demand depends on the level of income.

5   The consumption function relates consumption spending to income. Income that is not consumed is saved, so that the saving function can be derived from the consumption function.

6   The multiplier is the amount by which a one-dollar change in autonomous spending changes the equilibrium level of output. The greater the propensity to consume, the higher the multiplier.

7   Government purchases and government transfer payments act like increases in autonomous spending in their effects on the equilibrium level of income. A proportional income tax has the same effects on the equilibrium level of income as a reduction in the propensity to consume. A proportional income tax thus reduces the multiplier.

8   The budget surplus is the excess of government receipts over its expenditure. When the government is spending more than it receives, the budget is in deficit. The size of the budget surplus (deficit) is affected by the government's fiscal policy variables — government purchases, transfer payments, and tax rates.

9   The budget surplus is also affected by changes in taxes and transfers resulting from changes in the level of income occurring as a result of changes in private autonomous spending. The *cyclically adjusted* or *full-employment* (high-employment) budget surplus is accordingly frequently used as a measure of the active use of fiscal policy. The full-employment surplus measures the budget surplus that would exist if output were at its potential (full-employment) level.

10   When foreign trade is taken into account, exports add to and imports subtract from autonomous spending. The dependence of imports on income affects the size of the multiplier: the higher the marginal propensity to import, the lower the multiplier.

11   There are *repercussion effects* by which a change in foreign income eventually induces an increase in the demand for foreigners' goods

through exports. The size of these interdependence and repercussion effects depends on the relative size and openness of the economy. A small economy may be very dependent on a larger one, but a larger economy's level of income does not depend much on the income level in small foreign economies.

KEY TERMS

Aggregate demand
Equilibrium output
Unintended (undesired) inventory
    accumulation
Planned aggregate demand
Consumption function
Marginal propensity to consume
Marginal propensity to save
Multiplier

Automatic stabilizer
Budget surplus
Budget deficit
Balanced budget multiplier
Full-employment (high-employment)
    surplus
Marginal propensity to import
Repercussion effect

PROBLEMS

1   Here we investigate a particular example of the model studied in Sections 3-2 and 3-3 with no government. Suppose the consumption function is given by $C = 100 + 0.8Y$, while investment is given by $\bar{I} = 50$.
   (a)   What is the equilibrium level of income in this case?
   (b)   What is the level of saving in equilibrium?
   (c)   If, for some reason, output was at the level of 800, what would the level of involuntary inventory accumulation be?
   (d)   If $\bar{I}$ were to rise to 100 (we discuss what determines $\bar{I}$ in later chapters), what would the effect be on equilibrium income?
   (e)   What is the multiplier α here?
   (f)   Draw a diagram indicating the equilibria in both 1(a) and 1(d).

2   Suppose consumption behaviour were to change in problem 1 so that $C = 100 + 0.9Y$, while $\bar{I}$ remained at 50.
   (a)   Would you expect the equilibrium level of income to be higher or lower than in 1(a)? Calculate the new Y' to verify this.
   (b)   Now suppose investment increases to $\bar{I} = 100$ just as in 1(d). What is the new equilibrium income?
   (c)   Does this change in investment spending have more or less of an effect on Y than in problem 1? Why?
   (d)   Draw a diagram indicating the change in equilibrium income in this case.

3 We showed in the text that the equilibrium condition $Y = AD$ is equivalent to the $S = \bar{I}$, or saving = investment, condition. Starting from
$S = \bar{I}$ and the saving function, derive the equilibrium level of income,
as in Equation (10).

4 This problem relates to the so-called *paradox of thrift*. Suppose that
$I = \bar{I}$ and that $C = \bar{C} + cY$.
(a) What is the savings function, that is, the function that shows
how saving is related to income?
(b) Suppose individuals want to save more at every level of income.
Show, using a figure like Figure 3-5, how the saving function is
shifted.
(c) What effect does the increased desire to save have on the new
equilibrium level of saving? Explain the paradox.

5 Now let us look at a model which is an example of the one presented
in Sections 3-4 and 3-5; that is, it includes government purchases,
taxes, and transfers. It has the same features as the one in problems 1
and 2, except that it also has a government. Thus, suppose consumption is given by $C = 100 + 0.8YD$ and $\bar{I} = 50$, while fiscal policy is
summarized by $\bar{G} = 200$, $\overline{TR} = 62.5$, and $t = 0.25$.
(a) What is the equilibrium level of income in this more complete
model?
(b) What is the new multiplier $\bar{\alpha}$? Why is this less than the multiplier
in problem 1(e)?

6 Using the same model as in problem 5, determine the following:
(a) What is the value of the budget surplus BS when $\bar{I} = 50$?
(b) What is BS when $\bar{I}$ increases to 100?
(c) What accounts for the change in BS from 6(a) to 6(b)?
(d) Assuming that the full-employment level of income $\bar{Y}$ is 1,200,
what is the full-employment budget surplus BS^* when $\bar{I} = 50$?
100? (Be careful.)
(e) What is BS^* if $\bar{I} = 50$ and $\bar{G} = 250$, with $\bar{Y}$ still equal to 1,200?
(f) Explain why we use BS^* rather than simply BS to measure the
direction of fiscal policy.

7 Suppose we expand our model to take account of the fact that transfer payments TR do depend on the level of income Y. When income
is high, transfer payments such as unemployment benefits will fall.
Conversely, when income is low, unemployment is high and so are
unemployment benefits. We can incorporate this into our model by
writing transfers as $TR = \overline{TR} - bY$, $b > 0$. Remember that equilibrium
income is derived as the solution to $Y_0 = C + \bar{I} + \bar{G} = \bar{C} + cYD + \bar{I} + \bar{G}$,
where $YD = Y + TR - TA$ is disposable income.
(a) Derive the expression for Y_0 in this case, just as Equation (22) was
derived in the text.
(b) What is the new multiplier now?
(c) Why is the new multiplier less than the standard one, $\bar{\alpha}$?
(d) How does the change in the multiplier relate to the concept of
automatic stabilizers?

8 Now we look at the role taxes play in determining equilibrium income. Suppose we have an economy of the type in Sections 3-4 and 3-5, described by the following functions:

$$C = 50 + 0.8YD$$
$$\bar{I} = 70$$
$$\bar{G} = 200$$
$$\overline{TR} = 100$$
$$t = 0.20$$

(a) Calculate the equilibrium level of income and the multiplier in this model.
(b) Calculate also the budget surplus BS.
(c) Suppose that t increases to 0.25. What is the new equilibrium income? The new multiplier?
(d) Calculate the change in the budget surplus. Would you expect the change in the surplus to be more or less if $c = 0.9$ rather than 0.8?
(e) Can you explain why the multiplier is 1 when $t = 1$?

9 Suppose the economy is operating at equilibrium with $Y_0 = 1,000$. If the government undertakes a fiscal change so that the tax rate t increases by 0.05 and government spending increases by 50, will the budget surplus go up or down? Why?

10 Suppose the government decides to reduce transfer payments (such as welfare), but to increase government purchases of goods and services by an equal amount. That is, it undertakes a change in fiscal policy such that $\Delta \bar{G} = -\overline{TR}$.
(a) Would you expect equilibrium income to rise or fall as a result of this change? Why? Check out your answer with the following example: Suppose initially $c = 0.8$, $t = 0.25$, and $Y_0 = 600$. Now let $\Delta \bar{G} = 10$ and $\Delta \overline{TR} = -10$.
(b) Find the change in equilibrium income ΔY_0.
(c) What is the change in the budget surplus ΔBS? Why has BS changed?

*11 We have seen in problem 10 that an increase in G accompanied by an equal decrease in TR does not leave the budget unchanged. What would the effect on equilibrium income be if TR and G change to leave the budget surplus BS fixed? [Hint: Notice that $BS = TA - TR - G$. We want $\Delta BS = \Delta TA - \Delta TR - \Delta G = 0(*)$ so that $\Delta TR = \Delta TA - \Delta G$. Since t is constant, $\Delta TA = t\Delta Y_0(**)$. We also know that $Y_0 = \bar{\alpha}(\bar{C} + \bar{I} + \bar{G} + c \times \overline{TR})$ and $\Delta Y_0 = \bar{\alpha}(\Delta \bar{G} + c\Delta \overline{TR})$.

[Substituting (*) and (**) into this last equation, derive an expression for ΔY in terms of ΔG. Simplify that expression, using the fact that $\bar{\alpha} = \{1/[1 - c(1 - t)]\}$, to obtain the balanced budget result in the case of changes in transfers and government spending.]

*12 In the preceding problem and in the appendix we derived the bal-
     anced budget multiplier result. It states that if $\Delta G = \Delta TA$ from the
     initial to final equilibrium, then $\Delta Y = \Delta G$. Let us look at an example
     of this balanced budget multiplier in action.
     Consider the economy described by the following functions:

$$C = 85 + 0.75\,YD$$
$$\bar{I} = 50$$
$$\bar{G} = 150$$
$$\overline{TR} = 100$$
$$t = 0.20$$

(a) Derive the multiplier $\bar{\alpha}$ and the level of autonomous spending $\bar{A}$.
(b) From 12(a) calculate the equilibrium level of income and the
     budget surplus.
(c) Now suppose G rises to 250 while t increases to 0.28. Repeat step
     12(a) for the new fiscal policy.
(d) What are ΔTA, ΔG, ΔY, and ΔBS?
(e) In view of this result and that of problem 10, what do you think
     the effect on income would be if we had a balanced budget
     change where $\Delta TR = \Delta TA$?

*13 Suppose the aggregate demand function is as in the figure below.
     Notice that at Y_0 the slope of the aggregate demand curve is *greater*
     than 1. (This would happen if $c > 1$.) Complete this picture as is
     done in Figure 3-1 to include the arrows indicating adjustment
     when $Y \neq Y_0$ and show what IU is for $Y < Y_0$ and $Y > Y_0$. What is
     happening in this example, and how does it differ fundamentally
     from Figure 3-1?

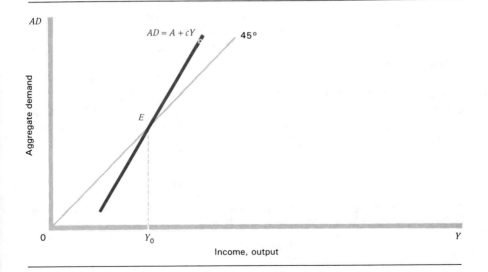

14 Let us look at the effect of the foreign sector by adding the following equations to the model in problem 8:

$$\overline{X} = 150$$
$$Q = 10 + .14Y$$

(a) Calculate the equilibrium level of income and the multiplier in this model.
(b) Why is the multiplier less than the one obtained in problem 8?
*(c) Derive an expression for the trade balance, NX, as a function of income and plot it in a diagram with Y on the horizontal axis.
*(d) Show the effect of a change in income on the trade balance, using your diagram. Show also the effect on the trade balance of a change in exports, given income.
*(e) Calculate the effect on equilibrium income and the trade balance of an increase in exports.

APPENDIX: THE BALANCED BUDGET MULTIPLIER

This appendix considers the balanced budget multiplier result mentioned earlier. The balanced budget multiplier refers to the effects of an increase in government purchases accompanied by an increase in taxes such that, in the new equilibrium, the budget surplus is exactly the same as in the original equilibrium. The result is that the multiplier of such a policy change, the balanced budget multiplier, is 1.

A multiplier of unity implies that output expands by precisely the amount of the increased government purchases with no induced consumption spending. It is apparent that what must be at work is the effect of higher taxes that exactly offset the effect of the income expansion, and that thus maintain disposable income, and hence consumption, constant. With no induced consumption spending, output expands simply to match the increased government purchases.

We can derive this result formally by noting that the change in aggregate demand ΔAD is equal to the change in government purchases plus the change in consumption spending. The latter is equal to the marginal propensity to consume out of disposable income, c, times the change in disposable income, ΔYD; that is, $\Delta YD = \Delta Y_0 - \Delta TA$, where ΔY_0 is the change in output. Thus:

$$\Delta AD = \Delta\overline{G} + c(\Delta Y_0 - \Delta TA) \tag{A1}$$

Since from one equilibrium to another the change in aggregate demand has to equal the change in output, we have

$$\Delta Y_0 = \Delta\overline{G} + c(\Delta Y_0 - \Delta TA)$$

or $$\Delta Y_0 = \frac{1}{1-c}(\Delta\overline{G} - c\Delta TA) \tag{A2}$$

Next we note that by assumption the change in government purchases between the new equilibrium and the old one is exactly matched by a change in tax collection so that $\Delta\overline{G} = \Delta TA$. It follows from this last equality, after substitution in Equation (A2), that with this particular restriction on fiscal policy we have

$$\Delta Y_0 = \frac{1}{1-c}(\Delta\overline{G} - c\Delta\overline{G}) = \Delta\overline{G} = \Delta TA \qquad (A3)$$

so that the multiplier is precisely unity.

Another way of deriving the balanced budget multiplier result is by considering the successive rounds of spending changes caused by the government policy changes. Suppose each of government purchases and taxes increased by \$1. Let $c(1 - t)$, the induced increase in aggregate demand caused by a \$1 increase in income in the presence of taxes, be denoted by $\bar{c}$.

TABLE A3-1   THE BALANCED BUDGET MULTIPLIER

| | CHANGE IN SPENDING RESULTING FROM | | | |
Spending round	$\Delta\overline{G} = 1$	$\Delta TA = 1$	Net this round	Total
1	1	$-\bar{c}$	$1 - \bar{c}$	$1 - \bar{c}$
2	$\bar{c}$	$-\bar{c}^2$	$\bar{c} - \bar{c}^2$	$1 - \bar{c}^2$
3	$\bar{c}^2$	$-\bar{c}^3$	$\bar{c}^2 - \bar{c}^3$	$1 - \bar{c}^3$
4	$\bar{c}^3$	$-\bar{c}^4$	$\bar{c}^3 - \bar{c}^4$	$1 - \bar{c}^4$
$\vdots$				
n	$\bar{c}^{n-1}$	$-\bar{c}^n$	$\bar{c}^{n-1} - \bar{c}^n$	$1 - \bar{c}^n$

Table A3-1 shows the spending induced by the two policy changes. The first column shows the changes in spending resulting from the change in government purchases and its later repercussions. The second column similarly gives the spending effects in successive rounds of the tax increase. The third column sums the two effects for each spending round, while the final column adds all the changes in spending induced so far. Since $\bar{c}$ is less than 1, $(\bar{c})^n$ becomes very small as the number of spending rounds, n, increases, and the final change in aggregate spending caused by the balanced budget increase in governmental spending is just equal to \$1.

Finally, the balanced budget multiplier can also be thought of from a somewhat different perspective. Consider the goods market equilibrium condition in terms of saving, taxes, investment, transfers, and government purchases:

$$S + TA - TR = \overline{I} + G \qquad (A4)$$

Now, using the definition of the budget surplus, $BS \equiv TA - TR - G$,

$$BS = \overline{I} - S \qquad (A5)$$

If there is no change in the budget deficit, nor a change in investment, the equilibrium change in saving is zero. For saving not to change, disposable income must remain unchanged. This says that $\Delta YD = \Delta Y - \Delta TA = 0$, and hence shows once more that the change in income equals the change in taxes. This in turn equals the change in government purchases.

Hence, the balanced budget multiplier, or more precisely, the multiplier associated with an unchanging budget surplus or deficit, is equal to unity. This perspective on the income determination process is very useful because it emphasizes the fact that a change in the surplus or deficit of one sector is matched by a corresponding change in the deficit or surplus of the remaining sectors. If the government surplus is constrained by fiscal policy to be unchanged, so too must be the private sector's surplus, $S - \bar{I}$.

CHAPTER 3: FOOTNOTES

[1]Because output is equal to income received in the economy, economists tend to use the terms *income* and *output* interchangeably when discussing the level of economic activity.

[2]The terms *autonomous* and *induced* are traditionally used to indicate spending that is independent of the level of income and dependent on the level of income, respectively. More generally, autonomous spending is spending that is independent of the other variables explained in a given theory.

[3]The assumption that prices are constant is made to simplify the exposition of Chaps. 3 and 4. In later chapters, we use the theories developed in Chaps. 3 and 4 to study the factors that determine the price level and cause it to change over time.

[4]From now on we shall assume that actual consumption is equal to planned consumption, so that all differences between actual and planned aggregate demand are reflected in unintended inventory changes. In practical terms, this means we are not considering situations where firms put ''Sold Out'' signs in their windows and customers cannot buy what they want.

[5]You may have noticed that the adjustment process we describe raises the possibility that output will temporarily exceed its new equilibrium level during the adjustment to an increase in aggregate demand. This is the *inventory cycle*. Suppose firms desire to keep on hand inventories which are proportional to the level of demand. When demand unexpectedly rises, inventories are depleted. In subsequent periods, the firms have to produce not only to meet the new higher level of aggregate demand, but also to restore their depleted inventories and to raise them to a higher level. While they are rebuilding their inventories and also producing to meet the higher level of demand, their total production will exceed the new level of aggregate demand.

[6]Equation (4) is special because consumption is assumed to be a *linear* function of income. That means that in terms of Fig. 3-2, we can show the consumption function as a straight line. You might want to experiment with nonlinear consumption functions. Note also that because income is equal to output, we use the same symbol, Y, for both income and output.

[7]In Chapter 4 investment spending will become a function of the rate of interest and will gain an important place in the transmission of monetary policy.

[8]We frequently use the subscript $_0$ to denote the equilibrium level of a variable.

[9]Do you see that there is once more the possibility of an inventory cycle? Refer to footnote 5.

[10]In problem 3 at the end of this chapter, we ask you to derive Eq. (10) for Y_0 by starting from $S = \bar{I}$ and substituting for S from Eq. (6).

[11]Recall that autonomous spending $\bar{A}$ is spending that is independent of the level of income. Note also that the answer to this question is contained in Eq. (10). Can you deduce the answer directly from Eq. (10)? This section provides an explanation of that answer.

[12]If you are familiar with the calculus, you will realize that the multiplier is nothing other than the derivative of the equilibrium level of income, Y_0, in Eq. (10) with respect to autonomous spending. Use the calculus on Eqs. (10) and (26) to check the statements of the text.

[13]*Two warnings:* (1) The multiplier is necessarily greater than 1 in this very simplified model of the determination of income, but as we shall see in the discussion of "crowding out" in Chap. 4, there may be circumstances in which it is less than 1. (2) The term *multiplier* is used more generally in economics to mean the effect on some endogenous variable (a variable whose level is explained by the theory being studied) of a unit change in an exogenous variable (a variable whose level is not determined within the theory being examined). For instance, one can talk of the multiplier of a change in the income tax rate on the level of unemployment. However, the classic use of the term is as we are using it here — the effects of a change in autonomous spending on equilibrium output.

[14]We are assuming no taxes are paid on transfers from the government. As a matter of fact, taxes are paid on some transfers, such as interest payments on the government debt, and not paid on other transfers, such as welfare and unemployment benefits.

[15]You should check Eq. (26) by using Eq. (22) to write out Y_0 corresponding to a tax rate of t, and Y'_0 corresponding to t'. Then subtract Y_0 from Y'_0 to obtain ΔY_0 as given in Eq. (26).

[16]We leave it to you to calculate the multiplier relating the change in equilibrium income to the total change in taxes received by the government.

[17]It might be helpful to note that all the results we have derived can be obtained in a straightforward manner by taking the change in aggregate demand at the initial level of income times the multiplier. (Check this proposition for each of the fiscal policy changes we have considered.) You should consider, too, the effect on equilibrium income of an increase in government purchases combined with an equal reduction in transfer payments, $\Delta \bar{G} = -\overline{TR}$. (See problem 10 at the end of this chapter.)

[18]In 1981 the theory that tax cuts would increase government revenue was advanced most strongly by Arthur Laffer of the University of Southern California. However, the argument depended on a different mechanism than that discussed here. Laffer did not depend on aggregate demand effects of tax cuts, but rather on the possibility that a tax cut would lead people to work more. This was a strand in supply-side economics, which we examine more closely in Chap. 17.

[19]In this case, $\bar{\alpha} = 1/[1 - 0.8(0.75)] = 2.5$. So $\Delta BS = -2.5(0.2)(0.75) = -0.375$.

[20]The effects of an increase in the tax rate on the budget surplus are examined in detail in problem 8 at the end of this chapter.

[21]Note that the balanced budget multiplier may well be less than 1 in the more sophisticated models of Chap. 4, in which investment spending depends on the interest rate.

[22]Rather than go through the analysis of changes in transfer payments, we leave it to you to work through an example of the effects on the budget of a change in transfer payments in problem 10 at the end of the chapter.

[23]The concept of the full-employment surplus was first used by E. Cary Brown, "Fiscal Policy in the Thirties: A Reappraisal," *American Economic Review*, December 1956.

[24]In practice, transfer payments, such as welfare and unemployment benefits, are also affected by the state of the economy, so that *TR* also depends on the level of income. But the major cause of differences between the actual surplus and the full-employment surplus is taxes.

[25]A very lucid discussion of the full-employment surplus and other measures — such as the weighted full-employment surplus — that attempt to adjust for the imperfections of the full-employment surplus measure is contained in Alan S. Blinder and Robert M. Solow, "Analytical Foundations of Fiscal Policy," in Alan S. Blinder et al. *The Economics of Public Finance* (Washington, D.C.: The Brookings Institution, 1974).

[26]The OECD (Organization for Economic Cooperation and Development) is a grouping of 24 industrialized countries, based in Paris, which serves as a framework for international policy discussion. Among the members are the few listed in Table 18-4, plus Italy, the United Kingdom, France, and seventeen others.

[27]Do you see why the relative effect on total OECD income (0.74 percent) of a 1 percent increase in U.S. autonomous spending is smaller than the relative effect on U.S. income (1.47 percent)? (*Hint*: Consider (*a*) on which OECD country the U.S. expansion has the largest effect and (*b*) the size of total OECD income relative to that of the United States.)

[28]There is, however, an offset to this, since a more open economy (as measured by the marginal propensity to import) will have a smaller multiplier, so that a given demand expansion will induce a smaller increase in imports. The net effect of more openness, though, is to increase the spillover effects.

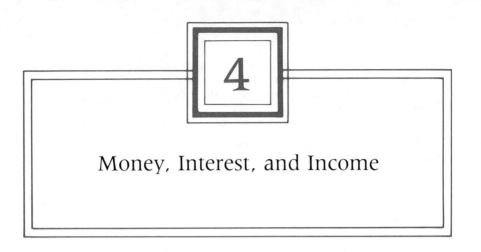

Money, Interest, and Income

The stock of money, interest rates, and the Bank of Canada seemingly had no place in the model of income determination developed in Chapter 3. Clearly, though, we know that money has an important role to play in the determination of income and employment. Interest rates are frequently mentioned as an important determinant of aggregate spending, and the Bank of Canada and monetary policy receive at least as much public attention as fiscal policy. For instance, the blame for the deep 1980–1982 recession and its extraordinarily high interest rates is often placed on the tight money policy pursued in the U.S. and Canada. This chapter introduces money and monetary policy, and builds an explicit framework of analysis in which the interaction of goods and assets markets can be studied.

This new framework leads to an understanding of the determination of interest rates and of their role in the business cycle. Figure 4-1 shows the interest rate on Treasury bills. The interest rate on Treasury bills represents the payment, per dollar per year, that someone receives who lends to the Government of Canada. Thus an interest rate of 10 percent means that someone who lends $100 to the government for 1 year will receive 10 percent, or $10, in interest. Figure 4-1 immediately suggests some questions: What factors cause the interest rate to increase, as occurred for example in 1980–1981, and what factors cause rates to decline as they did in 1982? Furthermore, when interest rates increase, what are the effects on output and employment?

The model we introduce in this chapter, the *IS-LM model*, is the core of modern macroeconomics. It maintains the spirit and, indeed, many details of the previous chapter. The model is broadened, though, by introducing the interest rate as an additional determinant of aggregate demand. In Chapter 3, autonomous spending and fiscal policy were the chief determinants of aggregate spending. Now we add the interest rate and argue that a reduction in the rate of interest raises aggregate demand. This seems a minor extension, which can readily be handled in the context of Chapter 3. This is not entirely correct, because we have to ask what determines the rate of interest. That question extends our model to include the markets for financial assets and forces us to study the interaction of goods and assets markets. Interest rates and income are jointly determined by equilibrium in goods and assets markets.

What is the payoff for that complication? The introduction of assets markets and interest rates serves three important purposes:

1   The extension shows how monetary policy works.
2   The analysis qualifies the conclusions of Chapter 3. Consider Figure 4-2, which lays out the logical structure of the model. So far we have looked at the submodel of autonomous spending and fiscal policy as determinants of aggregate demand and equilibrium income. Now the inclusion of assets markets — money demand and supply, as we shall see — introduces an additional channel. An expansionary fiscal policy, for example, would in the first place raise spending and income. That increase in income, though, would affect the assets markets by raising money demand and thereby raising interest rates. The higher interest rates in turn reduce aggregate spending and thus, as we shall show, dampen the expansionary impact of fiscal policy. Indeed, under certain conditions, the increase in interest rates may be sufficiently important to offset fully the expansionary effects of fiscal policy. Clearly, such an extreme possibility is an important qualification to our study of fiscal policy in Chapter 3.
3   Even if the interest rate changes just mentioned only dampen (rather than offset fully) the expansionary effects of fiscal policy, they nevertheless have an important side effect. The *composition* of aggregate demand between investment and consumption spending will depend on the rate of interest. Higher interest rates dampen aggregate demand mainly by reducing investment. Thus, an expansionary fiscal policy would tend to raise consumption through the multiplier, but it would tend to reduce investment through the induced increase in interest rates. The side effects of fiscal expansion on interest rates and investment continue to be a sensitive and important issue in policy making. An influential view is that fiscal expansion should not be used as a tool for demand management because the increase in government spending takes place at the expense of private investment. Government spending crowds out, or displaces, private investment because it tends to raise interest rates.

These three reasons justify the more complicated model we study in this chapter. There is the further advantage that the extended model helps us to understand the functioning of financial markets.

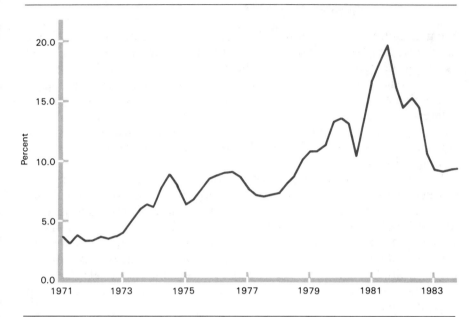

FIGURE 4-1   THE INTEREST RATE ON TREASURY BILLS (Percent per year) (*Source: Bank of Canada Review*)

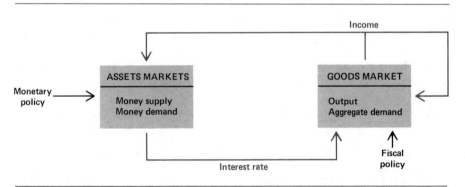

FIGURE 4-2   THE STRUCTURE OF THE *IS-LM* MODEL. The *IS-LM* model empha-sizes the interaction between goods and assets markets. The model of Chapter 3 looks at income determination by arguing that income affects spending, which in turn determines output and income. Now we add the effects of interest rates on spending and thus income, and the dependence of assets markets on income. Higher income raises money demand and thus increases interest rates. Higher interest rates lower spending and thus income. Spending, interest rates, and income are determined jointly by equilibrium in goods *and* assets markets.

Outline of the Chapter

We use Figure 4-2 once more to lay out the structure of this chapter. We start in Section 4-1 with a discussion of the link between interest rates and aggregate demand. Here we use the model of Chapter 3 directly, augmented to include an interest rate as a determinant of aggregate demand. We derive a key relationship, the *IS* curve, that shows combinations of interest rates and levels of income for which the goods markets clear. In this chapter, we restrict the analysis to the case of a closed economy with no foreign trade or capital flows. The open economy case is taken up in Chapters 5 and 6.

In section 4-2, we turn to assets markets and, in particular, to the money market. We show that the demand for money depends on interest rates and income and that there is a combination of interest rates and income levels, the *LM* curve, for which the money market clears.[1] In Section 4-3, we combine the two schedules to study the joint determination of interest rates and income. Section 4-4 lays out the adjustment process toward equilibrium. Monetary policy is discussed in Section 4-5. Fiscal policy and the important issue of the monetary-fiscal policy mix are considered in sections 4-6 and 4-7.

4-1   THE GOODS MARKET AND THE *IS* CURVE

In this section we derive a *goods market equilibrium schedule*. The goods market equilibrium schedule, or *IS* schedule, shows combinations of interest rates and levels of output such that planned spending equals income. The goods market equilibrium schedule is an extension of income determination with a 45° line diagram. What is new here is that investment is no longer fully exogenous but is also determined by the interest rate. To appreciate the extension of Chapter 3 we briefly review what we found there.

In Chapter 3 we derived an expression for equilibrium income:

$$Y_0 = \frac{\overline{A}}{1 - \overline{c}} \qquad \overline{c} = c(1 - t) \tag{1}$$

Equilibrium income in this simple Keynesian model has two determinants: autonomous spending, $\overline{A}$, and the propensity to consume out of income, $\overline{c}$. Autonomous spending includes government spending, investment spending, and autonomous consumption spending. The propensity to consume out of income, as seen from (1), depends on the propensity to consume out of disposable income, c, and on the fraction of a dollar of income retained after taxes, $1 - t$. The higher the level of autonomous spending and the higher the propensity to consume, the higher the equilibrium level of income.

Investment and the Interest Rate

So far, investment spending $\bar{I}$ has been treated as *entirely* exogenous — some number like $25 billion determined altogether outside the model of income determination. Now, as we make our macromodel more complete by introducing interest rates as part of the model, investment spending, too, becomes endogenous. The desired or planned rate of investment is lower the higher the interest rate.

A simple argument shows why. Investment is spending on additions to the capital stock (machinery, structures, inventories). Such investment is undertaken with the aim of making profits in the future by operating machines and factories. Suppose firms borrow to buy the capital (machines and factories) that they use. Then the higher the interest rate, the more firms have to pay out in interest each year from the earnings they receive from their investment. Thus, the higher the interest rate, the less the profits to the firm after paying interest, and the less it will want to invest. Conversely, a low rate of interest makes investment spending profitable and is, therefore, reflected in a high level of planned investment.

The Investment Demand Schedule

We specify an investment spending function of the form[2]

$$I = \bar{I} - bi \qquad b > 0 \tag{2}$$

where i is the rate of interest and b measures the interest response of investment. $\bar{I}$ now denotes autonomous investment spending, that is, investment spending that is independent of both income and the rate of interest.[3] Equation (2) states that the lower the interest rate, the higher is planned investment, with the coefficient b measuring the responsiveness of investment spending to the interest rate.

Figure 4-3 shows the investment schedule of Equation (2). The schedule shows for each level of the rate of interest the rate at which firms plan to spend on investment. The schedule is negatively sloped to reflect the assumption that a reduction in the rate of interest increases the profitability of additions to the capital stock and therefore leads to a larger rate of planned investment spending.

The position of the investment schedule is determined by the slope — the term b in Equation (2) — and by the level of autonomous investment spending $\bar{I}$. If investment is highly responsive to the interest rate, a small decline in interest rates will lead to a large increase in investment, so that the schedule is almost flat. Conversely, if investment responds little to interest rates, the schedule is more nearly vertical. Changes in autonomous investment spending $\bar{I}$ shift the investment schedule. An increase in $\bar{I}$ means that at each level of the interest rate firms plan to invest at a higher rate. This would be shown by a rightward shift of the investment schedule.

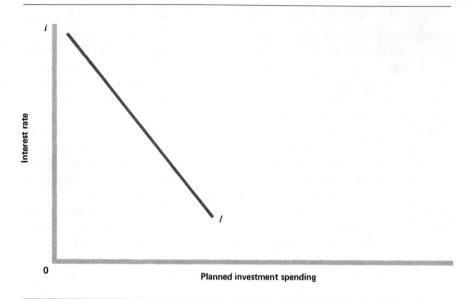

FIGURE 4-3   THE INVESTMENT SCHEDULE. The investment schedule shows the planned level of investment spending at each rate of interest. Because higher interest rates reduce the profitability of additions to the capital stock, higher interest rates imply lower planned rates of investment spending. Changes in autonomous investment shift the investment schedule.

The Interest Rate and Aggregate Demand: The *IS* Curve

We now modify the aggregate demand function of Chapter 3 to reflect the new planned investment spending schedule. Aggregate demand still consists of the demand for consumption, investment, and government spending on goods and services. Only now investment spending depends on the interest rate. We have

$$
\begin{aligned}
AD &\equiv C + I + G \\
&= \overline{C} + c\overline{TR} + c(1 - t)Y + \overline{I} - bi + \overline{G} \\
&= \overline{A} + \overline{c}Y - bi
\end{aligned} \tag{3}
$$

where

$$
\overline{A} \equiv \overline{C} + c\overline{TR} + \overline{I} + \overline{G} \tag{4}
$$

From Equation (3) we observe that an increase in the interest rate reduces aggregate demand at a given level of income because an interest rate increase reduces investment spending. Note that the term $\overline{A}$, which is the part of aggregate demand unaffected by either the level of income or the interest rate, does include part of investment spending, namely, $\overline{I}$. As noted earlier, $\overline{I}$ is the *autonomous* component of investment spending, which is independent of the interest rate (and income).

At any given level of the interest rate, we can still proceed as in Chapter 3 to determine the equilibrium level of income and output. As the interest rate changes, however, the equilibrium level of income changes. The relationship we now derive between the interest rate and the equilibrium level of income in the goods market is the *IS* curve.

Figure 4-4 is used to derive the *IS* curve. For a given level of the interest rate, say, i_1, the last term of Equation (3) is a constant (bi_1), and we can in Figure 4-4a draw the aggregate demand function of Chapter 3, this time with an intercept $\overline{A} - bi_1$. The equilibrium level of income obtained in the usual manner is Y_1 at point E_1. Since that equilibrium level of income was derived for a given level of the interest rate i_1, we can plot that pair (i_1, Y_1) in the bottom panel as point E_1. We now have one point, E_1, on the *IS* curve.

Consider next a lower interest rate, i_2. At a lower interest rate, aggregate demand would be higher at each level of income because investment spending is higher. In terms of Figure 4-4a, that implies an upward shift of the aggregate demand schedule. The entire aggregate demand schedule shifts upward by $-b\Delta i$, where Δi, the assumed change in the interest rate, is negative. The curve shifts upward because the intercept $\overline{A} - bi$ has been increased. Given the increase in aggregate demand, we note that the equilibrium level of income rises to point E_2, with an associated income level Y_2. At point E_2, in the bottom panel, we record the fact that an interest rate i_2 implies an equilibrium level of income, Y_2, — equilibrium in the sense that the goods market is in equilibrium (or that the goods market *clears*). Point E_2 is another point on the *IS* curve.

We can apply the same procedure to all conceivable levels of the interest rate and thereby generate all the points which make up the *IS* curve. They have in common the property that they are combinations of interest rates and income (output) such that the goods market clears. We therefore refer to the *IS* curve as the *goods market equilibrium schedule*.

Figure 4-4 shows that the *IS* curve is negatively sloped, reflecting the increase in aggregate demand associated with a reduction in the interest rate. We can also derive the *IS* curve by using the goods market equilibrium conditon, income equals planned spending, or:

$$Y = AD$$
$$= \overline{A} + \bar{c}Y - bi \tag{5}$$

which can be simplified to

$$Y = \bar{\alpha}(\overline{A} - bi) \qquad \bar{\alpha} = \frac{1}{1 - \bar{c}} \tag{6}$$

where $\bar{\alpha}$ is the multiplier of Chapter 3. Equation (6) should now be compared with (1) at the beginning of this chapter. From Equation (6), we note that a higher interest rate implies a lower level of equilibrium income for a given $\overline{A}$, as Figure 4-4 shows.

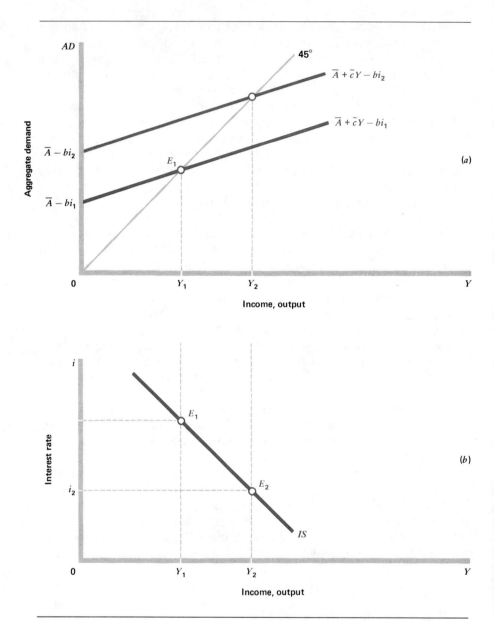

FIGURE 4-4   DERIVATION OF THE *IS* CURVE. At an interest rate i_1, equilibrium in the goods market obtains at point E_1 in the upper panel with an income level Y_1. In the lower panel this is recorded as point E_1. A fall in the interest rate to i_2 raises aggregate demand, shifting the level of spending upward at each income level. The new equilibrium income level is Y_2. In the lower panel, point E_2 records the new equilibrium in the goods market corresponding to an interest rate i_2.

The construction of the *IS* curve is quite straightforward and may even be deceptively simple. We can gain further understanding of the economics of the *IS* curve by asking and answering the following questions:

- What determines the slope of the *IS* curve?
- What determines the position of the *IS* curve, given its slope, and what causes the curve to shift?
- What happens when the interest rate and income are at levels such that we are not on the *IS* curve?

The Slope of the *IS* Curve

We have already noted that the *IS* curve is negatively sloped because a higher level of the interest rate reduces investment spending, therefore reducing aggregate demand and thus the equilibrium level of income. The steepness of the curve depends on how sensitive investment spending is to changes in the interest rate, and also on the multiplier $\bar{\alpha}$ in Equation (6).

Suppose that investment spending is very sensitive to the interest rate, so that b in Equation (6) is large. Then, in terms of Figure 4-4, a given change in the interest rate produces a large change in aggregate demand, and thus shifts the aggregate demand curve in Figure 4-4a up by a large distance. A large shift in the aggregate demand schedule produces a correspondingly large change in the equilibrium level of income. If a given change in the interest rate produces a large change in income, the *IS* curve is very flat. This is the case if investment is very sensitive to the interest rate, that is, if b is large. Correspondingly, with b small and investment spending not very sensitive to the interest rate, the *IS* curve is relatively steep.

The Role of the Multiplier

Consider next the effects of the multiplier $\bar{\alpha}$ on the steepness of the *IS* curve. Figure 4-5 shows aggregate demand curves corresponding to different multipliers. The coefficient $\bar{c}$ on the darker aggregate demand curves is smaller than the corresponding coefficient $\bar{c}'$ on the lighter aggregate demand curves. The multiplier is accordingly larger on the lighter aggregate demand curves. The initial levels of income, Y_1 and Y_1', correspond to the interest rate i_1 on the lower of each of the darker and lighter aggregate demand curves, respectively.

A given reduction in the interest rate, to i_2, raises the intercept of the aggregate demand curves by the same vertical distance, as shown in the top panel. However, the implied change in income is very different. For the lighter curve, income rises to Y_2', while it rises only to Y_2 on the darker line. The change in equilibrium income corresponding to a given change in the interest rate is accordingly larger as the aggregate demand curve is

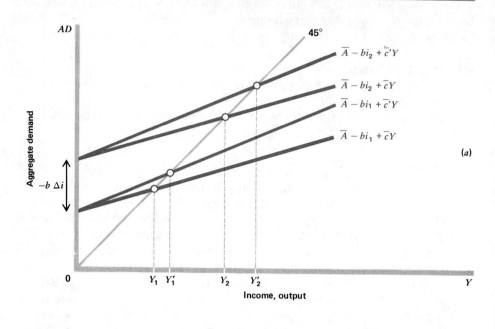

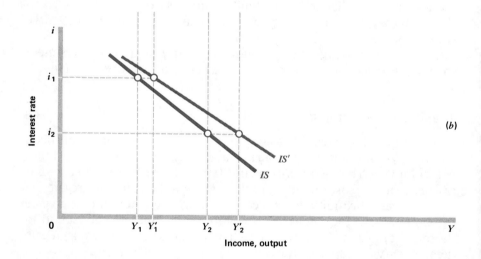

FIGURE 4-5   EFFECTS OF THE MULTIPLIER ON THE STEEPNESS OF THE *IS* CURVE. The diagram shows that corresponding to a higher marginal propensity to spend, and hence a steeper aggregate demand schedule, there is a flatter *IS* schedule.

steeper; that is, the larger the multiplier, the greater the rise in income. That should not be surprising since effectively the change in the interest rate and induced change in investment act in the same way on the aggregate demand curves as a change in autonomous spending $\overline{A}$. As we see from the lower figure, the smaller the multiplier, the steeper the IS curve. Equivalently, the larger the multiplier, the larger the change in income produced by a given change in the interest rate.

We have thus seen that the smaller the sensitivity of investment spending to the interest rate and the smaller the multiplier, the steeper the IS curve. This conclusion can be confirmed by using Equation (6). We can turn Equation (6) around to express the interest rate as a function of the level of income:

$$i = \frac{\overline{A}}{b} - \frac{Y}{\overline{\alpha}b} \tag{6a}$$

Thus, for a given change in Y, the associated change in i will be larger in size as b is smaller and $\overline{\alpha}$ is smaller.

Given that the slope of the IS curve depends on the multiplier, fiscal policy can affect that slope. The multiplier $\overline{\alpha}$ is affected by the tax rate: an increase in the tax rate reduces the multiplier. Accordingly, the higher the tax rate, the steeper the IS curve.[4]

The Position of the IS Curve

Figure 4-6 shows two different IS curves, the lighter one of which lies to the right and above the darker IS curve. What might cause the IS curve to be at IS' rather than at IS? The answer is an increase in the level of autonomous spending.

In Figure 4-6a we show an initial aggregate demand curve drawn for a level of autonomous spending $\overline{A}$ and for an interest rate i_1. Corresponding to the initial aggregate demand curve is the point E_1 on the IS curve in Figure 4-6b. Now, at the same interest rate, let the level of autonomous spending increase to $\overline{A}'$. The increase in autonomous spending increases the equilibrium level of income at the interest rate i_1. The point E_2 in Figure 4-6b is thus a point on the new goods market equilibrium schedule IS'. Since E_1 was an arbitrary point on the initial IS curve, we can perform the exercise for all levels of the interest rate and thereby generate our new curve IS'. We see that an increase in autonomous spending shifts the curve out to the right.

By now how much does the curve shift? The change in income, as a result of the change in autonomous spending, can be seen from the top

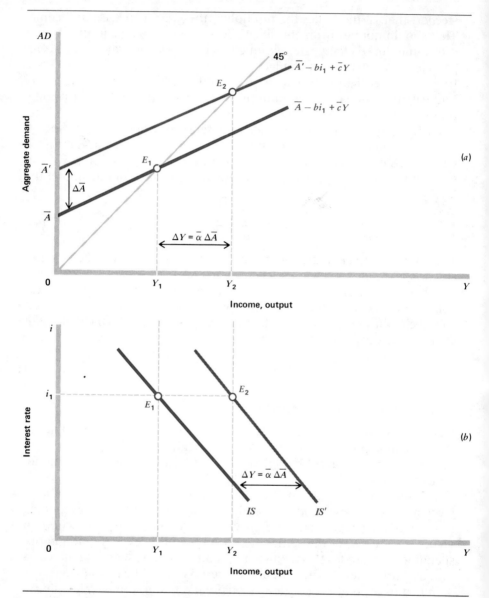

FIGURE 4-6   A SHIFT IN THE *IS* CURVE CAUSED BY A CHANGE IN AUTONO-MOUS SPENDING. An increase in aggregate demand due to higher autonomous spending shifts the aggregate demand curve in Figure 4-6(*a*) up, raising the equilibrium level of output at interest rate i_1. The *IS* schedule shifts. At each level of the interest rate, equilibrium income is now higher. The horizontal shift of the *IS* schedule is equal to the multiplier times the increase in autonomous spending.

panel to be just the multiplier times the change in autonomous spending. That means that the *IS* curve is shifted horizontally by a distance equal to the multiplier times the change in autonomous spending. This can be seen from the fact that the distance between E_1 and E_2, in the lower panel, is the distance between Y_1 and Y_2 in the upper panel.

Now the level of autonomous spending is, from Equation (4):

$$\overline{A} \equiv \overline{C} + c\overline{TR} + \overline{I} + \overline{G}$$

Accordingly, an increase in government purchases or transfer payments will shift the *IS* curve out to the right, the extent of the shift depending on the size of the multiplier. A reduction in transfer payments or in government purchases shifts the *IS* curve to the left.

Positions off the *IS* Curve

We gain understanding of the meaning of the *IS* curve by considering points off the curve. Figure 4-7 reproduces Figure 4-4, along with two additional points — the *dis*equilibrium points E_3 and E_4. Consider first the question of what is true for points off the schedule, points such as E_3 and E_4. In Figure 4-7*b* at point E_3 we have the same interest rate i_2 as at point E_2, but the level of income is lower than at E_2. Since the interest rate i_2 at E_3 is the same as at E_2, we must have the same aggregate demand function corresponding to the two points. Accordingly, looking now at Figure 4-7*a*, we find both points are on the same aggregate demand schedule. At E_3 on that schedule, aggregate demand exceeds the level of output. Point E_3 is therefore a point of *excess demand for goods*: the interest rate is too low or output is too low for the goods market to be in equilibrium. Demand for goods exceeds output.

Next, consider point E_4 in Figure 4-7*b*. Here we have the same rate of interest i_1 as at E_1, but the level of income is higher. Given the interest rate i_1, the corresponding point in Figure 4-7*a* is at E_4, where we have an *excess supply of goods* since output is larger than aggregate demand — that is, aggregate demand, given the interest rate i_1 and the income level Y_2.

The preceding discussion can be generalized by saying that points above and to the right of the *IS* curve — points like E_4 — are points of excess supply of goods. This is indicated by *ESG* (excess supply of goods) in Figure 4-7*b*. Points below and to the left of the *IS* curve are points of excess demand for goods (*EDG*). At a point like E_3, the interest rate is too low and aggregate demand is therefore too high, relative to output. *EDG* shows the region of excess demand in Figure 4-7.

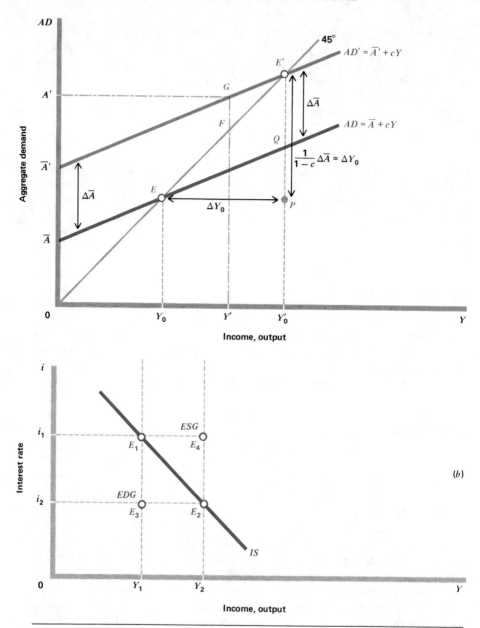

FIGURE 4-7 EXCESS SUPPLY (*ESG*) AND DEMAND (*EDG*) IN THE GOODS MARKET. Points above and to the right of the *IS* schedule correspond to an excess supply of goods, and points below and to the left to an excess demand for goods. At a point such as E_4, interest rates are higher than at E_2 on the *IS* curve. At the higher interest rates, investment spending is too low, and thus output exceeds planned spending and there is an excess supply of goods.

Summary

The major points about the *IS* curve are:

1 The *IS* curve is the schedule of combinations of the interest rate and level of income such that the goods market is in equilibrium.

2 The *IS* curve is negatively sloped because an increase in the interest rate reduces planned investment spending and therefore reduces aggregate demand, thus reducing the equilibrium level of income.

3 The smaller the multiplier and the less sensitive investment spending is to changes in the interest rate, the steeper the curve.

4 The *IS* curve is shifted by changes in autonomous spending. An increase in autonomous spending, including an increase in government purchases, shifts the *IS* curve out to the right.

5 At points to the right of the curve, there is excess supply in the goods market, and at points to the left of the curve, there is excess demand for goods.

We turn now to examine behaviour in the assets markets.

4-2   THE ASSETS MARKETS AND THE *LM* CURVE

In the preceding section, we discussed aggregate demand and the goods market. In the present section, we turn to the assets markets. The assets markets are the markets in which money, bonds, stocks, houses, and other forms of wealth are traded. Up to this point in the book, we have ignored the role of those markets in affecting the level of income, and it is now time to remedy the omission.

There is a large variety of assets, and a tremendous volume of trading occurs everyday in the assets markets. But we shall simplify matters by grouping all available financial assets into two groups, *money* and *interest-bearing assets*.[5] By analogy with our treatment of the goods market, we proceed in the assets markets as if there are only two assets, money and all others. It will be useful to think of the other assets as marketable claims to future income such as *bonds*.

A bond is a promise to pay to its holder certain agreed-upon amounts of money at specified dates in the future. For example, a borrower sells a bond in exchange for a given amount of money today, say, $100, and promises to pay a fixed amount, say, $6, each year to the person who owns the bond, and to repay the full $100 (the principal) after some fixed period of time, such as 3 years, or perhaps longer. In this example, the interest rate is 6 percent, for that is the percentage of the amount borrowed that the borrower pays each year.

BOX 4-1   ASSETS AND ASSET RETURNS

There are four kinds of assets in the economy: money, interest-bearing assets, equities or stocks, and real assets.

MONEY

The money stock consists of assets that can be immediately used for making payments. It includes currency (notes and coins) and deposits on which cheques can be written. There is no interest paid on currency and most chequable deposits. However, in recent years, interest-bearing chequing accounts have become more common, thus blurring the distinction between money and nonmonetary financial assets. The definition of the stock of money is discussed in more detail in Chapter 9.

INTEREST-BEARING ASSETS

These include savings accounts in banks and other financial institutions, mortgages and bonds. A bond is a promise by a borrower to pay the lender a certain amount (the principal) at a specified date (the maturity date of the bond) and in the meantime to pay a given amount of interest per year. Thus we might have a bond, issued by the Government of Canada, that pays $10,000 on June 1, 1985, and until that time pays 8 percent interest per year, or $800 each year. Bonds are issued by many types of borrower — the government, municipalities, corporations. The interest rates on bonds issued by different borrowers reflect the differing risk of default. Default occurs when a borrower is unable to meet the commitment to pay interest or principal. Corporations sometimes default, and during the great depression of the 1930s, so did some cities. In the early 1980s there was fear that many foreign governments would do so.

EQUITIES OR STOCKS

Equities or stocks are claims to a share of the profits in an enterprise. For example, a share in Alberta Energy entitles the owner to a share of the profits of that corporation. The shareholder or stockholder receives the return on equity in two forms. Most firms pay regular *dividends*, which means that stockholders receive a certain amount of dollars for each share they own. Firms may also decide not to distribute profits to the stockholders, but rather retain them and reinvest these profits by adding to their stock of machines and structures. When this occurs, the shares become more valuable since they now represent claims on the profits from a larger capital stock. Therefore, the price of the stock in the market will rise, and stockholders make *capital gains*. A capital gain is an increase, per period of time, in the price of an asset. Of course, when the outlook for a corporation turns sour, stock prices can fall and stockholders make capital losses.

Thus the return on stocks or the yield to a holder of a stock is equal to the dividend (as a percent of price) plus the capital gain.

Suppose we look at 1983 and 1984 and consider the yield on a stock in an imaginary company, BioMiracles, Inc. In 1983 the stock trades for $15. In 1984 the stock pays a dividend of $0.75 and the stock price increases to $16.50. What is the yield on the stock? The yield per year is equal to 15.0 percent, which is the dividend as a percent of initial price [5 percent = (0.75/15) × 100] plus 10.0 percent, which is the $1.50 capital gain as a percent of initial price.

REAL ASSETS

Real assets, or tangible assets, are the machines, land, and structures owned by corporations, and the consumer durables (washing machines, stereos, etc.) and houses owned by households. These assets carry a return that differs from one asset to another. Owner-occupied houses provide a return to owners who enjoy living in them and not paying monthly rent; the machines a firm owns contribute to producing output and thus making profits. The assets are called *real* to distinguish them from *financial* assets (money, stocks, bonds).

The value of equities and bonds held by individuals cannot be added to tangible wealth to get the total wealth of individuals. The reason is that the equities and bonds they hold are claims on part of the tangible wealth, that part held by corporations. The equity share gives an individual a part ownership in the factory and machinery.

In macroeconomics, to make things manageable, we lump assets into two categories. On one side we have money, with the specific characteristic that it is the only asset that serves as a means of payment. On the other side we have all other assets. Because money offers the convenience of being a means of payment, it carries a lower return than other assets, but that differential depends on the relative supplies of assets. As we see in this chapter, when the Bank of Canada reduces the money stock and increases the supply of other assets (we say "bonds"), the yield on other assets increases.

The Appendix to Chapter 8 develops the relationship between interest rates and asset prices or present values. The Appendix can be read independently of Chapter 8, and the interested student can study that material now.

The Wealth Constraint

At any given time, an individual has to decide how to allocate his or her financial wealth between alternative assets. The more bonds held, the more interest received on total financial wealth. The more money held, the less likely the individual is not to have money available when he or she wants to make a purchase. The person who has $1,000 in financial wealth has to decide whether to hold, say, $900 in bonds and $100 in money, or rather, $500 in each type of asset, or even $1,000 in money and none in bonds. Decisions on the form in which to hold assets are *portfolio decisions*.

The example makes it clear that the portfolio decision on how much money to hold and the decision on how many bonds to hold are really the same decision. Given the level of financial wealth, the individual who has decided how many bonds to hold has implicitly also decided how much money to hold. There is thus a *wealth budget constraint* which states that the sum of the individual's demand for money and demand for bonds has to add up to that person's total financial wealth.

Real and Nominal Money Demand

At this stage we have to reinforce the crucial distinction between *real* and *nominal* variables. The nominal demand for money is the individual's demand for a given number of dollars, and similarly, the nominal demand for bonds is the demand for a given number of dollars' worth of bonds. The real demand for money is the demand for money expressed in terms of the number of units of goods that money will buy: it is equal to the nominal demand for money divided by the price level. If the nominal demand for money is $100 and the price level is $2 per good — meaning that the representative basket of goods costs $2 — then the real demand for money is 50 goods. If the price level later doubles to $4 per good and the demand for nominal money likewise doubles to $200, the real demand for money is unchanged at 50 goods.

Real money balances — real balances for short — are the quantity of nominal money divided by the price level, and the real demand for money is called the *demand for real balances*. Similarly, real bond holdings are the nominal quantity of bonds divided by the price level.

The wealth budget constraint in the assets markets states that the demand for real balances, which we denote L, plus the demand for real bond holdings, which we denote DB, must add up to the real financial wealth of the individual. Real financial wealth is, of course, simply nominal wealth WN divided by the price level P:

$$L + DB \equiv \frac{WN}{P} \tag{7}$$

Note, again, that the wealth budget constraint implies, given an individual's real wealth, that a decision to hold more real balances is also a decision to hold less real wealth in the form of bonds. This implication turns out to be both important and convenient. It will allow us to discuss assets markets entirely in terms of the money market. Why? Because, given real wealth, when the money market is in equilibrium, the bond market will turn out also to be in equilibrium. We now show why that should be.

The total amount of real financial wealth in the economy consists of real money balances and real bonds in existence. Thus, total real financial wealth is equal to

$$\frac{WN}{P} \equiv \frac{M}{P} + SB \tag{8}$$

where M is the stock of nominal money balances and SB is the real value of the supply of bonds. Total real financial wealth consists of real balances and real bonds. The distinction between Equations (7) and (8) is that Equation (7) is a constraint on the amount of assets individuals wish to hold, whereas Equation (8) is merely an accounting relationship which tells us how much financial wealth there is in the economy. There is no implication in the accounting relationship in Equation (8) that individuals are necessarily happy to hold the amounts of money and bonds that actually exist in the economy.

Now we substitute Equation (7) into Equation (8) and rearrange terms to obtain

$$\left(L - \frac{M}{P}\right) + (DB - SB) \equiv 0 \qquad (9)$$

Let us see what Equation (9) implies. Suppose that the demand for real balances L is equal to the existing stock of real balances M/P. Then the first term in parentheses in Equation (9) is equal to zero, and therefore the second term in parentheses must also be zero. Thus, if the demand for real money balances is equal to the real money supply, the demand for real bonds DB must be equal to the supply of real bonds SB.

Stating the same proposition in terms of "markets," we can say the following: The *wealth budget constraint* implies that when the money market is in equilibrium ($L = M/P$), the bond market, too, is in equilibrium ($DB = SB$). Similarly, when there is excess demand in the money market, so that $L > M/P$, there is an excess supply of bonds; $DB < SB$. We can therefore fully discuss the assets markets by concentrating our attention on the money market.

The Demand for Money

We now turn to the money market and initially concentrate on the demand for real balances.[6] The demand for money is a demand for *real* balances because the public holds money for what it will buy. The higher the price level, the more nominal balances a person has to hold to be able to purchase a given quantity of goods. If the price level doubles, then an individual has to hold twice as many nominal balances in order to be able to buy the same amount of goods.

The demand for real balances depends on the level of real income and the interest rate. It depends on the level of real income because individuals hold money to finance their expenditures, which, in turn, depend on income. The demand for money depends also on the cost of holding money. The cost of holding money is the interest that is foregone by holding money rather than other assets. The higher the interest rate, the more costly it is to hold money, rather than other assets, and accordingly, the less cash will be held at each level of income.[7] Individuals can economize on their holdings of cash, when the interest rate rises, by being more careful in managing their money, by making transfers from money to bonds whenever their money holdings reach any appreciable magnitude. If the interest rate is 1 percent, then there is very little benefit from holding bonds rather than money. However, when the interest rate is 10 percent, one would probably go to some effort not to hold more money than needed to finance day-to-day transactions.

On these simple grounds, then, the demand for real balances increases with the level of real income and decreases with the interest rate. The demand for real balances is accordingly written[8]

$$L = kY - hi \qquad k > 0 \qquad h > 0 \tag{10}$$

The parameters k and h reflect the sensitivity of the demand for real balances to the level of income and the interest rate, respectively. A \$5 increase in real income raises money demand by $5k$ real dollars. An increase in the interest rate by 1 percentage point reduces real money demand by h real dollars.

The demand function for real balances, Equation (10), implies that for a given level of income, the quantity demanded is a decreasing function of the rate of interest. Such a demand curve is shown in Figure 4-8 for a level of income Y_1. The higher the level of income, the larger the demand for real balances, and therefore the further to the right the demand curve. The demand curve for a higher level of real income Y_2 is also shown in Figure 4-8.

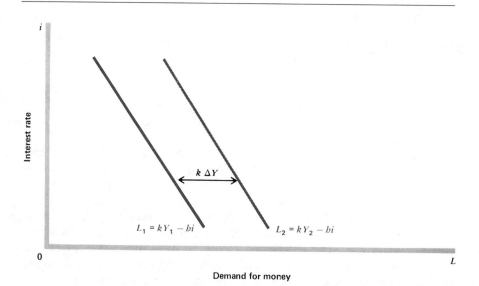

FIGURE 4-8   THE DEMAND FOR REAL BALANCES AS A FUNCTION OF THE INTEREST RATE AND REAL INCOME. The demand for real balances is drawn as a function of the rate of interest. The higher the rate of interest, the lower the quantity of real balances demanded, given the level of income. An increase in income raises the demand for money. This is shown by a rightward shift of the money demand schedule.

The Supply of Money, Money Market Equilibrium, and the *LM* Curve

Now we study equilibrium in the money market. For that purpose we have to say how the supply of money is determined. The nominal quantity of money M is controlled by the Bank of Canada, and we take it as given at the level $\overline{M}$. We assume the price level is constant at the level $\overline{P}$, so that the real money supply is at the level $\overline{M}/\overline{P}$.[9]

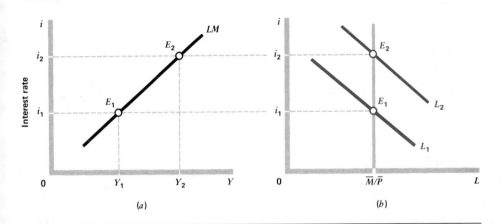

(a)   (b)

FIGURE 4-9 DERIVATION OF THE *LM* CURVE. The right-hand panel shows the money market. The supply of real balances is the vertical line $\overline{M}/\overline{P}$. The nominal money supply $\overline{M}$ is fixed by the Bank of Canada, and the price level $\overline{P}$ is assumed given. Demand for money curves L_1 and L_2 corresponds to different levels of income. When the income level is Y_1, L_1 applies, and the equilibrium interest rate is i_1. This gives point E_1 on the *LM* schedule in Figure 4-9(a). At income level Y_2, greater than Y_1, the equilibrium interest rate is i_2, yielding point E_2 on the *LM* curve.

In Figure 4-9, we show combinations of interest rate and income levels such that the demand for real balances exactly matches the available supply. Starting with the level of income Y_1, we have the corresponding demand curve for real balances L_1, in Figure 4-9b. It is drawn, as in Figure 4-8, as a decreasing function of the interest rate. The existing supply of real balances $\overline{M}/\overline{P}$ is shown by the vertical line, since it is given and therefore is independent of the interest rate. The interest rate i_1 has the property that it clears the money market. At that interest rate, the demand for real balances equals the supply. Therefore, point E_1 is an equilibrium point in the money market. That point is recorded in Figure 4-9a as a point on the *money market equilibrium schedule*, or the *LM* curve.

Consider next the effect of an increase in income to Y_2. In Figure 4-9b the higher level of income causes the demand for real balances to be higher at each level of the interest rate, and so the demand curve for real balances shifts up and to the right, to L_2. We require an increase in the interest rate to i_2 to maintain equilibrium in the money market at that higher level of income. Accordingly, our new equilibrium point is E_2. In Figure 4-9a we record point E_2 as a point of equilibrium in the money market. Performing the same exercise for all income levels, we generate a series of points that can be linked up to give us the *LM* schedule.

The *LM* schedule, or money market equilibrium schedule, shows all combinations of interest rates and levels of income such that the demand for real balances is equal to the supply. Along the *LM* schedule, the money market is in equilibrium.

The *LM* curve is positively sloped. An increase in the interest rate reduces the demand for real balances. To maintain the demand for real balances equal to the fixed supply, the level of income has, therefore, to rise. Accordingly, money market equilibrium implies that an increase in the interest rate is accompanied by an increase in the level of income.

The *LM* curve can be obtained directly by combining the demand curve for real balances, Equation (10), and the fixed supply of real balances. For the money market to be in equilibrium we require that demand equals supply, or that

$$\frac{\overline{M}}{P} = kY - hi \tag{11}$$

Solving for the interest rate, we have

$$i = \frac{1}{h}\left(kY - \frac{\overline{M}}{P}\right) \tag{11a}$$

The relationship (11a) is the *LM* curve.

Next we ask the same questions about the properties of the *LM* schedule that we asked about the *IS* curve.

The Slope of the *LM* Curve

The larger the responsiveness of the demand for money to income, as measured by k, and the lower the responsiveness of the demand for money to the interest rate h, the steeper the *LM* curve will be. This point can be established by experimenting with Figure 4-9. It can also be confirmed by examining Equation (11a), where a given change in income ΔY has a larger effect on the interest rate i, the larger is k and the smaller is h. If the demand for money is relatively insensitive to the interest rate, so that h is close to zero, the *LM* curve is nearly vertical. If the demand for money is very sensitive to the interest rate, so that h is large, then the *LM* curve is close to horizontal. In that case, a small change in the interest rate is accompanied by a large change in the level of income to maintain money market equilibrium.

The Position of the LM Curve

The real money supply is held constant along the *LM* curve. It follows that a change in the real money supply will shift the *LM* curve. In Figure 4-10, we show the effect of an increase in the real money supply. In Figure 4-10*b*, we draw the demand for real money balances for a level of income Y_1. With the initial real money supply $\overline{M}/\overline{P}$, the equilibrium is at point E_1, with an interest rate i_1. The corresponding point on the *LM* schedule is E_1.

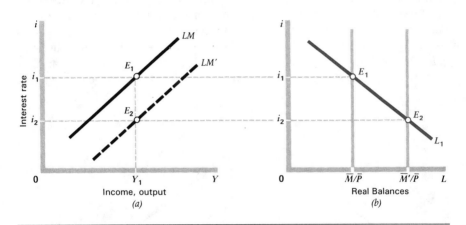

FIGURE 4-10 AN INCREASE IN THE SUPPLY OF MONEY FROM $\overline{M}$ to $\overline{M}'$ SHIFTS THE *LM* CURVE TO THE RIGHT. An increase in the stock of real balances shifts the supply schedule in the right panel from $\overline{M}/\overline{P}$ to $\overline{M}'/\overline{P}$. At the initial income level Y_1, the equilibrium interest rate in the money market falls to i_2. In the left panel we show point E_2 as one point on the new *LM* schedule, corresponding to the higher money stock. Thus an increase in the real money stock shifts the *LM* schedule down and to the right.

Consider the effect of an increase in the real money supply to $\overline{M}'/\overline{P}$, which is represented by a rightward shift of the money supply schedule. At the initial level of income and, hence, on the demand schedule L_1, we now have an excess supply of real balances. To restore money market equilibrium at the income level Y_1, the interest rate has to decline to i_2. The new equilibrium is, therefore, at point E_2. This implies that in Figure 4-10*a*, the *LM* schedule shifts to the right and down to *LM'*. At each level of income the equilibrium interest rate has to be lower to induce people to hold the larger real quantity of money. Alternatively, at each level of the interest rate the level of income has to be higher so as to raise the transactions demand for money and thereby absorb the higher real money supply. These points can be noted, too, from inspection of the money market equilibrium condition in Equation (11).

Positions off the *LM* Curve

Next we consider points off the *LM* schedule, to characterize them as points of excess demand or supply of money. For that purpose, we look at Figure 4-11, which reproduces Figure 4-9 but adds the disequilibrium points E_3 and E_4. Look first at point E_1, where the money market is in equilibrium. Next assume an increase in the level of income to Y_2. This will raise the demand for real balances and shift the demand curve to L_2. At the initial interest rate, the demand for real balances would be indicated by point E_4 in Figure 4-11b, and we would have an excess demand for money — an excess of demand over supply — equal to the distance E_1E_4. Accordingly, point E_4 in Figure 4-11a is a point of excess demand for money: the interest rate is too low and/or the level of income too high for

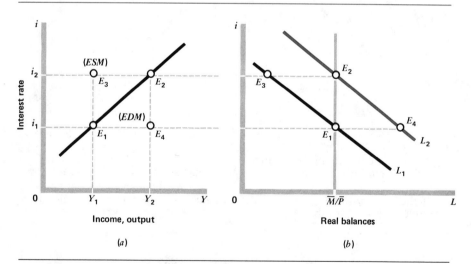

FIGURE 4-11   EXCESS DEMAND (*EDM*) AND SUPPLY (*ESM*) OF MONEY. Points above and to the left of the *LM* schedule correspond to an excess supply of real balances; points below and to the right to an excess demand for real balances. Starting at point E_1 in the left panel, an increase in income takes us to E_4. At E_4 in the right panel, there is an excess demand for money — and thus at E_4 in the left panel there is an excess demand for money. By a similar argument, we can start at E_2 and move to E_3, at which the level of income is lower. This creates an excess supply of money.

the money market to clear. Consider, next, point E_3 in Figure 4-11b. Here we have the initial level of income Y_1, but an interest rate that is too high to yield money market equilibrium. Accordingly, we have an excess supply of money equal to the distance E_3E_2. Point E_3 in Figure 4-11a therefore corresponds to an excess supply of money.

More generally, any point to the right and below the LM schedule is a point of excess demand for money, and any point to the left and above the LM curve is a point of excess supply. This is shown by the EDM and ESM notations in Figure 4-11a.

Summary

The following are the major points about the LM curve.

1　The LM curve is the schedule of combinations of the interest rate and level of income such that the money market is in equilibrium.

2　When the money market is in equilibrium, so is the bond market in equilibrium. The LM curve is, therefore, also the schedule of combinations of the level of income and the interest rate such that the bond market is in equilibrium.

3　The LM curve is positively sloped. Given the fixed money supply, an increase in the level of income, which increases the quantity of money demanded, has to be accompanied by an increase in the interest rate. This reduces the quantity of money demanded and thereby maintains money market equilibrium.

4　The LM curve is shifted by changes in the money supply. An increase in the money supply shifts the LM curve out to the right.

5　At points to the right of the LM curve, there is an excess demand for money, and at points to its left, there is an excess supply of money.

We are now ready to discuss the joint equilibrium of the goods and assets markets.

4-3　EQUILIBRIUM IN THE GOODS AND ASSETS MARKETS

We have so far studied the conditions that have to be satisfied for the goods and money markets, respectively, to be in equilibrium. These conditions are summarized by the IS and LM schedules. The task now is to determine how these markets are brought into *simultaneous* equilibrium. For simultaneous equilibrium, interest rates and income have to be such that *both* the goods market *and* the money market are in equilibrium. That condition is satisfied at point E in Figure 4-12. The equilibrium interest rate is therefore i_0, and the equilibrium level of income is Y_0, given the exogenous variables, in particular, the real money supply and fiscal policy.[10] At point E, both the goods market and the assets markets are in equilibrium.

Figure 4-12 summarizes our analysis: the interest rate and the level of output are determined by the interaction of the assets (LM) and goods (IS) markets.

It is worth stepping back now to review our assumptions and the meaning of the equilibrium at E. The major assumption that we are making is that the price level is constant and that firms are willing to supply whatever amount of output is demanded at that price level. Thus, we assume the level of output Y_0 in Figure 4-12 will be willingly supplied by firms at the price level $\overline{P}$. We repeat again that this assumption is one that is temporarily needed for the development of the analysis; it will be dropped in Chapter 13 when we begin to study the determinants of the price level.

At the point E, in Figure 4-12, the economy is in equilibrium, given the price level, because both the goods and money markets are in equilibrium. The demand for goods is equal to the level of output on the IS curve. And on the LM curve, the demand for money is equal to the supply of money.

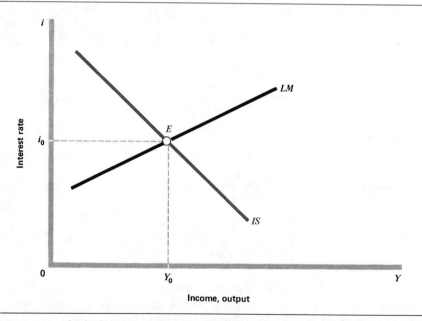

FIGURE 4-12   GOODS AND ASSETS MARKET EQUILIBRIUM. Goods and assets markets clear at point E. Interest rates and income are such that the public holds the existing stock of money and planned spending equals output.

That also means the supply of bonds is equal to the demand for bonds, as our discussion of the wealth budget constraint showed. Accordingly, at point E, firms are producing the amount of output they plan to (there is no unintended inventory accumulation or decumulation), and individuals have the portfolio compositions they desire.

Changes in the Equilibrium Levels of Income and the Interest Rate

The equilibrium levels of income and the interest rate will change when either the IS or the LM curve shifts. Figure 4-13, for example, shows the effects of an increase in the rate of autonomous consumption $\overline{C}$ on the equilibrium levels of income and the interest rate. Such an increase raises autonomous spending $\overline{A}$, and therefore shifts the IS curve to the right. That results in a rise in the level of income and an increase in the interest rate at point E'.

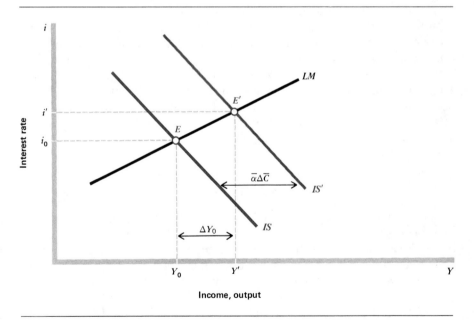

FIGURE 4-13   EFFECTS OF AN INCREASE IN AUTONOMOUS SPENDING ON INCOME AND THE INTEREST RATE. An increase in autonomous spending shifts the IS schedule out and to the right. Income increases, and the equilibrium income level rises. The increase in income is less than is given by the simple multiplier $\overline{\alpha}$. This is because interest rates increase and dampen investment spending.

We recall that an increase in autonomous spending, equal to $\Delta\overline{C}$, shifts the IS curve to the right by the amount $\overline{\alpha}\Delta\overline{C}$, as we show in Figure 4-13. In Chapter 3, where we dealt only with the goods market, we would have argued that $\overline{\alpha}\Delta\overline{C}$ would be the change in the level of income resulting from the change of $\Delta\overline{C}$ in autonomous spending. But it can be seen in Figure 4-13 that the change in income here is only ΔY_0, which is clearly less than the shift in the IS curve $\overline{\alpha}\Delta\overline{C}$.

What explains the fact that the increase in income is smaller than the increase in autonomous spending $\Delta\overline{C}$ times the simple multiplier $\overline{\alpha}$? Diagrammatically, it is clear that it is the slope of the LM curve. If the LM curve were horizontal, there would be no difference between the extent of the horizontal shift of the IS curve and the change in income. If the LM curve were horizontal, then the interest rate would not change when the IS curve shifts.

What is the economics of what is happening? The increase in autonomous spending does tend to increase the level of income. But an increase in income increases the demand for money. With the supply of money fixed, the interest rate has to rise to ensure that the demand for money stays equal to the fixed supply. When the interest rate rises, investment spending is reduced because investment is negatively related to the interest rate. Accordingly, the equilibrium change in income is less than the horizontal shift of the IS curve, $\overline{\alpha}\Delta\overline{C}$.

We have now provided an example of the use of the IS-LM apparatus. That apparatus is most useful for studying the effects of monetary and fiscal policy on income and the interest rate, and we so use it in Sections 4-5 through 4-7. Before we do, however, we discuss how the economy moves from one equilibrium, such as E to another, such as E'.

4-4   ADJUSTMENT TOWARD EQUILIBRIUM

Suppose the economy were initially at a point like E in Figure 4-13, and that one of the curves then shifted, so that the new equilibrium was at a point like E'. How would that new equilibrium actually be reached? The adjustment will involve changes in both the interest rate and the level of income. To study how they move over time, we make two assumptions:

1   Output increases whenever there is an excess demand for goods and contracts whenever there is an excess supply of goods. This assumption reflects the adjustment of firms to undesired decumulation and accumulation of inventories.

2   The interest rate rises whenever there is an excess demand for money and falls whenever there is an excess supply of money. This adjust-

ment occurs because an excess demand for money implies an excess supply of other assets (bonds). In attempting to acquire more money, people sell off bonds and thereby cause their prices to fall or their yields (interest rate) to rise.

A detailed discussion of the relationship between the price of a bond and its yield is presented in the Appendix to Chapter 8. Here we give only a brief explanation. For simplicity, consider a bond which promises to pay the holder of the bond $5 per year forever. The $5 is known as the bond *coupon*, and a bond which promises to pay a given amount to the holder of the bond forever is known as a *perpetuity*. If the yield available on other assets is 5 percent, the perpetuity will sell for $100 because at that price it too yields 5 percent (= $5/$100). Now suppose that the yield on other assets rises to 10 percent. Then the price of the perpetuity will drop to $50, because only at that price does the perpetuity yield 10 percent; that is, the $5 per year interest on a bond costing $50 gives its owners a 10 percent yield on their $50. This example makes it clear that the price of a bond and its yield are inversely related, given the coupon.

In point 2 above we assumed that an excess demand for money causes asset holders to attempt to sell off their bonds, thereby causing their prices to fall and their yields to rise. Conversely, when there is an excess supply of money, people attempt to use their money to buy up other assets, raising their prices and lowering their yields.

In Figure 4-14 we apply the analysis to study the adjustment of the economy. Four regions are represented, and they are characterized in Table 4-1. We know from Figure 4-11 that there is an excess supply of money above the *LM* curve, and hence we show *ESM* in regions I and II in Table 4-1. Similarly, we know from Figure 4-7 that there is an excess demand for goods below the *IS* curve. Hence, we show *EDG* for regions II and III in Table 4-1. You should be able to explain the remaining entries of Table 4-1.

The adjustment directions specified in assumptions 1 and 2 above are represented by arrows. Thus, for example, in region IV we have an excess demand for money that causes interest rates to rise as other assets are sold off for money and their prices decline. The rising interest rates are represented by the upward-pointing arrow. There is, too, an excess supply of goods in region IV, and, accordingly, involuntary inventory accumulation to which firms respond by reducing output. Declining output is indicated by the leftward-pointing arrow. The adjustments shown by the arrows will lead ultimately, perhaps in a cyclical manner, to the equilibrium point E. For example, starting at E_1 we show the economy moving to E, with income and the interest rate increasing along the *adjustment path* indicated.

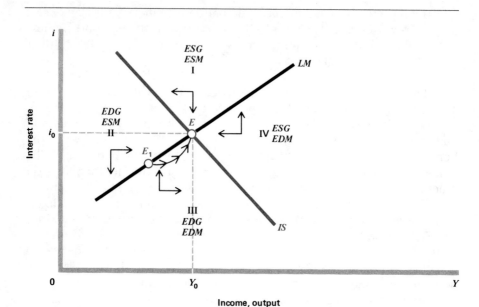

FIGURE 4-14   DISEQUILIBRIUM AND DYNAMICS IN THE GOODS AND MONEY MARKETS. Income and interest rates adjust to the disequilibrium in goods markets and assets markets. Specifically, interest rates fall when there is an excess supply of money and rise when there is an excess demand. Income rises when aggregate demand for goods exceeds output and falls when aggregate demand is less than output. The system converges over time to the equilibrium at E.

TABLE 4-1   DISEQUILIBRIUM AND ADJUSTMENT

	GOODS MARKET		MONEY MARKET	
Region	Disequilibrium	Adjustment: Output	Disequilibrium	Adjustment: Interest rate
I	ESG	Falls	ESM	Falls
II	EDG	Rises	ESM	Falls
III	EDG	Rises	EDM	Rises
IV	ESG	Falls	EDM	Rises

Rapid Asset Market Adjustment

For many purposes it is useful to restrict the dynamics by the reasonable assumption that the money market adjusts very quickly and the goods market adjusts relatively slowly. Since the money market can adjust merely through the buying and selling of bonds, the interest rate adjusts rapidly and the money market effectively is always in equilibrium. Such an assumption implies that we are always on the *LM* curve: any departure from the equilibrium in the money market is almost instantaneously eliminated by an appropriate change in the interest rate. In disequilibrium, we therefore move along the *LM* curve, as is shown in Figure 4-15.

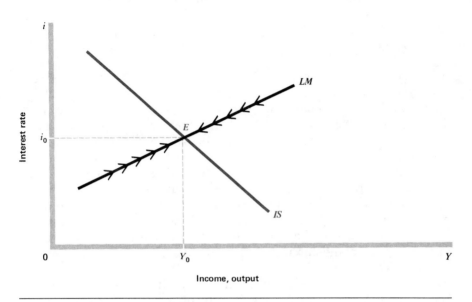

FIGURE 4-15   ADJUSTMENT TO EQUILIBRIUM WHEN THE MONEY MARKET ADJUSTS QUICKLY. If the money market adjusts very rapidly, then the economy is always in monetary equilibrium. In the diagram this corresponds to always being on the *LM* schedule. When there is excess demand for goods, output and interest rates are rising, and when there is excess supply of goods, output and interest rates are falling.

The goods market adjusts relatively slowly because firms have to change their production schedules, which takes time. For points below the *IS* curve, we move up along the *LM* schedule with rising income and interest rates, and for points above the *IS* schedule, we move down along the *LM* schedule with falling output and interest rates until point *E* is reached. The adjustment process is *stable* in that the economy does move to the equilibrium position at *E*.

The adjustment process shown in Figure 4-15 is very similar to that of Chapter 3. To the right of the *IS* curve, there is an excess supply of goods, and firms are therefore accumulating inventories. They cut production in response to their inventory buildup, and the economy moves down the *LM* curve. The difference between the adjustment here and in Chapter 3 is the following: here, as the economy moves toward the equilibrium level of income, with a falling interest rate, desired investment spending is actually rising.[11]

Now that we have established that the economy does adjust toward its equilibrium position, we turn to examine the effects of monetary and fiscal policy on the equilibrium interest rate and level of income.

4-5   MONETARY POLICY

In this section we are concerned with the effect of an increase in the real quantity of money on the interest rate and level of income. We break up that inquiry into two separate questions. First, what is the ultimate effect of the increase in the money supply when the new equilibrium is reached? Second, how is that new equilibrium reached, or what is the transmission mechanism?

Through monetary policy the Bank of Canada affects the quantity of money and thereby the interest rate and income. The chief instrument, studied in more detail in Chapter 10, is *open market operations*. In an open market operation the Bank of Canada purchases bonds in exchange for money, thus increasing the stock of money, or it sells bonds in exchange for money paid by the purchasers of the bonds, thus reducing the money stock.

We take here the case of an open market purchase of bonds. The purchase is made by the Bank of Canada, which pays for its purchases with money that it can create. One can usefully think of the Bank printing money with which to buy bonds, even though that is not strictly accurate, as we shall see in Chapter 10. The purpose of an open market operation is to change the available *relative* supplies of money and bonds and thereby change the interest rate or yield at which the public is willing to hold this modified composition of assets. When the Bank buys bonds, it reduces the supply of bonds available in the market and thereby tends to increase their price, or lower their yield. Only at a lower interest rate will the public be prepared to hold a larger fraction of their given wealth in the form of money, and a lower fraction in the form of bonds.

In Figure 4-16 we show graphically how the open market purchase works. The initial equilibrium at point E is on the initial *LM* schedule that corresponds to a real money supply, $\overline{M}/\overline{P}$. Consider next an open market operation that increases the nominal quantity of money, and given the price level, the real quantity of money. We showed before that, as a consequence, the *LM* schedule will shift to *LM'*. Therefore, our new equilibrium will be at point E' with a lower interest rate and a higher level of income. The equilibrium level of income rises because the open market purchase reduces the interest rate and thereby increases investment spending.

By experimenting with Figure 4-16, you will be able to show that the steeper the LM schedule, the larger the change in income. If money demand is very sensitive to the interest rate, then a given change in the money stock can be absorbed in the assets markets with only a small change in the interest rate. The effects of an open market purchase on investment spending would then be small. By contrast, if the demand for money is not very sensitive to the interest rate, a given change in the money supply will cause a large change in the interest rate and have a big effect on investment demand.[12] Similarly, if the demand for money is very sensitive to income, a given increase in the money stock can be absorbed with a relatively small change in income.

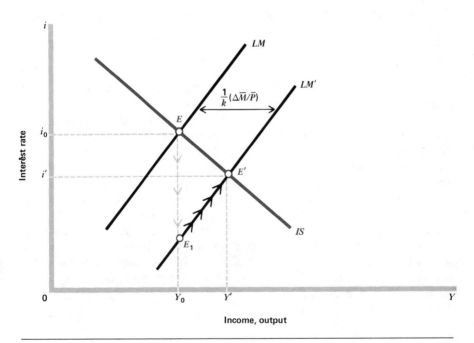

FIGURE 4-16   THE ADJUSTMENT PATH OF THE ECONOMY FOLLOWING AN INCREASE IN THE MONEY STOCK. An increase in the real money stock shifts the LM schedule down and to the right. Interest rates immediately decline from E to E_1, and then, through their effect on investment, cause spending and income to rise until a new equilibrium is reached at E'. Once all adjustments have taken place, a rise in the real money stock raises equilbrium and lowers equilibrium interest rates.

Consider next the adjustment process to the monetary expansion. At the initial equilibrium point E, the increase in the money supply creates an excess supply of money to which the public adjusts by attempting to reduce its money holdings by buying other assets. In the process, asset prices increase and yields decline. By our assumption that the assets markets adjust rapidly, we move immediately to point E_1, where the money market clears, and where the public is willing to hold the larger real quantity of money because the interest rate has declined sufficiently. At point E_1, however, there is an excess demand for goods. The decline in the interest rate, given the initial income level Y_0, has raised aggregate demand and is causing inventories to run down. In response, output expands and we start moving up the LM' schedule. Why does the interest rate rise in the adjustment process? Because the increase in output raises the demand for money and that increase has to be checked by higher interest rates.

Thus the increase in the money stock first causes interest rates to fall as the public adjusts its portfolio and then, through lower interest rates, increases aggregate demand.

The Transmission Mechanism

Two steps in the *transmission mechanism* — the process by which changes in monetary policy affect aggregate demand — are essential. The first is that an increase in real balances generates a *portfolio disequilibrium* — at the prevailing interest rate and level of income, people are holding more money than they want. This causes portfolio holders to attempt to reduce their money holdings by buying other assets, thereby changing asset prices and yields. In other words, the change in the money supply changes interest rates. The second stage of the transmission process occurs when the change in interest rates affects aggregate demand.

These two stages of the transmission process are essential in that they appear in almost every analysis of the effects of changes in the money supply on the economy. The details of the analysis will often differ — some analyses will have more than two assets and more than one interest rate; some will include an influence of interest rates on other categories of demand, such as consumption.[13]

TABLE 4-2   THE TRANSMISSION MECHANISM

(1)	(2)	(3)	(4)
Change in real money supply	Portfolio adjustments lead to a change in asset prices and interest rates	Spending adjusts to the change in interest rates	Output adjusts to the change in aggregate demand

Table 4-2 provides a summary of the stages in the transmission mechanism. The process starts with a change in the real money stock which, in the first place, leads to portfolio disequilibrium and changes in interest rates. From here the disturbance spills from assets markets to goods markets, as spending adjusts to the change in interest rates. The change in spending or aggregate demand in turn leads to income adjustments.

There are two critical links between the change in real balances and the ultimate effect on income. First, the change in real balances, by bringing about portfolio disequilibrium, must lead to a change in interest rates. Second, that change in interest rates must change aggregate demand. Through those two linkages, changes in the real money stock affect the level of output in the economy. But that immediately implies the following: if portfolio imbalances do not lead to significant changes in interest rates, for whatever reason, or if spending does not respond to changes in interest rates, the link between money and output does not exist.[14] We now study these linkages in more detail.

The Liquidity Trap

In discussing the effects of monetary policy on the economy, two extreme cases have received much attention. The first is the *liquidity trap*, a situation in which the public is prepared, at a given interest rate, to hold whatever amount of money is supplied. This implies that the *LM* curve is horizontal and that changes in the quantity of money do not shift it. In that case, monetary policy carried out through open market operations[15] has no effect on either the interest rate or level of income. In the liquidity trap, monetary policy is powerless to affect the interest rate.

There is a liquidity trap at a zero interest rate. At a zero interest rate, the public would not want to hold any bonds, since money, which also pays zero interest, has the advantage over bonds of being usable in transactions. Accordingly, if the interest rate ever, for some reason, was zero, increases in the quantity of money could not induce anyone to shift into bonds and thereby reduce the interest rate on bonds even below zero. An increase in the money supply in that case would have no effect on the interest rate and income, and the economy would be in a liquidity trap.

The belief that there was a liquidity trap at low positive (rather than zero) interest rates was quite prevalent during the forties and fifties. It was a notion associated with the Keynesian followers and developers of the theories of the great English economist John Maynard Keynes, although Keynes himself did state that he was not aware of there ever having been such a situation.[16] The importance of the liquidity trap stems from its presenting a circumstance under which monetary policy has no effect on the interest rate and thus on the level of real income. Belief in the trap, or at least the strong sensitivity of the demand for money to the interest rate, was the basis of the Keynesian belief that monetary policy has no effects on the economy. There is no strong evidence that there ever was a liquidity trap, and there certainly is not one now.

The Classical Case

The polar opposite of the horizontal *LM* curve — which implies that monetary policy cannot affect the level of income — is the vertical *LM* curve. The *LM* curve is vertical when the demand for money is entirely unresponsive to the interest rate. Under those circumstances, any shift in the *LM* curve has a maximal effect on the level of income. Check this by moving a vertical *LM* curve to the right and comparing the resultant change in income with the change produced by a similar horizontal shift of a nonvertical *LM* curve.

The vertical *LM* curve is called the *classical case*. It implies that the demand for money depends only on the level of income and not at all on the interest rate. The classical case is associated with the classical *quantity theory of money*, which argues that the level of nominal income is determined solely by the quantity of money. As we shall see, a vertical *LM* curve implies not only that monetary policy has a maximal effect on the level of income, but also that fiscal policy has no effect on income. The vertical *LM* curve, implying the comparative effectiveness of monetary policy over fiscal policy, is sometimes associated with the view that "only money matters" for the determination of output. Since the *LM* curve is vertical only when the demand for money does not depend on the interest rate, the interest sensitivity of the demand for money turns out to be an important issue in determining the effectiveness of alternative policies.

These two extreme cases, the liquidity trap and the classical case, suggest that the slope of the *LM* curve is a key determinant of the effectiveness of monetary policy in affecting output. The slope of the *LM* curve in turn depends on the interest sensitivity of money demand. The more sensitive to the interest rate is the quantity of money demanded, the flatter the *LM* curve.

4-6   FISCAL POLICY AND CROWDING OUT

Whenever governments run budget deficits, borrowing to pay for the excess of their spending over the tax revenue they receive, the talk turns to *crowding out*. Crowding out occurs when expansionary fiscal policy causes interest rates to rise, thereby reducing private spending, particularly investment.

When we introduced fiscal policy in Chapter 3, we had not yet included the assets markets in the analysis. Thus we could not discuss the effects of changes in fiscal policy on interest rates. In this chapter we consider how fiscal policy works when the interdependence of goods and assets markets is taken into account in the *IS-LM* model.

Our aim is to see how explicit consideration of the role of interest rates affects the conclusions we reached in Chapter 3 about fiscal policy. Is it still the case that an increase in government spending raises output and employment? Do tax cuts still increase output, or is it possible that the effects of fiscal policy on interest rates are so important that our previous conclusions about the effects of fiscal policy on the economy are reversed?

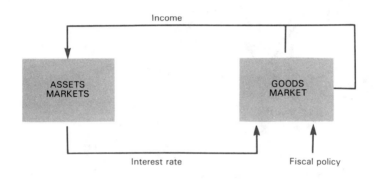

FIGURE 4-17   FISCAL POLICY IN THE *IS-LM* MODEL. Fiscal policy affects aggregate demand and thus has an impact on output and income. But changes in income affect the demand for money and thereby equilibrium interest rates in assets markets. These interest rate changes feed back to the goods market and dampen the impact of fiscal policy.

Figure 4-17 shows how fiscal policy fits into the *IS-LM* model. Fiscal policy affects aggregate demand directly. For instance, an increase in government spending increases aggregate demand, tending to raise output. But the higher output level raises the interest rate in the assets markets, and thereby dampens the effects of the fiscal policy on output. The higher interest rates reduce the level of investment spending, or crowd out investment. Thus a fiscal policy that increases output may actually reduce the rate of investment.

An Increase in Government Spending

At unchanged interest rates, higher levels of government spending will increase the level of aggregate demand. To meet the increased demand for goods, output must rise. In Figure 4-18 we show the effect of a shift of the *IS* schedule. At each level of the interest rate, equilibrium income must rise by $\bar{\alpha}$ times the government spending. For example, if government spending rises by 100 and the multiplier is 2, then equilibrium income must increase at each level of the interest rate by 200. Thus the *IS* schedule shifts to the right by 200.

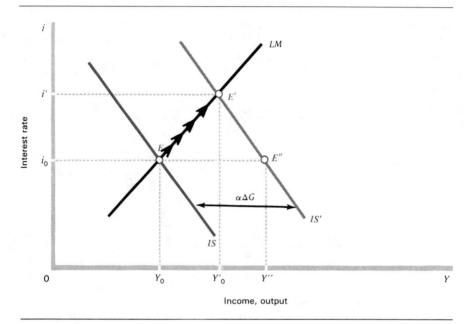

FIGURE 4-18   EFFECTS OF AN INCREASE IN GOVERNMENT SPENDING. An increase in government spending raises aggregate demand at each level of the interest rate and thus shifts the *IS* schedule out and to the right to *IS'*. At point *E* there is now an excess demand for goods. Output rises, and with it the interest rate, because the income expansion raises money demand The new equilibrium is at point *E'*. The increase in income ($Y'_0 - Y_0$) is less than the amount indicated by the simple multiplier ($Y'' - Y_0$) because higher interest rates crowd out some investment spending.

If the economy is initially in equilibrium at point *E* and now government spending rises by 100, we would move to point *E''* *if the interest rate stayed constant.* At *E''* the goods market is in equilibrium in that planned spending equals output. But the assets market is no longer in equilibrium. Income has increased, and therefore money demand now is higher. At interest rate i_0, the demand for real balances now exceeds the given real money supply. Because there is an excess demand for real balances, the interest rate rises. But as interest rates rise, private spending is cut back. Firms' planned investment spending declines at higher interest rates, and thus aggregate demand falls off.

What is the complete adjustment, taking into account the expansionary effect of higher government spending and the dampening effects of higher interest rates on private spending? Figure 4-18 shows that only at point E' do *both* the goods and assets markets clear. Only at point E' is planned spending equal to income and, at the same time, the quantity of real balances demanded equal to the given real money stock. Point E' is therefore the new equilibrium point.

The Dynamics of Adjustment

We continue to assume that the money market clears fast and continuously, while output adjusts only slowly. This implies that as government spending increases, we stay initially at point E, since there is no disturbance in the money market. The excess demand for goods, however, leads firms to increase output, and that increase in output and income raises the demand for money. The resulting excess demand for money, in turn, causes interest rates to be bid up, and we proceed up along the LM curve with rising output and rising interest rates, until the new equilibrium is reached at point E'.

The Extent of Adjustment

Comparing E' to the initial equilibrium at E, we have seen that increased government spending raises both income and the interest rate. But another important comparison is between points E' and E'', the equilibrium in the goods market at unchanged interest rates. Point E'' corresponds to the equilibrium we studied in Chapter 3 where we neglected the impact of interest rates on the economy. In comparing E'' and E' it becomes clear that the adjustment of interest rates and their impact on aggregate demand dampen the expansionary effect of increased government spending. Income, instead of increasing to the level Y'', rises only to Y'_0. This leads us to the following question: What factors determine the extent to which interest rate adjustments dampen the output expansion induced by increased government spending?

The extent to which a fiscal expansion raises income and the interest rate depends on the slopes of the IS and LM schedules and on the size of the multiplier. By drawing for yourself different IS and LM schedules you will be able to show the following:

1   Income increases more, and interest rates increase less, the flatter the LM schedule.
2   Income increases less, and interest rates increase less, the flatter the IS schedule.
3   Income and interest rates increase more the larger the multiplier $\bar{\alpha}$ and thus the larger the horizotnal shift of the IS schedule.

To illustrate these conclusions, we turn to the two extreme cases we discussed in connection with monetary policy, the liquidity trap and the classical case.

The Liquidity Trap

If the economy is in the liquidity trap so that the LM curve is horizontal, then an increase in government spending has its full multiplier effect on the equilibrium level of income. There is no change in the interest rate associated with the change in government spending, and thus no investment spending is cut off. There is therefore no dampening of the effects of increased government spending on income.

You should draw your own IS-LM diagrams to confirm that if the LM curve is horizontal, monetary policy has no impact on the equilibrium of the economy and fiscal policy has a maximal effect on the economy. Less dramatically, if the demand for money is very sensitive to the interest rate, so that the LM curve is almost horizontal, fiscal policy changes have a relatively large effect on output, while monetary policy changes have little effect on the equilibrium level of output.

So far, we have taken the money supply to be constant at the level $\overline{M}$. It is possible that the Bank of Canada might instead manipulate the money supply so as to keep the interest rate constant. In that case the money supply is responsive to the interest rate. We could talk of a money supply function which is elastic with respect to the interest rate. More simply, the Bank increases the money supply whenever there are signs of an increase in the interest rate, and reduces the money supply whenever the interest rate seems about to fall. If the money supply function is very elastic with respect to the interest rate, the LM curve will be very flat and fiscal policy will again have large impacts on the level of output.

The Classical Case and Crowding Out

If the LM curve is vertical, then an increase in government spending has *no* effect on the equilibrium level of income. It only increases the interest rate. This case is shown in Figure 4-19a, where an increase in government spending shifts the IS curve to IS' but has no effect on income. If the demand for money is not related to the interest rate, as a vertical LM curve implies, then there is a unique level of income at which the money market is in equilibrium.

Thus with a vertical LM curve, an increase in government spending cannot change the equilibrium level of income, but only raises the equilibrium interest rate. But if government spending is higher and output is unchanged, there must be an offsetting reduction in private spending. The increase in interest rates *crowds out* private investment spending. Crowding out, as defined earlier, is the reduction in private spending (and particularly investment) associated with the increase in interest rates caused by fiscal expansion. There will be full crowding out if the *LM* curve is vertical.[17]

In Figure 4-19 we show the crowding out in panel (*b*), where the investment schedule of Figure 4-3 is drawn. The fiscal expansion raises the equilibrium interest rate from i_0 to i' in panel (*a*). In panel (*b*), as a consequence, investment spending declines from the level I_0 to I'. Now it is easy to verify that if the *LM* schedule were positively sloped rather than vertical, interest rates would rise less with a fiscal expansion and as a result investment spending would decline less. The extent of crowding out thus depends on the slope of the *LM* curve and therefore on the interest responsiveness of money demand. The less interest-responsive is money demand, the more a fiscal expansion crowds out investment rather than raising output.

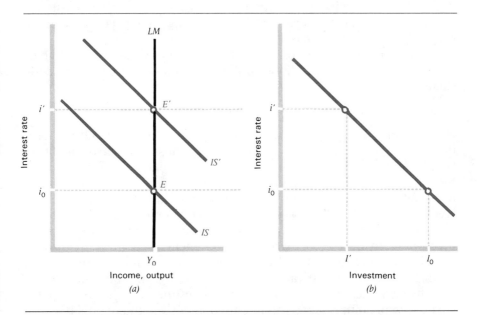

FIGURE 4-19   FULL CROWDING OUT. With a vertical *LM* schedule, a fiscal expansion, shifting out the *IS* schedule, raises interest rates, not income. Government spending displaces, or crowds out, private spending, one-for-one.

The view that increased government spending crowds out private spending, largely or even completely, is held by most monetarists.[18] They believe money determines income or, as we saw above, that money demand does not depend on the interest rate, implying a vertical *LM* schedule. However, there is also another case where crowding out can be complete, as we shall see in Chapter 15. If the economy is at full employment so that output cannot expand, then, of course, increased purchases of goods by the government must mean that some other sector uses less goods and services. Interest rates increase to crowd out private spending by an amount exactly equal to the higher level of government spending.

Is Crowding Out Likely?

How seriously must we take the possibility of crowding out? Here three points must be made. First, in an economy with unemployed resources there will *not* be full crowding out because the *LM* schedule is not, in fact, vertical. A fiscal expansion will raise interest rates, but income will also rise. Crowding out thus, rather than being full, is a matter of degree. In terms of the above quote, the increase in aggregate demand raises income, and with the rise in income, it raises the level of saving. This expansion in saving, in turn, makes it possible to finance a larger budget deficit without *completely* displacing private borrowing or investment.

We can look at this proposition with the help of Equation (12), which states the equilibrium condition in the goods market already studied in Chapter 3[19]:

$$S \equiv I + (G + TR - TA) \tag{12}$$

Here the term $G + TR - TA$ is the budget deficit. Now from (2) it is clear that an increase in the deficit, given saving, must lower investment. In simple terms, when the deficit rises, the government has to borrow to pay for its excess spending. That borrowing "uses up" part of saving, leaving less available for firms to borrow to further their investment plans. But it is equally apparent that if saving rises with a government spending increase, because income rises, then there need not be a one-for-one decline in investment. In an economy with unemployment, crowding out is incomplete because increased demand for goods raises real income and output; savings rise and interest rates do not rise enough (because of interest-responsive money demand) to choke off investment.

The second point is that, with unemployment and thus a possibility for output to expand, interest rates need not rise at all when government spending rises, and there need not be any crowding out. This is because the monetary authorities can *accommodate* the fiscal expansion by an increase in the money supply. Monetary policy is *accommodating* when, in the course of a fiscal expansion, the money supply is increased so as to prevent interest rates from increasing. Monetary accommodation is also referred to as *monetizing budget deficits*, meaning that the Bank of Canada prints money to buy the bonds with which the government pays for its deficit.[20] When the Bank accommodates a fiscal expansion, both the *IS* and the *LM* schedule shift to the right as in Figure 4-20. Output will clearly increase, but interest rates need not rise. Accordingly, there need not be any adverse effects on investment.

The third comment on crowding out is an important warning. So far we are assuming an economy with given prices and less than full employment. When we talk about fully employed economies in Chapter 15, crowding out becomes a much more realistic possibility, and accommodating monetary policy may turn into an engine of inflation.

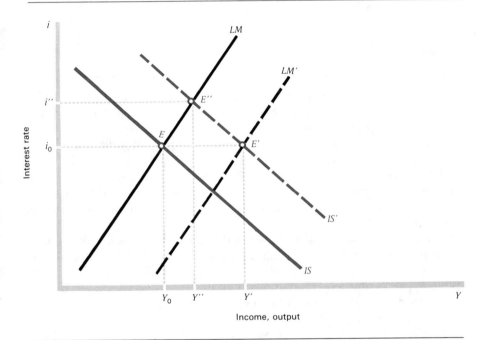

FIGURE 4-20   MONETARY ACCOMMODATION OF FISCAL EXPANSION. A fiscal expansion shifts the *IS* curve to *IS'*, and moves the equilibrium of the economy from *E* to *E"*. Because the higher level of income has increased the quantity of money demanded, the interest rate rises from i_0 to $i"$, thereby crowding out investment spending. However, the Bank of Canada can accommodate the fiscal expansion, creating more money and shifting the *LM* curve to *LM'*, and the equilibrium of the economy to *E'*. The interest rate remains at level i_0, and the level of output rises to *Y'*.

4-7   THE COMPOSITION OF OUTPUT

We have now seen that both monetary and fiscal policy can be used to expand aggregate demand and thus raise the equilibrium level of output.

Since the liquidity trap and the classical case represent, at best, extremes useful for expositional purposes, it is apparent that policy makers can use either monetary or fiscal policy to affect the level of income.

Table 4-3 summarizes the effects of expansionary monetary and fiscal policy on output and the interest rate. These are the effects shown in Figures 4-16 and 4-18.

TABLE 4-3   SUMMARY: POLICY EFFECTS ON INCOME AND INTEREST RATES

Policy	Equilibrium income	Equilibrium interest rate
Monetary expansion	+	−
Fiscal expansion	+	+

We now examine the policy choices of an economy that is in equilibrium with an output level Y_0, below the full-employment level $\overline{Y}$. What can be done to raise output? From the preceding analysis and Table 4-3, it is obvious that we could use an expansionary monetary policy. By increasing the money supply, we could shift the *LM* curve down and to the right, lower interest rates, and raise aggregate demand. Alternatively, we can use an expansionary fiscal policy to shift the *IS* curve up and to the right. Finally, we can use a combination of monetary and fiscal policy. What package should we choose?

The choice of monetary and fiscal policy as tools of stabilization policy is an important and controversial topic. In Chapter 11 we address some technical issues that deal with the flexibility and speed with which these policies can be implemented and can take effect. Here we do not discuss speed and flexibility, but rather look at what these policies do to the composition of aggregate demand.

In that respect, there is a sharp difference between monetary and fiscal policy. Monetary policy operates by stimulating interest-responsive components of aggregate demand, primarily investment spending and, in particular, residential construction. There is strong evidence that the earliest and strongest effect of monetary policy is on residential construction.

Fiscal policy, by contrast, operates in a manner that depends on precisely what goods the government buys or what taxes and transfers it changes. Here we might be talking of government purchases of goods and services such as defence spending, or a reduction in the corporate profits tax, or in sales taxes, or social insurance contributions. Each policy affects the level of aggregate demand and causes an expansion in output, except that the type of output and the beneficiaries of the fiscal measures differ. An investment subsidy, discussed below, increases investment spending. An income tax cut has a direct effect on consumption spending. Given the quantity of money, all expansionary fiscal policies have in common is that they will raise the interest rate.

An Investment Subsidy

Table 4-4 shows examples of the impact of different fiscal policies on key variables. One interesting case is an *investment subsidy*, shown in Figure 4-21. When the government subsidizes investment, it essentially pays part of the cost of each firm's investment. A subsidy to investment shifts the investment schedule in panel (*a*). At each interest rate, firms now plan to invest more. With investment spending higher, aggregate demand increases.

TABLE 4-4   ALTERNATIVE FISCAL POLICIES

	Interest rate	Consumption	Investment	GNP
Income tax cut	+	+	−	+
Government spending	+	+	−	+
Investment subsidy	+	+	+	+

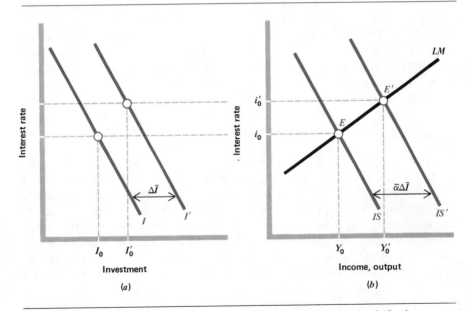

FIGURE 4-21   AN INVESTMENT SUBSIDY. An investment subsidy shifts the investment schedule in panel (*a*) at each interest rate out and to the right. The increase in planned investment shows in panel (*b*) as a shift of the *IS* curve. Equilibrium income rises to Y'_0, and the interest rate increases to i'_0. At the higher interest rate, investment is still higher, I'_0, than it was initially. Thus an investment subsidy raises interest rates, income, and investment.

In panel (b), the IS schedule shifts by the multiplier times the increase in autonomous investment brought about by the subsidy. The new equilibrium is at point E', where goods and money markets are again in balance. But note now that although interest rates have risen, we see in panel (a) that investment is higher. Investment is at the level I'_0 up from I_0. The interest rate increase thus has only dampened but not reversed the impact of the investment subsidy. Here is an example where both consumption, induced by higher income, and investment rise as a consequence of fiscal policy.

The Policy Mix

In Figure 4-22 we show the policy problem of reaching full-employment output $\overline{Y}$ for an economy that is initially at point E with unemployment. Should we choose a fiscal expansion, moving to point E_1 with higher income and higher interest rates, or should we choose a monetary expansion, leading to full employment with lower interest rates at point E_2? Or should we pick a policy mix of fiscal expansion and accommodating monetary policy, leading to an intermediate positon?

Once we recognize that all the policies raise output but differ significantly in their impact on different sectors of the economy, we open up a problem of political economy. Given the decision to expand aggregate demand, who should get the primary benefit? Should the expansion take place through a decline in interest rates and increased investment spending, or should it take place through a cut in taxes and increased personal spending, or should it take the form of an increase in the size of government?

Questions of speed and predictability of policies apart, the issues raised above have been settled by political preferences. Conservatives will argue for a tax cut anytime. They will favour stabilization policies that in a recession cut taxes and in a boom cut government spending. Over time, given enough cycles, the government sector becomes very small, just as a conservative would want it to be. The counterpart view belongs to those who feel that there is much scope for government spending on education, environment, job training and rehabilitation, and the like, and who, accordingly, favour expansionary policies in the form of increased government spending. Growth-minded people and the construction industry finally argue for expansionary policies that operate through low interest rates.

The recognition that monetary and fiscal policy changes have different effects on the composition of output is important. It suggests that policy makers can choose a policy mix that will both get the economy to full employment and also make a contribution to solving some other policy problem. We anticipate here several subsequent discussions in which we point out two other targets of policy which have been taken into account

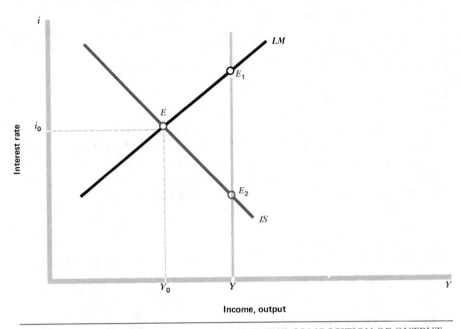

FIGURE 4-22   EXPANSIONARY POLICIES AND THE COMPOSITION OF OUTPUT.
In an economy with output Y_0 below the full-employment level $\overline{Y}$, there is a
choice of using monetary or fiscal expansion to move to full employment.
Monetary expansion would move the LM curve to the right, putting the
equilibrium at E_2. Fiscal expansion shifts the IS curve, putting the new
equilibrium at E_1. The expansionary monetary policy reduces the interest rate,
while the expansionary fiscal policy raises it. The lower interest rate in the case of
monetary policy means that investment is higher at E_2 than it is at E_1.

in setting monetary and fiscal policy — growth and balance of payments
equilibrium.

*4-8   A FORMAL TREATMENT OF THE *IS-LM* MODEL

Our exposition so far has been verbal and graphic. We now round off the
analysis with a more formal treatment that uses the equations of the IS and
LM schedules to derive and discuss fiscal and monetary policy multipliers.

Equilibrium Income and the Interest Rate

The intersection of the IS and LM schedules determines equilibrium income and the equilibrium interest rate. We can derive expressions for
these equilibrium values by using the equations of the IS and LM schedules.

From Section 4-1 we remember the equation of the *IS* schedule or goods market equilibrium schedule as

IS schedule: $$Y = \bar{\alpha}(\bar{A} - bi) \qquad (13)$$

and the equation describing money market equilibrium as[21]

LM schedule: $$i = \frac{1}{h}\left(kY - \frac{\overline{M}}{\overline{P}} \right) \qquad (14)$$

The intersection of the *IS* and *LM* schedules in the diagrams corresponds to a situation where both the *IS* and *LM* equations hold — the *same* interest rate and income levels assure equilibrium in *both* the goods and money market. In terms of the equations, that means we can substitute the interest rate from the *LM* Equation (14) into the *IS* Equation (13):

$$Y = \bar{\alpha}\left[\overline{A} - \frac{b}{h}\left(kY - \frac{\overline{M}}{\overline{P}} \right) \right] \qquad (15)$$

Collecting terms and solving for the equilibrium level of income, we obtain

$$Y_0 = \frac{h\bar{\alpha}}{h + kb\bar{\alpha}}\,\overline{A} + \frac{b\bar{\alpha}}{h + kb\bar{\alpha}}\frac{\overline{M}}{\overline{P}} \qquad (15a)$$

Equation (15a) shows the equilibrium level of income depending on two exogenous variables: autonomous spending $\overline{A}$, including fiscal policy parameters ($\overline{C}$, $\overline{I}$, $\overline{G}$, t, $\overline{TR}$) and the real money stock $\overline{M}/\overline{P}$. Equilibrium income is higher the higher the level of autonomous spending $\overline{A}$ and the higher the stock of real balances.

The equilibrium rate of interest, i_0, is obtained by substituting the equilibrium income level Y_0 from (15a) into the equation of the *LM* schedule, (14):

$$i_0 = \frac{k\bar{\alpha}}{h + kb\bar{\alpha}}\,\overline{A} - \frac{1}{h + kb\bar{\alpha}}\frac{\overline{M}}{\overline{P}} \qquad (16)$$

Equation (16) shows that the equilibrium interest rate depends on the parameters of fiscal policy captured in the multiplier and the term $\overline{A}$, and on the real money stock. A higher real money stock implies a lower equilibrium interest rate.

For policy questions we are interested in the precise relation between changes in fiscal policy or changes in the real money stock and the resulting changes in equilibrium income. The *monetary* and *fiscal policy multipliers* provide the relevant information.

The Fiscal Policy Multiplier

The fiscal policy multiplier tells us how much an increase in government spending changes the equilibrium level of income, holding the real money supply constant. Examine Equation (15a) and consider the effect of an increase in government spending on income. The increase in government spending $\Delta\bar{G}$ is a change in autonomous spending, so that $\Delta\bar{A} = \Delta\bar{G}$. The effect of the change in $\bar{G}$ is given by

$$\frac{\Delta Y_0}{\Delta\bar{G}} = \frac{h\bar{\alpha}}{h + bk\bar{\alpha}} \qquad (17)$$

We note that the expression in Equation (17) is zero if h is very small and will be equal to $\bar{\alpha}$ if h approaches infinity. This corresponds, respectively, to vertical and horizontal LM schedules. Similarly, a large value of either b or k serves to reduce the effect on income of government spending. Why? A high value of k implies a large increase in money demand as income rises and hence a large increase in interest rates in order to maintain money market equilibrium. In combination with a high b, this implies a large reduction in private aggregate demand. Equation (17) thus presents the algebraic analysis that corresponds to the graphical analysis of Figures 4-18 and 4-19.

The Monetary Policy Multiplier

The monetary policy multiplier tells us by how much an increase in the real money supply increases the equilibrium level of income, keeping fiscal policy unchanged. Using Equation (15a) to examine the effects of an increase in the real money supply on income, we have

$$\frac{\Delta Y_0}{\Delta(\overline{M/P})} = \frac{b\bar{\alpha}}{h + bk\bar{\alpha}} \qquad (18)$$

The smaller h and k and the larger b and $\bar{\alpha}$, the more expansionary the effect of an increase in real balances on the equilibrium level of income. Large b and $\bar{\alpha}$ correspond to a very flat IS schedule. Equation (18) thus corresponds to the graphical analysis presented in Figure 4-16.

The Classical Case and the Liquidity Trap

We now turn to two special cases that demonstrate the role of the demand function for real balances in the effectiveness of monetary and fiscal policies. Consider first the possibility that money demand does not depend at all on interest rates and is simply proportional to real income. This happens if the parameter h is zero, so that real money demand is simply

$$L = kY \qquad (19)$$

In this case monetary equilibrium, equating the demand and supply of money, leads to [22]

$$Y = (1/k)\frac{\overline{M}}{\overline{P}} \qquad (20)$$

This case is called the *classical case* because classical (that is, nineteenth century) economists did not give much emphasis to the interest response of money demand. The case is important because it has the following implication: If money demand does not depend on the interest rate and only on the level of income, as in (19), the money supply alone determines income.

In this classical case the level of nominal income, $\overline{P}Y$, is proportional to the nominal money stock. Changes in the nominal money stock lead to changes in income in the same proportion. Furthermore, while income does respond to money, it is *totally* unresponsive to fiscal policy. We also can see the point from (15a) by setting $h = 0$.

Interest Rates and Fiscal Policy

How is it possible that fiscal policy should have no effect at all on income? After all, if the government were to spend more, how is it possible that the increased spending should *not* raise income? The reasoning is as follows. An increase in government spending does lead to an incipient rise in aggregate demand and income, but that immediately raises the demand for money. With the money supply unchanged, interest rates will shoot up to clear the money market. But the rise in interest rate does nothing to reduce the quantity of money demanded. It does, however, have an impact on private investment spending. As interest rates rise because of the excess demand for money, investment spending declines. The fall in investment spending compensates exactly for the higher government spending, and the level of income is unchanged.

We can see this by looking at the investment equation (21), obtained by substituting in the equilibrium interest rate from (16):

$$I = \overline{I} - bi_0 = \overline{I} - \frac{bk\overline{\alpha}}{h + bk\overline{\alpha}}\overline{A} + \frac{b}{h + bk\overline{\alpha}}\frac{\overline{M}}{P} \tag{21}$$

In the case where $h = 0$, the coefficient multiplying $\overline{A}$ in (11) is 1. This means that a \$1 increase in $\overline{A}$, given the real money stock, leads to an equal reduction of investment. That is what we call *full* crowding out. In general, with h not equal to zero, the coefficient of $\overline{A}$ is a fraction, as shown in (21). The larger h, the smaller the fraction of an extra dollar of government spending that is offset by reduced investment spending.

Liquidity Trap

The other extreme for monetary and fiscal policy is represented by a world where h is infinite. Then money and other assets are effectively perfect substitutes. In such a world, Equation (15a) reduces to

$$Y = \overline{\alpha}\overline{A} \tag{22}$$

This is the "multiplier world" of Chapter 3, where autonomous spending entirely determines the level of real income. It occurs if the economy is in a liquidity trap.

In the liquidity trap, money does not matter for income determination because money demand is *so* responsive to interest rates. The smallest change in interest rates is sufficient to eliminate imbalances in the money market that might arise from changes in money supply or in income. And because these corrective changes in interest rates are so small, they do not even affect aggregate demand. The interest rate effect can be verified from (11). With *h* extremely high, investment spending is not influenced by either monetary or fiscal policy.

4-9   SUMMARY

1   The *IS-LM* model presented in this chapter is the basic model of aggregate demand that incorporates the assets markets as well as the goods market. It lays particular stress on the channels through which monetary and fiscal policy affect the economy.

2   The *IS* curve shows combinations of the interest rate and level of income such that the goods market is in equilibrium. Increases in the interest rate reduce aggregate demand by reducing the demand for investment goods. Thus at higher interest rates, the level of income at which the goods market is in equilibrium is lower: the *IS* curve slopes downward.

3   The demand for money is a demand for *real* balances. The demand for real balances increases with income and decreases with the interest rate, the cost of holding money rather than other assets. With an exogenously fixed supply of real balances, the *LM* curve, representing money market equilibrium, is upward-sloping. Because of the wealth constraint, equilibrium of the money market implies equilibrium of the remaining assets markets, summarized here under the catchall "bond market."

4   The interest rate and level of output are jointly determined by simultaneous equilibrium of the goods and money markets. This occurs at the intersection point of the *IS* and *LM* curves.

5   Assuming that output is increased when there is an excess demand for goods, and that the interest rate rises when there is an excess demand for money, the economy does move toward the new equilibrium when one of the curves shifts. Typically we think of the assets markets as clearing rapidly, so that in response to a disturbance, the economy tends to move along the *LM* curve to the new equilibrium.

6   Monetary policy affects the economy in the first instance by affecting the interest rate, and then by affecting aggregate demand. An increase in the money supply reduces the interest rate, increases investment demand and aggregate demand, and thus increases equilibrium output.

7   There are two extreme cases in the operation of monetary policy. In the classical case the demand for real balances is independent of the rate of interest. In this case monetary policy is highly effective. The other extreme is the liquidity trap, where the public is willing to hold *any* amount of real balances at the going interest rate. In that case changes in the supply of real balances have no impact on interest rates and therefore do not affect aggregate demand and output.

8   Taking into account the effects of fiscal policy on the interest rate modifies the multiplier results of Chapter 3. Fiscal expansion, except in extreme circumstances, still leads to an income expansion. However, the rise in interest rates that comes about through the increase in money demand caused by higher income dampens the expansion.

9   Fiscal policy is more effective the smaller are the induced changes in interest rates and the smaller is the response of investment to these interest rate changes.

10   In the liquidity trap, the interest rate is constant because money demand is completely elastic with respect to the interest rate. Monetary policy has no effect on the economy, whereas fiscal policy has its full multiplier effect on output, and no effect on interest rates.

11   In the classical case, the demand for money is independent of the interest rate. In that case, changes in the money stock change income, but fiscal policy has no effect on income — it affects only the interest rate. In this case there is complete crowding out of private spending by government spending.

12   Neither the liquidity trap nor the classical case applies in practice. But they are useful cases to study in order to show what determines the magnitude of monetary and fiscal policy multipliers.

13   A fiscal expansion, because it leads to higher interest rates, displaces or crowds out some private investment. The extent of crowding out is a sensitive issue in assessing the usefulness and desirability of fiscal policy as a tool of stabilization policy.

14   In an economy that is less than fully employed, crowding out need not occur. The monetary authorities can provide an accommodating monetary policy that avoids the rise in interest rates associated with the output expansion.

15 The question of the monetary-fiscal policy mix arises because expansionary monetary policy reduces the interest rate while expansionary fiscal policy increases the interest rate. Accordingly, expansionary fiscal policy increases output while reducing the level of investment; expansionary monetary policy increases output and the level of investment.

16 Governments have to choose the mix in accordance with their objectives for economic growth, or increasing consumption, or from the viewpont of their beliefs about the desirable size of the government.

KEY TERMS

IS Curve
LM Curve
Bond
Money
Portfolio decisions
Real balances (real money balances)
Wealth budget constraint

Open market operation
Transmission mechanism
Liquidity trap
Classical case
Crowding out
Monetary-fiscal policy mix
Investment subsidy

PROBLEMS

1 The following equations describe an economy. (Think of C, I, G, etc., as being measured in billions and i as percent; a 5 percent interest rate implies $i = 5$.)

$$C = 0.8(1 - t)Y \qquad 1$$
$$t = 0.25 \qquad 2$$
$$I = 400 - 20i \qquad 3$$
$$G = 500 \qquad 4$$
$$L = 0.25Y - 30i \qquad 5$$
$$\frac{M}{P} = 350 \qquad 6$$

(a) What is the equation that describes the IS curve?
(b) What is the general definition of the IS curve?
(c) What is the equation that describes the LM curve?
(d) What is the general definition of the LM curve?
(e) What are the equilibrium levels of income and the interest rate?
(f) Describe in words the conditions that are satisfied at the intersection of the IS and LM curves, and why this is an equilibrium.

2 Continue with the same equations.
(a) What is the value of $\bar{\alpha}$, which corresponds to the simple multiplier (with taxes) of Chapter 3?

(b) By how much does an increase in government spending of $\Delta \bar{G}$ increase the level of income in this model, which includes the assets markets?

(c) By how much does a change in government spending of $\Delta \bar{G}$ affect the equilibrium interest rate?

(d) Explain the difference between your answers to 2(a) and (b).

3 (a) Explain in words how and why the multiplier $\bar{\alpha}$ and the interest sensitivity of aggregate demand affect the slope of the *IS* curve.

(b) Explain why the slope of the *IS* curve is a factor in determining the working of monetary policy.

4 Explain in words how and why the income and interest sensitivities of the demand for real balances affect the slope of the *LM* curve.

5 (a) Why does a horizontal *LM* curve imply that fiscal policy has the same effects on the economy as we derived in Chapter 3?

(b) What is happening in this case in terms of Figure 4-2?

(c) Under what circumstances might the *LM* curve be horizontal?

6 We mentioned in the text the possibility that the interest rate might affect consumption spending. An increase in the interest rate could, in principle, lead to increases in saving and therefore a reduction in consumption, given the level of income. Suppose that consumption were in fact reduced by an increase in the interest rate. How would the *IS* curve be affected?

7 Suppose that the money supply, instead of being constant, increased (slightly) with the interest rate. How would this change affect the construction of the *LM* curve?

8 (a) How does an increase in the tax rate affect the *IS* curve?

(b) How does it affect the equilibrium level of income?

(c) How does it affect the equilibrium interest rate?

9 Draw a graph of how i and Y respond over time (that is, use time as the horizontal axis) to an increase in the money supply. You may assume that the money market adjusts much more rapidly than the goods market.

10 (a) Show that a given change in the money stock has a larger effect on output the less interest sensitive the demand for money.

(b) How does the response of the interest rate to a change in the money stock depend on the interest sensitivity of money demand?

11 The economy is at full employment. Now the government wants to change the composition of demand toward investment and away from consumption without, however, allowing aggregate demand to go beyond full employment. What is the required policy mix? Use the *IS-LM* diagram to show your policy proposal.

12 Discuss the role of the parameters $\bar{\alpha}$, h, b, and k in the transmission mechanism linking an increase in government spending to the resulting change in equilibrium income. In developing the analysis use the following table:

(1)	(2)	(3)
Increase in G raises aggregate demand and output	The increase in income raises money demand and hence interest rates	The increase in interest rates reduces investment spending and hence dampens the output expansion

13 Consider an economy where the government considers two alternative programs for contraction. One is the removal of an investment subsidy; the other is a rise in income tax rates. Use the IS-LM schedule and the investment schedule, as shown in Figure 5-5, to discuss the impact of these alternative policies on income, interest rates, and investment.

*14 Suppose the parameters k and $\bar{\alpha}$ are 0.5 and 2, respectively. Assume there is an increase of $1 billion in government spending. By how much must the real money stock be increased to hold interest rates constant?

CHAPTER 4: FOOTNOTES

[1]The terms IS and LM are shorthand representations, respectively, of investment equals saving (goods market equilibrium) and money demand (L) equals money supply (M), or money market equilibrium. The classic article that introduced this model is J. R. Hicks, "Mr. Keynes and the Classics: A Suggested Interpretation," *Econometrica*, 1937, pp. 147–159.

[2]Here and in other places in the book, we specify linear (straight-line) versions of behavioural functions. We use the linear specifications to simplify both the algebra and the diagrams. The linearity assumption does not lead to any great difficulties so long as we confine ourselves to talking about small changes in the economy. You should often draw nonlinear versions of our diagrams to be sure you can work with them.

[3]In Chap. 3, investment spending was defined as autonomous with respect to income. Now that the interest rate appears in the model, we have to extend the definition of autonomous to mean independent of *both* the interest rate and income. To conserve notation, we continue to use $\bar{I}$ to denote autonomous investment, but recognize that the definition is broadened.

[4]In problem 3 we ask you to relate this fact to the discussion of automatic stabilizers in Chap. 3.

[5]We assume in this section that certain assets, such as the capital that firms use in production, are not traded. That too is a simplification. A more complete treatment of the assets markets would allow for the trading of capital and would introduce a relative price for the capital operated by firms. This treatment is usually reserved for advanced graduate courses. For such a treatment of the assets markets, see James Tobin, "A General Equilibrium Approach to Monetary Theory," *Journal of Money, Credit and Banking*, February 1969, pp. 15–29, and by the same author, "Money, Capital, and Other Stores of Value," *American Economic Review*, May 1961, pp. 26–37.

[6]The demand for money is studied in depth in Chap. 9; here we only briefly present the arguments underlying the demand for money.

[7]In recent years, it has become more common to pay interest on some forms of money holdings. Nevertheless there do remain sizable parts of money holding, including currency, on which no interest is paid, so that overall, money earns less interest than other assets and the analysis of this chapter is still applicable.

[8]Once again, we use a linear equation to describe a relationship. You should experiment with an alternative form, for example, $L = kY + h'/i$, where k and h' are positive. How would the equivalent of Figure 4-8 look for this demand function?

[9]Since for the present we are holding constant the money supply and price level, we refer to them as exogenous and denote that fact by a bar.

[10]Recall that exogenous variables are those whose values are not determined within the system being studied.

[11]In a more detailed analysis, one would want to allow for the possibility that desired investment would be cut back in response to excess inventories. This again raises the possibility of the inventory cycle, referred to in Chap. 3.

[12]In problem 3 we ask you to provide a similar explanation of the role of the slope of the *IS* curve, which is determined by the multiplier and the interest sensitivity of investment demand, in determining the effect of monetary policy on income.

[13]Some analyses also include a mechanism by which changes in real balances have a direct effect on aggregate demand through the real balance effect. The argument is that wealth affects consumption demand (as we shall see in Chap. 7) and that an increase in real balances increases wealth and therefore consumption demand. This effect would not apply in the case of an open market purchase, which merely exchanges one asset for another (bonds for money) without changing wealth. The real balance effect is not very important empirically because the relevant real balances are only a small part of wealth.

[14]We refer to the responsiveness of aggregate demand, rather than investment demand, to the interest rate because consumption demand may also respond to the interest rate. Higher interest rates may lead to more saving and less consumption at a given level of income. Empirically, it has been difficult to isolate such an interest rate effect on consumption.

[15]We say "through open market operations" because an increase in the quantity of money carried out simply by giving the money away increases individuals' wealth and, through the real balance effect, has some effect on aggregate demand. An open market purchase, however, increases the quantity of money and reduces the quantity of bonds by the same amount, leaving wealth unchanged.

[16]J. M. Keynes, *The General Theory of Employment, Interest and Money* (New York: Macmillan, 1936), p. 207.

[17]Note again that, in principle, consumption spending could be reduced by increases in the interest rate, and then both investment and consumption would be crowded out.

[18]We discuss monetarism in Chap. 17.

[19]We have simply rearranged Eq. (1*a*) in Chap. 3, cancelling consumption on both sides.

[20]The term *accommodation* is also used more generally. For instance, when oil prices increased in the 1970s, there was much discussion of whether central banks should accommodate the higher prices by raising the money stock. This issue, and the meaning of *accommodation* in that context, are discussed in Chap. 15.

[21]To deal with the case where liquidity preference is not only high but at some rate, say i', *perfectly* elastic, we could rewrite the *LM* equation as $\overline{M}/\overline{P} = kY - h(i - i')$, so that real money demand depends on the excess of the interest rate above some floor level i'. With this formulation, (4) becomes $i = i' + (1/h)[kY - \overline{M}/\overline{P}]$. If h is extremely high, the interest rate is $i = i'$ or the *LM* schedule is horizontal at the level i'.

[22]The demand for real balances is $L = kY$ and the supply $\overline{M}/\overline{P}$. Thus with demand equal to supply, $\overline{M}/\overline{P} = kY$ or $Y = (1/k)\overline{M}/\overline{P}$.

5

Macroeconomics in the Open Economy: Trade and Capital Flows with Fixed Exchange Rates

This is the first of two chapters analysing foreign trade and its effects on the economy. It extends the macroeconomics we have learned to open economies — economies that trade with others. International transactions include not only trade in goods and services — Canadians buy Japanese cars and foreign countries buy our wheat, but also borrowing and lending and trade in assets — Canadians buy American stocks and sell bonds to foreign investors. Since Canada exports about 25 percent of national output and makes substantial use of foreign capital to finance investment, transactions with other countries are of major importance in our economy.

This chapter begins with a brief description of the balance of payments accounts — the record of the country's transactions with other economies. Section 5-1 also describes the two basic exchange rate systems: the fixed and flexible rate systems. In a *fixed exchange rate system*, central banks fix the prices of foreign currencies and stand ready to buy and sell foreign currencies at those prices. Canada was on a fixed exchange rate from 1962 to 1970 and most other countries were on a fixed rate system from 1946 to 1973, though there were occasional adjustments of exchange rates during that period. In the *flexible exchange rate system*, the exchange rate is determined in the foreign exchange market and can change from moment to moment.

The rest of this chapter analyses trade in goods and international capital flows in a fixed exchange rate system. Section 5-2 examines the way in which foreign trade affects goods market equilibrium and Section 5-3 discusses the effects of a devaluation. Capital flows are studied in Sections 5-4 and 5-5, as are the implications of such flows for the effectiveness of monetary and fiscal policy. Chapter 6 presents an analysis of trade and capital flows under flexible exchange rates.

5-1   THE BALANCE OF PAYMENTS AND EXCHANGE RATE REGIMES

The *balance of payments* is the record of the transactions of the residents of a country with the rest of the world. There are two main accounts in the balance of payments: the current account and the capital account.

The *current account* records trade in goods and services, as well as transfer payments. Services include freight, royalty payments, and interest payments. Transfer payments consist of remittances, gifts, and grants. We talk of a current account surplus if exports exceed imports plus net transfers to foreigners, that is, if receipts from trade in goods and services and transfers exceed payments on this account.

The *capital account* records borrowing and lending as well as purchases and sales of assets, such as stocks, bonds, and land. There is a capital account surplus, or a net capital *inflow*, when our receipts from borrowing and the sale of stocks, bonds, land, bank deposits, and other assets exceed our payments for lending and purchases of foreign assets.

Closely related to the current account are certain subaccounts that we mention here for completeness. The *merchandise trade balance* simply records trade in goods. Adding trade in services to the trade balance, we arrive at the *balance on goods and services*. Finally, adding net transfers, we arrive at the current account balance.

Surpluses and Deficits

The simple rule for balance of payments accounting is that any transaction that gives rise to the disbursement of foreign currency is recorded as a payment. Thus, imports of goods, foreign travel, purchase of foreign stocks and lending to foreigners are all payment items. Conversely, any transactions that give rise to the acquisition of foreign exchange are recorded as receipts .Such transactions include exports of goods and borrowing from foreigners.

The overall *balance of payments* is the sum of the current and capital accounts. If both the current account and the capital account are in deficit, then the overall balance of payments is in deficit. When one account is in surplus and the other is in deficit to precisely the same extent, the overall balance of payments is zero — neither in surplus nor in deficit. We record these relationships in Equation (1)[1]:

Balance of payments surplus
$$= \text{current account surplus} + \text{capital account surplus} \qquad (1)$$

Table 5-1 shows the details of Canada's balance of payments in 1983 and Figure 5-1 shows the movements in the major categories since 1961. During the 1960s and 1970s, the typical pattern was a surplus on merchan-

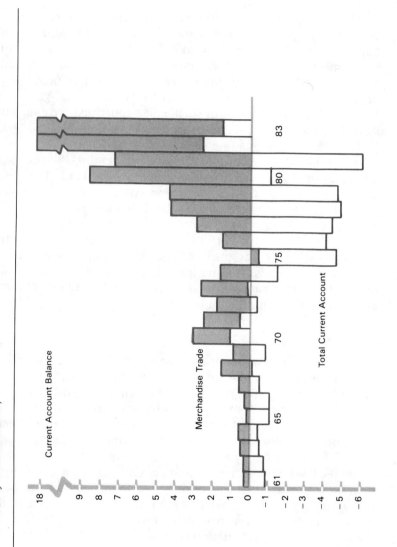

FIGURE 5-1 CANADA'S BALANCE OF INTERNATIONAL PAYMENTS, BILLIONS OF DOLLARS
(*Source: Bank of Canada Review*)

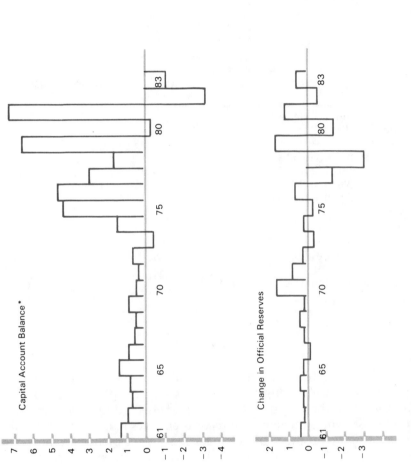

*Includes net errors and omissions

dise trade more than offset by a deficit on services and transfers, leaving a substantial current account deficit. Much of this deficit was attributable to a large outflow of dividend and interest payments associated with accumulated foreign indebtedness and foreign ownership of Canadian businesses. More recently, the merchandise trade surplus has risen sharply and the overall current account has moved into a surplus position.

TABLE 5-1   CANADIAN BALANCE OF INTERNATIONAL
PAYMENTS, 1983 (billions of dollars)

	Receipts (+)	Payments (−)	Balance
Current account			
Merchandise trade	$91.3	$73.2	
Travel	3.9	5.9	
Interest and dividends	1.9	11.3	
Freight and shipping	4.0	3.6	
Other services and transfers	9.9	15.4	
Balance on current account			$1.6
Capital account			
Long-term capital			
Direct investment	$0.2	$2.5	
Portfolio investment, net	5.1		
Short-term capital, net[1]		3.8	
Balance on capital account			$−1.0
Change in official reserves			$0.6

[1] Includes net errors and omissions
Source: Bank of Canada Review.

As shown in Table 5-1, capital flows can be divided into movements of long-term capital and movements of short-term capital. The long-term flows can be further divided into *direct investment* and *portfolio investment*. Direct investment is the item that records changes in nonresident ownership of domestic business and changes in resident ownership of foreign businesses. Thus, direct investment in Canada is capital investment in a branch plant or subsidiary in Canada in which the investor has voting control. Alternatively, it may be in the form of a takeover in which a controlling interest is acquired in a business previously controlled by residents. Portfolio investment, on the other hand, is investment in bonds or a minority holding of shares that does not involve legal control.

In 1983 there was a small net inflow of direct investment. Portfolio investment provided the source of surplus on long-term capital, primarily as a result of borrowing by private Canadian corporations, provinces, and provincially owned corporations such as Quebec Hydro. This pattern has been typical since 1975, but is in marked contrast to the fifties and sixties when direct investment accounted for a major fraction of long-term capital inflows.

Making International Payments

An overall deficit in the balance of payments — the sum of the current and capital accounts — means that Canadian residents make more payments to foreigners than they receive from foreigners. The foreign currency required to fill the gap is supplied out of the *official reserves* held by the Bank of Canada on behalf of the government of Canada. As can be seen in Figure 5-1, there have been wide swings in the overall balance of payments in recent years. There were very large deficits and losses of reserves in 1977 and 1978, and large surpluses and accumulations of reserves in 1970 and 1979.

Fixed Exchange Rates

We now examine in more detail the way in which central banks, through their official transactions, *finance*, or provide the means of paying for, balance of payments surpluses and deficits. At this point we distinguish between fixed and floating exchange rate systems, which we defined above.

In a fixed rate system, central banks stand ready to buy and sell their currencies at a fixed price in terms of dollars. For example, from May 1962 to June 1970 the Bank of Canada would buy or sell any amount of foreign currency at 92.5 U.S. cents per Canadian dollar.[2] The fact that the Bank was prepared to buy or sell *any* amount of Canadian dollars at this fixed price or exchange rate meant that the market price would indeed be equal to 92.5 U.S. cents. Why? Clearly, nobody who wanted to buy Canadian dollars with U.S. dollars would pay more than 92.5 U.S. cents if they could be gotten at that price from the Bank of Canada. Conversely, nobody would part with Canadian dollars for less than 92.5 U.S. cents if the Bank of Canada was prepared to buy them at that price.

In a fixed rate system, the central banks have to finance any balance of payments surplus or deficit that arises at the official exchange rate. They do that simply by buying or selling all the foreign currency that is not supplied in private transactions.

Fixed exchange rates thus operate like any other price support scheme, such as in agricultural markets. Given market demand and supply the price fixer has to make up the excess demand or take up the excess supply. In order to be able to ensure that the price (exchange rate) stays fixed, it is obviously necessary to hold an inventory of foreign exchange that can be sold in exchange for domestic currency. Thus, the Bank of Canada holds *reserves* of U.S. dollars, and gold that can be sold for U.S. dollars, for the purpose of exchange market intervention.

Intervention

Intervention is the buying or selling of foreign exchange by the central bank. What determines the amount of intervention that a central bank has to do in a fixed exchange rate system? We already have the answer to that question. The balance of payments measures the amount of foreign exchange intervention needed from the central banks. So long as the foreign central bank has the necessary reserves, it can continue to intervene in the foreign exchange markets to keep the exchange rate constant. However, if a country persistently runs deficits in the balance of payments, the central bank eventually will run out of reserves of foreign exchange and will be unable to continue its intervention.

Before that point is reached, the central bank is likely to decide that it can no longer maintain the exchange rate, and will devalue the currency. In 1967, for instance, the British devalued the pound from $2.80 per pound to $2.40 per pound. That meant it became cheaper for foreigners to buy British pounds, and the devaluation thus affected the balance of payments. We shall study the way in which devaluation affects the balance of payments in Section 5-3.

Flexible Exchange Rates

We have seen that the central banks have to provide whatever amounts of foreign currency are needed to finance payments imbalances under fixed exchange rates. In flexible rate systems, by contrast, the central banks allow the exchange rate to adjust to equate the supply and demand for foreign currency. If today's exchange rate were 85 U.S. cents per Canadian dollar, and imports from the United States increased, thus increasing the demand for U.S. dollars by Canadians, the Bank of Canada could simply stand aside and let the exchange rate adjust. In this particular case, the exchange rate could move from 85 U.S. cents to a level such as 84 U.S. cents, making American goods more expensive in terms of Canadian dollars and thus reducing the demand for them by Canadians. We shall in Chapter 6 examine the way in which exchange rate changes under floating rates affect the balance of payments. The terms *flexible rates* and *floating rates* are used interchangeably.

Floating, Clean and Dirty

In a system of *clean floating*, central banks stand aside completely and allow exchange rates to be freely determined in the foreign exchange markets. The central banks do not intervene in the foreign exchange markets in a system of clean floating, and official reserve transactions would, accordingly, be zero in such a situation. That means the balance of payments would be zero in a system of clean floating: The exchange rate would adjust to make the current and capital accounts sum to zero.

In practice, the flexible rate system has not been one of clean floating. Instead, the system has been one of *managed*, or *dirty, floating*. Under managed floating, central banks intervene to buy and sell foreign currencies, in attempts to influence exchange rates. Official reserve transactions are, accordingly, not equal to zero. The reasons for this central bank intervention under floating rates are discussed in Chapter 6.

Terminology

The use of language with respect to exchange rates can be very confusing. In particular, the terms *depreciation* and *appreciation* and *devaluation* and *revaluation* will recur throughout this chapter and the next.

A *devaluation* takes place when the price of foreign currencies under a fixed rate regime is increased by official action. A devaluation thus means that foreigners pay less for the devalued currency or that residents of the devaluing country pay more for foreign currencies. The opposite of a devaluation is a *revaluation*.

Changes in the price of foreign exchange under flexible exchange rates are referred to as *currency depreciation* or *appreciation*. A currency *depreciates* when, under floating rates, it becomes less expensive in terms of foreign currencies. For instance, if the exchange rate of the Canadian dollar moves from 90 U.S. cents to 84 U.S. cents, we talk of a depreciation of the Canadian dollar. Conversely, an appreciation means that the value of our currency rises in terms of foreign exchange.

Summary

1   The balance of payments accounts are a record of the transactions of the economy with other economies. The capital account describes transactions in assets, while the current account covers transactions in goods and services and transfers.

2   Transactions that give rise to the disbursement of foreign exchange are recorded as payments, while those that give rise to the acquisition of foreign exchange are recorded as receipts. The balance of payments deficit (or surplus) is the sum of the deficits (or surpluses) on current and capital accounts.

3   Under fixed exchange rates, central banks stand ready to meet all demands for foreign currencies arising from balance of payments deficits or surpluses at a fixed price in terms of the domestic currency. They have to *finance* the excess demands for, or supplies of, foreign currency (that is, the balance of payments deficits or surpluses, respectively), at the pegged (fixed) exchange rate by running down, or adding to, their reserves of foreign currency.

4   Under flexible exchange rates, the demands for, and supplies of, foreign currency can be made equal through movements in exchange

rates. Under clean floating, there is no central bank intervention and the balance of payments is zero. Central banks sometimes intervene in a floating rate system, engaging in so-called dirty floating.

5-2 TRADE IN GOODS, MARKET EQUILIBRIUM, AND THE BALANCE OF TRADE

We now study the effects of trade in goods on the level of income, and the effects of various disturbances on both income and the trade balance — which, from now on, we use as shorthand for the current account. We also examine policy problems which arise when the balance of trade and the level of income require different corrective actions. We do not at this stage include the capital account, so that for the present the current account and the balance of payments are the same.

In this section we fit foreign trade into the *IS-LM* framework. As in Chapters 3 and 4, we assume that the price level is given, and that output that is demanded will be supplied. A word of warning is in order before you start working through the following sections. The exposition assumes you are thoroughly at home with the *IS-LM* analysis and therefore proceeds quite rapidly. However, the material is not more difficult than that of the previous chapters and should be accessible with careful reading.

Domestic Spending and Spending on Domestic Goods

In this subsection we want to establish how foreign trade fits into the *IS* schedule. In an open economy, part of domestic output is sold to foreigners (exports), and part of spending by domestic residents falls on foreign goods (imports). We accordingly have to modify our analysis of aggregate demand developed in Chapter 4.

The most important change is that it is no longer true that domestic spending determines domestic output. What is true now is that *spending on domestic goods* determines domestic output. Spending by domestic residents falls in part on domestic goods but also in part on imports. On the other hand, demand for domestic goods includes exports.

The way in which external transactions affect the demand for domestic output was examined in Section 3-6. Aggregate demand for domestically produced goods is

$$AD \equiv C + I + G + NX \tag{2}$$

where NX is the trade balance (net exports). Assuming that exports are fixed and that imports depend on income, we have

$$NX \equiv X - Q \equiv \overline{X} - \overline{Q} - mY \tag{3}$$

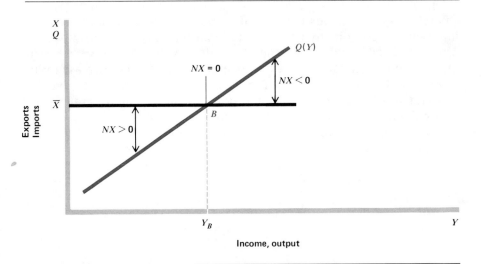

FIGURE 5-2   THE TRADE BALANCE AS A FUNCTION OF INCOME. The level of exports is given and equal to $\overline{X}$. Imports depend on the level of income. The schedule $Q(Y)$ shows that imports increase with the level of income. The slope of the schedule is the marginal propensity to import. For income levels less than Y_B, export earnings exceed import spending, and hence the trade surplus, equal to the vertical distance between the schedules, is positive. At Y_B there is trade balance equilibrium, and for higher income levels there are increasingly larger deficits.

The relationship expressed in Equation (3) is illustrated in Figure 5-2. Imports are small at low levels of income, so that given the fixed level of exports, there is a trade surplus, $NX > 0$. As income rises, import spending increases until we reach income level Y_B, where imports match exports, so that trade is balanced. A further increase in income gives rise to a trade deficit.

Goods Market Equilibrium

With these modifications, the equation for the IS curve becomes

$$Y = \overline{\overline{\alpha}}(\overline{A} - bi) \tag{4}$$

where autonomous spending now includes exports minus the autonomous component of imports and is thus given by

$$\overline{A} = \overline{C} + c\overline{TR} + \overline{I} + \overline{G} + \overline{X} - \overline{Q} \tag{5}$$

and the open economy multiplier is

$$\overline{\overline{\alpha}} = 1/[1 - c(1 - t) + m] \tag{6}$$

Figure 5-3 illustrates the goods market equilibrium condition (4). We still refer to it as a goods market equilibrium, or *IS* curve, although it is important to recognize that now the trade surplus appears as a component of demand for output. The schedule is downward-sloping because an increase in output causes an excess supply of goods: the increase in income is only partly spent on domestic goods, the rest being either saved or spent on imports. To compensate for the excess supply, interest rates have to decline to induce an increase in aggregate demand, and the *IS* curve therefore slopes down. The *IS* schedule is drawn for the given level of foreign demand $\bar{X}$.

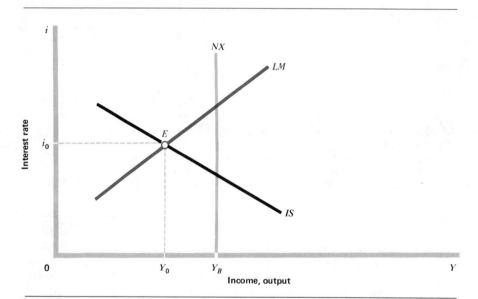

FIGURE 5-3   GOODS AND MONEY MARKET EQUILIBRIUM. The *LM* schedule is familiar from the closed economy. The *IS* schedule represents goods market equilibrium but now includes net exports *NX* as a component of demand. Given exports, there is a unique level of income Y_B at which trade is balanced. This is shown by the vertical *NX* schedule. Equilibrium obtains at point *E*, where goods and money markets clear. At *E* there is a trade surplus associated with the goods and money market equilibrium.

We have also shown, in Figure 5-3, the trade balance equilibrium schedule *NX*. Given exports, we see from Figure 5-2 and Equation (3) that there is some level of income, Y_B, at which import spending exactly matches export revenue, so that trade is balanced. Points to the left of the *NX* schedule are points of trade surplus. Here income and hence import spending are low relative to exports. Exports accordingly exceed imports. Points to the right of the *NX* schedule, by contrast, are deficit points. Here income and hence import spending are too high relative to exports for trade to be balanced. Finally, we have drawn, too, the *LM* schedule, which is precisely the same as in our study of the closed economy.

Equilibrium Income and the Balance of Trade

The next question to address, using Figure 5-3, is where the short-run equilibrium of the economy will be. It will be at point *E*, the intersection of the *IS* and *LM* curves. At point *E*, demand for domestic goods equals supply, and money demand equals money supply. Therefore, both the goods and money markets are in equilibrium.

The trade balance need not be in equilibrium since a deficit can be financed by running down foreign exchange reserves, and a surplus can be financed by building up reserves. The assumption is that the central bank finances the trade deficit by selling foreign exchange and thus maintains the exchange rate at its pegged level in the face of a trade and balance of payments deficit, or that the bank purchases foreign exchange if there is a surplus.[3] We assume the goods and money markets clear sufficiently quickly so that equilibrium is determined at point *E* in Figure 5-3. As we have drawn the equilibrium, the trade balance is in surplus.

Disturbances

How do internal and external disturbances — shifts in the level or composition of spending, or changes in exports — affect equilibrium income and the balance of trade? To answer that question, it is important to remember that both the *IS* and the trade balance schedules are drawn for a given level of exports, $\overline{X}$.

We can think of three types of disturbances, the effects of which we will briefly analyse in turn: (1) an increase in autonomous domestic spending that falls on our own goods, (2) an increase in exports, and (3) a shift in demand from domestic goods to imports.

Before going through the exercises, we indicate the results we expect to find. First, any autonomous increase (decrease) in spending on our goods should result in an increase (decrease) in equilibrium output and income. But we would expect the trade balance to worsen if domestic income expands because the higher income leads to increased import spending.

TABLE 5-2   THE EFFECT OF DISTURBANCES ON INCOME
AND ON THE TRADE BALANCE

	Autonomous increase in spending on domestic goods	Autonomous increase in exports	Shift in demand from imports to domestic goods
Income	+	+	+
Trade Balance	−	+	+

Second, it is not so clear how an increase in exports affects the trade balance. Say exports increase, and as a consequence, domestic income rises. This income increase, in turn, raises import spending, and we are not certain whether the net effect on the trade balance is an improvement or a worsening. In fact we can show that the net effect is actually an improvement — induced import spending dampens but does not offset the trade balance improvement resulting from an increase in exports. Table 5-2 summarizes those results.

The Effects of an Increase in Autonomous Spending

We now proceed to our analysis. First, consider an autonomous increase in our spending on domestic goods, perhaps because of expansionary fiscal policy. In Figure 5-4, we show the effect to be a shift in the *IS* curve. At the initial equilibrium *E* there is an excess demand for goods, and accordingly, the equilibrium income level increases. The new equilibrium is at point *E'*, where output and interest rates have risen and where we have a reduction in the trade surplus. The expansion in output increases import spending, and thus at *E'* the trade surplus is less than at *E*. The first lesson is, therefore, that expansionary domestic policies or autonomous

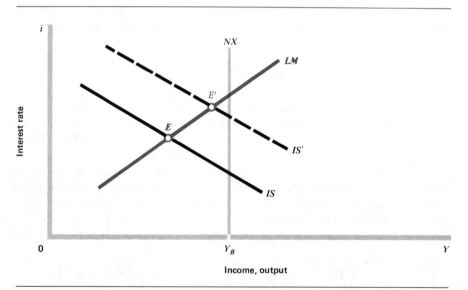

Income, output

FIGURE 5-4   THE EFFECTS OF AN INCREASE IN DOMESTIC SPENDING. Starting from equilibrium at *E*, there is an increase in our spending that falls on domestic goods. Accordingly, the *IS* schedule shifts to the right to *IS'*, and the new equilibrium is at point *E'*, where goods and assets markets clear. The increase in demand raises income. It also worsens the trade balance because of increased import spending.

increases in spending raise income but cause a worsening of the trade balance.

A second point worth making concerns the size of the income expansion induced by an expansionary policy, that is, the size of the multiplier. By comparison with a closed economy, we have less of an expansion in an open economy. Multipliers are smaller because induced spending on domestic goods is less. Part of an increase in income is now spent on imports rather than domestic goods. Imports are a *leakage* from the domestic multiplier process. Indeed, the larger the fraction of an increase in income that is spent on imports, the smaller the multiplier, because there is relatively little induced spending on domestic goods.

The Effects of an Increase in Exports

The next disturbance we consider is an increase in exports. An increase in exports raises the demand for domestic goods and thus shifts the *IS* curve to the right (to *IS'*), as shown in Figure 5-5. At the same time, the increase in exports implies that at each level of income the trade balance is improved.

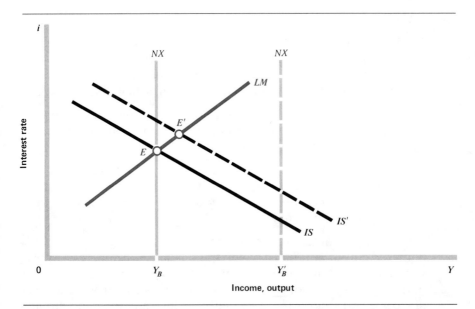

FIGURE 5-5   THE EFFECT OF AN INCREASE IN EXPORTS. Starting from an equilibrium at *E*, there is an increase in exports. The trade balance improves at each income level. It now takes a higher level of income to induce enough import spending to match the higher level of exports. Accordingly, the trade balance equilibrium schedule shifts to the right to *NX'*. Higher exports means increased demand for domestic goods. Therefore the *IS* schedule also shifts to the right. But it shifts by less than the trade balance schedule. The new equilibrium is at point *E'*. Interest rates and income rise. At the same time, the trade balance improves.

Given the higher exports, trade will now be balanced at a higher level of income. Thus, the trade balance schedule shifts to *NX'*.

Starting from a position of balanced trade at point *E*, we find that the increase in exports raises equilibrium income and improves the balance of trade at point *E'*. The first part is quite intuitive. Higher demand for our goods leads to an increase in equilibrium output. The trade balance improvement, though, is less intuitive. The increase in exports by itself improves the trade balance, but the increase in income leads to increased import spending, which, it seems, could perhaps offset the direct improvement from the export increase. This is, in fact, not the case, and we leave the demonstration of that result to Problem 1 at the end of this chapter.

A Shift in the Composition of Demand

The last disturbance we consider is a shift in demand from imports to domestic goods. You will recognize that this has the same effects as an increase in exports. It means increased demand for domestic goods and also an improvement in the trade balance.

Summary

1   The introduction of trade in goods means that spending by domestic residents is no longer equal to the demand for domestically produced goods. Some of our demand for goods goes for imports, and some of the demand for our goods comes from foreigners, to whom we export.

2   There is equilibrium in the goods market when the demand for our goods, consisting of spending by domestic residents, plus net exports, is equal to the output of domestic goods.

3   In equilibrium, there is no guarantee that trade balances. In our simplest model, there is a unique level of income at which trade balances, and this is not necessarily the income level at which the economy comes into equilibrium.

4   An increase in autonomous demand for domestic goods increases domestic output and worsens the trade balance. An increase in exports increases domestic income and reduces the trade deficit. A shift in demand toward domestically produced goods increases the level of income and reduces the trade deficit, or increases the trade surplus.

5-3   INTERNAL AND EXTERNAL BALANCE

We have now constructed and used, in Figures 5-3 through 5-5, our basic diagrammatic apparatus for embodying trade in the *IS-LM* model. We draw on the analysis of income and trade balance determination to ask about economic policy making. From a policy perspective we would want to be able to achieve both *internal* and *external balance*. Internal balance means that output is at the full-employment level $\overline{Y}$. External balance occurs when the trade balance is zero.

It is clear enough why internal balance should be an aim of policy, but why is external balance desirable? In a fixed exchange rate world, a balance of payments deficits cannot be maintained indefinitely, as the financing of the deficits requires the country to use its reserves of foreign currency. Such reserves will run out in the face of continual deficits. Hence, a country on a fixed exchange rate cannot aim to run a balance of payments deficit indefinitely. On the other side, a country on fixed rates wants to avoid running a permanent surplus, because that causes it to acquire foreign currencies to add to its reserves indefinitely. Since the foreign exchange could be used to buy and consume foreign goods, the country is permanently forgoing some consumption it could otherwise have had, when it chooses to run permanent balance of payments surpluses.

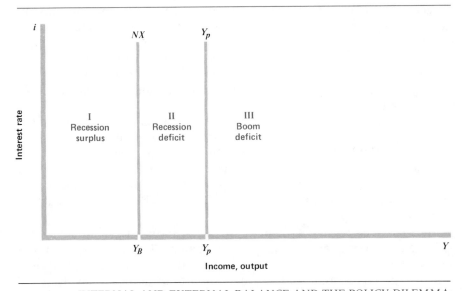

FIGURE 5-6 INTERNAL AND EXTERNAL BALANCE AND THE POLICY DILEMMA

The policy problem is illustrated in Figure 5-6. The problem is that for a given level of exports we may not be able to achieve *both* internal and external balance. In Figure 5-6, we have drawn the trade balance schedule, *NX*, for the given level of exports. We have drawn, too, the full-employment level of output $\overline{Y}$, and the two lines do not coincide.

We can break up Figure 5-6 into three regions. To the left of the trade balance schedule, we have a trade surplus, and to the right we have a deficit. To the left of the $\overline{Y}$ schedule, we have unemployment, and to the right we have overemployment, or a boom.

From a policy viewpoint, regions I and III present no problem. In region I we want to pursue an expansionary policy so as to raise employment *and* reduce the trade surplus. Until we get to trade balance equilibrium, there is no issue, since both the internal and external targets call for expansionary policies. Similarly, in region III we want to pursue restrictive policies to reduce overemployment and the trade deficit. Until we get to full employment, there is no issue.

Policy Dilemmas

The dilemma area is region II. Here we have to choose whether we want to use tight policies to achieve trade balance equilibrium or expansionary policies to achieve full employment. Not only are we unable to reach both targets simultaneously by manipulating aggregate demand, but any attempt to reach one target gets us further away from the other. Such a situation is called a *policy dilemma,* and it can always arise when there are more targets of policy than instruments with which to move the economy toward its targets. In our case we have only one policy instrument — aggregate demand policies — but we have two independent targets — external and internal balance.

The policy dilemma can be solved by finding another policy instrument to cope with the multiple targets. What is needed is some policy that shifts the trade balance schedule to the right until it overlaps with the full-employment level of output line, $\overline{Y}$. An obvious policy would be to cut down on imports at each level of income. Such a policy would reduce import spending at each level of income and thus shift the trade balance schedule to the right.

How can we cut import spending? We can use any of a number of tools, among them tariffs and exchange rate changes. Tariffs are taxes on imported goods. A tariff raises the cost of imports to domestic residents and thereby diverts demand away from imports to domestic goods. A 10 percent tariff on imported shoes, for instance, makes imported shoes more expensive relative to domestically made shoes. However, tariffs cannot be freely used to adjust the balance of trade, partly because there are international organizations and agreements such as GATT (General Agreement on Tariffs and Trade) and the IMF (International Monetary Fund) that outlaw, or at least frown on, the use of tariffs. Tariffs have generally fallen in the post-World War II period as the industrialized world has moved to desirable freer trade between countries.

Devaluation

An alternative to tariffs for reconciling internal and external balance is a *devaluation* that achieves the same effect by increasing the domestic currency price of foreign exchange.

Devaluation and Relative Prices

Assuming that nominal prices in the home currency in each country are fixed, a devaluation increases the relative price of imported goods in the devaluing country and reduces the relative price of exports from the devaluing country. These effects are illustrated in Table 5-3. We assume that Canada produces and exports rye whiskey and Britain produces and exports Scotch whiskey. Scotch is priced at £6.00 and rye at $10.00. These prices, in terms of the respective producer's currencies, are assumed to remain constant. Now, at an exchange rate of $2.00 per pound, the relative price of Scotch in terms of rye is $12.00/$10.00 = 6/5, meaning that Scotch costs 20 percent more than rye. Next, consider a devaluation of the Canadian dollar by 25 percent. The table shows that the Canadian dollar price of Scotch rises and that the sterling price of rye declines. Both in Canada and Britain, rye becomes *relatively* cheaper, or Scotch becomes relatively more expensive. The Canadian dollar devaluation lowers the sterling price of Canadian goods and raises the dollar price of British goods. The exchange ratio for Scotch and rye now becomes $15.00/$10.00 = 3/2, so that Scotch now costs 50 percent more than rye. Clearly, the decrease in the relative price of Canadian goods will affect the pattern of demand, increasing both Canadian and British demands for rye at the expense of the demand for Scotch.

TABLE 5-3   THE EFFECT OF EXCHANGE RATE CHANGES ON RELATIVE PRICES

	Scotch Whiskey	Rye Whiskey
Canadian dollar price		
(a) $2.00/pound	$12.00	$10.00
(b) $2.50/pound	$15.00	$10.00
Sterling price		
(a) $2.00/pound	£6.00	£5.00
(b) $2.50/pound	£6.00	£4.00

Effect of a Devaluation

The analysis of a devaluation is complicated by the fact that policies that shift spending from imports to domestic goods generally also affect aggregate demand in the goods market. Accordingly, policies to shift the *NX* line generally have to be accompanied by policies that adjust aggregate demand.

Figure 5-7 shows a situation in which the level of output in the economy is at $\overline{Y}$, but the balance of payments is in deficit, since the *NX* line is to the left of $\overline{Y}$. As we saw earlier in this chapter, aggregate demand policies cannot, in this case, both keep us at full employment and reduce the trade deficit. Consider using a devaluation which shifts demand from imports to domestic goods and shifts the trade balance line to the right until it coincides with the full-employment line.

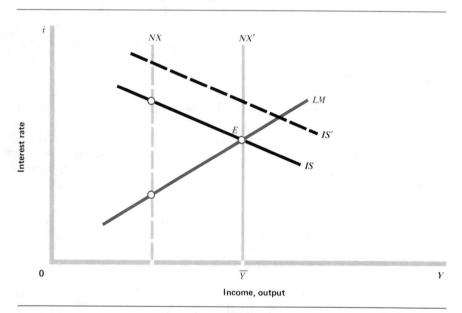

FIGURE 5-7   THE POLICY DILEMMA WITH A TRADE DEFICIT. An initial equilibrium at *E* involves a trade deficit. To correct the external balance a tariff is imposed, and this policy move shifts demand from imports to domestic goods. The trade balance equilibrium schedule shifts to *NX'* = 0 because imports are reduced at each income level. The *IS* schedule shifts right to *IS'* because of increased demand for domestic goods. A further policy change is now required to avoid the overemployment equilibrium at the intersection of *IS'* and *LM*. A reduction in money, shifting the *LM* schedule up and to the left, could restore full-employment equilibrium.

However the tariff will also affect the demand for domestic goods. The spending which at a given level of income no longer goes to imports goes to domestic goods instead. We are simply *switching* expenditures from imports to domestic goods. Accordingly, the *IS* curve shifts out to the right to *IS'*. We therefore have to use a further policy to offset the expansionary effect of the devaluation in the domestic goods market. We could use either monetary or fiscal policy to shift the economy's equilibrium back to the full-employment level $\overline{Y}$.

The important point is: In general it is necessary to combine both *expenditure switching policies*, which shift demand between domestic and imported goods, and *expenditure reducing* (or *expenditure increasing*) *policies*, to cope with the targets of internal and external balance. This point is of general importance and continues to apply when we take account of capital flows and other phenomena omitted in this section.

Targets and Instruments of Policy

In general we cannot secure both external and internal balance following a disturbance by using just one instrument of policy. A general rule of policy making is that we need to use as many policy instruments as we have policy targets. Thus, if a disturbance occurs that causes a trade deficit, it will, in general, not be enough just to have a devaluation.

To make that point we look at a reduction in saving or an autonomous increase in spending at home. The increased spending, by assumption, falls entirely on imports. Interest rates and income at home are unchanged because demand for domestic goods is unchanged, but there is now a trade deficit.

Since we are no longer in external balance, corrective action requires some measure to improve the trade balance. Suppose a devaluation is used and successfully shifts demand from imports to domestic goods. External balance now is secured, but we have done so by shifting demand to domestic goods. If initially there was full employment, the higher level of demand now means overemployment. Accordingly, we need a further policy, in addition to the devaluation, that ensures maintenance of full employment. A restrictive monetary or fiscal policy would do the job. Thus external balance adjustment involves an adjustment of the entire economy.

We should not fool ourselves into believing that just because full employment can be maintained, current account adjustment with a devaluation is costless. Current account adjustment involves not only a cut in spending to the level of income, but also, in many instances, a worsening of the *terms of trade*—the price of exports relative to imports. Foreign goods become more expensive, thus reducing the purchasing power of the goods we produce. Therefore our standard of living falls.

Finally, a comment on the role of the exchange rate in a fixed rate system: In the fixed rate system, the exchange rate is an *instrument of policy*. The central bank can change the exchange rate for policy purposes, devaluing when the current account looks as though it will be in for a prolonged deficit. In a system of clean floating, by contrast, the exchange rate moves freely to equilibrate the balance of payments. In a system of dirty floating, the central bank attempts to manipulate the exchange rate while not committing itself to any given rate. The dirty floating system is thus intermediate between a fixed rate system and a clean floating system.

5-4   CAPITAL MOBILITY

In this section we consider the role of the capital account in determining the balance of payments and equilibrium income. It plays an important role because of the high degree of international integration of capital markets. For example, yields on Canadian assets are closely linked to yields on comparable assets in the United States. If Canadian interest rates fall relative to U.S. rates, there will be a capital outflow from Canada as lenders move their funds out of Canada and borrowers attempt to raise funds in the domestic market rather than abroad.

The recognition that interest rates affect capital flows and the balance of payments has important implications for stabilization policy. First, because monetary and fiscal policy affect interest rates, they have an effect on the balance of payments through the capital account as well as through the trade account as discussed above. Second, the effect of interest rates on the balance of payments makes it possible to use a monetary-fiscal policy mix to achieve internal and external balance.

The Balance of Payments and Capital Flows

In introducing capital flows, we assume that the foreign rate of interest (i^*) is given and that capital flows into the home country at a rate that is higher, the higher the home country's rate of interest. In Figure 5-8 we show the rate of capital inflow CF, or the capital account surplus, as an increasing function of the rate of interest. At the foreign interest rate, the capital flow is zero. If the domestic interest rate is higher, there will be an inflow, and conversely, if the domestic rate is lower, there will be an outflow.

Under the assumptions given above, the capital account surplus is given by a relationship of the form:

$$CF = a(i - i^*) \tag{7}$$

Combining this with Equation (3) from Section 5.2 above we obtain the overall balance of payments surplus BP as:

$$BP = \overline{X} - \overline{Q} - mY + a(i - i^*) \tag{8}$$

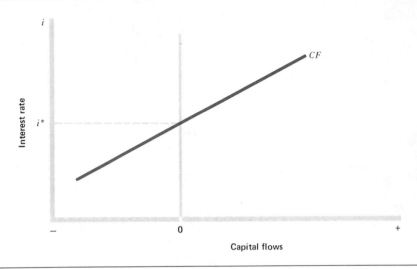

FIGURE 5-8   INTEREST-RESPONSIVE CAPITAL FLOWS

Equation (8) shows that an increase in income worsens the trade balance and reduces the overall surplus, while an increase in the interest rate increases the capital inflow and increases the overall surplus.

If we set the overall balance of payments surplus equal to zero, we obtain from Equation (8) the combinations of income and the interest rate for which we have balance of payments equilibrium. This relationship is illustrated in Figure 5-9 as the positively sloped BP curve. It is drawn for given exports and a given foreign interest rate. To derive the slope, start with an income expansion that raises imports and worsens the balance of payments. To restore balance of payments equilibrium, interest rates must be raised to attract capital inflows and offset the trade deficit. Thus a higher level of income must be matched by higher interest rates to maintain a zero balance of payments surplus.

As shown in Figure 5-9, at points above the BP curve we have a balance of payments surplus and at points below the curve we have a deficit. To see why this is so, consider what happens if we hold income constant and vary the domestic interest rate. At the interest rate for which we are on the curve, we have a zero balance. At a higher rate the trade balance will be the same but there will be a higher net capital inflow (or smaller net outflow) and therefore an overall surplus. Conversely, a lower interest rate will reduce the capital account surplus (or increase the deficit) and lead to an overall deficit.

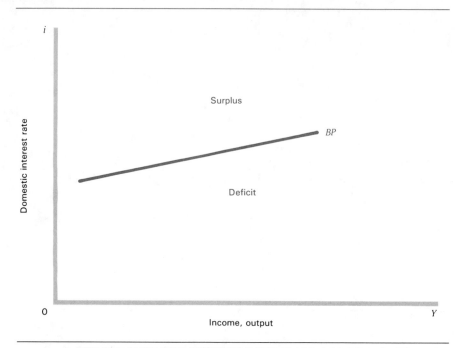

FIGURE 5-9   THE BALANCE OF PAYMENTS EQUILIBRIUM SCHEDULE. Along the *BP* curve the balance of payments is in equilibrium. A rise in income worsens the trade balance, and therefore higher interest rates are required to attract capital inflows that offset the trade deficit. Points above and to the left of the *BP* schedule correspond to surpluses and points below and to the right to deficits in the balance of payments. The higher the degree of capital mobility, the flatter the *BP* schedule, since then a small increase in our interest rates creates large capital inflows.

Equilibrium Income and the Balance of Payments

Figure 5-10 illustrates the equilibrium of an economy with both trade and capital flows. As was the case in Section 5-2 above, the intersection of the *IS* and *LM* curves determines the equilibrium income and interest rate. Since the balance of payments need not be in equilibrium, the *BP* curve serves to determine whether there will be a balance of payments surplus or deficit. The case illustrated in Figure 5-10 involves a surplus at equilibrium.

The Slope of the BP Curve

The slope of the *BP* curve depends on the marginal propensity to import and the degree of capital mobility as measured by the effect on capital

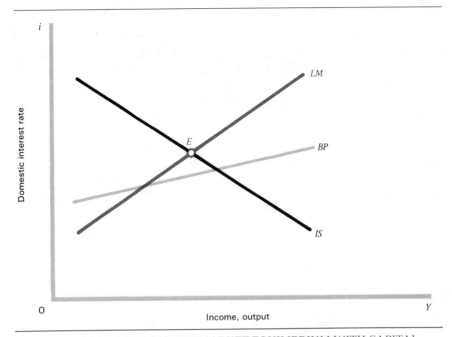

i

Domestic interest rate

LM

E

BP

IS

O

Y

Income, output

FIGURE 5-10   GOODS AND MONEY MARKET EQUILIBRIUM WITH CAPITAL FLOWS. Equilibrium income and the interest rate are determined by the intersection of the *IS* and *LM* schedules. The position of the *BP* schedule determines whether there is a surplus of deficit in the balance of payments. At the point *E* there is a surplus.

flows of a change in the domestic interest rate. The higher the degree of capital mobility, the flatter is the schedule. If capital flows are highly responsive to interest rates, then a small increase in the interest rate will bring about very large flows and thus allow a large increase in the trade deficit. The larger the marginal propensity to import, the steeper is the schedule. An increase in income worsens the trade balance by the increase in income times the marginal propensity to import. Thus a high propensity means that a given increase in income produces a large deficit and requires a large increase in interest rates to bring about a matching increase in capital inflow.

Since the *BP* and *LM* curves are both positively sloped, the assumption made as to which is steeper may have an important effect on the conclusions of our analysis. In Figure 5-10, we have made the *BP* curve relatively flat under the assumption that there is a high degree of capital mobility. This is likely to be appropriate for a country like Canada whose financial markets are closely integrated with those in the United States. This assumption is maintained throughout this section and is discussed further in Section 5-5 below.[4]

Monetary and Fiscal Policy

The effect of an expansionary fiscal policy on income and the balance of payments is illustrated in Figure 5-11. For simplicity we assume that we begin with *IS* and *LM* curves that intersect at the point *E* which is on the *BP* curve; that is, we assume that we begin at an equilibrium at which we have a zero balance of payments surplus. The *IS* curve shifts to the right and the new equilibrium is at *E'* where income and the interest rate are higher.

What will be the effect of expansionary fiscal policy on the balance of payments? The answer to this question is complicated by the fact that both the trade account and the capital account are affected. As in Section 5-2 above, the trade balance worsens because the higher income increases import spending. On the other hand, the higher interest rate increases the

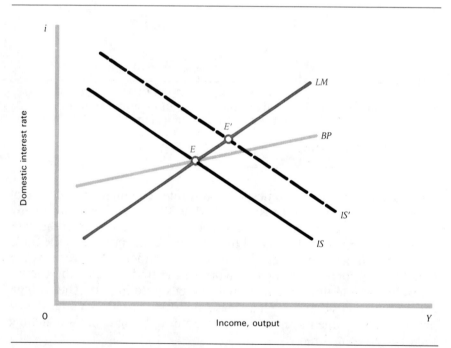

FIGURE 5-11   FISCAL POLICY AND THE BALANCE OF PAYMENTS. Expansionary fiscal policy shifts the *IS* curve up and to the right and the economy moves from *E* to *E'* where both income and the interest rate are higher. The trade account worsens since higher income increases imports, while the capital account improves since higher interest rates attract capital inflows. The net effect is an improvement since *E'* is above the *BP* schedule. This reflects the assumption that capital is highly mobile.

net capital inflow and improves the balance of payments. Since the point *E'* in Figure 5-11 is above the *BP* curve, the net effect is an *improvement* in the overall balance of payments. The capital account effect dominates the trade account effect because of our assumption that capital is highly mobile.

Monetary Policy

Turning to monetary policy, Figure 5-12 shows the effect of an increase in the money supply. The *LM* curve shifts to the right and the equilibrium income and interest rate both fall as we move from *E* to *E'*. The new equilibrium point is below the *BP* curve so that an expansionary monetary policy leads to a balance of payments deficit. In this case, the trade account and capital account effects work in the same direction. The higher level of income causes a worsening of the trade account and the lower interest rate causes a worsening of the capital account.

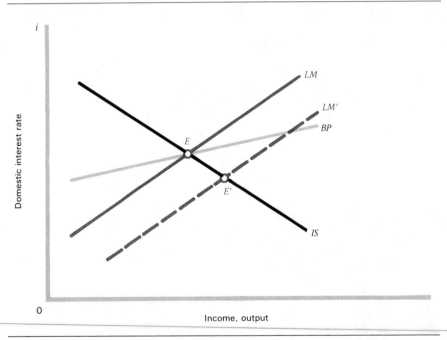

FIGURE 5-12   MONETARY POLICY AND THE BALANCE OF PAYMENTS. An increase in the money supply shifts the *LM* curve down and to the right so that income rises and the interest rate falls. The balance of payments worsens since the higher income increases imports and the lower interest rate reduces the net capital inflow.

Internal and External Balance

Figure 5-13 illustrates internal and external balance in an economy with capital flows. The full-employment output is shown as $\overline{Y}$ so that at the point E, we have both full employment and balance of payments equilibrium. The four quadrants represent the four possible policy problems. For example if we are at point E_1, we have unemployment and a balance of payments deficit. The appropriate policy to produce internal and external balance requires a higher level of employment for internal balance and higher interest rates and/or a lower level of income for external balance.

In terms of the earlier analysis there is a policy dilemma at E_1 because employment considerations suggest income should be raised and balance of payments considerations suggest it should be reduced. However, now there is a way out of the dilemma. Suppose we reduce the money supply and thus raise interest rates. To offset the effects of the higher interest rates on income, we could use expansionary fiscal policy. Clearly, we would keep income constant and reach balance of payments equilibrium by getting interest rates high enough. However, we can do better. We can use fiscal policy to get us all the way to full employment and use tight money,

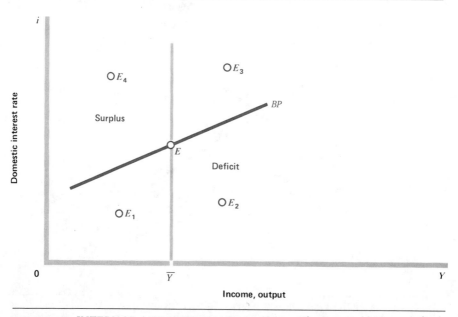

FIGURE 5-13   INTERNAL AND EXTERNAL BALANCE. The internal balance schedule is a vertical line at the full employment level of income. Along the BP schedule, the overall balance of payments is zero. The four quadrants represent the four possible policy problems. An appropriate combination of monetary and fiscal policy can be used to move the economy to the point E.

in the form of higher interest rates, to achieve balance of payments equilibrium. Thus we can get to point E with both internal and external balance.[5]

The lesson we have just derived is that under fixed exchange rates, we should expand income through fiscal policy whenever there is unemployment and use tight money whenever there is a balance of payments deficit. The combination of policies moves us to both internal and external balance. With a situation like point E_4, we want to use the same principle, but the economic conditions are different. Here we have a surplus and unemployment. Accordingly, we need expansionary fiscal policy to achieve full employment and expansionary monetary policy to reduce interest rates. Point E_4 is actually *not* a dilemma situation, since any form of expansionary policy moves us in the right direction with respect to both targets.

We leave it to you to work through the remaining cases and note here merely the principle: Under fixed exchange rates and with capital mobility, we use monetary policy to achieve external balance and fiscal policy to achieve full employment. What is the experience with such a rule? There is little doubt that tight money, for balance of payments reasons, is the oldest remedy in the policy maker's medicine chest. Since monetary policy is a flexible tool, attainment of external balance in the short run through tight money is relatively easy.

Limitations of the Policy Mix

The argument for a fiscal-monetary policy mix to handle both internal and external balance problems is persuasive, but it overlooks two important limitations. The first problem is that a country will typically not be indifferent to the level of domestic interest rates. Even if fiscal policy were sufficiently flexible to implement the policy mix, it would still be true that the composition of domestic output would depend on the mix. Thus, a country that attempts an expansion in aggregate demand, together with tight money, effectively restricts the construction sector and investment spending in general. The notion of a policy mix with monetary policy devoted to the balance of payments therefore overlooks the fact that the interest rate determines the composition as well as the level of aggregate spending.

The second consideration concerns the composition of the balance of payments. Countries are not indifferent about the makeup of their balance of payments between the current account deficit and the capital account surplus. Even if the overall balance is in equilibrium so that one target is satisfied, there is still the problem that a capital account surplus or capital inflow means net external borrowing: our country's debts to foreigners are increasing. Those debts will eventually have to be repaid.

Under a system of fixed exchange rates, there are circumstances under which a country, much like an individual, will find it useful to borrow in order to finance, say, a transitory shortfall of export earnings. But continued large-scale borrowing from abroad is not consistent with a fixed exchange rate over long periods. Large-scale borrowing eventually places the country in a position where the interest payments to foreigners become a major burden. Faced with the prospect of continued foreign borrowing on a large scale in order to maintain its fixed exchange rate, a country would be well advised to implement adjustment policies that improve the current account balance. Such policies would typically be a devaluation accompanied by restrictive monetary and/or fiscal policy to reduce domestic demand.

---

*5-5   BALANCE OF PAYMENTS AND MONEY SUPPLY

The analysis in the preceding sections has been based on the assumption that there is no link between the domestic money supply and the foreign exchange market intervention that is required to maintain a fixed exchange rate when the balance of payments is not in equilibrium. However, such a link does exist since intervention involves buying and selling foreign currency in exchange for domestic currency.

Consider, for example, the foreign exchange transactions required when there is a balance of payments deficit. The central bank offsets the excess demand for foreign currency by selling foreign currency out of its reserves. It receives domestic currency in payment and thus withdraws money from circulation.[6] In general, a balance of payments deficit leads to a decline in the domestic money supply and a surplus leads to an increase in the money supply.

Sterilization

It is possible, of course, for the central bank to offset the effects of foreign exchange transactions and insulate the domestic money supply from the balance of payments. The process by which offsetting open market operations are used for this purpose is called *sterilization*.[7] For example, if the Bank of Canada sells U.S. dollars in exchange for Canadian dollars, it can prevent a reduction in the money supply by simultaneously purchasing an equal Canadian dollar amount of bonds. Thus we can say that in the preceding sections we have assumed that the central bank breaks the link between the balance of payments and the money supply through sterilization.

The Adjustment Process without Sterilization

Suppose we assume that the central bank does not carry out sterilization operations and permits the money supply to be determined by the balance of payments surplus or deficit. How will this affect the analysis of monetary and fiscal policy carried out in Section 5-4?

Monetary Policy

We consider first the effect of an increase in the money supply as illustrated in Figure 5-12 of the previous section. The *LM* curve shifts to the right and the economy moves from *E* to *E'* where there is a balance of payments deficit. In the absence of sterilization, the money supply will fall and the *LM* curve will shift back until balance of payments equilibrium is restored at the starting point *E*. Thus we conclude that in the absence of sterilization, monetary policy has no effect since the money supply is automatically determined by the balance of payments and cannot be controlled by the central bank.

Fiscal Policy

The effect of an expanionary fiscal policy is illustrated in Figure 5-14. As in Figure 5-11, the *IS* curve shifts to the right and the economy moves to *E'* where there is a balance of payments surplus. In the absence of sterilization, the money supply will rise, the *LM* curve will shift to the right, and the economy will move along the adjustment path shown to the new equilibrium at *E''*. In this case the effect of fiscal policy is reinforced by the

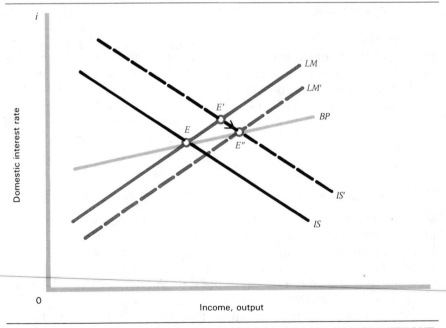

FIGURE 5-14   ADJUSTMENT TO AN EXPANSIONARY FISCAL POLICY WITHOUT STERILIZATION. An expansionary fiscal policy moves the economy to the point *E'* where there is a balance of payments surplus. As a result the money supply increases until a new equilibrium is reached at *E''*.

automatic adjustment of the money supply so that we get a larger increase in income than occurs with sterilization.

In general, if no sterilization operations are undertaken by the central bank, the equilibrium point is determined by the intersection of the *IS* and *BP* curves. The *LM* curve shifts automatically as the money supply changes in response to balance of payment surpluses or deficits.

The Monetary Approach to the Balance of Payments

The adjustment process described above highlights monetary considerations in explaining balance of payments problems. A balance of payments deficit can be interpreted as a reflection of an excessive quantity of money in the economy. This view of the problem is called the *monetary approach to the balance of payments*.

The monetary approach has been used extensively by the International Monetary Fund (IMF) in its analysis and design of economic policies for countries in balance of payments trouble. It starts with a division of the determinants of the domestic money supply into two basic factors. These are foreign exchange transactions, as described above, and *domestic credit* creation. The latter involves open market purchases of government securities and other central bank operations which provide credit to the private sector.

Given this framework, a policy plan can be drawn up by specifying a balance of payments target and projecting the demand for money. This determines the amount of domestic credit creation that will produce the level of the money supply required to attain the balance of payments target. The adoption of a limit on domestic credit creation helps the central bank avoid the temptation to expand the money supply by purchasing government bonds in the face of rising interest rates or government budget deficits.

Perfect Capital Mobility

We conclude this chapter with a discussion of the special case in which international capital is *perfectly mobile*. This means that there will be very large capital flows whenever the domestic interest rate deviates from the foreign rate so that we can have balance of payments equilibrium only when the domestic rate is equal to the foreign rate. For many purposes this is a useful approximation to the Canadian case.

The assumption of perfect capital mobility leads to a considerable simplification of our model of the balance of payments. Since the domestic interest rate is constrained to be equal to the foreign rate, Equation (8) which describes the *BP* schedule is replaced by:

$$i = i^* \tag{8a}$$

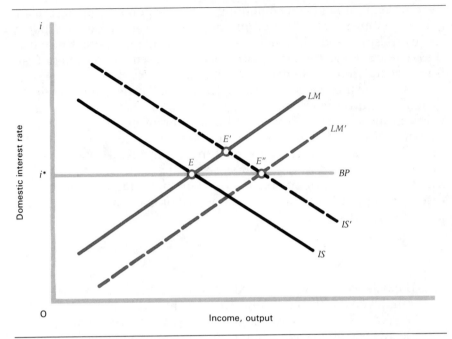

FIGURE 5-15   THE EFFECT OF FISCAL POLICY WITH PERFECT CAPITAL MOBIL-
ITY. With perfect capital mobility, the *BP* schedule is horizontal at the foreign
interest rate. An expansionary fiscal policy moves the economy from E to E'' and
has a full multiplier effect. The money supply must expand to maintain the
domestic interest rate equal to the foreign rate and prevent a massive capital
inflow.

As illustrated in Figure 5-15 the *BP* curve will be a horizontal line at the
interest rate $i = i^*$.

The implications of this assumption are very strong. To begin with,
under fixed exchange rates and perfect capital mobility, sterilization is not
possible and the central bank has no control over the domestic money
supply. This follows from the fact that at any point off the *BP* curve, there
will be a very large capital account surplus or deficit. The central bank is
forced to allow the money supply to adjust so as to maintain the domestic
interest rate equal to the foreign rate, and the equilibrium must be at a
point like E in Figure 5-15 where all three curves intersect at the same
point. This will be assured by the automatic adjustment of the money
supply and the *LM* curve.

Fiscal Policy with Perfect Capital Mobility

The effect of an expansionary fiscal policy is illustrated in Figure 5-15. The
IS curve shifts to the right and intersects the *LM* curve at E'. However, at E'

the economy cannot be in equilibrium since the domestic interest rate is above the foreign rate. To prevent a massive capital inflow, the money supply must expand, shifting the *LM* curve to the right until it intersects the *IS* curve at *E"*. At this point, income has increased, but the interest rate is unchanged from the initial equilibrium level.

Thus we find that under fixed exchange rates and perfect capital mobility, there is no crowding out and fiscal policy changes have a full multiplier effect on income. The effect of an increase in government spending as shown in Figure 5-15 is exactly the same as we obtained in Figure 4-20 of the previous chapter. There we assumed, in the context of a closed economy, that the fiscal expansion was *accommodated* by a discretionary money supply increase so as to maintain a constant interest rate. In the present case, the monetary accommodation is forced on the central bank for balance of payments reasons.

5-6   SUMMARY

1   The balance of payments accounts are a record of the international transactions of the economy. The current account records trade in goods and services, as well as transfer payments. The capital account records borrowing and lending and purchases and sales of assets.

2   The overall balance of payments is the sum of the current and capital accounts. If the overall balance is in deficit, we have to make more payments to foreigners than they make to us. The foreign currency for making these payments is supplied by central banks.

3   Under fixed exchange rates, the central bank maintains constant the price of foreign currencies in terms of the domestic currency. It does this by buying and selling foreign exchange at that fixed exchange rate. For that purpose, it has to keep reserves of foreign currency.

4   Under floating or flexible exchange rates, the exchange rate may change from moment to moment. In a system of clean floating, the exchange rate is determined by supply and demand without central bank intervention to affect the rate. Under dirty floating, the central bank intervenes by buying and selling foreign exchange in an attempt to influence the exchange rate.

The remainder of the chapter studies the role of trade in goods and capital flows under fixed exchange rates:

5   The introduction of trade in goods means that some of the demand for our output comes from abroad and that some spending by our residents is on foreign goods. There is equilibrium in the goods mar-

ket when the demand for domestically produced goods is equal to the output of those goods.

6   In equilibrium, the trade account may be in deficit. If there are no capital flows, there may be a policy dilemma in that trade balance and full employment cannot be attained using monetary and fiscal policy. An expenditure switching policy, such as a devaluation, is needed to change the allocation of spending between imports and domestic goods.

7   When capital flows are introduced with a high degree of capital mobility, an expansionary fiscal policy leads to an improvement in the balance of payments as a result of the effect of a higher interest rate on capital inflows. An expansionary monetary policy causes a worsening of both the trade account and the capital account.

8   Policy dilemmas can be handled by combining restrictive monetary policy that improves the capital account through higher interest rates with expansionary fiscal policy that increases domestic employment. However, if the balance of payments problem is not temporary then ultimately the imbalance must be dealt with by an alternative policy such as devaluation.

9   The domestic money supply can be insulated from foreign exchange transactions by sterilization operations. If there is no sterilization, then the money supply is automatically determined by the balance of payments and cannot be controlled by the central bank.

10   With perfect capital mobility, sterilization is not possible. The money supply must be allowed to adjust so as to maintain the domestic interest rate equal to the foreign rate. In this case there is no crowding out effect from changes in fiscal policy.

KEY TERMS

Fixed exchange rates
Flexible exchange rates
Balance of payments
Current account
Capital account
Trade balance
Intervention
Clean floating
Dirty (managed) floating
Devaluation
Revaluation

Currency depreciation
Currency appreciation
Internal and external balance
Targets and instruments of policy
Capital mobility
Policy mix
Sterilization
Monetary approach to the balance of payments
Perfect capital mobility

PROBLEMS

1 This problem formalizes some aspects of income and trade balance determination in the open economy. We assume, as a simplification, that the interest rate is given ($i = i_0$). In terms of Figures 5-3 and 5-4, the central bank holds the interest rate constant at i_0 so that the LM curve is effectively horizontal at this level. We assume aggregate demand is

$$AD = \overline{A} + cY - hi + X - Q$$

Import spending is given by

$$Q = \overline{Q} + mY$$

where $\overline{Q}$ is autonomous import spending. Exports are given and equal to

$$X = \overline{X}$$

(a) What is the balance of trade?
(b) What is the equilibrium level of income?
(c) What is the balance of trade at that equilibrium level of income?
(d) What is the effect of an increase in exports on the equilibrium level of income? What is the multiplier?
(e) What is the effect of increased exports on the trade balance?

2 Suppose that, in problem 1,

$\overline{A} = 400$ $c = 0.8$ $h = 30$ $i_0 = 5$ (percent) $\overline{Q} = 0$
$m = 0.2$ $\overline{X} = 250$

(a) Calculate the equilibrium level of income.
(b) Calculate the balance of trade.
(c) Calculate the open economy multiplier, that is, the effect of an increase in $\overline{A}$ on equilibrium output.
(d) Assume there is a reduction in export demand of $\Delta \overline{X} = 1$ (billion). By how much does income change? By how much does the trade balance worsen?
(e) How much does a 1 percentage point increase in the interest rate (from 5 to 6 percent) improve the trade balance? Explain why the trade balance improves when the interest rate rises.
(f) What policies can the country pursue to offset the impact of reduced exports on domestic income and employment as well as on the trade balance?

3 Consider a country that is in a position of full employment and balanced trade. Which of the following types of disturbance can be remedied with standard aggregate demand tools of stabilization? Indicate in each case the impact on external and internal balance as well as the appropriate policy response.
(a) A loss of export markets

(b) A reduction in saving and a corresponding increase in demand for domestic goods

(c) An increase in government spending

(d) A shift in demand from imports to domestic goods

(e) A reduction in imports with a corresponding increase in saving.

4 (a) Use the formula for the foreign trade multiplier to discuss the impact on the trade balance of an increase in autonomous domestic spending.

(b) Comment on the proposition that the more open the economy, the smaller the domestic income expansion.

5 Consider an economy with capital flows that is initially in internal and external balance. (Draw the *IS*, *LM*, and *BP* schedules.) Assume there is an increase in the foreign interest rate.

(a) Show the effect on the *BP* schedule.

(b) What policy reponse would immediately restore internal and external balance?

(c) If the central bank did not undertake sterilization operations, what would be the adjustment process?

6 Given the existence of capital flows, what mix of monetary and fiscal policy should be pursued to offset the following disturbances?

(a) A temporary gain in exports

(b) A permanent gain in exports

(c) A decline in autonomous spending

(d) An increased rate of capital outflow (at each level of the domestic interest rate)

7 Suppose we have a limited degree of capital mobility so that the *BP* curve is steeper than the *LM* curve. What would be the effects on the following of an increase in government spending?

(a) Income and the domestic interest rate

(b) Trade balance

(c) Capital account balance

(d) Overall balance of payments

*8 Reinterpret the conditions of Problem 1 as a case with perfect capital mobility rather than a discretionary monetary policy to maintain a constant interest rate. Illustrate graphically the effect on income of an increase in exports. What would be the effect on the trade account and the capital account?

CHAPTER 5: FOOTNOTES

1In using Eq. (1), recall that a deficit is a negative surplus.

2The Bank of Canada was not committed to maintaining exactly this rate. Under the rules of the International Monetary Fund in effect at that time, countries on fixed exchange rates maintained the value of their currencies within one percent of the stated fixed rate.

[3]We are abstracting here from a complication discussed in Section 5-5. Foreign exchange transactions will have an effect on the domestic money supply unless offsetting action is taken by the central bank. At this point we are assuming that there is no link between the balance of payments and the money supply.

[4]In problem 7 at the end of this chapter you are asked to consider the opposite case in which the *BP* curve is steeper than the *LM* curve.

[5]The idea of the policy mix for internal and external balance was suggested by Robert Mundell in his important paper, "The Appropriate Use of Monetary and Fiscal Policy under Fixed Exchange Rates," *I.M.F. Staff Papers*, March 1962. Mundell's work on international macroeconomics has been extraordinarily important, and the adventurous student should certainly consult his two books: *International Economics* (New York: Macmillan, 1967) and *Monetary Theory* (Pacific Palisades, Calif.: Goodyear, 1971).

[6]Strictly speaking, it is the *monetary base* rather than the total money supply that is affected. The change in the money supply is then determined by the multiplier process discussed in Chapter 10.

[7]*Open market operations* are purchases and sales of bonds by the central bank. The process by which these transactions affect the money supply is described in detail in Chapter 10.

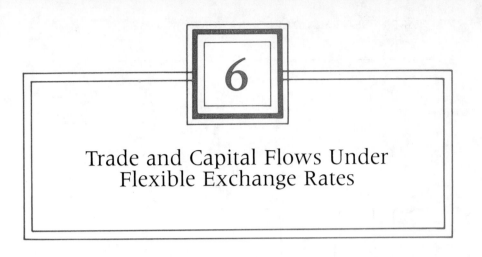

Trade and Capital Flows Under Flexible Exchange Rates

The Canadian economy has operated at various times under both fixed and flexible exchange rate regimes. Figure 6-1 shows the fluctuations in the value of the Canadian dollar since 1926. Between 1926 and 1929, Canada and most other countries fixed their rates by maintaining convertibility into gold at a fixed price. A floating rate was in effect during the 1930s until the outbreak of World War II when a fixed rate of 90.5 U.S. cents was established. The Canadian dollar was revalued to 100 U.S. cents in 1946 and this rate was abandoned in 1950 in favour of a floating rate. Under the influence of market forces, our dollar soon rose above 100 U.S. cents and remained there until 1961.

After a rapid downward movement of the Canadian dollar in 1961 and early 1962, the government decided to return to a fixed rate and a value of 92.5 U.S. cents was established in May 1962. In 1970, the Canadian dollar came under strong upward pressure and a floating rate was adopted again. By 1972, the rate had risen above 100 U.S. cents and was close to 104 cents in 1974. Since then the value of the Canadian dollar has drifted down and in early 1984 it dropped below 80 U.S. cents for the first time.

This chapter is concerned with macroeconomic adjustment under flexible exchange rates. We begin with the development of a model that simultaneously determines income, the interest rate and the exchange rate. In the light of this theory, we then review the experience of the Canadian economy under a flexible exchange rate in the 1950s. The chapter concludes with a discussion of the role of exchange rate expectations.

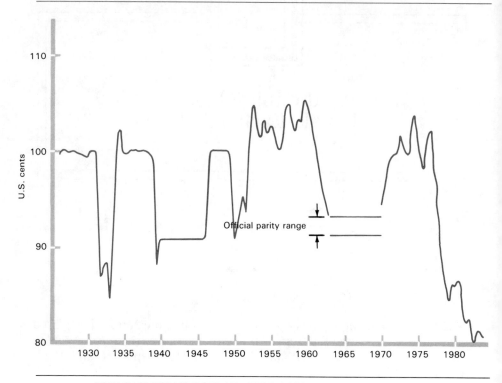

FIGURE 6-1   THE CANADIAN DOLLAR, 1926–1983
(*Source: Bank of Canada Review, Federal Reserve Bulletin*)

6-1   EXCHANGE RATES AND EQUILIBRIUM INCOME

Under a flexible exchange rate regime, the external value of the country's currency is determined by market forces and thus becomes a variable that is simultaneously determined along with income and interest rates. In this section we consider how the analysis of the previous chapter can be extended to the flexible rate case.

The Exchange Rate and Goods Market Equilibrium

As we indicated in our discussion of devaluation in Section 5-3, the exchange rate affects the trade balance and aggregate demand through its effect on the relative price of foreign and domestic goods. Assuming that nominal prices in the home currency are given in each country, a depreciation increases the relative price of imported goods in the home market and lowers the relative price of exports in the foreign market.

This relationship can be summarized in terms of the international competitiveness of the domestic economy. An exchange rate depreciation leads to a gain in home country competitiveness, and an appreciation leads to a loss in home country competitiveness. Thus a depreciation will cause an increase in net exports and an appreciation will cause a decrease in net exports.

As we have seen, aggregate demand for domestic goods consists of total spending by residents (including spending on imports) plus net exports. Thus the level of aggregate demand and the position of the *IS* curve depend on the exchange rate. We show in Figure 6-2 the *IS* schedule that represents goods market equilibrium, given the level of the exchange rate. What happens to the schedule if there is a depreciation?

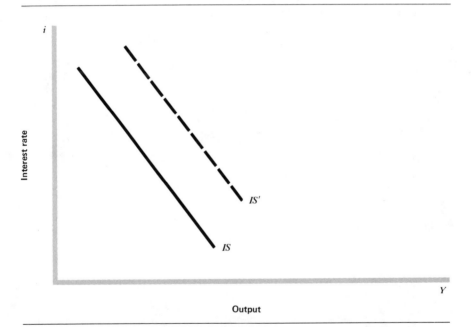

FIGURE 6-2   EFFECT OF EXCHANGE RATE DEPRECIATION ON THE IS CURVE. Each *IS* curve is drawn for a given exchange rate. A depreciation which makes us more competitive and thus increases aggregate demand shifts the *IS* curve to the right. The shift is larger the larger the response of the trade balance to a change in competitiveness and the larger the multiplier.

Exchange rate depreciation will improve competitiveness and increase the net export component of aggregate demand. Thus, for a given interest rate and income level, there will be excess demand for domestic goods. To restore equilibrium, output must rise or the interest rate must rise.

Accordingly, in Figure 6-2 we show that a depreciation shifts the *IS* schedule up and to the right. An appreciation would, of course, lead to an excess supply of domestic goods and a shift of the schedule down and to the left.

Monetary Equilibrium and Payments Balance

The condition for money market equilibrium is the familiar *LM* schedule as shown in Figure 6-3. For the present, we draw the balance of payments equilibrium schedule under the simplifying assumption of *perfect capital mobility*. This means that there will be very large capital flows whenever the domestic interest rate deviates from the foreign rate so that we can have balance of payments equilibrium only when the domestic rate is equal to the foreign rate. This implies that the *BP* curve will be a horizontal line at the foreign interest rate.

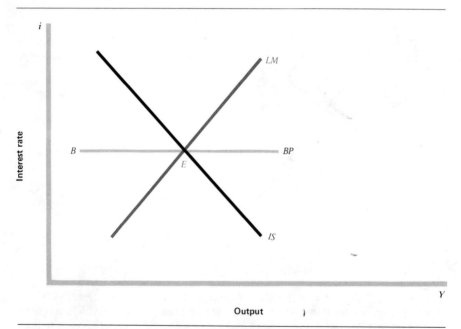

FIGURE 6-3   EQUILIBRIUM OF THE GOODS AND MONEY MARKETS AND THE BALANCE OF PAYMENTS. The *LM* schedule is familiar from the closed economy. The *IS* schedule is drawn for a given exchange rate. The schedule *BP* shows equilibrium in the balance of payments with capital flows matching trade imbalances. The schedule is horizontal in the case of perfect capital mobility where any divergence of home interest rates from those abroad leads to unlimited capital flows. Only at an interest rate $i = i^*$ can the balance of payments then be in equilibrium.

The Effect of an Increase in Exports

We have now completed the specification of our model as represented by Figure 6-3, and can ask how the economy will adjust to disturbances. The first change we look at is an exogenous increase in foreign demand for our goods, or an increase in exports.

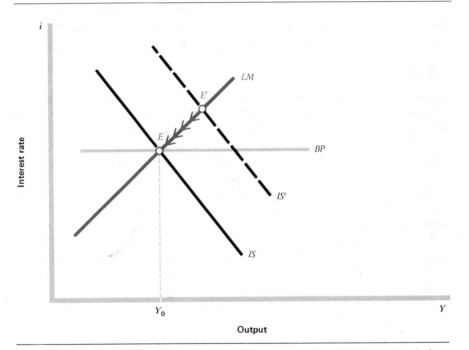

FIGURE 6-4   EFFECTS OF AN INCREASE IN THE DEMAND FOR EXPORTS. A rise in foreign demand for our goods, at the initial exchange rate and interest rate at point E, creates an excess demand for goods. The IS schedule shifts out to IS', and the new goods and money market equilibrium is at point E' where our interest rate exceeds that abroad. Capital will tend to flow into our country in response to the increased interest rate, and the resulting balance of payments surplus leads to currency appreciation. The appreciation means that we become less competitive. The IS schedule starts shifting back as a result of the appreciation, and the process continues until the initial equilibrium at E is reached again. In the end, increased exports (or a fiscal expansion) do not change output. They simply lead to currency appreciation and thereby to an offsetting change in net exports.

Starting from an initial equilibrium at point E in Figure 6-4, we see that the increase in foreign demand implies an excess demand for our goods. At the initial interest rate, exchange rate, and output level, demand for our goods now exceeds the available supply. For goods market equilibrium, at the initial interest rate and exchange rate, we require a higher level of output. Accordingly, the *IS* schedule shifts out and to the right.

Now consider for a moment point *E'*, where the goods and money markets clear. Here output has increased to meet the increased demand. The rise in income has increased money demand and thus raised equilibrium interest rates. Is point *E'* an equilibrium? It is not, because the balance of payments is not in equilibrium. In fact, we would not reach point *E'* at all. The tendency for the economy to move in that direction, as we show now, will bring about an exchange rate appreciation that will take us all the way back to the initial equilibrium at *E*.

The Adjustment Process

Suppose, then, that the increase in foreign demand takes place and that, in response, there is a tendency for output and income to increase. The induced increase in money demand will raise interest rates and thus will bring us out of line with interest rates internationally. The resulting capital inflows immediately put pressure on the exchange rate. The capital inflow causes our currency to appreciate.

The exchange appreciation means, of course, that import prices fall and that domestic goods become relatively more expensive. Demand shifts away from domestic goods, and net exports decline. In terms of Figure 6-4, the appreciation implies that the *IS* schedule shifts back from *IS'* to the left. Next, we have to ask how far the exchange appreciation will go and to what extent it will therefore dampen the expansionary effect of increased net exports.

The exchange rate will keep appreciating as long as our interest rate exceeds the world level. This implies that the exchange appreciation must continue until the *IS* schedule has shifted back all the way to its initial position. Thus adjustment is shown by the arrows along the *LM* schedule. Only when we return to point *E* will output and income have reached a level consistent with monetary equilibrium at the world rate of interest.

We have now shown that under conditions of perfect capital mobility, an expansion in exports has no lasting effect on equilibrium output. With perfect capital mobility the tendency for interest rates to rise, as a result of the increase in export demand, leads to currency appreciation and thus to a complete offset of the increase in exports. Once we return to point *E*, net exports are back to their initial level. The exchange rate has, of course, appreciated. Imports will increase as a consequence of the appreciation, and the initial expansion in exports is in part offset by the appreciation of our exchange rate.

Fiscal Policy

We can extend the usefulness of this analysis by recognizing that it is valid not only for an increase in exports. The same analysis applies to a fiscal expansion. A tax cut or an increase in government spending would lead to an expansion in demand in just the same way as increased exports do. Again, the tendency for interest rates to rise leads to appreciation and therefore to a fall in exports and increased imports. There is, accordingly, complete crowding out here. The crowding out takes place not as in Chapter 4 because higher interest rates reduce investment, but because the appreciation reduces competitiveness and causes a decline in net exports.

The important lesson here is that disturbances to the goods market do not affect equilibrium income under flexible rates with perfect capital mobility. This is in contrast to the effect of a fiscal expansion under fixed rates. In section 5-5, we showed that with a fixed exchange rate and perfect capital mobility, there is no crowding out and fiscal policy changes have a full multiplier effect on income. With a flexible rate, fiscal policy has no effect on income. Instead, it merely causes an offsetting loss of competitiveness and a shift in the composition of spending towards domestic goods and away from net exports.

Adjustment to a Monetary Disturbance

We now show that under flexible exchange rates, an increase in the money stock leads to an increase in income and a depreciation of the exchange rate. The analysis uses Figure 6-5. We start from an initial position at point E and consider an increase in the nominal quantity of money, M. Since prices are given, we have an increase in the real money stock, M/P. At E there will be an excess supply of real balances. To restore equilibrium, interest rates would have to be lower or income would have to be larger. Accordingly, the LM schedule shifts down and to the right to LM'.

We ask once again whether point E' is the new equilibrium. At E', goods and money markets are in equilibrium (at the initial exchange rate), but it is clear that interest rates have fallen below the foreign level. Capital outflows will therefore put pressure on the exchange rate. The exchange depreciation caused by the low level of interest rates implies that import prices increase, domestic goods become more competitive and, as a result, demand for our output expands. The exchange depreciation therefore shifts the IS curve out and to the right. As the arrows indicate, exchange depreciation continues until the relative price of domestic goods has fallen enough to raise demand and output to the level indicated by point E''. Only at E'' do we have goods and money market equilibrium compatible with the foreign rate of interest. Consequently, there is no further tendency for exchange rates and relative prices, and hence demand, to change.[1]

We have now shown that a monetary expansion leads to an increase in output and a depreciation of the exchange rate under flexible rates. One way of thinking about this result is that with P fixed, an increase in M increases M/P. The demand for real balances is, from Equation (4), equal to $L(i, Y)$. Since i cannot differ from the world rate of interest, Y has to rise to equate the demand for money to the supply. The exchange depreciation raises net exports, and that increase in net exports, in turn, sustains the higher level of output and employment. One interesting implication of our analysis, then, is the proposition that monetary expansion improves the current account through the induced depreciation.

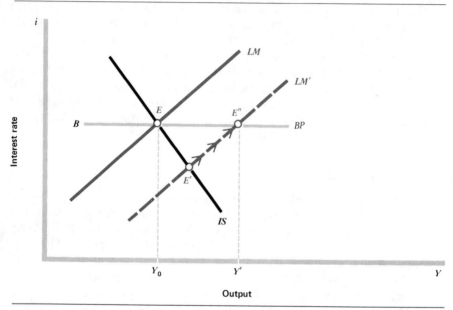

FIGURE 6-5   EFFECTS OF AN INCREASE IN THE MONEY STOCK. A monetary expansion shifts the LM schedule to LM'. At point E' the goods and money markets clear, but our interest rate is below the world level. Therefore capital will tend to flow out, the balance of payments goes into deficit, and the currency depreciates. The depreciation means that we become more competitive. Net exports rise, and therefore the IS curve shifts out and to the right. The process continues until we reach point E''. Interest rates are again at the foreign level, and the depreciation has led to a higher level of income. Monetary policy thus works by increasing net exports.

How do our results compare with those of the fixed exchange rate case? We argued in Section 5-5 that under fixed rates and perfect capital mobility, the central bank cannot control the money supply. An attempt to expand the money supply will merely lead to a reserve loss as the central bank attempts to prevent a depreciation of the currency in response to declining interest rates. Under flexible rates, by contrast, there is no intervention and the money supply increase is not reversed through foreign exchange transactions.

The fact that the central bank *can* control the money stock under flexible exchange rates is one of the most important aspects of the flexible rate system. As we shall see, it has important implications for the ability of the Bank of Canada to carry out an independent monetary policy. Under a fixed exchange rate the money supply in Canada is largely determined by monetary policy in other countries, particularly the United States.

Beggar-Thy-Neighbour Policy and Competitive Depreciation

It is useful to extend our analysis to a brief discussion of the international implications of exchange rate depreciation and changes in net exports. We showed that a monetary expansion in the home country leads to exchange depreciation, an increase in net exports, and therefore an increase in output and employment. But our increased net exports correspond to a deterioration in the trade balance abroad. The domestic depreciation shifts demand from foreign goods toward domestic goods. Abroad, output and employment therefore decline. It is for this reason that the depreciation-induced change in the trade balance has been called a *beggar-thy-neighbour policy* — it is a way of exporting unemployment or of creating domestic employment at the expense of the rest of the world.

The recognition that exchange depreciation is mainly a way of shifting demand from one country to another, rather than changing the level of world demand, is important. It implies that exchange rate adjustment can be a useful policy when countries find themselves in different stages of a business cycle — for example, one in a boom (with overemployment) and the other in a recession. In that event, a depreciation by the country experiencing a recession would shift world demand in that direction and thus work to reduce divergences from full employment in each country.

By contrast, when countries' business cycles are highly synchronized, such as in the 1930s or in the aftermath of the oil shock in 1973, exchange rate movements will not contribute much toward world full employment. The problem is then one of the level of total world spending being deficient or excessive while exchange rate movements affect only the allocation of a *given* world demand between countries. Nevertheless, from the point of view of an individual country, exchange depreciation works to attract world demand and raise domestic output. If every country tried to depreciate to attract world demand, we would have *competitive depreciation* and a shifting around of world demand rather than an increase in the world level of spending. Coordinated monetary and/or fiscal policies are needed to increase demand and output in each country.

*Imperfect Capital Mobility

In Chapter 5, we considered the effects of monetary and fiscal policy under fixed exchange rates in the more general model in which capital is not perfectly mobile. In this case, the rate of capital flow increases as the interest differential increases, but at a finite rate, so that there can be equilibrium with the domestic rate different from the foreign rate.

How would policy work with flexible exchange rates and imperfect capital mobility? We leave as an exercise at the end of the chapter the demonstration of the following results: First, a fiscal expansion at home raises our interest rate and increases our income. With the higher interest rate, there will be an increased inflow of capital. This implies a deterioration in the current account, since the sum of the current and capital accounts is zero. However, the current account deteriorates by less than the fiscal expansion. There is less than full crowding out, and hence, income rises.

In the case of a monetary expansion, our interest rate falls, income rises, and the current account must improve. We know that the current account must improve since the lower interest rate implies increased capital outflows which, for payments to balance, must be offset by an improvement in the current account.

The case of imperfect capital mobility clearly qualifies our earlier results. Now both monetary and fiscal policies are effective and the extent to which fiscal policy can affect income depends on the extent to which changes in interest differentials affect capital flows.

Summary

An examination of goods market and monetary disturbances under flexible exchange rates, and perfect capital mobility gave us the following results, summarized in Table 6-1.

TABLE 6-1   THE EFFECTS OF MONETARY AND FISCAL POLICY
           UNDER PERFECT CAPITAL MOBILITY

	Fixed rates	Flexible rates
Monetary expansion	No output change; reserve losses equal to money increase	Output expansion; trade balance improves; exchange depreciation
Fiscal expansion	Output expansion; trade balance worsens	No output change; reduced net exports; exchange appreciation

1   A fiscal expansion leaves output unchanged. The fiscal expansion tends to increase income and raise interest rates. The tendency for interest rates to rise leads to appreciation of the exchange rate as capital is attracted from abroad. The appreciation, by lowering import prices, shifts demand away from our goods and thus offsets the expansionary effect of fiscal policy.

2   This result is the opposite of that derived under fixed exchange rates. The difference results from the fact that under flexible rates, the money stock is exogenous and is kept fixed when fiscal policy changes, while under fixed rates, exchange rate stabilization makes money endogenous and thus accommodates the fiscal expansion.

3   For a monetary expansion, conclusions were also opposite to those for fixed rates. A monetary expansion leads to an increase in income and to exchange depreciation. The tendency for interest rates to fall as a consequence of monetary expansion leads to a capital outflow that causes the exchange rate to depreciate and thereby to raise demand for domestic output.

4   In the case of a fiscal expansion, the induced appreciation of the exchange rate leads to a reduction in net exports, offsetting the increased domestic spending. With a monetary expansion, the depreciation that ensues leads to an improvement in net exports. The trade balance effects of the two policies are thus quite different.

5   With imperfect capital mobility, interest rates can differ internationally, and both monetary and fiscal policies can affect the level of output.

6-2   CANADIAN EXPERIENCE WITH FLEXIBLE EXCHANGE RATES IN THE 1950s

Since World War II, Canada has operated under both fixed and flexible exchange rate regimes. A flexible rate was in effect from 1950 to mid-1962 and from mid-1970 to the present. In this section we examine the performance of the Canadian economy in the earlier period. A discussion of the more recent experience is postponed to Chapter 18 after we have introduced inflation into our analysis.

Figure 6-6 shows the performance of the Canadian economy over the period 1953–1961. There was a sharp but brief recession in 1954 followed by an investment boom in 1955 and 1956, which resulted in rapid growth in GNP and a decline in the unemployment rate below 4 percent. In 1957 the growth rate slowed and the unemployment rate rose sharply. The entire period from 1957 to 1961 was characterized by slow growth and relatively high unemployment.

The Natural Resource Boom of the Mid-1950s

During the mid-1950s Canada experienced boom conditions fueled by high world demand for natural resources. Further, the attractive investment opportunities that existed in Canada attracted large capital inflows. As can be seen in Figure 6-1, the effect of the capital account surplus was to push up the value of the Canadian dollar which remained above 100

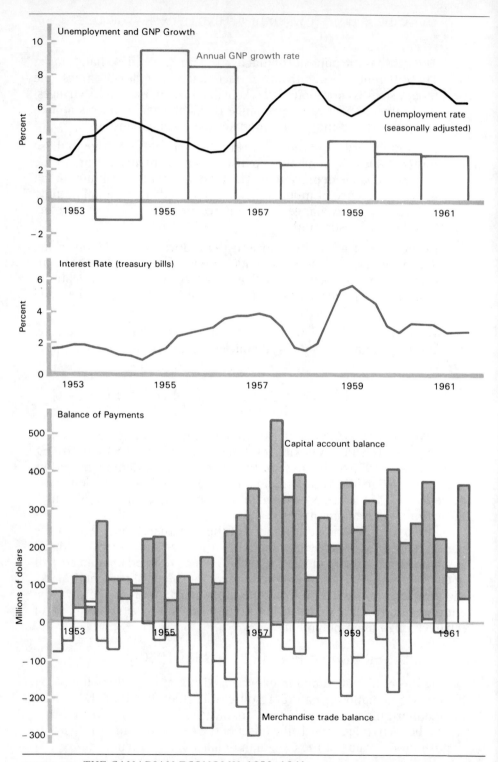

FIGURE 6-6   THE CANADIAN ECONOMY, 1953–1961
(*Source*: Department of Finance, *Economic Review*; Statistics Canada, 11-206)

U.S. cents and at times rose as high as 105 U.S. cents. This in turn had the effect of reducing exports and increasing imports so that there were deficits in merchandise trade.

This appreciation of the Canadian dollar acted as a stabilizer and had a desirable dampening effect on aggregate demand. The economy was subject to expansionary disturbances as represented by the outward shift in the *IS* schedule shown in Figure 6-4. At the point *E'* we have a balance of payments surplus which causes an appreciation and a movement of the *IS* back to *E*.

The question that remains is why did the Canadian economy go through a prolonged period of slow growth and high unemployment during the years 1957 to 1961? We now turn to a detailed examination of that period.

The slow growth period, 1957–1961

During 1957 the Canadian economy weakened and the unemployment rate rose, subsequently reaching a peak of 7.9 percent in mid-1958. There was an effort to stimulate the economy in 1958 and 1959 through expansionary fiscal policy and the cyclically adjusted federal budget balance moved into a deficit position. However, as we have seen, we would not expect fiscal policy to have a lasting effect on income under a flexible exchange rate. An increase in the government deficit leads to a crowding out of private demand in the form of net exports. Clearly, it is necessary for a country with a flexible exchange rate to use monetary policy for stabilization purposes.

How was monetary policy used in this period? During 1958, the money supply was expanded at a rapid rate, but this policy was reversed in 1959 and 1960. During these two years there was virtually no growth in the money supply and as a result interest rates rose sharply in 1959 and remained relatively high until mid-1961. Thus, the period 1959 to 1961 was characterized by a very restrictive monetary policy in spite of a clear need for economic stimulus.

A review of statements by the Bank of Canada during this period suggests that the restrictive monetary policy being followed was based on two major concerns. First, rising inflation was seen as an important threat to the Canadian economy even after 1957 when it was clear that a recession had taken hold. Second, the Governor placed great emphasis on what he regarded as the unsatisfactory state of Canada's balance of payments. In his *Annual Report* for 1959 (pp. 7–8) he stated:

> For some years, as I see it, the Canadian economy has been under the influence of excessive overall spending, which even in periods of relatively high unemployment resulted in a net inflow of imports from other countries. . . . The attempt to accomplish too much too fast has given rise to huge deficits in our international balance of payments on current account, . . . to a large and growing volume of foreign debt, . . . and has gone hand-in-hand with a growing degree of foreign predominance in Canadian business.

Continuing this theme in his *Annual Report* for 1960 (p. 22), he concluded that:

> . . . to engage in further large over-all monetary expansion in an attempt to drive down interest rates generally, with or without the motive of thereby reducing the inflow of capital from abroad, is an unsound and dangerous approach. . . .

It appears that the Bank of Canada's prescription for these supposed ills was to maintain high interest rates so as to reduce imports by curtailing overall aggregate demand, and to reduce the capital inflows by encouraging domestic saving. In retrospect, it is clear that this policy was at odds with the theory of an open economy under a flexible exchange rate.

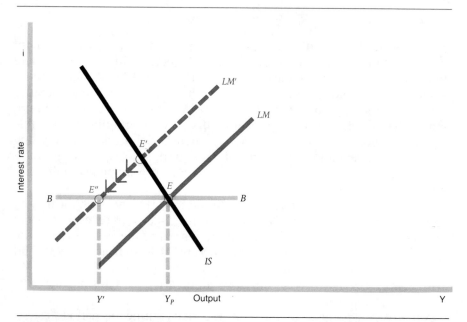

FIGURE 6-7   EFFECTS OF A RESTRICTIVE MONETARY POLICY. The adjustment process is the same as that shown in Figure 6-5 except that in this case we have a decrease in the money supply.

Consider Figure 6-7 in which the point *E* is assumed to represent equilibrium at the full-employment level of output. The adoption of restrictive monetary policy means the *LM* schedule shifts up and to the left to *LM'*. At *E'*, output is below the initial (full-employment) level and the domestic interest rate is above the foreign rate. The higher interest rate induces a capital account surplus and an appreciation of the Canadian dollar. As a result, the trade account moves toward a deficit position so that the *IS* curve shifts in and to the left and the economy moves toward *E''*. This adjustment process is quite consistent with the observed behaviour of the Canadian economy over the period 1959 to 1961.

Thus we conclude that mistakes in monetary policy were a major cause of the stagnation of the Canadian economy in the late fifties and early sixties. There was indeed considerable controversy at the time, and in 1960, a group of academic economists called upon the Minister of Finance to dismiss the Governor of the Bank of Canada. Subsequently, there was an acrimonious confrontation between the Minister and the Governor, and the latter finally resigned in July of 1961.[2]

*6-3   EXCHANGE RATE EXPECTATIONS AND THE INTEREST PARITY CONDITION

A cornerstone of our theoretical model of exchange rate determination in Section 6-1 was international capital mobility. In particular, we assumed that capital markets were highly integrated so that interest rates would be equalized across countries. How does this assumption stand up to the facts?

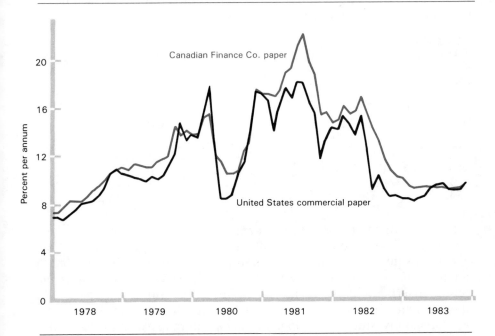

FIGURE 6-8   INTEREST RATES ON 90-DAY PAPER
(*Source: Bank of Canada Review*)

In Figure 6-8, we show Canadian and U.S. interest rates on 90-day paper. These rates follow a similar pattern over time but they are by no means equalized. Exchange rate expectations provide the key to squaring this fact with our theory.

Exchange Rate Expectations

The theory that implies international equalization of interest rates is incomplete in a world where exchange rates frequently do and are expected to change. For example, consider a situation where the German mark is expected to appreciate by 5 percent over the next year relative to the Canadian dollar. Suppose the interest rate in Germany is 6 percent. Then anyone buying German bonds will earn a return in marks of 6 percent. Suppose now that the Canadian interest rate is 10 percent. A German investing in Canada for a year will, at the beginning of the year, exchange his marks for dollars, and then earn 10 percent on his dollars. At the end of the year, he will want to change his dollars back into marks to spend in Germany. But he expects that by the end of the year, each dollar will be worth 5 percent less in terms of marks, as a result of the expected depreciation. Therefore, in terms of marks, he will expect to earn only 5 percent (10 percent minus 5 percent) by investing in Canadian bonds, whereas he earns 6 percent by investing in German bonds. He will naturally prefer to invest in German bonds.[3]

TABLE 6-2 INTEREST RATES AND EXCHANGE DEPRECIATION (in percentages)

	Domestic interest rate (1)	Foreign interest rate (2)	Depreciation (3)	Adjusted interest differential (1) − (2) − (3)
1.	10	5	0	5
2.	10	15	−5	0
3.	10	15	−2	−3
4.	10	15	−10	5

It is clear, therefore, that we must extend our discussion of interest rate equalization to incorporate expectations of exchange rate changes. Table 6-2 gives some combinations of the domestic interest rate, the foreign interest rate, and exchange rate changes. Suppose we want to know the return, in terms of domestic currency, of investments here compared with those abroad. For domestic investments we just look at our interest rate. For foreign investments, we look at the foreign rate, *and* at the exchange depreciation. Suppose foreign interest rates were 5 percent and exchange rates did not change. This is the case of row 1, and the *adjusted* interest differential is 5 percent in favour of the home country. Row 2 considers the case where interest rates abroad are high (15 percent), but where our currency appreciates at the rate of 5 percent or the foreign currency depreciates by that amount. Here the depreciation exactly offsets the higher foreign interest rates and the adjusted differential is zero—what would be gained in interest is lost through the foreign depreciation. Cases 3 and 4 show circumstances where the foreign depreciation falls short of, and exceeds, the interest differential, respectively. Clearly, in cases 1 and 4, we would want to invest in the home country; in case 2 we are indifferent; and case 3 favours the foreign country.

The trouble, of course, is that we do not know ahead of time how the exchange rate will move. We know the interest rates on, say, three-month treasury bills in Canada and the United Kingdom, so that we can compute the interest differential, but we do not know whether the pound will appreciate or depreciate over the next three months. Even if we somehow knew the direction, we would certainly not know the precise amount.

Investors then have to form *expectations* about the behaviour of the exchange rate; that is, in deciding whether to invest at home or abroad, they have to make forecasts of the future behaviour of the exchange rate. Given these forecasts, we would expect that in a world of high capital mobility, the interest differentials, adjusted for expected depreciation, should be negligible. That means that a country that is certain to depreciate will have interest rates above the world level, and conversely, a country that is expected to appreciate will have interest rates below the world level.

The Interest Parity Condition

The introduction of exchange rate expectations modifies our condition for balance of payments equilibrium. We maintain the assumption of perfect capital mobility, but replace the condition that the domestic rate i is equal to the foreign rate i^* with

$$i = i^* + x \qquad (1)$$

where x is the expected rate of depreciation of the domestic currency. This condition is called the *interest parity condition*.

Using this equation to describe the balance of payments equilibrium implies that the *BP* schedule will still be horizontal but its position will depend on exchange rate expectations. This implies that speculative capital flows related to expectations of changes in exchange rates will have macroeconomic consequences. In Figure 6-9, the *BP* schedule is drawn for a given foreign interest rate and a given expected rate of depreciation, say, zero. Suppose that we start in full equilibrium at point E and that the market develops the expectation that the home currency will appreciate. This implies that even with a lower home interest rate, domestic assets are

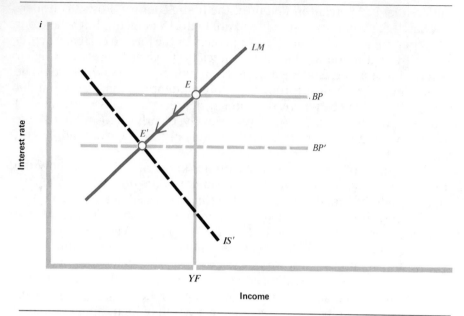

FIGURE 6-9   RESPONSE TO AN EXPECTED APPRECIATION OF THE CURRENCY.
The initial equilibrium at E is disturbed by the expectation that the home
currency will appreciate. The BP schedule shifts down to BP', reflecting the fact
that people are willing to hold domestic assets at a reduced interest rate since they
are compensated for the differential by anticipated appreciation. At E' there is
now a capital inflow that leads to currency appreciation. The IS schedule (not
drawn) shifts to IS', and the economy moves into a recession. The capital inflow
has brought about a loss of trade competitiveness and thus unemployment at
point E'.

attractive, and so the BP schedule shifts down by the amount of expected
appreciation.

Point E is no longer an equilibrium, given the shift of the BP schedule to
BP', but rather a position of surplus with large-scale capital inflows moti-
vated by the anticipation of appreciation. (This might well describe the
case of the United Kingdom after awareness of British oil discoveries spread
in the market.) The surplus causes the exchange rate to start appreciating,
and we move in a southwesterly direction, as indicated by the arrow. The
speculative attack causes appreciation, a loss in competitiveness, and,
consequently, falling output and employment.

This analysis confirms that exchange rate expectations, through their
impact on capital flows and thus on actual exchange rates, are a potential
source of disturbance to macroeconomic equilibrium.

Exchange Rate Overshooting

The interest parity condition also has important implications for the adjustment process in response to monetary changes. Consider the adjustment path shown in Figure 6-5. It is drawn under our usual assumption that the money market adjusts instantaneously so that the adjustment path is along the *LM* curve from *E'* to *E''*. Along this path, the currency is depreciating while the domestic interest rate is below the foreign rate. However, to the extent that this depreciation is anticipated, the interest parity condition is violated since we have $x > 0$ and $i - i^* < 0$.

Figures 6-10 and 6-11 illustrate an adjustment process that is consistent with the interest parity condition. Figure 6-11 shows the time paths of the money supply, the exchange rate and income. Note that the exchange rate is measured by the domestic currency price of foreign exchange so that a depreciation is shown as an increase.

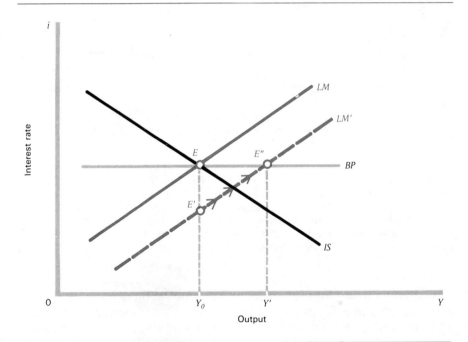

FIGURE 6-10   INTEREST PARITY AND THE ADJUSTMENT TO AN INCREASE IN MONEY. When the money supply is increased, the economy initially moves to *E'* where $i < i^*$ and investors anticipate an appreciation of the currency. As we move to *E''*, income increases, the currency appreciates, and *i* rises back to the level of i^*.

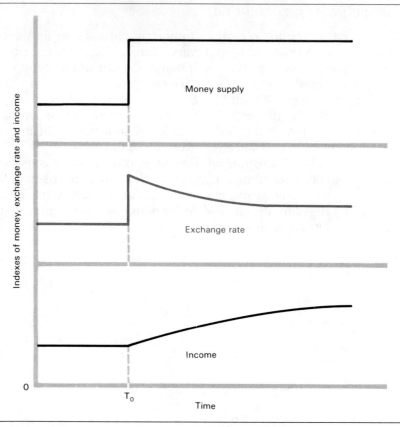

FIGURE 6-11 EXCHANGE RATE OVERSHOOTING. The diagram shows indexes of
the money supply, exchange rate and income to illustrate the time paths
corresponding to the adjustment process shown in Figure 6-10. An increase in the
money stock at time T_0 causes an immediate depreciation. The gain in
competitiveness leads to an increase in income over time while the currency
appreciates partially reversing the initial overshooting.

When the money supply is increased at time T_0, there is an immediate
depreciation and a fall in the domestic interest rate. As shown in Figure
6-11 this depreciation *overshoots* the final equilibrium value. Thereafter,
the domestic currency *appreciates* towards its new equilibrium. Meanwhile
in Figure 6-10, the economy moves initially to E'. At this point, the interest
parity condition holds since we have $i - i^* < 0$ and $x < 0$ (i.e., investors
anticipate an appreciation). As we move towards the new equilibrium,
income increases in response to the initial improvement in competitiveness,
the currency appreciates, and the interest rate rises back to the level of the
foreign rate.

At the new equilibrium, income is higher, the domestic interest rate is unchanged, and the currency has depreciated. However, the exchange rate overshoots the new equilibrium level since, in response to the disturbance, it initially moves beyond the equilibrium it ultimately will reach and then gradually returns to the new equilibrium. Overshooting means that changes in monetary policy produce large changes in exchange rates.

6-4 SUMMARY

1 Under flexible exchange rates, without government intervention, the exchange rate adjusts to ensure equilibrium in the overall balance of payments. The sum of the current and capital account deficits is zero with floating rates and no intervention.

2 The demand for our goods depends on the exchange rate which, given foreign and domestic prices, affects the relative price of imports versus exports. An increase in the exchange rate — a depreciation — increases the demand for domestically produced goods by reducing imports and increasing exports.

3 When capital is perfectly mobile, so that the interest rate essentially cannot differ from the foreign rate, fiscal policy becomes totally ineffective in changing the level of income. An increase in government spending merely reduces net exports, with the trade deficit being matched by a capital inflow.

4 Monetary policy retains its effectiveness when capital is very mobile. An increase in the money stock leads to a depreciation of the exchange rate and an improved trade balance, which increases demand for domestic output.

5 If an economy finds itself with unemployment, the central bank can intervene to depreciate the exchange rate and increase net exports and thus aggregate demand. Such policies are known as beggar-thy-neighbour policies, because the increase in demand for domestic output comes at the expense of demand for foreign output.

6 When exchange rate expectations are taken into account, balance of payments equilibrium is described by the interest parity condition which equates the domestic interest rate with the foreign rate plus the expected rate of depreciation.

7 The interest parity condition implies that there will be exchange rate overshooting in response to a change in the money supply. An increase in money causes a depreciation beyond the final equilibrium value

followed by an appreciation along an adjustment path to the new equilibrium.

KEY TERMS

Competitiveness
Perfect capital mobility
Beggar-thy-neighbour policy

Interest parity condition
Exchange rate overshooting

PROBLEMS

1 Explain why the belief that a devaluation is imminent makes a devaluation more likely in a fixed exchange rate system.

2 Explain why an expansionary fiscal policy "beggars our neighbours" less than direct intervention by the central bank in the foreign exchange markets to depreciate the exchange rate.

3 Assume that capital is perfectly mobile, the price level is fixed, and the exchange rate is flexible. Now let the government increase purchases. Explain first why the equilibrium levels of output and the interest rate are unaffected. Then show whether the current account improves or worsens as a result of the increased government purchases of goods and services.

4 Assume that there is perfect mobility of capital. How does the imposition of a tariff affect the exchange rate, output, and the current account? (Hint: Given the exchange rate, the tariff reduces our demand for imports.)

5 Explain how and why monetary policy retains its effectiveness when there is perfect mobility of capital.

6 Consult The Globe and Mail or some other newspaper which has foreign exchange rates listed on its financial pages. For some countries, such as Britain and the United States, you should find future prices listed. This is the price to be paid today to receive one unit of the foreign currency in the future. A 30-day future price for the pound sterling, say, is the price paid today to receive £1 30 days from now. Explain why the future prices are not generally equal to the spot prices — the price paid today to receive the foreign currency today.

7 Assume you expect the pound to depreciate by 6 percent over the next year. Assume that the Canadian interest rate is 8 percent. What interest rate would be needed on pound securities, such as government bonds, for you to be willing to buy those securities with your dollars today, and then sell them in a year in exchange for dollars?

Can you relate your answer to this question to your answer to problem 6?

8 This problem deals with the current account effect of an expansion in the money stock, given prices, perfect capital mobility, and flexible exchange rates.

(a) Given the interest rate i^*, the real money stock M/P, and the money market equilibrium condition

$$\frac{M}{P} = kY - hi$$

solve for the equilibrium level of income Y_0 that is compatible with monetary equilibrium.

(b) Consider next the goods market equilibrium condition:

$$Y = A(Y,i) + NX$$

Let $A = \overline{A} + cY - bi$. Substitute for $i = i^*$ and the equilibrium level of income from (a). What is the equilibrium value of the trade balance NX?

9 Assume capital is imperfectly mobile, so that the higher the interest rate at home, the higher the rate of capital inflow, but that the flows remain finite. Then we can write the balance of payments as

$$BP = NX(e, Y) + CF(i - i^*)$$

where CF denotes the net rate of capital inflow, i^* is the given foreign interest rate, and e is the exchange rate.

(a) Suppose the exchange rate adjusts to maintain payments equilibrium. Then $BP = 0$, and the current account surplus equals the capital account deficit:

$$NX(e, Y) = -CF(i - i^*)$$

Suppose the goods market is *also* in equilibrium, so that

$$Y = A(i, Y) + NX(Y, e)$$

Substituting for the current account in the goods market equilibrium condition yields

$$Y = A(i, Y) - CF(i - i^*)$$

Show this equation graphically in i, Y space and interpret it.

(b) Also draw an LM schedule in the same space and interpret the intersection point.

(c) Show now the effect of a fiscal expansion in the home country on interest rates, income, and the current account.

(d) Show the effect of a monetary expansion on income, interest rates, and the current account.

10 This problem draws on the discussion of stabilization policy and beggar-thy-neighbour policy in Section 6-1. Suppose we have two

countries with full-employment output levels of $\overline{Y}$ and $\overline{Y}*$ at home and abroad, respectively.

(a) Draw a diagram with actual output levels, Y and $Y*$, on the axes. Draw also lines corresponding to potential output levels. Label the resulting four quadrants I, II, III, and IV.

(b) Identify for each of the quadrants the state of demand in each country as boom or recession.

(c) Which policies can be pursued when output exceeds potential in each country? When output exceeds potential in one but falls short of potential in another?

(d) In which quadrants are beggar-thy-neighbour policies particularly dangerous? Where is coordination of policies essential?

CHAPTER 6: FOOTNOTES

[1]In Problem 8 at the end of this chapter, we ask you to show that the current account improves between E and E'', even though the increased level of income increases imports.

[2]See H. Scott Gordon, *The Economists Versus the Bank of Canada* (Toronto: The Ryerson Press, 1961).

[3]You should confirm that a Canadian who expects the dollar to depreciate by 5 percent would, given the 6 percent and 10 percent interest rates, also prefer to buy German bonds.

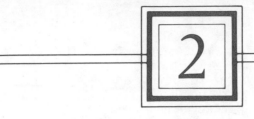

2

Aggregate Demand and Stabilization Policy

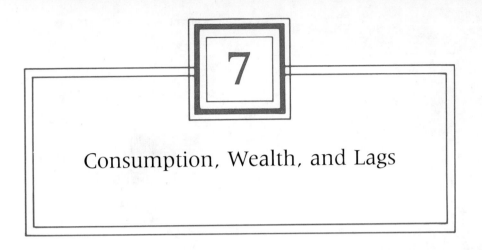

7

Consumption, Wealth, and Lags

The *IS-LM* model developed in Chapter 4 provides a framework which enables us to understand the interaction of some of the main macroeconomic variables. Now we retrace our steps to present a more detailed and more sophisticated treatment of the key equations in the *IS-LM* model. The present chapter deals with the consumption function. The following three chapters deal with investment, money demand, and money supply. As a unit, these chapters flesh out the behavioural equations of the *IS-LM* model and thus move us toward a more realistic and reliable understanding of the working of the economy.

Our starting point in examining consumption behaviour is the consumption function we have been using in the previous chapters. Thus far, we have been assuming that consumption is a linear function of disposable income:

$$C = \overline{C} + cYD \quad \overline{C} > 0 \quad 1 > c > 0 \tag{1}$$

Now what does the empirical evidence show? Do the data for the post-World War II period bear out the hypothesis of a consumption function such as Equation (1)? We plot consumption and disposable income (both in 1971 dollars) for each of the years from 1961 through 1983 in Figure 7-1. The diagram clearly reveals a close positive relationship between consumption and disposable income. To find numerical estimates of the intercept $(\overline{C})$ and the marginal propensity to consume (c) we "fit" a regression line to the observations. The regression line is fitted to the data using the method of least squares, which produces the linear equation that best characterizes the relation between consumption and disposable income contained in the data.[1]

The estimated regression line is shown in Figure 7-1 as the solid line and is reported in Equation (2). The estimate of the intercept is .70 and the estimate of the marginal propensity to consume is .88.

$$C = .70 + .88YD \quad \text{(annual data 1961–83)} \tag{2}$$

223

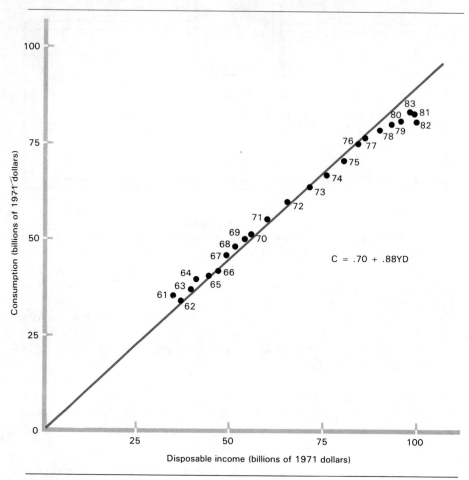

FIGURE 7-1   THE CONSUMPTION-INCOME RELATION, 1961–1983

Two characteristics of a consumption function such as Equation (1) are borne out by the empirical Equation (2). There is a positive intercept and the marginal propensity to consume is positive and less than unity.

If we divide through by YD in Equation (2), we obtain an equation that gives the average propensity to consume (C/YD) as a function of disposable income:

$$\frac{C}{YD} = \frac{.70}{YD} + 0.88$$

(3)

Equation (3) indicates that the average propensity to consume declines as disposable income rises.[2] However, although the intercept, .70, is positive, it

264   '81

is very small relative to disposable income, which is $98 billion ~~1971~~
dollars, in 198~~3~~.[3] If the intercept were actually zero, then we see from
Equations (1) and (3) that consumption would be proportional to disposable income, with $C/YD = c$. The marginal and average propensities to
consume would be equal. The relationship shown by Figure 7-1 and
Equation (2) is essentially one of proportionality, with the average and
marginal propensities to consume out of disposable income equal to each
other, at about 0.9.

Inspection of the regression line in Figure 7-1 suggests that the estimated
equation fits well. There are no points far off the fitted line. As a first
approximation then, Equation (2) provides a reasonable summary of consumption behaviour. The next step is to ask whether Equation (2) can be
improved upon, and if so, to determine how.

FIGURE 7-2   ACTUAL AND PREDICTED CHANGES IN CONSUMPTION

Figure 7-2 shows the annual *percentage changes* in consumption compared with the percentage changes calculated from Equation (2). The
errors are quite large, particularly in the last 6 years of the period. In
addition, the predicted change remains above the actual change from

1972 to 1975 and below the actual change from 1978 to 1981. It appears that the simple consumption function in Equation (2) can be improved upon.

In this chapter, we shall explore three more sophisticated formulations of the consumption function than Equation (1). These are the *life-cycle theory of consumption*, the *permanent-income hypothesis*, and the *relative-income formulation*, described in Sections 7-2 through 7-4. Before we examine those theories, though, we outline in Section 7-1 an empirical puzzle about the consumption function that was historically important in leading to the new theories of the consumption function.

7-1   A CONSUMPTION FUNCTION PUZZLE

The puzzle we describe consists of two types of evidence that made their appearance in the late 1940s and that were apparently in conflict. The first type of evidence came from estimates of the standard consumption function, Equation (1), using annual U.S. data for the 1929–1941 period. (No earlier data were available then.) The estimated equation (in 1972 dollars) is

$$C = 47.6 + 0.73Y_D \quad \text{(annual data, U.S., 1929–1941)} \qquad (4)$$

Using Canadian data for the period 1926–1940, the estimated equation (in 1971 dollars) is

$$C = 3.0 + .69Y_D \quad \text{(annual data, Canada, 1926–1940)} \qquad (4a)$$

These equations clearly imply that the average propensity to consume falls as the level of income rises. They also have low marginal propensities to consume. If we used Equation (4a) to predict today's average propensity to consume in Canada, the estimate would be around .72, which of course is far off the actual ratio of about .85.

The second piece of evidence was the finding by Simon Kuznets, using averages of U.S. data over long periods — 10 and 30 years — that there was near proportionality between consumption and income.[4] This is consistent with the intercept term in Equation (1) being zero. The average propensity to consume that he found for three overlapping 30-year periods is shown in Table 7-1. The Kuznets results suggest, using long-term averages, that there is little variation in the ratio of consumption to income and, in particular, that there is no tendency for the average propensity to decline.

There is clearly a conflict between the implications of the consumption function in Equations (4) and (4a) and Kuznets' findings. The Kuznets results suggest that the average propensity to consume is constant over long periods whereas Equations (4) and (4a) suggest it falls as income rises. It is also clear that the consumption function estimated in Equation (4a) on the basis of the prewar data is inconsistent with the same function estimated on the basis of postwar data, that is Equation (2).

TABLE 7-1   THE KUZNETS FINDING

	1869–1898	1884–1913	1904–1933
Average propensity	.867	.867	.879

Source: Simon Kuznets, *National Income, A Summary of Findings*, (New York: National Bureau of Economic Research, 1946), table 16.

The puzzle of the discrepancy between Kuznets' findings and Equation (4) was well known by the time the three alternative theories we outline below were developed. In resolving the puzzle, all three theories draw on the notion that consumption is related to a broader income measure than just current income. As already noted, the broader measures go under the names of *lifetime income, permanent income,* and *relative income.* These concepts have in common the recognition that consumption spending is maintained relatively constant in the face of fluctuations of current income. Consumption spending is not geared to what we earn today, but to what we earn on average. The important question obviously is what "average" means in this context.

The theories we present all imply that there is a difference between the marginal propensity to consume in the short run and the marginal propensity to consume in the long run. The short-run consumption function — the relationship between consumption spending and *current* disposable income — is indeed quite flat. However, this consumption function shifts upward over time. These shifts in the relationship between consumption and current disposable income bring into the discussion the roles of *wealth* and *permanent income* in affecting consumer spending.[5] These considerations are taken up in the next two sections.

7-2   THE LIFE-CYCLE THEORY OF CONSUMPTION AND SAVING

The consumption function (1) is based on the simple notion that individuals' consumption behaviour in a given period is related to their income in that period. The *life-cycle hypothesis* views individuals, instead, as planning their consumption and saving behaviour over long periods with the intention of allocating their consumption in the best possible way over their entire lifetimes.

The life-cycle hypothesis views savings as resulting mainly from individuals' desires to provide for consumption in old age. As we shall see, the theory points to a number of unexpected factors affecting the savings rate of the economy; for instance, the age structure of the population is, in principle, an important determinant of consumption and savings behaviour.

To anticipate the main results of this section, we can already state here that we will derive a consumption function of the form

$$C = aWR + cYL \qquad (5)$$

where WR is real wealth, a is the marginal propensity to consume out of wealth, YL is labour income, and c is the marginal propensity to consume out of labour income. *Labour income* is the income that is earned by labour, as opposed to the income earned by other factors of production, such as the rent earned by land or the profits earned by capital.

In developing the life cycle hypothesis of saving and consumption, we show what determines the marginal propensities a and c in Equation (5), why wealth should affect consumption, and how the life-cycle hypothesis helps explain the Kuznets puzzle described above.

Consider a person who expects to live for NL years, work and earn income for WL years, and be in retirement for (NL – WL) years. The individual's year 1 is the first year of work. We shall, in what follows, ignore any uncertainty about either life expectancy or the length of working life. We shall assume, too, that no interest is earned on savings, so that current saving translates dollar for dollar into future consumption possibilities. With these assumptions, we can approach the saving or consumption decision with two questions. First, what are the individual's lifetime consumption possibilities? Second, how will the individual choose to distribute consumption over his or her lifetime?

Consider now the consumption possibilities. For the moment we ignore property income (income from assets) and focus attention on labour income YL. Income, YL, and consumption, C, are measured in real terms. Given WL years of working, *lifetime income* (from labour) is (YL × WL), income per working year times the number of working years. Consumption over the individual's lifetime cannot exceed this lifetime income unless he or she is born with wealth, which we initially assume is not the case. Accordingly, we have determined the first part of the consumer's problem in finding the limit of lifetime consumption.

We assume the individual will want to distribute consumption over his or her lifetime so that there is a flat or even flow of consumption. Rather than consume a lot in one period and very little in another, the preferred profile is to consume exactly equal amounts in each period.[6] Clearly, this assumption implies that consumption is not geared to *current* income (which is zero during retirement), but rather to *lifetime income*.

Lifetime consumption equals lifetime income. This means that the planned level of consumption C, which is the same in every period, times the number of years in life NL equals lifetime income:

$$C \times NL = YL \times WL \qquad (6)$$

where WL is working life. Lifetime income is equal to (YL × WL). Dividing through by NL, we have planned consumption per year, C, which is proportional to labour income:

$$C = \frac{WL}{NL} \times YL \qquad (7)$$

The factor of proportionality in Equation (7) is WL/NL, the fraction of lifetime spent working. Accordingly, Equation (7) states that in each year of working life a fraction of labour income is consumed, where that fraction is equal to the proportion of working life in total life.

Numerical Example

Suppose a person starts working at age 20, plans to work till 65, and will die at 80. The working life WL is thus 45 years ($= 65 - 20$) and the number of years of life, NL, is 60 years ($= 80 - 20$). Annual labour income YL is $20,000.

Then

$$\text{Lifetime income} = YL \times WL$$
$$= \$20,000 \times 45$$
$$= \$900,000$$

This person will receive a total of $900,000 over his or her working lifetime.

The lifetime income, $900,000, has to be spread over the 60 years of life. The consumer wants to spread it evenly, and so

$$C = \frac{\$900,000}{60} = \$15,000 = \frac{WL}{NL} \times YL$$

$$= \frac{45}{60} \times 20,000$$

$$= 0.75 \times 20,000$$

In this example, 0.75 of labour income is consumed each year the person works. Why is the propensity to consume out of labour income in this example equal to 0.75? Because that is the fraction of lifetime that the person works.

Saving and Dissaving

The counterpart of Equation (7) is the saving function. Remembering that saving is equal to income less consumption, we have

$$S \equiv YL - C = YL \left(\frac{NL - WL}{NL} \right) \qquad (8)$$

Equation (8) states that saving during the period in which the individual works is equal to a fraction of labour income, with that fraction being equal to the proportion of life spent in retirement.

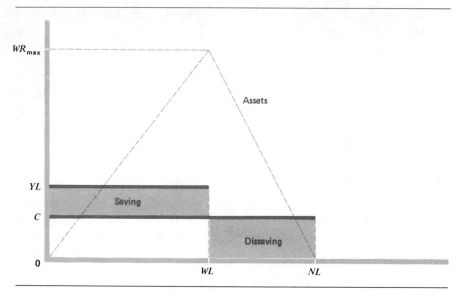

FIGURE 7-3   LIFETIME INCOME, CONSUMPTION, SAVINGS, AND WEALTH IN THE LIFE-CYCLE MODEL. During the working life, lasting *WL* years, the individual saves, building up assets. At the end of the working life, the individual begins to live off her assets, dissaving for the next (*NL* − *WL*) years, till the end of life. Consumption is constant at level *C* throughout the lifetime. All assets have been used up at the end of life.

Figure 7-3 shows the lifetime pattern of consumption, saving, and *dissaving*.[7] Over the whole lifetime, there is an even flow of consumption at the rate of *C*, amounting in total to *C* × *NL*. That consumption spending is financed during working life out of current income. During retirement the consumption is financed by drawing down the savings that have been accumulated during working life. Therefore the shaded areas (*YL* − *C*) × *WL* and *C* × (*NL* − *WL*) are equal, or equivalently, saving during working years finances dissaving during retirement.

The important idea of lifetime consumption theory is apparent from Figure 7-3. It is that consumption plans are made so as to achieve a smooth or even level of consumption by saving during periods of high income and dissaving during periods of low income. This is, therefore, an important departure from consumption based on current income. It is an important difference because, in addition to current income, the whole future profile of income enters into the calculation of lifetime consumption. Before developing that aspect further, however, we return to Figure 7-3 to consider the role of assets.

During the working years, the individual saves to finance consumption during retirement. The savings build up assets, and we accordingly show in Figure 7-3 how the individual's wealth or assets increase over working life and reach a maximum at retirement age. From that time on, assets decline because the individual sells assets to pay for current consumption.

What is the maximum level that assets reach? Remember that assets are built up to finance consumption during retirement. Total consumption during retirement is equal to $C \times (NL - WL)$. All that consumption is financed out of the assets accumulated by the date of retirement, which is when assets are at their peak.

Denote the maximum level of assets by $WR_{max.}$. Then,

$$WR_{max.} = C \times (NL - WL)$$

For instance, in the numerical example above, where C was $15,000 and $(NL - WL)$ was equal to 15, the individual would have $15,000 \times 15 = $225,000 saved at the date of retirement. Equivalently, the person has worked for 45 years, saving $5,000 each year. That too means he or she has accumulated $225,000 at age 65.

This simple case gives the spirit of the life-cycle hypothesis of consumption and saving. People do not want to consume over their lifetimes at precisely the same times and amounts they earn income. Thus they save and dissave so as to consume their lifetime incomes in the pattern they want. Typically, the theory argues, they will save while working, and then use the savings to finance spending in their retirement years.

Introducing Wealth

The next step is to extend this model and allow for initial assets, assuming the individual is born to wealth.[8] We can draw on the previous insight that the consumer will spread any existing resources to achieve an even lifetime consumption profile. The individual who has assets in addition to labour income will plan to use these assets to add to lifetime consumption. A person who is at some point T in life, with a stock of wealth WR and labour income accruing for another $(WL - T)$ years at the rate of YL, and with a life expectancy of $(NL - T)$ years to go, will behave as follows. The person's lifetime consumption possibilities are

$$C(NL - T) = WR + (WL - T)YL \tag{9}$$

where we have included wealth WR along with lifetime labour income as a source of finance for lifetime consumption. From Equation (9), consumption in each period is equal to

$$C = aWR + cYL \qquad a \equiv \frac{1}{NL - T} \qquad c \equiv \frac{WL - T}{NL - T} \qquad WL > T \tag{10}$$

where the coefficients a and c are, respectively, the marginal propensities to consume out of wealth and out of labour income.

In the numerical example above we considered a person starting to work at age 20, who will retire at 65 and die at 80. Thus $WL = 65 - 20 = 45$; and $NL = 80 - 20 = 60$. We also assumed $YL = \$20,000$.

Now suppose the person is 40 years old. Accordingly $T = 20$, meaning that the person is in the twentieth year of working life. We can calculate the propensity to consume out of wealth a and the propensity to consume out of income c from Equation (10). For this person, at age 40 (i.e., for $T = 20$):

$$a = \frac{1}{NL - T} = \frac{1}{60 - 20} = .025$$

$$c = \frac{WL - T}{NL - T} = \frac{45 - 20}{60 - 20} = .625$$

Suppose now that the individual's wealth is \$200,000. Then from the consumption function, Equation (10), we find:

$$\begin{aligned} C &= (.025 \times 200,000) + (.625 \times 20,000) \\ &= 5000 + 12,500 \\ &= 17,500 \end{aligned}$$

Note that the consumption level here is higher than in the previous example. That is because this individual has more wealth at age 40 than he or she would have if all his or her wealth came from saving out of labour income. (That amount, at age 40, would from the previous example be \$100,000 — since the individual in the previous example saved \$5,000 per year, and at $T = 20$ this person has been working 20 years.) We can conclude that we are dealing here with someone who inherited wealth and started out working life with some wealth.

Thus, in our model of individual lifetime consumption, we have derived a consumption function like Equation (5), where both wealth and labour income affect the individual's consumption decisions. It is important to recognize from Equation (10) that the marginal propensities are related to the individual's position in the life cycle. The closer a person is to the end of lifetime, the higher the marginal propensity to consume out of wealth. Thus, a person with 2 more years of life will consume half his or her remaining wealth in each of the remaining 2 years. The marginal propensity to consume out of labour income is related both to the remaining number of years during which income will be earned, $WL - T$, and to the number of years over which these earnings are spread, $NL - T$. It is quite clear from Equation (10) that an increase in either wealth or labour income will raise consumption expenditures. It is apparent, too, that lengthening working life relative to retirement will raise consumption because it increases lifetime income and reduces the length of the period of dissaving. The most basic point, however, is that Equation (10) shows both (lifetime) income and wealth as determinants of consumption spending.

To summarize where we have come so far, we note that in this form of the life-cycle model:

1 Consumption is constant over the consumer's lifetime.
2 Consumption spending is financed by lifetime income plus initial wealth.
3 During each year a fraction $1/(NL - T)$ of wealth will be consumed.
4 Current consumption spending depends on current wealth and lifetime income.

Extensions

The model as outlined makes very strong simplifying assumptions. It can be extended to remove most of the strong assumptions without affecting the underlying result of Equation (10), that consumption is related to both labour income and wealth.

First, it is necessary to take account of the possibility that saving earns interest, so that a dollar not consumed today will provide more than a dollar's consumption tomorrow. Second, the analysis has to be extended to allow for the fact that individuals are uncertain of the length of their lifetimes, and also that they sometimes want to leave bequests to their heirs. In this latter case, they would not plan to consume all their resources over their own lifetimes. Similarly, the model has to be extended to take account of the composition of the family over time, so that some consumption is provided for children before they begin to work. But, to repeat, these extensions do not change the basic results contained in Equation (10).

A final extension is very important. In practice, one never knows exactly what one's lifetime labour income will be, and lifetime consumption plans have to be made on the basis of predictions of future labour income. This, of course, raises the issue of how income is to be predicted. We do not pursue this important issue here, but leave it to the next section on permanent income, which is an estimate of lifetime income. However, *expected* lifetime labour income would be related to *current* disposable labour income, leading to a form of the consumption function like Equation (5), perhaps with other variables also included.

Indeed, it is useful to think of the life-cycle and permanent-income theories as being fundamentally the same, with the life-cycle theory developing most carefully the implications of the model for the role of wealth and other variables in the consumption function,[9] and the permanent-income theory concentrating on the best way to predict lifetime income.

Aggregate Consumption and Saving

The theory as so far outlined is strictly a theory about consumption and saving by individuals over the course of their lifetimes. How does it relate to aggregate consumption, which is, after all, the focus of macroeconomic interest in consumption? Imagine an economy in which population and the GNP were constant through time. Each individual in that economy would go through the life cycle of saving and dissaving outlined in Figure 7-3. The economy as a whole, though, would not be saving. At any one time, the saving of working people would be exactly matched by the dissaving of retired people. However, if the population were growing, there would be more young people than old, thus more saving in total than dissaving, and there would be net saving in the economy. Thus, aggregate consumption depends in part on the age composition of the population. It also depends on such characteristics of the economy as the average age of retirement and the presence or absence of government pensions. These surprising implications of the theory indicate the richness of the approach.

Implications

We want to return to Equation (5) to emphasize again the role of wealth. Note from Equation (5) that if there were an increase in wealth, the ratio of consumption to disposable income would rise. This has a bearing on the puzzle described in Section 7-1, where the average propensity to consume seems, on the basis of Equation (4), to decline with income, and on the basis of Kuznets' findings, to remain constant on average over long periods.

If we divide through in Equation (5) by YD, we obtain

$$\frac{C}{YD} = a\frac{WR}{YD} + c\frac{YL}{YD} \tag{11}$$

Now, if the ratio of wealth to disposable income and the ratio of disposable labour income to total disposable income are constant, then Equation (11) shows that the ratio of consumption to disposable income will be constant. However, if the ratio of wealth to disposable income is changing, the average propensity to consume will also be changing.

This suggests, as an explanation of the Kuznets puzzle, the possibility that the ratio of wealth to disposable income is roughly constant over long periods, and that it varied considerably during the 1930s, to which period the consumption function, Equation (4), applies. Similarly, Equation (11) suggests that the variability of consumption behavior in the short run, as seen in Figure 7-2, is explained in part by fluctuations in the ratio of wealth to disposable income. Indeed, the ratio of wealth to disposable income is reasonably constant in the long run, but fluctuates considerably in the short run in a way that helps explain the fluctuations in consumption shown in Figure 7-2.[10]

One further interesting implication of the life-cycle hypothesis is that it provides a route for the stock market to affect consumption behaviour.

The value of stocks held by the public is part of wealth and is included in *WR* in Equation (5). When the value of stocks is high — when the stock market is booming — *WR* is high and tends to increase consumption, and the reverse occurs when the stock market is depressed.

We continue now to the permanent-income theory of consumption, bearing in mind that we have not yet discussed the determinants of expected lifetime labour income in Equation (10) in any detail, and recalling that the two theories should be thought of as complementary rather than competing.

7-3   PERMANENT-INCOME THEORY OF CONSUMPTION

In the long run, the consumption-income ratio is very stable, but in the short run, it fluctuates. The behaviour of the propensity to consume implied by the standard consumption function, Equation (1), appears to differ when the equation is fitted over different periods. The life-cycle approach explains these observations by pointing out that people want to maintain a smooth profile of consumption even if their lifetime income profile is uneven, and thus emphasizes the role of wealth in the consumption function. Another explanation, which differs in details but entirely shares the spirit of the life-cycle approach, is the permanent-income theory of consumption.

The theory, which is the work of Milton Friedman,[11] argues that people gear their consumption behaviour to their permanent or long-term consumption opportunities, not to their current level of income. A suggestive example provided by Friedman involves someone who is paid or receives his or her income only once a week, on Fridays. We do not expect that individual to concentrate consumption on the one day on which income is received, with zero consumption on every other day. Again we are persuaded by the argument that individuals prefer a smooth consumption flow rather than plenty today and scarcity tomorrow or yesterday. On that argument, consumption on any one day of the week would be unrelated to income on that particular day but would rather be geared to average daily income — that is, income per week divided by the number of days per week. It is clear that in this extreme example, income for a period longer than a day is relevant to the consumption decision. Similarly, Friedman argues, there is nothing special about a period of the length of one quarter or one year that requires the individual to plan consumption within the period solely on the basis of income within the period; rather, consumption is planned in relation to income over a longer period.

The idea of consumption spending that is geared to long-term or average or permanent income is appealing and essentially is the same as the life-cycle theory. It leaves two further questions. The first concerns the precise relationship between current consumption and permanent income.

The second question is how to make the concept of permanent income operational, that is, how to measure it.

In its simplest form the permanent-income hypothesis of consumption behaviour argues that consumption is proportional to permanent income:

$$C = cYP \tag{12}$$

where YP is permanent (disposable) income. From Equation (12), consumption varies in the same proportion as permanent income. A 5 percent increase in permanent income raises consumption by 5 percent. Since permanent income should be related to long-run average income, this feature of the consumption function is clearly in line with the observed long-run constancy of the consumption-income ratio.

Estimating Permanent Income

The next problem is how to think of and measure permanent income. We define permanent income as follows:[12] *Permanent income* is the steady rate of consumption a person could maintain for the rest of his or her life, given the present level of wealth and income earned now and in the future.

To think about the measurement of permanent income, imagine someone trying to figure out what his or her permanent income is. The person has a current level of income, and has formed some idea of the level of consumption he or she can maintain for the rest of his or her life. Now income goes up. The decision must be made whether that income increase represents a permanent increase, or merely a *transitory* change, one that will not persist. In any particular case, the individual may know whether the increase is permanent or transitory. A government official who is promoted one grade will know that the increase in income is likely to be maintained. Or the worker who has exceptionally high overtime in a given year will likely regard that year's increased income as transitory. But in general, a person is not so certain about what part of any change in income is likely to be maintained, and is therefore permanent, and what part is not likely to be maintained, and is therefore transitory. Transitory income is assumed not to have any substantial effect on consumption.

The question of how to infer what part of an increase in income is permanent is resolved in a pragmatic way by assuming that permanent income is related to the behaviour of current and past incomes. To give a simple example, we might estimate permanent income as being equal to last year's income plus some fraction of the change in income from last year to this year:

$$\begin{aligned} YP &= Y_{-1} + \theta(Y - Y_{-1}) \qquad 0 < \theta < 1 \\ &= \theta Y + (1 - \theta)Y_{-1} \end{aligned} \tag{13}$$

where θ is a fraction and Y_{-1} is last year's income. The second line in Equation (13) writes permanent income as a *weighted average* of current and past income. The second formulation is, of course, equivalent to that in the first line. To understand Equation (13), assume we had a value of $\theta = 0.6$ and that this year's income was $Y = \$12,000$ and last year's income was $Y_{-1} = \$11,000$. The value of permanent income would be $YP = \$11,600$ ($= 0.6 \times \$12,000 + 0.4 \times \$11,000$). Thus, permanent income is an average of the two income levels. Whether it is closer to this year's or last year's income depends on the weight θ given to current income. Clearly, in the extreme with $\theta = 1$, permanent income is equal to current income.

Some special features of Equation (13) deserve comment. First, if $Y = Y_{-1}$, that is, if this year's income is equal to last year's, then permanent income is equal to the income earned this year and last year. This guarantees that an individual who had always earned the same income would expect to earn that income in the future. Second, note that if income rises this year compared with last year, then permanent income rises by *less* than current income. The reason is that the individual does not know whether the rise in income this year is permanent. Not knowing whether the increase in income will be maintained or not, the individual does not immediately increase the expected or permanent income measure by the full amount of the actual or current increase in income.

Rational Expectations and Permanent Income

An estimate of permanent income that uses only current and last year's income is likely to be an oversimplification. Friedman forms the estimate by looking at incomes in many earlier periods, as well as current income, but with weights that are larger for the more recent, as compared with the more distant, incomes.[13]

There is no simple theory that would tell us how expectations are or should be formed without looking at how income changes in practice. If, in practice, changes in income are typically permanent or long-run changes, then a consumer who sees a given change in his income will believe that it is mostly permanent. Such a consumer would have a high θ as in Equation (13). If the consumer's income is usually very variable, then he will not pay much attention to current changes in income in forming his estimate of permanent income. Such a consumer will have a low value of θ.[14]

This argument—that expectations are likely to be formed on the basis of the actual behaviour of variables — is part of the theory of rational expectations, on which we shall focus further in Chapters 15 and 18. The theory suggests that the estimate of permanent income in Equation (13) should be based on how income in the economy actually changes over time.

At the same time, any sensible theory of expectations, including rational expectations, would emphasize that a formula like (13), based on the behaviour of income in the past, cannot include all the factors that influence a person's beliefs about future income. The discovery of a vast amount of oil in a country, for instance, would raise the permanent incomes of the inhabitants of the country as soon as it was announced, even though a (mechanical) formula like Equation (13) based on past levels of income would not reflect such a change.

Permanent Income and the Dynamics of Consumption

Using Equations (12) and (13), we can now rewrite the consumption function:

$$C = cYP = c\theta Y + c(1 - \theta)Y_{-1} \tag{14}$$

The marginal propensity to consume out of *current* income is then just $c\theta$, which is clearly less than the long-run average propensity to consume, c. Hence, the permanent-income hypothesis implies that there is a difference between the short-run marginal propensity to consume and the long-run marginal (equal to the average) propensity to consume.

We shall see shortly that this implication is supported by the data. But first we explore it in more detail. The reason for the lower short-run marginal propensity to consume is that when current income rises, the individual is not sure that the increase in income will be maintained over the longer period on which he or she bases consumption plans. Accordingly, the person does not fully adjust consumption spending to the higher level that would be appropriate if the increase in income were permanent. However, if the increase turns out to be permanent, that is, if next period's income is the same as this period's, then the person will (next year) fully adjust consumption spending to the higher level of income. Note, though, that the adjustment here is completed in 2 years only because we have assumed, in Equation (13), that permanent income is an average of 2 years' income. Depending on how expectations of permanent income are formed, the adjustment could be much slower.

The argument is illustrated in Figure 7-4. Here we show the long-run consumption function as a straight line through the origin with slope c, which is the constant average and marginal propensity to consume out of permanent income. The lower flat consumption function is a short-run consumption function drawn for a given history of income which is reflected in the intercept $c(1 - \theta)Y_0$ and consumption therefore equal to cY_0, as is shown at the intersection of long-run and short-run consumption functions at point E. Assume next that income increases to the level Y'. In the short run, which means during the current period, we revise our estimate of permanent income upward by θ times the increase in income and consume a fraction c of that increase in permanent income. Accordingly, consumption moves up along the short-run consumption function to point E'.

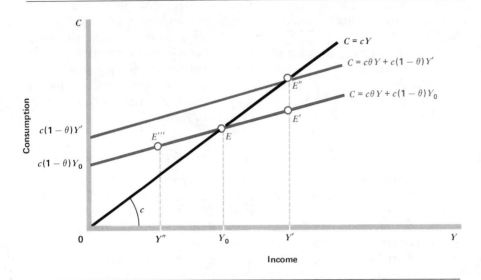

FIGURE 7-4   THE EFFECTS ON CONSUMPTION OF A SUSTAINED INCREASE IN INCOME. The short-run consumption functions, shown in red, have marginal propensity to consume of $c\theta$. The position of the short-run consumption function depends on the level of income in the previous period. The long-run consumption function is shown by the black line, and has average and marginal propensity to consume equal to c. When the level of income rises from Y_0 to Y', consumption rises only to E' in the short run, because consumers are not sure the change in income is permanent. But with income remaining at Y', the short-run consumption function shifts up and consumption rises to point E'', as consumers realize their permanent income has changed.

Note immediately that in the short run the ratio of consumption to income declines as we move from point E to E'. Going one period ahead and assuming that the increase in income persists so that income remains at Y', we get a shift in the consumption function. The consumption function shifts upward because, as of the given higher level of income, the estimate of permanent income is now revised upward to Y'. Accordingly, consumers want to spend a fraction of c of their new estimate of permanent income Y'. The new consumption point is E'', where the ratio of consumption to income is back to the long-run level. The example makes clear that in the short run, an increase in income causes a decline in the average propensity to consume because people do not anticipate that the increase in income will persist or be permanent. Once they do observe that the increase in income does persist, however, they fully adjust consumption to match their higher permanent income.

Like the life-cycle hypothesis, the permanent-income hypothesis has some unexpected and interesting implications. For instance, we noted above that an individual whose income is very unstable would have a low value of θ, whereas one whose income is more stable would have a higher value of θ. Looking at Equation (14), this means that the short-run marginal propensity to consume of someone whose income is very variable will be relatively low — because the short-run marginal propensity to consume is $c\theta$. Friedman shows that this implication is borne out by the facts. Farmers, for instance, have very variable incomes and a low marginal propensity to consume out of current income.

The Life-Cycle and Permanent-Income Hypotheses

To conclude this section, it is worth considering again the relationship between the life-cycle and permanent-income hypotheses briefly. The two hypotheses are not mutually exclusive. The life-cycle hypothesis pays more attention to the motives for saving than the permanent-income hypothesis does, and provides convincing reasons to include wealth as well as income in the consumption function. The permanent-income hypothesis, on the other hand, pays more careful attention to the way in which individuals form their expectations about their future incomes than the original life-cycle hypothesis does. Recall that current labour income entered the life-cycle consumption function to reflect expectations of future income. The more detailed analysis of the determinants of expected future income that is provided by the permanent-income hypothesis can be, and has been, included in the life-cycle consumption function.

Indeed, modern theories of the consumption function combine the expectations formation emphasized by the permanent-income approach with the emphasis on wealth and demographic variables suggested by the life-cycle approach. A simplified version of a modern consumption function would be

$$C = aWR + b\theta YD + b(1 - \theta)YD_{-1} \tag{15}$$

where YD in Equation (15) would be disposable labour income. Equation (15) combines the main features that are emphasized by modern consumption theory.[15] It also shows the role of wealth, which is an important influence on consumption spending.

Recent research on consumption has combined the two theories and has been aimed particularly at checking the implications of the permanent-income, and life-cycle, theory that transitory changes in income have little effect on consumption.[16] Some of this research is described in Box 7-1.

We end this section by repeating a warning that is important enough for us to risk overstating. An equation like (15) performs quite well on average in predicting consumption. But it is always important to remember the underlying theory when using it. Equation (15) embodies the estimate of permanent income implied by Equation (13). If we have knowledge about some particular change in income—for example, that it is transitory —then we should use that knowledge in predicting consumption. For instance, a temporary 1-year tax increase that reduced current disposable income would reduce current consumption by much less than a tax increase of the same size that was known to be permanent, even though Equation (15) does not show that.

BOX 7-1   MODERN CONSUMPTION FUNCTION PUZZLES

No theory explains all the facts, or is the last word to be written on a topic. Research continually turns up new questions and puzzles, which lead to further research, and to revised theories. Research of the late 1970s and early 1980s has revealed some aspects of consumption behaviour that do not fit well with the life-cycle and permanent-income theories of consumption. Over the next few years either research will show that the new facts are not quite the problem they seem now, or the existing theories will be amended.

We briefly discuss these modern consumption puzzles.

1   The Life-Cycle Hypothesis, Consumption of the Elderly, and Bequests

The life-cycle hypothesis assumes that people want to smooth consumption over their lifetimes. This leads to the conclusion that people save mainly for retirement, and draw down their savings during retirement.

Two recent papers question the assumed motive for saving and the implication that people draw down their savings when old. Laurence Kotlikoff and Lawrence Summers[*] have made calculations suggesting that most saving is done to provide bequests rather than to provide for consumption when old. Of course, the savings are there for the old to use in retirement, but, they argue, the amount of wealth in the economy is far too large for people to have been saving only for their retirement. Rather, they conclude, people are saving mainly to pass wealth on to their descendants.

A detailed examination of the consumption propensities of the elderly by Sheldon Danziger, Jacques van der Gaag, Eugene Smolensky, and Michael Taussig[†] contains the remarkable conclusion that the elderly save a higher proportion of their incomes than the young. This fact is inconsistent with the simple form of the life-cycle hypothesis set out in the chapter.

How might this evidence be reconciled with existing theories? The facts are not yet definitive. For instance, the Kotlikoff-Summers argument that most of savings is undertaken to provide bequests is based on complicated calculations and assumptions that will likely be disputed by adherents of the life-cycle theory. Explanation of the consumption behaviour of the elderly will probably have to take into account their increasing fears of being left alone without financial help from family, and with possibly large medical expenses, as they get older.

2   Excess Sensitivity of Consumption to Current Income

Recent tests of the permanent-income hypothesis conclude that consumption is excessively sensitive to changes in current income.[‡] Consumption does react more to permanent than to transitory changes in current income. But these tests show that the reaction to transitory changes is larger than the theory predicts.

Suppose the propensity to consume out of permanent income is 0.9. The permanent income theory predicts that the propensity to consume out of a change in income that is expected to last only 1 year should be very small, perhaps something like 0.05. In fact, though, the propensity to consume out of transitory income is much higher, more like 0.25.

This is the puzzle that is described as the excess sensitivity of consumption to changes in income. The candidate to explain the puzzle is *liquidity constraints*. Recall that someone with temporarily low income is supposed to use up savings to maintain the level of consumption, or else to borrow. But many people do not have the savings to draw down, nor can they borrow to finance consumption. Thus, it is argued, they cannot find the liquidity (that is, available funds) to pay for the consumption they would like. When income goes up, such people increase their consumption more than the permanent-income theory would predict, because they are no longer so constrained.

The excess sensitivity finding does not mean the permanent-income theory is irrelevant to understanding consumption behaviour. It only means that there is more that determines consumption than the factors stressed by the simple permanent-income and life-cycle models.

---

*"The Role of Intergenerational Transfers in Aggregate Capital Accumulation," *Journal of Political Economy*, August 1981.

†In their research paper from the University of Wisconsin, "The Life Cycle Hypothesis and the Consumption Behavior of the Elderly," 1982.

‡For example, Marjorie Flavin, "The Adjustment of Consumption to Changing Expectations about Future Income," *Journal of Political Economy*, October 1981.

7-4 FURTHER ASPECTS OF CONSUMPTION BEHAVIOUR

In this section we briefly review three topics in consumption behaviour, starting with the relative-income hypothesis.

The Relative-Income Hypothesis

Modern theories of the consumption function have in common the objective of explaining short-run fluctuations in the ratio of consumption to disposable income combined with virtual constancy of the ratio of consumption to disposable income in the long run. Life-cycle and permanent-income theories explain this behaviour as an attempt to maintain a smooth flow of consumption that is geared to long-run consumption opportunities, as measured by lifetime income and wealth or by permanent income.

An earlier and influential theory along much the same lines is the relative-income hypothesis that was advanced by James Duesenberry.[17] The theory argues that current consumption depends not only on current income but also on the history of income. Individuals build up consumption standards that are geared to their peak income levels. If income declines relative to past income, then individuals will not immediately sacrifice the consumption standard they have adopted. There is a ratchet effect, and they will only adjust to a small extent to the decline in current income. However, there is an asymmetry, because an increase in income relative to past peaks immediately raises the consumption level.

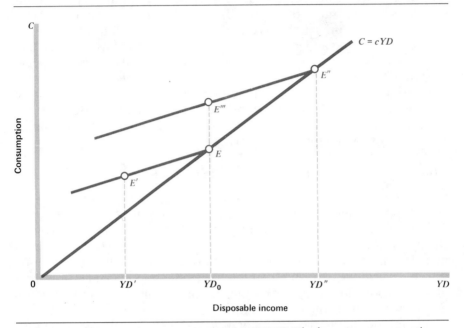

FIGURE 7-5   THE RELATIVE-INCOME HYPOTHESIS. The long-run consumption function is shown by the dark line. But previous peak levels of income or consumption affect current consumption in the short run. Thus if individuals initially are at income level YD_0, a decline in income to YD' will take them to point E'—they are reluctant to cut consumption because they have got used to the higher consumption level at E. An *increase* of income from YD_0 to YD'' would lead to point E'' on the long-run consumption function.

Figure 7-5 shows consumption behaviour according to the relative-income hypothesis. The dark line is the consumption function if current income is the peak level of income. Thus, if current income is YD_0 and exceeds previous levels of income, then consumption would be at point E on the consumption function $C = cYD$. If income declined from the level YD_0 to YD', then consumption would adjust along the light schedule to E'. The peak level of income YD_0 would continue to influence consumption because it determines the consumption standard that individuals seek to maintain. In the short run, therefore, saving adjusts so as to allow consumption to be maintained close to the habitual level. Assume next that income rose to the level YD''. This would be a new peak level of income, and consumption accordingly would rise to E''. If income were then to decline to YD_0, the new peak level YD'' would continue to influence consumption, so that we would find ourselves at point E'''.

The theory is very suggestive again of the attempt to smooth consumption in the face of income fluctuations. It has an intuitive appeal in its emphasis on consumption standards geared to peak income. It lacks, perhaps, the economic richness that the later theories of the life cycle and permanent income added. Its main shortcoming is the asymmetry that suggests that a current increase in income, if it exceeds a previous peak, immediately induces a new consumption standard. Here the alternative theories are more persuasive in that they suggest a partial adjustment for both an increase and a decrease in income. But the theory does suggest that as the level of income rises over time, consumption will rise roughly in proportion, along the line $C = cYD$.

Consumption, Saving, and Interest Rates

Consumers in Canada and the United States save a lower proportion of their disposable income than consumers in many other countries, as Table 7-2 shows. One question, which we do not attempt to answer, is why saving rates in North America are so low. Another question is why it matters. The answer is that the amount of investment in the economy, which determines how much capital — factories and machines — is available for production, depends on the saving rate. If an economy is at full employment, then an increase in the saving rate will lead to more investment and to more future production, as we see in Chapter 19 when we discuss supply-side economics. It is thus not a coincidence that the countries with low savings rates in Table 7-2 are also the slower growing among the seven major economies listed there.

TABLE 7-2   NET HOUSEHOLD SAVING AS A PERCENTAGE OF
DISPOSABLE HOUSEHOLD INCOME
(Average, 1960–1980)

United States	Japan	Germany	France	U.K.	Italy	Canada
7.6	19.0	15.3	12.8	6.7	19.5	7.7

Source: OECD Economic Outlook, Historical Statistics 1960–1980 (Paris: Organization for Economic Co-Operation and Development, 1982), p. 65.

The next question is what could be done about a low saving rate? One suggestion is to make saving more worthwhile for the saver. Anyone who saves receives a return in the form of interest, or dividends and capital gains (an increase in the price) on stocks. It seems, then, that the neutral way to raise saving is to raise the return available to savers. Think of someone saving and receiving an interest rate of 5 percent each year for each dollar saved. Surely an increase in the interest rate to, say, 10 percent would make that person save more.

Should we really expect an increase in the interest rate to increase savings? It is true that when the interest rate rises, saving is made more attractive. But it is also made less necessary. Consider someone who has decided to save an amount that will ensure $10,000 per year is available for retirement. Suppose the interest rate is now 5 percent, and the person is saving $1,000 per year. Now let the interest rate rise to 10 percent. With such a high interest rate, the individual needs to save less now to provide the given $10,000 per year during retirement. It may be possible to provide the same retirement income by saving only about $650 a year. Thus an increase in the interest rate might reduce saving.

What do the facts show? Does saving rise when the interest rate increases, because every dollar of saving generates a higher return? Or does saving fall because there is less need to save to provide a given level of future income? The answer from the data is ambiguous. Many researchers have examined this question, but few have found strong positive effects of interest rate increases on saving. Typically, research suggests the effects are small and certainly hard to find.[18]

Consumption, Consumption Purchases, and Durables

The theories we have examined so far are theories about the rate at which consumers consume rather than spend on goods and services. For most consumption, such as that of eating meals, or watching movies, or using gasoline, consumption follows purchase quite closely. But for some goods, such as automobiles, or TV sets — called consumer durables because they last for a long time — the act of consumption may be separated by months or years from the purchase of the good.

The item "Consumption" in the GNP accounts and in Figure 7-1 is actually the *purchases* of consumption goods, including, for example, cars, food, refrigerators, and toasters. Obviously, though, someone who owns and uses a car is consuming automobile services in a given year even if he or she does not buy a new car. So there is a difference between consumption and purchases of consumption goods.

The distinction matters because the component of consumption in the national accounts that fluctuates most is purchases of consumer durables. It is not surprising that consumer durable purchases fluctuate more than purchases of other consumption goods, because someone whose income is temporarily low can easily make do with the same car for a short while. Thus actual consumption would fluctuate less than purchases.

This argument suggests that durable purchases may be affected more than other components of consumers' purchases by transitory changes in income. There is indeed evidence to that effect.[19] In addition, durable purchases more than other categories of consumption spending show signs of being affected by the interest rate. In particular, high interest rates reduce automobile purchases.

7-6   CONSUMPTION AND THE *IS-LM* FRAMEWORK

In this section we discuss briefly how the more sophisticated theories of consumption we have developed in this chapter affect the *IS-LM* analysis of Chapter 4. We focus on two implications. The first is that consumption is a function of wealth, and not only income as we assumed previously. The second is that the response of consumption to various changes, for instance, in autonomous spending, may take time as individuals gradually adjust their estimates of permanent income.

Wealth in the Consumption Function

The life-cycle hypothesis, and estimated consumption functions of a form like Equation (15), show that the rate of consumption depends on the level of wealth, as well as disposable income. This means that the position of the *IS* curve, representing equilibrium in the goods market, depends on the level of wealth.

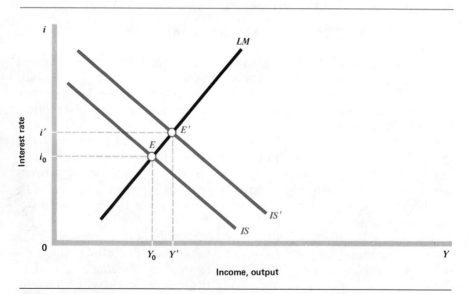

FIGURE 7-6   THE EFFECTS OF A SHIFT IN WEALTH. An increase in wealth shifts the consumption function, raising consumption demand at any level of income. Accordingly, the *IS* curve shifts to *IS'*, the level of output rises from Y_0 to Y', and the interest rate rises from i_0 to i'.

Figure 7-6 shows how an increase in the level of wealth affects equilibrium output and the interest rate. The economy is initially in equilibrium at point E. There is then an increase in wealth: perhaps the stock market has gone up, because everyone is optimistic that the economy is recovering from a recession. The higher wealth raises consumption spending, and the IS curve thus shifts up to IS'. The new equilibrium is at E'.

At E', the interest rate and level of output are higher than at E. Thus an increase in wealth raises equilibrium output. Since the increase in wealth was assumed to result from expectations that the economy was recovering from a recession, we see that the expectation is partly self-fulfilling. A self-fulfilling prophecy is one which, purely as a result of being made, produces the prophesied result.

The Dynamics of Adjustment

In Section 7-3 and Figure 7-4, we examined the dynamic response of consumption spending to a shift in disposable income. Now we want to embody that dynamic adjustment in a full IS-LM model. The slow adjustment of consumption to a given change in disposable income will mean that income itself adjusts slowly to any given shift in autonomous spending that is not at first recognized as permanent, as we now show.

We assume here that people do not know whether the shift in autonomous demand is permanent or transitory. Rather, the only way they can figure that out is by seeing whether the change in demand persists or goes away. Figure 7-7 illustrates the effects of a permanent shift in autonomous demand, the nature of which (permanent or transitory) is not known to consumers.

Suppose that the economy is initially in equilibrium at point E. Now there is a shift in autonomous investment demand. In the long run, such a shift will move the IS curve to IS'. The extent of the shift is determined by the *long-run* multiplier $[1/(1 - c)]$, where c is the long-run propensity to consume. When expectations of income have fully adjusted, the economy will be at position E', with output level Y' and interest rate i'.

But in the short run the marginal propensity to consume is not c, but only $c\theta$. Thus the short-run multiplier is only $[1/(1 - c\theta)]$. In the short run, the IS curve shifts only to IS''. Thus the immediate effect of the shift in investment demand is to raise income to Y'' and the interest rate to i''.

Next period, the IS curve shifts again. It does not shift all the way to IS' though. Consumers have adjusted upward their estimate of permanent income, but they have not yet adjusted it all the way to Y', because income last period was only Y'' and not Y'. (To keep the diagram simple, we do not show the IS curve for the second or later periods.) Income and the interest rate will rise above Y' and i', but still fall short of Y'' and i''.

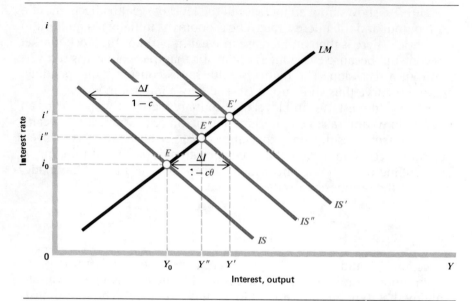

FIGURE 7-7   THE DYNAMICS OF ADJUSTMENT TO A SHIFT IN INVESTMENT
DEMAND. Autonomous investment demand rises by amount ΔI, but it is not
known whether the shift is permanent or transitory. It is in fact permanent,
so that the IS curve will eventually be at IS', shifted by an amount $[\Delta I/(1 - c)]$ to the
right, where $[1/(1 - c)]$ is the long-run multiplier. But in the first period, the IS
curve shifts only to IS", by amount $[\Delta I/(1 - c\theta)]$, determined by the short-run
consumption function and multiplier. Over time, the economy moves gradually
from E" to E', as individuals come to recognize that the shift in investment
demand is permanent.

This process continues, with the consumption function gradually shifting up over time, as people come to realize that their permanent incomes
have risen. A single shock to autonomous demand therefore produces a
slow, or *distributed lag*, effect on output. Figure 7-8 shows how income
adjusts gradually to its new equilibrium level. The time pattern of changes
in income caused by the increase in investment demand is called the
dynamic multiplier of income with respect to autonomous investment.

Policy Implications

Suppose we have a permanent decline in investment expenditure. As we
have seen, the decline in spending would lead to a fall in output and
employment, occurring over a period of time.

Suppose the government wants to offset the reduction in aggregate demand by using tax cuts to keep income at the full-employment level. Since
consumption adjusts only gradually to the changes in income resulting

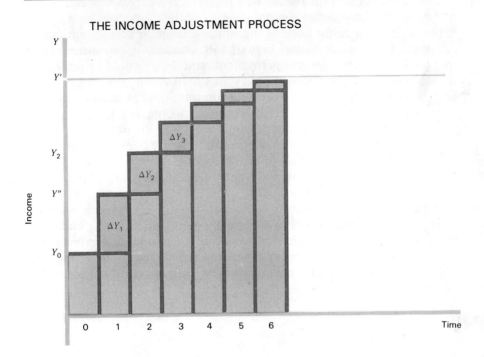

FIGURE 7-8   THE INCOME ADJUSTMENT PROCESS. The figure shows the *dynamic multiplier* of investment spending on income. This is how a given change in autonomous investment spending affects the level of output over time. Income rises in the first period from Y_0 to Y''. Then in subsequent periods it continues to rise toward its long-run equilibrium level Y'.

from both the initial fall in investment and tax cuts, the policy maker who wants to stabilize output *over time* will have to know about the adjustment pattern of consumption so as not to overreact. The problems may be further complicated, as we discuss in Chapter 11, by the fact that frequently the policy maker too reacts only with a lag to changed circumstances.

In the short run, consumption does not respond fully to changes in income. Therefore it takes a relatively large tax cut to obtain a given change in consumption with which to offset the decline in investment. Over time, though, consumption adjusts to the change in disposable income, and the tax cut that was initially just sufficient to offset reduced investment now turns out to be too generous. The compensating policy must therefore be one of a tax cut that is *front-loaded* and gradually phased down to the long-run level. The difference between the short-run and long-run tax cuts is determined by the relative size of the short-run and long-run tax multipliers.

Indeed, the observant reader will recall that we assumed consumers had no special knowledge about the nature of the changes in income they experienced as a result both of the initial change in investment and of subsequent tax adjustments. Remarkably enough, if consumers knew that the investment shift was permanent, and if they could be persuaded that the change in government policy was permanent, a one-time reduction in taxes, calculated using the long-run multiplier implied by the consumption function, would precisely stabilize income. For, in that case, the response to the fall in investment would recognize the permanent nature of the change, implying the long-run multiplier is relevant, and the response to the tax change would also recognize the permanent nature of the change. Consumption would adjust immediately, rather than gradually over the course of time.

The conclusion of this section is that policy making, and understanding of the behaviour of the economy cannot be successful unless careful attention is paid to expectations formation — bearing in mind that expectations depend in part on how the policy makers are perceived to be acting. This is the message of rational expectations, to which we return in Chapters 15 and 17.

7-7 SUMMARY

1   The simple Keynesian consumption function

$$C = .70 + 0.88YD \tag{2}$$

accounts well for observed consumption behaviour. The equation suggests that out of an additional dollar of disposable income, 88 cents is spent on consumption. The consumption function implies, too, that the ratio of consumption to income, C/YD, declines somewhat with the level of income.

2   Early empirical work on short-run consumption behaviour showed that the marginal propensity to consume was lower than that found in longer-period studies. The evidence revealed also that the average propensity to consume declined with the level of income. Postwar studies, by contrast, find a relatively constant average propensity to consume of about 0.9.

3   The evidence is reconciled by a reconsideration of consumption theory. Individuals want to maintain relatively smooth consumption profiles over their lifetime. Their consumption behaviour is geared to their long-term consumption opportunities — permanent income or lifetime income plus wealth. With such a view, current income is only one of the determinants of consumption spending. Wealth and ex-

pected income play a role, too. A consumption function that represents this idea is

$$C = aWR + b\theta YD + b(1 - \theta)YD_{-1} \qquad (15)$$

which allows for the role of real wealth WR, current disposable income YD, and lagged disposable income YD_{-1}.

4   The life-cycle hypothesis suggests that the propensities of an individual to consume out of disposable income and out of wealth depend on the person's age. It also suggests that aggregate saving depends on the growth rate of the economy and on such variables as the age distribution of the population.

5   The permanent-income hypothesis emphasizes the formation of expectations of future income. It implies that the propensity to consume out of permanent income is higher than the propensity to consume out of transitory income.

6   Both theories do well, in combination, in explaining aggregate consumption behaviour. But there are still some consumption puzzles, including the excess sensitivity of consumption to current income and the fact that the aged do not appear to draw down their savings as they age.

7   The relative-income hypothesis argues that current consumption is related not only to current income but also to previous peak income. The argument for this is that individuals find it difficult to reduce rates of consumption to which they have become accustomed.

8   The rate of consumption, and thus of savings, could in principle be affected by the interest rate. But the evidence for the most part shows little effect of interest rates on saving.

9   Lagged adjustment of consumption to income results in a gradual adjustment of the level of income in the economy to changes in autonomous spending and other economic changes. An increase in autonomous spending raises income. But the adjustment process is spread out over time because the rising level of income raises consumption only gradually. This adjustment process is described by dynamic multipliers that show by how much income changes in each period following a change in autonomous spending (or other exogenous variables).

10   The dynamic adjustment of the economy to changes in policy variables, such as a change in government spending or transfers, creates a problem for policy making. The analysis of Section 7-6 shows that the policy maker needs detailed information about the dynamic responses

of the economy, if policy is not to result in income levels that differ from the target levels. In a dynamic setting, the making of policy requires the policy maker to consider how much any particular policy action will affect income in each time period and to calculate *time paths* for policy variables that will bring about the desired performance.

KEY TERMS

Life-cycle hypothesis
Dissaving
Permanent income
Rational expectations

Liquidity constraints
Relative-income hypothesis
Dynamic multiplier

PROBLEMS

1 What is the significance of the ratio of consumption to GNP in terms of the level of economic activity? Would you expect it to be higher or lower than normal during a recession (or depression)? Do you think the ratio would be higher in developed or underdeveloped countries? Why?

The Life-Cycle Hypothesis

2 The text implies that the ratio of consumption to accumulated savings declines over time until retirement.
   (a) Why? What assumption about consumption behaviour leads to this result?
   (b) What happens to this ratio after retirement?

3 (a) Suppose you earn as much as your neighbour but are in much better health and expect to live longer. Would you consume more or less than your neighbour? Why? Derive your answer from Equation (7).
   (b) According to the life-cycle hypothesis, what would the effect of the Canada Pension Plan system be on your average propensity to consume out of (disposable) income?
   (c) How would Equation (10) be modified for an individual who expects to receive $X per year of retirement benefits? Verify your result in 3(b).

4 Give an intuitive interpretation of the marginal propensity to consume out of wealth and income at time T in the individual's lifetime in Equation (10).

*5 In Equation (7), consumption in each year of working life is given by

$$C = \frac{WL}{NL} \times YL \qquad (7)$$

In Equation (10), consumption is given as

$$C = aWR + cYL \qquad a \equiv \frac{1}{NL - T} \qquad c \equiv \frac{WL - T}{NL - T} \qquad (10)$$

Show that Equations (7) and (10) are consistent for an individual who started life with zero wealth and has been saving for T years. [*Hint*: First calculate the individual's wealth after T years of saving at rate $YL - C$. Then calculate the level of consumption implied by Equation (10) when wealth is at the level you have computed.]

Permanent-Income Hypothesis

6 In terms of permanent-income hypothesis, would you consume more of your Christmas bonus if:
   (a) You knew there was a bonus every year, or
   (b) This was the only year such bonuses were given out?

7 Suppose that permanent income is calculated as the average of income over the past 5 years; that is,

$$YP = \frac{1}{5}(Y + Y_{-1} + Y_{-2} + Y_{-3} + Y_{-4})$$

Suppose, further, that consumption is given by $C = 0.9YP$.
   (a) If you have earned $10,000 per year for the past 10 years, what is your permanent income?
   (b) Suppose next year (period $t + 1$) you earn $15,000. What is your new YP?
   (c) What is your consumption this year and next year?
   (d) What is your short-run MPC? Long-run MPC?
   (e) Assuming you continue to earn $15,000 starting in period $t + 1$, graph the value of your permanent income in each period using the equation above.

8 Explain why good gamblers (and thieves) might be expected to live very well even in years when they don't do well at all.

*9 The accompanying graph shows the lifetime earnings profile of a person who lives for four periods and earns income of $30, $60, and $90 in the first three periods of the life cycle. There are no earnings during retirement. Assume that the interest rate is 0.
   (a) You are asked to determine the level of consumption, compatible with the budget constraint, for someone who wants an even consumption profile throughout the life cycle. Indicate in which periods the person saves and dissaves and in what amounts.

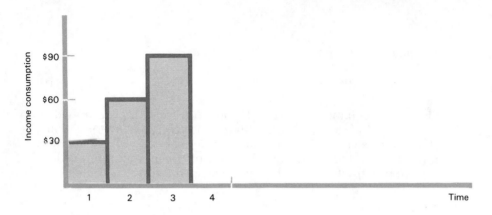

(b) Assume now that, contrary to 9(a), there is no possibility for borrowing. The credit markets are closed to the individual. Under this assumption, what is the flow of consumption the individual will pick over the life cycle? In providing an answer, continue to assume that if possible, an even flow of consumption is preferred. (*Note*: You are assuming here that there are liquidity constraints.)

(c) Assume next that the person described in 9(b) receives an increase in wealth or nonlabour income. The increase in wealth is equal to $13. How will that wealth be allocated over the life cycle with and without access to the credit market? How would your answer differ if the increase in wealth were $23?

(d) Relate your answer to the problem of excess sensitivity of consumption to current income.

*10 Consider the consumption function in Equation (15). Assume autonomous investment spending is constant, as is government spending. The economy is close to full employment and the government wishes to maintain aggregate demand precisely constant. In these circumstances, assume there is an increase in real wealth of $10 billion. What change in income taxes will maintain constant the equilibrium level of income in the present period? What change is required to maintain income constant in the long run?

11 Equation (15) shows consumption as a function of wealth and current and lagged disposable income. To reconcile that consumption function with permanent-income expectations formation, you are asked to use Equation (13) and the consumption function

$$C = 0.045WR + 0.55YD + 0.17YD_{-1}$$

to determine the magnitude of θ and $(1 - \theta)$ that is implied by Equation (15).

12 (a) Explain why the interest rate might affect saving.
   (b) Why does it matter?

*Adjustment and Dynamics

13 Here is a challenge to your ability to develop diagrams. You are asked to show short-run and long-run income determination in the 45° diagram of Chapter 3. Assume that investment demand is totally autonomous and does not respond to the interest rate. Thus you do not need to use the full *IS-LM* model.
   (a) Draw the short-run and long-run consumption functions and the aggregate demand schedule with $I = \bar{I}$.
   (b) Show the initial full equilibrium.
   (c) Show the short-run and long-run effects of increased investment on equilibrium income.

CHAPTER 7: FOOTNOTES

[1]It is frequently useful to summarize a relationship, such as that of Chart 7-1, between consumption expenditures and disposable income by writing an equation such as Eq. (2), which has specific numerical values in it, rather than the more general form of Eq. (1), which does not specify numerical values of the coefficients $\bar{C}$ and c. The line drawn in Chart 7-1 is the line represented by Eq. (2). That line is calculated by minimizing the sum of the squares of the vertical distance of the points in Chart 7-1 from the line, and it provides a good description of the general relationship between the two variables. For further details on the fitting of such lines, called least-squares regression lines, see Robert S. Pindyck and Daniel L. Rubinfeld, *Econometric Models and Economic Forecasts* (New York: McGraw-Hill, 1976.)

[2]You should check the *Canadian Statistical Review* to see how well Equation (2) predicts consumption for 1984. Disposable income in 1971 dollars can be obtained by dividing the current dollar figure by the implicit price index (deflator) for personal consumption expenditure.

[3]Technically, the intercept is statistically not significantly different from zero. See Pindyck and Rubinfeld, *op. cit.*, for the meaning of tests of significance.

[4]Simon Kuznets, *National Product Since 1869* and *National Income, A Summary of Findings* (New York: National Bureau of Economic Research, 1946).

[5]The theories of the consumption function developed hereafter are also useful for explaining another empirical puzzle that we shall not go into in detail. In *cross-sectional* studies of the relationship between consumption and income — studies in which the consumption of a sample of families is related to their income — the marginal propensity to consume out of disposable income also appears to be lower than the average propensity to consume, with the average propensity to consume falling as the level of income rises. If you are interested in the reconciliation of this evidence with the long-run evidence of Kuznets, you should look at the ingenious explanation advanced by Milton Friedman through the permanent-income hypothesis. Follow up the reference given in footnote 11.

[6]Why? The basic reason is the notion of diminishing marginal utility of consumption. Consider two alternative consumption plans. One involves an equal amount of consumption in each of two periods; the other involves consuming all in one period and none in the other. The principle of diminishing marginal utility of income implies that in the latter case, we would be better off by transferring some consumption from the period of plenty toward that of starvation. The loss in utility in the period of plenty is *more* than compensated by the gain in utility in the period of scarcity. And there is a gain to be made by transferring consumption so long as there is any difference in consumption between the two periods. The principle of diminishing marginal utility of consumption conforms well with the observation that most people choose stable life-styles — not, in general, saving furiously in one period to have a big bust in the next, but rather, consuming at about the same level every period.

[7]Figure 7-3 was developed by Franco Modigliani in "The Life Cycle Hypothesis of Saving, the Demand for Wealth and the Supply of Capital," *Social Research*, vol. 33, no. 2, 1966. Modigliani, together with Richard Brumberg and Albert Ando, formulated the life-cycle theory.

[8]The individual may receive wealth early in life through gifts or bequests. In the fully developed life-cycle model, the individual, in calculating lifetime consumption, has also to take account of any bequests he or she may want to leave. We discuss the role of bequests in Box 7-1.

[9]The other variables indicated here will be discussed in the next paragraph.

[10]The life-cycle theory also suggests why the simple consumption function of Eq. (2) would look different when estimated over different time periods, for example, 1961–1983 and 1926–1940. Equation (2) omits a variable, wealth, which should be in the consumption function. This means that the estimates we get for the intercept and the marginal propensity to consume will depend on how wealth changes in the period for which we are fitting the line. As a difficult problem, see whether you can show that the estimated average propensity to consume will be constant if the ratio of wealth to disposable income is constant, but is omitted from the equation when it is fitted. Similarly, show that when wealth is constant but is omitted when fitting Eq. (2), the estimated average propensity to consume will decline with income.

[11]Milton Friedman, *A Theory of the Consumption Function* (Princeton, N.J.: Princeton University Press, 1957).

[12]There is no standard definition of permanent income in Friedman's exposition of his theory. The definition given above is similar to average lifetime income. But it is not quite the same, because it effectively converts wealth into income in defining permanent income. Someone with no labour income, and only wealth, is defined as having permanent income equal to the amount he could consume each year by using up his wealth at a steady rate over the remainder of his life.

[13]Friedman also adjusted permanent income by taking into account the growth of income over time.

[14]Recall that although we restricted our measure of permanent income to a 2-year average, there is no reason why the average should not be taken over longer periods. If current income is unstable, an appropriate measure of permanent income may well be an average over 5 or more years.

[15]To fix ideas, you should draw a graph of Eq. (15) with consumption on the vertical axis and current disposable labour income on the horizontal axis. What is the intercept? How does the diagram differ from Fig. 7-4? Show the effects of (1) a transitory increase in income, (2) a sustained increase in income, and (3) an increase in wealth.

[16]See, for example, Robert E. Hall, "Stochastic Implications of the Life Cycle–Permanent Income Hypothesis: Theory and Evidence," *Journal of Political Economy*, December 1978. This is difficult reading.

[17]See James Duesenberry, *Income, Savings and the Theory of Consumer Behavior* (Cambridge, Mass.: Harvard University Press, 1952).

[18]The best known study finding positive interest rate effects is that of Michael Boskin, "Taxation, Saving, and the Rate of Interest," *Journal of Political Economy*, pt. 2, April 1978. For more typical results, see Gerald A. Carlino, "Interest Rate Effects and Intertemporal Consumption," *Journal of Monetary Economics*, March 1982.

[19]For example, Michael Darby, "The Allocation of Transitory Income among Consumers' Assets," *American Economic Review*, December 1972.

Investment Spending

Consumption spending in Canada is on average about 60 percent of real GNE, and thus accounts for much of aggregate demand. Investment spending is typically about 20 percent of real GNE, but it fluctuates more than consumption. Table 8-1 shows how the components of aggregate demand changed in the most recent recession which began in the third quarter of 1981 and reached a trough in the fourth quarter of 1982. Real GNE fell sharply, mainly because of the large decline in investment spending. The fall in consumption was smaller than the decline in income as would be predicted by the permanent income theory.[1]

TABLE 8-1 REAL GNE AND ITS COMPONENTS IN THE 1981–82 RECESSION (billions of 1971 dollars)

	1981 II	1982 IV	Change
GNE	$135.3	$128.4	−6.9
Consumption	83.9	81.4	−2.5
Investment	29.1	19.6	−9.5
Government	26.8	27.3	1.9
Net exports	−4.1	−.1	4.0

Source: Statistics Canada, 11-003.

The cyclical importance of investment spending, shown in Table 8-1, goes back a long way. For instance, in the Great Depression, gross investment fell to less than 4 percent of GNP in 1933. Understanding investment, then, is of prime importance in understanding the business cycle.

In this chapter we continue our in-depth analysis of the components of aggregate demand. We both provide a foundation for the essential component of the simple investment function of Chapter 4 — that investment demand is reduced by increases in the interest rate — and go further than that investment function, by discussing the roles of output and taxes in

determining investment. While much of the reason for studying investment spending is that its fluctuations help account for the business cycle,
another reason is that investment spending can be significantly affected
by policy. High interest rates, caused by restrictive monetary policy and
expansive fiscal policy, reduce investment spending; policies that reduce
interest rates and provide tax incentives for investment can increase
investment spending.

One simple relationship is vital to the understanding of investment.
Investment is spending devoted to increasing or maintaining the stock of
capital. The stock of capital consists of the factories, machines, offices,
and other durable products used in the process of production. The capital
stock also includes residential housing as well as inventories. Investment
is spending that adds to these components of capital stock. Recall the
distinction drawn in Chapter 2 between *gross* and *net investment*. Gross
investment represents total additions to the capital stock. Net investment
subtracts depreciation — the reduction in the capital stock that occurs each
period through wear and tear and the simple ravages of time — from gross
investment. Net investment thus measures the increase in the capital stock in
a given period of time.

In this chapter, we disaggregate investment spending into three categories.
The first consists of spending by business firms on productive capital in
the form of *machinery and equipment* and *nonresidential construction*. The second is *residential construction* which consists of spending on houses and
apartment buildings. These two categories comprise *fixed investment* as
opposed to the third one, *inventory investment*, some aspects of which were
discussed in Chapter 3.

TABLE 8-2   GROSS BUSINESS INVESTMENT, 1983
            (billions of 1971 dollars)

Machinery and equipment	$9.3
Nonresidential construction	8.6
Residential construction	5.8
Total fixed investment	$23.7
Change in inventories	− .1
Gross business investment	$23.6

Source: Statistics Canada, 11-003.

Table 8-2 shows investment spending in these categories for 1983, and
Figure 8-1 shows the components of investment since 1961. Although
inventory investment is a small fraction of GNP it shows wide fluctuations.
Note that the large negative inventory investment in the recession year
1982 is unusual, since in most years it is positive.

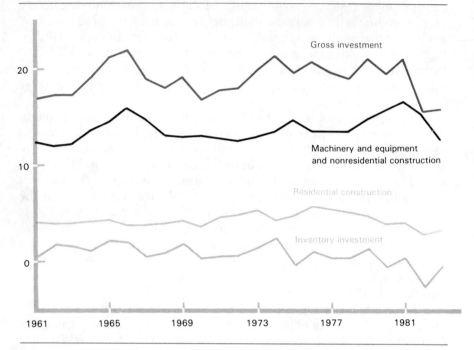

FIGURE 8-1   COMPONENTS OF INVESTMENT SPENDING AS A PERCENTAGE OF
GNP
(*Source*: Department of Finance, *Economic Review*)

In the remainder of this chapter, we develop theories and discuss evidence about the determinants of the rate of investment in each of the three major categories shown in Table 8-2 and Figure 8-1. We will develop what look like different models to explain each of the categories of investment spending. However, as we discuss in Section 8-5, the theories are essentially similar, sharing a common view of the interaction between a desired capital stock and the rate at which the economy adjusts toward that desired stock.

8-1 BUSINESS FIXED INVESTMENT: THE NEOCLASSICAL APPROACH

The machinery, equipment, and structures used in the production of goods and services constitute the *stock* of business fixed capital. Our analysis of business fixed investment in this section proceeds in two stages. First, we ask how much capital firms would like to use, given the costs and returns of using capital and the level of output they expect to produce. That is, we ask what determines the *desired capital stock*. The desired capital stock is the capital stock that firms would like to have in the long run, abstracting from the delays they face in adjusting their use of capital. However, because it takes time to order new machines, build factories, and install the machines, firms cannot instantly adjust the stock of capital used in production. Second, therefore, we discuss the rate at which firms adjust from their existing capital stock toward the desired level over the course of time. The rate of adjustment determines how much firms spend on adding to the capital stock in each period; that is, it determines the rate of investment.

The Desired Capital Stock: Overview

Firms use capital, along with labour, to produce goods and services for sale. The firms' goal is, of course, to maximize their profits. In deciding how much capital to use in production, they have to balance the contribution that more capital makes to their revenues against the cost of using more capital. The *marginal product of capital* is the increase in output produced by using one more unit of capital in production. The *rental (user) cost of capital* is the cost of using one more unit of capital in production.

To derive the rental cost of capital, we think of the firm as financing the purchase of the capital (whether the firm produces the capital itself or buys it from some other firm) by borrowing, at an interest cost i. In order to obtain the services of an extra unit of capital, in each period the firm must pay the interest cost i for each dollar of capital that it buys. Thus the basic measure of the rental cost of capital is the interest rate.[2] Later we shall go into more detail about the rental cost of capital, but, for the meantime we shall think of the interest rate as determining the rental cost.

In deciding how much capital they would like to use in production, firms compare the value of the marginal product of capital with the user or rental costs of capital. The value of the marginal product of capital is the increase in the *value* of output obtained by using one more unit of capital. For a competitive firm, it is equal to the price of output times the marginal product of capital. So long as the value of the marginal product of capital is above the rental cost, it pays the firm to add to its capital stock. Thus the firm will keep investing until the value of the output produced by adding one more unit of capital is equal to the cost of using that capital — the rental cost of capital. In equilibrium, we must have:

$$\text{Value of marginal product of capital} = \text{rental cost of capital} \qquad (1)$$

To give content to this relationship, we have to specify what determines the productivity of capital and what determines the user (rental) cost of capital. The marginal product of capital is examined next, and then we turn to the rental cost of the capital.

The Marginal Productivity of Capital

In understanding the marginal productivity of capital, it is important to note that firms can substitute capital for labour in the production of output. Different combinations of capital and labour can be used to produce a given level of output. If labour is relatively cheap, the firm will want to use relatively more labour, and if capital is relatively cheap, the firm will want to use relatively more capital.

The general relationship among the desired capital stock (K^*), the rental cost of capital (rc), and the level of output is given by

$$K^* = g(rc, Y) \qquad (2)$$

Equation (2) indicates that the desired capital stock depends on the rental cost of capital and the level of output. The lower the rental cost of capital, the larger the desired capital stock. And the greater the level of output, the larger the desired capital stock.

The relationship shown in Equation (2) makes complete sense. It says that firms want to have more capital on hand if they have to produce more output, and that they want to have more capital the cheaper it is to

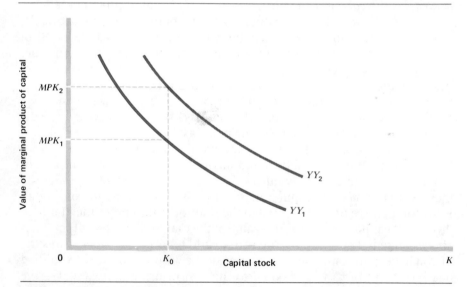

FIGURE 8-2   THE MARGINAL PRODUCT OF CAPITAL IN RELATION TO THE LEVEL OF OUTPUT AND THE CAPITAL STOCK. The marginal product of capital decreases as relatively more capital is used in producing any given level of output. Thus the schedules YY_1 and YY_2 are downward sloping. The higher the level of output, for any given capital input, the higher the marginal product of capital. Thus schedule YY_2, with output level Y_2 greater than Y_1, is above schedule YY_1.

use capital. We now explain in more detail the factors underlying Equation (2).

As the firm combines progressively more capital with relatively less labour in the production of a *given* amount of output, the marginal product of capital declines. This relation is shown in the downward-sloping schedules in Figure 8-2. Those schedules show how the marginal product of capital falls as more capital is used in producing a given level of output. The schedule YY_1 is drawn for a level of output Y_1. The schedule YY_2 is drawn for the higher output level Y_2. The marginal product of capital, given the capital stock, say, K_0, is higher on the schedule YY_2 than on YY_1. That is because more labour is being used in combination with the given amount of capital K_0 to produce the level of output Y_2 than to produce Y_1.

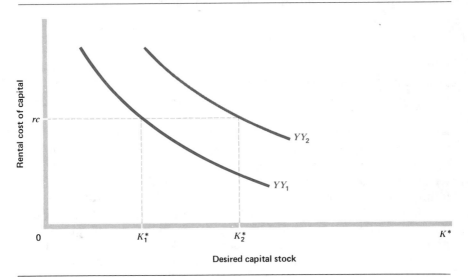

FIGURE 8-3   THE DESIRED CAPITAL STOCK IN RELATION TO THE LEVEL OF OUTPUT AND THE RENTAL COST OF CAPITAL. Firms' desired capital stock is chosen at the point at which the value of the marginal product of capital is equal to the rental cost of capital. At rental cost rc and output level Y_1, the firm's desired capital stock is K_1^*. An increase in the level of output to Y_2 raises the desired capital stock to K_2^*. An increase in the rental cost of capital (not shown) would reduce the desired capital stock at each level of output.

Figure 8-2 shows the marginal product of capital in relation to the level of output and the amount of capital being used to produce that output. Figure 8-3 is a similar diagram which shows the desired capital stock as related to the rental cost of capital and the level of output. Given the level of output, say, Y_1, the firm will want to use more capital the lower the rental cost of capital — because at low rental costs of capital, it can afford to use capital even when its marginal productivity is quite low. If the rental cost of capital is high, the firm will be willing to use capital only if its marginal productivity is high — which means that the firm will not want to use very much capital and will instead substitute labour for capital. In producing a higher level of output, say, Y_2, the firm will use both more capital and more labour, given the rental cost of capital.[3] Therefore, at higher levels of output, the desired capital stock is higher.

The Cobb-Douglas Production Function

While Equation (2) provides the general relationship determining the desired capital stock, a particular form of the equation, based on the *Cobb-Douglas production function*,[4] is frequently used in studies of investment behaviour. The particular equation that is used is[5]

$$K* = \frac{\gamma Y}{rc} \tag{3}$$

where γ is a constant. In this case, the desired capital stock varies in proportion to output. Given output, the desired capital stock varies inversely with the rental cost of capital.

Expected Output

In determining the desired stock, we have to specify the relevant time period for which the decision on the capital stock applies. In this section we are discussing the capital stock that the firm desires to hold at some future time. Accordingly, the level of output in Equations (2) and (3) should be the level of output which firms expect to be producing at that time. For some investments the future time at which the output will be produced is a matter of months or only weeks. For other investments, such as power stations, the future time at which the output will be produced is years away.

This suggests that the notion of permanent income (in this case, permanent output) introduced in Chapter 7 is relevant to investment as well as consumption. For longer-lived investments, the firm's capital demand is governed primarily by its views on the level of output it will be producing on average in the future. The firm's long-run demand for business fixed capital, depending on the normal or permanent level of output, is thus relatively independent of the current level of output, and depends on *expectations* of future output levels. However, it is affected by current output to the extent that current output affects expectations of permanent output.[6]

Summary on the Desired Capital Stock

It is worthwhile stepping back for a moment to summarize the main results so far:

1 The firm's demand for capital — the desired capital stock K^* — depends on the rental cost of capital, rc, and the expected level of output.
2 Firms balance the costs and benefits of using capital. The lower the rental cost of capital, the larger the optimal level of capital relative to output. This relation reflects the lower marginal productivity of capital when it is used relatively intensively. The intensive use of capital will be profitable only if the rental cost of capital is low.
3 The higher the level of output, the larger the desired capital stock.
4 The firm plans its capital stock in relation to expected future or permanent output.
5 Current output affects capital demand to the extent that it affects expectations about future output.

The Rental Cost of Capital Again

We have already introduced the notion of the rental or user cost of capital in determining the firm's desired capital stock. As a first approximation, we identified the rental cost of capital with the interest rate, on the argument that firms would have to borrow to finance their use of capital. Now we go into more detail on the cost per period of using capital.

To use capital for a single period, say a year, the firm can be thought of as buying the capital with borrowed funds and paying the interest on the borrowing. At the end of the year, the firm will still have some of the capital left. But the capital is likely to have depreciated over the course of the year. We shall assume that the firm intends to continue using the remaining capital in production in future years and that its depreciation simply represents the using up of the capital in the process of production — physical wear and tear. We now examine the rental cost, taking into account interest costs and depreciation. Later we will show that taxes also affect the rental cost of capital.

Leaving aside taxes, we now examine the two elements in the rental cost of capital in more detail. For the moment, let us write the interest cost i. Insofar as depreciation is concerned, we assume that a fixed proportion d of the capital is used up per period. The depreciation cost, per dollar of capital, is d.[7] The rental cost, or user cost, of capital, per dollar's worth of capital, which we denote by rc, is therefore

$$rc = i + d \qquad (4)$$

A numerical example should help in understanding Equation (4). Suppose the interest rate is 10 percent per year and the rate of depreciation is 15 percent. That means that by the end of the year, the firm will have had to spend 15 cents per dollar of capital to maintain capital's production efficiency in the face of depreciation. The costs to the firm of using the capital for the year are then the interest cost, 10 cents per dollar of capital, and the depreciation cost, 15 cents per dollar of capital. The cost of using capital for a year is thus 25 cents per dollar's worth of capital.

The Real Rate of Interest

We have to distinguish carefully between the *real* and the *nominal* rates of interest. The *real interest rate* is the nominal (stated) rate of interest minus the rate of inflation. In general, someone borrowing at a stated nominal rate of interest, say 10 percent, does not know what the rate of inflation over the period of the borrowing will be. Accordingly, the real rate of interest relevant when a loan transaction is entered into is the *expected* real rate of interest—the stated nominal interest rate minus the rate of inflation expected over the period of the loan.

The notion of the real rate of interest is extremely important. Suppose that the nominal interest rate, the rate stated in the loan agreement, is 10 percent. Then suppose also that prices are rising at 10 percent. Someone borrowing $100 at the beginning of the year pays back $110 at the end of the year. But those dollars in which repayment is made buy less goods than the dollars lent at the beginning of the year when the loan was made. If the inflation rate is 10 percent, then the $110 paid at the end of the year buys the same amount of goods that could have been bought with the original $100 at the beginning of the year. In *real* terms, in terms of the goods which the money can buy, the lender has no more at the end than at the beginning of the year. Thus the *real* interest rate actually received was zero, even though the *nominal* interest rate was 10 percent. Given the nominal interest rate, the real interest rate is lower the higher the rate of inflation becomes. In practice, nominal interest rates tend to be higher when inflation is higher.

It is the *expected real* rate of interest that should enter the calculation of the rental cost of capital. Why? The firm is borrowing in order to produce goods for sale. On average, across all firms, it is reasonable to believe that the prices of the goods the firms sell will be rising along with the general price level. Thus the value of what the firm will be producing in the future will be rising with the price level, but the nominal amount of interest it has to pay back on account of its borrowings does not rise with the price level. The real value of the debt it has incurred by borrowing will be falling over time, as a result of inflation, and it should take that reduction in the real value of its outstanding debts into account in deciding how much capital to employ.

Accordingly, we can be more precise in the way we write Equation (4) for the rental cost of capital. We write the rental cost of capital, taking account of expected inflation at the rate π^*, as

$$rc \equiv r + d \equiv i - \pi^* + d \qquad (5)$$

where r is the real interest rate, i the nominal interest rate, and

$$r \equiv i - \pi^* \qquad (6)$$

Equation (6) states that the real rate of interest is the nominal interest rate minus the expected rate of inflation. Implicitly, Equation (6) refers to the expected real rate of interest.[8] At the end of the period, when the rate of inflation is known, we can also state what the *actual* or realized real rate of interest for the period was — namely, the nominal interest rate i minus the actual rate of inflation.

To reiterate, it is important to note that the interest rate relevant to the firm's demand for capital is the *real* rate, and not the nominal rate. This makes it clear that the nominal rate of interest is not a good guide to the rental cost of capital. If the rate of inflation is zero and is expected to be zero and the nominal interest rate is 5 percent, then the real interest rate is 5 percent. By contrast, if the nominal interest rate is 10 percent and inflation is at the rate of 10 percent, the real interest rate is zero. Other things equal, the desired capital stock in this example would tend to be higher with the nominal interest rate of 10 percent than with the nominal rate of 5 percent — because those rates correspond to real rates of zero and 5 percent, respectively. As you have no doubt deduced, and as we shall show, investment spending tends to be higher when the rental cost of capital is lower. But because of the distinction between real and nominal interest rates, that is *not* the same as saying that investment tends to be higher when the nominal rate of interest is lower.

Taxes and the Rental Cost of Capital

The rental cost of capital is affected by tax variables as well as by the interest rate and depreciation. The two main tax variables that affect the rental cost of capital are the corporate income tax and the investment tax credit. The corporate income tax is an essentially proportional tax on profits, whereby the firm pays a proportion, say t, of its profits in taxes. The investment tax credit allows firms to deduct from their taxes a certain fraction, say, τ, of their investment expenditures in each year. Thus a firm spending $1 million for investment purposes in a given year can deduct 10 percent of the $1 million, or $100,000, from the taxes it would otherwise have to pay the federal government.

We want to know what effects the corporate income tax and the investment tax credit have on the rental cost of capital. The easier case is the investment tax credit. The investment tax credit reduces the price of a capital good to the firm by the ratio τ, since the government returns to the firm a proportion τ of the cost of each capital good. Equivalently, we can say that the rental cost is reduced by the factor τ. The investment tax credit therefore reduces the rental cost of capital.

To a first approximation, the corporate income tax, surprisingly, has no effect on the desired stock of capital. In the presence of the corporate income tax, the firm will want to equate the *after-tax* value of the marginal product of capital with the *after-tax* rental cost of capital in order to ensure that the marginal contribution of the capital to profits is equal to the marginal cost of using it.

Let us focus on the interest component of the rental cost. The basic point is that interest cost is treated as a deduction from revenues in the calculation of the corporation's taxes. Suppose there were no corporate income tax, no inflation, no depreciation, and an interest rate of 10 percent. The desired capital stock would be that level of the capital stock, say, K_0^*, such that the marginal product of capital was 10 percent. Now suppose that the corporate income tax rises to 46 percent and the interest rate remains constant. At the capital stock K_0^*, the after-tax marginal product of capital is now 5.4 percent (since 46 percent of the profits are paid in taxes). But if the interest rate stays at 10 percent and the firm gets to deduct 46 percent of its interest payments from taxes, the after-tax cost of capital will be 5.4 percent too. In this case, the desired capital stock is unaffected by the rate of corporate taxation.

However, there are complexities in the tax laws, which we do not go into here, which make the total effect of the corporate income tax on the desired capital stock ambiguous. The ambiguities arise when the special tax treatment of depreciation,[9] of inflation, and of investment financing other than through borrowing is taken into account.[10]

We conclude by noting the two main points. The investment tax credit reduces the rental cost of capital and increases the desired stock of capital. The corporate income tax has ambiguous effects on the desired stock of capital.

Summary and Effects of Fiscal and Monetary Policy on the Desired Capital Stock

We summarize, using Equation (2), which gives the desired capital stock as a function of the rental cost of capital and the expected level of output, and the preceding discussion of the rental cost of capital. From Equation (2) we note that the desired capital stock increases when the expected level of output rises and when the rental cost of capital falls.

The rental cost of capital falls when the real interest rate and the rate of depreciation fall. It likewise falls when the investment tax credit rises. Changes in the rate of corporate taxation have ambiguous effects on the desired capital stock.

The major significance of these results is their implication that monetary and fiscal policy affect the desired capital stock. Fiscal policy exerts an effect through both the corporate tax rate t and the investment tax credit τ. Both these instruments are used to affect capital demand and thus investment spending.

Fiscal policy affects capital demand by its overall effects on the position of the IS curve, as we discussed in Chapter 4. A high tax–low government spending policy keeps the real interest rate low and encourages the demand for capital. (At this point you want to refer to Figure 4-22.) A high government spending–low tax policy that produces large deficits raises the real interest rate and discourages the demand for capital.

Monetary policy affects capital demand by affecting the market interest rate.[11] A lowering of the nominal interest rate by the Bank of Canada (given the expected inflation rate), as reflected in a downward shift in the *LM* curve of Chapter 4, will induce firms to desire more capital. This expansion in capital demand, in turn, will affect investment spending, as we shall now see.

From Desired Capital Stock to Investment

We have now put more content into the general form of Equation (2) for the desired capital stock by discussing the rental cost of capital in detail. The actual capital stock will often differ from the capital stock firms would like to have. At what speed do firms change their capital stocks in order to move toward the desired capital stock? In particular, is there any reason why firms do not attempt to move to their desired capital stocks immediately?

Since it takes time to plan and complete an investment project, and because attempts to invest quickly are likely to be more expensive than gradual adjustment of the capital stock, it is unlikely that firms would attempt to adjust their capital stocks to the long-run desired level instantaneously. Very rapid adjustment of the capital stock would require crash programs by the firm which would distract management from its routine tasks and interfere with ongoing production. Thus, firms generally plan to adjust their capital stocks gradually over a period of time rather than immediately.

Capital Stock Adjustment

There are a number of hypotheses about the speed with which firms plan to adjust their capital stock over time; we single out the *gradual adjustment hypothesis* here.[12] The basic notion behind the gradual adjustment hypothesis is that the larger the gap between the existing capital stock and the desired capital stock, the more rapid a firm's rate of investment. The hypothesis is that firms plan to close a fraction λ of the gap between the desired and actual capital stocks each period. Denote the capital stock at the end of the last period by K_{-1}. The gap between the desired and actual capital stocks is $(K^* - K_{-1})$. The firm plans to add to last period's capital stock K_{-1}, a fraction λ of the gap $K^* - K_{-1}$ so that the capital stock at the end of current period, K, will be

$$K = K_{-1} + \lambda(K^* - K_{-1}) \tag{7}$$

Equation (7) states that the firm plans to have the capital stock at the end of the period (K) be such that a fraction λ of the gap (between the desired capital stock K^* and the capital stock K_{-1} that existed at the end of last period) is closed. To increase the capital stock from K_{-1} to the level of K indicated by Equation (7), the firm has to achieve an amount of net investment, $I \equiv K - K_{-1}$, indicated by Equation (7). We can therefore write net investment as

$$I = \lambda(K^* - K_{-1}) \qquad (8)$$

which is the gradual adjustment formulation of net investment. Notice that Equation (8) implies that investment is larger, the larger the gap between actual and desired capital stocks.[13] With a zero gap net investment is zero.

In Figure 8-4 we show the adjustment process of capital in a circumstance where the initial capital stock is K_1 and the given desired capital stock is K^*. The assumed speed of adjustment is $\lambda = 0.5$. Starting from K_1, one-half the discrepancy between target capital and current actual capital is made up in every period. First-period net investment is therefore $0.5(K^* - K_1)$. In the second period, investment will be less because the previous period's investment reduces the gap. Investment continues until the actual capital stock reaches the level of target capital. The speed with which this process allows actual capital to reach target is determined by λ. The larger λ is, the faster the gap is reduced.

In Equation (8), we have reached our goal of deriving an investment function that shows current investment spending determined by the desired stock of capital K^* and the actual stock of capital K_{-1}. According to the flexible accelerator hypothesis, any factor that increases the desired stock increases the rate of investment. Therefore an increase in expected output, or a reduction in the real interest rate, or an increase in the investment tax credit will each increase the rate of investment. We thus have derived a quite complete theory of business fixed investment that includes many of the factors we should expect to affect the rate of investment. And the theory of investment embodied in Equation (8) also contains aspects of *dynamic behaviour* — that is, of behaviour that depends on values of economic variables in periods other than the current period.

There are two sources of dynamic behaviour in Equation (8). The first arises from expectations. The K^* term depends on the firm's estimate of future or permanent output. To the extent that the firm forms its estimates of permanent output as a weighted average of past output levels, there will be lags in the adjustment of the level of permanent output to the actual level of output. In turn, investment will therefore also adjust slowly to a change in the level of output. The second source of dynamic behaviour arises from adjustment lags. Firms plan to close only a proportion of the gap between the actual and desired capital stocks each period, as shown in Figure 8-4. The adjustment lags produce lagged response of investment to change in the variables that affect the desired capital stock.

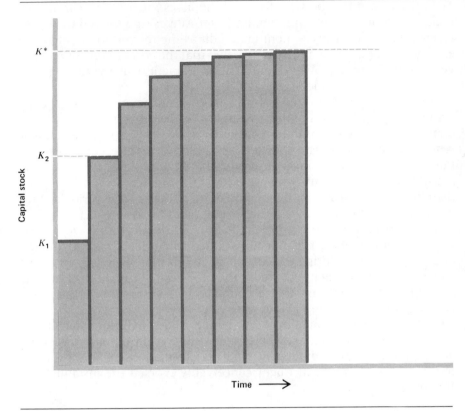

FIGURE 8-4   THE GRADUAL ADJUSTMENT OF THE CAPITAL STOCK. The desired capital stock is K^*, and the current capital stock is K_1. The firm plans to close half the gap between the actual and the desired capital stock each period ($\lambda = 0.5$). Thus, in period one it moves to K_2, with (net) investment equal to $(K_2 - K_1)$, which in turn is equal to one half of $(K^* - K_1)$. In each subsequent period it closes half the gap between the capital stock at the beginning of the period and the desired capital stock, K^*.

The Timing of Investment and the Investment Tax Credit

The flexible accelerator model provides a useful summary of the dynamics of investment. But it does not sufficiently emphasize the *timing* of investment. Because investment is undertaken for the long run and often requires several years to complete, there is flexibility in the dates on which the actual investment is undertaken. For example, suppose a firm wanted to have some machinery in place within 3 years. Suppose that it knew the investment tax credit would be raised substantially a year from now.

Then the firm might be wise to delay the investment for a year and to make or acquire the machinery at a faster rate during the next 2 years, receiving the higher investment tax credit as the reward for waiting the extra year. Similarly, if a firm anticipated that the cost of borrowing next year would be much lower than this year, it might wait a year to undertake its investment project.

The flexibility in the timing of investment leads to an interesting contrast between the effects of the investment tax credit and the income tax on investment and consumption, respectively. We saw in Chapter 7 that a *permanent* change in the income tax has a much larger effect on consumption than a *transitory* change. However, the rate of investment *during the period* that a *temporary* investment tax credit is in effect would be higher than the rate of investment that would occur over the same period during which a *permanent* credit of the same magnitude was in effect. Why? If firms knew the investment tax credit was temporary, they would advance the timing of their planned investments in order to take advantage of the higher credit during the current period. If there were a permanent change in the investment tax credit, then the desired capital stock would rise, and there would on that account be more investment. But there would not be a bunching of investment.

It is for this reason that temporary changes in the investment tax credit have been suggested as a highly effective countercyclical policy measure. However, this is not a simple policy tool, as expectations about the timing and duration of the credit might conceivably worsen the instability of investment.

Summary on the Neoclassical Theory of Business Fixed Investment

The main conclusions of the theory of business fixed investment as developed here are:

1 Over time, net investment spending is governed by the discrepancy between actual and desired capital.

2 Desired capital depends on the rental (user) cost of capital and the expected level of output. Capital demand rises with expected output and the investment tax credit, and declines with an increase in *real* interest rates.

3 Monetary and fiscal policies exert effects on investment via the desired capital stock, although the short-run impact is likely to be minor. The longer-run effects are larger. The lags with which these investment effects occur are important to bear in mind in shaping stabilization policy.

4 Investment theory, like consumption theory, emphasizes the role of expected or permanent income or output as a determinant of capital demand.

8-2 BUSINESS FIXED INVESTMENT: ALTERNATIVE APPROACHES AND EMPIRICAL RESULTS

In this section we briefly discuss the way a firm typically approaches its investment decisions, and also describe the standard *accelerator theory of investment*. Then we go on to examine the empirical evidence on investment.

The Business Investment Decision: The View from the Trenches

Business people making investment decisions typically use *discounted cash flow analysis*. The principles of discounting are described in the Appendix to this chapter. Consider a business person deciding whether to build and equip a new factory. The first step is to figure out how much it will cost to get the factory into working order, and how much revenue the factory will bring in each year after it starts operation.

For simplicity we consider a very short-lived project, one that costs $100 in the first year to set up and that then generates $50 in revenue (after paying for labour and raw materials) in the second year and a further $80 in the third year. By the end of the third year the factory has disintegrated.

The manager wants to know whether to undertake such a project. Discounted cash flow analysis says that the revenues received in later years should be *discounted* to the present in order to calculate their present value. As the Appendix on discounting shows, if the interest rate is 10 percent, $110 a year from now is worth the same as $100 now. Why? Because if $100 were lent out today at 10 percent, a year from now the lender would end up with $110. Thus to calculate the value of the investment project, the business person calculates its present discounted value at the interest rate at which the business can borrow. If the present value is positive, then the project is undertaken.

Suppose that the relevant interest rate is 15 percent.[14] The calculation of the present discounted value of the investment project is shown in Table 8-3. The $50 received in year 2 is worth only $43.50 today: $1 a year from now is worth $1/1.15 = 0.87 today, and so $50 a year from now is worth $43.50. The present value of the $80 received in year 3 is calculated similarly. The table shows that the present value of the net revenue received from the project is positive ($3.98) and thus that the firm should undertake the project.

TABLE 8-3   DISCOUNTED CASH FLOW ANALYSIS
            AND PRESENT VALUE, $

	Year 1	Year 2	Year 3	Present discounted value
Cash or revenue	−100	+50	+80	
Present value of 1 dollar	1	1/1.15 = 0.870	(1/1.15²) = 0.756	
Present value of costs or revenue	−100	50 × 0.870 = 43.50	80 × 0.756 = 60.48	(−100 + 43.50 + 60.48) = 3.98

Note that if the interest rate had been much higher, say 18 percent, the decision would have been *not* to undertake the investment decision. We thus see how the interest rate affects the investment decision of the typical firm. The higher the interest rate, the less likely the firm will be to undertake any given investment project.

Each firm has at any time an array of possible investment projects, and estimates of the costs and the revenues from those projects. Depending on the level of the interest rate, it will want to undertake some of the projects and not undertake others. Taking all firms in the economy together and adding their investment demands, we obtain the total demand for investment in the economy at each interest rate.

This approach to the investment decision, which, of course, can be applied to investment projects of any duration and complexity, seems far from the description of Section 8-1 in terms of a desired capital stock and rate of adjustment.

Actually, the two approaches are quite consistent. First, we should think of the desired capital stock as being the stock of capital that will be in place when the firms have their factories and new equipment on-line. Second, the adjustment speed tells us how rapidly firms on average succeed in installing that capital.

We started with formulation in terms of the desired capital stock because the framework provides a very clear way of including the different factors that affect investment. For instance, it is easy to see how expectations of future output and taxes affect investment.

But because the two approaches are consistent, the same factors could be included using discounted cash flow analysis. The effects of expectations of future output can be analysed using the discounted cash flow approach by asking what determines the firms' projections of their future revenues (corresponding to the $50 in year 2 and $80 in year 3 in the example above); expected demand for their goods and their output must be relevant. Similarly, taxes can be embodied by analysing how taxes affect the amount of revenue the firm has left after taxes in each future year; the investment tax credit reduces the amount the firm has to lay out in the early years when it is actually building the project — because the government provides a refund of part of the cost of the project through taxes.

Finally, the firm makes decisions about the speed of adjustment by considering the cash flows associated with building the project at different speeds. If the project can be built more rapidly, the firm will decide on the speed with which it wants the project brought on-line by considering the present discounted costs and revenues associated with speeding it up.

The Accelerator Model of Investment

The *accelerator model of investment* asserts that the rate of investment is proportional to the *change* in the economy's output. To derive the accelerator model of investment, assume that there is complete adjustment of the capital stock to its desired level within one period (that is, that $\lambda = 1$), so that $K = K^*$; that there is no depreciation, so that $d = 0$; and that the desired capital-output ratio is a constant, independent of the rental cost of capital:

$$K^* = vY \tag{9}$$

In Equation (9), v is a constant equal to the desired capital-to-output ratio. Substituting Equation (9) into Equation (8), setting $\lambda = 1$, and noting that $K_{-1} = K^*_{-1}$, we obtain

$$I = v(Y - Y_{-1}) \tag{10}$$

which is precisely the accelerator model of investment.

The accelerator model creates the potential for investment spending to fluctuate a good deal. If investment spending is proportional to the *change* in GNP, then when the economy is in a recovery, investment spending is positive, and when the economy is in a recession, investment will be negative.[15] Thus the accelerator model predicts that investment will fluctuate considerably, as Figure 8-1 shows it does.

Empirical Results

We now examine how the investment models we have developed, particularly the neoclassical model summarized in Equation (8), perform empirically.

To use Equation (8), it is necessary to substitute some specific equation for K^*, the desired capital stock. Frequently the Cobb-Douglas form is chosen. Using Equation (3) in Equation (8) yields a (net) investment function of the form

$$I = \lambda\left(\frac{\gamma Y}{rc} - K_{-1}\right) \tag{11}$$

The rental cost of capital, rc in Equation (11), is as in Equation (5), but adjusted for taxes.

Early empirical evidence, in particular that of Dale Jorgenson and his associates,[16] showed that an investment function including the variables in Equation (11) provided a reasonable explanation of the behaviour of business fixed investment. However, the form shown in Equation (11) could be improved upon by allowing more scope for investment to respond slowly to changes in output. The empirical evidence suggests that the adjustment of investment to output takes the bell-shaped form in Figure 8-5. The major impact of a change in output on actual investment occurs with a 2-period (year) lag. The impact in the first year is less than the impact 2 years later.

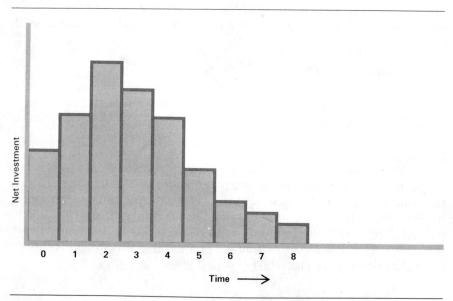

FIGURE 8-5   EFFECTS OF AN INCREASE IN OUTPUT IN PERIOD ZERO ON NET INVESTMENT IN SUBSEQUENT PERIODS (Years)

There are two, not mutually exclusive, explanations for the behaviour shown in Figure 8-5, corresponding to the two sources of dynamic behaviour in Equation (8) that we discussed above. The first possibility is that the lag pattern of Figure 8-5 reflects the way in which expectations about future output, and thus the long-run desired capital stock, are formed. In that view, only a sustained increase in output will persuade firms that the capital stock should be increased in the long run. Figure 8-5 would then imply that it takes about 2 years for changes in the variables that determine the desired capital stock to have major impact on expectations.

The second explanation relies less on expectations and more on the physical delays in the investment process. That interpretation would be that Figure 8-5 reflects the long time it takes for a change in the desired capital stock to be translated into investment spending. In industries in which investment can be undertaken quickly, there may be some response within a year. In other industries there may be long lags between the time machinery is ordered and the time it is ready to be delivered. In the economy as a whole, the maximum impact on investment of a change in the desired capital stock happens only 2 years after the change in the desired stock.

For many purposes, it does not matter which explanations of the form of Figure 8-5 is correct, and it is difficult to tell the explanations apart empirically. It is undoubtedly true that both explanations are relevant. The important point is that lags in the determination of the level of business fixed investment are long.

The Accelerator Model Again

Subsequent empirical research has suggested that the accelerator model of Equation (10), somewhat expanded, does about as good a job at explaining investment behaviour as the neoclassical model.[17] The accelerator model is expanded in empirical work to make the rate of investment depend not only on the change in income this period, but also on the change in income in earlier periods. In empirical applications, this simple accelerator model differs therefore from the neoclassical model mainly in that it omits the cost of capital.

At least on evidence through 1979, it seems that the cost of capital empirically does not much affect investment and that accordingly the simple accelerator model does as well as the neoclassical model at explaining investment. Events since 1979 should, though, provide a good test of whether the cost of capital affects investment. Real interest rates and the rental cost of capital were extremely high in 1981 and 1982, and the rate of investment fell sharply. Future empirical work is thus quite likely to confirm the importance of the rental cost of capital, as well as the level of output, in determining investment spending. Certainly, theory suggests that the rental cost should play an important role in affecting investment.

We now discuss some other aspects of investment behaviour.

Sales and Profits as Determinants of Investment

Some studies of investment find either the level of sales or total profits to be factors explaining the level of investment. The level of sales could be interpreted as affecting expectations of future output and thus affecting the desired capital stock. Note that output and sales differ by the amount of inventory accumulation.

The role of profits can be interpreted similarly. High profits may provide an indication of future demand for the firm's product, and thus of future output. Alternatively, it is often argued that firms prefer to use retained profits to finance investment, rather than borrow. The preference might result from the expense of having to raise outside funds relative to using inside funds. However, in using its retained profits to finance investment rather than borrow, the firm has also to consider the possibility of paying out its profits to the firm's owners, who can invest in other firms. Thus even when using retained earnings, firms have to take into account the level of interest rates as a measure of the returns their owners could receive if the earnings were paid out.

Why Does Investment Fluctuate?

The facts with which we started this chapter show that investment fluctuates much more than consumption spending. The accelerator model provides one explanation of these fluctuations. There are two other basic explanations: the uncertain basis for expectations and the flexibility of the timing of investment.

Uncertain Expectations

Keynes, in the *General Theory*, emphasized the uncertain basis on which investment decisions are made. In his words, " . . . we have to admit that our basis of knowledge for estimating the yield ten years hence of a railway, a copper mine, a textile factory, the goodwill of a patent medicine . . . amounts to little and sometimes to nothing. . . . "[18] Thus, he argued, investment decisions are very much affected by how optimistic or pessimistic the investors feel.

The term "animal spirits" is sometimes used to describe the optimism or pessimism of investors, where "animal spirits" indicates that there may be no good basis for the expectations on which investors base their decisions. If there is no good basis for the expectations, then they could change easily and the volume of investment would also change.

The Timing of Investment Decisions

The second possible reason for fluctuations in investment is that, as noted in Section 8-1, investment decisions can be delayed if the project will take a long time to come on-line. Suppose a firm has an investment project it would like to undertake, but the economy is currently in a recession and the firm is not sure when the recession will end. Further, at the current time it cannot even usefully fully employ all the capital it already has. Such a firm might choose to wait until the prospects for the economy look better — when the recovery gets under way — before deciding to start the investment project.

Either or both of these factors could help account for the substantial fluctuations that are seen in business investment spending. Indeed, they may also explain the success of the accelerator theory of investment, for if firms wait for a recovery to get under way before investing, their investment will be closely related to the change in GNP.

8-3   RESIDENTIAL CONSTRUCTION

We study residential construction separately from other fixed investment both because somewhat different theoretical considerations are relevant[19] and because institutional features of the economy make residential construction especially sensitive to changes in interest rates.

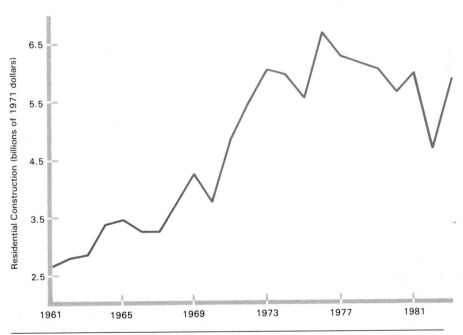

FIGURE 8-6   RESIDENTIAL CONSTRUCTION SPENDING
(*Source*: Department of Finance, *Economic Review*)

Figure 8-6 shows residential construction spending in constant (1971) dollars for the period 1961–1983. Residential construction declines in recession periods such as 1970, 1974–75, 1980, and 1982. There was also a decline in 1966 as a result of the tight monetary policy of that year.

Theory

Residential construction consists of the building of single-family and multi-family dwellings which we shall call housing. Housing is distinguished as an asset by its long life. Consequently, investment in housing in any one year tends to be a very small proportion of the existing stock of housing — about 3 percent. The theory of residential investment starts by considering the demand for the existing stock of housing. Housing is viewed as one among the many assets that a wealth holder can own.

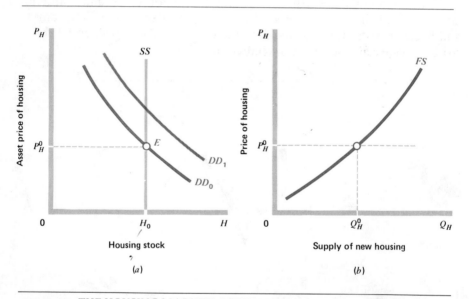

FIGURE 8-7   THE HOUSING MARKET: DETERMINATION OF THE ASSET PRICE OF HOUSING AND THE RATE OF HOUSING INVESTMENT. The supply and demand for the stock of housing determine the asset price of housing (P_H^0) in panel (a). The rate of housing investment (Q_H^0) is determined by the flow supply of housing at price P_H^0, in panel (b).

In Figure 8-7a we show the demand for the stock of housing in the downward-sloping DD_0 curve. The lower the price of housing (P_H), the greater the quantity demanded. The position of the demand curve itself depends on a number of economic variables. First, the greater wealth is, the greater the demand for housing. The more wealthy individuals are, the more housing they desire to own. Thus an increase in wealth would shift the demand curve from DD_0 to DD_1. Second, the demand for housing as an asset depends on the real return available on other assets. If returns on other forms of holding wealth, such as bonds, are low then housing looks like a relatively attractive form in which to hold wealth. The lower the return on other assets, the greater the demand for housing. A reduction in the return on other assets, such as bonds or common stock, shifts the demand curve from DD_0 to DD_1.

Third, the demand for the housing stock depends on the net real return obtained by owning housing. The gross return, before taking costs into account, consists of rent if the housing is rented out, or the implicit return that the homeowner receives by living in the home, plus capital gains arising from increases in the value of the housing. In turn, the costs of owning the housing consist of interest cost, typically the mortgage interest rate, plus any real estate taxes, and depreciation. These costs are deducted from the gross return and, after tax adjustments, constitute the net return. An increase in the net return on housing, caused, for example, by a reduction in the mortgage interest rate, makes housing a more attractive form in which to hold wealth and shifts up the demand curve for housing from DD_0 to DD_1

The price of housing is determined by the interaction of this demand with the stock supply of housing. At any time the stock supply is fixed — there is a given stock of housing that cannot be adjusted quickly in response to price changes. The supply curve of the stock of housing is the SS curve of Figure 8-7a. The equilibrium *asset price of housing*, P_H^0, is determined by the intersection of the supply and demand curves. The asset price of housing is the price of a typical house or apartment. At any one time, the market for the stock of housing determines the asset price of housing.

The Rate of Investment

We now consider the determinants of the rate of investment in housing, and for the purpose turn to Figure 8-7b. The curve FS represents the supply of new housing as a function of the price of housing. This curve is the same as the regular supply curve of any industry. The supply curve shows the amount of a good that suppliers want to sell at each price. In this case, the good being supplied is new housing. The position of the FS curve is affected by the costs of factors of production used in the construction industry and by technological factors affecting the cost of building.

The curve FS is sometimes called the flow supply curve, since it represents the *flow* of new housing into the market in a given time period. In contrast, the *stock* supply curve SS represents the total amount of housing in the market at a moment of time.

Given the price of housing established in the asset market, P_H^0, building contractors supply the amount of new housing, Q_H^0, for sale at that price. The higher the asset price, the greater the supply of new housing. Now the supply of new housing is nothing other than gross investment in housing — total additions to the housing stock. Figure 8-7 thus represents our basic theory of the determinants of housing investment.

Any factor affecting the demand for the existing stock of housing will affect the asset price of housing, P_H, and thus the rate of investment in housing. Similarly, any factor shifting the flow supply curve FS will affect the rate of investment. We have already investigated the major factors shifting the DD demand curve for housing, but will briefly repeat that analysis.

Suppose the interest rate — the rate potential homeowners can obtain by investing elsewhere — rises. Then the asset demand for housing falls and the price of housing falls; that, in turn, induces a decline in the rate of production of new housing, or a decline in housing investment. Or suppose that the mortgage interest rate rises: once again there is a fall in the asset price of housing and a reduction in the rate of construction.

Because the existing stock of housing is so large relative to the rate of investment in housing, we can ignore the effects of the current supply of new housing on the price of housing in the short run. However, over time, the new construction shifts the SS curve of the left-hand panel to the right as it increases the housing stock. The long-run equilibrium in the housing industry would be reached, in an economy in which there was no increase in population or wealth over time, when the housing stock was constant. Constancy of the housing stock requires gross investment to be equal to depreciation, or net investment to be equal to zero. The asset price of housing would have to be at the level such that the rate of construction was just equal to the rate of depreciation of the existing stock of housing in long-run equilibrium. If population or income and wealth were growing at a constant rate, the long-run equilibrium would be one in which the rate of construction was just sufficient to cover depreciation and the steadily growing stock demand. In an economy subjected to continual nonsteady changes, that long-run equilibrium is not necessarily ever reached.

Minor qualifications to the basic theoretical structure arise chiefly because new housing cannot be constructed immediately in response to changes in P_H; rather, it takes a short time for that response to occur. Thus, the supply of new housing responds, not to the actual price of housing today, but to the price expected to prevail when the construction is completed. However, the lags are quite short; it takes less than a year to build a typical house. Another qualification stems from that same construction delay. Since builders have to incur expenses before they sell their output, they need financing over the construction period, and hence the position of the flow supply curve is affected by the interest rate.

Monetary Policy and Residential Construction

Monetary policy has powerful effects on the housing market. Most of the loans obtained to finance new construction are mortgages provided by financial institutions, particularly life insurance companies, trust companies, mortgage loan companies, and chartered banks. When interest rates rise, the supply of mortgage funds is affected in two ways. First, the interest cost to financial institutions of attracting deposits rises as the return on alternative investments increases. Second, the proportion of their assets channelled into mortgages falls as the yields on other securities rise.

TABLE 8-4   MONTHLY PAYMENTS ON MORTGAGES

Interest rate	5%	10%	15%
Monthly payment	$292	$454	$640

Note: The assumed mortgage is a loan for $50,000, paid back over 25 years, with equal monthly payments for those 25 years.

The demand for housing is sensitive to interest rates, and the reason for this can be seen in Table 8-4. It shows the monthly payment that has to be made to repay a $50,000 mortgage with a 25 year amortization period at various interest rates. The monthly payment approximately doubles when the interest rate doubles. Thus an essential component of the cost of owning a house rises almost proportionately with the interest rate. It is therefore not surprising that the demand for housing is very sensitive to the interest rate.

Homeowners are affected not only by real interest rates, but also by nominal rates. The reason has to do with the form of the mortgage. Normally the borrower pays a fixed amount each month over the amortization period of the mortgage. If the interest rate rises only because the expected rate of inflation has risen, and thus the real rate is constant, the payments that have to be made *today* by a borrower go up even though the inflation has not yet happened. Thus the real payments made today by a borrower rise when the *nominal* interest rate rises, even if the real rate does not rise.[20]

8-4   INVENTORY INVESTMENT

Inventories consist of raw materials, goods in the process of production, and completed goods held by firms in anticipation of their sale. The ratio of inventories to monthly shipments in Canadian manufacturing has been in the range of 1.5 to 2.5 over the past 30 years.

The inventories of interest to us are those held to meet future demands for goods. Firms hold such inventories because goods cannot be instantly manufactured or obtained from the manufacturer to meet demand. Some inventories are held as an unavoidable part of the production process; there is an inventory of meat and sawdust inside the sausage machine during the manufacture of sausage, for example. Inventories are also held because it is less costly for a firm to order goods less frequently in large quantities than to order small quantities frequently, just as the average household finds it useful to keep several days' supplies on hand in the house so as not to have to visit the supermarket daily.

Firms have a desired ratio of inventories to final sales that depends on economic variables. The smaller the cost of ordering new goods and the greater the speed with which such goods arrive, the smaller the inventory–sales ratio. The more uncertainty about the demand for the firm's goods, given the expected level of sales, the higher the inventory–sales ratio. The inventory–sales ratio may also depend on the level of sales, with the ratio falling with sales because there is relatively less uncertainty about sales as sales increase. Finally, there is the interest rate. Since firms carry inventories over time, they must tie up money to buy and hold them. There is an interest cost involved in such inventory holding, and the desired inventory–sales ratio should be expected to fall with increases in the interest rate. However, such a link has been difficult to establish empirically.

Anticipated versus Unanticipated Inventory Investment

The most interesting aspect of inventory investment lies in the distinction between anticipated (desired) and unanticipated (undesired) investment. Inventory investment could be high in two circumstances. First, if sales are unexpectedly low, firms would find unsold inventories accumulating on their shelves; that constitutes unanticipated inventory investment. This is the type of inventory investment discussed in Chapter 3. Second, inventory investment could be high because firms plan to restore depleted inventories. The two circumstances obviously have very different implications for the behaviour of aggregate demand. Unanticipated inventory investment is a result of unexpectedly low aggregate demand. On the other hand, planned inventory investment can be a response to recent, unexpectedly high aggregate demand. That is, rapid accumulation of inventories could be associated with either rapidly declining aggregate demand or rapidly increasing aggregate demand.

Inventories in the Business Cycle

Inventory investment fluctuates substantially in the business cycle — proportionately more than any other component of aggregate demand, as shown in Figure 8-1. Inventory behaviour over the business cycle is well illustrated in the 1981–1982 recession. In Figure 8-8, we show sales by

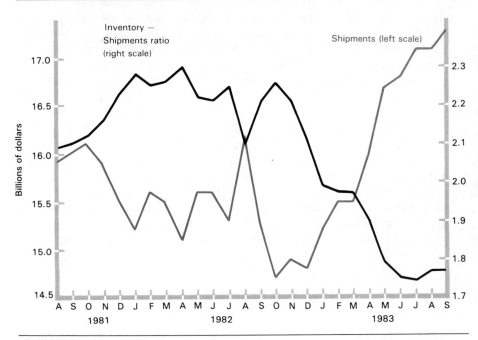

FIGURE 8-8   MANUFACTURING SHIPMENTS AND INVENTORY — SHIPMENTS
RATIO
(*Source*: Statistics Canada, 11-003, 11-206)

Canadian manufacturing industries as measured by shipments and the
ratio of inventories to shipments. As we move into the recession in the last
quarter of 1981, sales begin to decline. Initially, however, there is relatively little adjustment in production, so there is an *unintended* buildup of
inventories and the inventory–sales ratio increases. As the recession
proceeds, production is cut back and the inventory–sales ratio stops rising.
As demand picks up again at the beginning of 1983, increases in production lag behind, allowing inventories to decline. Thus the inventory–sales
ratio decreases as the economy moves out of the recession.

Note that this behaviour of inventories reflects the adjustment mechanism for output that we discussed in Chapter 3. When there is a fall in
aggregate demand, firms unanticipatedly accumulate inventories. They
cut back production in order to get output back in line with demand. As
we noted in the footnotes in Chapter 3, though, in the process of reducing
production to cut back inventories, firms may cause a larger reduction in
GNP for a while than would have happened had inventories not been
unintentionally accumulated. This is known as the *inventory cycle*.

To understand the inventory cycle, consider the case of a hypothetical automobile dealer who sells, say, thirty cars per month, and holds an average of 1 month's sales, namely thirty cars, in inventory. As long as sales stay steady at thirty cars per month, the dealer will be ordering thirty cars per month from the factory. Now suppose sales drop to twenty-five cars per month, and it takes the dealer 2 months to respond to the change. During those 2 months his or her inventory will have climbed to forty cars. In the future he or she will want an inventory of only twenty-five cars on hand. Thus when the dealer does respond to the fall in demand orders from the factory are cut from thirty to ten in the third month, to get the inventory back to 1 month's sales. After the desired inventory–sales ratio has been restored, the dealer will then order twenty-five cars per month from the factory. We see in this extreme case how the drop in demand of five cars, instead of leading to a simple drop in car output of five cars per month, causes a drop in output of twenty cars in 1 month, followed by the longer-run drop in output of five cars per month.

8-5   COMPARISON OF THE MODELS

We have presented several different models to explain the different categories of investment behaviour in this chapter. Nonetheless, there is a basic common element in the models, the interaction of the demand for the stock of capital with investment. In each case we started by examining the determinants of the desired stock — capital or housing. The discussion of inventory investment started by examining the determinants of the desired inventory–sales ratio. Then, in each case, we went on to analyse or describe the determinants of the rate per year of that type of investment.

We come now to the question of why there is a difference between the theoretical models used to explain the level of business fixed investment and residential investment. The fundamental difference arises from the degree of standardization of the capital and the associated question of the existence of a good market for the used capital goods. Much of business fixed investment is in capital that is specifically designed for a given firm and is not of much use to other firms. It is, accordingly, difficult to establish a market price for the stock of that type of capital, and the theory used in discussing residential construction would be difficult to apply in that case. Although housing too varies a good deal, it is, nonetheless, possible to talk of a price of housing. Further, used housing is a very good substitute for new housing, whereas that is less often true for many capital goods.[21] If we disaggregated business fixed investment further than we have, we might well find that the model used to study housing investment is readily applicable for certain categories of business fixed investment, for which the capital good in question is relatively standard and has a good secondhand market.

8-6 SUMMARY

1 Investment constitutes less than 20 percent of aggregate demand, but fluctuations in investment account for a large share of business cycle movements in GNP. We analyse investment in three categories: business fixed investment, residential construction, and inventory investment.

2 Investment is spending that adds to the capital stock.

3 The neoclassical theory of business fixed investment sees the rate of investment being determined by the speed with which firms adjust their capital stocks toward their desired levels. The desired capital stock is larger the more output the firm expects to produce, and the smaller is the rental or user cost of capital. Since investment is undertaken for *future* production, it is expected future (permanent) output that determines the desired capital stock.

4 The real interest rate is the nominal (stated) interest rate minus the inflation rate.

5 The rental cost of capital is higher, the higher the real interest rate and the higher the rate of depreciation of capital. Taxes also affect the rental cost of capital, in particular through the investment tax credit. The investment tax credit is, in effect, a government subsidy for investment.

6 In practice, firms decide how much to invest using discounted cash flow analysis. This analysis gives answers that are consistent with those of the neoclassical approach.

7 The accelerator model of investment is a special case of the gradual adjustment model of investment. It predicts that investment demand is proportional to the *change* in GNP.

8 Empirical results show that business fixed investment responds with long lags to changes in output. The accelerator model, which does not take into account changes in the rental cost of capital, does almost as good a job of explaining investment as the more sophisticated neoclassical model.

9 The theory of housing investment starts from the demand for the *stock* of housing, affected by wealth, the interest rates available on alternative investments, and the mortgage rate. The latter is the cost

of borrowing to buy a house. Increases in wealth increase the stock demand for housing; increases in either the interest rate on alternative assets or the mortgage rate reduce the stock demand. The price of housing is determined by the interaction of the stock demand and the given stock supply of housing available at any given time.

10   The rate of housing investment is determined by the rate at which builders supply housing at the going price.

11   Housing investment is affected by monetary policy because housing demand is sensitive to the interest rate (real and nominal), and also because it affects the supply of mortgage funds.

12   Inventory investment fluctuates proportionately more than any other class of investment. Firms have a desired inventory-to-sales ratio. The actual ratio may get out of line if sales are unexpectedly high or low, and then firms change their production levels to adjust inventories. For instance, when aggregate demand falls at the beginning of a recession, inventories build up. Then when firms cut back production, output falls even more than did aggregate demand. This is the inventory cycle.

13   We now summarize the common elements of the different models. First, aggregate investment is the sum of the different types of investment spending. Thus any variable that affects any of the categories of investment analysed also affects aggregate investment. Second, monetary and fiscal policy both affect investment, particularly business fixed investment and housing investment. The effects take place through changes in the real (and nominal in the case of housing) interest rates and through tax incentives for investment. Third, there are substantial lags in the adjustment of investment spending to changes in output and other determinants of investment. This is true particularly for business fixed investment and inventory investment. Such lags are likely to increase fluctuations in GNP.

KEY TERMS

Business fixed investment
Residential construction
Inventory investment
Desired capital stock
Marginal product of capital
Rental (user) cost of capital
Cobb-Douglas production function

Real interest rate
Gradual adjustment hypothesis
Discounted cash flow analysis
Accelerator model of investment
Inventory cycle
Present discounted value

PROBLEMS

1 We have seen in Chapters 7 and 8 that *permanent* income and output, rather than current income and output, determine consumption and investment.
   (a) How does this affect the *IS-LM* model built in Chapter 4? (Refer to Figure 7-4.)
   (b) What are the policy implications of the use of the "permanent" measures?

2 In Chapter 4 it was assumed that investment rises during periods of low interest rates. That, however, was not the case during the 1930s, when investment and interest rates were both very low. Explain how this can occur. What would have been appropriate fiscal policy in such a case?

3 According to the description of business fixed investment in this chapter, how would you expect a firm's investment decisions to be affected by a sudden increase in demand for its product? What factors would determine the speed of its reaction?

4 It is often suggested that investment spending is dominated by "animal spirits" — the optimism or pessimism of investors. Is this argument at all consistent with the analysis of Sections 8-1 and 8-2?

5 Here are the cash flows for an investment project:

Year 1	Year 2	Year 3
− 200	100	120

Should this firm undertake the project:
   (a) If the interest rate is 5 percent?
   (b) If the interest rate is 10 percent?

6 Is there any relation between the neoclassical theory of investment and the way firms make their investment decisions in practice?

7 Explain how the two panels of Figure 8-7 react together over time. What would happen if the demand for housing stock (*DD*) shifts up and to the right over time?

8 Trace carefully the step-by-step effects on the housing market (using Figure 8-7) of an increase in interest rates. Explain each shift and its long-run and short-run effects.

9 In the past, restrictive monetary policy seriously hurt the housing industry in an effort to avoid excess aggregate demand. What is the mechanism by which this happened?

10 (a) Explain how final sales and output can differ.
   (b) Point out from Figure 8-8 periods of planned and unplanned inventory investment and decumulation.
   (c) During a period of slow but steady growth, how would you expect final sales and output to be related? Explain. Draw a hypothetical figure like Figure 8-8 for such a period.

11 Suppose that an explicitly temporary tax credit is enacted. The tax credit is at the rate of 10 percent and lasts only 1 year.
   (a) What is the effect of this tax measure on investment in the long run (say, after 4 or 5 years)?
   (b) What is the effect in the current year and the following year?
   (c) How will your answers under (a) and (b) differ if the tax credit is permanent?

*12 For this question use the Cobb-Douglas production function and the corresponding desired capital stock given by Equation (3). Assume that $\gamma = 0.3$, $Y = 2.5$ trillion, and $rc = 0.15$.
   (a) Calculate the desired capital stock K^*
   (b) Now suppose that Y is expected to rise to 3 trillion. What is the corresponding desired capital stock?
   (c) Suppose that the capital stock was at its desired level before the change in income was expected. Suppose further that $\lambda = 0.4$ in the gradual adjustment model of investment. What will the rate of investment be in the first year after expected income changes? In the second year?
   (d) Does your answer in (c) refer to gross or net investment?

---

*APPENDIX: INTEREST RATES, PRESENT VALUES, AND DISCOUNTING

In this Appendix we deal with the relationships among bond coupons, interest rates and yields, and the prices of bonds. In doing so, we shall introduce the very useful concept of present discounted value (PDV).

Section 1

We start with the case of a perpetual bond, or perpetuity. Such bonds have been issued in a number of countries, including the United Kingdom, where they are called Consols. The Consol is a promise by the British government to pay a fixed amount to the holder of the bond every year and forever. Let us denote the promised payment per Consol by Q_c, the coupon.[22]

The yield on a bond is the return per dollar that the holder of the bond receives. The yield on a savings account paying 5 percent interest per year is obviously just 5 percent. Someone paying $25 for a Consol that has a coupon of $2.5 obtains a yield of 10 percent [($2.5/25) × 100%].

The yield on a Consol and its price are related in a simple way. Let us denote the price of the Consol by P_c and the coupon by Q_c. Then, as the above example suggests, the yield i is just

$$i = \frac{Q_c}{P_c} \qquad\qquad (A1)$$

which says that the yield on a perpetuity is the coupon divided by the price. Alternatively, we can switch Equation (A1) around to

$$P_c = \frac{Q_c}{i} \qquad\qquad (A2)$$

which says that price is the coupon divided by the yield. So, given the coupon and the yield, we can derive the price, or given the coupon and the price, we can derive the yield.

None of this is a theory of the determination of the yield or the price of a perpetuity. It merely points out the relationship between price and yield. Our theory of the determination of the yield on bonds is presented in Chapter 4. The interest rate in Chapter 4 corresponds to the yield on bonds, and we tend to talk interchangeably of interest rates and yields.

We shall return to the Consol at the end of this Appendix.

Section 2

Now we move to a short-term bond. Let us consider a bond which was sold by a borrower for $100, on which the borrower promises to pay back $108 after 1 year. This is a 1-year bond. The yield on the bond to the person who bought it for $100 is 8 percent. For every $1 lent, the lender obtains both the $1 principal and 8 cents extra at the end of the year.

Next we ask a slightly different question. How much would a promise to pay $1 at the end of the year be worth? If $108 at the end of the year is worth $100 today, then $1 at the end of the year must be worth $100/108, or 92.6 cents. That is the value today of $1 in 1 year's time. In other words, it is the present discounted value of $1 in 1 year's time. It is the present value because it is what would be paid today for the promise of money in 1 year's time, and it is discounted because the value today is less than the promised payment in a year's time.

Denoting the 1-year yield or interest rate by i, we can write that the present discounted value of a promised payment Q_1, 1 year from now, is

$$PDV = \frac{Q_1}{1+i} \qquad\qquad (A3)$$

Let us return to our 1-year bond and suppose that the day after the original borrower obtained the money, the yield on 1-year bonds rises. How much would anyone now be willing to pay for the promise to receive $108 after 1 year?

The answer must be given by the general formula (A3). That means that the price of the 1-year bond will fall when the interest rate or yield on such bonds rises. Once again, we see that the price of the bond and the yield are inversely related, given the promised payments to be made on the bond.

As before, we can reverse the formula for the price in order to find the yield on the bond, given its price and the promised payment Q_1. Note that the price P is equal to the present discounted value, so that we can write

$$1 + i = \frac{Q_1}{P} \qquad (A4)$$

Section 3

Next we consider a 2-year bond. Such a bond would typically promise to make a payment of interest, which we shall denote Q_1, at the end of the first year, and then a payment of interest and principal (usually the amount borrowed), Q_2, at the end of the second year. Given the yield i on the bond, how do we compute its PDV, which will be equal to its price?

We start by asking first what the bond will be worth 1 year from now. At that stage, it will be a 1-year bond, promising to pay the amount Q_2 in 1 year's time, and yielding i. Its value 1 year from now will accordingly be given by Equation (A3), except that Q_1 in Equation (A3) is replaced by Q_2. Let us denote the value of the bond 1 year from now by PDV_1, and note that

$$PDV_1 = \frac{Q_2}{1 + i} \qquad (A5)$$

To complete computing the PDV of the 2-year bond, we can now treat it as a 1-year bond, which promises to pay Q_1 in interest 1 year from now, and also to pay PDV_1 1 year from now, since it can be sold at that stage for that amount. Hence, the PDV of the bond, equal to its price, is

$$PDV = \frac{Q_1}{1 + i} + \frac{PDV_1}{1 + i} \qquad (A6)$$

or

$$PDV = \frac{Q_1}{1 + i} + \frac{Q_2}{(1 + i)^2} \qquad (A6a)$$

As previously, given the promised payments Q_1 and Q_2, the price of the bond will fall if the yield rises, and vice versa.

It is now less simple to reverse the equation for the price of the bond to find the yield than it was before; that is because from Equation (A6), we obtain a quadratic equation for the yield, which has two solutions.

Section 4

We have now provided the outline of the argument whereby the present discounted value of *any* promised stream of payments for any number of years can be computed. Suppose that a bond, or any other asset, promises to pay amounts $Q_1, Q_2, Q_3, \ldots, Q_n$ in future years, 1, 2, 3, $\ldots, n$ years away. By pursuing the type of argument given in Section 3, it is possible to show that the *PDV* of such a payments stream will be

$$PDV = \frac{Q_1}{1 + i} + \frac{Q_2}{(1 + i)^2} + \frac{Q_3}{(1 + i)^3} + \ldots + \frac{Q_n}{(1 + i)^n} \qquad (A7)$$

As usual, the price of a bond with a specified payments stream will be inversely related to its yield.

Section 5

The formula (A7) is the general formula for calculating the present discounted value of any stream of payments. Indeed, the payments may also be negative. Thus in calculating the *PDV* of an investment project, we expect the first few payments, for example, Q_1 and Q_2, to be negative. Those are the periods in which the firm is spending to build the factory or buy machinery. Then in later years the Q_i become positive as the factory starts generating revenues.

Firms undertaking discounted cash flow analysis are calculating present values using a formula such as (A7).

Section 6

Finally, we return to the Consol. The Consol promises to pay the amount Q_c forever. Applying the formula, we can compute the present value of the Consol by

$$PDV = Q_c \left[\frac{1}{(1 + i)} + \frac{1}{(1 + i)^2} + \frac{1}{(1 + i)^3} + \ldots + \frac{1}{(1 + i)^n} + \ldots \right] \qquad (A8)$$

The contents of the parentheses on the right-hand side are an infinite series, the sum of which can be calculated as $1/i$. Thus,

$$PDV = \frac{Q_c}{i} \qquad (A9)$$

This section casts a slightly different light on the commonsense discussion of Section 1 of this Appendix. Equations (A8) and (A9) show that the Consol's price is equal to the *PDV* of the future coupon payments.

CHAPTER 8: FOOTNOTES

[1] The increase in net exports reflects the depreciation of the Canadian dollar and the greater severity of the recession in Canada as compared with the United States.

[2] Even if the firm finances the investment out of profits it has made in the past — retained earnings — it should still think of the interest rate as the cost of using the

new capital, since it could otherwise have lent out those funds and earned interest on them, or paid them out as dividends to shareholders.

[3]Throughout this discussion, we have implicitly been assuming that the real wage paid to labour is given and does not change as the rental cost of capital changes.

[4]The Cobb-Douglas production function is written in the form

$$Y = N^{1-\gamma}K^{\gamma} \qquad 1 > \gamma > 0$$

where N is the amount of labour used. This production function is particularly popular because it is easy to handle, and also because it appears to fit the facts of economic experience quite well. The coefficient γ appearing in Eq. (3) is the same as the γ of the production function. The reader trained in calculus will want to show that γ is the share of capital in total income.

[5]We draw attention here to a very subtle point: Equation (3) gives the marginal product of capital (MPK) when the *input of labour* is held fixed, while in Figs. 8-2 and 8-3 we work with the MPK when labour is being adjusted so that *output* is kept fixed. The desired capital stock that corresponds to Figs. 8-2 and 8-3 is

$$K^* = \left[\frac{\gamma w}{(1-\gamma)rc} \right]^{1-\gamma} Y \qquad (3a)$$

where w is the real wage.

Equation (3a), like Eq. (3), implies that desired capital is proportional to Y and varies inversely with the rental cost of capital. We use Eq. (3) rather than Eq. (3a) in the text because it is the form that has been used in empirical studies.

[6]The role of permanent income in investment has been emphasized by Robert Eisner. Much of his work is summarized in his book *Factors in Business Investment* (Cambridge, Mass.: Ballinger, 1978).

[7]Why is depreciation considered as a cost? The firm continues using the capital and therefore has to devote expenditures to maintaining the productive efficiency of capital and thus offsetting wear and tear. We are assuming that, per dollar of capital, d dollars per period are required to maintain productive efficiency.

[8]Some loans to firms carry *variable* interest rates, so that the amount of interest the firm has to pay changes over time as the general level of interest rates changes. In these cases the rate i in Equation (6) would be the expected interest rate over the life of the loan.

[9]For tax purposes depreciation is counted as a business expense, but these allowances follow complicated rules and are not generally equal to the depreciation that the capital stock actually undergoes.

[10]Some investment is financed through the sale of equities. Part of the return to equity holders typically takes the form of dividend payments. However, dividends are not treated as a deduction from profits in the calculation of corporate income taxes. Thus the basic argument presented in the case of interest payments, that the corporate income tax does not affect the desired capital stock, would not apply for equity-financed investment.

[11]We should note that the Bank of Canada is able to affect *nominal* interest rates directly by its sales and purchases of bonds. Its ability to control *real* interest rates is more limited.

[12]The gradual adjustment hypothesis is a generalized form of the older *accelerator* model of investment, in which investment is proportional to the change in the level of *GNP*. The accelerator model is examined in Sec. 8-2.

[13]Gross investment, as opposed to net investment described in Eq. (8), includes, in addition, depreciation. Thus, gross investment is $I + dK_{-1}$, where d is again the rate of depreciation.

[14]The interest rate here is nominal, because we are calculating the present value of dollars to be received in the future.

[15]The accelerator is not in practice a complete model of investment, for gross investment spending cannot be negative.

[16]See Dale W. Jorgenson, "Econometric Studies of Investment Behavior: A Survey," *Journal of Economic Literature*, December 1971. For an application of the theory with Canadian data, see G.O. Gaudet, J.D. May, and D.G. McFetridge, "Optimal Capital Accumulation: The Neoclassical Framework in a Canadian Context," *Review of Economics and Statistics*, August 1976.

[17]Peter K. Clark, "Investment in the 1970's: Theory, Performance, and Prediction," *Brookings Papers on Economic Activity*, 1979:1 (Washington, D.C.: The Brookings Institution, 1979).

[18]J.M. Keynes, *The General Theory of Employment, Interest and Money* (New York: Macmillan, 1936), pp. 149–150.

[19]In the concluding section of this chapter, we explain why slightly different theoretical models are used in explaining business fixed investment and residential construction.

[20]How can the real payments rise if the real interest rate stays the same? The explanation is that today's real payments rise, but the real present value of future payments falls: the repayment stream tilts toward the present. For more on this feature, see Franco Modigliani and Donald Lessard (eds.), *New Mortgage Designs for Stable Housing in an Inflationary Environment*, Federal Reserve Bank of Boston, Conference Series #14, 1975.

[21]The two models look very different. However, you may be able to see a way of casting the analysis of the housing market in terms of the theory used in discussing business fixed investment. You can define the desired capital stock of housing as that stock which the economy will eventually reach when the price of housing reaches a constant level. Then the level of investment will be an increasing function of the difference between that stock and the existing stock. Similarly, the model we have used for housing investment can be transformed into a model of business fixed investment. This is the so-called *Tobin's q* theory of investment. See James Tobin, "A General Equilibrium Approach to Monetary Theory," *Journal of Money, Credit and Banking*, February 1969. Modern analysis of investment behaviour frequently uses the q approach. For example, see Lawrence H. Summers, "Taxation and Corporate Investment: A q-Theory Approach," *Brookings Papers on Economic Activity*, 1981: 1. (This paper is not easy reading.)

[22]The *coupon rate* is the coupon divided by the face value of the bond, which is literally the value printed on the face of the bond. Bonds do not necessarily sell for their face value, though customarily the face value is close to the value at which the bonds are sold when they first come on the market.

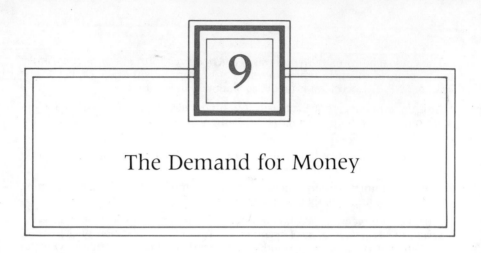

9

The Demand for Money

The assets markets and the goods market receive equal billing in the *IS-LM* model we studied in Chapter 4. In the previous two chapters we concentrated on the goods market, examining the demands for consumption and investment goods. Now we move to the assets markets, starting with the demand for money.

Money is a means of payment or medium of exchange. Since money is used for purchasing goods, individuals are interested in the purchasing power of their money holdings — the value of their cash balances in terms of the goods the cash will buy. In other words, they are concerned with their *real balances* rather than their *nominal* money holdings. What this means in practice is that (1) *real* money demand is unchanged when the price level increases, but *all* real variables, such as the interest rate, real income, and real wealth, remain unchanged; and (2) *nominal* money demand increases in proportion to the increase in the price level, given the constancy of the real variables just specified.[1]

We have a special name for behaviour that is not affected by changes in the price level, all real variables remaining unchanged. An individual is free from *money illusion* if a change in the level of prices, holding all real variables constant, leaves real behaviour, including real money demand, unchanged. By contrast, an individual whose real behaviour is affected by a change in the price level, all real variables remaining unchanged, is said to suffer from money illusion.

We shall see that empirical evidence supports the theoretical argument that the demand for money is a demand for real balances — or that the demand for nominal balances, holding real variables constant, is proportional to the price level.

In Chapter 4, we also assumed that the demand for money increases with the level of real income and decreases with the nominal interest rate. Recall that the interest elasticity of the demand for money is important in determining the effectiveness of fiscal policy. Changes in fiscal variables, such as tax rates or government spending, affect the level of income if the demand for money changes when the interest rate changes — if the demand for money is interest-elastic. If the demand for money does not react at all to changes in the interest rate, increases in government spending totally *crowd out* private spending and leave the level of income unaffected.

The demand for money has been studied very intensively at both the theoretical and empirical levels. There is by now almost total agreement that the demand should, as a theoretical matter, increase as the level of real income rises and decrease as the nominal interest rate rises. Empirical work bears out these two properties of the demand-for-money function.

9-1   COMPONENTS OF THE MONEY STOCK

The money supply definitions currently provided by the Bank of Canada are shown in Table 9-1.[2] The most widely used concept is $M1$ which includes currency and demand deposits. Currency consists of notes and coin in circulation outside the banking system, and demand deposits are chequing accounts at the chartered banks. $M1A$ is a slightly broader measure of the money supply that includes daily interest chequable savings accounts and nonpersonal notice deposits.[3]

TABLE 9-1   COMPONENTS OF THE MONEY STOCK,
            JANUARY 1984
            (millions of dollars, average of Wednesdays)

(1) Currency	$ 11,891
(2) Demand deposits	16,901
$M1 = (1) + (2)$	$ 28,792
(3) Daily interest chequable savings	3,412
(4) Nonpersonal notice deposits	5,541
$M1A = M1 + (3) + (4)$	$ 37,745
(5) Other personal savings deposits	56,521
(6) Personal term deposits	41,409
$M2 = M1A + (5) + (6)$	$135,675
(7) Other nonpersonal term deposits	37,575
(8) Foreign currency deposits*	10,024
$M3 = M2 + (7) + (8)$	$183,274

*Deposits of residents booked in Canada.
Source: Bank of Canada Review

Although $M1A$ includes the major assets that serve as a means of payment, it does not encompass all chequing accounts. For example, it includes only deposits in the chartered banks and it can be argued that chequable deposits in other financial institutions such as trust companies and credit unions should be included. Similarly, there is a question as to whether credit cards should not be regarded as means of making payment. If so, and the argument is certainly compelling, we should probably count the amount that people are allowed to charge by using their credit cards as part of the money stock.

Historically, there have often been changes in the type of assets which can be used as means of payment, and simultaneous disagreements about what constitutes money in those circumstances. When cheques first began to be widely used in England early in the nineteenth century, there was a disagreement over whether demand deposits should be regarded as part of the money stock. Now that point is not disputed. We can expect there to be continuing changes in the financial structure over the years, with consequent changes in the definitions of the various money supply concepts.

Table 9-1 also shows the broader definitions of the money supply, $M2$ and $M3$. $M2$ adds a variety of interest bearing savings accounts to $M1A$. The components of $M2$ that are not part of $M1$ are in general less *liquid* than $M1$ in that they cannot immediatley and conveniently be used for making payments. However, they are assets that are close to being money in the sense that they are available with only a little difficulty for making payments. $M3$ includes all Canadian dollar deposits in chartered banks and foreign currency deposits held by residents.

In summary, there is no unique set of assets which will always constitute the money supply. At present, there are arguments for using a broader definition of the money stock than $M1$ and even arguments for using a less broad definition — should $1,000 bills be included, for example? Further, over the course of time, the particular assets that serve as a medium of exchange, or means of payment, will certainly change further.

9-2   THE FUNCTIONS OF MONEY

Money is so widely used that we rarely step back to think how remarkable a device it is. It is impossible to imagine a modern economy operating without the use of money or something very much like it. In a mythical barter economy in which there is no money, every transaction has to involve an exchange of goods (and/or services) on both sides of the transaction. The examples of the difficulties of barter are endless. The economist wanting a haircut would have to find a barber wanting to listen to a lecture on economics; the peanut farmer wanting a suit would have to find a tailor wanting peanuts; and so on. Without a medium of exchange, modern economies could not operate.

Money, as a medium of exchange, makes it unnecessary for there to be a "double coincidence of wants" in exchanges. By the double coincidence, we have in mind the above examples. The wants of two individuals would have to be identically matched for the exchange to take place. For instance, the person selling peanuts would have to find a buyer whose goods he or she wanted to buy (the suit) while, at the same time, the person selling suits would have to find a buyer whose goods he or she wanted to buy (the peanuts).

There are four traditional functions of money, of which the medium of exchange is the first.[4] The other three are store of value, unit of account, and standard of deferred payment. These stand on a different footing from the medium of exchange function.

A *store of value* is an asset that maintains value over time. Thus, an individual holding a store of value can use that asset to make purchases at a future date. If an asset were not a store of value, then it would not be used as a medium of exchange. Imagine trying to use ice cream as money, in the absence of refrigerators. There would hardly ever be a good reason for anyone to give up goods for money (ice cream) if the money were sure to melt within the next few minutes. And if the seller were unwilling to accept the ice cream in exchange for his or her goods, then the ice cream would not be a medium of exchange. But there are many stores of value other than money — such as bonds, stocks, and houses.

The *unit of account* is the unit in which prices are quoted and books kept. Prices are quoted in dollars and cents, and dollars and cents are the units in which the money stock is measured. Usually, the money unit is also the unit of account, but that is not essential. In the German hyperinflation of 1922–1923, dollars were the unit of account for some firms, whereas the mark was the medium of exchange.

Finally, as a *standard of deferred payment*, money units are used in long-term transactions, such as loans. The amount that has to be paid back in 5 or 10 years is specified in dollars and cents. Dollars and cents are acting as the standard of deferred payment. Once again, though, it is not essential that the standard of deferred payment be the money unit. For example, the final payment of a loan may be related to the behaviour of the price level, rather than being fixed in dollars and cents. This is known as an indexed loan.

The last two of the four functions of money are, accordingly, functions which money *usually* performs, but not functions that it *necessarily* performs. The store of value function is one that many assets perform.

There are fascinating descriptions of different types of money that have existed in the past that we do not have room to review here,[5] but there is one final point we want to emphasize. *Money is whatever is generally accepted in exchange.* However magnificently a piece of paper may be engraved, it will not be money if it is not accepted in payment. And however unusual the material of which it is made, anything that is generally accepted in payment is money. The only reason money is accepted in payment is that the recipient believes that it can be spent at a later time. There is thus an inherent circularity in the acceptance of money. Money is accepted in payment because it is believed that it will also be accepted in payment by others.

9-3   THE DEMAND FOR MONEY: THEORY

In this section we review the three major motives underlying the demand for money. In doing so, we will concentrate on the effects of changes in income and changes in the interest rate on money demand.

The three theories we are about to review correspond to Keynes's famous three motives for holding money[6]: (1) the transactions motive, which is the demand for money arising from the use of money in making regular payments; (2) the precautionary motive, which is the demand for money to meet unforeseen contingencies; and (3) the speculative motive, which arises from the uncertainties about the money value of other assets that an individual can hold. In discussing the transactions and precautionary motives, we are mainly discussing $M1$, whereas the speculative motive refers more to $M2$, as we shall see.

Although we examine the demand for money by looking at the three motives for holding it, we cannot separate out a particular person's money holdings, say, $500, into three neat piles of, say, $200, $200, and $100, that are being held from each motive. Money being held to satisfy one motive is always available for another use. The person holding unusually large balances for speculative reasons also has those balances available to meet an unexpected emergency, so that they serve too as precautionary balances. All three motives influence an individual's holdings of money, and as we shall see, each leads to the prediction that the demand for money should fall as the interest rate on other assets increases.

This final point is worth emphasizing. Money ($M1$) generally earns no interest (currency and some chequable deposits) or less interest than other assets. Anyone holding money is giving up interest that could be earned by holding some other asset, such as a savings deposit or a bond. The higher the interest loss from holding a dollar of money, the less money we expect the individual to hold. The demand for money will thus be higher, the greater the interest rate on money itself if interest is paid on demand deposits, and will be lower, the higher the interest rate on alternative assets. In practice, we can measure the cost of holding money as the difference between the interest rate paid on money (perhaps zero) and the interest rate paid on the most nearly comparable other asset, such as a savings deposit or, for corporations, a certificate of deposit or commercial paper.

For most of the remainder of the chapter, we shall write as if money earns no interest. This is true of much of the $M1$ stock. Further, it is easy to modify the analysis to take account of the payment of interest on other parts of $M1$. All that is necessary is to substitute the difference between the interest rate on the alternative asset and the interest rate on money in places we mention only the interest rate on the alternative asset.

The Transactions Demand

The transactions demand for money arises from the use of money in making regular payment for goods and services. In the course of each month, an individual makes a variety of payments for such items as rent or mortgage, groceries, the newspaper, and other purchases. In this section we examine how much money an individual would hold for such purchases.

In analysing the transactions demand, we are concerned with a tradeoff between the amount of interest an individual forgoes by holding money and the costs and inconveniences of holding a small amount of money. To make the problem concrete, consider a person who is paid, say, $1,200 each month. Assume that he or she spends the $1,200 evenly over the course of the month, at the rate of $40 per day. Now at one extreme, the individual could simply leave the $1,200 in cash (whether currency or demand deposits) and spend it at the rate of $40 per day. Alternatively, on the first day of the month the individual could take his or her $40 to spend that day and put the remaining $1,160 in a daily-interest savings account. Then every morning the person could go to the bank to withdraw that day's $40 from the savings account. By the end of the month he or she would have earned interest on the money that was held each day in the savings account. This would be the *benefit* of keeping money holdings down as low as $40 at the beginning of each day. The *cost* of keeping money holdings down is simply the cost and inconvenience of the trips to the bank to withdraw the daily $40. To decide on how much money to hold for transactions purposes, the individual has to weigh the costs of holding small balances against the interest advantage of doing so.

We now study the tradeoff in more detail and derive a formula for the demand for money. Suppose the nominal monthly income[7] of the individual is Y_N. We make the simplifying assumption that Y_N is paid to his or her savings account, rather than a chequing account, each month. The money is spent at a steady rate over the course of the month. To spend it, the individual has to get it out of the savings account and into cash, which may be currency or a chequing account. If left in the savings account, the deposit earns interest at a rate of i per month. It earns zero interest as cash. The cost to the individual of making a transfer between cash and the savings account (which we henceforth call bonds for convenience) is tc. That cost may be the individual's time, or it may be a cost that he or she explicitly pays someone else to make the transfer. For convenience we refer to it as a broker's fee.

The Inventory Approach

The approach we are describing to the demand for money is known as the *inventory-theoretic approach.*[8] Although we are describing an individual's transactions demand, similar considerations apply for firms deciding how to manage their money. You should think of the inventory-theoretic approach applying equally well, with small changes in terminology and assumptions, to firms and households.

The individual has to decide how many transactions to make between bonds and cash each month. If he or she makes just one transaction, transferring Y_N into cash at the beginning of the month, the cash balance over the course of the month will be as shown in Figure 9-1a. It starts at Y_N, is spent evenly over the month, and is down to zero by the end of the month, at which time a new payment is received by the individual and transferred into his or her chequing account. If the individual makes two withdrawals from the savings account, he or she first transfers $Y_N/2$ into cash at the beginning of the month, resulting in a cash balance that is run down to zero in the middle of the month, at which time another $Y_N/2$ is transferred into cash and spent evenly over the rest of the month.[9] Figure 9-1b shows the individual's cash holdings in that case.

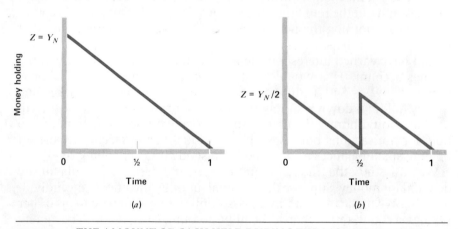

FIGURE 9-1   THE AMOUNT OF CASH HELD DURING THE MONTH RELATED TO THE NUMBER OF WITHDRAWALS. Panel (*a*) shows the pattern of money holding during the month when the individual makes just one transaction from the savings account to cash during the month. At the beginning of the month he transfers the entire amount to be spent, Y_N, into cash, and then spends it evenly over the month. Panel (*b*) shows the pattern of money holding when there are two transactions, one at the beginning of the month and one in the middle of the month. In panel (*a*), average cash holdings for the month are $Y_N/2$; in panel (*b*) they are $Y_N/4$.

We shall denote the size of a cash withdrawal from the bond portfolio (savings account) by Z and the number of withdrawals from the bond portfolio by n. Thus, n is the number of times the individual adds to the cash balance during the month. If he or she makes n equal-sized withdrawals during the month, transferring funds from the savings account to his or her chequing account, then the size of each transfer is Y_N/n, since a total of Y_N has to be transferred from the savings account into cash. For example, if Y_N is $1,200, and n, the number of transactions, is 3, then Z, the amount transferred to cash each time, is $400. Accordingly, we can write

$$nZ = Y_N \qquad (1)$$

Suppose that the amount Z is transferred from bonds to cash at each withdrawal. What then is the *average* cash balance over the course of the month? We want to find the size of the average cash balance in order to measure the interest that is lost as a result of holding cash; if that amount were not held as cash, it could be held as interest-earning bonds. In Figure 9-1a, the average cash balance held during the month is $Y_N/2 = Z/2$, since the cash balance starts at Y_N and runs down in a straight line to zero.[10] In the case of Figure 9-1b, the average cash balance for the first half of the month is $Y_N/4 = Z/2$, and the average cash balance for the second half of the month is also $Z/2$. Thus, the average cash balance for the entire month is $Y_N/4 = Z/2$. Similarly, if three withdrawals were made, the average cash balance would be $Y_N/6 = Z/2$. In general, the average cash balance is $Z/2$, as you might want to confirm by drawing diagrams similar to Figure 9-1 for $n = 3$ or other values of n.

The interest cost of holding money is the interest rate times the average cash balance, or $iZ/2$. From Equation (1), that means the total interest cost is $iY_N/2n$. The other component of the cost of managing the portfolio is the brokerage cost, or the cost in terms of the individual's time and inconvenience in managing his money. That cost is just the number of withdrawals made, n, times the cost of each withdrawal, tc, and is thus equal to $n \cdot tc$. The total cost of managing the portfolio is the interest cost plus the total brokerage cost:

$$\text{Total cost} = n \cdot tc + \frac{iY_N}{2n} \qquad (2)$$

Equation (2) shows formally that the brokerage cost $n \cdot tc$ increases as the number of withdrawals (transactions between bonds and money) rises, and that the interest cost decreases as the number of withdrawals increases. It thus emphasizes the tradeoff faced in managing money, and suggests that there is an optimal number of withdrawals the individual should make to minimize the total cost of holding money to meet transactions requirements for buying goods.

To derive that optimal point, we want to find the point at which the benefit of carrying out another withdrawal is less than, or just equal to, the cost of making another transaction between bonds and money. If the benefit of making another transaction were greater than the cost, then another withdrawal should be made, and the original point could not have been optimal. The cost of making another transaction is always equal to *tc*. In Figure 9-2, we show the costs of making a further transaction by the marginal cost curve *MC*, which is horizontal at the level *tc*. The financial benefit from making another transaction is represented by the *MB* (marginal benefit) curve in Figure 9-2, which represents the interest *saved* by making another withdrawal and thus having a smaller cash balance on average during the month.

The more transactions between money and bonds an individual makes, the lower is the total interest cost. But the reduction of the interest cost that is obtained by making more transactions falls off rapidly as the number of withdrawals increases. There is a substantial saving in interest costs by making two withdrawals rather than one, but very little saving in interest costs by making thirty-one transactions rather than thirty.

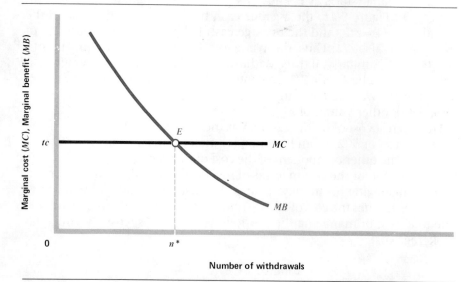

FIGURE 9-2   OPTIMAL CASH MANAGEMENT DETERMINING THE OPTIMAL NUMBER OF WITHDRAWALS. The marginal cost of making another transaction is the constant amount, *tc*, as shown by the *MC* curve. The marginal benefit of making another transaction is the amount of interest saved by holding smaller money balances. The marginal benefit decreases as the number of withdrawals from the savings account increases. Point *E* is the point at which the cost of managing money holdings is minimized. Corresponding to point *E* is n^*, the optimal number of transactions to make between the savings account and money.

This suggests that the marginal benefit of making more withdrawals decreases as the number of withdrawals becomes large. The *MB* curve in Figure 9-2 is, accordingly, downward-sloping.[11]

In Figure 9-2, the optimal number of transactions is given by n^*, the number at which the marginal benefit in terms of interest saved is equal to the marginal cost of making a transaction. Given the number of transactions and the individual's income, we also know the average cash balance M, using the relationship between average money holdings and the size of each transfer which we derived earlier:

$$M = \frac{Z}{2} = \frac{Y_N}{2n} \tag{3}$$

Properties of Money Demand

From Figure 9-2 we can see two important results. First, suppose the brokerage cost rises. That shifts the *MC* curve up, decreases the number of withdrawals n, and therefore [from Equation (3), where M is inversely related to n] *increases* the average holding of money. Second, an increase in the interest rate shifts up the *MB* curve, therefore increases n, and thus [again, from Equation (3)] reduces the holding of money: when the interest rate is higher, the individual is willing to make more trips to the bank to earn the higher interest now available. Figure 9-2 thus shows one of the key results we wanted to establish — that the demand for money is inversely related to the interest rate.

In the case of an increase in income, Figure 9-2 is unfortunately less useful. An increase in income shifts up the *MB* curve and increases the number of transactions. But from Equation (3), we see that an increase in the number of transactions accompanying an increase in income does not necessarily imply that the demand for money rises, since it seems that n could increase proportionately more than Y_N. However, more complete algebraic analysis of the individual's optimal behaviour will show that the demand for money in this model rises when income rises.

The famous *square-root formula* for money demand, developed by William Baumol and James Tobin,[12] both makes the results of the graphical analysis of Figure 9-2 more precise and resolves the ambiguity about the effects of income on the demand for money. The formula gives the demand for money that is obtained as a result of minimizing the total costs in Equation (2) with respect to the number of withdrawals and then using Equation (3) to derive the cash balance.[13] The formula is

$$M^* = \sqrt{\frac{tc \cdot Y_N}{2i}} \tag{4}$$

Equation (4) shows that the transactions demand for money increases with the brokerage fee, or the cost of transacting, and with the level of income. The demand for money decreases with the interest rate.

Money Demand Elasticities

Equation (4) also shows that an increase in income raises the demand for money proportionately less than the increase in income itself. To put the same point somewhat differently, the ratio of income to money, Y_N/M, rises with the level of income. A person with a higher level of income than another holds proportionately less money than the other person. This point is sometimes put in different words by saying that there are *economies of scale* in cash management.

Yet another way of saying the same thing is that the income elasticity of the demand for money is less than 1 [it is equal to ½ in Equation (4)]. The income elasticity measures the percentage change in the demand for money due to a 1 percent change in income.[14]

Similarly, Equation (4) implies that the elasticity of the demand for money with respect to the brokerage fee is ½, and the elasticity with respect to the interest rate is $-$ ½.

What accounts for the fact that people can somehow manage with less cash per dollar of spending as income increases? The reason is that cash management is more effective at high levels of income because the average cost per dollar of transaction is lower with large-size transactions. In turn, the lower average cost of transactions results from the fixed brokerage fee per transaction; it costs as much to transfer $10 as $10 million, so that the average cost per dollar transferred is lower for large transfers.

However, in the case of households, we should recognize that the "brokerage cost" *tc*, the cost of making withdrawals from a savings account, is in part the cost of time and the nuisance of having to go to the bank. Since the cost of time to individuals is likely to be higher the higher their income, *tc* may rise with Y_N. In that case, an increase in income would result in an increase in the demand for money by more than the income elasticity of ½ indicates because *tc* goes up together with Y_N.

The Demand for Real Balances

We started this chapter by emphasizing that the demand for money is a demand for real balances. It is worth confirming that the inventory theory of the demand for money implies that the demand for real balances does not change when all prices double (or increase in any other proportion). When all prices double, both Y_N and *tc* in Equation (4) double — that is, both nominal income and the nominal brokerage fee double. Accordingly, the demand for nominal balances doubles, so that the demand for real balances is unchanged. The square-root formula does not imply any money illusion in the demand for money. Thus we should be careful when saying the income elasticity of demand for money implied by Equation (4) is ½. The elasticity of the demand for *real* balances with respect to *real* income is

½. But if income rises only because all prices (including *tc*) rise, then the demand for *nominal* balances rises proportionately.

Integer Constraints

So far we have ignored the important constraint that it is possible to make only an integral number of transactions, such as 1, 2, 3, etc., and that it is not possible to make 1.25 or 3.57 transactions. However, when we take account of this constraint, we shall see that it implies that many people do not make more than the essential one transaction between money and bonds within the period in which they are paid.[15] Consider our previous example of the person who received $1,200 per month. Suppose, realistically, that the interest rate per month on savings deposits is ½ percent. The individual cannot avoid making one initial transaction, since income initially arrives in the savings account. The next question is whether it pays to make a second transaction. That is, does it pay to keep half the monthly income for half a month in the savings account and make a second withdrawal after half a month? With an interest rate of ½ percent per month, interest for half a month would be ¼ percent. Half the income would amount to $600 and the interest earnings would, therefore, be $600 × ¼ percent = $1.50.

Now if the brokerage fee exceeds $1.50, the individual will not bother to make more than one transaction. And $1.50 is not an outrageous cost in terms of the time and nuisance of making a transfer from the savings to the chequing account. Thus, for many individuals whose monthly net pay is below $1,200, we do not expect formula (4) to hold exactly. Their cash balance would instead simply be half their income. They would make one transfer into cash at the beginning of the month; Figure 9-1a would describe their money holdings. For such individuals, the income elasticity of the demand for money is 1, since their demand for money goes up precisely in proportion with their income. The interest elasticity is zero, so long as they make only one transaction, because they transfer all their income into cash immediately as they receive it.

The very strong restrictions on the income and interest elasticities of the demand for money of Equation (4) are not valid when the integer constraints are taken into account. Instead, the income elasticity is an average of the elasticities of different people, some of whom make only one transaction from bonds to money, and the elasticity is therefore between ½ and 1. Similarly, the interest elasticity is also an average of the elasticities across different individuals, being between − ½ and zero.[16] Because firms deal with larger amounts of money, they are likely to make a large number of transactions between money and bonds, and their income and interest elasticities of the demand for money are therefore likely to be close to the ½ and − ½ predicted by Equation (4).

The Payment Period

Once the integer constraints are taken into account, it can also be seen that the transactions demand for money depends on the frequency with which individuals are paid (the payment period). If one examines the square-root formula (4), the demand for money does not seem to depend on how often a person is paid, since an increase in the payments period increases both Y_N and i in the same proportion. Thus the demand for money appears unaffected by the length of the period. However, consider a person who makes only one transaction from bonds to money at the beginning of each month. His or her money demand is $Y_N/2$. If such a person were paid weekly, his or her demand for money would be only one-quarter of the demand with monthly payments. Thus we should expect the demand for money to increase with the length of the payment period.

Summary

The inventory-theoretic approach to the demand for money gives a precise formula for the transactions demand for money: The income elasticity of the demand for money is ½, and the interest elasticity is − ½. When integer constraints are taken into account, the limits on the income elasticity of demand are between ½ and 1, and the limits on the interest elasticity are between − ½ and zero. We have outlined the approach in terms of an individual's demand for money, but a similar approach is relevant for firms.

Some of the assumptions made in deriving the square-root formula are very restrictive. People do not spend their money evenly over the course of the month, and they do not know exactly what their payments will be. Their cheques are not paid into savings accounts, and so on. It turns out, though, that the major results we have derived are not greatly affected by the use of more realistic assumptions. There is thus good reason to expect the demand for money to increase with the level of income and to decrease as the interest rate on other assets (or, generally, the cost of holding money) increases.

The Precautionary Motive

In discussing the transactions demand for money, we focussed on transactions costs and ignored uncertainty. In this section, we concentrate on the demand for money that arises because people are uncertain about the payments they might want to, or have to, make.[17] Suppose, realistically, that an individual did not know precisely what payments he or she would be receiving in the next few weeks and what payments would have to be made. He or she might decide to have a hot fudge sundae, or need to take a cab in the rain, or have to pay for a prescription. If the person did not have money with which to pay, he or she would incur a loss. The loss could be missing a fine meal, or missing an appointment, or having to come back the next day to pay for the prescription. For concreteness, we shall denote the loss incurred as a result of being short of cash by $q. The loss clearly varies from situation to situation, but as usual we simplify.

The more money the individual holds, the less likely he or she is to incur the costs of illiquidity (that is, not having money immediately available). But the more money the person holds, the more interest is given up. We are back to a tradeoff situation similar to that examined in relation to the transactions demand. Somewhere between holding so little money for precautionary purposes that it will almost certainly be necessary to forgo some purchase (or to borrow in a hurry) and holding so much money that there is little chance of not being able to make any payment that might be necessary, there must be an optimal amount of precautionary balances to hold. That optimal amount will involve the balancing of interest costs against the advantages of not being caught illiquid.

Once more, we write down the total costs of holding an amount of money M.[18] This time we are dealing with expected costs, since it is not certain what the need for money will be. We denote the probability that the individual is illiquid during the month by $p(M, \sigma)$. The function $p(M, \sigma)$ indicates that the probability of the person's being illiquid at some time during the month depends on the level of money balances M being held and the degree of uncertainty σ about the net payments that will be made during the month. The probability of illiquidity is lower, the higher is M, and higher, the higher is the degree of uncertainty σ. The *expected cost* of illiquidity is $p(M, \sigma)q$ — the probability of illiquidity times the cost of being illiquid. The interest cost associated with holding a cash balance of M is just iM. Thus, we have

$$\text{Expected costs} = iM + p(M, \sigma)q \qquad (5)$$

To determine the optimal amount of money to hold, we compare the marginal costs of increasing money holding by $1 with the expected marginal benefit of doing so. The marginal cost is again the interest forgone, or i. That is shown by the MC curve in Figure 9-3. The marginal benefit of increasing money holding arises from the lower expected costs of illiquidity. Increasing precautionary balances from zero has a large marginal benefit, since that takes care of small, unexpected disbursements that are quite likely. As we increase cash balances further, we continue to reduce the probability of illiquidity, but at a decreasing rate. We start to hold cash to insure against quite unlikely events. Thus, the marginal benefit of additional cash is a decreasing function of the level of cash holdings — more cash on hand is better than less, but at a diminishing rate. The marginal benefit of increasing cash holdings is shown by the MB curve in Figure 9-3.

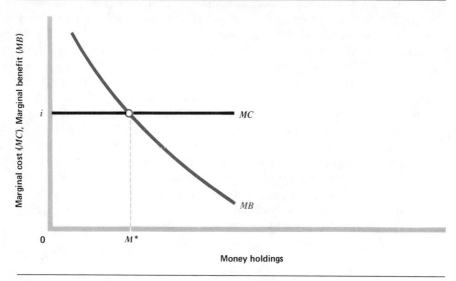

FIGURE 9-3   THE PRECAUTIONARY DEMAND FOR MONEY. The *MC* schedule shows the marginal cost of holding an extra dollar of money: holding an extra dollar means losing interest, and so the *MC* curve is horizontal at a level equal to the interest rate (or, more generally, the difference between the interest rate on money and alternative assets). The marginal benefit (*MB*) of holding an extra dollar is that the consumer is less likely to be short of money when it is needed. The marginal benefit declines with the amount of money held. The optimal amount of money to hold is shown by *M**, where marginal cost is equal to marginal benefit.

The optimal level of the precautionary demand for money is reached where the two curves intersect. That level of money is shown as *M** in Figure 9-3. Now we can use Figure 9-3 to examine the determinants of the optimal level of the precautionary demand. It is, first, apparent that precautionary balances will be larger when the interest rate is lower. A reduction in the interest rate shifts the *MC* curve down and increases *M**. The lower costs of holding money makes it profitable to insure more heavily against the costs of illiquidity. An increase in uncertainty leads to increased money holdings because it shifts up the *MB* curve. With more uncertainty about the flow of spending, there is more scope for unforeseen payments and thus a greater danger of illiquidity. It therefore pays to insure more heavily by holding larger cash balances. Finally, the lower the costs of illiquidity, *q*, the lower the money demand. A reduction in *q* moves the *MB* curve down. Indeed, if there were no cost to illiquidity, no one would bother to hold money. There would be no penalty for not having it, while at the same time, holding it would mean a loss of interest.

The model of precautionary demand can be applied to goods other than money. It is a broad theory that applies to any commodity inventory that is held as insurance against contingencies. For instance, cars carry spare tires. You can work out circumstances under which one would want to have more than one spare tire in a car, and even circumstances in which zero would be the optimal number. The idea of the precautionary demand for money or for goods is quite general. So, too, are the determinants of the precautionary demand: the alternative cost in terms of interest forgone, the cost of illiquidity, and the degree of uncertainty that determines the probability of illiquidity.

The Speculative Demand for Money

The transactions demand and the precautionary demand for money emphasize the medium of exchange function of money, for each refers to the need to have money on hand to make payments. Each theory is more relevant to the $M1$ definition of money than any other, though the precautionary demand could certainly explain part of the holding of savings accounts and other relatively liquid assets which are part of $M2$. Now we move over to the store of value function of money and concentrate on the role of money in the investment portfolio of an individual.

An individual who has wealth has to hold that wealth in specific assets. Those assets make up a *portfolio*. One would think an investor would want to hold the asset which provides the highest returns. However, given that the return on most assets is uncertain, it is unwise to hold the entire portfolio in a single *risky asset*. You may have the hottest tip that a certain stock will surely double within the next 2 years, but you would be wise to recognize that hot tips are far from infallible, and that you could lose a lot of money in that stock as well as make money. A prudent, risk-averse investor does not put all his or her eggs in one basket. Uncertainty about the returns on risky assets leads to a diversified portfolio strategy.

As part of that diversified portfolio, the typical investor will want to hold some amount of a safe asset as insurance against capital losses on assets whose prices change in an uncertain manner. The safe asset would be held precisely because it is safe, even though it pays a lower expected return than risky assets. Money is a safe asset in that its nominal value is known with certainty.[19] In a famous article, James Tobin argued that money would be held as the safe asset in the portfolios of investors.[20] The title of the article, "Liquidity Preference as Behavior towards Risk," explains the essential notion. In this framework the demand for money, the safest asset, depends on the expected yields, as well as on the riskiness of the yields, on other assets. The riskiness of the return on other assets is measured by the variability of the return. Using reasonable assumptions, Tobin shows that an increase in the expected return on other assets — an increase in the opportunity cost of holding money (that is, the return lost by holding money) — lowers money demand. By contrast, an increase in the riskiness of the returns on other assets increases money demand.

An investor's aversion to risk certainly generates a demand for a safe asset. The question we want to consider is whether that safe asset is money. That is, we want to ask whether considerations of portfolio behaviour do generate a demand for money. The relevant considerations in the portfolio are the returns and the risks on assets. From the viewpoint of the yield and risks of holding money, it is clear that term or savings deposits have the same risks as currency or chequable deposits. However, they generally pay a higher yield. The risks in both cases are the risks arising from uncertainty about inflation. Given that the risks are the same, and with the yields on time and savings deposits higher than on currency and demand deposits, portfolio diversification explains the demand for assets such as time and savings deposits better than the demand for $M1$. We therefore regard the speculative demand as applying primarily to $M2$.

The implications of the speculative, or risk-diversifying, demand for money are similar to those of the transactions and precautionary demands. An increase in the interest rate on nonmoney assets, such as long-term bond yields or equity yields, will reduce the demand for $M2$. An increase in the rate paid on savings accounts will increase the demand for savings accounts, perhaps even at the cost of the demand for $M1$, as people take advantage of the higher yields they can earn on their investment portfolios to increase the size of those portfolios. One important difference between the speculative and the other two categories of demand is that here the level of wealth is clearly relevant to the demand for $M2$. The level of wealth determines the size of the total portfolio, and we expect that increases in wealth lead to increases in the demand for the safe asset, and thus in $M2$ demand.

One final point on the speculative demand. Many individuals with relatively small amounts of wealth will indeed hold part of that wealth in savings accounts in order to diversify their portfolios. But bigger investors are sometimes able to purchase other securities which pay higher interest and also have fixed (that is, risk-free) nominal values. Large CDs (in excess of $100,000) are sometimes an example of such assets, as are treasury bills on occasion. For such individuals or groups, the demand for a safe asset is not a demand for money.

9-4   EMPIRICAL EVIDENCE

This section examines the empirical evidence — the studies made using actual data — on the demand for money. We noted in Chapter 4, and again at the beginning of Section 9-3, that the *interest elasticity* of the demand for money plays an important role in determining the effectiveness of monetary and fiscal policies. We then showed in Section 9-3 that there are good theoretical reasons for believing the demand for real balances should depend on the interest rate. The empirical evidence supports that view very strongly. Empirical studies have established that the demand for money is responsive to the interest rate. An increase in the interest rate reduces the demand for money.

The theory of money demand also predicts that the demand for money should depend on the level of income. The response of the demand for money to the level of income, as measured by the *income elasticity* of money demand, is also important from a policy viewpoint. The income elasticity of money demand provides a guide to the Bank of Canada as to how fast to increase the money supply to support a given rate of growth of GNP without changing the interest rate.

Suppose that the aim is for GNP growth of 10 percent, 6 percent real growth and 4 percent inflation. If the Bank of Canada wants to provide a sufficient growth rate of money to prevent interest rates from rising, it has to know the income elasticity of the demand for real balances. Suppose the real income elasticity is ½. Then we would require monetary growth of 7 percent to prevent an increase in interest rates. Why? First, the demand for nominal money increases in proportion to the price level, since money demand is a demand for real balances. Thus 4 percent growth in money is needed to meet the increased demand from the 4 percent increase in the price level. The 6 percent growth in real income would increase the demand for real balances by 3 percent (= 6 percent × ½), given the real income elasticity of ½. Hence, the needed 7 percent (= 4 + 3) growth in the nominal money supply to meet the increased demand arising from the increase in income.

Lagged Adjustment

The empirical work on the demand for money has introduced one complication that we did not study in the theoretical section — that the demand for money adjusts to changes in income and interest rates *with a lag*. When the level of income or the interest rate changes, there is first only a small change in the demand for money. Then, over the course of time, the change in the demand for money increases, slowly building up to its full long-run change. Reasons for this lag are not yet certain. The two usual possibilities exist in this case too. The lags may arise because there are costs of adjusting money holdings, or they may arise because money holders' expectations are slow to adjust. If people believe that a given change in the interest rate is temporary, they may be unwilling to make a major change in their money holdings. As time passes and it becomes clearer that the change is not transitory, they are more willing to make a larger adjustment.

Empirical Results

There are several published studies of the demand for money in Canada using postwar quarterly data.[21] The results of the most recent one are fairly typical and are summarized in Table 9-2. The table shows the elastici-ties of the demand for real balances with respect to real income Y (real GNP) and the rate on commercial paper i. This interest rate is relevant to the demand for money because commercial paper is an asset which is very liquid for corporations that hold it instead of money for short periods of time.

TABLE 9-2 ELASTICITIES OF REAL MONEY DEMAND ($M1$)

	Y	i
Short run	0.22	-0.054
Long run	0.73	-0.18

Source: S. Poloz, "Simultaneity and the Demand for Money in Canada," *Canadian Journal of Economics*, August 1980, p. 413.

In the short run (one quarter), the elasticity of demand with respect to real income is 0.22. This means that a 1 percent increase in real income raises money demand by 0.22 percent, which is considerably less than proportionately. The table shows that the interest elasticity of money demand with respect to interest rates is negative: an increase in interest rates reduces money demand. The short-run interest elasticity is quite small. An increase from 8 percent to 10 percent, that is, a 25 percent increase ($10/8 = 1.25$), reduces the demand for money by only 1.35 per-cent ($ = 0.054 \times 25$ percent).

The long-run elasticities exceed the short-run elasticities by a factor of more than 3, as Table 9-2 shows. The long-run real income elasticity is 0.73, meaning that in the long run the increase in real money demand occurring as a result of a given increase in real income is only 73 percent as large as the increase in income. Real money demand thus rises less than proportionately to the rise in real income. The long-run interest elasticity is -0.18, meaning that an increase in i from 8 to 10 percent would reduce the demand for money by 4.5 percent.

TABLE 9-3 DYNAMIC PATTERNS OF ELASTICITIES OF MONEY DEMAND WITH RESPECT TO REAL INCOME AND INTEREST RATES

Quarters elapsed	Y	i
1	0.22	-0.054
2	0.37	-0.092
3	0.48	-0.119
4	0.55	-0.138
8	0.69	-0.172
Long run	0.73	-0.182

Source: Calculated using the elasticities shown in Table 9-2 and reported by Poloz, *op. cit.*

How long is the long run? That is, how long does it take the demand for money to adjust from the short-run elasticities of Table 9-2 to the long-run elasticities shown in the table? Actually, it takes forever for the full long-run position to be reached. Table 9-3, however, shows the elasticities of the demand for real balances in response to changes in the level of income and interest rates after one, two, three, four, and eight quarters. Three-fourths of the adjustment is complete within the first year, and over 90 percent of the adjustment is complete within the first two years.

In summary, we have so far described three essential properties of money demand:

1 The demand for real money balances responds negatively to the rate of interest. An increase in interest rates reduces the demand for money.
2 The demand for money increases with the level of real income. However, the income elasticity of money demand is less than 1 so that money demand increases less than proportionately with income.
3 The short-run responsiveness of money demand to changes in interest rates and income is considerably less than the long-run response. The long-run elasticities are estimated to be over three times the size of the short-run elasticities.

There is one more important question to be considered. This is the question of how money responds to an increase in the level of prices. Here a number of researchers have found strong evidence that an increase in prices raises nominal money demand in the same proportion. We can add, therefore, a fourth conclusion:

4 The demand for nominal money balances is proportional to the price level. There is no money illusion; in other words, the demand for money is a demand for *real* balances.

Financial Innovation and Money Demand

Over the past ten years there have been a number of innovations in Canadian financial markets that have affected the demand for money.[22] Some of these have affected individual depositors and others have affected the banking business of corporations.

For individual depositors, the major change has been the introduction of daily interest accounts. Prior to 1979, the standard savings account in a chartered bank paid interest on the minimum balance held over each calendar month. Most individuals were unable to earn interest on funds available for periods of less than a month and thus were likely to keep funds received from salary payments in chequing accounts. The introduction of savings accounts which pay interest on daily balances provided a new option which reduced the demand for $M1$.

In 1981, banks and other financial institutions began offering daily interest chequing accounts. Typically these accounts pay a higher rate on balances above some minimum such as $2,000, and a much lower rate on balances below the minimum. The Bank of Canada has attempted to allow for the effect of these deposits by including them in the $M1A$ definition of the money supply.

The major innovation affecting corporate depositors has been the provision of more cash management services that enable the banks' customers to reduce their holdings of transactions balances and earn more interest. For example, there are arrangements under which surplus funds are automatically shifted at the end of each day to higher interest accounts. Such practices further reduce the demand for $M1$.

9-5   THE INCOME VELOCITY OF MONEY

The *income velocity of money* is the number of times the stock of money is turned over per year in financing the annual flow of income. Thus in 1983 GNP was $388.7 billion, the money stock ($M1$) averaged $28.2 billion, and velocity was therefore about 14. The average dollar of money balances financed $14 of spending on final goods and services, or the public held on average just under $0.07 of $M1$ per dollar of income. While we usually calculate velocity for the economy as a whole, we can also calculate it for an individual. For instance, for someone earning $12,000 per year, who has average money balances during the year of $1,000, the income velocity of money holdings is 12.

Income velocity (from now on we shall refer to velocity rather than income velocity) is defined, as in Section 4-8, as

$$V \equiv \frac{Y_N}{M} \tag{6}$$

the ratio of nominal income to nominal money stock. An alternative way of writing Equation (6) recognizes that Y_N, nominal GNP, is equal to the price level P times real income Y. Thus

$$M \cdot V = P \cdot Y \tag{7}$$

The Quantity Theory

Equation (7) is the famous *quantity equation*, linking the product of the price level and the level of output to the money stock. The quantity equation became the (classical) *quantity theory of money* when it was argued that both V, the income velocity of money,[23] and Y, the level of output, were fixed. Real output was taken to be fixed because the economy was at full employment, and velocity was assumed not to change much. Neither of these assumptions holds in fact, but it is nonetheless interesting to see where they lead. *If both V and Y are fixed, then it follows that the price level is proportional to the money stock.* Thus the classical quantity theory was a theory of inflation. The classical quantity theory argued that the price level was proportional to the money stock. We return to the quantity theory in Chapter 15.

Velocity and Policy

Velocity is a useful concept in economic policy making. We see how to use it by rewriting (6) as

$$Y_N \equiv VM \tag{6a}$$

Given the nominal money stock (M) and given velocity, we know the level of nominal GNP. Thus if we can predict the level of velocity, we can predict the level of nominal income, given the money stock.

Further, *if* velocity were constant, changing the money supply would result in proportionate changes in nominal income. Any policies, including fiscal policies, that did not affect the money stock would not affect the level of income. You will probably now recognize that we have previously discussed a case of constant velocity. In Chapter 4, we discussed the effectiveness of fiscal policy when the demand for money is not a function of the interest rate and the *LM* curve is therefore vertical. That vertical *LM* curve is the same as the assumption of constant velocity.

Velocity and the Demand for Money

The discussion of constant velocity is closely related to the behaviour of the demand for money. Indeed, the notion of velocity is important because it is a convenient way of talking about money demand.

We now examine the relationship between velocity and the demand for money. Let the demand for real balances be written $L(i, Y)$, consistent with Chapter 4. Recall that Y is real income. When the supply of money is equal to the demand for money, we have

$$\frac{M}{P} = L(i, Y) \tag{8}$$

or $M = PL(i, Y)$. Now we can substitute for the nominal money supply into Equation (6) to obtain

$$V = \frac{Y_N}{PL(i, Y)} = \frac{Y}{L(i, Y)} \tag{6b}$$

where we have recognized that Y_N/P is the level of real income. Income velocity is the ratio of the level of real income to the demand for real balances.

From Equation (6b) we note that velocity is a function of real income and the interest rate. Consider first the effects of a change in the interest rate on velocity. An increase in the interest rate reduces the demand for real balances and therefore increases velocity: when the cost of holding money increases, money holders make their money do more work, and thus turn it over more often.

The way in which changes in real income affect velocity depends on the income elasticity of the demand for money. If the income elasticity of the demand for real balances were 1, then the demand for real balances would change in the same proportion as income. In that case, changes in real income would not affect velocity. For, suppose that real income Y increased by 10 percent. The numerator Y in Equation (6b) would increase by 10 percent as would the denominator, and velocity would be unchanged. However, we have seen that the income elasticity of the demand for money is less than 1. That means that velocity *increases* with increases in real income. For example, suppose that real income rose 10 percent, and the demand for real balances increased only by 7.3 percent (= .73 × 10 percent), as Poloz's results suggest. Then the numerator of Equation (6b) would increase by more than the denominator, and velocity would rise.

The empirical work reviewed in Section 9-4 makes it clear that the demand for money and, therefore, also velocity do react systematically to changes in interest rates and the level of real income. The empirical evidence therefore decisively refutes the view that velocity is unaffected by changes in interest rates and that fiscal policy is, accordingly, incapable of affecting the level of nominal income. In terms of Equation (6b), and using the analysis of Chapter 4, expansionary fiscal policy can be thought of as working by increasing interest rates, thereby increasing velocity, and thus making it possible for a given stock of money to support a higher level of nominal GNP.

Velocity in Practice

The empirical evidence we reviewed in Section 9-4 is useful in interpreting the behaviour of velocity shown in Figure 9-4. The figure shows a striking and steady increase in velocity. The velocity of $M1$ has increased from under 8 in the early sixties to 14 in 1983. The average dollar finances 75 percent more income flow now than it did in the early sixties. This increase in velocity can of course be explained by the same factors that explain the demand for money. Velocity has risen because income has risen (since the income elasticity of demand is less than 1) and because interest rates have risen.

9-6   VELOCITY AND INFLATION

We begin to discuss inflation systematically only in Chapter 13, but we can take up here an important and fascinating aspect of inflation. The question is, How does inflation affect the demand for money? It is espe-

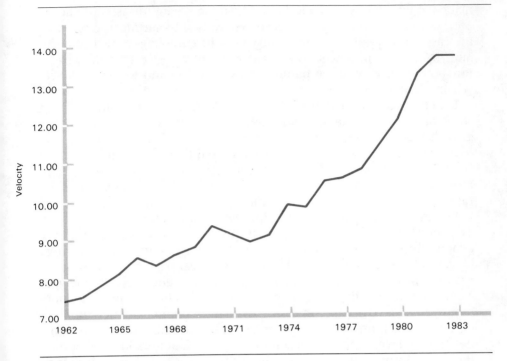

FIGURE 9-4   THE INCOME VELOCITY OF MONEY (M1)
(*Source*: *Bank of Canada Review*)

cially important to distinguish beween the demand for *nominal* and *real*
money balances. Earlier in the chapter we have seen that (1) an increase
in the price level, all real variables remaining unchanged, leaves the demand for real balances unchanged and increases the demand for nominal
balances in proportion to the increase in the price level, and (2) an increase in the rate of interest increases the cost of holding money and
reduces the demand for real balances.

These two points are relevant in discussing the effects of expected inflation — expected continuing increases in prices — on the demand for real
balances. We have seen that a one-time increase in the price level, all real
variables remaining unchanged after this increase, leaves the demand for
real balances unaffected. But now assume that prices increase and that the
public interprets the price increases as merely the prelude to further continuing price increases. That is, the public anticipates inflation. Inflation
reduces the purchasing power of money. Thus, inflation at the rate of
5 percent reduces the real value of a nominal dollar that is held for a period
of 1 year by 5 percent. Inflation acts as a tax on real balances.[24] Someone
holding $100 for a year during which inflation is 5 percent in effect pays
$5 for holding that money during the year. If that person held less money,

he or she would pay a smaller tax; if he or she reduced cash holdings to $50, the tax would be only $2.50. There is thus an incentive, when increased inflation is expected, to try to reduce holdings of real balances and, instead, hold assets whose value is not as adversely affected by inflation. That is why the public reduces the demand for real balances when inflation is expected.

The effects of expected inflation on the demand for real balances have a strong influence on the behaviour of the price level when money supply growth increases. Suppose that the money supply has been growing at 5 percent, that real income was constant, and that the inflation rate had been a steady 5 percent. Then let the money supply start growing more rapidly, say, at 10 percent. Ultimately, prices will increase at a 10 percent rate as well. But with 10 percent inflation expected, the demand for real balances is lower than when the expected inflation rate is only 5 percent. This means that at some stage during the process by which the economy adapts from an inflation rate of 5 percent to a rate of 10 percent, real balances have to be reduced. The only way real balances can fall is for prices to increase more rapidly than the money supply. Accordingly, at some point during the adjustment process, prices have to increase more rapidly than at 10 percent, the rate at which the nominal money supply is growing, which means that an increase in the growth rate of money to a new higher level produces, at some point, a rate of inflation higher than the rate of growth of money. The adjustment of real balances during an inflationary period will imply that prices increase more rapidly than the nominal money stock.

How does this observation link up with evidence on money demand during inflationary periods? Phillip Cagan of Columbia University studied the demand for real balances during *hyperinflations* — extremely rapid inflations — in an interesting and famous article.[25] His evidence shows that the demand for real balances declines dramatically as inflation reaches very high levels. As we noted earlier, expected inflation reduces the demand for money because it is a cost of holding money. For instance, during the Austrian hyperinflation in 1922–1923, the *monthly* rate of inflation rose from roughly zero to more than 80 percent. This extraordinary increase in inflation brought about a decline in real money demand to *one-fifth* the level that had been held at zero inflation. Velocity increased by a factor of 5. The evidence for other countries is, if anything, even more striking.

Cagan's evidence raises the question of how real money demand, or velocity, can be so flexible. How do people manage to reduce their money holdings per dollar, or crown, of income by so much? As inflation increases, the public takes more care in how it manages its cash balances. Money is spent more rapidly after it is received. Firms begin to pay their workers more frequently. Money becomes like a hot potato, with people anxious to pass it on rapidly. One can almost see the velocity of circulation increasing as people scurry to get rid of cash. These changes in payments patterns and shopping habits do impose costs on money holders that are the major costs of expected inflation, as we shall see in Chapter 16.

Inflation and Interest Rates

The adjustment of the demand for money to expected inflation is, in principle, no different from the adjustment to changes in the interest rate, which also increase the cost of holding money. Indeed, in countries with sufficiently well-developed capital markets, expected inflation is reflected in nominal interest rates. When inflation is expected, borrowers know that they will repay their debts in money that has lower purchasing power than the money they originally borrowed, and lenders know that too. Lenders, accordingly, become more reluctant to lend at any given level of the nominal interest rate, and borrowers become more anxious to borrow at a given nominal interest rate. The result is that the *nominal* interest rate rises when inflation is expected, thus compensating lenders for the loss of purchasing power of money.

The rise in the nominal interest rate that we are talking about reminds us of the distinction between *real* and *nominal* interest rates made in Chapter 8. When the expected rate of inflation rises, nominal interest rates — interest rates which specify how many dollars to be repaid — increase. The real interest rate — the nominal interest rate minus the expected rate of inflation — need not rise and may even fall. Undoubtedly, one of the major reasons for the increase in nominal interest rates between the 1960s and 1982 was the increase in the expected rate of inflation. This relationship is investigated in more detail in Chapter 16. In some Latin American countries where inflation rates have reached 100 percent per year or more, no one is surprised by bank loan rates of, say, 80 percent.

In talking about both the expected rate of inflation itself and nominal interest rates, we raise the question of whether each is a separate influence on the demand for money. In well-developed capital markets, in which interest rates are free to move to reflect expected inflation, the nominal interest rate is the relevant opportunity cost of holding money. That is because individuals could make investments at that interest rate. In markets where interest rates are controlled and rates do not rise to reflect expected inflation, individuals begin to think of the alternative of buying goods rather than holding money when the expected rate of inflation rises. The expected inflation rate itself then becomes a separate influence on the demand for money. Franco Modigliani has offered the following useful rule of thumb to decide whether the nominal interest rate or the expected rate of inflation should be included as determining the demand for money: If the nominal interest rate exceeds the expected rate of inflation, the nominal interest rate should be thought of as the cost of holding money. If the expected inflation rate exceeds the nominal interest rate, the expected inflation rate should be thought of as the cost of holding money.

9-7   SUMMARY

1   The demand for money is a demand for real balances. It is the purchasing power, not the number, of their dollar bills that matters to holders of money.

2   The money supply ($M1$) is made up of currency and demand deposits. $M2$ and $M3$ are broader measures that include savings accounts, and term and notice deposits.

3   The chief characteristic of money is that it serves as a means of payment.

4   There are two broad reasons why people hold money and thus forgo interest that they could earn by holding alternative assets. These reasons are transactions costs and uncertainty.

5   Transactions costs are an essential aspect of money demand. If it were costless to move (instantaneously) in and out of interest-bearing assets, nobody would hold money. Optimal cash management would involve transfers from other assets (bonds or saving deposits) just before outlays, and it would involve immediate conversion into interest-bearing form of any cash receipts. The existence of transactions costs — brokerage costs, fees, and time costs — makes it optimal to hold some money.

6   The inventory-theoretic approach shows that an individual will hold a stock of real balances that varies inversely with the interest rate but increases with the level of real income and the cost of transactions. The income elasticity of money demand is less than unity, implying that there are economies of scale.

7   Transactions costs, in combination with uncertainty about payments and receipts, give rise to a precautionary demand for money. Money holdings provide insurance against illiquidity. Optimal money holdings are higher, the higher the variability of net disbursements and the higher the cost of illiquidity. Since holding money implies forgoing interest, optimal money holdings will vary inversely with the rate of interest.

8   Portfolio diversification involves the tradeoff between risk and return. Saving accounts form part of an optimal portfolio because they are not risky — their nominal value is constant. Savings accounts dominate currency or demand deposits, which are also safe nominal assets, because they bear interest. Thus the speculative portfolio demand for money is a demand for saving or term deposits.

9   The empirical evidence provides strong support for a negative inter-
    est elasticity of money demand and a positive income elasticity. Be-
    cause of lags, short-run elasticities are much smaller than long-run
    elasticities. The long-run income elasticity is about 0.7, and the long-
    run interest elasticity is about -0.2.

10 Over the past ten years the demand for money ($M1$) declined as a
    result of both the introduction of new assets and improvements in
    cash management methods.

11 The income velocity of money is defined as the ratio of income to
    money or the rate of turnover of money. Since the sixties, velocity
    has increased to a level of about 14.

12 The empirical evidence implies that an increase in real income raises
    velocity, as does an increase in the rate of interest. At higher levels of
    income or at higher interest rates, there is a lower demand for money
    in relation to income. Higher interest rates lead people to economize
    on cash balances.

13 Inflation implies that money loses purchasing power, and inflation
    thus creates a cost of holding money. The higher the rate of inflation,
    the lower the amount of real balances that will be held. Hyperinfla-
    tions provide striking support for this prediction. Under conditions of
    very high expected inflation, money demand falls dramatically rela-
    tive to income. Velocity rises as people use less money in relation to
    income.

KEY TERMS

Real balances	Transactions demand
Money illusion	Inventory-theoretic approach
M1	Square-root formula
M2	Precautionary demand
Liquidity	Speculative demand
Medium of exchange	Income velocity of money
Store of value	Quantity equation
Unit of account	Quantity theory of money
Standard of deferred payments	Hyperinflation

PROBLEMS

1 To what extent would it be possible to design a society in which there
   was no money? What would the problems be? Could currency at

least be eliminated? How? (Lest all this seems too unwordly, you should know that some people are beginning to talk of a "cashless economy" in the next century.)

2 Evaluate the effects of the following changes on the demand for $M1$ and $M2$. Which of the functions of money do they relate to?
   (a) "Instant cash" machines which allow 24-hour withdrawals from savings accounts at banks.
   (b) The employment of more tellers at your bank
   (c) An increase in inflationary expectations
   (d) Widespread acceptance of credit cards
   (e) Fear of an imminent collapse of the government
   (f) A rise in the interest rate on nonchequable savings deposits

*3 The assumption was made in the text that in the transactions demand for cash model, it is optimal to space transactions evenly throughout the month. Prove this as follows in the case where $n = 2$. Since one transaction must be made immediately, the only question is when to make the second one. For simplicity, call the beginning of the month $t = 0$, and the end of the month $t = 1$. Then consider a transaction strategy which performs the second transaction at time t_0. If income is Y_N, then this will require moving $t_0 Y_N$ into cash now, and $(1 - t_0)Y_N$ at time t_0. Calculate the total cost incurred under this strategy, and try various values of t_0 to see which is optimal. (If you are familiar with calculus, prove that $t_0 = \frac{1}{2}$ minimizes total cost.)

*4 For those students with calculus, derive Equation (4) from Equation (2) by minimizing total costs with respect to n.

5 (a) Determine the optimal strategy for cash management for the person who earns $1,600 per month, can earn 0.5 percent interest per month in a savings account, and has a transaction cost of $1.
   (b) What is the individual's average cash balance?
   (c) Suppose income rises to $1,800. By what percentage does the person's demand for money rise? (Pay attention to the integer constraints.)

6 Discuss the various factors that go into an individual's decision regarding how many traveller's cheques to take on a vacation.

7 In the text, we said that the transactions demand-for-money model can also be applied to firms. Suppose a firm sells steadily during the month and has to pay its workers at the end of the month. Explain then how it would determine its money holdings.

8 This chapter emphasizes that the demand for money is a demand for

real balances. At the same time, inflation causes the real demand to fall. Explain how these two assertions can both be correct.

9 "Muggers favour deflation." Comment.

CHAPTER 9: FOOTNOTES

[1]Be sure you understand that (1) and (2) say the same thing in slightly different ways.

[2]For a detailed description of the definitions, see *Bank of Canada Review*, Table 9 and the appended notes. Details concerning recent revisions are given in the March 1983 issue.

[3]A notice deposit is an account on which the bank reserves the right to require notice before a withdrawal can be made. Personal savings accounts have such a provision, but it is not normally enforced. (Look at the small print in your passbook!)

[4]See W.S. Jevons, *Money and the Mechanism of Exchange* (London: Routledge & Kegan Paul 1910).

[5]See Paul Einzig, *Primitive Money* (New York: Pergamon Press, 1966).

[6]J.M. Keynes, *The General Theory of Employment, Interest and Money* (New York: Macmillan, 1936), Chap. 13.

[7]As a reminder, nominal income Y_N is defined as real income Y times the price level P: $Y_N \equiv PY$.

[8]The approach was originally developed to determine the inventories of goods a firm should have on hand. In that context, the amount Y_N would be the monthly sales of the good, tc the cost of ordering the good, and i the interest rate for carrying the inventory. The analogy between money as an inventory of purchasing power, standing ready to buy goods, and an inventory of goods, standing ready to be bought by customers, is quite close. The inventory-theoretical approach to the demand for money is associated with the names of William Baumol and James Tobin. (William Baumol, "The Transactions Demand for Cash: An Inventory Theoretic Approach," *Quarterly Journal of Economics*, November 1952; and James Tobin, "The Interest Elasticity of Transactions Demand for Cash," *Review of Economics and Statistics*, August 1956.) The most famous result of Baumol's and Tobin's work is the *square-root law* of the demand for money, which is presented later in Eq. (4).

[9]With simple interest being paid on the savings account, the individual's transactions between bonds and cash should be evenly spaced over the month. We leave the proof of that for the case where there are two transactions to the problem set.

[10]The average cash balance is the average of the amount of cash the individual holds at each moment during the month. For instance, if he held $400 for 3 days and zero for the rest of the month, the average cash balance would be $40, or one-tenth (3 days divided by 30 days) of the month times $400.

[11]Two points about Fig. 9-2: First, note that we have, for convenience, drawn the curves as continuous, even though you will recognize that it is only possible to make an integral number of transactions, and not, for example, 1.6 or 7.24 transactions. Second, if you can use the calculus, try to derive the equation of the

marginal benefit curve from the component of costs in Eq. (2) that is due to interest lost.

[12]See the references in footnote 8.

[13]If you can handle calculus, try to derive Eq. (4) by minimizing total cost in Eq. (2).

[14]The income elasticity of demand is $\dfrac{\Delta(M/P)}{M/P} \bigg/ \dfrac{\Delta Y}{Y}$. Similarly, the interest elasticity is $\dfrac{\Delta(M/P)}{M/P} \bigg/ \dfrac{\Delta i}{i}$.

[15]If we had assumed that individuals were paid in cash, it would turn out that many people would not make any transactions between money and bonds in managing their transactions balances.

[16]See Robert J. Barro, "Integer Constraints and Aggregation in an Inventory Model of Money Demand," *Journal of Finance*, March 1976.

[17]See Edward H. Whalen, "A Rationalization of the Precautionary Demand for Cash," *Quarterly Journal of Economics*, May 1966.

[18]This paragraph contains technical material that is optional and can easily be skipped.

[19]Of course, when the rate of inflation is uncertain, the real value of money is also uncertain, and money is no longer a safe asset. Even so, the uncertainties about the values of equity are so much larger than the uncertainties about the rate of inflation that money can be treated as a relatively safe asset.

[20]James Tobin, "Liquidity Preference as Behavior towards Risk," *Review of Economic Studies*, February 1958.

[21]See for example K. Clinton, "The Demand for Money in Canada, 1955–70," *Canadian Journal of Economics*, February, 1973; N. Cameron, "The Stability of Canadian Demand for Money Functions," *Canadian Journal of Economics*, May, 1979; S. Poloz, "Simultaneity and the Demand for Money in Canada," *Canadian Journal of Economics*, August 1980.

[22]See C. Freedman, "Financial Innovation in Canada: Causes and Consequences," *American Economic Review*, May 1983.

[23]Why do we say income velocity and not plain velocity? There is another concept, transactions velocity, that is, the ratio of total transactions to money balances. Total transactions far exceed GNP for two reasons. First, there are many transactions involving the sale and purchase of assets that do not contribute to GNP. Second, a particular item in final output typically generates total spending on it that exceeds the contribution of that item to GNP. For instance, 1 dollar's worth of wheat generates transactions as it leaves the farm, as it is sold by the miller, as it leaves the baker for the supermarket, and then as it is sold to the household. One dollar's worth of wheat may involve several dollars of transactions before it is sold for the last time. Transactions velocity is thus higher than income velocity.

[24]We explore the notion of inflation as a tax on real balances in more detail in Chap. 17, which deals with the budget.

[25]Phillip Cagan, "The Monetary Dynamics of Hyperinflation," in Milton Friedman (ed.), *Studies in the Quantity Theory of Money* (Chicago: The University of Chicago Press, 1956).

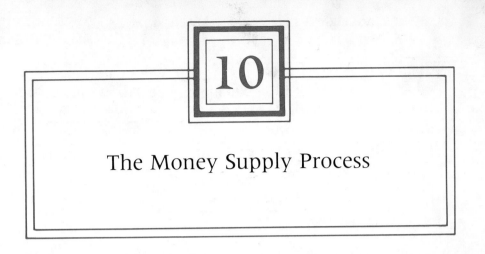

The Money Supply Process

We have so far taken the money supply to be given and determined by the Bank of Canada. By and large, the Bank is indeed able to determine the money supply quite accurately, but it does not set it directly. In this chapter we study the ways in which the actions of the Bank of Canada, the chartered banks, and the public interact in determining the stock of money.

In conducting monetary policy, the Bank of Canada pays attention to the behaviour of both interest rates and the money supply. We will show that the Bank of Canada cannot simultaneously set both the money supply and the interest rate at whatever level it wants, though it can set either the money supply or the interest rate. In addition, we shall examine in some detail the way in which the Bank of Canada operates monetary policy.

10-1 DEFINITIONS

We noted in Chapter 9 that the money supply measure $M1$ is the sum of demand deposits, DD, and currency held by the public, CU.

$$M1 = CD + CU \qquad (1)$$

A broader measure of the money supply is $M2$, which includes personal savings and term deposits and nonpersonal notice deposits, SD.

$$M2 = M1 + SD \qquad (2)$$

Table 10-1 summarizes the data in Table 9-1 and shows the components of the money stock in January 1984. $M1$ was \$28.8 billion of which about 41 percent was currency. $M2$ was over four times as large with personal

TABLE 10-1   COMPONENTS OF THE MONEY STOCK, JANUARY 1984 (millions of dollars, average of Wednesdays)

(1)	(2)	(3)	(4)	(5)	(6)
Currency	Demand deposits	$M1 =$ (1) + (2)	Personal savings & term dep.	Nonpersonal notice deposits	$M2 =$ (3) + (4) + (5)
11,891	16,901	28,792	101,342	5,541	135,675

Source: Bank of Canada Review

savings and term deposits making up the major portion of the difference between $M1$ and $M2$. Since these deposits have been growing more rapidly than $M1$, $M2$ has been growing more rapidly than $M1$. This can be seen in Figure 10-1 which shows the behaviour of these aggregates since 1968.

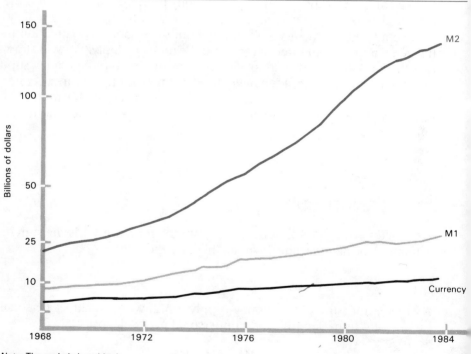

Note: The scale is logarithmic.

FIGURE 10-1   MONETARY AGGREGATES
(Source: Bank of Canada Review)

For simplicity, we shall now ignore the distinction between demand and savings deposits and consider the money supply process as if there were only a uniform class of deposits D. Using that simplification, we define money as deposits plus currency:

$$M \equiv CU + D \tag{3}$$

Starting from Equation (3), we now begin to develop the details of the process of money stock determination. It is apparent from Equation (3) that both the public and the chartered banks have an influence on the determination of the money supply. The public has a role because its demand for currency affects the currency component CU. The banks have a role because the other component of the money stock, deposits D, is a liability of the banks, that is, a debt the banks owe their customers. We know too that the Bank of Canada has a part (the most important) in determining the money supply. The interactions among the actions of the public, the chartered banks, and the Bank of Canada determine the money supply, and we shall summarize their behaviour in the money supply process by three separate variables.

The Public

From the viewpoint of money supply determination, the variable on which we concentrate as representing the behaviour of the public is the *currency-deposit ratio* (*cu*), that is, the ratio of the public's holding of currency (CU) to their holdings of deposits (D). Using the broader definition of the money supply ($M2$), the value of this ratio in January 1984 was .096 (equals $11.9 billion of currency divided by $123.8 billion of deposits).

The Chartered Banks

The behaviour of the chartered banks is summarized by the *cash reserve ratio*. Cash reserves are assets held by the chartered banks to meet (1) the demands of their customers for currency and (2) payments their customers make by cheques which are deposited in other banks. Cash reserves consist of notes held by the chartered banks (till money) and also of deposits held by the chartered banks at the Bank of Canada.

The chartered banks have accounts at the Bank of Canada which they can use to make payments among themselves. Thus when my bank has to make a payment to your bank because I paid you with a cheque drawn on my bank account, it makes the payment by transferring money from its account to your bank's account at the Bank of Canada.[1]

We examine the determinants of the banks' demand for cash reserves, RE, in more detail in Section 10-5, but in the meantime we summarize that behaviour by the ratio of cash reserves to deposits, $re \equiv RE/D$. The cash reserve ratio is less than 1 since banks hold other assets such as securities and loans they make to individuals and firms. In January 1984, the chartered banks held cash reserves of $6.3 billion so that the cash reserve ratio was $6.3/123.8 = .051$.

The Bank of Canada

The Bank of Canada's behaviour is summarized by the stock of *high-powered money*, or the *monetary base*, H. High-powered money consists of currency and deposits of the chartered banks at the Bank of Canada. Part of the currency is held by the public — the $11.9 billion previously referred to. The remainder is held by the chartered banks as till money. The notes that constitute most of the outstanding stock of currency are issued by the Bank of Canada, and the cash reserves held by chartered banks as Bank of Canada deposits are a liability of the Bank of Canada, that is a debt of the Bank of Canada to the chartered banks.

10-2   THE MONEY MULTIPLIER

In this section we develop a simple approach to money stock determination. The approach is organized around the supply of and the demand for *high-powered money*. The Bank of Canada can control the *supply* of high-powered money. The total *demand* for high-powered money comes from the public, who want to use it as currency, and the chartered banks, who need it as cash reserves. Because the public has a preferred ratio of currency to deposits and because the banks have a desired ratio of reserves to deposits, we can calculate the total money stock that can be supported by any given stock of high-powered money.

Before we go into the details, we want to think briefly about the relationship between the money stock and the stock of high-powered money. Figure 10-2 illustrates the relationship. At the top of the figure we show the stock of high-powered money. At the bottom we show the stock of money. They are related by the *money multiplier*. The money multiplier is the ratio of the stock of money to the stock of high-powered money.

The money multiplier is larger than 1. It is clear from the diagram that the multiplier is larger the larger are deposits as a fraction of the money stock. That is because currency uses up 1 dollar of high-powered money per dollar of money. Deposits, by contrast, use up only the amount re of high-powered money (in reserves) per dollar of money stock. For instance, if the reserve ratio re is 11 percent, every dollar of the money stock in the form of deposits uses up only 11 cents of high-powered money.

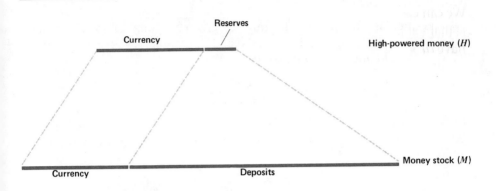

FIGURE 10-2   THE MONEY MULTIPLIER. The money multiplier is the ratio of the money stock (the base of the diagram) to high-powered money. The multiplier is larger than 1. It is larger, the smaller the ratio of currency to deposits and the smaller the ratio of cash reserves to deposits.

It is thus clear that (1) *the money multiplier is larger, the smaller is the reserve ratio re*. In addition, (2) *the money multiplier is larger, the smaller is the currency deposit ratio cu*. That is because the smaller is *cu*, the smaller the proportion of the high-powered money stock that is being used as currency (which translates high-powered money only one for one into money) and the larger the proportion that is available to be reserves (which translate much more than one for one into money).

The precise relationship between the money stock M, the stock of high-powered money H, the reserve-deposit ratio *re*, and the currency-deposit ratio *cu* is derived in the Appendix to this chapter. Here we present the resulting expression for the money supply expressed in terms of its principal determinants, *re*, *cu*, and H:

$$M = \frac{1 + cu}{re + cu} H \equiv mm \cdot H \qquad (4)$$

where *mm* is the money multiplier given by

$$mm \equiv \frac{1 + cu}{re + cu} \qquad (5)$$

Careful examination of the formula for the money multiplier (5) shows that the multiplier is higher the smaller the reserve ratio and the smaller the currency-deposit ratio — as our earlier discussion suggested.

Numerical Example

We can calculate the money multiplier as given by Equation (5) using the actual values of the two ratios that existed in January 1984. For $M2$, we have $cu = .096$ and $re = .051$, so that

$$mm = \frac{1 + .096}{.051 + .096} = 7.46$$

The same result can be obtained by taking the ratio of the $M2$ money stock ($135.7 billion) to the sum of currency ($11.9 billion) and reserves ($6.3 billion).

Graphical Analysis

Figure 10-3 shows graphically how the money multiplier works. The supply of high-powered money, $\overline{H}$, is shown by the horizontal black line. The demand for high-powered money, HD, is an upward-sloping line with slope equal to 1 over the money multiplier. The intersection point E is the point at which the demand for high-powered money is equal to the supply. The corresponding money supply is shown by M_0.

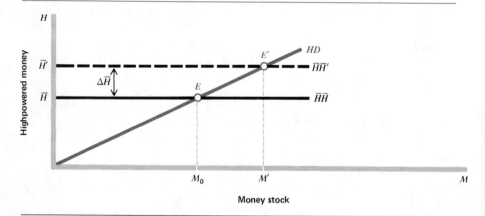

FIGURE 10-3   THE MONEY MULTIPLIER AND AN INCREASE IN THE MONETARY BASE. The HD schedule shows the demand for high-powered money, as related to the money stock M. The slope of the HD schedule is 1 over the money multiplier [see Equation (4)]. The supply of high-powered money is shown by the $\overline{H}\overline{H}$ schedule. At point E the demand for high-powered money is equal to supply. The corresponding money supply is M_0. An increase in the stock of high-powered money by $\Delta\overline{H}$ shifts the $\overline{H}\overline{H}$ schedule up to $\overline{H}\overline{H}'$, resulting in a new equilibrium money stock M'. The ratio of the distance $(M' - M_0)$ (the increase in the money stock) to $\Delta\overline{H}$ (the increase in the base) is equal to the money multiplier.

Now suppose the stock of high-powered money increases to H'. The $\overline{HH}$ schedule moves up by amount $\Delta\overline{H}$ to $\overline{HH}'$. The money supply increases until we reach point E', with new money stock M'. Because the slope of the HD schedule is less than 1, the distance between M_0 and M' is greater than $\Delta\overline{H}$. Indeed, the ratio of the distance $(M' - M_0)$, which is the increase in the money stock, to $\Delta\overline{H}$ is equal to the money multiplier.[2]

The Multiplier in Practice

The behaviour of the money multipliers over the period 1968 to 1984 is shown in Figure 10-4. A glance at this chart shows that they are far from constant. Since the Bank of Canada controls $\overline{H}$, it would be able to control

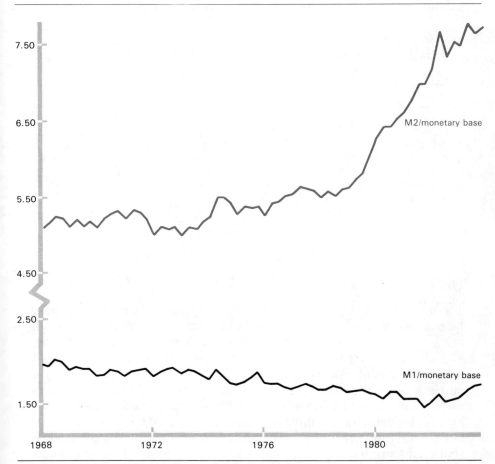

FIGURE 10-4   THE MONEY MULTIPLIERS, 1968–1983
(*Source: Bank of Canada Review*)

M exactly if the multiplier were constant or fully predictable. However, the money multiplier varies, not entirely predictably, and the Bank of Canada cannot always set the money supply at precisely the level it wants. In the rest of this chapter we take a closer look at the reasons the money multiplier varies.

10-3   THE STOCK OF HIGH-POWERED MONEY

Table 10-2 shows the balance sheet of the Bank of Canada. The components of the monetary base appear on the liability side and high-powered money is created when the Bank of Canada acquires assets or reduces its liability in the form of Government of Canada deposits.

TABLE 10-2   BALANCE SHEET OF THE BANK OF CANADA, JANUARY 1984 (millions of dollars)

Assets		**Liabilities**	
Government of Canada		Notes in circulation	
securities	$16,863	Held by chartered banks	$ 2,573
Advances	1	Other	10,704
Net foreign currency		Chartered bank deposits	3,700
assets	221	Government of Canada	
Other assets, net	270	deposits	378
Total assets	$17,355	Total liabilities	$17,355

Source: Bank of Canada Review

Open Market Operations

The major means by which the Bank of Canada changes the monetary base is *open market operations*. We will examine the mechanics of an open market *purchase*, an operation in which the Bank of Canada buys, say, $1 million of government bonds from individuals or businesses which comprise the nonbank private sector. The accounting for the open market purchase is shown in Table 10-3. The Bank of Canada's holdings of government securities rise by $1 million and the nonbank private sector's holdings fall by the same amount. How does the Bank of Canada pay for the bonds? It writes a cheque on itself and the seller deposits the cheque in a chartered bank which in turn sends the cheque to the Bank of Canada. Thus, chartered bank reserves held in the form of Bank of Canada deposits increase by $1 million. The Bank of Canada owns more government securities, and the stock of high-powered money has been increased by the amount of the open market purchase. That increase in high-powered money shows up as an increase in chartered bank deposits at the Bank of Canada. Later, as the money stock increases, the demand for currency will rise, and part of the increase in $\overline{H}$ will show up on the Bank of Canada's balance sheet as currency. Chartered bank deposits will fall by the amount that currency rises on the ("Liabilities") side of Table 10-3. You should now trace the way in which an open market sale reduces the stock of high-powered money.

TABLE 10-3   EFFECTS ON BALANCE SHEETS OF AN OPEN MARKET PURCHASE FROM THE NONBANK PRIVATE SECTOR

Nonbank private sector

Assets	Liabilities	
Government securities	− 1	
Deposits	+ 1	

Chartered Banks

Assets	Liabilities	
Cash reserves	+ 1 Deposits	+ 1

Bank of Canada

Assets	Liabilities	
Government securities	+ 1 Chartered bank deposits	+ 1

The only strange part of the story of the open market purchase is that the Bank of Canada can write cheques on itself. The cheque instructs the Bank to pay $1 million to the order of the seller of the bond. The payment is made by giving the eventual owner of the cheque a deposit at the Bank of Canada. That deposit can be used to make payments to other banks, or it can be exchanged for currency. Just as the ordinary deposit holder at a chartered bank can obtain currency in exchange for deposits, the chartered bank deposit holder at the Bank of Canada can acquire currency in exchange for its deposits. When the Bank of Canada pays for the bond with a deposit, it creates high-powered money with a stroke of the pen. Further, since it is the issuer of currency, it also creates high-powered money with the printing press. In either event, the Bank of Canada can create high-powered money at will merely by buying assets, such as government bonds, and paying for them with its liabilities.

We have assumed so far that the open market purchase is made from the nonbank private sector. What will happen if the seller is a chartered bank? This case is illustrated in Table 10-4. The chartered bank receives a cheque from the Bank of Canada and exchanges it for a deposit. Thus chartered bank cash reserves and the stock of high-powered money increase as in the previous case, but the transaction has no direct effect on the nonbank private sector.

TABLE 10-4   EFFECTS ON BALANCE SHEETS OF AN OPEN
            MARKET PURCHASE FROM A CHARTERED
            BANK

Chartered Banks

Assets		Liabilities
Government Securities	− 1	
Cash reserves	+ 1	

Bank of Canada

Assets		Liabilities	
Government securities	+ 1	Chartered bank deposits	+ 1

Government of Canada Deposits and the Base

As shown in Table 10-2, the Government of Canada maintains deposits with the Bank of Canada and it uses this account for government receipts and payments. If this were the only bank account maintained by the government, fluctuations in government revenues and expenditures would be reflected in fluctuations in the stock of high-powered money. For example, in a period in which the government receives more than it spends, there would be a transfer of deposits from the chartered banks to the government's account at the Bank of Canada so that cash reserves would be reduced. To avoid these effects, the Government of Canada maintains deposits with the chartered banks as well as with the Bank of Canada. Transfers of these deposits between the chartered banks and the Bank of Canada can then be used to offset the effects of government transactions and provide an alternative means of controlling the stock of high-powered money.

Borrowed Reserves

The chartered banks can increase their cash reserves by borrowing from the Bank of Canada at a rate of interest known as the *bank rate*. This arrangement is designed to provide a ''lender of last resort'' and advances are made to the chartered banks only occasionally. Rather than relying on advances from the Bank of Canada, the chartered banks typically meet their cash requirements by varying their holdings of interest-earning liquid assets or bidding for blocks of funds available for investment by large corporations. Earning liquid assets consist of treasury bills, Government of Canada bonds, day-to-day loans and other short-term loans.

Purchase and Resale Agreements

When a chartered bank varies its holdings of *day-to-day loans* for the purpose of managing its cash position, there can be an indirect effect on the monetary base. These loans are made to a group of investment dealers who carry inventories of Government of Canada securities. When necessary, these dealers can in turn obtain financing from the Bank of Canada under *purchase and resale agreements (PRA)*; that is, they can sell securities to the Bank of Canada with an agreement to repurchase them within a stated maximum time period.

Thus, when the chartered banks reduce their day-to-day loans they may induce an increase in PRA, so that the end result is the same as if the banks had borrowed from the Bank of Canada directly. Of the $16,863 million of government securities held by the Bank of Canada in January 1984 (see Table 10-2), $113 million were held under PRA.

10-4   THE SIZE OF THE MONEY MULTIPLIER

As we have seen, the size of the money multiplier depends on the currency-deposit ratio and the cash reserve ratio. We now consider the determinants of these two ratios.

The Currency-Deposit Ratio

The currency-deposit ratio reflects the behaviour of the public and is determined primarily by payment habits. It has a strong seasonal pattern and is highest around Christmas. It increases when the ratio of consumption to GNP increases, since currency demand is more closely linked to consumption than GNP, while deposit demand is more closely linked to GNP.

The ratio of currency to demand deposits has shown a rising trend and this accounts for some of the decline in the $M1$ multiplier shown in Figure 10-4.

The Cash Reserve Ratio

The banking system affects the money multiplier through the ratio of cash reserves to deposits. The major determinants of this ratio are the *minimum required cash reserve ratios* prescribed under the Bank Act. Under the provisions of the 1980 changes to the Bank Act, the ratio for demand deposits is currently set at 10 percent. For notice deposits, the ratio is 2 percent for the first $500 million of deposits in each bank, and 3 percent for the remainder. The foreign currency component of $M3$ is also subject to a 3 percent minimum reserve ratio.

Excess Cash Reserves

A second factor affecting the cash-reserve ratio is the amount of *excess cash reserves* held by the chartered banks beyond the level of required cash reserves. In deciding how much excess reserves to hold, a bank's economic problem is very similar to the problem of the individual in deciding on a precautionary demand for money. Banks hold reserves to meet demands on them for currency or payments to other banks. The opportunity cost of holding excess cash reserves is the interest foregone and in principle we might expect the demand to depend on the rate of interest. However, since chartered bank holdings of excess cash reserves are typically very small (less than one-tenth of one percent of total deposits) this relationship is not of much importance in determining the money mutiplier.

10-5   BANK LENDING AND THE MONEY MULTIPLIER

As can be seen from the balance sheet in Table 10-5, loans and investments make up a substantial fraction of chartered bank assets. In this section, we show how the process of bank lending plays an important role in the operation of the money multiplier and the determination of the money supply.

TABLE 10-5   BALANCE SHEET OF THE CHARTERED BANKS, JANUARY 1984 (billions of dollars)

Assets		Liabilities	
Bank of Canada notes		Demand deposits	$ 16.8
and deposits	$ 6.3	Personal savings deposits	101.3
Loans and investments		Nonpersonal term and	
Government of Canada		notice deposits	43.1
securities	15.3	Government of Canada	
Loans	149.3	deposits	6.0
Other securities	12.9	Other liabilities, net	16.6
Total Canadian dollar			
major assets	$183.8	Total	$183.8

Source: Bank of Canada Review

When banks make loans or purchase securities, they pay for the assets they acquire by creating deposits. A bank that makes a loan to a customer does not give the customer currency, but rather gives the loan in the form of a deposit at the bank and allows the customer to draw on the deposit either by taking out currency or writing a cheque on the account.

The Adjustment Process

For purposes of illustration we assume a currency-deposit ratio of .25 and a cash reserve ratio of .10. Suppose the stock of high-powered money has been increased by 1 dollar through an open market purchase. We start by considering the individual who sold the bond to the Bank of Canada. That person is paid with a cheque which he or she takes to the bank. Since this person, like all asset holders, has a currency-deposit ratio of cu, he or she will keep a fraction $cu/(1 + cu)$ as currency and deposit the balance. With $cu = .25$, he or she keeps 20 cents ($= .25/1.25$ dollars) as currency and deposits 80 cents.

At this stage the money stock has increased by only 1 dollar as a result of the increase in the stock of high-powered money. The effect of the deposit on the bank's balance sheet is shown in Table 10-6a. The bank has increased its cash reserves by 80 cents as a result of depositing at the Bank of Canada the cheque received from its customer and then paying out 20 cents in currency.

Now comes the crucial stage. The bank does not want to hold the *entire* extra 80 cents as cash reserves. The bank's reserve ratio is only re, so that it will hold only re of an extra dollar of deposits it receives in the form of cash reserves and lend out the rest to earn interest. Given $re = .10$, it will lend out 72 cents ($= .90 \times 80$ cents).

This loan is shown in Table 10-6b. For simplicity we assume the borrower receives the loan of 72 cents in the form of currency. *It is at this stage that the bank's lending activities have increased the money supply by more than the increase in high-powered money.* The person who sold the bond to the Bank of Canada has 1 more dollar of money, but the person who borrowed from the bank also has more money holdings — the 72 cents lent by the bank. The money supply has increased by $1.72.

The person receiving the 72 cents will now want to hold a fraction $cu/(1 + cu)$ as bank deposits, but when this amount is deposited in a bank, the bank will want to lend out a fraction $1 - re$. Clearly the process can keep going through many stages.

TABLE 10-6   EFFECTS OF LENDING ON BANK BALANCE SHEETS*

(a)			(b)			
Assets		**Liabilities**	**Assets**		**Liabilities**	
Cash reserves	80	Deposits 80	Cash reserves	8	Deposits	80
			Loans	72		

*In (a), reserves and deposits both increase by $1/(1 + cu)$. In (b), the bank lends out the fraction $1 - re$ of the reserves. The values of cu and re are .25 and .10 respectively.

TABLE 10-7 MULTIPLE EXPANSION OF BANK DEPOSITS, BANK LOANS, AND THE MONEY MULTIPLIER

Increase in H	Increase in currency	Increase in deposits	Increase in reserves	Increase in bank loans	Stage
1	$\dfrac{cu}{1+cu}$	$\dfrac{1}{1+cu}$	$\dfrac{re}{1+cu}$	$\dfrac{1-re}{1+cu}$	Round 1
	$\dfrac{cu}{1+cu}\left(\dfrac{1-re}{1+cu}\right)$	$\dfrac{1}{1+cu}\left(\dfrac{1-re}{1+cu}\right)$	$\dfrac{re}{1+cu}\left(\dfrac{1-re}{1+cu}\right)$	$\dfrac{1-re}{1+cu}\left(\dfrac{1-re}{1+cu}\right)$	Round 2
	$\dfrac{cu}{1+cu}\left(\dfrac{1-re}{1+cu}\right)^2$	$\dfrac{1}{1+cu}\left(\dfrac{1-re}{1+cu}\right)^2$	$\dfrac{re}{1+cu}\left(\dfrac{1-re}{1+cu}\right)^2$	$\dfrac{1-re}{1+cu}\left(\dfrac{1-re}{1+cu}\right)^2$	Round 3
	$\dfrac{cu}{1+cu}\left(\dfrac{1-re}{1+cu}\right)^n$	$\dfrac{1}{1+cu}\left(\dfrac{1-re}{1+cu}\right)^n$	$\dfrac{re}{1+cu}\left(\dfrac{1-re}{1+cu}\right)^n$	$\dfrac{1-re}{1+cu}\left(\dfrac{1-re}{1+cu}\right)^n$	Round $n+1$
	$\dfrac{cu}{1+cu}SUM$	$\dfrac{1}{1+cu}SUM$	$\dfrac{re}{1+cu}SUM$	$\dfrac{1-re}{1+cu}SUM$	Total*
	$\dfrac{cu}{cu+re}$	$\dfrac{1}{cu+re}$	$\dfrac{re}{cu+re}$	$\dfrac{1-re}{cu+re}$	After substituting for SUM from Equation (7)

*SUM is defined by Equation (7).

Table 10-7 shows the successive steps by which the money multiplier builds up as a result of the decisions of individuals to deposit part of their increased money holdings in the banks, and the decision of the banks to make loans (or buy securities). Round 1 is the process described in Table 10-6, ending with the bank making a loan. Round 2 starts when the borrower spends the loan, and the person receiving the proceeds holds some of that amount as currency and deposits the rest in a bank. Round 2 ends once again with a bank loan, and so forth.

We can now add up the increases in currency, deposits, reserves, and bank credit occurring over all the rounds together, that is, during the entire process. As in the Appendix to Chapter 8, we are now dealing with the sum of an infinite series, denoted here as *SUM*. That sum is given by[3]

$$SUM = 1 + \left(\frac{1-re}{1+cu}\right) + \left(\frac{1-re}{1+cu}\right)^2 + \left(\frac{1-re}{1+cu}\right)^3 + \dots$$

$$= \frac{1+cu}{cu+re} \tag{7}$$

We use Equation (7) in arriving at the bottom row of Table 10-7, which shows that currency increases by the fraction $[cu/(cu+re)]$ of \$1 following the increase in H of \$1, that deposits increase by $[1/(cu+re)]$, that reserves increase by $[re/(cu+re)]$, and finally, that credit increases by $[(1-re)/(cu+re)]$.

Adding the increases in currency and deposits, we discover that the two together have risen by the amount $[(1+cu)/(cu+re)]$, which is nothing other than the money multiplier. Table 10-7 thus provides another way of thinking about the money multiplier. The table also shows how, and by how much, the banking system creates loans (or buys securities) when the central bank increases high-powered money.

In our numerical example, currency increases by \$0.714 $[cu/(cu+re)]$, deposits by \$2.857 $[1/(cu+re)]$, reserves by \$0.286 $[re/(cu+re)]$, and bank loans by \$2.571 $[(1-re)(cu+re)]$. The money stock increases by \$3.571 or 3.571 times the increase in the stock of high-powered money. This is the value that can be obtained directly from the sum of the infinite series shown in Equation (7).

Multiple Expansion of Bank Deposits

Table 10-7 illustrates the process known as the *multiple expansion of bank deposits*. It shows how an increase in deposits leads to further deposits, and therefore how the money multiplier works. There is one further interesting aspect of the results shown in Table 10-7. It is possible to say that the banking system creates money in the sense that if there were not a banking system, a \$1 increase in H would increase the money stock only by \$1.

With the banking system, the \$1 increase in H leads to more than a \$1 increase in M.[4]

The interesting point is that at each stage of the process, no one bank believes it is, or can be said to be, creating money. At each stage, each bank in the process is only lending out money that has been deposited with it. Each bank manager would rightly, and no doubt vehemently, deny that the bank is creating money. The system as a whole, though, is creating money through the successive rounds of loans and subsequent further bank deposits.

10-6   CONTROL OF THE MONEY STOCK AND CONTROL OF THE INTEREST RATE

We make a simple but important point in this section: The Bank of Canada cannot simultaneously set both the interest rate and the stock of money at any given target levels that it may choose. If the Bank of Canada wants to achieve a given interest rate target, such as 8 percent, it has to supply the amount of money that is demanded at that interest rate. If it wants to set the money supply at a given level, say \$30 billion in the month of June 1984, it has to allow the interest rate to adjust to equate the demand for money to that supply of money.

Figure 10-5 illustrates the point. Suppose that the Bank of Canada, for some reason, decides that it wants to set the interest rate at a level i^* and the money stock at the level M^*, but that the demand for money function is as shown in $L(i, Y_0)$. The Bank is able to move the money supply around but it is not able to move the money demand function around. It therefore has to accept that it can set only the combinations of the interest rate and the money supply that lie along the money demand function. At the interest rate i^*, it can have the money supply $M_0/\overline{P}$. At the target money supply $M^*/\overline{P}$, it can have the interest rate i_0. But it cannot have both $M^*/\overline{P}$ and i^*.

The point is sometimes put more dramatically as follows. When the Bank of Canada decides to set the interest rate at some given level and keep it fixed — a policy known as *pegging* the interest rate — it loses control over the money supply. It has to supply whatever amount of money is demanded at that interest rate. If the money demand curve were to shift, because of income growth, say, the Bank would have to increase the stock of high-powered money to increase the money supply.

As an operational matter, the Bank of Canada in its day-to-day operations can more easily control interest rates exactly than it can control the money stock exactly. The Bank buys and sells government securities — primarily treasury bills — on a regular basis. If the Bank of Canada wants to raise the price of government securities (lower the interest rate), it can

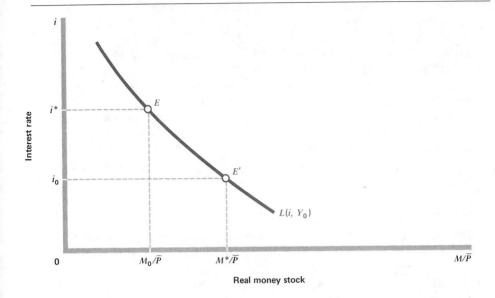

CONTROLLING THE MONEY STOCK AND INTEREST RATES. The Bank of Canada cannot simultaneously set both the interest rate and the money stock levels it wants. Suppose it wanted the interest rate to be i^* and the money stock to be M^*. These two levels are inconsistent with the demand for money. If the Bank insists on the interest rate level i^*, it will have to accept a money stock equal to M_0. If instead the Bank wants to set the money stock at M^*, it will end up with an interest rate equal to i_0.

buy the securities at the price it wants. If it wants to reduce the price of government securities (raise the interest rate), it can sell a sufficient amount of securities from its large portfolio. Thus, on a day-to-day basis, the Bank can determine interest rates quite accurately.

10-7 OTHER INSTRUMENTS OF MONETARY POLICY

The above discussion has focussed on the operation of monetary policy through control of the monetary base using open market operations. The Bank of Canada also makes use of changes in the bank rate and *secondary reserve requirements* to influence credit markets.

Changes in the Bank Rate

As indicated in Section 10-3 above, the bank rate is the rate of interest at which the Bank of Canada makes advances to the chartered banks. In principle, an increase in the bank rate can affect the money supply by raising the chartered bank's demands for excess cash reserves. Banks might be induced to maintain a larger cushion in view of the higher cost of borrowing if they suffer a loss of cash and are forced to seek accommodation from the Bank of Canada to meet their reserve requirements. It is not likely that this mechanism is of much importance in Canada, since the chartered banks rarely borrow from the Bank of Canada. On the other hand, the bank rate still plays a role as a signal of the Bank's view concerning the appropriate level of interest rates and its intentions with regard to monetary tightness or ease. These "announcement effects" of bank rate changes can be used to reinforce changes in other instruments of monetary policy.

The Floating Bank Rate

During the period 1956–1962 and more recently beginning in March 1980, the Bank of Canada has used a floating bank rate system under which the rate is automatically set each week at one-quarter of one percent above the rate of interest on 91-day treasury bills. At other times the bank rate has been fixed at the discretion of the Bank of Canada.

The main advantage of the floating rate is that it automatically maintains a small penalty cost to a chartered bank that makes use of Bank of Canada advances to replenish its cash reserves rather than selling some of its earning liquid assets. However, this system has been a subject of considerable controversy in the financial community. The objections are misguided to the extent that they are based on the notion that the Bank of Canada can control interest rates as a separate objective of policy while at the same time independently controlling the money supply. As we saw in the previous section, this is clearly not possible.

A legitimate argument is that the floating bank rate eliminates the information concerning Bank of Canada intentions provided by announced changes. On the other hand, these announcement effects are a somewhat clumsy and inefficient means of transmitting information. In periods of rapidly changing interest rates, bank rate changes have frequently followed rather than led changes in market rates. The volatility of interest rates during 1980 is cited by the Bank of Canada as the major reason for the return to a floating rate.[5]

Secondary Reserve Requirements

At times when the Bank of Canada is attempting to restrain inflationary forces, it may wish to dampen expenditures not only through higher interest rates but also through some form of direct control over the expansion of bank loans. Restricting the supply of cash reserves will not restrain the banks from extending credit if they have substantial quantities of liquid assets that can be sold off to finance new loans. The Bank of Canada is empowered to restrict the ability of the chartered banks to expand their loans through the imposition of a required minimum secondary reserve ratio within the range of 0 to 12 percent of deposits. Secondary reserves are defined as holdings of treasury bills, day-to-day loans, and excess cash reserves.

A required minimum ratio of 9 percent was set in July 1970. Over the period 1971 to 1981, it was lowered in stages to 4 percent and it has remained at that level since.

---

*10-8 SHORT-RUN CONTROL OF THE MONEY SUPPLY

The discussion of bank deposit expansion given above neglected some institutional features of reserve requirements that influence the short-run response of the banking system to changes in the supply of high-powered money.[6]

Reserve Averaging Period

An individual bank is subject to erratic day-to-day fluctuations in its cash position as cheques are cleared and deposits are transferred from one bank to another. In view of this, the required reserve ratios apply not to each day's holdings of cash reserves, but to the average level over some specified period. Since 1969, this reserve averaging period has been two weeks. Thus, banks do not need to adjust to changes in their cash reserves on a particular day unless they are approaching the end of a two-week period with an average level of reserves below the minimum requirement.

Furthermore, the level of required cash reserves in effect at any time is not based on the current volume of deposits, but rather on the average volume of deposits during the *preceding* month. Thus, an expansion of loans and deposits will not affect total excess reserves during the current month, but will increase the level of required reserves that must be held in the following month. Of course, to the extent that the banks are not all expanding their loans at the same rate, deposits and cash will be redistributed, so that the faster growing banks will tend to lose reserves to the slower growing ones.

Chartered bank holdings of Bank of Canada notes that can be counted towards reserve requirements are also calculated as an average over the preceding month. This means that changes in the public's demand for currency have no effect on a bank's reserve position in the current month unless they induce the bank to reduce or replenish its till money by respectively increasing or running down its deposits at the Bank of Canada.

Actual Versus Desired Excess Cash Reserves

Under the circumstances described above, the Bank of Canada can control not only the total base, but also the reserve component of the base. Further, since required cash reserves are determined by deposits in the preceding month, effective control can be exercised over the excess cash reserves of the chartered banks.

The method by which the Bank of Canada induces changes in the money supply is to cause the actual level of excess reserves to diverge from the level which the banks find it desirable to maintain.[7] Suppose that the Bank of Canada wishes to bring about a contraction of the money supply. By setting the level of excess cash reserves below the level regarded by the banks as a minimum acceptable one, it will induce the banks to sell liquid assets in an attempt to increase their holdings of cash. However, the banking system as a whole will be frustrated in this attempt, since the assets it sells will be paid for by cheques drawn on the banks; assets and deposits will fall but cash reserves will remain the same. In addition, interest rates will rise since the banks will have to offer increased yields to induce nonbank investors to increase their holdings of securities at the expense of their holdings of bank deposits. As long as the supply of excess cash reserves is kept below the level desired by the banks, the money supply will continue to fall and interest rates will continue to rise.

Thus, if the Bank of Canada wishes to reduce the money supply by some target amount, it keeps the banks in a tight cash position until the target is achieved, and then restores the supply of cash reserves to the level desired by the banks. Similarly, an increase in the money supply is brought about by injecting additional cash into the banking system and inducing the banks to bid for additional liquid assets. In practice, this control of the money supply through cash reserve management by the Bank of Canada is a process of successive approximation, because the level of cash desired by the banks varies and cannot easily be predicted. By testing the reaction of the banks to a particular supply of cash, the Bank of Canada can estimate the target levels of cash that the banks are attempting to achieve and adjust the supply accordingly.

10-8 SUMMARY

1   The stock of money is determined by the Bank of Canada through its control of the monetary base (high-powered money); the public through its preferred currency-deposit ratio; and the chartered banks through the cash reserve ratio.

2   The money multiplier is the ratio of the money stock to high-powered money. It is larger the smaller the cash reserve ratio and the smaller

the currency-deposit ratio. The major determinants of the cash reserve ratio are the minimum required cash reserve ratios.

3   The Bank of Canada controls the money supply primarily through open market operations. These are purchases and sales of government securities that have a direct affect on the stock of high-powered money.

4   The adjustment to a change in the stock of high powered money takes place in stages as banks lend out the excess reserves which arise from deposit creation at the previous stage.

5   The Bank of Canada cannot set both the interest rate and the stock of money at independently chosen target levels. It chooses only those combinations that are consistent with the demand for money.

6   Other instruments of monetary policy are changes in the bank rate and secondary reserve requirements. Beginning in 1980, the Bank of Canada adopted a floating bank rate which is automatically set each week at one-quarter of one percent above the treasury bill rate.

7   Since required cash reserves depend on average deposits in the preceding month, the Bank of Canada can exercise control over the money supply in the short run by setting the supply of excess cash reserves. Changes in the money supply are induced by purchases or sales of liquid assets by the chartered banks in response to deviations of actual cash reserves from the desired level.

KEY TERMS

Currency-deposit ratio
Cash reserve ratio
High-powered money (monetary base)
Money multiplier
Open market operation

Bank rate
Excess cash reserves
Multiple expansion of bank deposits
Secondary reserve requirements
Floating bank rate

PROBLEMS

1   Use Figure 10-3 to show how (a) an increase in the currency-deposit ratio and (b) an increase in the cash reserve ratio affect the money stock, given the monetary base.

2 Show the effects on the balance sheets of the Bank of Canada and the chartered banks of a change in the monetary base brought about by a transfer of government deposits from the chartered banks to the Bank of Canada.

3 Table 10-3 shows the initial impact on the Bank of Canada's balance sheet of an open market purchase. As noted in the text, at the end of the process both currency and chartered bank deposits at the Bank of Canada rise. What is the final increase in currency? Use the ratios cu and re in arriving at your answer.

4 A proposal for "100 percent banking" involves a reserve-deposit ratio of unity. Such a scheme has been proposed in order to enhance control over the money supply. Indicate (a) why such a scheme would help monetary control and (b) what bank balance sheets would look like under this scheme. (c) How would banking remain profitable, under 100 percent money?

5 Suppose a bank has excess reserves and makes a loan to someone who immediately withdraws the deposit the bank has given him and holds it as currency. Why does the bank's granting of the loan increase the money supply?

6 Discuss the impact of credit cards on the money multiplier.

7 This problem extends the analysis of the chapter by further distinguishing between $M1$ and $M2$. Assume a currency-demand deposit ratio cu and a desired ratio of demand to notice deposits of the public, $d = DD/ND$. Assume, too, that banks have reserve ratios, described by r_d and r_n, with respect to demand and notice deposits, where the reserve ratio for notice deposits r_n is lower than that for demand deposits r_d.
   (a) Use the definition of $M1$ and the ratios d, r_d and r_n to derive an expression for the equilibrium stock of $M1$.
   (b) Use the definition of $M2$ and the ratios to derive an expression for the equilibrium stock of $M2$.
   (c) Show the effects of an increase in the demand-notice deposit ratio on credit.

8 Use Figure 10-3 and an $IS\text{-}LM$ diagram to show the effect of an increase in required reserves on:
   (a) The equilibrium money supply
   (b) Interest rates
   (c) The equilibrium level of income

9 The Canada Deposit Insurance Corporation insures chartered bank deposits against bank default. Discuss the implications of that deposit scheme for the money multiplier.

10 Assume required reserves were zero. Would banks hold any reserves?

APPENDIX

We derive the equilibrium money stock and the multiplier by looking at the demand and supply of money and of high-powered money. Consider, first, equilibrium between the supply of money and the demand for money, which, in turn, equals currency plus deposits:

$$M = CU + D \equiv (cu + 1)D \qquad \text{(A1)}$$

where we have substituted for $CU = cuD$, noting the public's desired ratio of currency to deposits cu.

Equilibrium between the supply of high-powered money and the demand for high-powered money which equals currency plus reserves implies:

$$\overline{H} = CU + RE \equiv (cu + re)D \qquad \text{(A2)}$$

Again we have expressed the demand side in terms of the desired ratio of currency to deposits and of the banks' cash reserve ratio re. When (A1) and (A2) both hold, we are in monetary equilibrium because people hold the composition of their money balances in the preferred ratio and banks hold just the right ratio of reserves to deposits.

Dividing (A2) by (A1) yields an expression for the money multiplier:

$$M/\overline{H} = mm \equiv \frac{1 + cu}{cu + re} \qquad \text{(A3)}$$

The money multiplier thus depends on the cu ratio and the re ratio. We can also use (A3), multiplying both sides by $\overline{H}$, to obtain the money supply in terms of the principal determinants mm and $\overline{H}$:

$$M = mm\,\overline{H} \qquad \text{(A4)}$$

In writing (A4) we remember that mm is dependent on the currency-deposit preferences of the public and the cash reserve ratio of banks. It thus takes into account preferences about the composition of balance sheets.

CHAPTER 10: FOOTNOTES

[1]Since the establishment of the Canadian Payments Association in 1980, other financial institutions such as trust companies have also been able to participate in the cheque clearing system by maintaining deposits at the Bank of Canada.

[2]In problem 1, we ask you to use Fig. 10-3 to show the effects of increases in the currency-deposit ratio (cu) and the reserve-deposit ratio (re) on the money multiplier and the money stock. Changes in these ratios change the slope of the HD line in Fig. 10-3.

[3] *Technical note*: The formula for the sum of a geometric series, which can in general be written

$$SUM = 1 + a + a^2 + \ldots$$

where a is a number between minus and plus 1, is

$$SUM = \frac{1}{1 - a}$$

If you have not met geometric series before, you may want to take an example, say, $a = \frac{1}{4}$, and start adding the terms in the first formula in the footnote. You will soon find your answer coming close to $\frac{4}{3}$, which is the answer given by the second formula in the footnote.

[4] Bank loans and purchases of securities are described as *bank credit*. It is the existence of bank credit that makes the money stock larger than the stock of high-powered money. If banks did not extend credit (that is, did not make loans or buy securities), the entire multiple expansion process would never get off the ground, and we would have $M = H$.

[5] See *Annual Report* of the Bank of Canada for 1980, p. 9, 34.

[6] For a detailed description of the requirements under the Bank Act, see *Bank of Canada Review*, notes to Table 14.

[7] For a detailed discussion of this mechanism, see J.F. Dingle, G.R. Sparks and M.A. Walker, "Monetary Policy and the Adjustment of Chartered Bank Assets," *Canadian Journal of Economics*, Nov., 1972.

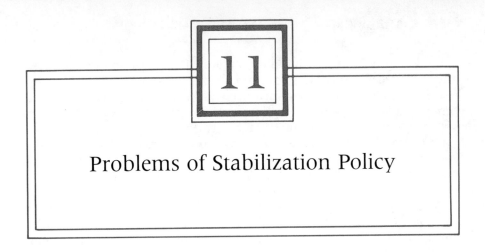

Problems of Stabilization Policy

This chapter discusses the problems of macroeconomic policy making. An understanding of the general difficulties of carrying out successful stabilization policies — policies to reduce the fluctuations of the economy — helps explain economic performance over the past 30 years. Figure 11-1, which shows the unemployment rate over the period 1931–1983, gives the clear impression that stabilization policy has left something to be desired.

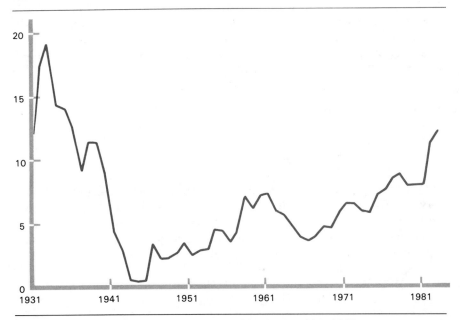

FIGURE 11-1   UNEMPLOYMENT RATE IN CANADA, 1931–1983
(*Source*: Statistics Canada, 11-505; Department of Finance, *Economic Review*)

The reason for discussing the problems of stabilization policy here is that the preceding chapters have laid out a clear body of theory that seems to show exactly the policy measures that can be used to maintan full employment. We saw that high unemployment, or a large GNP gap, can be reduced by an expansion in aggregate demand. An increase in aggregate demand in turn can be achieved by expansionary monetary or fiscal policies: an increase in the money supply, a reduction in taxes, an increase in government spending, or an increase in transfers. Similarly, a boom can be contained by restrictive monetary or fiscal policies.

The policies needed to prevent the fluctuations in unemployment shown in Figure 11-1 accordingly appear to be simple and obvious. The policy maker knows the full-employment level of output. If there is unemployment, he or she can use a model, such as the *IS-LM* model, to calculate the level of government spending or taxes needed to get income to the full-employment level. But if it is so simple, how did the fluctuations in Figure 11-1 occur? The answer must be that policy making is far from simple. Part of the difficulty arises from the possible *conflict between the maintenance of full employment and the target of low inflation*. That important issue is discussed in Chapters 15 and 16. Other difficulties are described in this chapter.

We begin by discussing the types of disturbance that cause the economy to move away from the full-employment level of output in the first place. Then we briefly describe *econometric models*, models of the economy with specific numerical values for parameters and multipliers, that can be used to assist policy making. The bulk of the chapter is taken up by a discussion of three factors that in large measure account for the failure of policy continually to achieve its targets. The three *handicaps of policy making* are:

1 Lags in the effects of policy
2 The role of expectations in determining private sector responses to policy
3 Uncertainty about the effects of policy

In a nutshell, we are going to argue that a policy maker who (1) observes a disturbance, (2) does not know whether it is permanent or not, (3) takes time to develop a policy which (4) takes still more time to affect behaviour and (5) has uncertain effects on aggregate demand is very poorly equipped to do a perfect job of stabilizing the economy.

11-1   ECONOMIC DISTURBANCES

Before identifying in detail the obstacles in the way of successful policy making, we discuss economic disturbances in terms of their sources, persistence, and importance for policy. Disturbances are shifts in aggregate demand or aggregate supply, or shifts in money demand or money supply, that cause output, interest rates, or prices to diverge from their target paths.

We return to the *IS-LM* model as the framework for the discussion of economic disturbances in this chapter. In Figure 11-2 we show the *IS* and *LM* schedules and also the full-employment level of output, $\overline{Y}$. The economy is initially at full employment at point *E*. Now what disturbances might cause the economy to move away from full employment? Obviously, anything that shifts the *IS* and/or *LM* curves would disturb the economy and move it away from *E*.

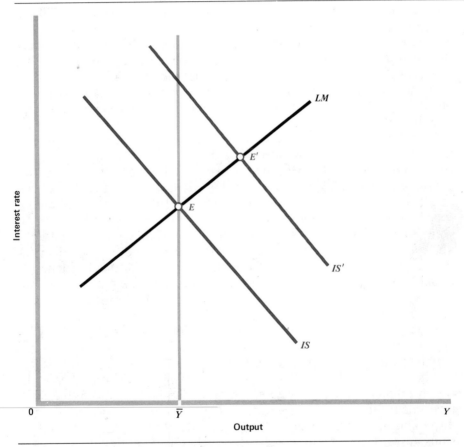

FIGURE 11-2   AN AGGREGATE DEMAND DISTURBANCE. The economy is initially in equilibrium at point *E*, with level of output $\overline{Y}$. An increase in government spending shifts the *IS* curve to *IS'*. This disturbance tends to raise the level of output above the full-employment level. Monetary and/or fiscal policy, or even rationing, may be used to keep the level of demand in check, shifting the *IS'* curve back to *IS* and/or shifting the *LM* curve up and to the left.

In terms of overall economic impact, the major disturbances to the economy — the forces moving the *IS* and *LM* curves — have been wars. The effects of the increases in government spending associated with World War II and the Korean War can be seen in Chart 11-1 in the very low unemployment rates in those periods. Of these, World War II had the largest impact on the economy. At the height of the war, in 1944, federal government spending exceeded 40 percent of GNP.

As shown in Figure 11-2, an increase in government spending would shift the *IS* schedule upward and therefore lead to an excess demand for goods. To contain aggregate spending to the full-employment level of output, increased government spending would have to be offset by a reduction in private demand, that is, a reduction in investment and/or consumption spending. Investment spending can be reduced by allowing the interest rate to rise, and consumption spending can be reduced by increasing income taxes. These conventional economic policies may not be sufficient in wartime, however. In World War II more direct methods of reducing investment and consumption were used. A system was set up in which investment projects had to be approved. That system served to reduce the overall rate of private investment and also to direct investment toward areas helpful for the war effort. There was also some rationing of consumption goods, which reduced consumption expenditure as some of the rationed demand spilled over into increased saving rather than being diverted toward other goods. Thus, the aggregate level of consumption spending was reduced by using rationing to reduce the consumption of various goods essential for the war effort (gasoline, tires, shoes, etc.).[1]

Changes in government spending or tax policies not connected with wars may also constitute economic disturbances. Government spending or taxes may be increased or reduced for reasons which have to do with the government's view of desirable social policies. Those changes too may affect the level of aggregate demand if not accompanied by appropriate monetary and fiscal policies. In a country like Canada that is heavily dependent on foreign trade, changes in foreign demand for our exports may be an important source of disturbances.

Other economic disturbances that lead to changes in aggregate demand, which originate in the private sector, are shifts in the consumption or investment function. If consumers decide to consume more out of their disposable income at any given level of income, the *IS* curve of Figure 11-2 shifts upward, tending to increase the level of income. If there is no economic explanation for the shift in the consumption function, then it is attributed to a change in the tastes of consumers between consumption and saving. In such a case, we describe the shift as a disturbance.

Similarly, if investment spending increases for no apparent economic reason, then we attribute the increase to an unexplained change in the optimism of investors about the returns from investment. Again, we regard that change in investment behaviour as a disturbance to the system.

Changes in the optimism of investors are sometimes described as changes in their *animal spirits* — a term that suggests that there may be little rational basis for those spirits.[2] Some shifts in the investment function are caused by new inventions that require large amounts of investment for their successful marketing, such as the development of the railways in the nineteenth century and the spread of the automobile in the 1920s.

Shifts in the demand for money may affect the interest rate, and thus indirectly affect the rate of investment; they, too, constitute a possible source of private sector economic disturbances.

Disturbances that we have not yet incorporated in our basic theoretical framework also affect the level of income. These include changes in supply conditions, such as the oil embargo of 1973–1974, which will affect the level of income and are discussed in Chapter 13. In Chapter 15, we also discuss the possibility that the behaviour of wages may constitute a source of economic disturbances.

Finally, there is the interesting possibility that disturbances may be caused by the policy makers themselves. There are two different arguments concerning this possibility. First, since policy making is difficult, it is entirely possible that the attempts of policy makers to stabilize the economy could be counterproductive. Indeed, a forcefully stated and influential view of the causes of the Great Depression[3] argues that an inept monetary policy in the United States was chiefly responsible for the severity of the depression. The argument of Friedman and Schwartz is basically that the officials in charge of the American central bank in the early 1930s did not understand the workings of monetary policy and therefore carried out a policy that made the depression worse rather than better.

The second argument that policy makers themselves may be responsible for economic disturbances arises from the relationship between election results and economic conditions in the period before the election.[4] If it appears that incumbents tend to be reelected when economic conditions, primarily the unemployment rate, are improving in the year before the election, it is tempting for them to try to *improve* economic conditions in the period before the election; their efforts may involve tax reductions or increases in government spending. It is not quite common to talk of the *political business cycle*. The political business cycle consists of economic fluctuations produced by economic policies designed to help win elections.

It has been argued that election results are significantly affected by the growth rate, rather than the level, of income, in the year leading up to an election. If that is so, then it is tempting indeed for governments to start an expansion in an election year. Despite the difficulties of policy making, it is always easy to start an economic expansion in the short run — though not to control it later when its inflationary consequences appear. While there is some evidence to support the notion of a political business cycle, the argument should be regarded as tentative because the link between economic conditions and election results is not yet firmly established.

We proceed next to discuss econometric models and the three factors that make the task of policy makers far more difficult than an overliteral interpretation of the simple *IS-LM* model in Figure 11-2 might suggest.

11-2 ECONOMETRIC MODELS FOR POLICY MAKING AND FORECASTING

In Figure 11-3 we show the typical situation facing economic policy makers. Something has happened that created a recession. Output is at level Y_0 rather than full-employment level $\bar{Y}$. How should policy makers react if they want to get output back to the full-employment level? The *IS-LM* model gives a number of choices. One possibility is to increase the money stock. Or taxes could be reduced, or government spending increased.

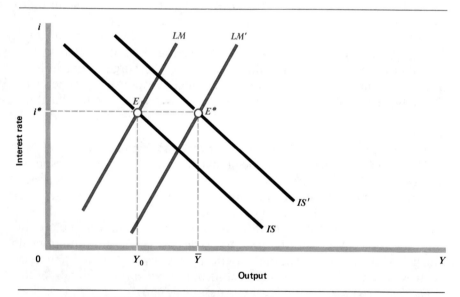

FIGURE 11-3 POLICIES TO END A RECESSION. The economy is in a recession at point *E*. Policy makers plan to return to full-employment output at the interest rate *i**, at point *E**. The *IS* curve has to be shifted to *IS'* and the *LM* curve to *LM'*. This requires expansionary fiscal and monetary policy. The precise amounts to increase government spending and the money stock can be calculated from the government spending and monetary policy multipliers.

Suppose the decision has been made to attempt to return to full employment at point *E**, with the interest rate remaining at *i**. Suppose also that the plan is to do this by increasing government spending and at the same time expanding the money supply. The *IS* curve has to be shifted to *IS'* and the *LM* curve to *LM'*.

Such plans are, however, not detailed enough. The policy makers need to know not only in what direction to shift government spending and the money stock, but also *how much* to change them. If government spending should be increased by $5 billion, it will not do much good to increase it by $1 billion. But if it should be increased by only $1 billion, an increase in government spending of $5 billion will push the economy well beyond the point of full employment and create inflationary pressures. The policy makers have to know not only the medicines to prescribe, but also the right doses.

In other words, they have to know the *multipliers*, associated with monetary and fiscal policy. To calculate these multipliers, they typically rely on *econometric models*. An econometric model is an equation or a set of equations with numerical values for parameters, based on the past behaviour of the economy, describing the behaviour of some specific sectors of the economy or the economy as a whole.

Econometric Models of Canada

A considerable number of econometric models of the Canadian economy have been constructed and are used regularly for forecasting and policy analysis. Within the federal government, there are models at the Bank of Canada, Department of Finance and the Economic Council of Canada. Models are also maintained by John Helliwell at the University of British Columbia and the Institute of Policy Analysis at the University of Toronto. Models are operated as private commercial enterprises by Chase Econometrics, Data Resources of Canada and Informetrica.

These models describe aggregate demand using an extended *IS-LM* framework. Equations are estimated for the components of aggregate demand using theories similar to those described in Chapters 7–10. The consumption function, for instance, would be similar to the sophisticated function we discussed in Chapter 7, although in most cases it would be disaggregated into several components.

To be useful, the models must also include equations to predict the rate of inflation as well as output. For this purpose the models have aggregate supply sectors along the lines described in Chapters 13 to 15.

Fiscal and monetary policy multipliers for two of the Canadian models are shown in Table 11-1. CANDIDE is the Economic Council of Canada model and RDXF is one of the models at the Bank of Canada. The table shows *dynamic multiplier* effects which take place in stages over time and reflect the various lags built into the models. For fiscal policy, the CANDIDE model shows a larger effect on real GNE in the third year compared with the initial year while the RDXF model shows declining multiplier effects. In both cases we see crowding out occurring so that by the tenth year the changes in output are much smaller.

For both policy changes, the multiplier effects are quite different in magnitude and lag pattern between the two models. This reflects differences in size and degree of disaggregation between the two models as well as differences in the theoretical assumptions used in constructing the equations. At the present time there is clearly no consensus on the exact structure of the economy and thus there is considerable variation among the models.

TABLE 11-1   REAL GNE MULTIPLIERS FROM TWO ECONOMETRIC MODELS

Policy change		Year			
		1	3	5	10
Fiscal policy: increase in government spending (multiplier effect)	CANDIDE	1.98	2.25	1.85	.77
	RDXF	1.09	.58	.34	.06
Monetary policy: 1 percent decrease in money supply (percent change in output)	CANDIDE	0	−.17	−.33	−.21
	RDXF	−.22	−.13	−.06	−.06

Source: B. O'Reilly, G. Paulin, and P. Smith, *Responses of Various Econometric Models to Selected Policy Shocks*, Bank of Canada Technical Report 38, July 1983. CANDIDE and RDXF are models constructed by the Economic Council of Canada and the Bank of Canada, respectively.

11-3 LAGS IN THE EFFECTS OF POLICY

Suppose that the economy was at full employment and has been affected by an aggregate demand disturbance that reduces the equilibrium level of income below full employment in Figure 11-3 toward point E. Suppose further that there was no advance warning of this disturbance and that, consequently, no policy actions were taken in anticipation of its occurrence. Policy makers now have to decide *whether at all* and *how* to respond to the disturbance.

The first concern, and the first difficulty, should be over the permanence of the disturbance and its subsequent effects. Suppose the disturbance is only transitory, such as a one-period reduction in consumption spending. When the disturbance is transitory so that consumption rapidly reverts to its initial level, the best policy may be to do nothing at all. Provided suppliers or producers do not mistakenly interpret the increase in demand as permanent but, rather, perceive it as transitory, they will absorb it by production and inventory changes rather than capacity adjustments. The disturbance will affect income in this period but will have very little permanent effect. Policy actions generally do not affect the economy immediately. Any policy actions taken to offset the disturbance this period, for example, a tax reduction, will have their impact on spending and income only over time. In later periods, however, the effects of the initial fall in demand on the level of income will be very small, and without the policy action the economy would tend to be very close to full employment. The effects of a tax cut, therefore, would be to raise income in later periods and move it away from the full-employment level. Thus, if the disturbance is temporary and it has no long-lived effects and policy operates with a lag, then the best policy is to do nothing.

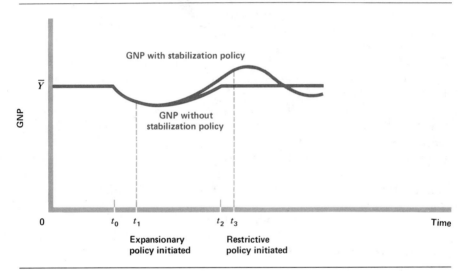

FIGURE 11-4   LAGS AND DESTABILIZING POLICY. A disturbance at time t_0 reduces output below the full-employment level. It takes until t_1 before policy responds, and there is a further lag until the policy starts working. By the time the full effects of the policy are evident, output would already have returned to the full-employment level even without policy. But because a policy action has been taken, output now rises *above* the full-employment level and then fluctuates around $\bar{Y}$. The lags in policy thus have made policy a source of fluctuations in output that would not otherwise have happened.

Figure 11-4 illustrates the main issue. Assume an aggregate demand disturbance reduces output below potential, starting at time t_0. Without active policy intervention output declines for a while but then recovers and reaches the full-employment level again at time t_2. Consider next the path of GNP under an active stabilization policy, but one that works with the disadvantage of lags. Thus, expansionary policy might be initiated at time t_1 and start taking effect some time after. Output now tends to recover faster as a consequence of the expansion and, because of poor dosage and/or timing, actually overshoots the full-employment level. By time t_3, restrictive policy is initiated, and some time after, output starts turning down toward full employment and may well continue cycling for a while. If this is an accurate description of the potency or scope of stabilization policy, then the question must seriously arise whether it is worth trying to stabilize output or whether the effect of stabilization policy is, in fact, to make things worse. Stabilization policy may actually *destabilize* the economy.

One of the main difficulties of policy making is in establishing whether or not a disturbance is temporary. It was clear enough in the case of World War II that a high level of defence expenditures would be required for some years. However, in the case of the Arab oil embargo of 1973–1974, it was not clear at all how long the embargo would last or whether the high prices for oil that were established in late 1973 would persist. At the time, there were many who argued that the oil cartel would not survive and that oil prices would soon fall—that is, that the disturbance was temporary. That did not turn out to be true. Let us suppose, however, that it is known that the disturbance will have effects that will last for several quarters, and that the level of income will, without policy, be below the full-employment level for some time. What lags do policy makers encounter?

We now consider the steps required before a policy action can be taken after a disturbance has occurred, and then the process by which that policy action affects the economy. There are delays, or lags, at every stage. It is customary and useful to divide the lags into an *inside* lag, which is the time period it takes to undertake a policy action—such as a tax cut, or an increase in the money supply — and an *outside* lag, which describes the timing of the effects of the policy action on the economy. The inside lag, in turn, is divided into recognition, decision, and action lags.

The Recognition Lag

The *recognition lag* is the period that elapses between the time a disturbance occurs and the time the policy makers recognize that action is required. This lag could in principle be *negative* if the disturbance could be predicted and appropriate policy actions considered *before* it even occurs. For example, we know that seasonal factors affect behaviour. Thus it is known that at Christmas the demand for currency is high. Rather than allow this to exert a restrictive effect on the money supply, the Bank of Canada will accommodate this seasonal demand by an expansion in high-powered money. In other cases the recognition lag has been positive, so that some time has elapsed between the disturbance and the recognition that active policy was required.

The major reason that there is any recognition lag at all, apart from the delay in collecting statistical data, is that it is never certain what the consequences of a disturbance will be. That uncertainty in turn is a result of economists' lack of knowledge of the workings of the economy (which was discussed above) as well as political uncertainties.

The Decision and Action Lags

The recognition lag is the same for monetary and fiscal policy. The Bank of Canada and the Department of Finance are in constant contact with one another and share their predictions about the future course of the economy. For the *decision* lag — the delay between the recognition of the need for action and a policy decision — by contrast there is a difference between monetary and fiscal policy. Once the need for a policy action has been recognized by the Bank of Canada, the decision lag for monetary policy is short. Further, the action lag — the lag between the policy decision and its implementation — for monetary policy is also short.

However, fiscal policy actions are less rapid. Once the need for a fiscal policy action has been recognized, the government has to prepare legislation for that action. Next, the legislation has to be considered and approved by Parliament before the policy change can be made. Even after the legislation has been approved, the policy change has still to be put into effect. If the fiscal policy takes the form of a change in tax rates, it may be some time before the changes in tax rates begin to be reflected in paycheques — that is, there may be an action lag.

Built-In Stabilizers

The existence of the inside lag of policy making focusses attention on the built-in or automatic stabilizers that we discussed in Chapter 3. One of the major benefits of automatic stabilizers is that their inside lag is zero. Recall from Chapter 3 that the most important automatic stabilizer is the income tax. It stabilizes the economy by reducing the multiplier effects of any disturbance to aggregate demand. The multiplier for the effects of changes in autonomous spending on GNP is inversely related to the income tax rate. The higher the tax rate, the smaller the effects of any given change in autonomous demand on GNP. Similarly, unemployment compensation is another automatic stabilizer. When workers become unemployed and reduce their consumption, that reduction in consumption demand tends to have multiplier effects on output. Those multiplier effects are reduced when a worker receives unemployment compensation because disposable income is reduced by less than the loss in earnings.

Although built-in stabilizers have desirable effects, they cannot be carried too far without also affecting the overall performance of the economy. The multiplier could be reduced to 1 by increasing the tax rate to 100 percent, and that would appear to be a stabilizing influence on the economy. But with 100 percent marginal tax rates, the desire to work and consequently the level of GNP, would be reduced. Thus there are limits on the extent to which automatic stabilizers are desirable. Nonetheless, automatic stabilizers play an important role in the economy; it has been argued that the absence of significant unemployment compensation in the 1930s was one of the major factors making the Great Depression so severe, and that the existence of the stabilizers alone makes the recurrence of such a deep depression unlikely.

The Outside Lag

The inside lag of policy is a *discrete* lag in which policy can have no effect on the economy until it is implemented. The outside lag is generally a *distributed* lag: once the policy action has been taken, its effects on the economy are spread over time. There is usually a small immediate effect of a policy action, but other effects occur later.

The idea that policy operates on aggregate demand and income with a distributed lag is shown in Figure 11-5. The process illustrated is the same as that represented by the numerical results from the econometric models shown in Table 11-1.

Suppose that we are considering a once-for-all increase in high-powered money in period 1, as shown in Figure 11-5a. This increase in high-powered money, by affecting interest rates and therefore aggregate spending, changes the level of income in subsequent periods by the amounts indicated in Figure 11-5b. The height of the bars shows the amount by which GNP exceeds the level that it would have had in the absence of the policy change. The main point to be made is that monetary or fiscal actions taken now affect the economy over time.

If we measure time in quarters, the impact in the initial period is likely to be relatively small with most of the affect coming later in the adjustment period as illustrated in Figure 11-5b. Thus if it were necessary to increase the level of employment rapidly to offset a demand disturbance, a large policy change would be necessary. However, in later quarters large effects on GNP would be built up so that there would probably be an overcorrection of the unemployment leading to inflationary pressures. It would then be necessary to reverse policy and undertake contractionary actions to avoid the inflationary consequences of the initial expansionary policy.

It should thus be clear that when policy acts slowly, with the impacts of policy building up over time, considerable skill is required of policy makers if their own attempts to correct an initially undesirable situation are not to lead to problems that themselves need correcting. Recall also that we have been talking here about the *outside* lag, and that the policy action we are

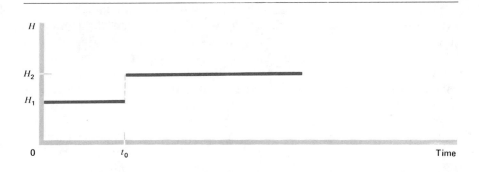

FIGURE 11-5a   TIME PATH OF HIGH-POWERED MONEY

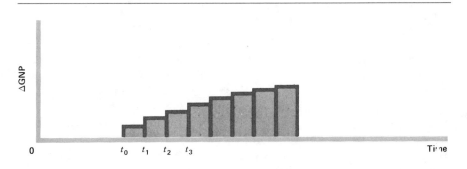

FIGURE 11-5b   DYNAMIC MULTIPLIERS FOR THE EFFECTS OF A CHANGE IN HIGH-POWERED MONEY ON GNP. An increase in the stock of high-powered money causes GNP to increase by successively larger amounts as we move through time. The height of the bars shows the amount by which GNP exceeds the level that it would have been in the absence of the policy change.

considering would be taken only six months after the initial disturbance if the inside lag is six months long.

Why are there such long inside lags? We have already discussed some of the reasons for these lags in Chapter 7 on the consumption function, where current consumption depends on lagged income, and also in Chapter 8 on investment, where the accelerator models imply that investment depends on lagged and current income. Similar lags are also present in the financial sector of the economy, where the demand for money depends on lagged income. Each of these sources of lags creates an outside lag, and their interaction generally produces longer lags than each of the underlying lags.

Because the point is so important, let us describe in more detail how the lags of monetary policy arise. Suppose the Bank of Canada conducts an open market purchase. Because aggregate demand depends heavily on lagged values of income, interest rates, and other economic variables, the open market purchase initially has effects mainly on short-term interest rates and not on income. Short-term interest rates, such as the treasury bill rate, affect long-term interest rates with a lag. The long-term interest rates in turn affect investment with a lag, and also affect consumption by affecting the value of wealth.[4] Then when aggregate demand is affected by the initial open market purchase, the increase in aggregate demand itself produces lagged effects on subsequent aggregate demand through the fact that both consumption and investment depend on past values of income. So the effects of an initial open market purchase will be spread through time, as in Figure 11-5.

Monetary and Fiscal Policy Lags

The discussion in the previous paragraph suggests that fiscal policy and certainly changes in government spending, which act directly on aggregate demand, may affect income more rapidly than monetary policy. This is indeed the case. However, the fact that fiscal policy acts faster on aggregate demand than monetary policy must not lead us to overlook the fact that fiscal policy has a considerably longer inside lag. Moreover, the inside lag for government spending is longer than that for taxes because, when the government purchases goods and services, it has to decide what goods to buy, have bids for the sale of those goods submitted by the private sector, and then decide on the award of the contracts. In summary, therefore, fiscal policy is attractive because of the short outside lag, but that advantage is more than offset by a potentially long inside lag.

Our analysis of lags indicates clearly one difficulty in undertaking stabilizing short-term policy actions: it takes time to set the policies in action, and then the policies themselves take time to affect the economy. But that is not the only difficulty. Further difficulties considered in Sections 11-4 and 11-5 arise from uncertainty about the exact timing and magnitude of the effects of policy.

11-4   THE ROLE OF EXPECTATIONS

We have discussed the two basic sources of lags in economic behaviour in earlier chapters. The first source is the costs of rapid adjustment. For example, in Chapter 8 we showed how the costs of adjusting the actual capital stock to the desired capital stock led to lags in the investment function. The second source of lags is expectations. In this section we focus on expectations, their formation, and the effects they have on policy and its effectiveness.

While it is undoubtedly true that the past behaviour of a variable influences expectations about its future behaviour, it is also true that consumers and investors will sometimes use more information than is contained in the past behaviour of a variable when trying to predict its future behaviour. Consider, in particular, forecasts of permanent income — long-run average income. In Chapter 7, as in Friedman's original work on the consumption function, permanent income is estimated as an average of income in the recent past. Suppose, however, that you were a resident of a small country that had just discovered vast gold deposits. You would then take the information about the gold discovery into account in forming an estimate of your permanent income. You would *immediately* estimate a permanent income substantially higher than your historical average income. Alternatively, suppose that you have been estimating the expected rate of inflation as an average of past rates of inflation, at a time when the inflation rate is high and a new government is elected on a strictly anti-inflationary platform. Then you would lower your estimate of the inflation rate; that is, you would use more information in predicting it than is contained solely in its past behaviour. It should be clear that it is in general very difficult to incorporate *all* relevant information that is used by economic agents within a simple economic model. That means there will inevitably be errors in what the models predict for the consequences of various policy actions, meaning in turn that it is difficult to control the economy precisely.

It is particularly important to consider the effects of a given policy action itself on expectations, since it is possible that a new type of policy will affect the way in which expectations are formed.[5] Suppose that the Bank of Canada announced a new monetary policy designed to stabilize the average level of income and avoid booms and recessions. The new policy would be to reduce the money supply whenever the income level rose and to increase the money supply whenever the income level fell. Such a countercyclical rule has implications for expectations. Clearly, it would be inappropriate in the presence of such monetary policy to use an expectations mechanism that implies that an increase in income will persist. The monetary policy rule implies that the money supply should be reduced following an increase in income, and one expects the reduction in money to exert at least a dampening effect on income.

While correct expectations mechanisms must therefore use information about policy responses to disturbances, such care is difficult to apply in practice. Most expectations mechanisms embodied in econometric models of the economy and used for the assessment of policies assume that expectations affecting consumption and investment spending are based entirely on past values.

Econometric Policy Evaluation

The preceding discussion of the effects of a change in policy on expectations is part of a wider *econometric policy evaluation critique* formulated by Robert E. Lucas, of the University of Chicago, intellectual leader of the rational expectations approach to macroeconomics.[6] Lucas argues that existing macroeconometric models cannot be used to study the effects of policy changes *because the way private agents (firms and consumers) respond to changes in income and prices depends on the types of policy being followed.*

For example, suppose there is a change in income this period. How does consumption react? If policy is successful in keeping income always very close to potential, the change in income will be viewed as transitory, and there will be almost no change in consumption. But if policy is such that deviations of output from potential are typically prolonged, the change in income will be regarded as more permanent and the consumption response will be large. The key point is that the consumption response to changes in income depends on the types of policy being followed. Therefore one cannot use a consumption function which does not allow for this change in behaviour to examine the effects of policy changes.

Lucas argues that problems of this sort are pervasive in macroeconometric models. He does not argue that it will never be possible to use econometric models to study policy, only that existing models cannot be used for that purpose.

Accordingly, the Lucas critique is not one that rules out the use of econometric models. It suggests rather that very careful modelling of the responses of consumers and firms to changes in income and prices is necessary. For instance, the consumption example above would not be impossible to handle, so long as permanent income were estimated as a weighted average of past incomes that changed appropriately as the behaviour of income itself changed with policy.

Summary

This section has made two important points about the role of expectations in explaining the difficulties of policy making. First, the general point is that the difficulties of modelling the way in which expectations are formed will inevitably lead to errors in economists' forecasts of the effects of particular policy actions on the economy. The second point, a particular one, is that expectations themselves are likely to be affected by policy measures, and that failure to take account of the effects of policy on expectations will lead to mistaken predictions of the effects of those policies.

11-5 UNCERTAINTY AND ECONOMIC POLICY

So far in this chapter we have described the disturbances that affect the economy, econometric models that are used in policy making, the difficulties of making policy when there are long lags in the effects of policy, and the problem of modelling expectations. We can summarize most of the implied problems for policy making by saying that it is impossible to predict the effects of any given policy action exactly.

How should a policy maker react in the face of these uncertainties? We want to distinguish here between uncertainty about the correct model of the economy and uncertainty about the precise values of the parameters or coefficients within a given model of the economy, even though the distinction is not watertight.

First, there is considerable disagreement and therefore uncertainty about the correct model of the economy, as evidenced by the large number of macroeconometric models. Reasonable economists can and do differ about what theory and empirical evidence suggest are the correct behavioural functions of the economy. Generally, each economist will have reasons for favouring one particular form and will use that form. But, being reasonable, the economist will recognize that the particular formulation being used may not be the correct one, and will thus regard its predictions as subject to a margin of error. In turn, policy makers will know that there are different predictions about the effects of a given policy, and will want to consider the range of predictions that are being made in deciding on policy.

Second, as we noted in Section 11-2, even within the context of a given model there is uncertainty about the values of parameters and multipliers. The statistical evidence does allow us to say something about the likely range of parameters or multipliers,[7] so that at least we can get some idea of the type of errors that could result from a particular policy action.

Uncertainty about the size of the effects that will result from any particular policy action is known as *multiplier uncertainty*. For instance, our best estimate of the multiplier of an increase in government spending might be 1.2. If GNP has to be increased by $6 billion, we would increase government spending by $5 billion. But the statistical evidence might be better interpreted as saying only that we can be quite confident the multiplier is between 0.9 and 1.5. In that case, when we increase government spending by $5 billion, we expect GNP to rise by some amount between $4.5 and $7.5 billion.

What is optimal behaviour in the face of such multiplier uncertainty? The more precisely policy makers are informed about the relevant parameters, the more activist the policy can afford to be. Conversely, if there is a considerable range of error in the estimate of the relevant parameters — in our example, the multiplier — then policy should be more modest. With poor information, very active policy runs a large danger of introducing unnecessary fluctuations in the economy.

11-6 ACTIVIST POLICY

We started this chapter asking why there are any fluctuations in the economy when the policy measures needed to iron out those fluctuations seem to be so simple. The list of difficulties in the way of successful policy making that we have outlined may have raised a different question: Why should one believe that policy can do anything to reduce fluctuations in the economy?

Indeed, considerations of the sort spelled out in the previous four sections have led Milton Friedman and others to argue that there should be no use of active countercyclical monetary policy,[8] and that monetary policy should be confined to making the money supply grow at a constant rate. The precise value of the constant rate of growth of money, Friedman suggests, is less important than the fact that monetary growth be constant and that policy should *not* respond to disturbances. At various times, he has suggested growth rates for money of 2 percent or 4 percent or 5 percent. As Friedman has expressed it, "By setting itself a steady course and keeping to it, the monetary authority could make a major contribution to promoting economic stability. By making that course one of steady but moderate growth in the quantity of money, it would make a major contribution to avoidance of either inflation or deflation of prices."[9] Friedman thus advocates a simple monetary rule in which the central bank does not respond to the condition of the economy. Policies that respond to the current or predicted state of the economy are called *activist policies*.

In discussing the desirability of active monetary and fiscal policy, we want to distinguish between policy actions taken in response to major disturbances to the economy and *fine tuning* in which policy variables are continually adjusted in response to small disturbances to the economy. We see no case for arguing that monetary and fiscal policy should not be used actively in the face of major disturbances to the economy. Most of the considerations of the previous sections of this chapter indicate some uncertainty about the effects of policy, but there are still clearly definable circumstances in which there can be no doubt that the appropriate policy is expansionary or contractionary. A government coming to power in 1933 should not have worried about the uncertainties associated with expansionary policy that we have outlined. The economy does not move from 25 percent unemployment to full employment in a short time (precisely because of those same lags that make policy difficult). Thus, expansionary measures, such as a rapid growth of the money supply, or increased government expenditures, or tax reductions, or all three, would have been appropriate policy since there was no chance they would have an impact only after the economy was at full employment. Similarly, contractionary policies for private demand are called for in wartime. In early 1977, with unemployment over 8 percent and rising rapidly and forecasts of unemployment for the next two years being very high, policies designed to reduce unemployment were appropriate.[10] In the event of large disturbances in the future, active monetary and/or fiscal policy should once again be used.[11]

Fine tuning presents more complicated issues. The basic question is whether policy variables should be adjusted at frequent intervals to attempt to smooth out minor disturbances to the economy. For example, should an increase of 0.5 percent in the unemployment rate lead to a small tax reduction, or a small increase in the rate of growth of the money supply, or should policy simply not respond to such disturbances? One possibility is that the initial increase in the unemployment rate is transitory and that policy action is therefore inappropriate; the other is that the initial disturbance is permanent and perhaps even the first sign of a major disturbance, in which case a policy reaction is suitable. If the disturbance is permanent, the appropriate policy response to a small disturbance is a small change in the course of policy. Thus, even if it turned out that the policy action was inappropriate because the disturbance was transitory, the (undesirable) consequences of the policy action would be limited because only a small adjustment had been made. Accordingly, we believe that fine tuning is appropriate provided that policy responses are always kept small in response to small disturbances.

However, we should emphasize that the argument for fine tuning is a controversial one. The major argument against it is that in practice policy makers cannot behave as suggested — making only small adjustments to small disturbances. Rather, it is argued they tend to try to do too much, if allowed to do anything. Instead of merely trying to offset disturbances, they attempt to keep the economy always at full employment and therefore undertake inappropriately large policy actions in response to small disturbances.

The major lesson of the previous sections of this chapter is not that policy is impossible, but that policy that is too ambitious in trying to keep the economy always at full employment (with zero inflation) is impossible. The lesson is to proceed with extreme caution, always bearing in mind the possibility that policy itself may be destabilizing. We see no reason why the Bank of Canada should try to keep the money supply always growing at the same rate; we believe, on the contrary, that the stability of the economy would be improved by its following a careful countercyclical policy. Similarly, if fiscal policy were not subject to a long inside lag, we would believe it possible for cautiously used fiscal policy to be stabilizing.

Rules versus Discretion

Finally, in this section, we want to discuss an issue that has perhaps had more attention in the economics literature than it deserves. This is the issue of "rules versus discretion." The issue is whether the monetary authority and also the fiscal authority should conduct policy in accordance with a preannounced rule that describes precisely how their policy variables will be determined in all future situations, or whether they should be allowed to use their discretion in determining the values of the policy variables at different times. One example is the rule establishing the constant growth rate — say, at 4 percent — for monetary policy. The rule is that *no matter what happens*, the money supply will be kept growing at 4 percent. Another example would be a rule that the money supply growth rate will be increased by 2 percent per year for every 1 percent unemployment in excess of, say, 5 percent. Algebraically, such a rule would be expressed as

$$\frac{\Delta M}{M} = 4.0 + 2(u - 5.0) \tag{1}$$

where the growth rate of money $\Delta M/M$ is at an annual percentage rate and u is the percentage unemployment rate.

The activist monetary rule of Equation (1) is shown in Figure 11-6. On the horizontal axis, we show the unemployment rate, and on the vertical axis, the growth rate of the money stock. At 5 percent unemployment, monetary growth is 4 percent. If unemployment rises above 5 percent, monetary growth is *automatically* increased. Thus, with 7 percent unemployment, monetary growth would be 8 percent. Conversely, if unemployment dropped below 5 percent, monetary growth would be lowered below 4 percent. The rule therefore gears the amount of monetary stimulus to an indicator of the business cycle. By linking monetary growth to the unemployment rate, an activist, anticyclical monetary policy is achieved, but this is done without any discretion.

The issue of rules versus discretion has been clouded by the fact that most proponents of rules have been nonactivists, whose preferred monetary rule is a constant growth rate rule.[12] Consequently, the argument has tended to centre on whether activist policy is desirable or not. The fundamental point to recognize is that we can design *activist rules*. We can design rules that have countercyclical features without at the same time leaving any discretion in their actions to policy makers. The point is made by Equation (1), which is an activist rule because it expands money when

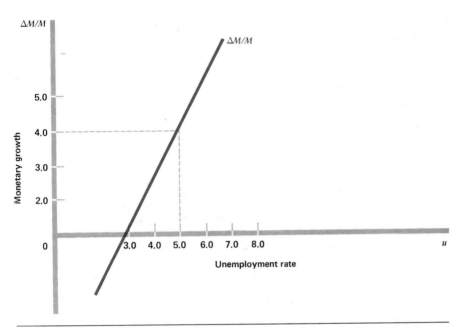

FIGURE 11-6   AN ACTIVIST MONETARY RULE. The figure describes an activist monetary rule. The growth rate of money is high when the unemployment rate is high and is low when unemployment is low. That way monetary policy is expansionary at times of recession and contractionary in a boom.

unemployment is high and reduces it when unemployment is low. It leaves no room for policy discretion and in this respect is a rule.

Given that the economy and our knowledge of it are both changing over time, there is no case for stating permanent policy rules that would tie the hands of the monetary and fiscal authorities permanently. The practical issue in rules versus discretion then becomes that of whether the policy makers should announce in advance what policies they will be following for the foreseeable future. This would seem to be a desirable development in that it would aid private individuals in forecasting the future course of the economy.

*11-7   TARGETS AND INSTRUMENTS OF MONETARY POLICY

We conclude this chapter with a discussion of some operational problems in the implementation of monetary policy that arise from the existence of uncertainty. We begin with the issue of money supply targets.

Interest Rate Versus Money Supply Targets

Prior to the early 1970s, the Bank of Canada's monetary policy was formulated primarily in terms of target levels of interest rates and other measures of the cost and availability of credit. By 1973, the Bank had become dissatisfied with this approach and was beginning to move towards greater emphasis on control of the money supply. In his Annual Report for 1973, Governor Gerald Bouey commented as follows (page 7):

> Looking back on the experience of Canada and other countries over a longer period, . . . there have been more substantial and persisting departures from reasonably steady monetary growth than would appear in retrospect to have been desirable. Since the lags associated with monetary policy are rather long, the full effects of such departures do not become apparent until well after the event. . . . In the light of these considerations, I have a certain amount of sympathy with the case that is often made for more stable monetary growth over time. . . . The Bank of Canada certainly has no intention of basing its operations on any mechanistic formula, but . . . it has been giving considerable weight to underlying rates of monetary growth.

Although the governor had rejected the idea of a "mechanistic formula" for monetary growth in 1973, two years later the Bank of Canada announced that it would henceforth follow the practice of establishing target ranges for the rate of growth of the narrowly defined money supply ($M1$). The initial target was established in late 1975 at 10 to 15 percent a year. As can be seen in Table 11-2, the target was subsequently reduced in stages to the range of 4 to 8 percent which was announced in February 1981. The practice of announcing target ranges was discontinued in 1982.

TABLE 11-2   BANK OF CANADA TARGET GROWTH RATES
OF $M1$, 1975–1981

Base Period	Target Band	Base Period	Target Band
2nd Qtr. 1975	10–15%	June 1978	6–10%
Feb.–Apr. 1976	8–12	2nd Qtr. 1979	5–9
June 1977	7–11	Aug.–Oct. 1980	4–8

Targets in the IS-LM *Framework*

Let us assume that the Bank of Canada's policy objective is to reach a particular level of output. The question is whether it can do that more accurately by targeting the money stock or by fixing interest rates.[13] We should think of the analysis as applying to a time horizon of 3 to 6 months over which the Bank of Canada could achieve money supply targets with a small margin of error.

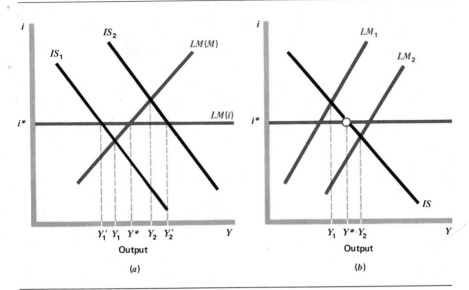

FIGURE 11-7   MONEY AND INTEREST RATE TARGETS. In panel (*a*), the *IS* curve shifts. If the Bank of Canada targets the money stock, the *LM* curve is shown by *LM*(*M*). *LM*(*i*) is the *LM* curve when the interest rate is held constant. The aim of policy is to hit output level *Y**. If the *LM* curve is *LM*(*M*), the output levels will be either Y_1 or Y_2, depending on where the *IS* curve turns out to be. In the case of an interest rate target, the corresponding levels of output are Y'_1 and Y'_2, both further from the desired level of output Y^*. Thus monetary targeting leads to more stable output behaviour. In panel (*b*) it is the *LM* curve that is shifting, because of shifts in the demand for money. With *LM* shifting and the *IS* curve stable, output will be at the target level Y^* if the interest rate is held constant at i^*, but will be at either Y_1 or Y_2 if the money stock is held constant. Therefore the Bank should target the interest rate if the demand-for-money function is unstable.

Figure 11-7*a* starts with the *IS* and *LM* curves. Recall that the *LM* curve shows combinations of the interest rate and output at which the money market is in equilibrium. The *LM* curve labelled *LM*(*M*) is the *LM* curve that exists when the Bank of Canada fixes the money stock. The *LM* curve labelled *LM*(*i*) describes money market equilibrium when the Bank fixes the interest rate. It is horizontal at the chosen level of the interest rate i^*.

The problem for policy is that the *IS* and *LM* curves shift in ways that cannot be predicted. When they shift, output ends up at a level different from the target level. In Figure 11-7*a* we show two alternative positions for the *IS* curve, IS_1 and IS_2. We assume that the Bank does not know in advance which *IS* curve will obtain: the position depends, for instance, on investment demand, which is difficult to predict. The Bank's aim is to have income come out as close as possible to the level Y^*.

In Figure 11-7a we see that the level of output stays closer to Y^* if the LM curve is $LM(M)$. In that case the level of output will be Y_1 if the IS curve is IS_1 and Y_2 if the IS curve is IS_2. If policy had kept the interest rate constant, we would in each case have a level of income that is further from Y^*: Y'_1 instead of Y_1, and Y'_2 instead of Y_2.

Thus we have our first conclusion: If output deviates from its equilibrium level mainly because the IS curve shifts about, then output is stabilized by keeping the money stock constant. The central bank should, in this case, have monetary targets.

We can see from Figure 11-7a why it is more stabilizing to keep M than i constant. When the IS curve shifts to the right and the $LM(M)$ curve applies, the interest rate rises, thereby reducing investment demand and moderating the effect of the shift. But if the $LM(i)$ curve applies, there is no resistance from monetary policy to the effects of the IS shift. Monetary policy is thus automatically stabilizing in Figure 11-7a when the IS curve shifts, and the money stock is held constant.

In Figure 11-7b we assume that the IS curve is stable. Now the uncertainty about the effects of monetary policy results from shifts in the LM curve. Assuming that the Bank of Canada can fix the money stock, the LM curve shifts because the money demand function shifts. The Bank does not know when it sets the money stock what the interest rate will be. The LM curve could end up being either LM_1 or LM_2. Alternatively the Bank could simply fix the interest rate at level i^*. That would ensure that the level of output is Y^*.

If the Bank were to fix the money stock, output could be either Y_1 or Y_2. If it fixes the interest rate, output will be Y^*. Thus we have our second conclusion: If output deviates from its equilibrium level mainly because the demand-for-money function shifts about, then the central bank should operate monetary policy by fixing the interest rate. That way it automatically neutralizes the effects of the shifts in money demand. In this case the central bank should have interest rate targets.

Implications for Bank of Canada Policy

The above analysis indicates that the shift to money supply targeting by the Bank of Canada was appropriate if the main source of disturbances is thought to be the goods market rather than the money market. This assumption may well be a good approximation much of the time given the proposition that asset markets achieve equilibrium quickly while goods markets are characterized by more sluggish adjustment.[14]

On the other hand, the argument depends on the existence of a stable demand for money. During the late 1970s and early 1980s, the financial innovations discussed in Chapter 9 caused a breakdown in the stability of this relationship and ultimately led to the abandonment of monetary targeting by the Bank of Canada.

The Instrument Problem

The above analysis focusses on a 3 to 6 month time horizon over which the Bank of Canada can achieve money supply targets. As we argued in Chapter 10, the Bank cannot control the money supply in the short run. The variables over which the Bank of Canada does have direct control are called policy instruments and the choice of the appropriate variable to control in the face of unpredictable disturbances is known as the instrument problem.

The short-run operating problem can be described as follows. Having chosen its money supply target, should the Bank of Canada implement its policy by setting the level of the interest rate or the monetary base? The analysis of Figure 11-7 can be applied in this context by assuming that the upward sloping *LM* curve in Figure 11-7a is drawn for a given level of the monetary base *H*, rather than the money supply. The shifts in the *LM* curve shown in Figure 11-7b then reflect shifts in the money multiplier as well as the demand for money.

The conclusions from the analysis become:

1 If the demand for money and the money multiplier are stable, then the Bank of Canada should use *H* as the instrument and allow interest rates to fluctuate in response to shifts in the *IS* curve.
2 If the *IS* curve is stable, then the Bank should use the interest rate as the instrument and allow *H* to fluctuate in response to shifts in the demand for money and the money multiplier.

The Bank of Canada's Operating Procedure

During the period 1975 to 1982 when the Bank of Canada was setting targets for the money supply, its operating procedure was as follows. Having set its money target, a projection was made for income and the price level, and a money demand function was used to infer the appropriate setting for the interest rate.[15] Thus the Bank used the interest rate as the instrument.

The rationale for this procedure is that the goods market is relatively predictable in the short run but the money market is not. In particular, as we argued in Section 10-8 of Chapter 10, the money multiplier is likely to be unstable in the short run.[16]

11-8 SUMMARY

1 Despite the apparent simplicity of policies needed to maintain continuous full employment, the historical record of the behaviour of

unemployment, shown in Figure 11-1, implies that successful stabilization policy is difficult to carry out.

2   Many of the complications in the execution of stabilization policy are a result of the tradeoff between inflation and unemployment in the short run. This important topic is deferred to Chapter 15. The present chapter concentrates on other sources of difficulty for stabilization policy.

3   The potential need for stabilizing policy actions arises from economic disturbances. Some of these disturbances, such as changes in money demand, consumption spending, or investment demand, arise from within the private sector. Others, such as wars, may arise for non-economic reasons.

4   Inappropriate economic policy may also tend to move the economy away from full employment. Policy may be inappropriate because policy makers make mistakes or because policy is manipulated for political reasons, leading to the political business cycle.

5   Policy makers work with econometric models in predicting the effects of their policy actions. Econometric models are typically statistical descriptions of the types of model we have worked with in earlier chapters and also include an aggregate supply sector. Existing econometric models vary considerably in structure and thus imply widely varying numerical values for policy multipliers.

6   The first difficulty of carrying out successful stabilization policy is that policy works with lags. The inside lag — divided into recognition, decision, and action lags — is the period between which an action becomes necessary and when it is taken. The outside lag is the period between which a policy action is taken and when it affects the economy. The outside lag is generally a distributed lag: the effects of a policy action build up over the course of time.

7   The behaviour of expectations is a further source of difficulty for policy making. First, it is difficult to know exactly what determines expectations and to capture those factors in a simple formula. Second, policy actions themselves are likely to affect expectations.

8   More generally, there is always uncertainty about the effects of a given policy action on the economy. Economists are not agreed on the "correct" model of the economy, and evidence is not likely to be at hand soon to decisively settle disagreements over some behavioural functions — such as the consumption function. Even if we did know the form of the behavioural functions, the statistical evidence would be insufficient to pinpoint the values of the relevant parameters.

9 There are clearly occasions on which active monetary and fiscal policy actions should be taken to stabilize the economy. These are situations in which the economy has been affected by major disturbances.

10 Fine tuning — continuous attempts to stabilize the economy in the face of small disturbances — is more controversial. If fine tuning is undertaken, it calls for small policy responses in an attempt to moderate the economy's fluctuations, rather than to remove them entirely. A very active policy in response to small disturbances is likely to destabilize the economy.

11 The real issue in rules versus discretion is whether policy actions should be announced as far in advance as possible. Such announcements are desirable in that they aid private individuals in forecasting the future behaviour of the economy.

12 During the period 1975 to 1981, the Bank of Canada operated monetary policy using target rates of growth of the money supply. This is an appropriate strategy if the money market is stable and the goods market is subject to substantial disturbances.

KEY TERMS

Economic disturbances
Political business cycle
Econometric models
Inside lag
Recognition lag
Decision lag
Action lag
Outside lag

Econometric policy evaluation critique
Multiplier uncertainty
Activist policy
Fine tuning
Rules versus discretion
Targets and instruments of monetary policy

PROBLEMS

1 Suppose that GNP is $4 billion below its potential level. It is expected that next period GNP will be $2 billion below potential, and two periods from now it will be back at its potential level. You are told that the multiplier for government spending is 2, and that the effects of the increased government spending are immediate. What policy actions can be taken to put GNP back on target each period?

2 The basic facts about the path of GNP are as above. But there is now a one-period outside lag for government spending. Decisions to spend

today are translated into actual spending only tomorrow. The multiplier for government spending is still 2 in the period that the spending takes place.

(a) What is the best that can be done to keep GNP as close to target as possible each period?

(b) Compare the path of GNP in this question with the path in problem (1), after policy actions have been taken.

3 Life has become more complicated. Government spending works with a distributed lag. Now when $1 billion is spent today, GNP increases by $1 billion this period and $1.5 billion next period.

(a) What happens to the path of GNP if government spending rises enough this period to put GNP back to its potential level this period?

(b) Suppose fiscal policy actions are taken to put GNP at its potential level this period. What fiscal policy will be needed to put GNP on target next period?

(c) Explain why the government has to be so active in keeping GNP on target in this case.

4 Suppose that you knew that the multiplier for government spending was between 1 and 2.5, but that its effects were all over in the period that spending was increased. How would you run fiscal policy if GNP would, without policy, behave as in problem 1?

5 Explain why monetary policy works with a distributed lag, as in Figure 11-5.

6 Evaluate the argument that monetary policy should be determined by a rule rather than discretion. How about fiscal policy?

7 Evaluate the arguments for a constant growth rate rule for money.

8 (a) What is the unemployment rate at the time you are reading this?

(b) Should either fiscal or monetary policy be changed to enable the economy to return more rapidly to full employment?

9 Use Figure 11-7 to analyse the short-run problem of instrument choice. What conclusions can you draw for the validity of the Bank of Canada's strategy of using the interest rate as the instrument?

CHAPTER 11: FOOTNOTES

[1]In passing, it is worth considering for a moment why partial rationing might work as a macroeconomic policy, that is, as a policy reducing aggregate demand. The reason must be that part of the expenditure that is precluded by rationing does not shift to other goods but instead increases saving, that is, future consumption.

[2]Keynes, in particular, argued that shifts in the investment function were a major cause of fluctuations in the economy. See J.M. Keynes, *The General Theory of Employment, Interest and Money* (New York: Macmillan, 1936), Chap. 22.

[3]See Milton Friedman and Anna J. Schwartz, *The Great Contraction* (Princeton, N.J.: Princeton University Press, 1965). We review the argument in Chapter 10.

[4]Recall that in Chapter 7 we discussed the life-cycle model of consumption demand, in which consumption is affected by the level of wealth. Part of wealth is the value of stock market assets; the value of stock market assets rises when the long-term interest rate falls. Thus, interest rates affect consumption through a wealth effect.

[5]The role of expectations in economics and the interaction between policy and expectations in particular have been the subject of much recent research. See, for example, Thomas J. Sargent and Neil Wallace, "Rational Expectations and the Theory of Economic Policy," *Journal of Monetary Economics*, April 1976. See also our discussion in Chapter 17.

[6]See "Econometric Policy Evaluation: A Critique," in R.E. Lucas, Jr., *Studies in Business Cycle Theory* (Cambridge, Mass.: M.I.T. Press, 1981).

[7]We are discussing here *confidence intervals* about estimates of parameters; see Robert S. Pindyck and Daniel L. Rubinfeld, *Econometric Models and Economic Forecasts* (New York: McGraw-Hill, 1976), for further discussion.

[8]See Milton Friedman, *A Program for Monetary Stability* (New York: Fordham University Press, 1959).

[9]Milton Friedman, "The Role of Monetary Policy," *American Economic Review*, March 1968.

[10]Because the inflation rate was high in 1977, policy making then required some judgment about the costs of inflation compared with those of unemployment, a topic discussed in Chap. 16. Policy making in 1977 was thus more difficult than policy making in 1933. Policy decisions in 1980 through 1982, with rising unemployment and very high inflation, were also very tough.

[11]Interestingly, in the article cited in footnote 9, Friedman argues for the use of active policy in the face of major disturbances.

[12]An assessment of the issues is provided in Arthur Okun, "Monetary-Fiscal Activism: Some Analytical Issues," *Brookings Papers on Economic Activity*, 1972:1 (Washington, D.C.: The Brookings Institution, 1972).

[13]The analysis presented here is based on William Poole, "Optimal Choice of Monetary Policy Instruments in a Simple Stochastic Macro Model," *Quarterly Journal of Economics*, May 1970.

[14]Another argument for money targeting arises from the distinction between real and nominal interest rates. The nominal interest rate can rise because inflation is expected. If the Bank fights this increase in the nominal rate by increasing the money stock, it is only feeding the inflation. We examine this argument in more detail in Chapter 15.

[15]In algebraic terms the value for the interest rate was obtained using an LM equation of the form shown in Equation 11a of Chapter 4 (page 124).

[16]For a statement of the Bank's strategy see *Annual Report of the Bank of Canada* for 1975. A critical view is given in T.J. Courchene, *Money, Inflation, and the Bank of Canada, Vol. II*, C.D. Howe Institute, 1981, pp. 157–183.

Fiscal Policy and Public Finance

This chapter is intended to serve two purposes. The first is to review the experience of the 1930s and the postwar period. The Great Depression is worth studying for purely historical interest, but of equal importance is the fact that the thirties and the war that followed molded many of the institutions and views of the modern economy. The role of government expanded markedly, and it was the experience of the thirties that led to the view, now taken for granted in practice, that the government has primary responsibility for satisfactory economic performance.

The second purpose of the chapter is to discuss a number of questions connected with the budget, government spending and taxes. In Section 12-3 we describe the financing of the federal government budget deficit, that is, how the government pays for the excess of its spending over its income from taxes. The issue of the burden of the debt is taken up at the conclusion of the chapter.

12-1 THE GREAT DEPRESSION

In this section we describe the experience of the 1930s and review the controversy over the causes of the depression. Data describing the performance of the Canadian economy are shown in Figure 12-1 and Table 12-1. As can be seen from the chart, between 1929 and 1933, real GNP fell by 30 percent and the price level fell by 20 percent. Investment collapsed; indeed, *net* investment was negative from 1932 to 1936. The unemployment rate rose to nearly 20 percent in 1933 and remained above 11 percent through the thirties, with the exception of 1937 when it dipped close to 9 percent. By 1933 the stock market had fallen almost to one-third of its 1929 value.

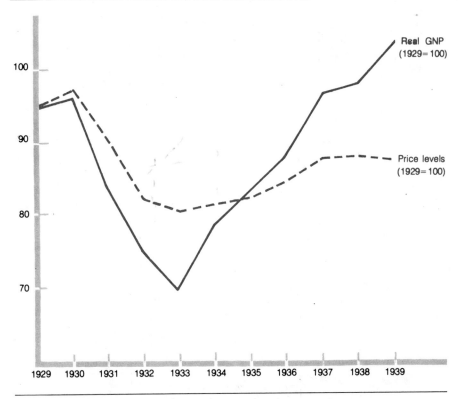

FIGURE 12-1   OUTPUT AND PRICES IN THE GREAT DEPRESSION
(*Source*: Statistics Canada, 11-505)

Events in Canada closely mirrored those in the United States and the economic collapse in the U.S. was a major cause of the decline in Canada. The sharp fall in our exports, shown in Table 12-1 resulted from the fall in income in the U.S. and other countries and the psychological impact was an important factor in the collapse of investment. In view of this it is necessary to examine events in the U.S. in order to obtain clues as to the causes of the depression.

American Experience in the 1930s

The depression and the stock market crash of October 1929 are popularly thought of as almost the same thing. In fact, the U.S. economy started turning down before the stock market crash. The peak of the business cycle is estimated to have been in August 1929, and the stock market itself peaked in September 1929. Using September 1929 as the base period,

TABLE 12-1   THE GREAT DEPRESSION IN CANADA

	GNP (billions of 1961 dollars)	Govt. Exp. (billions of 1961 dollars)	Exports	GNE Deflator (1961 = 100)	Gross Investment (% of GNP)	Budget Surplus (% of GNP)	Unemployment Rate (%)	Stock Market Index (1961 = 100)
1929	12.24	1.70	3.10	50.2	22.2	.2		49.0
1930	11.71	1.93	2.70	48.8	18.9	−3.9		35.0
1931	10.23	1.94	2.41	45.9	15.5	−6.6	11.6	21.9
1932	9.17	1.79	2.24	41.6	8.8	−7.3	17.6	14.2
1933	8.56	1.47	2.26	40.8	6.8	−5.0	19.3	17.6
1934	9.59	1.58	2.55	41.4	7.7	−4.7	14.5	22.1
1935	10.34	1.68	2.81	41.6	8.6	−4.0	14.2	23.6
1936	10.80	1.67	3.38	42.9	10.0	−.7	12.8	30.7
1937	11.89	1.79	3.46	44.1	11.8	−.6	9.1	32.6
1938	11.98	1.93	3.12	44.0	11.3	−2.8	11.4	26.8
1939	12.87	2.02	3.44	43.7	10.3	−.8	11.4	25.8

Source: Statistics Canada, 11-505.

Standard & Poor's composite stock price index fell from 100 in September to 66 in November. It rose again through March 1930, but then the collapse continued until the index fell to 15 in June 1932.

By early 1931, the U.S. economy was suffering from a very severe depression, but not one that was out of the range of the experience of the previous century.[1] It was in the period from early 1931 until Franklin Roosevelt became President in March 1933 that the depression became "Great."

Economic Policy

What was economic policy during this period? The money stock fell from 1929 to 1930, and then fell rapidly in 1931 and 1932 and continued falling through April 1933. At the same time, the composition of the money stock changed. In March 1931 the currency-demand deposit ratio was 18.5 percent; 2 years later, it was 40.7 percent.

The fall in the money stock was the result of large-scale bank failures. Banks failed because they did not have the reserves with which to meet customers' cash withdrawals, and in failing they destroyed deposits and hence reduced the money stock. But the failures went further in reducing the money stock, because they led to a loss of confidence on the part of depositors and hence to an even higher desired currency-deposit ratio. Furthermore, banks that had not yet failed adjusted to the possibility of a run by holding increased reserves relative to deposits. The rise in the currency-deposit ratio and the reserve-deposit ratio reduced the money multiplier and hence sharply contracted the money stock.

The American central bank, commonly referred to as the Fed (Federal Reserve System), took very few steps to offset the fall in the money supply; for a few months in 1932 it did undertake a program of open market purchases, but otherwise seemed to acquiesce in bank closings and certainly failed to understand that the central bank should act vigorously in a crisis to prevent the collapse of the financial system.[2]

Canadian experience was similar but for quite different reasons. There was little scope for monetary policy in Canada during the early years of the depression as there was no central bank (the Bank of Canada began operations in 1935). As in the U.S., the money supply fell sharply after the 1929 crash, but there were no bank failures. However the monetary base fell as a result of the institutional arrangements at the time under which the volume of bank reserves was determined primarily at the initiative of the chartered banks through a form of borrowing.[3] With the onset of the depression, the demand for loans by credit-worthy borrowers collapsed and the chartered banks responded by contracting their operations.

Fiscal policy in the U.S. was also not very vigorous. The natural impulse of politicians then was to balance the budget in times of trouble, and much rhetoric was devoted to that proposition. The presidential candidates in 1932 campaigned on balanced budget platforms. In fact, the federal government ran enormous deficits, particularly for that time, averaging 2.6 percent of GNP from 1931 to 1933, and even more later. The belief in budget balancing was more than rhetoric, however, for state and local governments raised taxes to match their expenditures, as did the federal government, particularly in 1932 and 1933. President Roosevelt tried seriously to balance the budget — he was no Keynesian. The full-employment surplus shows fiscal policy (combined state, local, and federal) as most expansionary in 1931, and moving to a more contractionary level from 1932 to 1934. In fact, the full-employment surplus was positive in 1933 and 1934, despite the actual deficits. Of course, the full-employment surplus concept had not been invented in the 1930s.

Economic activity recovered in the period from 1933 to 1937, with fiscal policy becoming more expansionary and the money stock growing rapidly. The growth of the money stock was based on an inflow of gold from Europe which provided an increase in high-powered money. This period also saw a program of legislative action to aid recovery known as the *New Deal*.

International Aspects

Another important aspect of the depression deserves mention: it was virtually worldwide. To some extent, this was the result of the collapse of the international financial system.[4] It resulted too from the mutual adoption of high tariff policies by many countries (including the United States), keeping out foreign goods to protect domestic producers. And, of course, if each country keeps out foreign goods, the volume of world trade declines, providing a contractionary influence on the world economy.

The experience of the thirties varied internationally. Sweden suffered its depression in the twenties and benefitted from expansionary policies in the thirties. Britain's economy too suffered more in the twenties than in the thirties. Germany grew rapidly after Hitler came to power and expanded government spending. China escaped the recession until after 1931, essentially because it had a floating exchange rate. As always, there is much to be learned from the exceptions.

12-2   THE GREAT DEPRESSION: THE ISSUES AND IDEAS

What caused the great depression, could it have been avoided, and could it happen again? The question of what caused the depression seems purely academic, but it is much more than that. The depression was the greatest economic crisis the Western world had experienced.

The classical economics of the time had no well-developed theory that would explain persistent unemployment, nor any policy prescriptions to solve the problem. Many economists of the time did, in fact, recommend government spending as a way of reducing unemployment, but they had no macroeconomic theory by which to justify their recommendations.

Keynes wrote his greatest work, *The General Theory of Employment, Interest and Money* in the 1930s, after Britain had suffered during the 1920s from a decade of double-digit unemployment and while the United States was in the depths of its depression. He was fully aware of the seriousness of the issues. As Don Patinkin of the Hebrew University puts it[5]:

> . . . the period was one of fear and darkness as the Western world struggled with the greatest depression that it had known. . . . [T]here was a definite feeling that by attempting to achieve a scientific under-standing of the phenomenon of mass unemployment, one was not only making an intellectual contribution, but was also dealing with a critical problem that endangered the very existence of Western civilization.

Keynesian theory explained what had happened, what could have been done to prevent the depression, and what could be done to prevent future depressions. The explanation soon became accepted by most macroeconomists, in the process described as the Keynesian revolution.

The Keynesian Explanation

The essence of the Keynesian explanation of the great depression is based on the simple aggregate demand model developed in Chapter 3. Growth in the twenties, in this view, was based on the mass production of the automobile and radio and was fueled by a housing boom. The collapse of growth in the thirties resulted from the drying up of investment opportunities and a downward shift in investment demand. Some researchers also believe there was a downward shift in the consumption function in 1930.[6] Poor fiscal policy, as reflected in the perverse behaviour of the full-employment surplus from 1931 to 1933, shares the blame, particularly for making the depression worse.

What does this view have to say about the monetary collapse? The Fed argued in the thirties that there was little it could have done to prevent the depression, because interest rates were already as low as they could possibly go. A variety of sayings of the type, "You can lead a horse to water but you can't make it drink," were used to explain that further reductions in interest rates would have had no effect if there was no demand for investment. Investment demand was thought to be very unresponsive to the rate of interest — implying a very steep *IS* curve. At the same time, the *LM* curve was believed to be quite flat, though not necessarily reaching the extreme of a liquidity trap. In this situation, as we saw in Chapter 4, monetary expansion would be relatively ineffective in stimulating demand and output.

It was also widely believed that the experience of the depression showed that the private economy was inherently unstable in that it could self-depress with no difficulty if left alone. The experience of the thirties, implicitly or explicitly, was the basis for the belief that an active stabilization policy was needed to maintain good economic performance.

The Keynesian model not only offered an explanation of what had happened, but also suggested policy measures that could have been taken to prevent the depression, and that could be used to prevent future depressions. Vigorous use of countercyclical fiscal policy was the preferred method for reducing cyclical fluctuations. If a recession ever showed signs of deteriorating into a depression, the cure would be to cut taxes and increase government spending. And those policies would, too, have prevented the depression from being as deep as it was.

There is nothing in the *IS-LM* model developed in Chapter 4 that suggests fiscal policy is more useful than monetary policy for stabilization of the economy. Nonetheless, it is true that until the 1950s, Keynesians tended to give more emphasis to fiscal than to monetary policy.

The Monetarist Challenge

The Keynesian emphasis on fiscal policy, and its downplaying of the role of money, was increasingly challenged by Milton Friedman and his coworkers[7] during the 1950s. During this period Friedman was developing much of the analysis and evidence that provided the basis for monetarism, which we describe in detail in Chapter 17. The main thrust was a heavy emphasis on the role of monetary policy in determining the behaviour of both output and prices.

If monetary policy was to be given an important role, though, it was necessary to dispose of the view that monetary policy had been tried in the great depression and had failed. In other words, the view that "You can lead a horse to the water, etc.," had to be challenged.

The view that monetary policy in the thirties had been impotent was attacked in 1963 by Friedman and Schwartz in their *Monetary History*. They argued that the depression, far from showing that money does not matter, "is in fact a tragic testimonial to the importance of monetary factors."[8] They argued, with skill and style, that the failure of the Fed to prevent bank failures and the decline of the money stock from the end of 1930 to 1933 was largely responsible for the recession being as serious as it was. This monetary view, in turn, came close to being accepted as the orthodox explanation of the depression.[9]

Synthesis

Both the Keynesian and the monetarist explanations of the great depression fit the facts, and both provide answers to the question of why it happened, and how to prevent it from happening again. Inept fiscal and monetary policies both made the great depression severe. If there had been prompt, strong, expansive monetary and fiscal policy, the economy would have suffered a recession but not the trauma it did.

On the question of whether it could happen again, there is agreement that it could not, except, of course, in the event of truly perverse policies. But these are less likely now than they were then. For one thing, we have history to help us avoid its repetition. Taxes would not again be raised in the middle of a depression, nor would attempts be made to balance the budget. The Bank of Canada would seek actively to keep the money supply from falling. In addition, the government now has a much larger role in the economy than it did then. The higher level of government spending, which is relatively slow to change, and automatic stabilizers, including the income tax,[10] unemployment insurance, and social insurance, give the economy more stability than it had then.[11]

There is no inherent conflict between the Keynesian and monetarist explanations of the great depression. The *IS-LM* model, augmented by the supply-side analysis of wage and price adjustment to be discussed in Chapters 13 to 15, easily combines both explanations. Why, then, has there been controversy over the causes of the great depression? The reason is that the thirties are seen as the period that set the stage for massive government intervention in the economy. Those opposed to an active role for government have to explain away the debacle of the economy in the thirties. If the depression occurred because of, and not despite, the government, the case for an active government role in economic stabilization is weakened. Further, the thirties are a period in which the economy behaved in such an extreme way that competing theories have to be subjected to the test of whether they can explain that period. Those are the main reasons the dispute over the causes of the great depression continues more than 50 years after it began.

12-3   FISCAL POLICY IN THE POSTWAR PERIOD

The experience of the Great Depression and World War II resulted in a fundamental change in the role of government expenditures and taxes as instruments of government policy. The 1945 White Paper on Employment and Income established the principle that the federal government had a responsibility to maintain high and stable levels of employment and income. Since then, consideration of the desired degree of fiscal stimulus or restraint has become an important element in the budgets presented to Parliament.

Both the achievements and failures of economic policy in the postwar period can be seen in Figure 12-2. In comparison with earlier eras, the fifties and sixties were years of prosperity and steady growth. The first

prolonged slump occurred during the years 1958 to 1961 when the unemployment rate reached a peak of 7.1 percent. By 1965, the economy was
operating at or near potential, but in retrospect, it appears that policy
makers misjudged the situation. As can be seen in Figure 12-3, rising
income had moved government budgets into a surplus position, but some
of the restraining effects of the built-in stabilizers were offset by tax cuts
introduced in the federal budget of April 1965. As a result, the cyclically
adjusted federal budget moved to a deficit position. Tax increases and
some expenditure cuts were imposed in the years 1966–1968, but fiscal
restraint came too late to prevent the entrenchment of inflationary forces.
The rate of inflation had crept up steadily during the sixties and by 1969
had reached 4.6 percent.

Perspectives on economic policy in the sixties appear to differ widely. It

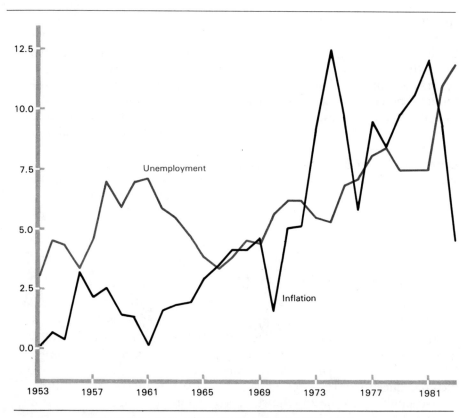

FIGURE 12-2   INFLATION AND UNEMPLOYMENT, 1953–1983
(*Source*: Statistics Canada, 11-206, 11-505, 71-201)

was a period in which faith in the efficiency of activist fiscal policy reached a peak. Although the analytical approach consisted basically of the Keynesian tools we have outlined in previous chapters, fiscal activism became known as the "New Economics" in the United States.[12] In one view, the period was one of high employment and prosperity, thanks to the activist stance of policy. An alternative view is that overexpansionist policies in that period were responsible for the inflation that was to prove to be the economic policy problem of the seventies. Actually, both views are correct. Policy in the early sixties was indeed successful, and economic policy in the second half of the period was overexpansionary or, equivalently, not sufficiently contractionary, in the face of increases in spending to a large extent related to the Vietnam war. Government spending in the U.S. rose rapidly, and rising income in the U.S. stimulated demand for Canadian exports, thereby contributing to inflationary pressure in Canada.

The decade of the 1970s began with the federal government in a surplus position, but there was a shift to an expansionary policy in view of the steep rise in unemployment that had occurred. With an unemployment rate in excess of 6 percent during most of 1971 and 1972, the federal budget was maintained in a deficit position. In 1974 the emphasis shifted to moderating the inflationary pressures that were building up. At mid-year the unemployment rate was down around 5 percent and the consumer price index was rising at a rate in excess of 10 percent. However, toward the end of the year there was a significant worsening of the outlook. Slower growth and rising unemployment occurred in Canada while the United States experienced a substantial *decline* in real GNP. In view of these conditions, an expansionary budget was brought down late in the year which provided for a reduction in personal income taxes of about $1.5 million in 1975.

As can be seen from Figure 12-3, the federal budget moved to a substantial deficit position in 1975 and 1976. This resulted from both the automatic response of tax revenues and unemployment insurance benefits to relatively low levels of economic activity, and the effects of discretionary policy as reflected in the cyclically adjusted federal balance. Further tax cuts were introduced in 1977 and 1978 in response to rising unemployment rates, but policy decisions were complicated by the emergence of two major dilemmas.

First, although the unemployment rate rose above 8 percent in 1977 for the first time since the 1930s, the rate of inflation continued at an unacceptably high level. By 1981, the consumer price index was rising at a 12 percent rate and unemployment was still over 7 percent of the labour force. In the third quarter of 1981 Canada plunged into the worst recession of the postwar period and the inflation rate finally eased as the unemployment rate reached 12 percent at the trough. The problem of the coexistence of high unemployment and a high inflation rate is taken up in Chapter 16.

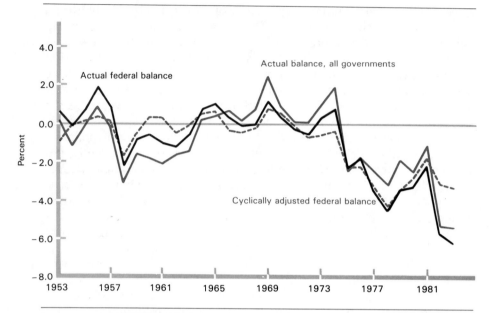

FIGURE 12-3   ACTUAL AND CYCLICALLY ADJUSTED BUDGET BALANCE AS A
PERCENTAGE OF GNP
(*Source*: Department of Finance, *Economic Review*)

The second dilemma that arose in the late 1970s was the rapid growth
of the government deficit. By 1982 the deficit of all levels of government
had risen above 5 percent of GNP. A substantial fraction of the deficit was
attributable to the 1981–1982 recession but as can be seen in Figure 12-3,
much of it was a cyclically adjusted or *structural deficit* arising from an
imbalance between tax rates and expenditure programs. The structural
deficit of the federal government in 1982 was over 3 percent of GNP as
compared with an average of less than .1 percent over the period 1953 to
1974. The issue of large deficits and a rising national debt are taken up in
Section 12-4 below. We conclude this section with a detailed look at
government revenue and expenditure.

Government Revenue and Expenditure

Table 12-2 shows the pattern of federal government revenues and expenditures during the 1970s and early 1980s. Revenues grew faster than GNP
from 1970 to 1974, reaching a peak of 20.3 percent of GNP. With the
exception of oil and gas taxes, revenues grew more slowly thereafter as a
result of a slowing down of income growth and the introduction of various tax reductions. As estimated by the Department of Finance, the cumu-

lative effect of the tax changes made in the budgets over the period 1972 to 1981 was a reduction of revenue in the 1982–83 fiscal year of nearly $25 billion. In relation to GNP this amounts to a loss of 7 percentage points.[13]

On the expenditure side, the most rapid growth has been in interest on the public debt and transfer payments. Subsidies under the oil import compensation program jumped from below $1 billion in 1974 to nearly $4 billion in 1980. Under this program, the federal government subsidized users of imported oil to compensate them for the difference between the world price and the controlled domestic price. With the rapid increase in world oil prices in 1979, this difference widened to more than $17 per barrel. More recently increases in the domestic price and reductions in the world price have eliminated much of the differential.

TABLE 12-2   FEDERAL GOVERNMENT REVENUE AND EXPENDITURE (billions of dollars)

	1970	1974	1980	1982
Revenue				
Personal income taxes	6.41	11.13	19.13	25.85
Other personal direct taxes	1.02	2.41	4.33	6.40
Corporate income taxes	2.28	5.01	8.00	5.10
Direct oil and gas taxes	—	—	—	1.65
Indirect oil and gas taxes	—	1.62	2.06	6.45
Other indirect taxes	4.03	6.88	10.07	10.87
Other revenue	1.78	2.93	7.06	8.55
Total revenue	15.52	29.98	50.65	64.87
(percent of GNP)	(18.1)	(20.3)	(17.0)	(18.1)
Expenditure				
Goods and services	5.01	8.38	14.81	20.13
Transfers to persons	4.06	8.71	16.47	24.64
Transfers to provinces and municipalities	3.40	6.16	12.83	15.77
Interest on the public debt	1.86	2.96	9.65	16.44
Petroleum compensation payments	—	.89	3.93	2.88
Other transfers	.93	1.77	3.11	6.10
Total expenditure	15.26	28.87	60.80	85.96
(percent of GNP)	(17.8)	(19.6)	(20.4)	(24.0)

Source: Dept. of Finance, *Economic Review*

Provincial and Municipal Governments

Table 12-3 shows the budgetary position of the provincial and municipal governments. Their expenditures grew at about the same rate as federal outlays during the 1970s but their revenues grew at a faster rate, and as a result their budget balance improved.

TABLE 12-3   PROVINCIAL AND MUNICIPAL REVENUE AND EXPENDITURE (billions of dollars)

	1970	1974	1980	1982
Revenue				
Own sources	15.10	26.47	59.36	74.24
Federal cash transfers	3.40	6.16	12.83	15.77
Total revenue	18.50	32.63	72.19	90.01
(percent of GNP)	(21.6)	(22.1)	(24.3)	(25.1)
Expenditure				
Goods and services	14.74	24.88	51.99	66.19
Transfers to persons	2.82	4.68	11.17	14.11
Interest on the public debt	1.39	2.46	6.24	8.80
Other transfers	.20	.69	1.82	2.25
Total expenditure	19.15	32.71	71.22	91.35
(percent of GNP)	(22.3)	(22.2)	(23.9)	(25.5)
Budget Balance				
Sask., Alberta, and B.C.	−.07	.80	3.25	0.00
Other provinces	−.58	−.88	−2.27	0.00
Total	−.65	−.08	.98	−1.34

Source: Dept. of Finance, Economic Review

One of the principal contributions to the growth of revenues has been natural resource royalties. By 1980, these accounted for over 7 percent of total revenues, as compared with less than 2 percent in 1970. Almost all of this revenue goes to Alberta, Saskatchewan, and British Columbia. As can be seen in Table 12-3, the surplus for provincial and municipal governments in 1980 arose from the net effect of a substantial surplus in these three provinces and a substantial deficit in the remainder. As in the case of the federal government, the low level of economic activity in 1982 lead to a marked deterioration in the financial position of the provinces and municipalities.

12-4   GOVERNMENT DEFICITS AND THE NATIONAL DEBT

As we indicated in the preceding section, in the early 1980s the structural (cyclically adjusted) deficit of the federal government had reached 3 percent of GNP. In view of the persistence of high unemployment, the fiscal plan adopted by the Minister of Finance in April of 1983 involved a "tilting" of the deficit track. The strategy was to allow some immediate increase in the structural deficit and then reduce it over time with the objective of bringing it down to the range of 1 to 2 percent of GNP by 1987.[14]

A similar problem existed in the U.S. as a result of substantial tax cuts introduced in 1981 as part of the "supply-side" program of the Reagan administration (see Box). Many economists on both sides of the border were expressing concern about the implications for the future. There was a fear that continued massive government borrowing would cause interest rates to rise and crowd out private investment. An alternative danger was that rising interest rates would induce the central banks to intervene to hold them down. This would involve increasing the money supply and creating inflationary pressure.

The emergence of unprecedented deficits raises a number of questions that we have not yet considered. We begin this section by examining the relationship between the federal government's deficit and changes in the stocks of money and government debt.

BOX 12-1   SUPPLY SIDE ECONOMICS AND THE LAFFER CURVE

At the time the tax cuts were introduced in the U.S., the Reagan administration and an associated group of *supply-side economists* argued that the tax cuts would not create any deficits. They argued that they would be self-financing because lower tax rates would cause people to work harder, so much harder that total income taxes would rise. Moreover, they argued that problems of crowding out would not occur because the tax cuts would induce people to save more.

Arthur Laffer, of the University of Southern California, is among the best known of the supply-side economists and originator of the *Laffer curve*. Figure 1 shows this curve which relates tax revenues to the tax rate. It shows total tax revenue first increasing as the tax rate rises and then eventually decreasing.

The argument supporting the shape of the curve is as follows. Assume that we are discussing the income tax rate. When the tax rate is zero, government tax revenue is certainly zero. Hence we have point A on the curve. Further, suppose the tax rate were 100 percent. Then the government would be taking all the income that people earn. There would be no point in working if the government took all earnings, and so income in that case too would be zero. Then tax revenue would also be zero. Accordingly, point B is also a point on the Laffer curve.

Between A and B, though, the government certainly takes in some revenue from taxes. Thus we expect the curve to start to rise from point A as the tax rate is increased from zero to some very small rate, such as 3 percent. Eventually, though, the curve has to come back down to B. Thus at some point it will turn around — perhaps at a tax rate of 60 percent, as shown in Figure 1. Point C is the dividing line: at tax rates below 60 percent, any increase in the tax rate *raises* total tax revenue. At tax rates above 60 percent, any increase in the tax rate *reduces* total revenue. Looking at the same relationship in the opposite direction, we find that at any tax rate above 60 percent, a *cut* in the tax rate will *increase* total tax revenue.

Supply-siders were thus arguing in 1981 that the American economy was to be right of the point where the Laffer curve turns down — say, at some point such as D. There was no evidence to support this assertion, and it does not appear to have been right. But it is a theoretical possibility.

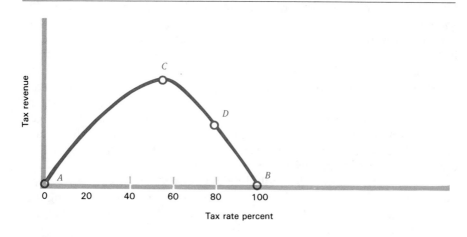

FIGURE 1   THE LAFFER CURVE. Total tax revenue is zero when the tax rate is either zero (point *A*) or 100 percent (point *B*). Tax revenue is positive at intermediate tax rates. At point *C* tax revenue is at a maximum. If tax rates are any higher, for instance, at point *D*, a *cut* in the tax rate will *increase* tax revenue.

Supply-siders made a similar claim about the effects of cuts in taxes on saving. When tax rates on saving are cut, the after-tax rate of return rises. For instance, suppose someone is earning 9 percent before tax on savings. The tax rate is 25 percent, implying an after-tax rate of return on savings of 6.75 percent (= 0.75 × 9 percent). Now suppose the tax rate is cut to 20 percent. The after-tax rate of return rises to 7.2 (= 0.8 × 9 percent). Surely, supply-siders argued, such a person will save more.* Then there will be more investment, a larger capital stock, and high output. With output higher, total tax revenue could be higher despite the cut in the tax rate.

Whatever the theoretical possibilities, the 1981 tax cuts did not lead to an increase in government revenue in the U.S. This excessively optimistic element in supply-side economics was never believed by any but a small minority of economists, and is now totally dismissed.† The emphasis on the role of incentives, though, is a valuable component of supply-side analysis and is discussed further in Chapter 19.

*There are conflicting income and substitution effects at work in this case too, and the theoretical effects of the cut in the tax rate on saving is uncertain.
†On the supply-side story, see Michael Evans, *The Truth about Supply-Side Economics* (New York: Basic Books, 1983), and Jude Wanniski, *The Way the World Works* (New York: Touchstone, 1978). For a critical view, see Robert Lekachman, *Greed Is Not Enough: Reganomics* (New York: Pantheon, 1982).

The Mechanics of Financing the Deficit

How does the government pay for its spending? Directly, it pays for most of its spending with cheques, drawn on the Bank of Canada. Aside from the fact that the cheque is drawn on a bank in which private individuals do not have accounts, a payment made by the government looks much like a cheque payment made by anyone else. Like an individual, the federal government must have funds in the account on which it writes cheques. So the question of how the federal government finances its spending is the same as the question of how it makes sure that it has funds in the bank account (at the Bank of Canada) on which it writes its cheques.

The federal government receives the bulk of its revenues from taxes and in some years taxes are less than expenditures so that it runs a budget deficit. Total government expenditures consist of purchases of goods and services, G, and transfers, TR. Denoting taxes by TA and the deficit by BD we know that

$$BD \equiv (G + TR) - TA \equiv -BS \tag{1}$$

Equation (1) reminds us that the deficit, BD is just the negative of the surplus, BS.

Now, how does the government make payments when its tax receipts are insufficient to cover its expenditures? The answer is that it has to borrow either from the public or the Bank of Canada. When the government finances its deficit by borrowing from the private sector, it is engaged in debt financing. It sells securities or debt to the private sector and, in return, receives cheques from individuals and firms (including banks) in exchange for the securities it sells them. The cheques are deposited in government accounts at the chartered banks or at the Bank of Canada, and can then be spent in the same way as tax receipts.

Alternatively, the government can borrow from the Bank of Canada by selling securities to the Bank. However, there is a major difference between government borrowing from the public and the Bank of Canada. When the Bank of Canada lends to the government by buying securities, it pays for them by giving the government a cheque on the Bank of Canada, that is, by creating high-powered money. When the government spends the deposit it has received at the Bank of Canada in exchange for its debt, it leaves the private sector with larger holdings of high-powered money. By contrast, when the government borrows from the public, it receives and then spends high-powered money, thus leaving the amount of high-powered money in the hands of the public unchanged, except for a brief transition period between the sale of securities and expenditures by the government. Since the stock of high-powered money is an important macroeconomic variable, the distinction between selling debt to the public and selling it to the Bank of Canada is in fact essential.

When the government borrows from the central bank to finance its deficit, it is engaged in money financing. Alternatively, the sale of securities to the Bank of Canada is referred to as *monetizing the debt*, meaning that the Bank creates (high-powered) money to finance the debt purchase.

Another way of looking at the difference between sales to (borrowing from) the Bank of Canada and the public is to ask: What is the net change in the private sector's portfolio after the government has made *and* financed its expenditures? Consider first the case of borrowing from the public or selling debt to the public. In this case, the public holds more debt and an unchanged quantity of high-powered money, since the government spends the money it obtains from the debt sale to cover its deficit. Consider next the case where the deficit is financed by sale of debt to the Bank of Canada. In this event, the private sector's debt holding is unchanged while its holding of high-powered money is increased. The reason is that expenditures were financed by the creation of high-powered money by the Bank of Canada.

The Government Budget Constraint

We have seen that the government deficit can be financed in two ways: by sales of securities to the private sector and by borrowing from the Bank of Canada. Let ΔB_p and ΔB_b be the change in the value of government bonds held by the private sector and the Bank of Canada, respectively. Writing H for the stock of high-powered money, we have

$$BD = \Delta B_b + \Delta B_p = \Delta H + \Delta B_p \qquad (2)$$

Equation (2) is called the government budget constraint. It states that the budget deficit is financed by borrowing either from the Bank of Canada or from the private sector. The change in Bank of Canada holdings of debt causes a corresponding change in high-powered money (ΔH), so that we can say that the budget deficit is financed either by selling debt to the public or by increasing the stock of high-powered money. It is in this sense that the Bank of Canada "monetizes" the debt.[15]

The view that the deficit is financed either by selling debt to the public or by increasing the stock of high-powered money looks at the government sector as a whole, including or "consolidating" the Bank of Canada along with the government in the government sector. When one thinks of the government sector as a whole, relative to the private sector, the transactions in which the Bank of Canada buys debt from or lends to the government are seen as mere bookkeeping entries within the government sector.

Although this consolidation is useful for some purposes, it is important to recognize that the institutional arrangements provide for a clear division of responsibility under which the Bank of Canada determines the division of the total deficit BD, in Equation (2), between the change in high-powered money and the change in government debt held by the private sector. There is no *necessary* association between the size of the government deficit in Canada and increases in the stock of high-powered money. If the Bank of Canada does not purchase securities when the government is borrowing, the stock of high-powered money is not affected by the deficit. On the other hand, there will be a more or less automatic association between Bank of Canada purchases of securities and government borrowing if the Bank of Canada commits itself to maintaining interest rates on government bonds at a constant level. As we saw in Chapter 4, an increase in the government deficit tends to increase the interest rate. If the Bank of Canada wishes to prevent this it must intervene in the market and purchase securities.

Prior to 1975, the Bank of Canada's policy focussed primarily on target interest rates, which could change from time to time, so that there was a link between deficits and Bank of Canada purchases of securities. More recently the Bank has shifted to a policy which concentrates on the behaviour of the money supply. A commitment to bringing about a given money stock breaks the link between government deficits and the creation of high-powered money. If the Bank of Canada creates high-powered money at a rate that should result in money's growing at the target rate, the change in the stock of high-powered money is not directly associated with the size of the government deficit.

Deficits and the National Debt

It follows from Equation (2) that when the budget is not balanced, the government changes the net amount of claims on it held by the private sector and the Bank of Canada. Those claims are the securities sold to the private sector and the Bank of Canada, and they represent claims for future interest payments. The total stock of government bonds (or claims on the government) outstanding constitutes the national, or public, debt. When the budget is in deficit, the national debt increases — the stock of claims against the government increases. When the budget is in surplus, the national debt decreases. The government takes in more taxes than it pays out, and can use the excess to retire (or buy back) previously issued debt.

The national debt is a direct consequence of past deficits in the federal budget. The national debt increases when there is a budget deficit and decreases when the budget is in surplus. The way the national debt is divided between private sector claims on the government and high-powered money depends on past monetary policy. If the Bank of Canada has financed only a small part of each deficit in the past, then the ratio of high-powered money to national debt is small.

The government sells securities more or less continuously. There is, for instance, a weekly treasury bill auction, at which prospective buyers of treasury bills (lenders to the federal government) submit sealed bids specifying how much they are prepared to lend at different interest rates. The government sells the amount of treasury bills it has offered at the auction to the bidders who offer the highest prices, or the lowest interest rates.[16]

Longer-term debt issues are less frequent. Issues of government debt are not all made for the purpose of financing the budget deficit. Most debt issues are made to refinance parts of the national debt that are maturing. For example, the government has to pay the amount it borrowed to a treasury bill holder when the treasury bill matures. Six months after a 180-day treasury bill is issued, the government has to pay the face amount of the treasury bill to the holder. Typically, the government obtains the funds to make those payments by further borrowing. The process by which the government (with the help and advice of the Bank of Canada) finances and refinances the national debt is known as *debt management*. Only a part of debt management is concerned with financing the current budget deficit. Most of it is concerned with the consequences of past budget deficits.

Figure 12-4 shows the growth of the national debt since the mid-fifties. Although the amount of debt has been steadily rising, it grew at a slower rate than GNP until 1975. This is reflected in the decline in the ratio of debt to GNP shown in Figure 12-5. As a result of the sharp increase in the size of

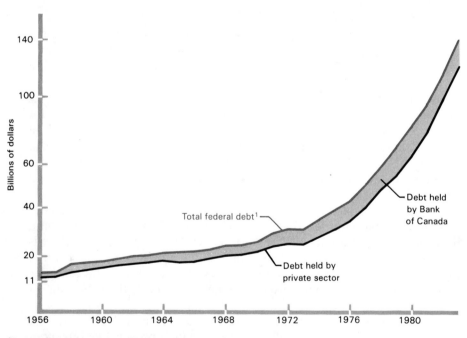

¹Excludes debts held in Government of Canada Accounts

FIGURE 12-4   THE NATIONAL DEBT
(*Source: Bank of Canada Review*)

the federal deficit, the ratio began to move up and by 1983 it was double the level of 1975, although it was still below the level of the early sixties.

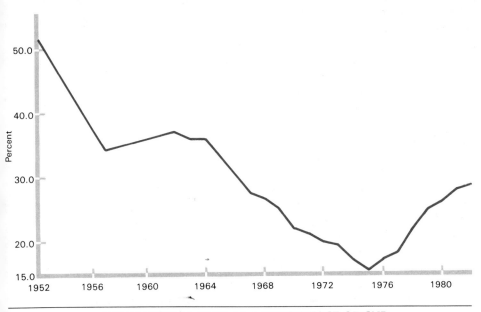

FIGURE 12-5   THE NATIONAL DEBT AS A PERCENTAGE OF GNP
(*Source*: Department of Finance, *Economic Review*)

The Burden of the Debt

To what extent is the national debt a burden? It must be recognized of course that corresponding to the liability that we all have as our share of the national debt, there are assets in the form of government securities held by Canadians. With the exception of debt held by foreigners, we owe the national debt to ourselves. Each individual shares in the public debt, but many individuals own claims on the government that are the other side of the national debt. If there is a debt for individuals taken together, it arises from prospective taxes to pay off the debt. The taxes that different individuals would pay to retire the debt would also vary among the population. To a first approximation, one could think of the liability that the debt represents as cancelling out the asset that the debt represents to the individuals who hold claims on the government.[17]

The question at issue then is whether the debt is counted as part of wealth for the population as a whole. It is not certain whether individuals take into account the future tax liabilities connected with paying off the debt. There certainly does not seem to be any argument that the liability represented by some possible paying off of the debt at some unknown future time outweighs the value of the assets that individuals hold at present. At this level, then, there is no persuasive argument that the debt is a burden in the sense that the economy as a whole regards the national debt as a reduction in its wealth.

The only factor ignored in the previous paragraph is that part of the debt is owned by foreigners. In that case, for the Canadian economy as a whole, part of the asset represented by the debt is held by foreigners, while the future tax liability accrues entirely to residents. Then that part of the debt held by foreigners might represent a net reduction in the wealth of Canadian residents.

Although the debt is not a burden in the fairly crude sense in which one asks whether individuals regard themselves as being poorer because of the existence of the debt (leaving aside the part of the debt owned by foreigners), there are more sophisticated senses in which it might be a burden. The most important sense in which there is a possible burden arises from the potential long-run effects of the debt on the capital stock. Since debt financing increases the interest rate and reduces investment, the capital stock would be lower with debt financing than otherwise. If individuals regard the debt as part of their wealth, then they tend to increase their consumption at a given level of income, which results in a smaller proportion of GNP being invested.

In the long run, that would result in a lower capital stock and thus a lower level of real output. In that sense, then, the debt could be a burden. Secondly, the debt might be a burden because debt servicing in the long run could require higher tax rates. If those tax rates have adverse effects on the amount of work that individuals do, then real output would be reduced. However, it is far from certain that higher tax rates in fact reduce the amount of work that individuals do. Thus we conclude that the major sense in which the national debt may be a burden is that it may lead to a decline in the capital stock in the long run.

12-5   SUMMARY

Six main points were made in the previous section.

1 Federal government spending is financed through taxes and through borrowing, which is necessary when the budget is in deficit.

2 Borrowing may be from the private sector or from the Bank of Canada.

3 Lending to the government by the Bank of Canada changes the stock of high-powered money, whereas lending by the private sector to the government to finance the deficit does not affect the stock of high-powered money.

4   The stock of claims held by the Bank of Canada and the private sector against the government — the national debt — changes with the budget deficit. The national debt increases when there is a budget deficit and decreases when there is a budget surplus.

5   Because the deficit can be financed in two ways, there is no *necessary* connection between the budget deficit and changes in the stock of high-powered money. Equation (2), the government budget constraint, says only that the *sum* of changes in the stock of debt and changes in high-powered money is approximately equal to the budget deficit.

6   With the exception of debt held by foreigners, the national debt is not a burden since we owe it to ourselves. However the debt may be a burden in the long run because it leads to a decline in the capital stock.

KEY TERMS

Structural deficit   *Government budget constraint*
Debt finance   *National debt*
Money finance   *Burden of the debt*
Monetizing the debt

PROBLEMS

1   Using *IS-LM* curves, describe the competing "autonomous spending" and "monetary" explanations for the Great Depression.

2   Explain why many people believe the inflationary problems of the 1970s have their roots in the 1960s. How can this be so? What would be the cause? What could have been done to avoid such "heating up" of the economy, in this view?

3   Government budget deficits are often a source of public concern. What would be the implications for stabilization policy of a commitment to a balanced budget every year?

4   Discuss the notion of the monetary-fiscal policy mix. What determines the mix that is chosen? Illustrate, using a *IS-LM* diagram, how the effects of the mixes of 1971 and 1981 differ, given the information below. (Ignore changes in the level of income.)

	1971	1981
Cyclically adjusted federal deficit (% of GNP)	0	−1.7
Increase in the treasury bill rate (percent)	−2.5	5.0

5 What effect does a federal government surplus have on the stock of money and the stock of debt? Explain in detail the mechanics of how the stocks of money and bonds are affected.

6 Suppose the government issues $1 billion in treasury bills which are bought by the public. Then the Bank of Canada conducts open market purchases of $300 million. Effectively, how has the debt been financed?

7 Under what circumstances are fiscal and monetary policy related rather than existing as two completely independent instruments in the hands of the government?

8 Some people say that a huge government debt is a burden while others point out that a large debt means individuals own large amounts of government securities and thus are wealthier. Who is right?

CHAPTER 12: FOOTNOTES

[1]Milton Friedman and Anna J. Schwartz, in *A Monetary History of the United States 1867–1960* (Princton, N.J.: Princeton University Press, 1963), give a very detailed account of the great depression, comparing it with other recessions and emphasizing the role of the Fed. For a more general economic history of the period, see Robert A. Gordon, *Economic Instability: The American Record* (New York: Harper & Row, 1974), Chap. 3.

[2]Friedman and Schwartz speculate on the reasons for the Fed's inaction; the whodunit or "who didn't do it" on pp. 407 to 419 of their book (cited in footnote 1) is fascinating.

[3]See T.J. Courchene, "An Analysis of the Canadian Money Supply: 1925–1934," *Journal of Political Economy*, May/June 1969.

[4]This aspect of the depression is emphasized by Charles Kindleberger, *The World in Depression, 1929–1939* (Berkeley: University of California Press, 1973), and Gottfried Haberler, *The World Economy, Money and the Great Depression* (Washington, D.C.: American Enterprise Institute, 1976).

[5]In "The Process of Writing *The General Theory*: A Critical Survey," in Don Patinkin and J. Clark Leith (eds.), *Keynes, Cambridge and the General Theory* (Toronto: University of Toronto Press, 1978), p. 3. For a short biography of Keynes, see D.E. Moggridge, *John Maynard Keynes* (New York: Penguin Books, 1976).

[6]Peter Temin, *Did Monetary Forces Cause the Great Depression?* (New York: Norton, 1976).

[7]See, in particular, Milton Friedman (ed.), *Studies in the Quantity Theory of Money* (Chicago: University of Chicago Press, 1956).

[8]Friedman and Schwartz, *op. cit.*, p. 300.

[9]Ben Bernanke, in "Nonmonetary Effects of the Financial Crisis in the Propagation of the Great Depression," *American Economic Review*, June 1983, takes issue with the monetary view, arguing instead that the destruction of the financial system made it difficult for borrowers to obtain funds needed for investment.

[10]Recall from Chap. 3 that a proportional income tax reduces the multiplier.

[11]See Martin Baily, "Stabilization Policy and Private Economic Behavior," *Brookings Papers on Economic Activity*, 1978:1 (Washington, D.C.: The Brookings Institution, 1978).

[12]See the history of the New Economics in W.W. Heller, *New Dimensions of Political Economy* (New York: Norton, 1967). Walter Heller, now a professor at the University of Minnesota, was one of the chief architects of the economic policies of the Kennedy-Johnson administration. With him, as members of the Council of Economic Advisers or staff economists, were highly distinguished economists: James Tobin, Kenneth Arrow, Robert Solow, Otto Eckstein, Gardner Ackley, and the late Arthur Okun. Paul A. Samuelson served as an unofficial adviser.

[13]See Department of Finance, *The Federal Deficit in Perspective*, 1983, Annex D. About three-fifths of this revenue loss was attributable to indexation of the personal income tax. Indexation is discussed in Chapter 16.

[14]See Department of Finance, *The Federal Deficit in Perspective*, 1983, p.3.

[15]Note that the government budget constraint (2) also shows that for a given value of the deficit, changes in the stock of high-powered money are matched by offsetting changes in the public's holdings of government debt. A positive ΔH matched by a negative ΔB_p is nothing other than an open market purchase.

[16]Technically, there is no interest paid on treasury bills. Instead, a treasury bill is a promise to pay a given amount on a given date, say $100 on June 30. Before June 30, the treasury bill sells for a *discount* at less than $100, with the discount implying a rate of interest. For instance, if the treasury bill just described sold for $97.50 on January 1, the holder of the bill for six months would earn a little more than 5 percent per annum, or 2.5 percent for six months.

[17]For an eclectic, but difficult, view of this argument, see Robert J. Barro, "Are Government Bonds Net Wealth?" *Journal of Political Economy*, December 1974.

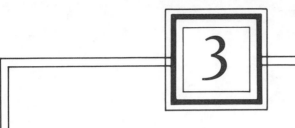

Output and the Price Level

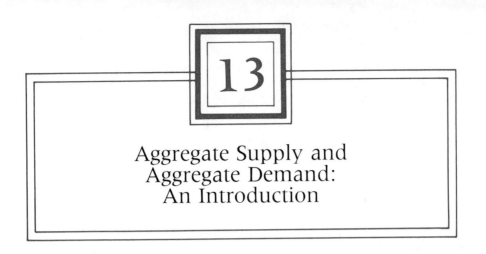

Aggregate Supply and
Aggregate Demand:
An Introduction

So far our analysis of the behaviour of the economy has assumed that the price level is fixed. We studied the impacts of changes in the money supply, or of taxes, or of government spending, assuming that whatever amount of goods was demanded would be supplied, *at the existing price level*.

To put the same point in different words, we have not yet analysed *inflation*. But, of course, inflation is one of the major concerns of macroeconomists, citizens, and policy makers. The time has therefore come to bring the price level and the inflation rate — the rate of change of the price level — into the centre of our analysis of the economy. We have to study the determination of both the level of output — on which we have concentrated thus far — and the price level.

Figure 13-1 shows the model of *aggregate demand and supply* that we shall use to study the joint determination of the price level and the level of output. The aggregate demand curve *AD*, which is downward-sloping, is based entirely on the material of the earlier chapters, in particular Chapter 4. We define the aggregate demand curve in this chapter, and show why it slopes down and what causes it to shift. The aggregate supply curve will be introduced in this chapter and developed further in Chapter 14. The intersection of the *AD* and *AS* schedules at E determines the equilibrium level of output, Y_0, and the equilibrium price level P_0. Shifts in either schedule cause the price level and the level of output to change.

The aggregate demand-supply model is the basic macroeconomic model for studying output and price level determination — just as in microeconomics, demand and supply curves are the essential tools for studying output and price determination in a single market. However, the aggregate demand and supply curves are not as simple as the microeconomic demand and supply curves, for there is more going on in the background of the aggregate curves than there is in that of the microeconomic curves. That is why it will take us two chapters to develop the aggregate curves.[1]

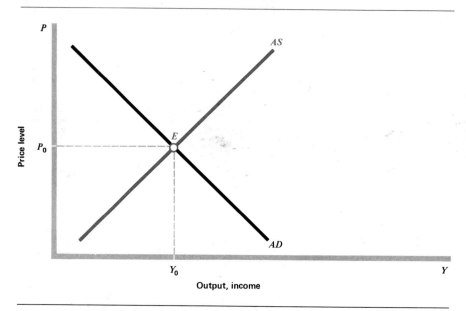

FIGURE 13-1   AGGREGATE SUPPLY AND DEMAND. The diagram shows the complete model of aggregate demand and supply that is developed in this and the next chapter to explain the joint determination of the levels of output and prices. The aggregate demand curve, AD, is based on the IS-LM model studied in earlier chapters. The aggregate supply curve AS is developed in this and the next chapter. Their intersection at point E determines the level of output Y_0 and the price level P_0.

13-1   INTRODUCING AGGREGATE DEMAND AND SUPPLY

Before we go deeply into the factors underlying the aggregate demand and supply curves, we show how the curves will be used. Suppose that the money supply is increased. What effects will that have on the price level and output? In particular, does an increase in the money supply cause the price level to rise, thus producing inflation? Or does the level of output rise, as it did in the analysis of earlier chapters? Or do both output and the price level rise?

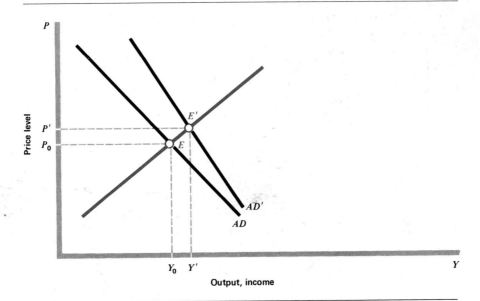

FIGURE 13-2   THE EFFECTS OF AN INCREASE IN THE NOMINAL MONEY STOCK. An increase in the money stock shifts the aggregate demand curve from AD to AD'. The equilibrium moves from E to E', resulting in higher levels of both prices and output. Thus an increase in the money stock in part results in higher prices, and not entirely in higher output.

Figure 13-2 shows that an increase in the money supply shifts the aggregate demand curve AD to the right, to AD'. We see later in this chapter why that should be so. The shift of the aggregate demand curve moves the equilibrium of the economy from E to E'. The price level rises from P_0 to P', and the level of output from Y_0 to Y'. Thus the answer to the questions we asked at the end of the previous paragraph is that an increase in the money stock causes both the level of output and the price level to rise.

The Slope of the Aggregate Supply Curve

What determines how much the price level rises and how much output increases? Looking at Figure 13-3a we see that if the aggregate supply curve is relatively flat, a shift in the AD curve raises output a lot and prices very little. By contrast, in Figure 13-3b we see that when the aggregate supply curve is nearly vertical, an increase in the money supply mainly causes prices to rise and hardly increases output at all.

If the aggregate supply curve is vertical, or nearly so as in Figure 13-3b, then the analysis of the earlier chapters that showed an increase in the money stock raising output could be very misleading. For example, if the aggregate supply curve is vertical, an increase in the money stock will lead only to higher prices, not to more output. Thus one of the key questions on which we shall concentrate is what determines the shape of the aggregate supply curve. When is it vertical, or nearly so as in Figure 13-3b? When is the aggregate supply curve more nearly horizontal as in Figure 13-3a?

Fully developing the answers will take the next two chapters. We start here by defining aggregate demand and supply.

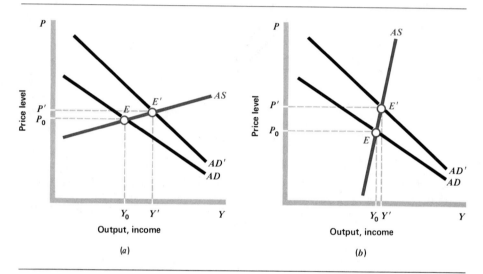

FIGURE 13-3   THE INTERACTION OF AGGREGATE SUPPLY AND DEMAND. The effects of a shift in the aggregate demand curve from *AD* to *AD'* depend on the slope of the aggregate supply curve. If the *AS* curve is relatively flat, as in Figure 13-3a, the shift in the aggregate demand curve results mainly in an increase in output. By contrast, in Figure 13-3b, the shift in the aggregate demand curve results almost entirely in an increase in the price level and very little in an increase in output.

Aggregate Demand and Supply Defined

The *aggregate demand curve* shows the combinations of the price level and level of output at which the goods and assets markets are simultaneously in equilibrium. At any point on the aggregate demand curve, for instance point B in Figure 13-4, we see that for the given price level, P_B in this case, the level of output at which the goods and assets markets are in equilibrium is Y_B.

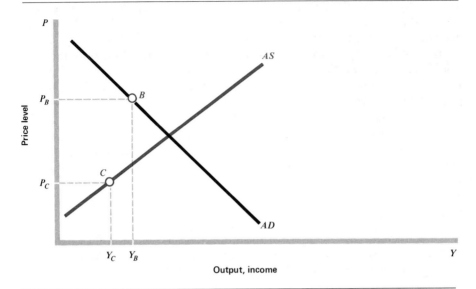

FIGURE 13-4   AGGREGATE DEMAND AND SUPPLY CURVES DEFINED. At any point on the aggregate demand curve, such as point B, both the goods and assets markets are in equilibrium. This is the equilibrium described by the intersection of IS and LM curves in Chapter 4. For instance, with price level P_B, the level of output at which both goods and assets markets are in equilibrium is Y_B. The aggregate supply curve AS describes the relation between the price level and the amount of output firms wish to supply. For instance, at price level P_C, firms want to supply output Y_C.

We can already give a preliminary explanation of why the aggregate demand curve slopes down, based on the discussion of monetary policy in Chapter 4. Suppose that the goods and assets markets are in equilibrium at a level of output like Y_B, with given price level P_B. Now suppose the price level falls. With a given nominal stock of money, a fall in the price level creates an increase in the quantity of *real balances*. We recall from Chapter 4 that an increase in the quantity of real balances reduces interest rates, increases investment demand, and therefore increases aggregate spending. Accordingly, when the price level falls, the equilibrium level of output rises; therefore the AD curve slopes down. We go into the details in Section 13-3.

We can also see, from the definition of the aggregate demand curve, why the analysis of the previous twelve chapters is not at all wasted. The aggregate demand curve describes the joint equilibrium of the goods and assets markets. That is precisely what the IS-LM analysis describes. Thus the material we studied in earlier chapters is an essential part of the aggregate demand and supply model we shall use to analyse the simultaneous determination of the levels of output and prices.

The *aggregate supply curve* describes the combinations of output and the price level such that firms are willing, at the given price level, to supply the given quantity of output. For instance, at point C in Figure 13-4, with price level P_C, firms are willing to supply output equal to Y_C. The amount of output firms are willing to supply depends on the prices they receive for their goods and the amounts they have to pay for labour and other factors of production. Accordingly, the aggregate supply curve reflects conditions in the factor markets, especially the labour market, as well as in the goods markets.

13-2   AGGREGATE SUPPLY: TWO SPECIAL CASES

In this chapter we concentrate on two special cases in discussing aggregate supply. The first, the *Keynesian case*, shown in Figure 13-5a, is a horizontal

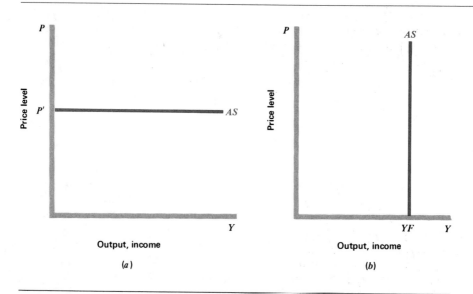

FIGURE 13-5   KEYNESIAN AND CLASSICAL SUPPLY FUNCTIONS. The Keynesian aggregate supply curve is horizontal, implying that any amount of output will be supplied at the existing price level. This is shown in panel (a), where the AS curve is horizontal at price level P'. The classical supply function is based on the assumption that there is always full employment of labour, and thus that output is always at the level of output corresponding to full employment of labour, $\overline{Y}$, and *independent of the price level*. This is shown by the vertical aggregate supply curve in panel (b).

aggregate supply curve. The *Keynesian aggregate supply curve* is horizontal, indicating that firms will supply at the existing price level whatever amount of goods is demanded.

The idea underlying the Keynesian aggregate supply curve is that because there is unemployment, firms can obtain as much labour as they want at the current wage. Their average costs of production therefore are assumed not to change as their output levels change, and they are accordingly willing to supply as much as is demanded at the existing price level.

The Classical Supply Curve

Figure 13-5b shows the opposite extreme, of a vertical supply curve. In the *classical* case, the *aggregate supply curve* is vertical, indicating that the same amount of goods will be supplied whatever the price level.

The classical supply curve is based on the assumption that the labour market is always in equilibrium with full employment of the labour force. If the entire labour force is being employed, then output cannot be raised above its current level even if the price level rises. There is no more labour available to produce any extra output. Thus the aggregate supply curve will be vertical at a level of output corresponding to full employment of the labour force, $\overline{Y}$ in Figure 13-5b.

Underlying the assumption that the labour market is always in equilibrium is another assumption — that the wage adjusts rapidly to maintain equilibrium. For example, suppose that the economy is in equilibrium and the aggregate demand curve shifts to the right, as in Figure 13-2. At the existing price level, the quantity of goods demanded increases.

Now firms try to obtain more labour. Each firm attempts to hire more labour, offering to pay higher wages if necessary. But there is no more labour available in the economy, and so firms are unable to obtain more workers. Instead, in competing against each other for workers, they merely bid up wages. Because wages are higher, the prices the firms charge for their output will also be higher. But output will be unchanged.

The essential difference in assumptions between the classical and Keynesian aggregate supply curves is that the classical supply curve is based on the belief that the labour market works smoothly, always maintaining full employment of the labour force. Movements in the wage are the mechanism through which full employment is maintained. The Keynesian aggregate supply curve is instead based on the assumption that the wage does not change much or at all when there is unemployment, and thus that unemployment can continue for some time.

These two cases — the classical, representing continuing labour market equilibrium, and the Keynesian, assuming wages do not adjust — are the two extremes. In the next chapter we show what determines the slope of the aggregate supply curve and discuss when it will be more like the classical extreme and when it will be more like the Keynesian extreme.

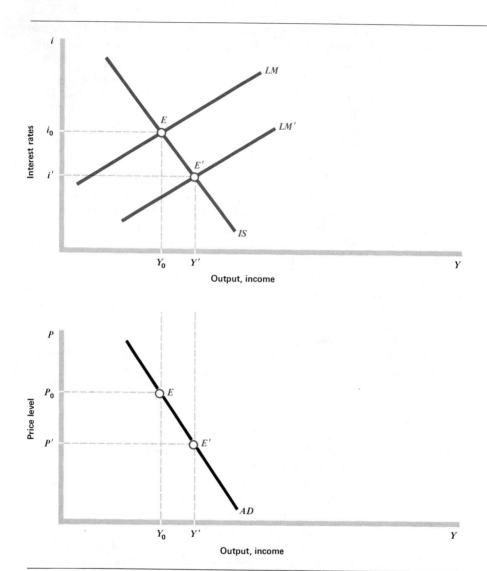

FIGURE 13-6   DERIVATION OF THE AGGREGATE DEMAND SCHEDULE. The
upper panel shows the *IS* schedule and the initial *LM* schedule drawn for the real
money stock M/P_0. Equilibrium is at point *E*. In the lower panel we record that at
a price level P_0 the equilibrium level of income and spending is Y_0. This is shown
by point *E*. At a lower level of prices, say, P', the real money stock is M/P', and
therefore the *LM* schedule shifts to *LM'*. Equilibrium income now is Y'. Again in
the lower panel we show at point E' the combination of the price level P' and the
corresponding equilibrium level of income and spending Y'. Considering
different levels of prices and connecting the resulting points such as *E* and E', we
derive the aggregate demand schedule *AD*. The schedule shows the equilibrium
level of spending at each level of prices, *given* the nominal money stock and fiscal
policy.

13-3   THE AGGREGATE DEMAND SCHEDULE

As noted earlier, the aggregate demand curve, or schedule, shows, for each price level, the level of output at which the goods and assets markets are simultaneously in equilibrium. At any given price level, we use the *IS-LM* model to determine the level of output at which the goods and assets markets are in equilibrium.

In Figure 13-6 we show the *IS-LM* model. The position of the *IS* curve depends on fiscal policy. The *LM* schedule is drawn for a given nominal money stock M and a given price level P_0 and thus for a given real money stock M/P_0. The equilibrium interest rate is i_0, and the equilibrium level of income and spending is shown as Y_0.

A Change in the Price Level

Consider the effect of a fall in the price level from P_0 to P'. This reduction in the price level increases the real money stock from M/P_0 to M/P'. To clear the money market with an increased real money stock, either interest rates must fall, inducing the public to hold more cash balances, or output must rise, thus increasing the transactions demand for money.

Accordingly, the *LM* curve shifts down and to the right, to *LM'*. The new equilibrium is shown at point E', where once again both the money market clears — because we are on the *LM* curve — and the goods market clears — because we are on the *IS* curve. The new equilibrium level of output is Y', corresponding to the lower price level P'. Thus a reduction in the price level, *given the nominal quantity of money*, results in an increase in equilibrium income and spending. The derivation of the *AD* schedule can be seen in Figure 13-6. The economy is initially in equilibrium at points E in both the upper and lower panels. The equilibrium interest rate is i_0, the level of output is Y_0, and the corresponding price level is P_0. Now the price level drops to P'. In the upper panel, the equilibrium moves to E', as a result of the shift of the *LM* curve to *LM'*. Corresponding to point E' in the upper panel is point E' in the lower panel, at price level P' and level of income and output Y'.

Thus E and E' in the lower panel are both points on the *AD* schedule. We could now consider all possible price levels and the corresponding levels of real balances. For each level of real balances there is a different *LM* curve in the upper panel. Corresponding to each *LM* curve is an equilibrium level of income, which would be recorded in the lower panel at the price level that results in the *LM* curve in the upper panel. Connecting all these points gives us a downward-sloping aggregate demand curve *AD*, as shown in Figure 13-6.

The *AD* curve is downward-sloped because there is a definite relation between equilibrium spending and the price level: the higher the price level, the lower are real balances, and hence the lower the equilibrium level of spending and output.

Properties of the *AD* Schedule

The *AD* schedule shows how the level of real spending changes with the level of prices, given fiscal policy, the quantity of money, and autonomous private spending. What are the precise properties of the *AD* schedule? We start with the slope, which tells us how much real spending changes in response to a change in the level of prices.

The Slope of the AD Schedule

In Figure 13-6 we derived the *AD* schedule by considering the effect of changes in the price level, and hence in real balances, on the *LM* schedule and hence on equilibrium income and spending. The slope of the *AD* curve therefore reflects the extent to which a change in real balances changes the equilibrium level of spending, taking both assets and goods markets into account.

But we have already examined the effects of a change in the stock of real balances on the level of output that equilibrates the goods and assets markets. In Chapter 4 we showed the effect of an increase in the nominal stock of money on equilibrium spending and output, with the price level given. Now we ask what is the effect of a change in real balances due to lower prices, given nominal money.

In discussing monetary policy in Chapter 4 we showed the following results using the *IS-LM* schedules:

1 An increase in real balances leads to a larger increase in equilibrium income and spending, the smaller the interest response of money demand and the higher the interest response of investment demand.
2 An increase in real balances leads to a larger increase in equilibrium income and spending, the larger the multiplier and the smaller the income response of money demand.

Because the slope of the AD curve is determined by the effect of a change in real balances on equilibrium spending and output, the same factors that determine the effects of a change in the stock of money on equilibrium output and spending also determine the slope of the AD curve. If a given change in real balances has a large impact on equilibrium spending, then the *AD* curve will be very flat — because a small change in the price level creates a large change in equilibrium spending. But if a given change in real balances has a small effect on equilibrium spending and output, then the *AD* curve will be steep: in that case it takes a large change in the price level to create a small change in spending and output.

Accordingly, we see that:

1 The *AD* curve is flatter (a) the smaller the interest responsiveness of the demand for money, and (b) the larger the interest responsiveness of investment demand.
2 The *AD* curve is flatter (a) the larger the multiplier, and (b) the smaller the income responsiveness of the demand for money.

To fix ideas further, it is useful to think for a moment about the *AD* schedule in terms of the extreme classical and liquidity trap cases that we learned about in Chapter 4. In the classical case, where money demand is entirely unresponsive to interest rates and the *LM* curve is vertical, changes in real balances have a big effect on income and spending. In Figure 13-7 that corresponds to a very flat *AD* schedule, such as *AD'*, as we should expect based on point 1 (*a*) above. Conversely, in the liquidity trap case, where the public is willing to hold any amount of real balances at unchanged interest rates, a fall in prices and a rise in the real money stock have very little effect on income and spending.[2] In Figure 13-7 that would correspond to an almost vertical *AD* curve, as suggested again by point 1 (*a*) above. A vertical *AD* curve means that the planned level of spending is unresponsive to the price level.

You should now experiment with alternative *IS* and *LM* schedules to see how the effects of a change in the price level depend on the slopes of the *IS* and *LM* curves and the factors underlying those slopes. In doing so you will confirm the points summarized under 1 and 2 above. In problem 4 at the end of the chapter, we ask you to demonstrate these links.

Next we consider the factors that determine the position of the *AD* curve.

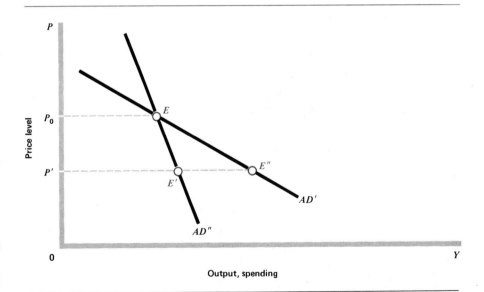

FIGURE 13-7   THE SLOPE OF THE AD SCHEDULE. The diagram shows two possible *AD* schedules. Along *AD"* a change in prices from P_0 to P' has a smaller effect on spending than along *AD'*. The former corresponds to the case where changes in real balances have little impact on equilibrium income and spending; the latter to the case where real balance changes exert significant effects.

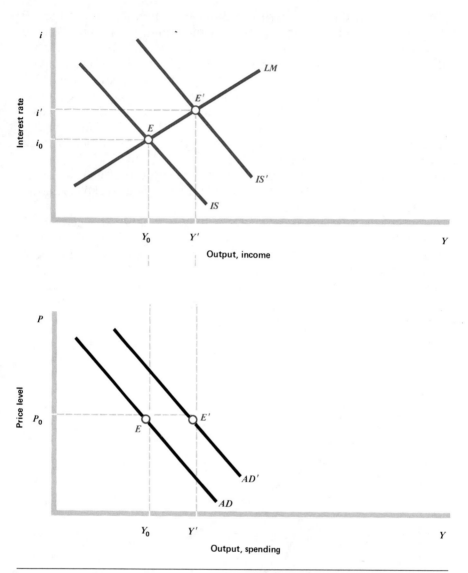

FIGURE 13-8   THE EFFECT OF A FISCAL EXPANSION ON THE AD SCHEDULE. A fiscal expansion, such as an increase in government spending, shifts the *IS* curve in the upper panel to *IS'*. At any given price level, such as P_0, the equilibrium in the upper panel shifts to E', with higher level of output Y' and higher interest rate i'. Point E' in the lower panel is a point on the new aggregate demand schedule AD' corresponding to price level P_0. We could similarly trace the effect of increased government spending on the equilibrium level of output and spending in the lower panel for every price level, and thus show that the *AD* curve shifts out to *AD'* when fiscal policy is expansionary.

The Effect of a Fiscal Expansion

We noted above that the same factors that determine the positions of the *IS* and *LM* schedules also determine the position of the *AD* curve. We now show how changes in fiscal and monetary policy shift the *AD* curve, starting with a fiscal expansion.

In Figure 13-8 the initial *LM* and *IS* schedules correspond to a given nominal quantity of money and the price level P_0. Equilibrium obtains at point *E*, and there is a corresponding point on the *AD* schedule in the lower panel.

Now the government increases the level of spending, say, on defence. As a consequence, the *IS* schedule shifts out and to the right. At the initial price level there is a new equilibrium at point *E'* with higher interest rates and a higher level of income and spending. Thus at the initial level of prices, P_0, equilibrium income and spending now are higher. We show this by plotting point *E'* in the lower panel. Point *E'* is a point on the new schedule *AD'* reflecting the effect of higher government spending.

Of course, we could have started with any other point on the original *AD* curve, and would then have shown how in the lower panel the rise in government spending leads to a higher equilibrium level of output at each price level. In that way we trace out the entire *AD'* schedule, which lies to the right of *AD*.

In fact, we can say more: At each level of prices, and hence of real balances, the *AD* schedule shifts to the right by an amount indicated by the fiscal policy multiplier developed in Chapter 4. As we saw there, a fiscal expansion leads to a higher level of income and spending, the larger the interest response of money demand, the smaller the interest response of aggregate demand, and the larger the marginal propensity to consume.

Thus if the fiscal policy multiplier derived in Chapter 4 was, for example, 1.5, then a $1 (billion) dollar increase in government spending would increase equilibrium income and spending by $1.5 billion, at the given price level. In response to any change in government spending, the *AD* schedule would shift to the right by 1.5 times the increase in *G*.[3]

The Effect of a Monetary Expansion on the AD Schedule

An increase in the nominal money stock implies, at each level of prices, a higher real money stock. In the assets markets interest rates decline to induce the public to hold higher real balances. That decline in interest rates, in turn, stimulates aggregate demand and thus raises the equilibrium level of income and spending. In Figure 13-9 we show that an increase in the nominal money stock shifts the *AD* schedule up and to the right.

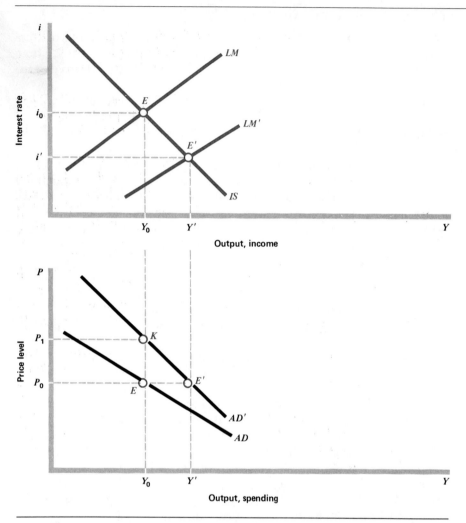

FIGURE 13-9   THE EFFECTS OF AN INCREASE IN THE MONEY STOCK ON THE
AD SCHEDULE.   An increase in the money stock shifts the *LM* curve to *LM'* in the
upper panel. The equilibrium level of income rises from Y_0 to Y' at the initial price
level P_0. Correspondingly, the *AD* curve moves out to the right, to *AD'*, with point
E' in the lower panel corresponding to E' in the upper panel. The *AD* curve shifts
up in exactly the same proportion as the money stock increases. For instance, at
point K the price level P_1 is higher than P_0 in the same proportion that the money
supply has risen. *Real balances* at K on *AD'* are therefore the same as at E on *AD*.

The extent to which an increase in nominal money shifts the *AD* schedule to the right depends on the monetary policy multiplier. If the monetary policy multiplier is large, say, because money demand is not very

interest elastic and goods demand is, the *AD* schedule will shift a lot. Conversely, if the *LM* schedule is nearly flat, in which case we know monetary policy is ineffective, the *AD* schedule will shift very little.

We can also ask about the *upward* shift of the schedule. Here an interesting and important point emerges. Recall that what matters for equilibrium income and spending is the *real* money supply *M/P*. If an increase in nominal money is matched by an equiproportionate increase in prices, *M/P* is unchanged, and hence interest rates, aggregate demand, and equilibrium income and spending will remain unchanged. This gives us the clue to the vertical shift of the *AD* schedule.

An increase in the nominal money stock shifts the AD *schedule up exactly in proportion to the increase in nominal money.* Thus if, starting at point *E* in the lower panel of Figure 13-9, we have a 10 percent increase in *M*, real spending will be unchanged only if prices also rise by 10 percent, thus leaving real balances unchanged. Therefore the *AD* schedule shifts upward by 10 percent. At point *K* in Figure 13-9, *real* balances are the same as at *E*, and therefore interest rates and equilibrium income and spending are the same as at *E*.

We now have completed the derivation of the aggregate demand schedule. The important points to recall are that the *AD* schedule is shifted to the right both by increases in the money stock and by expansionary fiscal policy. In the remainder of this chapter we show how to use this tool to discuss the effects of monetary and fiscal policy *on both the level of output and the price level* under alternative assumptions about the supply side. We thus begin to consider how the price level and the rate of inflation are determined and affected by monetary and fiscal policy. The discussion continues, again using the *AD* schedule, in the next chapter, where we look at macroeconomic adjustment over time.

13-4   MONETARY AND FISCAL POLICY UNDER ALTERNATIVE SUPPLY ASSUMPTIONS

In Figure 13-2 we showed how the aggregate supply and demand curves together determine the equilibrium level of income and prices in the economy. Now that we have shown how the aggregate demand curve is derived, and how it is shifted by policy changes, we use the aggregate demand and supply model to study the effects of monetary and fiscal policy in the two extreme supply cases — Keynesian and classical.

We should expect that the conclusions we reach in the Keynesian supply case are precisely the same as those reached in Chapters 4 and 5. In those chapters, in developing the *IS-LM* model, we assumed that whatever amount of goods was demanded would be supplied at the existing price level. And of course, as Figure 13-5*a* shows, the Keynesian supply curve implies that any amount of goods demanded will be supplied at the existing price level.

The Keynesian Case

In Figure 13-10 we combine the aggregate demand schedule with the Keynesian aggregate supply schedule. The initial equilibrium is at point *E*, where *AS* and *AD* intersect. At that point the goods and assets markets are in equilibrium.

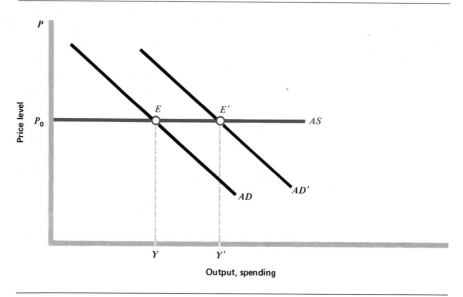

FIGURE 13-10   A FISCAL EXPANSION: THE KEYNESIAN CASE. In the Keynesian case, with output in perfectly elastic supply at a given price level, a fiscal expansion increases equilibrium income from *Y* to *Y'*. This is exactly the result already derived with *IS* and *LM* schedules.

Consider now a fiscal expansion. As we have already seen, increased government spending, or a cut in tax rates, shifts the *AD* schedule out and to the right from *AD* to *AD'*. The new equilibrium is at point *E'*, where output has increased. Because firms are willing to supply *any* amount of output at the level of prices P_0, there is no effect on prices. The only effect of higher government spending in Figure 13-10 is to increase output and employment. In addition, as we know from the *IS-LM* model that lies behind the *AD* schedule, the fiscal expansion will raise equilibrium interest rates. Because interest rates do increase, the fiscal expansion raises output less than suggested by the simple multiplier of Chapter 3.

We leave it to you to show that in the Keynesian case an increase in the nominal quantity of money likewise leads to an expansion in equilibrium output. With a horizontal AS schedule there is again no impact on prices. The magnitude of the output expansion then depends, in this Keynesian case, only on the monetary policy multiplier that determines the extent of the horizontal shift of the AD schedule.

Thus, as we expected, all our conclusions about the effects of policy changes in the Keynesian supply case are those of the simple IS-LM model.

The Classical Case: Fiscal Policy

In the classical case the aggregate supply schedule is vertical at the full-employment level of output. Firms will supply the level of output $\overline{Y}$ whatever the price level. Under this supply assumption we obtain results very different from those reached using the Keynesian model. Now the price level is not given, but rather depends on the interaction of supply and demand.

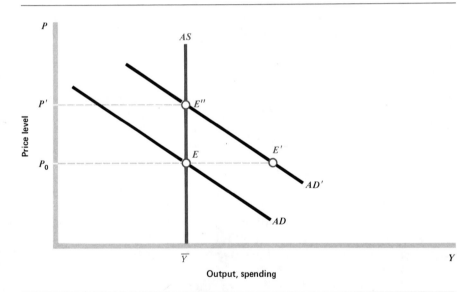

FIGURE 13-11   A FISCAL EXPANSION: THE CLASSICAL CASE. The supply of output is perfectly inelastic at the full-employment level of output, $\overline{Y}$. A fiscal expansion raises equilibrium spending, at the initial price level P_0, from E to E'. But now there is an excess demand because firms are unwilling to supply that much output. Prices increase, and that reduces real balances until we reach point E''. At E'' government spending is higher, but the higher price level means lower real balances, higher interest rates, and hence reduced private spending. At E'' increased government spending has crowded out an equal amount of private spending.

In Figure 13-11 we study the effect of a fiscal expansion under classical supply assumptions. The aggregate supply schedule is AS, with equilibrium initially at point E. Note that at point E there is full employment because, by assumption, firms supply the full-employment level of output at any level of prices.

The fiscal expansion shifts the aggregate demand schedule from AD to AD'. At the initial level of prices, P_0, spending in the economy rises to point E'. At price level P_0 the demand for goods has risen. But firms cannot obtain the labour to produce more output, and output supply cannot respond to the increased demand. As firms try to hire more workers, they only bid up wages and their costs of production, and therefore they charge higher prices for their output. The increase in the demand for goods therefore leads only to higher prices, and not to higher output.

The increase in prices reduces the real money stock and leads to an increase in interest rates and a reduction in spending. The economy moves up the AD' schedule until prices have risen enough, and real balances have fallen enough, to raise interest rates and reduce spending to a level consistent with full-employment output. That is the case at a price level P'. At point E'' aggregate demand, at the higher level of government spending, is once again equal to aggregate supply.

Crowding Out Again

Note what has happened in Figure 13-11: output is unchanged at the full-employment level $\bar{Y}$, but government spending is higher. That must imply less spending by the private sector. There is thus *full*, or complete, *crowding out*. Recall from Chapter 4 that crowding out occurs when an increase in government spending results in less spending by the private sector. Typically, as we showed in Chapter 4, government spending crowds out investment. In the case shown in Figure 13-11, with a classical supply curve, every dollar increase in real government spending is offset by a dollar reduction in private spending, so that crowding out is complete.

We thus reach the following important result: *In the classical case increased real government spending leads to full crowding out.* We now explain the mechanism through which crowding out occurs.

Figure 13-12 shows the IS-LM diagram, augmented with the line $\bar{Y}$ at the full-employment level of output. The initial equilibrium is at point E, where the money market clears and planned spending equals output. The fiscal expansion shifts the IS schedule to IS'. At an unchanged price level, and assuming firms were to meet the increase in demand by expanding production, we would move to point E', but this is not possible under classical supply assumptions. Faced with an excess demand for goods, firms end up raising prices rather than output. The price increase, in turn, reduces real balances and therefore shifts the LM schedule up. Prices will

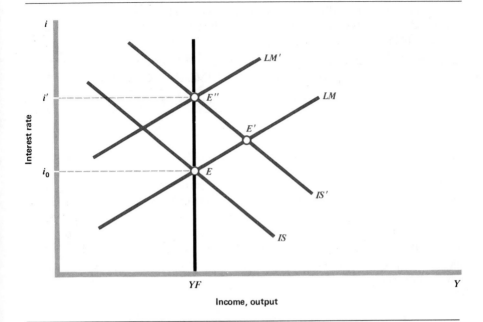

FIGURE 13-12   CROWDING OUT IN THE CLASSICAL CASE. A fiscal expansion in the classical case leads to full crowding out. The fiscal expansion shifts the *IS* schedule to *IS'*. At the initial price level the economy would move to point *E'*, but there is excess demand since firms only supply *Y*. Prices increase, shifting the *LM* schedule up and to the left until *LM'* is reached. The new equilibrium is at point *E''*, where interest rates have risen enough to displace an amount of private spending equal to the increased government demand.

increase until the excess demand has been eliminated. That means the *LM* schedule shifts up and to the left until we reach a new equilibrium at point *E''*.

At *E''* the goods market clears at the full-employment level of output. Interest rates have increased compared with the initial equilibrium at *E*, and that increase in interest rates has reduced private spending to make room for increased government purchases. Note that the money market is also in equilibrium. Output and income are the same as at point *E*. The higher interest rate reduces the demand for real balances, matching the decline in the real money stock.

Note that we have now seen two mechanisms that produce full crowding out. In Chapter 4, crowding out is complete if the *LM* curve is vertical. In that case, crowding out occurs because money demand is interest inelastic. In this chapter, full crowding out occurs because aggregate supply limits total output. In brief, in Chapter 4 crowding out is a demand phenomenon; here it is a supply phenomenon.

We summarize in Table 13-1 the effects of a fiscal expansion in the cases of classical and Keynesian supply conditions. In each case we show what happens to output, interest rates, and the price level.

TABLE 13-1   THE EFFECTS OF A FISCAL EXPANSION

Aggregate supply	Output	Interest rate	Prices
Keynesian	+	+	0
Classical	0	+	+

The table reinforces our understanding of the two models: in one case only prices adjust; in the other case only output. These models are clearly extremes, and we would expect that often adjustment occurs in both output and prices. That is the adjustment process we study in the next chapter. We shall see there that the Keynesian case comes close to describing the short-run effects of a fiscal expansion, while the classical case more accurately predicts what happens in the long run after all adjustments have taken place.

Monetary Expansion Under Classical Conditions

We have already seen the impact of monetary policy under Keynesian supply conditions: with prices given, a rise in the nominal money stock is a rise in the real money stock. Equilibrium interest rates decline as a consequence, and output rises. Consider now the adjustments that occur in response to a monetary expansion when the aggregate supply curve is vertical and the price level is no longer fixed.

In Figure 13-13 we study an expansion in the nominal money stock under classical supply conditions. The initial full-employment equilibrium is at point E, where the AD and AS schedules intersect. Now the nominal money stock is increased, and accordingly, the aggregate demand schedule shifts up and to the right to AD'. If prices were fixed, the economy would move to E', the Keynesian equilibrium, but now output is in fixed supply. The increase in aggregate demand leads to an excess demand for goods. Firms that attempt to expand, hiring more workers, bid up wages and costs. Prices increase in response to the excess demand, and that means real balances fall back toward their initial level. In fact prices keep rising until the excess demand for goods disappears. Thus they must increase until the economy reaches point E'', where AS intersects the new aggregate demand schedule AD'. Only when aggregate demand is again equal to full-employment supply does the goods market clear and the pressure for prices to rise disappear.

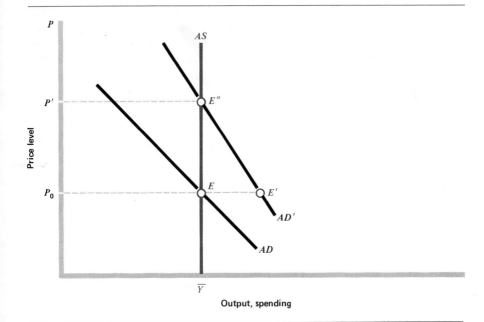

FIGURE 13-13   THE EFFECT OF A MONETARY EXPANSION UNDER CLASSICAL SUPPLY ASSUMPTIONS. Starting from the full-employment equilibrium at point *E*, an increase in the nominal money stock shifts the aggregate demand schedule to *AD'*. At the initial price level there is now an excess demand for goods. Prices increase, and thus the real money stock declines toward its initial level. Price increases continue until the economy reaches point *E''*. Here the *real* money stock has returned to its initial level, and with output unchanged, interest rates are again at their initial level. Thus a monetary expansion only affects prices, not output or interest rates.

Consider now the adjustment that takes place in moving from *E* to *E''*. There is no change in output, only a change in the price level. Note, moreover, that prices rise in exactly the same proportion as the nominal quantity of money.[4] This we know because we saw earlier that in response to an increase in nominal money the *AD* schedule shifts upward in the same proportion as the increase in money. Thus at point *E''* the real money stock *M/P* is back to its initial level. At *E''* both nominal money and the price level have changed in the same proportion, leaving real money and hence interest rates and aggregate demand unchanged. We thus have an important implication of the classical model: *Under classical supply conditions an increase in nominal money raises the price level in the same proportion, but leaves interest rates and real output unchanged.*

In Table 13-2 we summarize the effects of an increase in the nominal money stock under Keynesian and classical supply conditions. Once again we look at the effects on output, prices, and interest rates. In addition we show the effect on real balances M/P. The table brings out the fact that under classical supply conditions, none of the *real* variables, such as output, interest rates or real balances, are affected by a change in the nominal money stock. Only the price level changes.

TABLE 13-2   THE EFFECTS OF AN INCREASE IN THE
NOMINAL MONEY STOCK

Aggregate supply	Output	Interest rate	Prices	Real balances
Keynesian	+	−	0	+
Classical	0	0	+	0

13-5   THE QUANTITY THEORY AND THE NEUTRALITY OF MONEY

The classical model of supply, in combination with the *IS-LM* model describing the demand side of the economy, has extremely strong implications. Because, by assumption, output is maintained at the full-employment level by full price flexibility, monetary and fiscal policy do not affect output. Fiscal policy affects interest rates and the *composition* of spending between the government and the private sector and between consumption and investment. Monetary policy only affects the price level.

These implications about the effects of monetary policy on output are consistent with the *quantity theory of money*. The quantity theory of money in its strongest form asserts that the price level is proportional to the stock of money. For instance, in the case of the classical supply curve, an increase in the quantity of money produces, in equilibrium, a proportional increase in the price level. In this case, money is *neutral*.

The Neutrality of Money

Money is *neutral* when changes in the money stock lead only to changes in the price level, with no real variables (output, employment, and interest rates) changing. For instance, money is neutral in the second row of Table 13-2, where in response to a change in the money stock, only the price level changes, with output, interest rates, and real balances remaining unchanged.

We saw above that the classical supply curve has the powerful and important implication that fiscal poicy cannot affect output. The neutrality of money likewise has strong policy implications. For instance, if money were neutral, there would be an easy way to reduce the inflation rate if we ever wanted to do that. All we would have to do would be to reduce the rate at which the money stock is growing.

In practice, it is very difficult to change the inflation rate without producing a recession, as for instance in the period 1979–1983. When a lower growth rate of money leads first to unemployment, and only later to lower inflation, as it did in the recession in 1982, then we know that money is not neutral. Changes in the quantity of money then have real effects — monetary policy affects the level of output. This means that the aggregate supply curve cannot be vertical in the short run. In the next chapter we develop the aggregate supply curve, showing why in the short run it is quite flat, whereas over longer periods it is more nearly vertical.

The Modern Quantity Theory: Monetarism

We defined the strict quantity theory as asserting that the price level is proportional to the quantity of money. Although the quantity theory is centuries, and perhaps millennia, old, few have believed in the strict quantity theory. That is, few have believed that the price level is strictly proportional to the money stock, or that money is the *only* factor affecting the price level. Rather, quantity theorists argued and argue that the money stock is, in practice, the single most important factor producing inflation.

Box 13-1 presents quotations from Irving Fisher (1867–1947), widely thought to be the greatest American economist of his time, and from Milton Friedman, the leading exponent of the quantity theory and the importance of money in the modern era. The two differ in emphasis: Fisher comes close to asserting that only changes in the quantity of money affect the price level; Friedman is more clear in arguing that other factors can affect the price level, but that these other factors are of secondary importance.

Friedman is the recognized intellectual leader of an influential group of economists called *monetarists*, who emphasize the role of money and monetary policy in affecting the behaviour of output and prices. Leading monetarists include professors Karl Brunner of the University of Rochester, Allan Meltzer of Carnegie-Mellon University, Thomas Mayer of the University of California at Davis, David Laidler and Michael Parkin of the University of Western Ontario, and other scholars, both in North America and elsewhere. There is more to monetarism than the argument that money is the most important determinant of macroeconomic performance, but we leave the other tenets of monetarism for further discussion in Chapter 17.

BOX 13-1   THE QUANTITY THEORY OF MONEY

Irving Fisher (1867–1947) and Milton Friedman (born 1912) are two of the foremost monetary economists in the United States in this century. Both strongly advocated the quantity theory of money as the right model of price level determination.

Fisher stated*:

In recent popular discussions a great variety of reasons have been assigned for the "high cost of living," *e.g.,* "profiteering"; speculation; hoarding; the middleman; . . . the tariff; cold storage; longer hauls on railroads; marketing by telephone; the free delivery system; the individual package; the enforcement of sanitary laws; the tuberculin testing of cattle; the destruction of tainted meat; sanitary milk; the elimination of renovated butter and of "rots" and "spots" in eggs; food adulteration; advertising; unscientific management; extravagance; higher standards of living; the increasing cost of government; the increasing cost of old-age pensions, and of better pauper institutions, hospitals, insane asylums, reformatories, jails and other public institutions; . . .

I shall not discuss in detail this list of alleged explanations. While some of them are important factors in raising particular prices, none of them . . . has been important in raising the *general* scale of prices. . . .

The ups and downs of prices roughly correspond with the ups and downs of the money supply. Throughout all history this has been so. For this general broad fact the evidence is sufficient even where we lack the index numbers by which to make accurate measurements. Whenever there have been rapid outpourings from mines, following discoveries of the precious metals used for money, prices have risen with corresponding rapidity. This was observed in the sixteenth century, after great quantities of the precious metals had been brought to Europe from the New World; and again in the nineteenth century, after the Californian and Australian gold mining of the fifties; and, still again, in the same century after the South African, Alaskan, and Cripple Creek mining of the nineties. Likewise when other causes than mining, such as paper money issues, produce violent changes in the quantity or quality of money, violent changes in the price level usually follow.

Friedman wrote†:

Since men first began to write systematically about economic matters they have devoted special attention to the wide movements in the general level of prices that have intermittently occurred. Two alternative explanations have usually been offered. One has attributed the changes in prices to changes in the quantity of money. The other has attributed the changes in prices to war or to profiteers or to rises in wages or to some other special circumstance of the particular time and place and has regarded any accompanying change in the quantity of money as a common consequence of the same special circumstance. The first explanation has generally been referred to as the quantity theory of money, although that designation conceals the variety of forms the explanation has taken, the different levels of sophistication on which it has been developed, and the wide range of the claims that have been made for its applicability. . . .

In its most rigid and unqualified form the quantity theory asserts strict proportionality between the quantity of what is regarded as money and the level of prices. Hardly anyone has held the theory in that form, although statements capable of being so interpreted have often been made in the heat of argument or for expository simplicity. Virtually every quantity theorist has recognized that changes in the quantity of money that correspond to changes in the volume of trade or of output have no tendency to produce changes in prices. Nearly as many have recognized also that changes in the willingness of the community to hold money can occur for a variety of reasons and can introduce disparities between changes in the quantity of money per unit of trade or of output and changes in prices. What quantity theorists have held in common is the belief that these qualifications are of secondary importance for substantial changes in either prices or the quantity of money, so that the one will not in fact occur without the other.

---

*Irving Fisher, *Stabilizing the Dollar* (New York: Macmillan, 1920), pp. 10–11 and 29.
†Milton Friedman, "Money: The Quantity Theory," in *The International Encyclopedia of the Social Sciences*, Vol. X, 1968, pp. 432–447.

A Formal Statement

We can discuss the quantity theory more formally by drawing on the definition of the income velocity of money V presented in Chapter 9. Income velocity times the stock of money M is equal to nominal income, which in turn is equal to the price level P times real income Y:

$$MV = PY \tag{1}$$

or, dividing by real output Y,

$$P = \frac{MV}{Y} \tag{2}$$

Suppose that output is fixed at the full employment level $\overline{Y}$. Suppose also that the velocity of money is fixed. Then it follows from Equation (2) that changes in the money stock will cause proportionate changes in the price level. Thus, if (1) output is at the full-employment level, and (2) velocity is constant, the *strict* quantity theory holds.

We can also use (2) to see why modern quantity theorists argue, as does Friedman, that factors other than quantity of money may affect prices. Most important, and as the data in Figure 9-4 on page 319 confirm, the income velocity of money may change.

Recall from Chapter 9 that the income velocity of money is closely related to the demand for money. The more money people hold in relation to their income, the lower the income velocity of money. For instance, if people on average hold money balances equal to 2 months of their income, the income velocity of money (the ratio of annual income to the money stock) will be 6. We know that the lower the interest rate, the more real balances people hold. Thus we certainly expect velocity to be affected by interest rates: the higher the interest rate, the higher the velocity because the less real balances people will hold relative to their incomes.

Modern quantity theorists, or monetarists, recognize that interest rate movements do affect velocity. Similarly, velocity is affected by changes in the banking system that make it easier to economize on the holding of money. But in practice, monetarists assert, changes in interest rates and the structure of the banking system are not important enough to obscure the main message: The most important factor changing the price level is the quantity of money.

We return to monetarism and the evidence supporting it in Chapters 17 and 18.

Fiscal Policy and the Price Level

We can use Equation (2) to show how a change in fiscal policy affects the price level in the classical case. Assuming that the economy is at the full-employment level of output, we know that expansionary fiscal policy increases the interest rate. That means velocity rises. From Equation (2) we see that the price level must rise, given the nominal money stock M. This confirms the conclusion we reached in Figure 13-11 in discussing fiscal policy in the classical case.

The Long Run and the Short

Modern quantity theorists differ also from the strict quantity theory in not believing that the supply curve is vertical in the short run. Monetarists such as Milton Friedman argue that a reduction in the money stock does in practice *first* reduce the level of output, and only later have an effect on prices.

Thus Friedman and other monetarists make an important distinction between the short- and long-run effects of changes in money. They argue that in the long run money is more or less neutral. Changes in the money stock, after they have worked their way through the economy, have no real effects and only change prices: the quantity theory and the neutrality of money are, from this long-run perspective, not just theoretical possibilities, but instead a reasonable description of the way the world works. But in the short run, they argue, monetary policy and changes in the money stock can and do have important real effects.

The short-run versus long-run distinction is pursued in the next chapter, where we go more deeply into the aggregate supply curve.

13-7   SUMMARY

1   The aggregate supply and demand model is used to show the determination of the equilibrium levels of *both* output and prices.

2   The aggregate supply schedule *AS* shows at each level of prices the quantity of real output or GNP firms are willing to supply.

3   The Keynesian supply schedule is horizontal, implying that firms supply as much goods as are demanded at the existing price level. The classical supply schedule is vertical. It would apply in an economy that has full price and wage flexibility. In such a frictionless economy, employment and output are always at the full-employment level.

4   The aggregate demand schedule *AD* shows at each price level the level of output at which the goods and assets markets are in equilibrium. This is the quantity of output demanded at each price level. Along the *AD* schedule fiscal policy is given, as is the nominal quantity of money. The *AD* schedule is derived using the *IS-LM* model.

5   Moving down and along the *AD* schedule, lower prices raise the real value of the money stock. Equilibrium interest rates fall, and that increases aggregate demand and equilibrium spending.

6   A fiscal expansion or an increase in the nominal quantity of money shifts the *AD* schedule out and to the right.

7   Under Keynesian supply conditions, with prices fixed, both monetary and fiscal expansion raise equilibrium output. A monetary expansion lowers interest rates, while a fiscal expansion raises them.

8   Under classical supply conditions, a fiscal expansion has no effect on output. But a fiscal expansion raises prices, lowers real balances, and increases equilibrium interest rates.

9   Under classical supply conditions there is full crowding out. Private spending declines by exactly the increase in government demand.

10   A monetary expansion, under classical supply conditions, raises prices in the same proportion as the rise in nominal money. All real variables, specifically output and interest rates, remain unchanged. When changes in the money stock have no real effects, money is said to be *neutral*.

11   The strict quantity theory of money states that prices move in proportion to the nominal money stock. The strict quantity theory holds if velocity is constant and if output remains at the full-employment level. Neither of these conditions obtains in practice.

12   Modern quantity theorists, or monetarists, accept that there is no exact link between money and prices, but argue that changes in the money stock are, in practice, the most important single determinant of changes in the price level. They note, also, that changes in the money stock

have real effects in the short run, but, they argue, money is approximately neutral in the long run.

KEY TERMS

Aggregate supply curve
Aggregate demand curve
Keynesian aggregate supply curve
Classical aggregate supply curve

Full crowding out
Quantity theory of money
Neutrality of money
Monetarism

PROBLEMS

1 Define the aggregate demand and supply curves.

2 Explain why the classical supply curve is vertical and explain the mechanisms that ensure continued full employment of labour in the classical case.

3 Discuss, using the *IS-LM* model, what happens to interest rates as prices change along a given *AD* schedule.

4 Show graphically that the *AD* curve is steeper (a) the larger the interest responsiveness of the demand for money and (b) the smaller the multiplier.

5 Suppose full-employment output increases from $\overline{Y}$ to $\overline{Y}'$. What does the quantity theory predict will happen to the price level?

6 In goods market equilibrium, $S + T = I + G$. Use this equation to explain why, in the classical case, a fiscal expansion must lead to full crowding out.

7 Show, using *IS* and *LM* curves, why money is neutral in the classical supply case. (Refer to footnote 4 for hints.)

8 Suppose the government reduces the personal income tax rate from t to t'.
   (a) What is the effect on the *AD* schedule?
   (b) What is the effect on the equilibrium interest rate?
   (c) What happens to investment?

9 Suppose there is a decline in the demand for money. At each output level and interest rate the public now wants to hold lower real balances.
   (a) In the Keynesian case, what happens to equilibrium output and to prices?
   (b) In the classical case, what is the effect on output and on prices?

10 In problem 9, use the quantity theory of money to explain the effect of the money demand shift on prices.

11 Suppose the government undertakes a balanced budget increase in spending. Government spending rises from G to G', and there is an accompanying increase in tax rates so that at the initial level of output the budget remains balanced.
    (a) Show the effect on the AD schedule.
    (b) Discuss the effect of the balanced budget policy on output and interest rates in the Keynesian case.
    (c) Discuss the effect in the classical case.

12 (a) Define the strict quantity theory.
    (b) Define monetarism.
    (c) What type of statistical evidence would you need to collect to support or refute the major argument of monetarism presented in this chapter?

CHAPTER 13: FOOTNOTES

[1]The aggregate demand curve is sometimes referred to as the *macroeconomic demand curve*, both to emphasize that it is different from a regular demand curve in microeconomics and to distinguish it from the aggregate demand schedule in Chap. 3. We stay with the same name AD here after warning that the present AD schedule represents an extension of that in Chap. 3 since it makes interest rates endogenous along the curve.

[2]The reason a reduction in prices increases output in this case is the *real balance effect*: with lower prices, the value of real balances held by the public is higher, their wealth is accordingly higher, and therefore their consumption spending and output are higher. See footnote 13 in Chap. 4 for a related point. The real balance effect is central to monetary theory as developed in the classical treatise by Don Patinkin, *Money, Interest and Prices* (New York: Harper & Row, 1965).

[3]In Chap. 4 we showed that the fiscal policy multiplier is given by the expression $\beta \equiv h\bar{\alpha}/(h + kb\bar{\alpha})$, where h is the interest responsiveness of money demand, $\bar{\alpha}$ the simple Keynesian multiplier, k the income response of money demand, and b the interest response of investment demand.

[4]In problem 7 we ask you to use the IS and LM curves to show how the change in the money supply works. To answer the problem you have to use Fig. 13-9 along with the fact that the LM schedule shifts as the price level changes.

Aggregate Supply: Wages, Prices, and Employment

In this chapter we develop the aggregate supply side of the economy. We show the links between wages, prices, and employment and the adjustment process to disturbances in aggregate demand — monetary or fiscal policy changes or autonomous changes in spending. The development of the aggregate supply side of the economy also allows us to study the adjustment to supply shocks such as the increase in oil prices of 1973–1974 and 1979–1980 or the decline in oil prices in 1982–1983. The supply side of the economy is an essential part of the *dynamics* of prices (inflation) and output, that is, of the adjustment of prices and output over time when the economy is hit by a disturbance. For that reason we spend an entire chapter on the topic. The investment of time on this topic is worthwhile also because an understanding of aggregate supply is essential if we are to grasp the policy dilemma, described in later chapters, that comes from the short-run tradeoff between inflation and unemployment.

We start, in Section 14-1, with the *frictionless classical model* of output, prices, wages, and employment. This model provides a sensible general framework of analysis. But because the model makes a number of extremely strong assumptions about the working of goods and labour markets — in particular, *full* wage and price flexibility — it cannot explain recessions and booms.

We therefore move on, in Sections 14-2 and 14-3, to develop a more realistic framework that leads to an upward-sloping supply schedule such as the one in Chapter 13. However, we do not lose sight of the classical model because we also show that the supply schedule does not stay put, but rather moves over time in response to changes in wages which come about because of overemployment or underemployment. Three points emerge from that analysis.

1 Changes in aggregate demand lead in the short run to changes in both output and prices in the same direction. The extent to which the price level changes depends on the slope of the aggregate supply curve.

2 The extent to which changes in demand are met by changes in output as opposed to prices depends on the response of costs to an expansion in output and employment. If wage costs are very unresponsive in the short run, the supply curve is quite flat, and shifts in demand are met at essentially constant prices.

3 An expansion of output above normal will bring about overemployment and therefore rising wages and costs. Firms will pass on these cost increases by increasing their prices. The aggregate supply schedule shifts upward, thereby raising equilibrium prices and reducing equilibrium output along the aggregate demand schedule. The process continues until output declines to the level of full employment. There is, of course, a parallel story for a decline in demand.

The third point means that the classical model describes well the long-run response of output, employment, and prices to disturbances. It is thus an essential part of our understanding of the workings of the economy. But the frictionless model does not do a good job of explaining short-run responses of prices and output to disturbances. That is why we have to go beyond the classical model in this chapter.

Once the aggregate supply framework is developed, we use it to study the economy's adjustment to a change in monetary and fiscal policy. We show that both monetary and fiscal expansion in the short run lead to higher output and higher prices, just as in Chapter 13. In the long run, however, the economy returns to full employment. The chapter concludes with a discussion of the adjustment to supply shocks and some finer points of aggregate supply.[1]

14-1   THE FRICTIONLESS CLASSICAL MODEL

The relationship among wages, prices, and employment and between employment and output will now be studied in an idealized *frictionless* case. That is the case where wages and prices are *fully* flexible, where there are no costs either to workers in finding jobs or to firms in increasing or reducing their labour force, and where firms behave competitively and expect to sell all they produce at prevailing prices. That case both serves as a benchmark for the discussion of more realistic cases, and also allows us to introduce such useful concepts as the production function and the demand for labour. Throughout, we assume that labour is the only variable factor of production in the short run and that the capital stock is given.

The Production Function

A production function provides a relation between the quantity of factor inputs, such as the amount of labour used, and the maximum quantity of output that can be produced using those inputs.[2] The relation reflects only technical efficiency. In Equation (1) we write the production function

$$Y = F(N, \ldots) \tag{1}$$

where Y denotes real output, N is labour input, and the dots denote other cooperating factors (capital, for example) that are in short-run fixed supply. The production function is shown in Figure 14-1. The production function exhibits *diminishing returns* to labour, which means that the increase in output resulting from the employment of one more unit of labour declines as the amount of labour used increases.

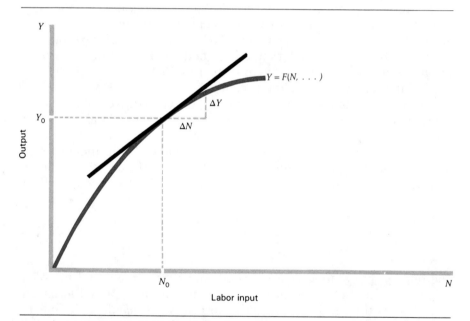

FIGURE 14-1   THE PRODUCTION FUNCTION AND THE MARGINAL PRODUCT OF LABOUR. The production function links the amount of output produced to the level of labour input, given other factors of production such as capital. The schedule shows diminishing returns. Successive increases in labour yield less and less extra output. The marginal product of labour is shown by the slope of the production function, $\Delta Y/\Delta N$, that is, the increase in output per unit increase in employment. The flattening of the slope shows that the marginal product of labour is declining.

Diminishing returns are shown in the production function by the fact that it is not a straight line through the origin (constant returns) or an upward-curling line (increasing returns). Diminishing returns are explained by the fact that as employment increases and other inputs remain constant, each labourer on the job has fewer machines with which to work and therefore becomes less productive. Thus, increases in the amount of labour progressively reduce the addition to output that further employment can bring. An increase in the labour force will always raise output, but progressively less so as employment expands. The marginal contribution of increased employment is indicated by the slope of the production function, $\Delta Y/\Delta N$. It is readily seen that the slope flattens out as we increase employment, thus showing that increasing employment makes a diminishing, but still positive, contribution to output.

Labour Demand

From the production function we proceed to the demand for labour. We are asking how much labour a firm would want to hire. The rule of thumb is to hire additional labour and expand production as long as doing so increases profits. A firm will hire additional workers as long as they will bring in more in revenue than they cost in wages.

The contribution to output of additional labour is called the *marginal product of labour*. It is equal, in Figure 14-1, to the slope of the production function. The marginal product, as we have seen, is both positive — additional labour is productive — and diminishing, which means that additional employment becomes progressively less productive. *A firm will employ additional labour as long as the marginal product of labour, MPN for short, exceeds the cost of additional labour.* The cost of additional labour is given by the real wage, that is, the nominal wage divided by the price level. The real wage measures the amount of real output the firm has to pay each worker. Since hiring one more worker results in an output increase of *MPN* and a cost to the firm of the real wage, firms will hire additional labour if the *MPN* exceeds the real wage. This point is formalized in Figure 14-2, which looks at the labour market.

The downward-sloping schedule in Figure 14-2 is the demand for labour schedule, which is the *MPN* schedule; firms hire labour up to the point at which the *MPN* is equal to the real wage. The *MPN* schedule shows the contribution to output of additional employment. It follows from our reasoning that the *MPN* is positive but that additional employment reduces it, so that the *MPN* schedule is negatively sloped.

Now consider a firm that currently employs a labour force, N_1, and assume the real wage is $(w/P)_0$, where w is the money wage and P the price of output. At an employment level N_1 in Figure 14-2, the firm is clearly employing too much labour since the real wage exceeds the *MPN* at that level of employment. What would happen if the firm should reduce employment by one unit? The reduction in employment would decrease output by the *MPN*, and therefore reduce revenue to the firm. On the other side of the calculation, we have the reduction in the wage bill. Per unit reduction in employment, the wage bill would fall at the rate of the real wage $(w/P)_0$. The net benefit of a reduction in the employment level is thus equal to the vertical excess of the real wage over the *MPN* in Figure 14-2. It is apparent that at the level of employment N_1, the excess is quite sizable, and it pays the firm to reduce the employment level. Indeed, it pays to reduce employment until the firm gets to point N_0. Only at that point does the cost of additional labour — the real wage — exactly balance the benefit in the form of increased output.

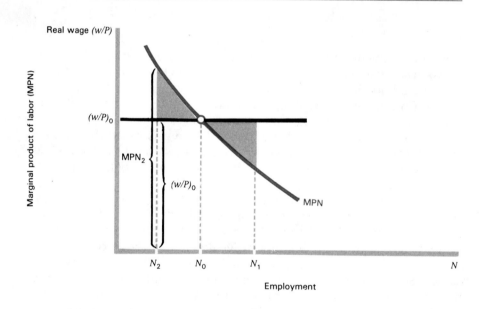

FIGURE 14-2   THE OPTIMAL EMPLOYMENT CHOICE FOR A GIVEN REAL WAGE. The marginal product of labour *MPN* is a declining function of the level of employment because of diminishing returns. Given a real wage $(w/P)_0$, the optimal employment choice is N_0. At N_1 the marginal product of labour is less than the real wage, so that the firm would save by reducing employment. Conversely, at N_2 the marginal product exceeds the real wage, so that the firm would gain by hiring an additional worker.

The same argument applies to the employment level N_2. Here employment is insufficient because the contribution to output of additional employment, MPN_2, exceeds the cost of additional employment, and it therefore pays to expand the level of employment. It is readily seen that with a real wage $(w/P)_0$, the firm's profits are maximized when employment is N_0. In general, given *any* real wage, the firm's demand for labour is shown by the *MPN* curve.

The firm's optimal employment position is formalized in Equation (2). At the optimal employment level the marginal product of labour (which is a declining function of employment) $MPN(N)$ is equal to the real wage:

$$MPN(N) = w/P \qquad (2)$$

Equilibrium in the Labour Market

We have now developed the relation between output and employment (the production function) and the optimal employment choice for a given real wage that is implied by the demand for labour. It remains to consider the determination of the real wage as part of labour market equilibrium. What we have not yet dealt with is the supply of labour.

We make a quite simple assumption concerning labour supply. We assume that the supply of labour is fixed at $\overline{N}$ and that it is independent of the real wage.[3] This is shown in Figure 14-3 as the vertical schedule, $\overline{NN}$. The equilibrium real wage is clearly $(w/P)_0$.

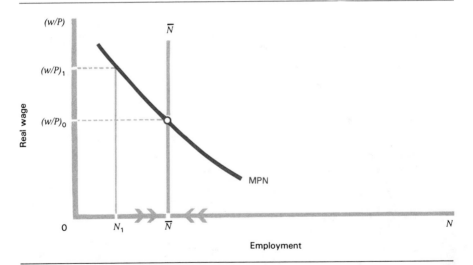

FIGURE 14-3　EQUILIBRIUM IN THE LABOUR MARKET. The labour supply is $\overline{N}$ and is independent of the real wage. The demand for labour is the marginal product schedule *MPN*. Labour market equilibrium obtains at a real wage $(w/P)_0$. At that real wage the demand for labour equals the quantity of labour supplied. At a lower real wage there is an excess demand for labour; at a higher real wage there is an excess supply or unemployment.

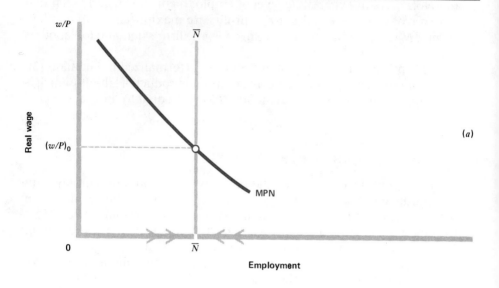

(a)

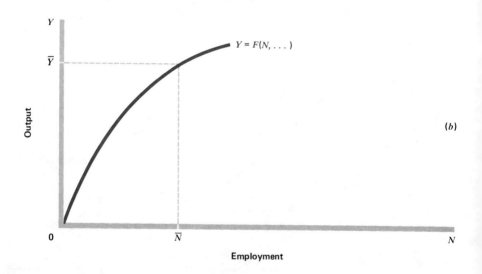

(b)

FIGURE 14-4   EQUILIBRIUM IN THE LABOUR MARKET AND FULL-EMPLOYMENT OUTPUT. Part (a) of the diagram repeats the labour market equilibrium of Figure 14-3. Part (b) shows the production function. The equilibrium employment level $\overline{N}$, also the full-employment level, leads to an output $\overline{Y}$, which is the full-employment level of output.

How would the labour market get to that equilibrium? Suppose that the real wage fell whenever there was an excess supply of labour and that it rose whenever there was an excess demand. In terms of Figure 14-3 this would mean that the real wage would decline whenever it was above $(w/P)_0$. At $(w/P)_1$, for example, labour demand is only N_1 and thus falls short of the labour supply. This would put downward pressure on the real wage, cause the real wage to fall, and make it profitable to expand employment. Exactly the reverse argument holds for real wages lower than $(w/P)_0$, where there is an excess demand for labour.

From Figure 14-3 we see that adjustment of the real wage would bring the labour market into full-employment equilibrium at a real wage $(w/P)_0$ and an employment level equal to the given labour supply $\bar{N}$. Figure 14-4 summarizes the complete equilibrium in the labour market and the corresponding level of *full-employment output* $\bar{Y}$, which is the level of output associated with employment equal to the given labour supply.

Classical Goods and Labour Market Equilibrium

We have now derived the full-employment supply of output and the corresponding *real* wage, and have to complete the classical model by asking how *money* wages and prices are determined. How can we be sure that goods produced can be sold? Here we make two important assumptions: (1) goods prices will rise or fall instantaneously to clear the goods market, and (2) money wages will instantaneously rise or fall to clear the labour market. How will those adjustments work?

In the labour market, the flexibility of money wages ensures that at each price level the money wage rises or falls to achieve the necessary level of the real wage. We are therefore continuously in labour market equilibrium, and whatever the level of prices, firms will employ the full-employment labour force $\bar{N}$ and supply the corresponding level of output $\bar{Y}$. This is shown in Figure 14-5 in the aggregate supply curve AS. The aggregate supply schedule is vertical to show that the equilibrium level of output supplied — when the labour market is in equilibrium — is independent of the price level. If prices rose relative to wages, firms would be making profits. In an attempt to secure even larger profits, they would attempt individually to expand their employment level at the going money wage. In the aggregate, though, all they would do would be to compete for the given labour force and drive up the money wage until it had risen in proportion to the increase in prices, thus leaving real output unchanged.

Figure 14-5 includes an aggregate demand curve AD along with the vertical classical aggregate supply function. Recall from Chapter 13 that the aggregate demand curve slopes downward because increases in the price level reduce real balances, increase the interest rate, and reduce aggregate demand. Aggregate demand and supply jointly determine the equilibrium price level P_0. We need not be concerned yet with a full understanding of the details of the adjustment process of the price level in response to shifts in aggregate supply or demand. We need only recognize that it is plausible that the economy will converge to a full-employment equilibrium with all markets in equilibrium. Given the equilibrium price level P_0, the nominal wage will adjust so that the real wage is $(w/P)_0$. Furthermore, *if* wages and prices adjust rapidly, and *if* firms respond rapidly in their production decisions to changing conditions, and *if* labour moves rapidly between jobs as some firms expand and others contract, we would expect to be in full-employment equilibrium continuously. Any disturbance, such as an increase in the nominal money supply or an improvement in technology, would immediately be reflected in changes in wages and prices that would restore the full-employment equilibrium.

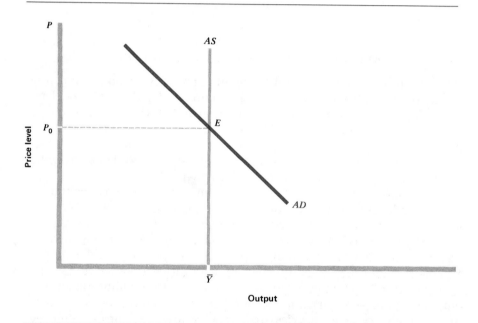

FIGURE 14-5   AGGREGATE DEMAND, AGGREGATE SUPPLY, AND THE EQUILIB-
RIUM PRICE LEVEL. The labour market equilibrium leads to an employment level $\bar{N}$ and implies an output level $\bar{Y}$. This is the full-employment output level shown by the vertical supply schedule AS. Aggregate demand is shown by the downward-sloping schedule AD. Equilibrium in the goods market obtains at a price level P_0. At that price level, demand for output equals the full-employment supply. Price and wage flexibility ensures that the economy reaches the equilibrium at point E.

The classical full equilibrium is a useful reference point for the study of more realistic descriptions of macroeconomics. We should expect to converge to the classical equilibrium in the long run. But in the short run, transactions costs and information problems associated with finding and taking jobs, together with simple stickiness of wages and prices due to contractual arrangements, will affect the adjustment process. If, for example, prices do not fall fast enough in response to a decline in the nominal quantity of money, we would expect to get transitory disequilibrium and unemployment. Such unemployment would not occur in the classical model. It is exactly the range of issues such as short-run adjustment and unemployment with which the macroeconomics of the short run is concerned. We therefore retain the classical analysis as a reference point and turn next to a discussion of the adjustment process under less ideal conditions.

14-2 THE WAGE FLOOR ASSUMPTION

We have seen that the classical model assumes fully flexible wages and prices which imply continual full employment. The classical model therefore cannot explain unemployment. A popular modification of the classical model that goes some way toward a satisfactory model is the *wage floor assumption*. The wage floor assumption states that in the short run money wages are *completely* rigid downward, but *fully* flexible upward.

In Figure 14-6 we show labour supply as a function of the *money* wage. Below full employment $\bar{N}$, the supply schedule is flat at the level of wages w_0. Whatever the level of unemployment, workers will not work for less. But the wage is fully flexible upward. Therefore, if more than $\bar{N}$ of labour were demanded, wages would immediately increase, moving up to the point where the quantity of labour demanded were again equal to the full-employment supply.

Aggregate Supply

How does the wage floor assumption modify the aggregate supply function AS of Figure 14-5? To answer that question we look in Figure 14-6 at the labour market and the production function. We show two labour demand schedules corresponding to two price levels, P' and a lower level P'', respectively. At a price level P', given the wage floor w_0, the value of the marginal product of labour at full employment, $P' \cdot MPN(N)$, far exceeds the wage floor. Equilibrium in the labour market obtains at point E' with a money wage w'. The corresponding levels of employment and output are $\bar{N}$ and $\bar{Y}$.

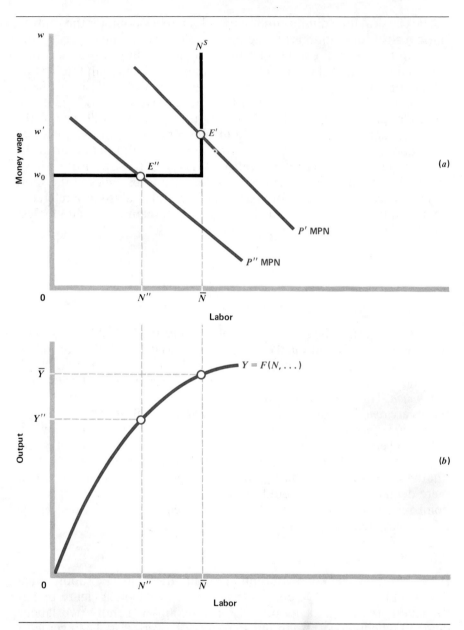

FIGURE 14-6   THE WAGE FLOOR MODEL. The upper part of the diagram shows the labour supply as a function of the *money* wage. Up to $\overline{N}$, any amount of labour is supplied at a given wage w_0. At $\overline{N}$, labour supply becomes completely unresponsive to the money wage, and the money wage is fully flexible upward. Labour demand schedules, the value of the marginal product $(P \cdot MPN(N))$, are shown for alternative price levels. At a price level P', the equilibrium wage is w', above the wage floor, and employment and output correspond to full employment. But at a lower price level P'', firms only hire N'' of labour, and accordingly, output supplied is only Y'', less than full-employment output $\overline{Y}$.

Suppose next that the price level were much lower, for example, P''. At each wage rate the demand for labour would be much lower. At any given level of employment, the value of the marginal product of labour is correspondingly lower. Thus at the wage rate w_0, the demand for labour is only N'', and accordingly, the amount of output produced and supplied is only Y'', less than the full-employment supply. How much less depends on the curvature of the production function, that is, on the extent of diminishing returns. If returns are nearly constant (a nearly straight production function), output declines by quite a bit. If returns are strongly diminishing, then a reduction in employment costs relatively little in terms of output lost. We thus find that if the price level falls below a certain level (the level at which the labour demand schedule passes through the kink at $\bar{N}$), prices are too low relative to the wage floor, and therefore employment and output decline. The lower are prices, the lower is output.[4]

In Figure 14-7 we show the aggregate supply schedule that embodies the wage floor assumption. Just as in the classical model, the aggregate supply schedule becomes vertical at the full-employment level of output $\bar{Y}$. This is because the wage is fully flexible upward. Any attempt by firms

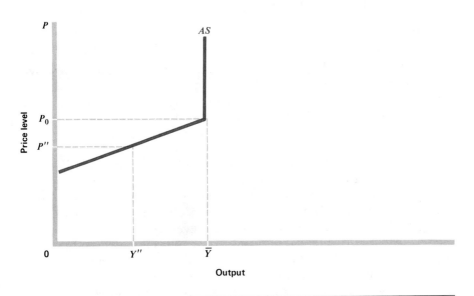

FIGURE 14-7   AGGREGATE SUPPLY IN THE WAGE FLOOR MODEL. With a wage floor w_0 the aggregate supply schedule has a kink. At high enough prices the value of the marginal product of labour exceeds the wage floor, and labour demand therefore is equal to the full-employment level. Thus the aggregate supply schedule, at high enough prices, becomes vertical just as in the classical case. But for lower prices firms find it profitable to hire less than the full-employment labour force. Output therefore is at Y'', below the full-employment $\bar{Y}$. The extent to which a reduction in prices leads to a reduction in output supplied depends on the production function.

to produce more than $\bar{Y}$ would require a labour input in excess of $\bar{N}$, and that would make wages rise.

But now the aggregate supply schedule has a kink. The level of that kink, P_0, depends on the given money wage floor w_0. If prices fall below P_0, say, to P'', the value of the marginal product of labour at full employment, $P''. MPN(N)$, is less than the given wage w_0. Firms therefore reduce employment because, at the margin, workers cost more than they add to the firms' revenue. With full wage flexibility the resulting unemployment would immediately lead to lower wages, and that would restore full employment. But now wages are entirely rigid downward. Thus when prices decline below P_0, firms must cut employment enough to restore profitability. Cutting employment does so, because as employment falls, the marginal product of labour rises. Therefore firms can afford to pay the same nominal wage, w_0, even though the price level is below P_0.

The upward-sloping segment of the aggregate supply schedule thus shows the supply of output in the unemployment region. Because the firm faces a given money wage, it cannot profitably supply the output level $\bar{Y}$, at *any* level of prices. Prices have to be high enough to pay the labour costs of producing the output. The lower the level of prices (relative to the given money wage), the less output can be profitably produced.

Effects of a Demand Disturbance

Consider now how the wage floor model affects our analysis of demand disturbances, say, a change in government spending. In Figure 14-8 we start in a full-employment equilibrium at point E. We look at two alternatives: an increase in government spending, leading to a rightward shift of the aggregate demand schedule to AD', and a reduction in spending, shifting the schedule to AD''. When demand increases, we observe the same result as in the classical model. Wages increase as firms compete in the labour market for the scarce labour supply. Prices increase because buyers are competing for the limited supply of goods. Equilibrium output and employment do not change, and the rise in prices, by reducing real balances and raising interest rates, leads to crowding out that restores aggregate demand to the full-employment level.

But consider now a reduction in government spending. The decline in demand leads to a new equilibrium at point E''. Both output and prices decline. The fall in demand means that firms cannot sell the full-employment level of output, and they therefore cut down on employment. But the fall in employment does not now lead to lower wages. Wages are rigid, and therefore, unlike in the classical case, we end up with some unemployment. It is no longer the case that wages and prices decline enough to raise real balances and lower interest rates to the point where private spending has risen enough to make up for reduced government spending. Wage stickiness, when demand declines, is therefore clearly a cause of unemployment.

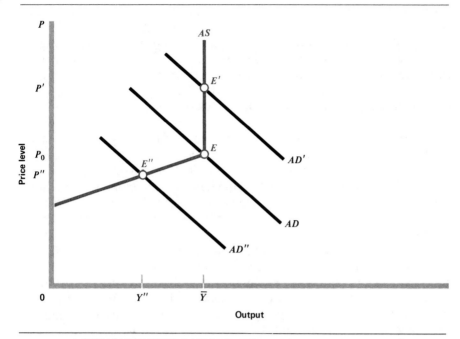

FIGURE 14-8   DEMAND DISTURBANCE IN THE WAGE FLOOR MODEL. The economy starts at an initial full-employment equilibrium at E. An increase in government spending shifts the aggregate demand schedule to AD' and leads to higher prices but no increase in output, just as in the classical case. However, a fall in demand shifts the aggregate demand schedule to AD'' and brings about an unemployment equilibrium at E''. There is some fall in prices and a decline in employment and output. Because wages are totally rigid, prices cannot fall enough to restore demand to the full-employment level.

Evaluation of the Wage Floor Model

The wage floor model is successful in explaining how a reduction in demand can lead to unemployment. In providing that explanation it is an important modification of the classical model, bringing the analysis much closer to realism. But the model is not quite realistic yet.

The main objection is to the overly sharp asymmetry between the behaviour of wages at full employment and below full employment. It is not in fact the case that the wage is fully flexible when labour demand exceeds the full-employment level. Output can be above the full-employment level $\overline{Y}$, for instance if labour works overtime. It is also not the case that money wages are totally rigid downward, whatever the level of unemployment.

Under the wage floor assumption nothing further happens once the economy is caught in an unemployment situation such as E'' in Figure 14-8. Specifically there is no link between unemployment and *changes* in wages.

What is more nearly the case, as we see in the next section, is that wages rise gradually when there is overemployment or fall gradually when there is unemployment. Our analysis will therefore use a model of *sticky* wages rather than the extreme right-angled labour supply schedule of Figure 14-6.

A second objection concerns the behaviour of real wages, w/P, that is implied by the wage floor model. This model assumes that when aggregate demand and output decline, for example, from E to E'' in Figure 14-8, prices fall but money wages remain unchanged. Therefore in a recession *real* wages rise. Conversely, in moving from a point like E'' to E, prices rise, and with unchanged money wages, that means real wages decline in an expansion.

The wage floor model thus implies that real wages move *countercyclically*, that is, they fall in an expansion and rise in a recession. Keynes originally advanced this idea, and it has been explored with data for various countries. The conclusion that emerges from all this work is that there is no clearcut evidence in support of the hypothesis of a significant cyclical behaviour of real wages. Some studies find that wages are mildly procyclical; others that wages are mildly countercyclical. There is no evidence that real wages move in a strongly countercyclical fashion. The facts thus do not support a key implication of the wage floor model.[5]

14-3   WAGES, EMPLOYMENT, AND OUTPUT

The wage floor model represents a significant modification of the classical model because it does at least allow the possibility of unemployment. Both the wage floor and the classical models build on two components, as can be seen in Figures 14-4 and 14-6. Those components are the production function, linking output to employment, and a relationship between employment and the wage. In the wage floor model, that is the labour supply curve N^S.

In this section we develop a theory of aggregate supply that builds on the same two elements. We examine first the link between output and employment in the short run, equivalent to the production function in Figures 14-4 and 14-6. And second we present a modified view of the relationship between employment and the wage rate. In particular we look at how unemployment causes wages to change, and thus study the link between wages and employment over time.

We start with the cyclical relationship between employment and output.

Employment and Output in the Short Run

Estimates of the production function typically do not show diminishing returns to labour, of the type seen in the production function in Figure 14-1. If anything, there seem to be constant returns to labour or even increasing returns over the cycle. The key to the short-run relationship between output and employment is found in the cyclical behaviour of capacity utilization.

The Cyclical Behaviour of Employment and Capacity Utilization

The employment rate is defined as the fraction of the labour force that is currently employed. (More on the definition is given in Chapter 16.) The rate of capacity (capital) utilization is measured similarly. The rate of capacity utilization represents the fraction of the capital stock that is currently being used. The behaviour of these two variables in the 1981–82 recession is shown in Figure 14-9. They both fell in the recession and then rose as the economy recovered in 1983.[6]

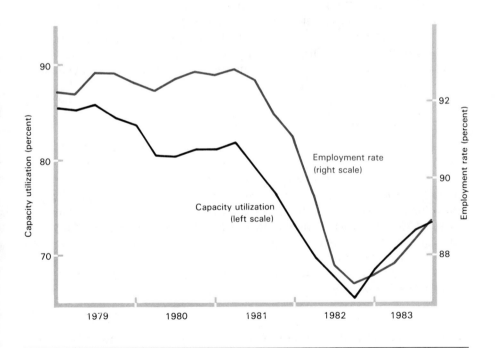

FIGURE 14-9   EMPLOYMENT RATE AND CAPACITY UTILIZATION IN THE 1981-1982 RECESSION
(*Source: Bank of Canada Review*)

Figure 14-9 shows that over the business cycle capital and labour input move together. This differs sharply from the assumption in the wage floor model that capital is given and fully utilized but employment varies. Here, with both inputs moving in the same direction, the ratio of capital to labour employed moves much less if at all. *Accordingly the marginal product of labour also is less variable, and with it so is the real wage.* The behaviour of capacity utilization thus explains why there is no consistent cyclical pattern of the real wage. The amount of capital *used* per worker is *not* higher in recessions than in booms; thus the marginal product of labour is not necessarily higher in recessions, and therefore the real wage should not be expected to be higher.

The observation that capital utilization and employment vary together leads to a quite different way of looking at the cyclical behaviour of employment. We now place less emphasis on the real wage as a determinant of cyclical employment and place more emphasis on the link between the demand for output and the level of employment.

In passing we note that the large variation in capacity utilization comes as a bit of a surprise. If firms own capital and it costs nothing (or little) to use, why do they not use it to full capacity at all times and thus save some on labour costs? A large part of the answer is that in the short run technology does not permit a lot of capital-labour substitution. For example, it takes a certain number of people to run a steel mill or to drive a truck. When demand declines, firms will work the plant for fewer shifts or even close down some plants for a time.

The Employment-Output Relationship

With the real wage and the capital-labour ratio both being relatively constant over the cycle, we cannot rely on movements in the real wage to generate changes in employment. Rather we now assume that the amount of labour that firms hire is determined by the amount of output that they produce. We assume that to produce a level of output Y, the firm needs an amount of labour aY.[7] The coefficient a denotes the labour requirement per unit of output. For example, if $a = 2$, it takes 2 hours of labour to produce 1 unit of output.[8]

With the assumption of a given unit labour requirement a, there is a direct link between employment and output:

$$N = aY \tag{3}$$

Equation (3) states that employment (or the demand for labour) is proportional to the level of output. The factor of proportionality is the unit labour requirement.

Equation (3) implies that employment varies one for one with the level of production. The implied short-run production function is shown in

Figure 14-10. This is a simplified view of the employment-production link, but it takes us far in understanding the supply side. Some qualifications follow at the end of the chapter. Until then, we maintain this useful simplification.

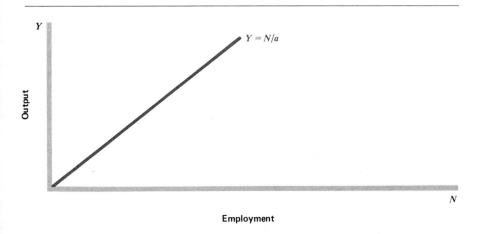

FIGURE 14-10   THE SHORT-RUN PRODUCTION FUNCTION. In the short run, the relationship between output and employment does not show diminishing returns. The short-run production function is assumed to have constant returns, with output proportional to the input of labour. The factor of proportionality is $1/a$, where a is the amount of labour needed to produce one unit of output. In the background, capital utilization is varying along with employment, as in Figure 14-9.

Employment and Wages

The second critical departure from the wage floor model comes with our assumptions about the behaviour of money wages. We reject the sharp asymmetry of the wage floor model and assume instead that money wages rise when there is overemployment and fall when there is unemployment. However, and this is critical, wages do not adjust rapidly. *Money wages move over time in response to disequilibrium in the labour market. They are neither totally rigid nor fully flexible.*

Wage behaviour is shown in Figure 14-11. We assume that money wages increase with current employment. Hence the *ww* curve, showing the wage-employment relationship, is upward-sloping. But we add a second, *dynamic*, element to the relationship. We assume that the *ww* curve *shifts* over time. If there is unemployment this period — if employment is less than $\overline{N}$ — then next period at any given employment level, the wage will be lower than it is this period. The dynamic assumption is that unemployment forces wages down over time. In terms of Figure 14-11, if there is unemployment this period, the *ww* curve shifts to *ww'* next period. If there is overemployment this period, the *ww* curve shifts to *ww''* next period.

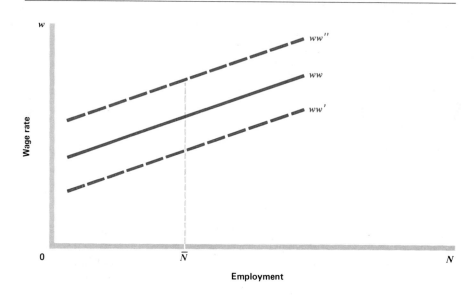

FIGURE 14-11　THE WAGE-EMPLOYMENT RELATIONSHIP. The short-run relationship between the wage rate and employment is shown by *ww*. The higher the level of employment this period, the higher the wage rate. In addition, there is a dynamic relationship between employment this period and the wage rate in the future. If output this period is below $\bar{N}$ (if there is unemployment this period) the *ww* curve shifts down to *ww'* next period. Thus unemployment reduces the wage over time. Similarly, if employment this period is above $\bar{N}$, the *ww* curve shifts up to *ww''*. Overemployment this period increases the wage over time. If unemployment continues from period to period, the *ww* curve keeps falling.

Figure 14-11 shows two implications of our assumptions about wage behaviour. First, to each level of employment today there is a corresponding money wage. Second, the present level of employment affects next period's wages. If there is unemployment, wages *keep falling*; if there is overemployment, wages *keep rising*.

These assumptions about wage behaviour are partway between the classical model of Section 14-1 and the wage floor model of Section 14-2. In the classical model wages adjust instantaneously in response to overemployment or unemployment. In the wage floor model wages do not fall at all in response to unemployment. In the model we are developing now, and in the real world, they are neither fully flexible nor totally rigid. Rather they adjust over time.

We formalize wage behaviour in Equation (4). The wage this period is equal to the wage that prevailed last period (say, last quarter), but with an adjustment for the state of employment:

$$w = w_{-1}[1 + \epsilon(N/\overline{N} - 1)] \qquad (4)$$

where w_{-1} is the wage that prevailed last period. The adjustment is shown by the term in brackets, which involves the ratio of employment N to the full-employment labour force $\overline{N}$. At full employment $N = \overline{N}$, and therefore wages do not change over time and the ww schedule does not shift. But when there is unemployment, $N/\overline{N}$ is less than 1. In that case the second term in Equation (4) is negative and wages today are less than they were last period. Further, because today's wage is below last period's, *next* period the ww schedule will be below this period's ww schedule. This Equation (4) implies that when there is unemployment, the ww schedule shifts down from period to period.

The extent to which wages respond to employment depends on the parameter ϵ. If ϵ is large, unemployment has a strong effect on wages. Conversely if ϵ is very small, wages are very sticky. The model of wage adjustment also implies that overemployment (unusually large amounts of overtime) leads to rising wages. The larger the adjustment coefficient ϵ, the more rapidly wages rise.

Why Wages Are Sticky

Wages are said to be sticky, or wage adjustment sluggish, when wages move slowly, over time, rather than being fully and immediately flexible so as to assure full employment at every point in time. The stickiness of wages is a well-established fact, but the reasons for that stickiness are much less established and remain the subject of intense research.

The central element in any explanation, however, is the following fact. The labour market involves long-term relations between firms and workers and an important role for *reputations*. These *long-term labour market relations* mean that one party will not take advantage of the other, because each gains from continuing reasonably trouble-free relations.[9] Workers who stay in the same job save themselves the trouble of quitting and searching for new jobs; firms save the costs of locating, screening, and training new workers. Each benefits if they can get on together.

In such a setting firms will not aggressively cut wages when there is unemployment, threatening workers with dismissal unless they take a cut. In turn, workers cannot threaten management with walkouts unless they immediately receive wage increases anytime the economy is doing well.

Of course there is *some* competition for a workplace between the unemployed and those who hold jobs. But that competition is *very* moderate. A firm that tries to cut its wage bill by threatening workers with unemployment gets a bad reputation and will lose workers the moment the economy improves. In the meantime work morale may deteriorate.

On the other side, to retain their labour force firms must be sure that the wages they pay match those that can, *on average*, be gotten elsewhere in the market. A worker who expects to come out, on average, as well in his or her current job as in another will not quit the job merely because the wage this month is below that in another firm. In the market for fresh fish the price must clear the market every day. The labour market is very different. It is not day-to-day fluctuations in the money wage that "clear" the labour market; rather, it is explicit or implicit long-term arrangements between firms and their work forces.

Another fact reinforces the slow adjustment of wages. Workers who are unemployed will receive benefits that allow them for some time to *search* for a job rather than just accept *any* kind of work to avoid starvation. They can wait for an opportunity that matches their skills. Thus competition from the unemployed is dampened by institutions that make unemployment less difficult to bear. If the unemployed were willing to accept work at any wage, however small, we would not observe unemployment for any length of time, but that clearly is not the case.

The implication of this view of the labour market is that wages move slowly. Unemployment leads only gradually to declining wages. High employment or overemployment leads only gradually to rising wages. There is a lot of inertia or stickiness in wages even if adjustment does take place over time. Both aspects of wage behaviour are central to modern macroeconomics. The short-run stickiness means that in the short run changes in aggregate demand lead to changes in output and employment. The long-run adjustments imply that these output and employment changes are only transitory.

BOX 14-1 THE PHILLIPS CURVE

When the demand for a commodity or service is high relatively to the supply of it we expect the price to rise, the rate of rise being greater the greater the excess demand. Conversely when the demand is low relatively to the supply we expect the price to fall, the rate of fall being greater the greater the deficiency of demand. It seems plausible that this principle should operate as one of the factors of determining the rate of change of money wage rates, which are the price of labour services.

This quote reproduces the opening lines to one of the most famous papers in macroeconomics. In 1958 A. W. Phillips, a professor at the London School of Economics, published a comprehensive study of wage behaviour in the United

Kingdom for the period 1861–1957.* The main finding is summarized in Figure 1 reproduced from his article: The higher the rate of unemployment, the lower the rate of increase of money wages, or in other words, there is a tradeoff between wage inflation and unemployment.

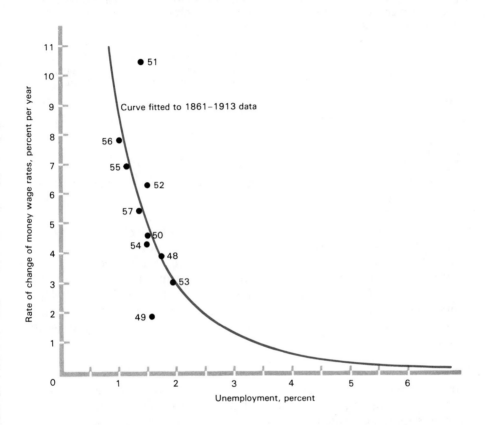

Today we call such a relation the *Phillips curve*. The Phillips curve very rapidly became a cornerstone of macroeconomic policy analysis. It suggested that policy makers could choose different combinations of unemployment and rates of wage inflation. For instance, they could have low unemployment so long as they recognized that that meant high wage inflation. Or they could have low wage inflation if they were willing to put up with high unemployment. Moreover, there appeared to be the possibility of improving the tradeoff. Specific policies (retraining, job banks, etc.) could make the labour market more efficient, thus shifting the Phillips curve in a way that reduced the rate of wage increases at each unemployment rate.

Economic policies in the 1960s led to a sustained expansion of activity, falling unemployment, and gradually rising inflation, as if the economy were moving up and along a Phillips curve. But attempts to reverse the inflation in the 1970s showed that there was much more to the inflation process than the simple Phillips curve suggests. Inflationary expectations in particular, as we shall see in Chapter 15, play a critical role. By the early 1970s the profession by and large recognized the proposition advanced by Milton Friedman and Edmund Phelps: *In the long run* there is no tradeoff between inflation and unemployment.[†] In other words, in the long run the economy moves to the full-employment rate of unemployment, whatever the rate of change of wages and prices.

*A. W. Phillips, "The Relation between Unemployment and the Rate of Change of Money Wages in the United Kingdom, 1861–1957," *Economica*, November 1958.

†Milton Friedman, "The Role of Monetary Policy," *American Economic Review*, March 1969, and Edmund Phelps, *Inflation Policy and Unemployment Theory* (New York: Norton, 1972).

The Phillips Curve

The *Phillips curve* relates the rate of change of wages to the level of unemployment (see Box 14-1). The lower the unemployment rate, the more rapid the rate of wage increase.

The link between wage changes and unemployment for nearly 100 years was documented for the United Kingdom in an important article written by A. W. Phillips in 1958. In some form or other, it has since become a cornerstone of modern macroeconomics. Our wage-employment model summarized in Equation (4) implies a Phillips curve. To derive the Phillips curve relation we use the definition of the unemployment rate as the percentage of the labour force that is not employed, $u \equiv 1 - N/\overline{N}$, in (4) to obtain:

$$w = w_{-1}(1 - \epsilon u) \tag{4a}$$

In the form of (4a), the wage equation states that wages are falling when there is unemployment and rising when there is overemployment (when the unemployment rate is negative).[10]

Wages and Output

In Figure 14-10 we show the relationship between output and employment. Figure 14-11 links the wage rate with employment. Putting the two relationships together in Figure 14-12, we obtain the wY relationship between money wages and output. The wage in the current period is higher, the higher the level of output. And if output this period is above the full-employment level, the wY curve shifts up to wY'' next period. Similarly, if output this period is below full employment, the wY curve will shift down to wY' next period.

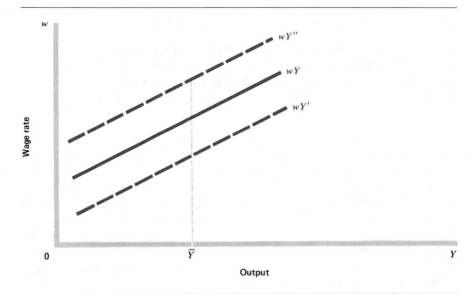

FIGURE 14-12   THE RELATIONSHIP BETWEEN WAGES AND OUTPUT. The relationship between the wage rate and output is derived from Figures 14-10 and 14-11. Because the wage rate rises with employment, and employment rises with output, the wage rate rises with output. Thus the wY curve is upward sloped. The wY curve shifts over time. If output is above the full-employment level this period, wY shifts next period to wY''. Similarly, if output is below $\overline{Y}$ this period, the wY curve will shift to a position like wY' next period.

We can formalize the link using Equations (3) and (4). Equation (3) states that $N = aY$. In particular, at the full-employment level we have $\overline{N} = a\overline{Y}$. Substituting for N and $\overline{N}$ in Equation (4) gives us the link between wages and output:

$$w = w_{-1}[1 + \epsilon(Y/\overline{Y} - 1)] \tag{5}$$

Equation (5) describes the wY curve in Figure 14-12. It states that wages increase when output is above the full-employment level and fall when output is below full employment. Thus Equation (5), like (4) and (4a), states that wages are rising or falling depending on the state of the business cycle.[11] Figure 14-12 [or Equation (5)] is one of the building blocks of the aggregate supply curve. We thus summarize the derivation of the wY schedule. It is based on the assumptions that labour input increases with the level of output (Figure 14-12), and that the wage both (a) increases in the current period with the level of output and (b) falls over time if there is unemployment or rises if there is overemployment.

14-4   THE AGGREGATE SUPPLY CURVE

Firms base the prices at which they sell on the costs of production, including a profit margin that constitutes the return to capital. We assume that the relation between prices and costs takes the simple *markup* form where price is equal to the unit labour cost plus a profit margin, z:

$$P = aw(1 + z) \qquad (6)$$

The term aw represents the labour costs of producing a unit of output. If it takes a hours of labour to produce a unit of output, the labour cost is a hours of labour times the wage per hour, or aw. For example, let $a = 2$ and $w = \$10$ per hour. Then the unit labour cost of the good is $20. Price exceeds unit labour cost because the firm must also earn a competitive rate of return on the capital that is employed. Therefore a markup over cost of z percent is charged.[12] We take the markup to be constant and given. If the markup is 15 percent or $z = 0.15$, then the firm would charge $23 ($= \$20 \times 1.15$) per unit of output.

The markup pricing assumption singles out three determinants of prices: the money wage; the unit labour requirement or its reciprocal, labour productivity[13]; and the markup rate. A rise in any of these three determinants will increase the price that firms set for their output. Conversely, a decline in wages, a rise in productivity, or a fall in the markup rate will lower costs and therefore lower prices.

We now are ready to derive the aggregate supply equation, by combining wage behaviour and the price equation. Substituting in (6) for the wage rate, using (5), we obtain the following equation:

$$P = a(1 + z)w_{-1}[1 + \epsilon(Y/\overline{Y} - 1)] \qquad (7)$$

This equation can be simplified to arrive at our basic supply curve by noting from (6) that $a(1 + z)w_{-1} = P_{-1}$ because last period, too, prices were set on the basis of the same markup pricing. Thus replacing the first term in (7) by P_{-1} we have arrived at the aggregate supply equation:

$$P = P_{-1}[1 + \epsilon(Y/\overline{Y} - 1)] \qquad (8)$$

Figure 14-13 shows the aggregate supply function implied by Equation (8). The supply curve is upward-sloping. Like the ww and wY schedules on which it is based, the AS curve shifts over time. If output this period is above the full-employment level, then next period the AS schedule will shift up to AS''. If output this period is below full employment, next period the AS schedule will shift down to AS'. Thus the properties of the AS curve are those of the wY curve. This is so because with the markup fixed at z, the price is just proportional to the money wage.

Equation (8) is an aggregate supply equation because it shows the price at which each level of output will be supplied. The aggregate supply equation (8) (and the AS schedule in Figure 14-13) shows a direct relation between prices today, prices last period, and the level of output. Prices today are equal to last period's prices with an adjustment for cyclical conditions. In a boom they exceed last period's prices; in a recession they fall below last period's price.

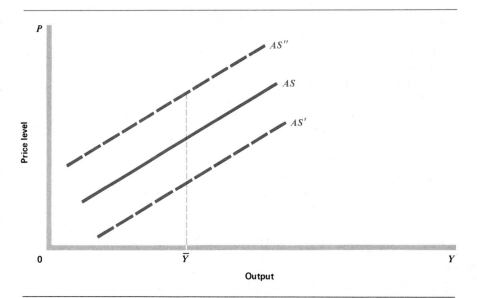

FIGURE 14-13   THE AGGREGATE SUPPLY CURVE. The aggregate supply curve is obtained from the wage-output curve wY of Figure 14-12, and from the assumption that the price level is a constant markup on the wage rate. AS is the aggregate supply curve in the current period. If output this period is above $\overline{Y}$, then next period the aggregate supply curve will shift to AS". If output is below the full-employment level this period, then next period the aggregate supply curve will shift down to AS'.

The AS curve is the aggregate supply curve of a world where wages are less than fully flexible. Prices increase with the level of output because increased output implies increased employment, reduced unemployment, and therefore increased labour costs. The fact that prices rise with output is entirely a reflection of the adjustments in the labour market where higher employment increases wages. Firms pass on these wage increases by raising prices, and for that reason prices rise with the level of supply.

Properties of the Aggregate Supply Curve

We now have derived the aggregate supply schedule AS used in Chapter 13 and can, with the help of (8), explore its properties more closely. We want to develop three points:

1 The aggregate supply schedule is flatter the smaller is the impact of output and employment changes on wages. If wages respond only slowly to unemployment, then the AS schedule in Figure 14-13 will be very flat. Conversely, if wages are highly responsive to unemployment, then a small change in unemployment will induce large wage changes and therefore price changes. The coefficient ϵ in Equations (5) and (8) captures this employment-wage change linkage.
2 The position of the aggregate supply schedule depends on the past level of prices. The schedule passes through the full-employment output level $\overline{Y}$ at $P = P_{-1}$. For higher output levels there is overemployment, and hence prices today exceed prices last period. Conversely, when there is unemployment, prices today are less than those of last period.
3 The aggregate supply schedule shifts over time. If output is maintained above the full-employment level $\overline{Y}$, then over time wages rise and the wage increases are passed on into increased prices.

Rather than discuss these three points in the abstract, we use the aggregate supply curve to examine the effects of a monetary expansion in Figure 14-14. This will give us a full understanding of both the short-run and long-run implications of our wage-price model.

14-5   THE EFFECTS OF A MONETARY EXPANSION

In Figure 14-14 we show the economy in full-employment equilibrium at point E. The aggregate supply schedule AS is drawn for a given past price level P_{-1}. It passes through the full-employment output level $\overline{Y}$ at the price level P_{-1} because when output is at the full-employment level, there is no tendency for wages to change, and hence costs and prices too are constant from period to period. The aggregate supply schedule is drawn relatively flat, suggesting a small effect of output and employment changes on wages.

Short-Run Effects

Suppose now that the nominal money stock is increased. At each price level real balances are higher, interest rates are lower, and hence the demand for output rises. The AD schedule shifts up and to the right, to AD'. At the initial price level $P = P_{-1}$ there is now an excess demand for goods. Firms find that their inventories are running down and accordingly hire more labour and raise output until point E', the short-run equilibrium, is

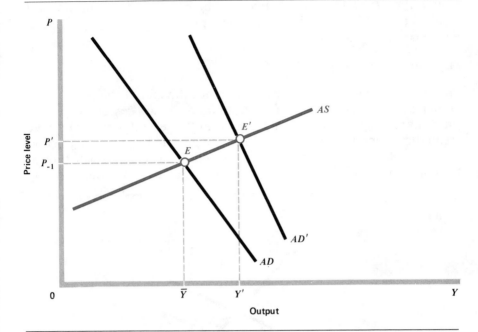

FIGURE 14-14   THE SHORT-RUN EFFECT OF AN INCREASE IN THE MONEY STOCK. The aggregate supply schedule AS is positively sloped and passes through the full-employment output level $Y = \overline{Y}$ at a price level equal to that prevailing last period, $P = P_{-1}$. The initial full-employment equilibrium at E is disturbed by an increase in the money stock that shifts aggregate demand to AD'. Short-run equilibrium is at point E' where *both* output and prices have increased. Prices are higher because the output and employment expansion have increased wages, and firms pass these cost increases into higher prices. The AS schedule is drawn quite flat, reflecting the assumption that wages are very sticky. Under these conditions prices rise little and most of the short-run effect is on output.

reached. Note that at E' both output and prices have risen. A monetary expansion has led to a short-run ir.....ase in output. The rise in prices is due to the increase in labour costs as production and employment rise.

Compare now the short-run result with the Keynesian and classical models of Chapter 13. Our new equilibrium at E' has a feature of each: output is higher, and prices have risen. Whether we are more nearly in the classical or Keynesian situation depends entirely on the slope of the aggregate supply schedule, that is, on the coefficient ϵ that translates employment changes into wage changes.

In moving from E to E' *real* balances have increased less than in a world where prices do not change. Therefore at E' output will have increased less than in the Keynesian case, though of course more than in the classical case, where output remains at the full-employment level and all adjustment takes place through prices.

Medium-Term Adjustment

The short-run equilibrium at point E' is not the end of the story. At E' output is above normal. Therefore, from (8) prices *will keep on rising*. Consider now in Figure 14-15 what happens in the second period. Once we are in the second period, looking back, the price in the preceding period was P' at point E'. Therefore the second-period supply curve passes through the full-employment output level at a price equal to P'. We show this by

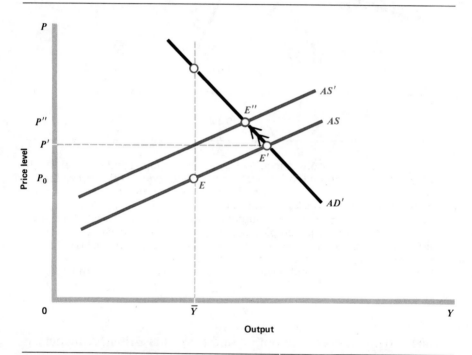

FIGURE 14-15   THE MEDIUM-TERM EFFECT OF AN INCREASE IN MONEY. The monetary expansion has led to a short-run equilibrium at point E'. But at E' output is above normal, and therefore wages are rising. The increase in wages shifts the AS schedule upward. Prices in the second period would be equal to those at E' if the economy were back at full employment. Thus, AS shifts up to AS' and we have a new equilibrium at E''. Output falls somewhat compared to E', and prices rise further. The adjustment from E' to E'' reflects cost pressures that arise in an overemployed economy. As these cost increases are passed on into higher prices, real balances fall, interest rates rise, and equilibrium income and spending fall.

shifting the aggregate supply schedule up to AS', reflecting the increase in wages that has taken place since last period in response to the high level of employment.

With the new aggregate supply schedule AS', and with the aggregate demand schedule unchanged at the higher level AD', the new equilibrium is at E''. Comparing E' and E'' we note that output now has fallen compared with the first period and prices have risen further. The increase in wages has been passed on by firms as an upward shift of the AS schedule, and the resulting price increase reduces real balances, raises interest rates, and lowers equilibrium income and spending. Thus, starting in the second period, we enter a phase of the adjustment process in which the initial expansion begins to be reversed. We continue this process by looking at the long-term adjustment.

Long-Term Adjustment

As long as output is above normal, employment is above normal, and therefore wages are rising. Because wages are rising, firms experience cost increases, and these are passed on, at each output level, as an upward shift of the aggregate supply schedule. As long as the short- and medium-term equilibrium positions of the economy (points E', E'', etc.) lie to the right of $\overline{Y}$, the AS schedule is shifting up and to the left. As a result, output will be declining toward the full-employment level and prices will keep rising. This adjustment is shown in Figure 14-16.

Figure 14-16 shows that the upward-shifting AS schedule gives us a series of equilibrium positions on the AD schedule, starting with E' and moving up toward E'''. During the entire adjustment process, output is above the full-employment level and prices are rising. But there is a long-run equilibrium at E''' in which the economy has returned to full employment.

Once prices have risen in the same proportion as the nominal money stock, the real money stock M/P is again at the initial level. This happens at E'''. When real balances and therefore interest rates are again at the initial level, so are aggregate demand, output, and employment. In the long run, once wages and prices have had time to adjust fully, the model has the same predictions as the classical case of Chapter 13 and Section 14-1. *The difference is only in the adjustment process.* In the classical case a monetary expansion leads immediately to an equiproportionate rise in prices with no real expansion. Here output and prices *both* rise in the short and medium term, and only in the long run do we reach the classical case. In the short run the predictions of our model more closely resemble the Keynesian case, and the more slowly wages adjust to changes in employment, the greater the resemblance.

Because the adjustments of wages and prices are in fact quite slow, the short- and medium-term adjustments are an important aspect of macroeconomics.

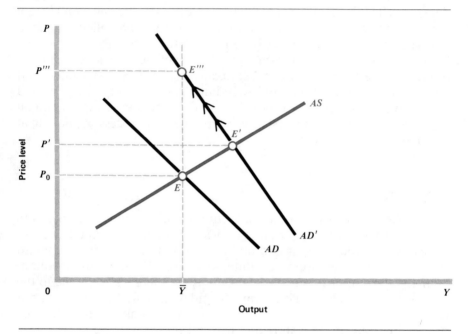

FIGURE 14-16   THE FULL ADJUSTMENT TO AN INCREASE IN THE MONEY STOCK. As long as output is above $\overline{Y}$, wages, costs, and equilibrium prices will be rising. From the short-run equilibrium at E', the upward-shifting aggregate supply schedule leads to declining output and rising prices as shown by the arrows. The adjustment continues until at E''' prices have risen in proportion to the increase in the money stock. At this point, output and employment have returned to the full-employment level. In the long run, therefore, a monetary expansion has no real effects.

14-6   ADJUSTMENT TO A DECLINE IN SPENDING

In Figure 14-17 we provide another application of the model. This time we look at a fall in autonomous spending, say, a reduction in investment due to a loss of business confidence. We start in full-employment equilibrium at E, with no tendency for prices to be changing because the labour market is in full-employment equilibrium and therefore exerts no cost pressures through changing wages.

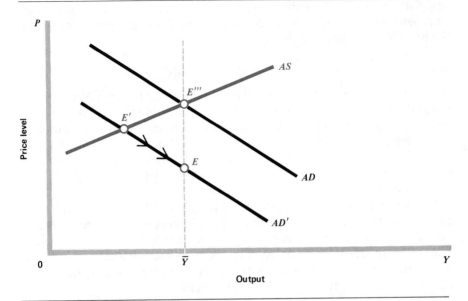

FIGURE 14-17   THE ADJUSTMENT TO A DECLINE IN AUTONOMOUS SPENDING. The initial equilibrium at E is disturbed by a decline in autonomous spending shifting the aggregate demand schedule to AD'. In the short run, both output and prices decline at point E'. Wage stickiness precludes an immediate return to full employment. Only as the recession and unemployment persist do wages decline, leading the supply schedule to shift down. Output recovers along with falling prices, as shown by the arrows. In the long run, the price level falls enough to lower interest rates and raise real spending back to the full-employment level.

The equilibrium is now disturbed by a decline in autonomous spending, shifting the aggregate demand schedule down from AD to AD'. Output and prices both fall as the economy moves from E to E' in the short run. Because wages are not fully flexible and firms set prices on the basis of costs, the price level cannot fall fast enough to raise real balances, lower interest rates, and thus restore full employment immediately. Now the economy is in recession at E'.

Unemployment at point E' implies that wages are falling. Therefore the aggregate supply schedule will start shifting down and to the right. Over time prices decline. The resulting rise in real balances gradually lowers interest rates and encourages aggregate demand. The process continues, with falling unemployment, until the economy reaches $\bar{Y}$ again.

In the long run, once again, the model has classical predictions. A decline in demand leads to a fall in prices, lower interest rates, and full employment. But in the short run the economy behaves very differently.

Sluggish or slowly adjusting wages are an obstacle to continuing full employment. Only by going through a recession and unemployment can the price level be brought down.

Summary

At the end of Section 14-4 we noted three features of the aggregate supply schedule: its slope, its position, and its movement over time. The description of the adjustment process to monetary changes or changes in autonomous demand has brought these three points into focus. Each plays an important role in determining how the sticky wage model compares with the two extremes of a fixed-price Keynesian model and a fully flexible-price classical model.

The flatter the AS schedule, the more Keynesian the model in the short run. But in the long run, that is, given enough time, the economy has fully flexible wages and prices and therefore *ultimately* reaches the classical full-employment equilibrium. However, because that adjustment can take a long time, there may be room for monetary and fiscal policy to help keep the economy more nearly at full employment.

14-7   SUPPLY SHOCKS

The macroeconomics story of the 1970s is incomplete without consideration of *supply shocks*. A supply shock is a disturbance to the economy whose first impact is to shift the aggregate supply curve. The two major supply shocks in the 1970s were the increases in the price of oil in 1973–1974 and 1979–1980. The first OPEC shock helped push the economy into the 1974–1975 recession, and the second OPEC price increase sharply accelerated the inflation rate. The high inflation led to tough monetary policy to fight inflation, with the eventual result that the economy went into a deep recession. Thus there is no doubt that supply shocks matter.

An Adverse Supply Shock

An *adverse supply shock* is one that shifts the aggregate supply curve up. Figure 14-18 shows the effects of such a shock. The AS curve shifts up to AS', and the equilibrium of the economy moves from E to E'. The immediate effect of the supply shock is thus to raise the price level and reduce the level of output. An adverse supply shock is doubly unfortunate: it causes *higher* prices and *lower* output.

There are two points to note about the impact of the supply shock. First, the shock is best thought of as an increase in the price of a raw material used in production. The *AS* curve shifts up because it now costs firms more to produce each unit of output. Second, we are assuming that the supply shock does not affect the level of potential output, which remains at $\overline{Y}$.[14]

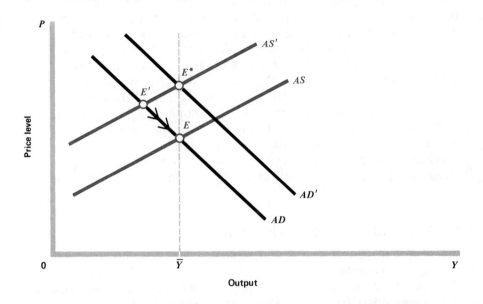

FIGURE 14-18   AN ADVERSE SUPPLY SHOCK. An increase in the real price of oil shifts the aggregate supply schedule up and to the left. The costs of production are higher at each level of output, and therefore *AS* shifts to *AS'*. In the short run, because wages do not decline enough, the economy moves into an unemployment equilibrium at *E'*. Prices are higher and output is lower because of the reduction in real balances. Over time, wages decline because of unemployment and the economy returns to the initial equilibrium at *E'*. Accommodating monetary or fiscal policies could shift the *AD* schedule to *AD'*, reducing the unemployment effects of the supply shock but increasing the inflationary impact.

What happens after the shock has hit? In Figure 14-18, the economy moves from *E'* back to *E*. The unemployment at *E'* forces wages and thus the price level down. The adjustment is slow because wages are slow to adjust. The adjustment takes place along the *AD* curve, with wages falling until *E* is reached.

At *E* the economy is back at full employment, with the price level the same as it was before the shock. But the nominal wage rate is lower than it was before the shock, because the unemployment in the meantime has forced the wage down. Thus the *real* wage too is lower than it was before the shock: the adverse supply shock reduces the real wage.

Accommodation of Supply Shocks

Could the unemployment required to bring down the wage rate be avoided by expansionary monetary and fiscal policy?

To answer that question, we look at Figure 14-18. If at the time of the oil price increase, aggregate demand could be increased by enough to move the economy to E^* rather than E', prices would rise to the full extent of the upward shift in the aggregate supply curve. Money wages would remain unchanged, and the economy would have stayed at full employment. Of course, the real wage would be lower, but it must fall in any case.

The monetary and fiscal policies that shift the AD curve to AD' in Figure 14-18 are known as *accommodating* policies. There has been a disturbance that requires a fall in the real wage. Policy is adjusted to make possible, or accommodate, that fall in the real wage *at the existing nominal wage*. Accommodation involves a tradeoff between the inflationary impact of a supply shock and its recessionary effects. The more accommodation there is, the greater the inflationary impact and the smaller the unemployment impact.

*Incorporating Materials Prices in the Analysis

In Equation (6) labour costs (and the markup) were the only determinants of output prices. Materials such as energy or copper or cotton were entirely neglected. But clearly the manufacturing sector does use these inputs whose prices have an impact on the prices of final goods.

We incorporate materials prices in our analysis by modifying the price equation to include not only labour costs and the markup, but also *materials prices*, which we denote by P_m:

$$P = aw(1 + z) + \lambda P_m \qquad (9)$$

In (9) the term λ denotes the material requirement per unit output, and hence λP_m is the component of unit costs that comes from materials inputs.

The wage rate, we recall, increases with the level of output. Hence from Equation (9) we get an upward-sloping supply curve. Further, any increase in the price of materials will increase the price level as of a given w. Thus an increase in P_m shifts the AS curve up, as in Figure 14-18.

We can alternatively write the price equation in terms of the *relative* or *real* price of materials, which we denote by the lower case p_m. The relative price is given by

$$p_m = P_m/P \qquad (10)$$

Substituting from (10) in (9) gives us a modified equation linking wages and prices[15]:

$$P = [a(1 + z)/(1 - \lambda p_m)]w \quad 1 > \lambda p_m \qquad (11)$$

Equation (11) shows that for given wages, profit margins, and labour productivity, a change in the real price of commodities will increase prices simply because it raises costs. The impact of a change in real commodity prices therefore is to shift the aggregate supply schedule upward at each level of output, as in Figure 14-18.

14-8 THE CYCLICAL BEHAVIOUR OF PRODUCTIVITY

In developing the sticky wage macroeconomic model we made a strong assumption about the link between output and employment, namely, $N = aY$. According to our assumption, labour productivity Y/N is equal to a constant $1/a$.

TABLE 14-1   THE CYCLICAL BEHAVIOUR OF PRODUCTIVITY

Recession (peak to trough)	Percent change peak to trough		Percent change in four quarters following trough	
	Output	Productivity	Output	Productivity
1974:1-74:3	−0.6	−2.3	1.8	0.3
1979:4-80:2	−1.5	−1.9	5.5	1.9
1981:2-82:4	−7.5	−2.6	7.1	3.7

Source: Department of Finance, *Economic Review*

That assumption is readily testable by looking at the cyclical behaviour of labour productivity or output per worker, Y/N. The data given in Table 14-1 shows that productivity falls as the economy moves into a recession and increases during the recovery. How do we explain these facts, and what implications do they have for our model? As we noted above, firms maintain long-term relations with their labour force. Part of that long-term relation is that during recessions firms are slow to dismiss personnel, especially highly specialized workers whom the firm does not want to risk losing permanently. This applies also to managers, because even if the firm produces only half the normal level of output, it is difficult to cut a manager in half.

Thus employment tends to fluctuate *less* than output or production. During a recession output falls, but employment falls relatively less. Hence productivity — the ratio of output to employment — falls. Conversely, in a recovery production rises, but because the firm has kept on or *hoarded* a lot of the work force, employment increases less. Thus productivity rises in a recovery.

The effects we have just described are reinforced by the fact that the firm bases its hiring and firing on expectations about future production. A firm will hire more workers and incur the expense of increasing employment only if there is an expectation that production and output will be higher for some time. Otherwise, paying overtime to the existing labour force would be a cheaper solution. Conversely, firms will lay off or dismiss workers only if they believe the decline in demand will last some time. Here then is another source of discrepancy between current employment and current production. Current production may be low but employment high because firms believe demand has declined only transitorily.

By assuming a tight link between output and employment, our model thus simplifies the complex relationships between a firm's production decisions and its employment decisions. For purposes of understanding aggregate supply, the simplification is justifiable, since output and employment do, in practice, move in the same direction, even if not exactly in lockstep.

14-9   SUMMARY

This chapter has covered a lot of hard ground. The major point to be established was that output variations along the short-run aggregate supply schedule are accompanied by only moderate price changes. In the short run, the price level varies little with the level of output. Over time, however, wages, costs, and prices will keep rising if output is above normal and keep falling if output is below normal.

We summarize the contents of the chapter as:

1   The classical theory of the demand for labour relates labour demand only to the real wage, given the quantity of other factors the firm is using. Competitive firms that are free to change the quantity of labour they use, costlessly and immediately, will hire labour up to the point where the real wage is equal to the marginal product of labour (*MPN*).

2   With wages and prices freely flexible, the equilibrium level of employment is determined in the labour market. The labour market is continuously in equilibrium at the full-employment level, and aggregate supply will therefore be the amount of output which that amount of labour produces. Given that the labour market is in equilibrium, the aggregate supply curve is vertical at the level of potential output — the aggregate supply curve is independent of the price level.

3   The wage floor model assumes that money wages are totally rigid downward, but entirely flexible upward. This leads to a kinked aggregate supply schedule. A rise in aggregate demand raises prices,

but not output. A fall in aggregate demand reduces both prices and output.

4   The wage floor model is unrealistic with its emphasis on the asymmetry between an increase and decrease in demand. It also fails with its prediction about the cyclical behaviour of real wages.

5   Firms and workers share an interest in stable long-term employment relations. Neither party benefits on average from frequent changes in employment and employment conditions. This environment makes for sluggish wage adjustment.

6   Nominal wages change in accordance with the state of excess demand in the labour market. When there is unemployment, wages fall, and when there is negative unemployment, wages rise. In this connection, it should be recalled that we abstract in this chapter from the existence of frictional unemployment.

7   Firms base the prices they charge on their costs of production. Thus, when wages rise because the level of employment is above the full-employment level, prices are increased too.

8   To assemble these elements: An increase in output is accompanied by an increase in prices. An increase in output resulting, say, from an increase in aggregate demand affects expected output, leading to an increase in employment. The increase in employment increases the nominal wage, which leads to some increase in the prices firms charge.

9   The full impact of changes in aggregate demand on prices occurs only over the course of time. A permanent increase in aggregate demand feeds slowly into an increased demand for labour, which in turn means wages rise slowly, which in turn means that prices are adjusted only over the course of time. If employment is somehow held above the full-employment level, wages and prices will continue to rise without end.

10 Materials prices, along with wages, are a determinant of costs and prices. Changes in materials prices are passed on as changes in prices and therefore changes in real wages. Materials price changes have been an important source of aggregate supply shocks.

11 Supply shocks, such as a material price increase, pose a difficult problem for macroeconomic policy. They can be accommodated through an expansionary aggregate demand policy with the effect of increased prices but stable output. Alternatively, they can be offset so that prices remain stable because of deflationary aggregate demand policy, but then output falls.

KEY TERMS

Frictionless classical model
Marginal product of labour
Wage floor assumption
Labour productivity
Long-term labour market relations
Sluggish wage adjustment

Phillips curve
Unit labour cost
Adverse supply shock
Accommodation of supply shocks
Real materials prices

PROBLEMS

1 Using Figures 14-14 to 14-16, analyse the effects of a reduction in the money stock on the price level and on output.

2 In problem 1, what happens to the level of real balances as a result of a reduction in the nominal money stock?

3 Suppose a new method of production is invented which increases the marginal product of labour at each level of employment.
   (a) What effect does this have on the (classical) demand for labour?
   (b) What effect does it have on the equilibrium real wage if the supply of labour is fixed and independent of the real wage?
   (c) How would your answer to (b) be affected if the supply of labour increased with the real wage?

4 Discuss the short-run and long-run adjustments to an increase in government spending using diagrams similar to Figures 14-14 to 14-16.

5 Suppose the economy is in a recession. How can monetary and fiscal policies speed up the recovery? What would happen in the absence of these policies?

6 The government increases income taxes. What are the effects on output, prices, and interest rates:
   (a) In the short run?
   (b) In the long run?

7 Consider a cut in aggregate demand because of reduced autonomous investment. Compare the effects in the sluggish wage model of Figure 14-17 with the wage floor model. Describe in detail what you see as the important differences.

8 Discuss why wages only move sluggishly.

9 Use the aggregate supply and demand framework to show the effect of a decline in the real price of materials. Show the effects:
   (a) In the short run
   (b) In the long run

10 Suppose a policy could be found to shift the *AS* curve down.
    (a) What are the effects?
    (b) Why do you think there is great interest in such policies? [In Chapter 16 we discuss TIP (tax-based incentive programs) that are intended to shift the *AS* schedule down.]

*11 Suppose that an increase in materials prices is accompanied by a fall in the level of potential output. There is no change in monetary or fiscal policy, and so the *AD* curve does not shift.
    (a) What is the long-run effect of the disturbance on prices and output? Compare the effect with the case in the text where potential output does not fall.
    (b) Assume the upward shift of the *AS* schedule leads initially to a decline in output below the new potential output level. Then show the adjustment process by which output and prices reach the new long-run equilibrium.

*12 Why does productivity move procyclically?

*13 Determine, using Equation (11), the long-run effect of an increased real price of materials on the real wage *w/P*. What effect would an energy conservation program have?

CHAPTER 14: FOOTNOTES

[1]The theory of aggregate supply is more difficult, less settled, and more controversial than the theory of aggregate demand. The student not concerned with the more difficult points can acquire the essentials of the theory by reading Sections 14-1 through 14-4.

[2]The production function was introduced in Chap. 8.

[3]The exposition of this chapter would be little affected if we assumed that labour supply increased as the real wage increased. The major change then would be that the full-employment level of employment would depend on the level of the real wage. You might want to experiment with an upward-sloping labour supply curve as you continue reading. The quantity of labour supplied does appear to increase with the real wages because new workers, particularly women, come into the labour force as the wage increases.

[4]Here is a more technical version of the argument. The firm maximizes profits when it chooses an employment level such that $w/P = MPN(N)$. From this equation there is a level of employment that corresponds to each wage and price level, $N = N(w/P)$. Using the production function, there is a level of output for each price level, given the wage floor. The higher the price level, the more output that is supplied, up to the level $\bar{Y}$.

[5]A study suggesting that wages and employment essentially are independent over the cycle, based on data from twelve countries, is "The Employment—Real Wage Relationship: An International Study," *Journal of Political Economy*, August 1982, by P. T. Geary and J. Kennan. Geary and Kennan also discuss why different researchers have come to different conclusions. A large part of the reason is that

they measure the real wage w/P using different measures for w (for example, average hourly wage versus average hourly wage excluding overtime) and different measures for P (for example, producer price index, consumer price index, GNP deflator).

[6]The two series are drawn on different scales. The average rate of capacity utilization in 1979–1983 was only 77.3 percent; that of labour was much higher and equal to 90.9 percent. Our interest here is only in the fact that the two series move together.

[7]At the end of the chapter we refine the analysis of the output-employment link. For the moment nothing is lost by assuming there is a tight proportional relationship between output and employment.

[8]The unit labour requirement is related to the average product of labour, or *labour productivity* for short. Labour productivity is defined as the ratio of output to labour input. The more productive is labour, the smaller is the labour requirement to produce a unit of output. In fact, labour productivity is simply the ratio of output to labour use, or $1/a$. We discuss labour productivity in more detail in Section 14-8.

[9]For an introduction to the literature see A. Okun, *Prices and Quantities* (Washington, D.C.: The Brookings Institution, 1981) and R. M. Solow, "On Theories of Unemployment," *American Economic Review*, March 1980.

[10]The measured unemployment rate is never negative. We must therefore interpret the unemployment rate in (4a), as the deviation of the unemployment rate from the unemployment rate at full employment, say, 6 percent. For further discussion see Chapter 16.

[11]Indeed, we can make the relationship between wage behaviour and the cycle even clearer by noting that $(Y/\overline{Y} - 1)$ is equal to the output gap. Then we can write:

$$w = w_{-1}(1 + \epsilon \text{ gap}) \tag{5a}$$

[12]Microeconomic theories of the competitive firm show that in equilibrium price is equal to marginal cost. With constant returns marginal and average cost are equal, so that price is equal to average cost. Similar relations, with an adjustment for the degree of monopoly, apply to non-competitive firms. Thus the markup equation is fully consistent with microeconomic theory of pricing.

Note also that in (6) the real wage w/P is equal to $1/a(1 + z)$. If z is constant, this implies a constant real wage over the cycle. But if z increases with output, then the real wage is lower the higher the level of output. This is consistent with the classical model that predicts an inverse relationship between output and real wages.

[13]See footnote 8.

[14]The increase in the price of oil in the seventies both shifted up the AS curve and reduced the level of potential output because firms reduced their use of oil and could not use capital as efficiently as before. But we are assuming in Figure 14-18 that the supply shock does not affect $\overline{Y}$.

[15]The analysis is easily extended to recognize the fact that the real price of commodities is *highly* cyclical. To do so we simply write $p_m = \overline{p}_m + \gamma$ gap, where γ denotes the cyclical response of the real commodity price and $\overline{p}_m$ is the full-employment real price.

Inflation and Unemployment

In this chapter we address the problem of inflation and unemployment, extending the analysis of Chapter 14. We ask why it is apparently inevitable that inflation stabilization should bring about unemployment. This question leads us to a distinction between short-run and long-run inflation-unemployment tradeoffs. In the short run, inflation cannot be reduced without creating unemployment; in the long run, though, the inflation rate is essentially independent of the rate of unemployment.

In Section 15-4 we explore the link between inflation and money growth. We concentrate on the question of whether money is all that matters for inflation, even in the short run. We reject that view and therefore, in Section 15-5, analyse other factors that play a role in determining short-run inflation.

15-1 THE PHILLIPS CURVE AND THE AGGREGATE SUPPLY CURVE

In Chapter 14 we introduced the aggregate supply curve and the Phillips curve. The Phillips curve, made famous by A. W. Phillips as described in Box 14-1, is a relationship between the rate of change of wages and the unemployment rate. The term *Phillips curve* is now used mainly to refer to a relationship between the rate of change of *prices* (the inflation rate) and the unemployment rate. We therefore refer to the Phillips curve as the *inflation*-unemployment relation unless we specify otherwise.

In this section we first show how the inflation-unemployment Phillips curve is derived. Then we show that *the Phillips curve and the aggregate supply curve are fully consistent with each other. The Phillips curve is a form of the aggregate supply curve that is convenient for studying ongoing inflation.*

The Phillips Curve

Our derivation of the aggregate supply curve in Chapter 14 started from the relation between the rate of wage change and unemployment. We argued, as did Phillips in 1958, that wages increase more rapidly the lower the unemployment rate. When unemployment is low, firms find it difficult to obtain the labour they demand, and accordingly offer higher wages to attract workers. Thus wages rise more rapidly when unemployment is low. On the other side, when unemployment is high, jobs are difficult to find, and firms can fill any vacancies they might have without raising wages — indeed wages may even be falling as workers compete for scarce jobs.

We briefly review the link between wages, prices, and the cyclical position of the economy. This time we look at unemployment rather than the GNP gap $Y/\bar{Y}$, but the analysis is entirely the same. In Chapter 14 we formalized wage behaviour by an equation that links current wages w to past wages w_{-1}, and the deviation of unemployment from the natural rate, $u - \bar{u}$.[1]

$$w = w_{-1}[1 - \epsilon(u - \bar{u})] \tag{1}$$

We also had a relation between wages and prices, $P = aw(1 + z)$, which in combination with (1) implies a link between prices today, past prices, and unemployment.[2]

$$P = P_{-1}[1 - \epsilon(u - \bar{u})] \tag{2}$$

Equation (2) states that prices today are above or below those last period, depending on the unemployment rate. When unemployment is high, prices are falling; when unemployment is low (relative to the natural rate), prices are rising.

In the last chapter we were interested in the level of prices and looked at the determination of output and prices over the adjustment period. In this chapter we examine the adjustment path further, looking at inflation, or a process of ongoing price increases. We can analyse inflation here because Equation (2) describes the inflation rate. Remember that the inflation rate is defined as the percentage increase in prices from one period to the next. With that definition in mind we can write

$$\text{Inflation rate} \equiv P/P_{-1} - 1 = gp \tag{3}$$

where gp is the growth rate of prices, or inflation. To fix ideas about calculating the inflation rate, suppose this period the price level index is 107 and last period it was 101. Then the inflation rate, using (3) is $gp = 5.9$ percent $[= (107 - 101)/(101) \times 100 \text{ percent}]$.

It is immediately clear from (2) and (3) that we already have a model of inflation. Dividing (2) by P_{-1} and subtracting 1 from both sides yields

$$gp = P/P_{-1} - 1 = -\epsilon(u - \bar{u}) \qquad (2a)$$

This model of inflation, $gp = -\epsilon(u - \bar{u})$, states that there is inflation when unemployment is below the natural rate, and there is deflation (falling prices) when unemployment exceeds the natural rate. Equation (2a) is the Phillips curve, and it is shown in Figure 15-2.

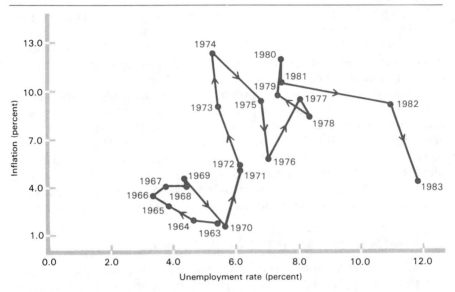

Note: Inflation is the rate of change over the year of the Consumer Price Index.

FIGURE 15-1   INFLATION AND UNEMPLOYMENT
(*Source*: Statistics Canada, 11-003, 11-206, 11-505, 71-201)

Properties of the Phillips Curve

Figure 15-2 shows the relation between the rate of inflation and the rate of unemployment as the schedule labelled *PC*. The Phillips curve has three properties that we want to draw out. First, the schedule is negatively sloped. When the slope is negative, lower unemployment rates imply higher inflation rates. This negative slope leads to the notion of a tradeoff: to have lower inflation we have to accept an increase in unemployment. This notion of a tradeoff occupies us in much of the chapter.

The second point concerns the intercept on the horizontal axis. The Phillips curve shows that at the natural rate of unemployment, $\bar{u}$, inflation is zero. At higher unemployment rates, prices are falling, or there is deflation. At lower unemployment rates, prices are rising, or there is inflation; the higher inflation, the lower is unemployment.

Finally, the schedule shows how responsive inflation is to the unemployment rate. A very flat Phillips curve implies that a given change in unemployment leads to only a small change in inflation. By contrast, a very steep Phillips curve implies that small unemployment changes have a major impact on the inflation rate.

The slope of the Phillips curve corresponds to the coefficient ϵ in (1) and (2a), which we remember as the parameter that tells us how responsive wages, and hence prices, are to unemployment. Highly sensitive wages imply a very steep Phillips curve; highly sluggish wages imply a very flat Phillips curve.

This is a good point to see the link between the aggregate supply schedule of Chapter 14 and the Phillips curve. In Chapter 14 a very flat aggregate supply curve meant that changes in aggregate demand have a big effect on output and little short-run effect on prices. Exactly the same can be said here in terms of the Phillips curve. If wages are highly sticky, so that the aggregate supply schedule is very flat, then the Phillips curve, too, is very flat. They are simply alternative ways of stating the link between wages and prices over time and the cyclical position of the economy.

Adjustment to a Fall in the Money Stock

We now use an example to show the precise link between the aggregate demand and supply analysis and the Phillips curve analysis of this chapter. We take the example of a reduction in the nominal money stock. The economy is initially in equilibrium with full employment and unchanging prices. Now the central bank reduces the nominal money stock through an open market operation. The impact effect, as we know from Chapter 14, is to reduce both prices and output.[3] In the short run, wages and hence prices are sluggish, and thus a recession results.

In Figure 15-3 we show the impact effect of the reduction in the nominal money stock which moves the economy from zero inflation at the natural rate to point A. At point A there is now excess unemployment, and therefore wages and prices are falling. Next we have to ask how the falling prices help restore full-employment equilibrium. This is easy to see.

The nominal money stock remains constant. Therefore falling prices imply that the *real* money stock moves back up over time. This, in turn, means interest rates are falling and aggregate demand is rising. Rising aggregate demand leads to rising output and employment, or to falling unemployment. Thus over time the economy moves from A toward the full-employment equilibrium. Prices will continue falling until they have declined enough to restore the *real* money stock to the initial level. At that

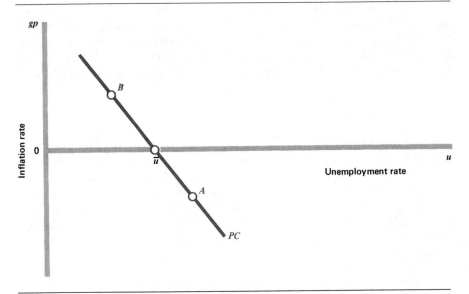

FIGURE 15-2   THE PHILLIPS CURVE. The Phillips curve is a negative relationship between the inflation rate and the unemployment rate. The Phillips curve *PC* shows a zero rate of inflation when unemployment is at the full-employment, or natural, rate $\bar{u}$. At higher unemployment rates, such as at point *A*, the inflation rate is negative. At lower unemployment rates, for example at point *B*, the inflation rate is positive. The slope of *PC* is equal to $-\epsilon$, which is the sensitivity of the rate of wage change to unemployment.

point interest rates, spending, output, and employment all have returned to the initial level, and the economy is back at $\bar{u}$. Thus movements along the Phillips curve represent the same adjustment process that we saw before in terms of the *AS* and *AD* schedules. Of course, without understanding the details of the earlier analysis we could not understand the present argument.

To round out the analysis we can also talk about the speed with which the economy returns to full employment. This depends simply on the slope of the Phillips curve. If wage changes and inflation are highly unresponsive to unemployment (a very flat Phillips curve), then the adjustment takes a long time, because prices are slow to fall and therefore have to fall for a long time. Conversely, if wage and price changes are extremely sensitive (a very steep Phillips curve), adjustment will be very rapid.

We can develop the same kind of analysis, using a diagram like Figure 15-3, to study the adjustment process, for example, to a fiscal expansion. Initially the expansion leads to a rise in employment, or a fall in unemployment, to a point on the Phillips curve to the left of the natural rate $\bar{u}$. There is now inflation. Given the nominal money stock, *real* balances will be falling, interest rates will be increasing, and thus crowding out takes place. As demand and employment decline, unemployment rises back up to the natural rate. The speed of adjustment of the process depends once again on the sensitivity of wages to unemployment, that is, on the slope of the Phillips curve.

The Phillips Curve as a Tradeoff

The adjustment process to monetary or real disturbances has been described in terms of movements along the Phillips curve, but we can also think of the Phillips curve as showing a tradeoff between inflation and unemployment. Policy makers, with this view, could pick monetary and fiscal policies to put the economy on a particular point on the Phillips curve, *and keep it there*. This tradeoff view of the Phillips curve was in the mind of policy makers in the early 1960s, and we now discuss why it had to be totally revised.

15-2   EXPECTATIONS AND SHORT-RUN PHILLIPS CURVES

After the appearance of Phillip's article in 1958, it was widely assumed that a Phillips curve such as *PC* in Figure 15-2 presented policy makers with a menu of inflation and unemployment rates from which to choose. Policy makers could choose a low unemployment – high inflation combination, such as point *B*, or if they preferred, they could be at a point such as *A*, with low inflation but high unemployment. Their choice between points such as *A* and *B* would depend on their estimates of the costs of inflation and unemployment.

Inflation and unemployment rates for the Canadian economy are shown in Figure 15-1. The observations for 1963 to 1964 display a Phillips curve tradeoff with the shape of the original Phillips curve of Box 14-1. Over that period, policy makers seemed to be choosing to trade off higher inflation for lower unemployment. However, the relationship that held in the 1960s clearly does not describe subsequent experience.

The Friedman-Phelps Argument

In 1967 and 1968, Edmund Phelps, of Columbia University, and Milton Friedman independently argued that a Phillips curve such as *PC* in Figure 15-2 did *not* represent a stable long-run relationship that could be used by policy makers. They predicted that a Phillips curve such as *PC* would *shift* upward if policy makers tried to keep the unemployment rate below the natural rate, and would shift downward if the unemployment rate were above the natural rate.

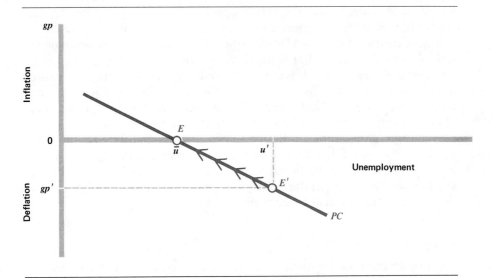

FIGURE 15-3   THE ADJUSTMENT TO A FALL IN THE NOMINAL MONEY STOCK.
A reduction in the nominal money stock leads immediately to a recession because
wages and prices are not fully flexible. The economy moves from E to a position
like point E' where we have unemployment and falling wages and prices. The
unemployment rate is u' and the rate of deflation is gp'. Over time, deflation or
falling prices raises the *real* money stock and therefore lowers interest rates,
increasing spending and employment. Through that adjustment process the
economy moves with falling unemployment from E' back to E. The process is
complete when prices have fallen far enough to restore the initial stock of real
balances and hence spending and employment.

Their argument started from the same point as that of Phillips, by discussing the adjustment of wages. Phillips, we recall, assumed that nominal wages rise more rapidly when the unemployment rate is low and less
rapidly when the unemployment rate is high. However, argued Friedman
and Phelps, neither workers nor firms are concerned with *nominal* wages.
Rather, both workers, in supplying labour, and firms, in demanding labour,
are concerned with the *real* wages they will be receiving and paying,
respectively.

When firms and workers bargain over the nominal wages to be paid for
the next several years, they take into account the inflation they expect
during that period. For instance, suppose both firms and workers expect
prices to be rising at 10 percent per year over the next 3 years. In fixing the
nominal wage rates to be paid during those years, they adjust for the
inflation they expect. With prices rising at 10 percent, wages are settled
now to rise at 10 percent too in order to keep the *real* wage constant.

Accordingly, argued Friedman and Phelps, the rate of wage change
should reflect two factors: (1) As in the regular Phillips curve, the lower

the unemployment rate, the more rapidly nominal wages rise. (2) The higher the expected inflation, the more rapidly nominal wages rise.

It is, of course, the second factor — the effects of expected inflation on the rate of wage change — that is the novel element in the Friedman-Phelps analysis of wage setting. It is clear why workers want wages to rise more rapidly when inflation is expected. Higher prices will reduce their real wages unless the nominal wage increases along with inflation. But what about the other side of the deal? Why do firms agree to raise wages more rapidly when they expect inflation? The reason is that they can afford to pay higher wages if the price of their output is rising. Indeed, when wages and prices are rising at the same rate, the real wage is constant. Both workers and firms are in the same position as they would be if there were no inflation and the real wage were constant.

Expected Inflation and the Phillips Curve

We modify the Phillips curve to include expected inflation by writing:

$$gp = gpe - \epsilon(u - \bar{u}) \tag{4}$$

In Equation (4), *gpe* is the expected rate of inflation. Equation (4) is known as the *expectations-augmented Phillips curve*, meaning simply that it is the standard Phillips curve with expectations of inflation added.

According to the expectations-augmented Phillips curve, if unemployment is above the natural rate, inflation is below the expected rate, and vice versa. Or to put the argument the other way around, the only way the unemployment rate can be reduced below the natural rate is by causing more inflation than was expected.

The link between the Friedman-Phelps arguments about wage behaviour and the Phillips curve equation (4) is again markup pricing. With unemployment at the natural rate, wages are rising at the expected rate of inflation. Prices, in turn, are based on wages, and are rising at the same rate as wages — equal to the expected rate of inflation. Thus with unemployment at the natural rate, prices are rising at the rate at which they were expected to rise. Similar arguments explain why prices rise more rapidly than expected when the unemployment rate is below the natural rate, and more slowly than expected when unemployment is above the natural rate.

Short-Run Phillips Curves

In Figure 15-4 we show how the inclusion of expectations of inflation affects the Phillips curve. On *PC"*, the expected inflation rate is 8 percent. We can tell that by the fact that when *u* is equal to *ū*, the natural rate, the inflation rate on *PC"* is equal to 8 percent (point *A*). On the Phillips curve *PC'*, the expected inflation rate is 3 percent. And on the Phillips curve *PC*, the expected inflation rate is zero.

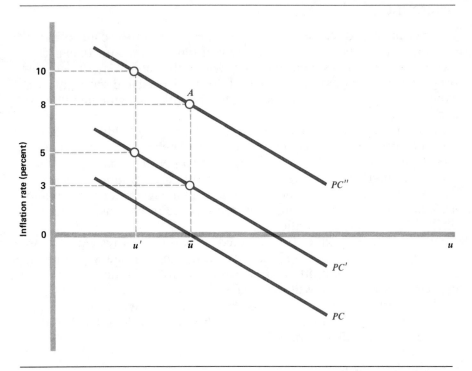

FIGURE 15-4   SHORT-RUN PHILLIPS CURVES. There is a short-run Phillips curve corresponding to each expected rate of inflation. For instance, on *PC"*, the expected rate of inflation is 8 percent. On *PC'* the expected inflation rate is only 3 percent, whereas on *PC* it is zero. If unemployment is at the natural rate, inflation is only 3 percent on *PC'*, but 8 percent on *PC"*. If the unemployment rate were lower, at *u'*, the inflation rate would be 5 percent on *PC'* but 10 percent on *PC"*.

Each of the three Phillips curves in Figure 15-4 is a *short-run Phillips curve*. The short-run Phillips curve shows the relationship between the inflation and unemployment rates when the expected inflation rate is held constant.

The slope of the short-run Phillips curve represents the short-run tradeoff that can be made between inflation and unemployment. In the short run, by which we mean the length of time it takes for expectations to adjust to inflation, the economy moves along a given short-run Phillips curve, such as *PC"*. On such a curve, the only way to reduce inflation is to have more unemployment.

The short-run Phillips curves in Figure 15-4 are quite flat. This reflects the evidence that in the short run of a few years, it typically takes a large amount of extra unemployment to produce just a small reduction in inflation. In Section 15-3, we examine the long-run tradeoff between inflation and unemployment.

Determinants of Expectations

We have already discussed the role of expectations in the context of the consumption function, where permanent income is a measure of expected income, and the investment function, where the rate of investment depends on expectations of future output. Now we need to discuss inflation expectations because of their role in the expectations-augmented Phillips curve.

How do people form expectations of inflation? Probably most of the time they base their expectations on the recent behaviour of the inflation rate. If the inflation rate has been around 10 percent for a while, then people are quite likely to believe it will continue at around 10 percent. Accordingly, economists frequently assume that expectations of inflation are equal to an average of inflation rates in the recent past. In normal times this is a good assumption.

But we cannot assume that expected inflation is always equal to an average of recent rates of inflation. For instance, if a new government comes to power committed to pursuing highly inflationary policies, expectations of inflation will rise because people expect economic policies to change. In this case the expected rate of inflation will change on the basis of expectations about economic policy, even if there has been no change in actual inflation rates.

Rational Expectations

The *rational expectations* hypothesis is the assumption that people base their expectations of inflation (or any other economic variable) on all the information available about the future behaviour of that variable.

The rational expectations approach to macroeconomics, associated primarily with the names of Robert Lucas of the University of Chicago and Thomas Sargent of Minnesota, was extremely influential in the 1970s. As we shall see in Chapter 17, the approach developed by Lucas, Sargent, and others involves much more than merely a theory of expectations. For now, though, we concentrate on the expectations part of the theory.

The rational expectations hypothesis implies that people do not make *systematic* mistakes in forming their expectations. Systematic mistakes — for instance, always underpredicting inflation — are easily spotted. According to the rational expectations hypothesis, people correct such mistakes and change the way they form expectations accordingly. On average, according to the rational expectations hypothesis, expectations are correct, because people understand the environment in which they work. People, of course, make mistakes from time to time, but they do not make *systematic* mistakes.

According to the rational expectations hypothesis, any policy that relies on people failing to understand what is happening in the economy is bound to fail eventually.

Perhaps policy makers can fool people once, by doing something un-expected. But policy makers cannot repeatedly fool people by doing the same thing. In the context of the expectations-augmented Phillips curve, this means that any policy that relies for its effects on systematic differ-ences between the actual and the expected inflation rates will not work very long.

Expectations and Contracts

The expectations that underlie the position of the short-run Phillips curve are not just the expectations that people have today about the inflation rate for the next year. Rather, expected rates of change of prices of the past few years are embodied in all the contracts, formal and informal, entered into in the past and in existence now. For instance, 3-year labour contracts specify wages to be paid over the next 3 years. Typically such contracts build in an increase in the wages to be paid each year. The increase in the wage rate year to year would have been 4 to 5 percent in the late fifties, but 9 to 10 percent in the late seventies. The difference results from the higher inflation expected in the seventies.

Thus the expected inflation rate term *gpe* in the expectations-augmented Phillips curve equation (4) has to be interpreted carefully. It represents expectations of inflation, *current and past*, that are present in existing con-tracts and affect today's economy. Shifts in the expected inflation rate *gpe* shift the short-run Phillips curve. However, there is inertia in wages and the curve does not shift quickly.

The Shifting Short-Run Phillips Curve

Friedman and Phelps argued that the Phillips curve would shift over time during the 1960s, when the experience seen in Figure 15-1 seemed to confirm that there was a stable Phillips curve. However, subsequent events provided strong support for the Friedman-Phelps view. There are periods of rising inflation combined with rising unemployment, and then from 1981 to 1983 a period that once again is similar to the 1960s' tradeoff, except that this time the tradeoff is taking place at a much higher rate of inflation.

What happened? As predicted by Friedman and Phelps, the short-run Phillips curve shifted. In the early 1960s, after a long period of low inflation, the expected inflation rate cannot have been more than 3 percent. Ac-cordingly, in the early 1960s the economy was on a short-run Phillips curve such as *PC'* in Figure 15-4, with expected inflation rate equal to 3 percent. By the mid-1970s, after a decade of rising inflation, the expected inflation rate was closer to 8 percent. At that stage the economy was on a short-run Phillips curve such as *PC"* in Figure 15-4, with an expected inflation rate of 8 percent. Between the early 1960s and the late 1970s, the short-run

Phillips curve shifted up as expectations of inflation changed and became embodied in the structure of contracts in the economy.

The shifts of the short-run Phillips curve meant that there was a higher inflation rate corresponding to a given rate of unemployment in the 1970s than in the early 1960s. For instance, with the unemployment rate at u', below the natural rate $\bar{u}$, the inflation rate in the late 1970s would have been 10 percent but in the early 1960s would have been only 5 percent. That is why the inflation rate corresponding to any given unemployment rate in the late seventies was higher than the inflation rate corresponding to the same unemployment rate in the early sixties.[4]

The conclusion of this section is the most important lesson economists and economic policy makers learned in the last 20 years. *The short-run Phillips curve shifts with the expected rate of inflation. The inflation rate corresponding to any given unemployment rate therefore changes over time as the expected inflation rate changes. The higher the expected inflation rate, the higher the inflation rate corresponding to a given unemployment rate.* This explains why we can have both higher inflation and more unemployment.

15-3 THE LONG-RUN PHILLIPS CURVE

Suppose that the expected inflation rate is initially 3 percent, as in the late fifties and early sixties. Then expansionary monetary and fiscal policies push the inflation rate up over the next 15 years to an average of 8 percent. The expected inflation rate too will be 8 percent after the actual inflation rate has been at that level for several years.

Thus after a period of years, the expected inflation rate will catch up to the actual inflation rate. *In the long run, the actual and expected inflation rates are equal.* Accordingly, we define the *long-run Phillips curve* as follows: The long-run Phillips curve describes the tradeoff, if any, between inflation and unemployment when the actual and expected inflation rates are equal. In working with this definition of the long-run Phillips curve, recall that the expectations embodied in the Phillips curve are expectations about inflation, current and past, that affect contracts currently in force in the economy.

What does the long-run Phillips curve look like? We can find that out using Equation (4), the expectations-augmented Phillips curve.

$$gp = gpe - \epsilon(u - \bar{u}) \tag{4}$$

In the long run, the actual and expected inflation rates are equal, and so $gp = gpe$. Thus in the long run

$$0 = -\epsilon(u - \bar{u})$$

or
$$u = \bar{u} \tag{5}$$

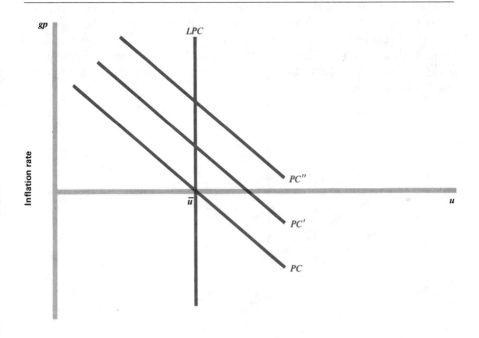

FIGURE 15-5   SHORT- AND LONG-RUN PHILLIPS CURVES. In the short run the economy moves along one of the short-run Phillips curves, such as *PC'*. The expected rate of inflation is constant on each of the short-run curves. In the long run, though, the expected rate of inflation is equal to the actual rate, and unemployment is the natural rate $\bar{u}$. In the long run the economy moves along *LPC*, with no tradedoff between inflation and unemployment.

Equation (5) implies that *in the long run, the actual unemployment rate is equal to the natural rate, whatever the rate of inflation.* In other words, *in the long run, there is no tradeoff between inflation and unemployment.* When expected inflation is equal to actual inflation, the unemployment rate is equal to the natural rate of unemployment.

Figure 15-5 shows the relationship between the short- and long-run Phillips curves. In the short run of a year or less, the economy moves along a short-run Phillips curve, such as *PC'*, with a given expected inflation rate. In the long run, though, expectations catch up to the actual inflation rate, and the economy will be at a point at which the actual and expected inflation rate are equal. That happens only along the vertical line *LPC*, the long-run Phillips curve.

Adjusting to a Higher Inflation Rate

Our understanding of the long-run Phillips curve is increased by asking how the economy moves over time from one long-run inflation rate to another. In Figure 15-6 the economy is initially at point E, with unemployment at the natural rate $\bar{u}$ and an inflation rate of 3 percent. Now monetary and fiscal policies become expansionary, moving the economy to a point such as E' on the short-run Phillips curve PC'. Because PC' is quite flat, there is only a small increase in the inflation rate and a substantial decline in the unemployment rate, to u'.

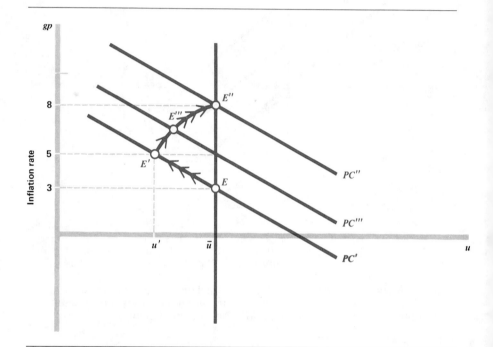

FIGURE 15-6   ADJUSTING TO HIGHER LONG-RUN INFLATION. The economy is initially at point E, with 3 percent inflation and unemployment at the natural rate $\bar{u}$. Expansionary monetary and fiscal policies move the economy in the short run to point E', on the short-run Phillips curve PC'. The unemployment rate drops to u', and the inflation rate increases to 5 percent. As a result of the higher inflation, expectations of inflation increase, shifting the short-run Phillips curve to PC'''. From E' the economy moves to E''', with higher inflation and more unemployment. Gradually, as expectations of inflation adjust, the short-run Phillips curve keeps shifting, and the economy moves to point E'', which is on both PC'' and LPC. The economy is back in equilibrium with a higher inflation rate and the same unemployment rate at which it started, $\bar{u}$. The adjustment process is shown by the arrows.

But now expectations of inflation begin to adjust. Wage increases in existing contracts were based on the assumption that the inflation rate would be 3 percent. But it is actually 5 percent. Workers adjust their expectations of inflation, say, to 5 percent, and that rate of wage increase is built into labour contracts.

The short-run Phillips curve moves up to a position such as *PC'''*. The expected inflation rate is 5 percent, and wages rise at a rate reflecting the higher expected inflation. The expansionary monetary and fiscal policies now show up more in higher inflation and less in lower unemployment, as the economy moves to a position such as *E'''*.

Once again expectations of inflation adjust, they become embodied in wages, and the short-run Phillips curve shifts up. We do not show how the short-run Phillips curve shifts from *PC'''*, to avoid cluttering the diagram. Eventually, though, expected and actual inflation are equal, and the economy is on both *PC''* and *LPC* at point *E''*. The path the economy takes to *E''* is shown by the arrows in Figure 15-6.

Eventually, then, expansionary aggregate demand policies produce a higher inflation rate and no reduction in the unemployment rate. But in the process of adjusting to the new inflation rate, there is a period in which output is higher than normal and unemployment is below the natural rate.

Stagflation

Note that as the economy moves from *E* to *E''*, we first see the inflation rate rising as the unemployment rate falls. Then, as expectations adjust to the higher inflation, the inflation rate and the unemployment rate increase together. That is, in the adjustment process of the economy to a higher inflation rate, there will be a period in which the inflation rate and the unemployment rate increase together.

A period of rising inflation together with rising unemployment is known as *stagflation*. Examining Figure 15-1, we see stagflationary episodes in 1970–1972 and 1976–1977. It is often believed that the Phillips curve implies that inflation and unemployment cannot increase together. That is not necessarily true, so long as we realize that the short-run Phillips curve can shift, and that in periods in which the short-run Phillips curve is shifting, the inflation rate and unemployment rate might well be moving in the same direction.

Anti-Inflationary Policies

The description in this section of how the economy moves from a lower to a higher inflation rate applies to the increasing inflation experienced by both Canada and the United States from the early sixties to the late seventies. A very similar analysis, moving in the opposite direction, applies when an attempt is made to reduce the inflation rate through tight monetary policy. In that case the restrictive policies first produce a sharp rise in the unemployment rate with little reduction in inflation. Later the inflation rate begins to fall, and eventually the economy starts moving back to full employment, with a lower rate of inflation. This was the story in both countries from 1979 to 1983.[5]

Is the Long-Run Phillips Curve Really Vertical?

The view that the long-run Phillips curve is vertical was initially controversial. Some economists argued that there was a long-run Phillips curve, steeper than the short-run curves, but not necessarily vertical. Curve *LPC'* in Figure 15-7 is an example. Part of the controversy arose because a curve such as *LPC* appears to suggest that *nothing* can be done about long-run unemployment, which will settle down to the rate $\bar{u}$ whatever aggregate demand policies are followed. *LPC'* does give a long-run tradeoff, leaving room for expansionary aggregate demand policies.

However, whether the long-run Phillips curve is vertical or negatively sloped, it may be possible to reduce the natural rate $\bar{u}$ through policies designed to make the labour market more efficient. Such policies would include, for instance, setting up job banks designed to improve the information available to both workers and employers about jobs and the workers available to fill them. Retraining programs for workers whose industries are in decline would be another example. In terms of Figure 15-7, these policies would shift the *LPC* curve to the left. They would also shift *LPC'* to the left, implying a lower rate of inflation at any given unemployment rate. Indeed, the idea of shifting the Phillips curve was discussed long before the issue of long-run vertical versus downward-sloping curves arose.

While there is now considerable agreement on a long-run vertical Phillips curve, that agreement is not unanimous.[6] Nor, for that matter, do we feel completely confident that the Phillips curve is vertical at *all* rates of inflation. We would not be surprised if the long-run Phillips curve has a shape such as that of *LPC"* in Figure 15-7. At positive rates of inflation (which are essentially what we have experienced since 1945), the curve is, for all practical purposes, vertical. At negative rates of inflation, it may well be virtually horizontal.

The basis for the long-run Phillips curve *LPC"* is the suggestion that money wage behaviour is asymmetrical. Wages rise in the face of excess demand for labour, or expected inflation, but do not fall at the same rate in the face of even heavy unemployment or expected deflation. There is some evidence for that view, and if it is correct, the long-run Phillips curve might well be kinked, like *LPC"*.

But even if *LPC"* did describe long-run tradeoffs, it offers little hope for manipulating the unemployment rate in the long run through changes in the inflation rate. Even on *LPC"*, any attempts to reduce the unemployment rate through expansionary aggregate demand policies soon produce inflation, rather than any further reductions in unemployment. The experi-

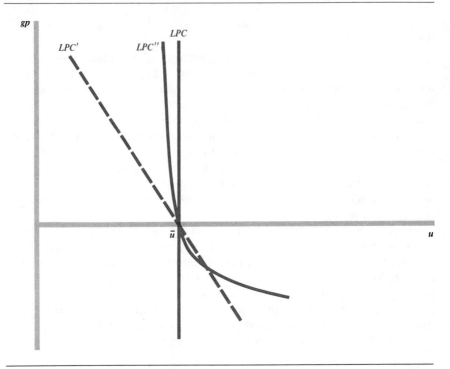

FIGURE 15-7   LONG-RUN PHILLIPS CURVES. *LPC* is the vertical long-run Phillips curve discussed earlier. In the sixties and early seventies some economists believed there was a long-run tradeoff between inflation and unemployment, as on *LPC'*, which is steeper than the short-run Phillips curves in earlier figures. This view is no longer widely held. A third possibility is that the long-run Phillips curve is practically vertical at positive rates of inflation, but quite flat at negative inflation rates, as on *LPC''*. This would be a result of downward wage stickiness. Because our experience since World War II is limited to positive rates of inflation, it is difficult to choose between *LPC* and *LPC''* on the basis of recent evidence.

ence of the last 20 years in Canada and elsewhere suggests two basic Phillips curve lessons: (1) In the short run, aggregate demand policies can reduce the unemployment rate, (2) but such policies cannot produce sustained reductions in the unemployment rate. For all practical purposes, the long-run Phillips curve is vertical.

15-4   MONEY AND INFLATION IN THE LONG RUN

In the previous section we discussed how the economy moves from a low to a higher inflation rate, from point *E* to *E''* in Figure 15-6. We suggested that expansionary aggregate demand policies would produce such a shift, but did not say precisely what sort of policies could produce an increase in the inflation rate in the long run.

It is often asserted, particularly by monetarists, that inflation is a monetary phenomenon. The claim that inflation is a monetary phenomenon means that sustained high rates of money growth produce high inflation, and that low rates of money growth will eventually produce low rates of inflation. Further, the statement that inflation is a monetary phenomenon means that high rates of inflation cannot long continue without high rates of money growth. The view that inflation is a monetary phenomenon is the implication of the quantity theory of money (described in Chapter 10), which is the backbone of monetarist macroeconomics. In this section we analyse the sense in which inflation is a monetary phenomenon, concentrating on long-run inflation.

Figure 15-8 presents evidence from Canada over the period since 1961, showing that the inflation rate and the growth rate of money have more or less moved together. Although the relationship is clearly positive, it is also obvious that the link between money growth and inflation is not precise. We examine the reasons the link is not precise in the next section.

The reason to expect a link between inflation and money growth derives from the fact that the demand for money is a demand for *real balances*. We write the demand function for real balances as

$$\frac{M}{P} = L(i, Y) \tag{6}$$

The demand function for real balances states that the demand depends on the nominal interest rate, i, and on real GNP, Y.

The long run is defined as the period in which the actual and the expected inflation rates are equal. In the long run, unemployment is at the natural rate $\bar{u}$, and thus output is at the full-employment level $\bar{Y}$. (For the moment assume that there is no growth in potential output, and so $\bar{Y}$ is constant over time.) Further, in the long run, when the economy is in equilibrium, the nominal interest rate is at some long-run equilibrium level, say, i^*. Thus in long-run equilibrium, both i and Y are at their constant equilibrium levels, i^* and $\bar{Y}$, respectively. Accordingly, *in long-run equilibrium in an economy in which potential output is constant, real balances are constant.*

When real balances are constant, the ratio M/P is constant. That means the nominal money stock M and the price level P are growing at the same rate. For instance, if the money stock is growing at 8 percent so are prices. Thus we conclude that *in the long-run equilibrium (with output constant), the inflation rate is equal to the growth rate of money (gm).* We write this long-run relationship as

$$gp = gm \tag{7}$$

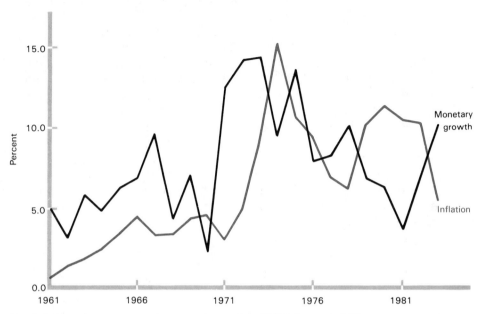

Note: Inflation and monetary growth are annual rates of the GNE deflator and of *M*1.

FIGURE 15-8   INFLATION AND MONETARY GROWTH
(*Source: Bank of Canada Review*)

The basic argument that in the long run inflation is a monetary pheno-menon thus comes from the recognition that in long-run equilibrium, real money demand and hence real balances will be constant if potential out-put is not growing. But there are several qualifications to the strong state-ment of Equation (7).

Output Growth and Inflation in the Long Run

Suppose that output, instead of being constant, grows in the long run at the growth rate of potential output, *gy**. In Canada *gy** has been about 4 percent. Some money growth is needed just to meet the increasing de-mand for real balances arising from growing income. Accordingly, the money growth rate will exceed the inflation rate in the long run.

The difference between money growth and inflation arises from the amount of money growth needed to meet the demand increases resulting from steadily rising income. How much money growth is that? Suppose the income elasticity of money demand is 0.7. Then for every 1 percent that income rises, the demand for real balances rises 0.7 percent. The

4 percent growth in potential output thus increases the demand for real balances by 2.8 percent a year.

If real money demand is rising, say at the rate of 2.8 percent per year, as a result of income growth, then monetary equilibrium requires that the real money supply increase at the same rate. The growth rate of the real money stock is just the difference between the growth rate of the nominal money stock and the rate of inflation. For instance, if the nominal money stock is increasing at 10 percent and the rate of inflation is 7.9 percent, the real money stock is increasing at 2.1 percent per year.

If the real money supply has to be growing at 2.8 percent per year to maintain monetary equilibrium, then the rate of inflation has to be 2.8 percent less than the rate of money growth, or, in symbols, $gp = gm - 2.8$.

More generally, with gy^* as the growth rate of potential output and η as the income elasticity of the demand for real balances, the relationship among the inflation rate, the growth rate of money, and the growth rate of output is

$$gp = gm - \eta gy^* \tag{8}$$

Changes in Velocity and Inflation

Table 15-1 shows the inflation rate, the growth rate of $M1$, and the growth rate of real GNP for six countries over the period 1953–1982. According to Equation (8), we should find that

$$gp - (gm - \eta gy) = 0 \tag{8a}$$

In column (4) of Table 15-1 we calculate $gp - (gm - gy)$, an amount which should be zero if the income elasticity of money demand is unity. Column (5) shows a similar calculation, assuming the income elasticity of money demand is 0.7.

The inflation experienced by Canada comes close to matching that predicted by Equation (8a). However, in the United Kingdom and the United States, inflation has been, on average, faster than predicted using Equation (8a). In Italy, and, depending on the correct income elasticity, perhaps Japan and Germany, inflation has been, on average, slower than predicted by Equation (8a).

The deviations of the inflation rate from the quantity theory predictions in Table 15-1 are a result of shifts in the demand for money over the last 30 years. In particular, the downward shifts of the demand function for $M1$ in the United States have reduced the amount of real balances individuals want to hold. If M/P demand falls, then P will rise, in the adjustment process, faster than M. That is why the inflation rate has exceeded the rate we would predict from knowledge of the growth rate of $M1$ and the growth rate of income.

TABLE 15-1   MONEY GROWTH AND INFLATION, 1953–1982

Country	(1) Inflation rate (CPI), gp	(2) Growth rate of M1, gm	(3) Growth rate of real GNP (or GDP), gy	(4) $gp - (gm - gy)$	(5) $gp - (gm - 0.7gy)$
Canada	4.8	7.7	4.0	1.1	−0.1
Germany	3.4	8.6	4.5	−0.7	−2.1
Italy	7.7	14.3	4.5	−2.1	−3.4
Japan	5.8	13.7	7.7	−0.2	−2.5
United Kingdom	7.3	6.9	2.3	2.7	2.0
United States	4.5	4.5	3.0	3.0	2.1

Source: International Financial Statistics.

Is Inflation a Monetary Phenomenon in the Long Run?

The answer to the question whether inflation is a monetary phenomenon in the long run is yes. No major inflation can take place without rapid money growth, and rapid money growth will cause rapid inflation. Further, any policy that determinedly keeps the growth rate of money low will lead eventually to a low rate of inflation.

But at the same time the long-run link between money growth and inflation is not precise, as the data of Table 15-1 show. There are two reasons for that. First, increases in output increase the demand for real balances and reduce the inflation rate corresponding to a given rate of money growth. And second, financial institutions change, the definition of money changes, and the demand for money may shift over time.

Having now recognized the special role of money growth in setting long-run inflation trends, we turn to the other factors mentioned in the above quote that can, *in the short run*, also influence the inflation rate.

15-5   OTHER CAUSES OF INFLATION

Figure 15-9 shows two short-run Phillips curves, *PC'* and *PC''*. We have already seen that expansionary monetary policy can move the economy from one Phillips curve to another. When the growth rate of money first increases, the economy moves from *E* to a position such as *E'*, moving along a short-run Phillips curve. But then, provided the money growth continues, expectations and contracts adjust, and the short-run Phillips curve moves up to *PC"*. If the new higher rate of money growth is maintained, the economy will end up with a higher inflation rate back at the natural rate of unemployment.

Increased money growth thus causes more inflation in both the short and the long run. But money growth is not the only source of inflation in the short run. In this section we briefly review three other potential sources of inflation in the short run: (1) expansionary fiscal policy, (2) supply shocks, and (3) wage disturbances. None of these can produce inflation *in the long run* unless money growth also increases. But here we are concentrating on the short run, not the long run.

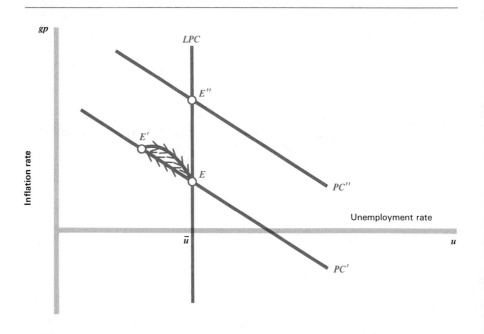

FIGURE 15-9   ADJUSTMENT TO A PERMANENT INCREASE IN GOVERNMENT SPENDING. A permanent increase in government spending shifts the economy in the short run along *PC'*, to point *E'*. Thus the initial impact of the fiscal expansion is to increase inflation and reduce unemployment. If expectations of inflation increase, the *PC'* curve may shift up (not shown). But eventually the economy returns to point *E* on *LPC*. This is because the fiscal expansion took place without any change in the growth rate of money — and in the long run the economy therefore has to come back to the same inflation rate from which it started. Curve *PC"* is included in the diagram to remind us of the contrast between the long-run effects of fiscal and monetary expansion on the inflation rate. (Figure 15-6 shows the long-run effects of an increase in the growth rate of money.)

Expansionary Fiscal Policy

Suppose there is an increase in government spending to a new higher level. In the short run, with wages and prices quite sticky, the increase in aggregate demand increases real output and reduces unemployment. The economy moves along a short-run Phillips curve such as PC' in Figure 15-9, to a position such as E'.

If people believe the increase in inflation caused by the expansionary fiscal policy is merely temporary, expectations will not adjust, and the economy will move back down the PC' curve. The adjustment after the initial expansion will involve a falling inflation rate and an unemployment rate that is still below the natural rate, but rising. Eventually the economy returns to the original inflation rate and the natural rate of unemployment.

However, people might believe that the new fiscal policy will have prolonged inflationary effects. In that case, because of inflationary expectations, the short-run Phillips curve will shift up after the move to point E'. From E' the inflation rate will increase while unemployment rises. But eventually the inflation rate will fall back to its original level as the economy moves back to the natural rate of unemployment. The arrows in Figure 15-9 show the adjustment path of the economy to the increase in government spending.

The inflation rate initially rises with the increase in government spending, but eventually the inflationary effect of the increase in government spending disappears. But the adjustment process takes a long time. Thus our analysis shows that a *permanent* increase in government spending has only *transitory* real expansionary and inflationary effects.

TABLE 15-2   THE EFFECTS OF INCREASED MONEY GROWTH AND PERMANENT FISCAL EXPANSIONS

	Inflation		Output	
	Short run	Long run	Short run	Long run
Increased money growth	+	+	+	0
Fiscal expansion	+	0	+	0

Table 15-2 summarizes the short- and long-run effects both of changes in the growth rate of money and of a fiscal expansion on output and on inflation. It serves to review the results we have derived so far. Note that the effects on unemployment are just the opposite of those on output.

Table 15-2 shows that neither increased money growth nor fiscal expansion can, in the long run, sustain output above full employment or reduce unemployment permanently below the natural rate. The table also shows that increased money growth permanently increases inflation, while fiscal expansion only transitorily raises inflation until the real money stock has declined enough to lead to full crowding out. In Chapters 17 and 18 we return to a discussion of the long-run effects of fiscal policy in the context of long-run supply-side issues.

Supply Shocks

In Figure 15-10 we examine the effects of a supply shock. Suppose the price of oil rises. An increase in a key material price, such as that of oil, takes time to be built into the prices charged by all the firms in the economy.

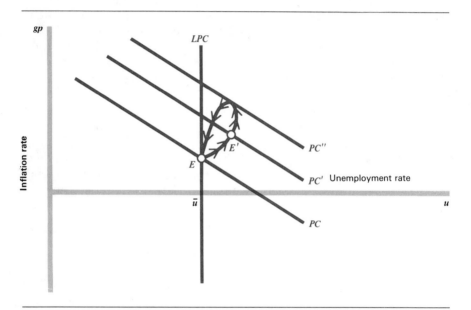

FIGURE 15-10   THE EFFECTS OF A SUPPLY SHOCK. A supply shock initially moves the short-run Phillips curve up, from *PC* to *PC'*. Because aggregate demand has not changed, the higher prices will force output down, thus causing unemployment. The economy moves in the short run from *E* to *E'*. From *E'* the short-run Phillips curve may shift up if workers demand higher rates of wage increase to compensate for the higher inflation. Eventually, though, the economy returns to point *E*. The arrows show the adjustment path followed after the supply shock.

While that adjustment is taking place, the short-run Phillips curve shifts up, for instance, from *PC* to *PC'*. There is a higher inflation rate corresponding to any given unemployment rate. If there is no change in monetary or fiscal policy, aggregate demand does not change. With prices higher, output has to fall, and unemployment therefore rises. The economy moves to *E'* on *PC'*. In the short run, inflation and unemployment increase together.

If the inflationary effects of the oil price shocks are slow in working their way into prices of all goods, then the short-run Phillips curve may stay at *PC'* for some time. Indeed, the short-run Phillips curve might even move up to a position such as *PC''* if expectations of inflation adjust, and workers begin to ask for higher rates of wage increase to compensate for the higher inflation they expect. With aggregate demand unchanged, this will lead to more unemployment along with the higher inflation.

Eventually though, the pressure of unemployment reduces the rate of increase of wages, the short-run Phillips curve begins to drop back toward *PC'* and then to *PC*, and the economy returns to full employment and lower inflation. But in the meantime, the economy has been through a recession caused by the supply shock.

Wage Push and the Policy Dilemma

Suppose that the economy were in a steady state and that workers ask for higher wages. A *wage push* takes place if workers claim wage increases that exceed those implied by the ongoing inflation rate on the short-run Phillips curve. A wage push might take place, for instance, in an economy which has large trade unions that have decided to mount a major campaign to increase wages.

The economic effects of a wage push are the same as those of any supply shock. If there is no response from monetary and fiscal policy, the inflation rate and unemployment rate will both rise in response to the wage push. Employed workers will get higher nominal wages. But because monetary and fiscal policy do not react, output falls as the price level rises. As a result of the higher unemployment, some workers who started out pushing for higher wages are out of a job and have lower rather than higher income.

If there were no response whatsoever from monetary and fiscal policy, the inflation rate and the unemployment rate would eventually return to their initial levels, as in Figure 15-10. But in the meantime the economy has been through a period of unemployment.

Accommodation

In both the case of a supply shock and the case of a wage push, the policy makers face the issue of whether to accommodate the inflation.[7] Policy makers *accommodate* supply shocks when they increase the growth rate of money to prevent unemployment that would otherwise occur as a result of a supply disturbance that shifts the short-run Phillips curve.

Accommodation of supply shocks results in higher inflation but has the benefits of reducing the unemployment rate. Since we have not yet examined the costs of inflation and unemployment, we are not in a position to evaluate the costs and benefits of accommodation.[8]

However, there is one important point to make about accommodation. We make it using the example of the wage push. Suppose that workers push for higher nominal wages, and that policy makers expand aggregate demand to accommodate that. The accommodation will produce an inflation rate above that expected by workers, and thus give them lower real wages than they expected. If their push is for higher *real* wages, next period they will push for yet higher increases in nominal wages to compensate for the greater inflation they expect. If policy makers try to accommodate real disturbances of this type, they end up in a process of ever-increasing inflation.

In Chapter 14 we discussed accommodation of an oil price shock that required a fall in the real wage. We argued there that the economy could adjust more easily to a shock of that type if monetary policy were expansionary. That would make it possible for the real wage to fall without the nominal wage having to fall. In that case accommodation would work, *because it is not attempting permanently to counteract a real change that the economy has to make.* Rather, it is helping the economy make the appropriate real adjustments more smoothly, by adjusting for the stickiness of nominal wages.

What is the general point about accommodation? It is that accommodation works when it is used to help move the economy toward the real adjustments it has to make to disturbances. Accommodation will not succeed if it tries to prevent real adjustments to real disturbances.

BOX 15-1   REAL WAGES AND UNEMPLOYMENT

Unemployment rates in North America and Europe in the early 1980s were far higher than they had been in the 1960s or even in the 1970s. Table 1 shows the data for different subperiods.

TABLE 1   UNEMPLOYMENT RATES IN NORTH AMERICA
AND EUROPE

	1970–1974	1975–1980	1980–1982
European community	2.5	5.3	7.9
United States	5.4	7.1	8.1
Canada	5.8	7.6	8.7

Source: European Economy, Economic Report of the President, 1983, and *Bank of Canada Review*

The high unemployment rates led to a discussion, especially in Europe, of whether excessively high real wages or insufficient aggregate demand was the chief source of the problem. Figure 1 helps sort out the issues. The figure shows the labour demand schedule — the marginal product of labour — with the real wage on the vertical axis and $\bar{N}$ as the full-employment labour supply. The full-employment real wage is $(w/P)_0$.

One interpretation of the unemployment problem of the early 1980s was that the economy was at a point such as A at a real wage $(w/P)'$. At point A firms hire only an amount of labour N' which falls short of full employment because the real wage is too high. The economy suffers from *classical*, or *real wage, unemployment*. The cure is either a reduction in the real wage to $(w/P)_0$ or else productivity growth or increased investment that shifts the *MPN* schedule out and to the right and thus reduces unemployment.

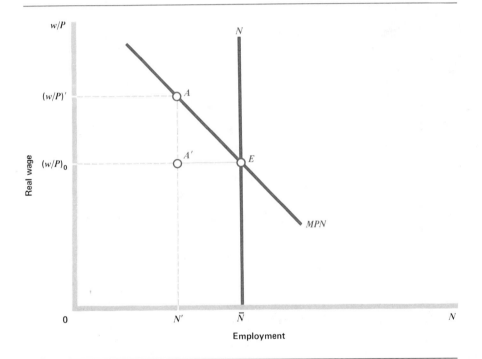

FIGURE 1   CLASSICAL OR KEYNESIAN UNEMPLOYMENT? The schedule *MPN* is the marginal product of labour or the demand curve for labour. The full-employment labour supply is *NN*. At a real wage $(w/P)'$ there is ''high real wage'' unemployment because firms only want to hire a labour force of N', which falls short of the supply N. But it is also possible that even at the lower wage $(w/P)^0$ firms only want to hire N' of labour because they cannot sell the output that would be produced by a larger labour force. The question is to know whether the unemployment results from high real wages, as at point A, or from insufficient aggregate demand, as at point A'.

An alternative interpretation is that the economy was at a point such as A'. Again there is unemployment, but this time the real wage is not the problem. Firms are not willing to hire more workers than N' because they cannot sell the output. Aggregate demand is insufficient to absorb more output than is produced by an employment level N'. Therefore firms do not hire more workers, and accordingly, there is *Keynesian unemployment*. The cure, in this case, is not a cut in real wages but rather an expansion in aggregate demand through monetary or fiscal stimulus.

In both cases there is unemployment. In both cases it is unprofitable for firms to hire more labour than N'. In one case the problem is that labour is too expensive; in the other there is no market for the increased output, but it is essential to identify what kind of unemployment the economy faces before designing policy action. Because we do not know the equilibrium real wage, there is no direct way to decide whether unemployment is Keynesian or classical.

In all likelihood in the early eighties, there was some classical unemployment in Europe, because real wages had not adjusted enough in response to the increased price of oil and reduced productivity growth. But in addition a dose of Keynesian unemployment was superimposed between 1980 and 1982, so that the economy was to the left of point A. In that case expansionary aggregate demand policies would have gone some way toward reducing unemployment, but there was also a need to cut labour costs relative to labour productivity.

15-7   SUMMARY

1   The inflation-unemployment Phillips curve is an alternative form of the aggregate supply curve introduced in Chapter 14. The choice of which to use is purely a matter of convenience.

2   The adjustment along a Phillips curve, given the nominal money stock, involves price changes, changes in real balances, and therefore changes in spending output and employment. In the long-run the economy will converge to the natural rate of unemployment unless policy makers attempt to maintain a different position.

3   Friedman and Phelps argued that the wage-unemployment Phillips curve would shift with the expected rate of inflation, as workers and firms adjust wages for the inflation expected over the period during which the wages will be paid. This leads to the expectations-augmented Phillips curve, which argues that the rate of price increase increases with the expected inflation rate and declines with the unemployment rate.

4   The expected inflation rate is constant on a short-run Phillips curve. The short-run Phillips curve is quite flat, reflecting the stickiness of wages and prices in the short run.

5   The expected rate of inflation in the Phillips curve should be interpreted as the inflation, current and past, that was expected when contracts relevant to current wages and prices were made.

6   The short-run Phillips curve shifts with the expected rate of inflation. The higher the expected rate of inflation, the higher the inflation rate corresponding to any given unemployment rate.

7   In the long run, expectations catch up with actual inflation. The long-run Phillips curve describes the tradeoffs, if any, between inflation and unemployment when the actual and expected inflation rates are equal. The long-run Phillips curve is essentially vertical, implying that the unemployment rate in the long run is equal to the natural rate, whatever the inflation rate.

8   Inflation is a monetary phenomenon in the sense that prolonged rapid inflation is impossible without high rates of money growth and that low rates of money growth will eventually reduce the inflation rate. The link between money growth and long-run inflation is not exact because of long-run growth in output and shifts in the demand for money.

9   Changes in monetary policy cause the inflation rate to change in both the short run and the long run. Fiscal policy changes and supply shocks change the inflation rate in the short run. A supply shock or a wage push creates a policy dilemma by raising the question of whether the inflation should be accommodated through expansionary monetary policy. Accommodation will be successful only when it helps the economy make real adjustments that would otherwise be impeded by wage and price stickiness.

KEY TERMS

Expectations-augmented Phillips curve   *Stagflation*
Short-run Phillips curve   *Wage push*
Rational expectations   *Accommodation*
Long-run Phillips curve

PROBLEMS

1   Use Figure 15-2 to discuss the adjustment process to a reduction in personal income tax rates. Specifically, use the insights gained from the aggregate demand and supply framework to determine the effects on the time path of unemployment and inflation.

2 Explain in words why the expected rate of inflation affects the position of the wage-unemployment Phillips curve.

3 (a) What determines the position and slope of the short-run Phillips curve?
   (b) Why does the short-run Phillips curve not shift immediately when a new policy to reduce inflation is introduced?

4 (a) In Figure 15-6 we show how the economy reaches a higher rate of inflation. Starting at an 8 percent inflation rate, show how the economy would shift back to 3 percent if the right policies were used.
   (b) What sort of policy would be needed to reduce the inflation rate from 8 to 3 percent?

5 (a) Define the long-run Phillips curve.
   (b) Explain why, according to the expectations-augmented Phillips curve, the long-run Phillips curve is vertical.

6 Suppose we have an economy where real output grows at the rate of 6 percent per year. The nominal quantity of money grows at the rate of 5 percent. The income elasticity of money demand is 0.5.
   (a) What is the rate of inflation in long-run equilibrium?
   (b) What is the rate of growth of nominal income? (Remember that nominal income can grow because prices increase, real output rises, or both.)
   (c) How would your answers to (a) and (b) change if the income elasticity of money demand was unity.

7 Figure 15-8 shows the long-run growth rate of $M1$ and the inflation rate in Canada from 1961 to 1983. The inflation rate differs from the growth rate of money (a) as a result of output growth, (b) when there are supply shocks, (c) when the demand function for money shifts. Discuss what parts of the relationship seen in Figure 15-8 can be explained using each of these factors.

8 (a) Show how a permanent increase in the price of oil affects inflation and unemployment in the short run.
   *(b) An increase in the price of oil results in a price level that is higher than it would otherwise have been. Explain. (*Hint:* During a period of higher than normal inflation, the price level is increasing relative to the level it would otherwise have been. Examine the adjustment path to the oil price shock and compare inflation rates with and without the shock.)

9 When would it be useful to accommodate a supply shock?

10 (a) Explain how the Canadian economy moved from low to high inflation between 1961 and 1980.

(b) Explain how the Canadian economy moved from high to low inflation between 1980 and 1983.

(c) In your view, was there any better way of reducing the inflation rate?

CHAPTER 15: FOOTNOTES

[1] We discuss the natural rate of unemployment, $\bar{u}$, in Chapter 16. In Chapter 14 we omitted the natural rate of unemployment, $\bar{u}$, noting in footnote 10 that we were measuring the unemployment rate relative to the full employment rate. Now we put in the natural or full employment rate because it begins to play an important role in the analysis.

[2] To get from Eq. (1) to Eq. (2) in this chapter, you can follow the same steps that took us from Eq. (6) to Eq. (8) in Chap. 14.

[3] It will be a good exercise for you and refresh your memory to draw the *AD* and *AS* schedules as you work through the argument.

[4] The experience shown in Figure 15-3 reflects more than changes in the expected rate of inflation. During this period there were also (1) supply shocks that shifted the short-run Phillips curve, (2) increases in the natural rate of unemployment, and (3) attempts to reduce the inflation rate by restrictive monetary policy. Later in this chapter and in the next we show how these other events affect the inflation and unemployment rates.

[5] In the problem set we ask you to show how a strongly anti-inflationary monetary policy affects the inflation and unemployment rates in the short and long runs.

[6] See, for example, Robert Solow, "Down the Phillips Curve with Gun and Camera," in David A. Belsley et al. (eds.), *Inflation, Trade and Taxes* (Columbus: Ohio State University Press, 1976). James Tobin, in "Stabilization Policy Ten Years After," *Brookings Papers on Economic Activity*, 1:1980, asks whether the natural rate of unemployment might not respond to recent unemployment experience, rather than being a constant or a slowly moving rate. We discuss the natural rate in Chapter 16.

[7] In Chapter 4 we discussed accommodation through fiscal policy where the monetary authorities prevent an increase in the interest rate and crowding out by allowing the money stock to rise in the course of a fiscal expansion.

[8] We discuss the costs of inflation and unemployment in Chap. 16.

16

The Tradeoffs Between Inflation and Unemployment

In 1982 and 1983, the Canadian economy experienced the highest unemployment rate since the Great Depression. More than one person in ten in the labour force was unemployed. At the same time there was a sharp decline in the rate of inflation from 12 percent to 5 percent. This experience provided a clear example of the short-run tradeoff between inflation and unemployment. In this chapter we discuss this tradeoff and the cost-benefit analysis that policy makers must bear in mind when designing stabilization policy.

We start with a discussion of unemployment and develop the concept of the natural rate of unemployment. We then consider the costs of unemployment and inflation and conclude the chapter with a discussion of alternative strategies for reducing the inflation rate.

16-1 THE ANATOMY OF UNEMPLOYMENT

The anatomy of unemployment is built around three central facts of unemployment behaviour:

1 There are substantial flows of individuals in and out of unemployment each month, and most people who become unemployed in any given month remain unemployed for only a short time.
2 Much of the unemployment is constituted of people who will be unemployed for quite a long time.
3 There is considerable variation of unemployment rates across different regions and groups in the labour force.

The first and second facts may seem contradictory. A numerical example should make it clear that there is no necessary contradiction. Suppose that the labour force consists of 100 people, and that five people become unemployed each month. Suppose that four of those people are unemployed for precisely one month, and one person will be unemployed for six months. Suppose also that the economy is in a steady state, so that this situation has repeated itself every month for years.

We ask first how many people are unemployed at any one time, say September 30. There will be five people who became unemployed September 1, one person who became unemployed August 1 (and who has been unemployed for two months), and so on, back to the person who became unemployed April 1, and whose six months of unemployment will end the next day, on October 1. In total, there will be ten people unemployed. So the unemployment rate is 10 percent. Of the ten, six will suffer a six-month spell of unemployment before they again become employed. This is consistent with the second fact, but remember that we started with five people becoming unemployed each month, four of whom remain unemployed for only a month. That is consistent with the first fact, that most people who become unemployed within a given month remain so for only a short time. We shall return to this example later in this section.

The third fact, variation of unemployment rates across different groups or regions in the labour force, can be examined using the relationship between the overall unemployment rate, u, and the unemployment rates, u_i, of groups within the labour force. The overall rate is a weighted average of the unemployment rates of the groups:

$$u = w_1u_1 + w_2u_2 + \ldots + w_nu_n \tag{1}$$

The weights, w_i, are the fraction of the labour force that falls within the specific group, say, teenagers.

Equation (1) makes it clear that the overall unemployment rate may conceal the dramatic differences in unemployment rates among regions or groups alluded to in Fact 3. For instance, in 1983, the aggregate unemployment rate was 11.9 percent. For the age group 15–24 the rate was 19.9 percent, while for the group aged 25 and over it was 9.4 percent. In terms of Equation (1), we have

$$11.9\% = (0.24)19.9\% + (0.76)9.4\%$$

where the shares of the two groups in the labour force are 24 percent and 76 percent respectively.

We now turn to a more detailed examination of the three central facts about the anatomy of unemployment.

Flows In and Out of Unemployment

An unemployed person is defined as one who is out of work *and* who (1) has either actively looked for work during the previous four weeks, or (2) is waiting to be recalled to a job after having been laid off, or (3) is waiting to report to a new job within four weeks.[1]

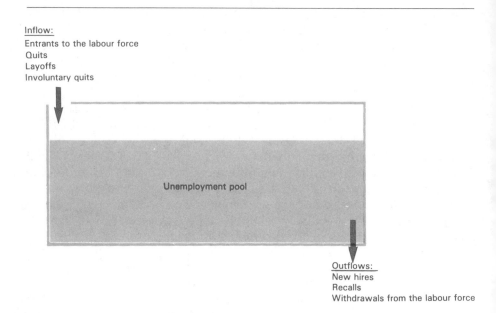

FIGURE 16-1 FLOWS IN AND OUT OF THE UNEMPLOYMENT POOL

Figure 16-1 shows how people enter and leave the *unemployment pool*. A person may become unemployed for one of four reasons: (1) The person may be a new entrant into the labour force, looking for work for the first time or else be a reentrant — someone returning to the labour force after not having looked for more than four weeks. (2) A person may leave a job in order to look for other employment and be counted as unemployed while searching. (3) The person may be laid off. A *layoff* means that the worker was not fired but rather, will return to the old job if demand for the firm's product recovers. A firm will typically adjust to a decline in product demand by laying off some labour. A firm may also rotate layoffs among its labour force so that the individual laid-off worker may expect a recall even before product demand has fully recovered. (4) A worker may lose a job to which there is no chance of returning, either because he is fired or because the firm closes down.

These sources of inflow into the pool of unemployment have a counterpart in the outflow from the unemployment pool. There are essentially three ways of moving out of the pool of unemployment. (1) A person may be hired into a new job. (2) Someone laid off may be recalled. (3) An unemployed person may stop looking for a job and thus, by definition, leave the labour force. Such a person may plan to look for a job again soon.

TABLE 16-1 FLOWS INTO UNEMPLOYMENT, 1983

	Number (thousands)	Percent of labour force
Job losers	859	7.1
Job leavers	200	1.6
New entrants	70	0.6
Reentrants	319	2.6
	1,448	11.9

Source: Statistics Canada, 71-001.

Table 16-1 shows the breakdown of the average flow into unemployment in 1983. Notice that a substantial fraction is accounted for by reentrants into the labour force. There is also a substantial flow from the unemployment pool out of the labour force. In June 1984, there were about 500,000 persons not in the labour force who had lost their jobs or had been laid off. This suggests that the distinction between being unemployed and being out of the labour force is not a very sharp one, and that individuals move quite easily in both directions — between being unemployed (meaning essentially that they looked for a job in the last four weeks) and not employed (out of the labour force).

TABLE 16-2 UNEMPLOYMENT RATE AND INCIDENCE OF UNEMPLOYMENT, 1982

Labour force and unemployment, annual average	
Total labour force (thousands)	11,958
Unemployed (thousands)	1,314
Unemployment rate (percent)	11.0
Incidence of unemployment	
In labour force at some time (thousands)	13,481
Unemployed at some time (thousands)	3,784
Incidence (percent)	28.1

Source: Statistics Canada, 71-001, Nov. 1983.

The data in Table 16-2 illustrates the fact that there are substantial flows of individuals in and out of unemployment. On average in 1982 there were 11,958,000 persons in the labour force and an average of 11 percent were unemployed. However, this unemployment rate does not represent a constant group of individuals who were unemployed for the whole year. Of the 13,481,000 individuals who were in the labour force at some time during the year, 28.1 percent experienced a spell of unemployment with a duration that averaged less than a year.

Consideration of the *duration* of spells of unemployment provides an alternative way of looking at flows in and out of unemployment. Given the unemployment rate, the shorter the average spell of unemployment — the time the individual is unemployed — the larger are the flows. For instance, in the example at the beginning of this section we had a 10 percent unemployment rate with five people becoming unemployed each month. We could also have a 10 percent unemployment rate if ten people became unemployed each month and each one remained unemployed for exactly one month. In the earlier example, the average spell is longer than a month, since four out of five spells end in a month, but one out of five lasts six months. (The average spell is thus two months.) The shorter the average duration, the larger the flows of labour through the unemployment pool, given the overall unemployment rate.

Table 16-3 shows the distribution of unemployment by duration in 1982. About one half of those surveyed had been unemployed for less than 14 weeks but one quarter had been unemployed for more than six months. These data establish that despite the substantial flows in and out of unemployment, much of aggregate unemployment is accounted for by people who remain unemployed for a substantial time. Thus, if one believes that unemployment is a more serious problem when it affects only a few people intensely, rather than many people a little, these data suggest that unemployment is a more severe problem than the aggregate unemployment rate indicates. The next set of data we review, those on the distribution of unemployment by age and region, support that view.

TABLE 16-3   DURATION OF UNEMPLOYMENT, 1982

Number of weeks	Number (thousands)	Percent
1–4	871	23.0
5–13	1,092	28.9
14–26	894	23.6
27–39	500	13.2
40 and over	426	11.3
	3,783	100.0

Note: Duration here refers to duration up to the end of the week of the survey rather than completed spells of unemployment.
Source: Statistics Canada, 71-001, Nov. 1983.

The Distribution of Unemployment

The third important fact about the anatomy of unemployment is that unemployment is distributed very unevenly across the population. Table

TABLE 16-4   UNEMPLOYMENT RATES BY AGE AND SEX,
1983

Age	Both sexes	Men	Women
15–24	19.9	22.4	17.0
25–44	10.4	10.3	10.5
45–54	7.6	7.4	8.0
55 and over	7.2	7.3	7.0
Total	11.9	12.1	11.6

Source: Statistics Canada, 71-001.

16-4 shows unemployment rates by age and sex. Unemployment is considerably higher in the age group 15–24 years, and it is lowest in the age group 45 years and over. Table 16-5 and Figure 16-2 show unemployment rates by region. The Atlantic Provinces have consistently shown the highest unemployment rates. In recent years, as a result of the oil and gas boom, the Prairie Provinces have experienced the lowest rates.

16-2   THE NATURAL RATE OF UNEMPLOYMENT

The *natural rate of unemployment* is also called the full-employment level of unemployment, or the long-run equilibrium level of unemployment, or the structural unemployment rate. In this section, we discuss the determinants of the natural rate of unemployment and then examine estimates of changes in the natural rate since the fifties.

Figure 16-1 points to the factors causing the unemployment rate to change. Increases in the rate of entry to the labour force, or quits, or layoffs, or other job losses cause the unemployment rate to rise. Increases in hiring, or recalls, or withdrawals from the labour force, cause the unemployment rate to fall. Each of these factors is in part determined by economic variables, such as the level of aggregate demand and the actual and expected real wage rate. When aggregate demand rises (at a given real wage), firms increase their hiring. When aggregate demand falls, firms lay off workers. Thus there is an immediate link between the factors emphasized in Figure 16-1 and aggregate demand. However, it should be noted that the relationship between aggregate demand and the variables affecting the rate of unemployment is not unambiguous. For instance, an increase in the demand for labour increases quits at the same time as it reduces layoffs. A person thinking of leaving one job to search for another would be more likely to quit when the job market is good and demand is

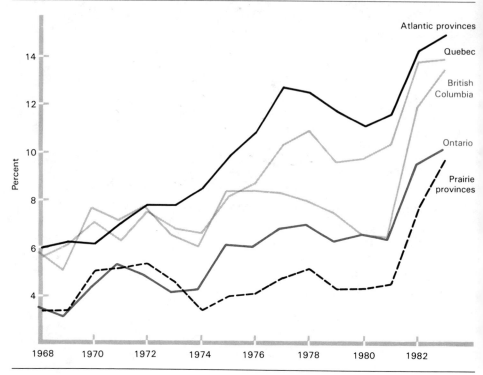

FIGURE 16-2 UNEMPLOYMENT RATES BY REGION
(*Source: Bank of Canada Review*)

TABLE 16-5 UNEMPLOYMENT RATES BY PROVINCE, 1983

Newfoundland	18.8	Prince Edward Island	12.2
New Brunswick	14.8	Alberta	10.8
Quebec	13.9	Ontario	10.4
British Columbia	13.8	Manitoba	9.4
Nova Scotia	13.2	Saskatchewan	7.4

Source: Statistics Canada, 11-003.

high than when there is heavy unemployment and the prospects of find-ing a good job quickly are low.

When the unemployment rate is constant, flows in and out of unem-ployment just balance each other. These flows can match at any level of unemployment. The *natural rate of unemployment*, however, is that rate of unemployment at which flows in and out of unemployment just balance,[2] *and* at which expectations of firms and workers as to the behaviour of prices and wages are correct.

The determinants of the natural rate of unemployment can be thought of in terms of the duration and frequency of unemployment. The duration depends on (1) the organization of the labour market, in regard to the presence or absence of employment agencies, youth employment services, etc.; (2) the demographic makeup of the labour force; (3) the ability and desire of the unemployed to keep looking for a better job; and (4) the availability and types of jobs. If all jobs are the same, an unemployed person will take the first one offered. If some jobs are better than others, it is worthwhile searching and waiting for a good one. If it is very expensive to remain unemployed, say, because there are no unemployment benefits, an unemployed person is more likely to accept a job offer than to continue looking for a better one. If unemployment benefits are high, then it may be worthwhile for the unemployed person to continue looking for a better job rather than to accept a poor job when one is offered.

The behaviour of workers who have been laid off is also important when considering the duration of unemployment. Typically, a worker who has been laid off returns to the original job and does not search for another job. The reason is quite simple: once a worker, say, has been with a firm for a long time, he or she has special expertise in the way that firm works which makes the worker valuable to that firm but is not of great benefit to another employer. In addition, he or she may have built up seniority rights, including a pension. That means that such an individual could not expect to find as good a job if he or she searched for a new one. The best course of action may be to wait to be recalled.

Frequency of Unemployment

The *frequency of unemployment* is the average number of times, per period, that workers become unemployed. There are two basic determinants of the frequency of unemployment. The first is the variability of the demand for labour across different firms in the economy. The second determinant is the rate at which new workers enter the labour force: The more rapidly new workers enter the labour force — the faster the growth rate of the labour force — the higher the natural rate of unemployment. Even when aggregate demand is constant, some firms are growing and some are contracting. The contracting firms lose labour and the growing firms hire more labour. The greater this variability of the demand for labour across different firms, the higher the unemployment rate. Further, the variability of aggregate demand itself will affect the variability of the demand for labour.

The four factors affecting duration and the two factors affecting frequency of unemployment are the basic determinants of the natural rate of unemployment.

You should note that the factors determining the level of the natural rate of unemployment are not immutable. The structure of the labour market and the labour force can change. The willingness of workers to remain unemployed while looking for, or waiting for, a new job can change. The variability of the demand for labour by different firms can shift. As Edmund Phelps has noted, the natural rate is not "an intertemporal constant, something like the speed of light, independent of everything under the sun."[3] Indeed, the natural rate is difficult to measure, and estimates of it have changed over the last few years from about 4 percent in the 1960s to 5.5 to 6 percent in the early eighties.

Estimates of the Natural Rate of Unemployment

Estimates of the natural rate of unemployment typically try to adjust for changes in the composition of the labour force, and perhaps for changes in the natural rate of unemployment of the various groups in the labour force. We can write an equation very similar to Equation (1) for the natural rate, $\bar{u}$;

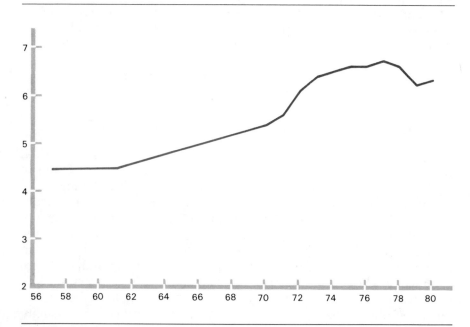

FIGURE 16-3   THE NATURAL RATE OF UNEMPLOYMENT, 1957–1980 (*Source*: See footnote 4.)

$$\bar{u} = w_1\bar{u}_1 + w_2\bar{u}_2 + \ldots + w_n\bar{u}_n \tag{2}$$

Equation (2) says that the natural rate is the weighted average of the natural rates of unemployment of the subgroups in the labour force.

Figure 16-3 shows the natural rate of unemployment as estimated in a study by P. Fortin and L. Phaneuf, who consider four labour force groups on the basis of age and sex.[4] Table 16-6 shows the changing structure of the labour force as reflected by the data for these groups. Over the period 1966 to 1975, the proportion of younger persons in the labour force grew and this is reflected in a rise in the overall natural rate of unemployment since this group has consistently experienced higher unemployment. The proportion of women in the labour force has grown steadily over the past 20 years as a result of growth in the female *participation rate* (the fraction of women who are in the labour force). Since the unemployment rate for females aged 25 and over rose during the 1970s, the increase in the participation rate for this group has contributed to the growth in the overall natural rate.

TABLE 16-6   THE CHANGING STRUCTURE OF THE LABOUR FORCE AND UNEMPLOYMENT, 1966–1983

	MALES			FEMALES			TOTAL
	Total	15–24	25 +	Total	15–24	25 +	
Proportion of Total Labour Force							
1966	68.7	13.7	55.0	31.3	10.5	20.8	100.0
1970	66.4	14.2	52.2	33.6	11.2	22.4	100.0
1975	63.1	14.9	48.2	36.9	12.2	24.7	100.0
1980	60.0	14.5	45.5	40.0	12.3	27.7	100.0
1983	58.3	12.7	45.6	41.7	11.3	30.4	100.0
Participation Rates							
1966	79.8	64.1	84.9	35.4	48.4	31.2	57.3
1970	77.8	62.4	83.3	38.3	49.4	34.5	57.8
1975	78.4	68.8	81.9	44.3	56.8	40.0	61.1
1980	78.3	72.0	80.5	50.3	62.6	46.2	64.0
1983	76.7	69.2	79.1	52.6	62.8	49.6	64.4
Average Unemployment Rate							
1966–1970	4.3	8.3	3.3	4.4	6.4	3.4	4.3
1971–1975	5.5	11.2	3.9	7.0	9.8	5.5	6.0
1976–1980	6.9	14.1	4.7	8.9	13.0	7.0	7.7
1981–1983	9.9	19.2	7.2	10.1	14.7	8.3	10.0

Source: Statistics Canada, 71-001, 71-529.

The sharp increase in the natural rate of unemployment in 1972 and 1973 reflects the estimated effects of liberalization of the benefits payable to the unemployed under the *Unemployment Insurance Act*. The provision of a high level of unemployment benefits makes it less urgent for an unemployed person to obtain a job. Further, the fact that a laid-off worker will not suffer a large loss from being unemployed makes it more attractive for an employer to lay off workers temporarily than to attempt to keep them on the job.

There seems to be little doubt that unemployment compensation does add to the natural rate of unemployment. This does not imply, though, that unemployment compensation should be abolished. What is appropriate is a scheme that will create less incentive for firms to lay off labour while at the same time ensuring that the unemployed are not exposed to economic distress. This is obviously a difficult trick to carry off.

16-3 THE COSTS OF UNEMPLOYMENT

The costs of unemployment are so obvious that this section might seem superfluous. Society on the whole loses from unemployment because total output is below its potential level. The unemployed as individuals suffer both from their income loss while unemployed and from the low level of self-esteem that long periods of unemployment cause.[5]

This section provides some estimates of the costs of forgone output resulting from unemployment, and clarifies some of the issues connected with the costs of unemployment and the potential benefits from reducing unemployment. We distinguish between cyclical unemployment, associated with short-run deviations of the unemployment rate from the natural rate and "permanent" or structural unemployment that exists at the natural rate.

Cyclical Unemployment

The fundamental cost of cyclical unemployment is the short-run loss of output. Are there any other costs of unemployment or, for that matter offsetting benefits? It is possible to imagine offsetting benefits. We do not discuss here the benefit arising from a temporary reduction in the inflation rate accompanying a temporary increase in unemployment, but rather, focus on the costs of unemployment taken by itself. A possible offsetting benefit occurs because the unemployed are not working and have more leisure. However, the value that can be placed on that leisure is small. In the first place, much of it is unwanted leisure.

Second, there is a fairly subtle issue that we shall have to explore. If a person were free to set his or her hours of work, he or she would work up to the point at which the individual judged the marginal value of leisure to be equal to the marginal return from working an extra hour. We would then be able to conclude that if the workday were slightly reduced, the overall loss would be extremely small. The reason is that the person acquires extra leisure from working less, at the cost of having less income, but he or she was previously at the point where the marginal value of leisure was equal to the after-tax marginal wage, so that the benefit of the increased leisure almost exactly offsets the private loss of income. However, the net marginal wage is less than the value of the marginal product of an employed person to the economy. The major reason is that society taxes the income of the employed person, so that society as a whole takes a share of the marginal product of the employed person. When the employed person in our example stops working, he or she loses only the *net* of tax wage he or she has been receiving. But society also loses the taxes this person has been paying. The unemployed person values leisure at the net of tax wage, and that value is smaller than the value of his or her marginal product for society as a whole. Therefore, the value of increased leisure provides only a partial offset to the cost of cyclical unemployment.

Note that we do not count both the individual's personal loss of income and the foregone output as part of the cost of unemployment. The reason is that the foregone output implicitly includes the individual's own loss of income — it estimates the total loss of output to the economy as a whole as a result of the reduction of employment. That loss could in principle be distributed across different people in the economy in many different ways. For instance, one could imagine that the unemployed person continues to receive benefit payments totalling close to his or her previous income while employed, with the benefit payments financed through taxes on working individuals. In that case, the unemployed person would not suffer an income loss from being unemployed, but society would still lose from the reduction in total output available.

However, the effects of an increase in unemployment are, in fact, borne heavily by the unemployed themselves. There is thus an extra cost to society of unemployment that is very difficult to quantify. The cost arises from the uneven distribution of the burden of unemployment across the population. Unemployment tends to be concentrated among the poor, and that makes the distributional aspect of unemployment a serious matter. It is not one that we can easily quantify, but it should not be overlooked. Further, there are many reports of the adverse psychic effects of unemployment that, again, are not easy to quantify but should not be ignored.[6]

"Structural" Unemployment

The benefits of reducing the natural rate of unemployment are more difficult to estimate than the costs of cyclical unemployment. We cannot use the short-run output-employment relationship since the increase in output associated with cyclical changes in unemployment results in part from the fact that the labour put back to work in the short run is able to use capital that had not been fully utilized when unemployment was high. However, in the long run, which is relevant when considering a reduction in the natural rate of unemployment, it would be necessary to invest to provide for the capital with which the newly employed would work.

The available estimates of the social benefits of a reduction in long-run unemployment cannot be narrowed down to very solid numbers. Even more difficult is the estimate of an "optimal" long-run unemployment rate. Here we ask the question whether any — and, if so, how much — unemployment is desirable in the long run. A first guess at the answer to that question is that all unemployment is wasteful, since the unemployed labour could usefully be employed. However, that answer is not totally persuasive. Those people who are unemployed in order to look for a better job are performing a valuable service not only for themselves. They are also performing a service for society by attempting to put themselves into a position in which they earn the most and are the most valuable. Because the composition of demand shifts over time, we can expect always to have some firms expanding and some contracting. This is true even with a stable level of aggregate demand. Those who lose their jobs will be unemployed and they benefit both society and themselves by not taking the very first job that comes along, but rather, searching for the optimal employment. Accordingly, we can conclude that some unemployment is a good thing in an economy in which the composition of demand changes over time. It is one thing to recognize this and quite another to pin down the optimal rate of unemployment numerically.

16-4   THE COSTS OF INFLATION

The costs of inflation are much less obvious than those of unemployment. There is no direct loss of output from inflation, as there is from unemployment. In studying the costs of inflation, we again want to distinguish the short run from the long run. In the case of inflation, though, the relevant distinction is between inflation that is *perfectly anticipated* and taken into account in economic transactions, and *imperfectly anticipated*, or unexpected inflation. We start with perfectly anticipated inflation because that case provides a useful bench mark against which to judge unanticipated inflation.

Perfectly Anticipated Inflation

Suppose that an economy has been experiencing a given rate of inflation, say 5 percent, for a long time, and that it is correctly anticipated that the rate of inflation will continue to be 5 percent. In such an economy, all contracts would build in the expected 5 percent inflation. Borrowers and lenders will both know and agree that the dollars in which a loan will be repaid will be worth less than the dollars which are given up by the lender when making the loan. Nominal interest rates would be 5 percent higher than they would be in the absence of inflation.[7] Long-term wage contracts will increase wages at 5 percent per year to take account of the inflation, and then build in whatever changes in real wages are agreed to. Long-term leases will take account of the inflation. In brief, any contracts in which the passage of time is involved will take the inflation into account. Inflation has no real costs in such an economy, except for a minor qualification to be noted below.

That qualification arises because the interest rate that is paid on money might not adjust to the inflation rate. No interest is paid on currency, that is notes and coin, throughout the world, and no interest is paid on demand deposits in many countries. It is very difficult to pay interest on currency, so that it is likely that the interest rate on currency will continue to be zero, independent of the perfectly anticipated inflation rate. Interest can be, and in some cases is already, paid on demand deposits. Thus it is reasonable to expect that in a fully anticipated inflation, interest would be paid on demand deposits, and the interest rate paid on demand deposits would adjust to the inflation rate. If so, the only cost of perfectly anticipated inflation is that the inflation makes it more costly to hold currency.

The cost to the individual of holding currency is the interest forgone by not holding an interest-bearing asset. When the inflation rate rises, the nominal interest rate rises, the interest lost by holding currency increases, and the cost of holding currency therefore increases. Accordingly, the demand for currency falls. In practice, this means that individuals economize on the use of currency by carrying less in their wallets and making more trips to the bank to cash smaller cheques than they did before. The costs of these trips to the bank are often described as the "shoe-leather" costs of inflation. They are related to the amount by which the demand for currency is reduced by an increase in the anticipated inflation rate, and they are small.

We should add that throughout this discussion, we are assuming inflation rates that are not too high to effectively disrupt the payments system. This disruption was a real problem in some instances of hyperinflation, but it need not concern us here. We are abstracting, too, from the cost of "menu change." This cost arises simply from the fact that with inflation, as opposed to price stability, people have to devote real resources to marking up prices and changing pay telephones and vending machines as well as cash registers. These costs are there, but one cannot get too excited about them. On balance, the costs of fully anticipated inflation are small.

The notion that the costs of fully anticipated inflation are trivial does not square well with the strong aversion to inflation reflected in policy making and politics. The most important reason for that aversion is probably that inflations in Canada have not been steady, and that our inflationary experience is one of imperfectly anticipated inflation, the costs of which are substantially different from those discussed in this section.

There is a further line of argument that explains the public aversion to inflation, even of the fully anticipated, steady kind we are discussing here. The argument is that such a state is not likely to exist, that it is a mirage to believe that policy makers could and would maintain a steady inflation rate at any level other than zero. The argument is that policy makers are reluctant to use restrictive policy to compensate for transitory increases in the inflation rate. Rather than maintain a constant rate of inflation in the face of inflation shocks, the authorities would accommodate these shocks and therefore validate them. Any inflationary shock would add to the inflation rate rather than being compensated by restrictive policy. In this manner inflation, far from being constant, would in fact be rising as policy makers validate any and every disturbance rather than use policy to rigidly enforce the inflation target. Zero inflation, it is argued, is the only target that can be defended without this risk.[8]

Although there are many examples of countries with long inflationary histories, there does not appear to be any tendency for the inflation rate of those countries to increase over time. The argument thus seems weak. However, it is true that the inflation rate has been more stable in countries with low rates of inflation than in countries with inflation rates that are on average higher,[9] perhaps providing a germ of validity to the notion.

Imperfectly Anticipated Inflation

The idyllic scene of full adjustment to inflation painted here does not describe economies that we actually know. Modern economies include a variety of institutional features representing different degrees of adjustment to inflation. Economies with long inflationary histories, such as those of Brazil and Israel, have made substantial adjustments to inflation through the use of indexing. Others in which inflation has been episodic, such as the Canadian economy, have made only small adjustments for inflation.

One of the important effects of inflation is to change the real value of assets fixed in nominal terms. A doubling of the price level, such as Canada experienced in the period from 1975 to 1983, cuts in half the purchasing power of all claims or assets fixed in money terms. Thus, someone who bought a 10-year government bond in 1975 and expected to receive a principal of, say, $100 in constant purchasing power at the 1985 maturity date, actually winds up with a $100 principal that has purchasing power of less than $50 in 1975 dollars. The more than doubling of the price level has effectively reduced the real value of the asset by over one-half. It has transferred wealth from creditors — holders of bonds — to debtors. This effect operates with respect to all assets fixed in nominal terms, in particular, money, bonds, savings accounts, insurance contracts, and some pensions. Obviously, it is an extremely important effect since it can certainly wipe out the purchasing power of a lifetime's saving that is supposed to finance retirement consumption.

These facts by themselves seem to explain the public concern over inflation. There appears to be a lot riding on each percentage-point change in the price level. That impression is slightly misleading. Many individuals are both debtors and creditors in nominal assets. Almost everyone has some money, and is thus a creditor in nominal terms. Many own housing, financed through mortgages whose value is fixed in nominal terms. Such individuals benefit from inflation because it reduces the real value of their mortgage. Other individuals have borrowed in nominal terms to buy consumer durables, such as cars, and to that extent have their real indebtedness reduced by inflation.

TABLE 16-7   IMPACT OF INFLATION ON RELATIVE NET ASSET POSITIONS OF HOUSEHOLDS, 1969–1975

Age group in 1969					
Under 25	25–34	35–44	45–54	55–64	65 and over
(Percent)					
21.1	14.5	4.4	−7.2	−10.8	−11.6

Income group			
Less than $4,000	$4,000–7,999	$8,000–14,999	$15,000 and over
(Percent)			
−10.8	5.1	10.9	−10.0

Source: Economic Council of Canada, *Thirteenth Annual Review*, p. 22.

Table 16-7 shows the estimated impact of inflation on the relative net asset positions of households classified by age and income. Over the period 1969 to 1975, the young gained in relation to the old because they typically had much larger debts. The middle-income groups gained because they typically had assets in the form of real estate financed by mortgage debt. Fewer poor families had the means to buy property or to incur debt, while wealthier families naturally had a larger fraction of their wealth in financial assets.

In addition to the redistribution among households shown in Table 16-7, inflation brings about transfers among the household, corporate and government sectors. However, the gains and losses from these wealth transfers basically cancel out over the economy as a whole. When the government gains from inflation, the private sector may have to pay lower taxes later. When the corporate sector gains from inflation, owners of corporations benefit at the expense of others. If we really did not care about the distribution of wealth among individuals, the costs of unanticipated inflation would be negligible. Included in the individuals of the previous sentence are those belonging to different generations, since the current owners of the national debt might be harmed by inflation, to the benefit of future taxpayers.

Inflation redistributes wealth between debtors and creditors because changes in the price level change the purchasing power of assets fixed in money terms. There is room, too, for inflation to affect income positions by changing the distribution of income. A popular line of argument has always been that inflation benefits capitalists or recipients of profit income at the expense of wage earners. Unanticipated inflation, it is argued, means that prices rise faster than wages and therefore allow profits to expand. For Canada in the postwar period, there is no persuasive evidence to this effect. There is evidence that the real return on common stocks, that is the real value of dividends and capital gains on equity, is reduced by unanticipated inflation. Thus, equity holders appear to be adversely affected by unanticipated inflation.[10]

The fact that unanticipated inflation acts mainly to redistribute wealth, the net effects of which redistribution should be close to zero, has led to some questioning of the reasons for public concern over inflation. The gainers, it seems, do not shout as loudly as the losers. Since some of the gainers (future taxpayers) have yet to be born, this is hardly surprising. There is also a notion that the average wage earner is subject to an illusion when both the nominal wage and the price level increase. Wage earners are thought to attribute increases in nominal wages to their own merit rather than to inflation, while the general inflation of prices is seen as causing an unwarranted reduction in the real wage they would otherwise have received. It is hard to know how to test the validity of this argument.

It does appear that the redistributive effects of unanticipated inflation are large, and that, accordingly, some parts of the population could be seriously affected by unanticipated inflation. It is difficult to be more precise in discussing this complicated question, which, like others in this chapter, remains the subject of ongoing research.

16-5   INFLATION, INTEREST RATES, AND INDEXATION

In this section we look at contracts that are especially affected by inflation. These are loan contracts, wage contracts, and the tax laws. In each case payments are fixed in nominal terms over some future period. However the future price level is not known ahead of time, and hence the *real* value of the payments can turn out to be very different from what had been anticipated.

Inflation and Interest Rates

Table 16-8 shows interest rates for several countries in 1980. The rates differ widely, ranging from under 5 percent in Switzerland to above 30 percent in Brazil and Colombia. Also shown are inflation rates for these countries for the preceding 4 years. This is a rough measure of the expected inflation rate in each country.

TABLE 16-8   INTEREST RATES AND EXPECTED
INFLATION, 1980*

Country	Average rate % per annum	Average inflation rate, 1976–1980
Australia	11.5	9.9
Brazil	33.0	53.6
Canada	12.8	9.1
Colombia	30.0†	25.4
France	11.9	10.6
Germany	9.1	4.0
Italy	17.2	16.2
Switzerland	4.8‡	2.5
United Kingdom	15.1	13.8
United States	11.6	9.7

*Interest rates are short-term market rates except as noted. The expected inflation rate is assumed to be the average of inflation rates over the previous 4 years.
†Central bank discount rate.
‡Government bond yield.
Source: International Financial Statistics.

The table shows a very strong relationship between a country's interest rate and its inflation rate. Figure 16-4 shows the same relationship over the period 1963 to 1983 in Canada. There is again a definite positive relationship, with interest rates rising as inflation increases. The positive relationship between expected inflation and the nominal interest rate is called the Fisher equation. It is named after the American economist Irving Fisher[11] and is based on the distinction between real and nominal interest rates:

Nominal interest rate = real interest rate + expected inflation rate[12]

Fisher argued that the real interest rate is roughly constant in long-run equilibrium. He regarded it as determined by the real factors in the economy, particularly the productivity of capital. *With the real interest rate approximately constant in the long run, and with expectations of inflation adjusting to actual inflation in the long run, the nominal interest rate adjusts with the inflation rate.* This is what we see in Table 16-8 and in Figure 16-4.

How does expected inflation get built into the interest rate? The reasoning is almost identical to that explaining how the expected inflation rate gets built into the rate of wage increase. Anyone making a loan when inflation is expected knows that he or she will be repaid in dollars of lower real value. For instance, suppose the expected inflation rate is 10 percent. Prices a year from now will be 10 percent above the price level today. One dollar will buy 10 percent less a year from now than a dollar buys today. Accordingly, the lender will want to be compensated by an extra 10 percent per year to adjust for the expected decline in the value of money. Someone lending at 3 percent when there is no inflation is effectively in

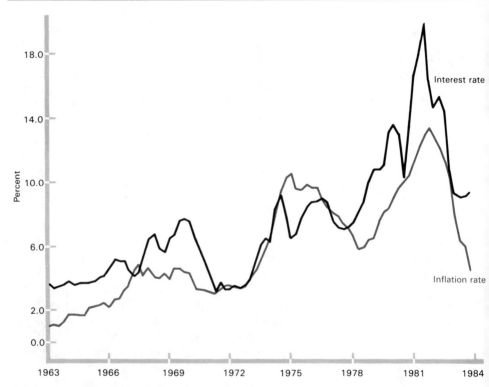

Note: Interest rate is the yield on 3-month Treasury bills. Inflation rate is the growth rate from the preceding year of the Consumer Price Index excluding food.

FIGURE 16-4   INTEREST RATES AND INFLATION
(*Source: Bank of Canada Review*)

the same situation as someone lending at 13 percent when there is 10 percent inflation.

But how can the borrower afford to pay the extra 10 percent? Suppose the borrower is a businessperson who plans to invest in machinery to produce goods for sale a year from now, and to repay the loan out of the proceeds. If prices are expected to rise by 10 percent, then the borrower will be able to sell the goods for 10 percent more next year than he or she could sell them if there were zero inflation. Thus the borrower will be willing to pay the extra 10 percent. He or she will also be in the same position with a 13 percent interest rate and 10 percent inflation as with 3 percent interest and zero inflation.

We make two points about the Fisher equation:

1   The real interest rate is not constant. It has, in particular, been extremely high in Canada and other countries in the period since 1980.[13]
2   Fisher believed that it took a long time for the economy to adapt to a new rate of inflation. His estimate was that it was 30 years before the interest rate fully adapted to higher inflation.

Indexation of Wages

Wages can be indexed by including automatic cost of living adjustment (COLA) provisions in wage contracts. COLA provisions link increases in money wages to increases in the price level. The adjustment may be complete — 100 percent indexation — or only partial. Partial indexation takes one of two forms. There may be a *threshold* or a *cap*. A threshold specifies a minimum increase in the price level before indexation comes into play. This implies that small price increases are not compensated, while larger ones are. A cap puts a limit on the extent to which price increases are compensated, say, 10 percent per year. COLA clauses are designed to allow workers to recover purchasing power lost through price increases.

Why Indexation?

Indexation in some form is a quite common feature of labour markets in many countries. Indexation strikes a balance between the advantages of long-term wage contracts and the interests of workers and firms in not having *real* wages get too far out of line. Bargaining for wages is costly because workers (unions) and the firm have to devote time and effort to arrive at a settlement and often work is disrupted through strikes. It is in the common interest of workers and firms therefore to hold to a minimum the number of times these negotiations take place.

Thus wages are not negotiated once a week or once a month, but rather they are negotiated in the form of 2- or 3-year contracts. However, over the term of these contracts the evolution of prices — consumer prices and the prices at which firms sell their output — is not known with certainty. Therefore real wages paid by firms or received by workers are not known even if money wages are. To remedy this uncertainty, some provision is made to adjust wages for inflation. Broadly, there are two possibilities. One is to index wages to the CPI and in periodic reviews, say quarterly, increase wages by the increase in prices over the period. The other is to schedule periodic, preannounced wage increases based on the expected rate of price increase. If inflation were known with certainty, the two methods would come to the same thing, but since inflation can differ from expectations, there will be discrepancies. Prefixed wage increases may turn out to be high or low relative to actual inflation. On that account indexation on the basis of actual inflation offers greater assurance of stable real wages for workers than do scheduled increases.

Supply Shocks and Indexation

Suppose real material prices increase, and firms pass these cost increases on into higher prices of final goods. Consumer prices will rise, and under a system of 100 percent indexation, wages would rise. This leads to further price and material costs, and wage increases. Indexation here leads to an inflation spiral that would be avoided under a system of prefixed wage increases because then real wages could fall as a consequence of higher material prices.

The example makes it clear that we must distinguish two possibilities in considering the effects of wage indexing, monetary disturbances and real disturbances. In the case of a monetary disturbance (a shift in the *LM* schedule), there is a "pure" inflation disturbance, and firms can afford to pay the same real wages and therefore would not mind 100 percent indexation. In the case of adverse real disturbances, however, real wages must fall, and full indexation is entirely the wrong system because it stands in the way of downward real wage flexibility.

From the two cases it is apparent that neither completely prefixed wage increases nor complete indexation is likely to be optimal. The best arrangement will depend on the relative importance of monetary and real shocks. Countries that had practised 100 percent indexation — for example, Italy and Brazil — have found in the 1970s that it is difficult to adjust to real shocks and that the indexation leads to a wage-price spiral that pushes up inflation with great speed.

Indexation of the Tax System

The contracts that would have to be adjusted for inflation to avoid distortion include the tax laws. For example, personal income tax rates are normally progressive and fixed in relation to nominal income so that

TABLE 16-9   EFFECTS OF INFLATION ON AFTER-TAX
INCOME

Price Level	Pretax income, nominal	Taxes, nominal	After-tax income, nominal	After-tax income, real
100	$20,000	$ 7,000	$13,000	$13,000
200	40,000	20,000	20,000	10,000

taxes rise as a proportion of income as income increases. Consider the taxpayer shown in Table 16-9 in which we are comparing an initial situation with a price level of 100 and pretax nominal income of $20,000 with a later situation in which both the price level and pretax nominal income have doubled. Initially, taxes of $7,000 are paid on nominal income of $20,000. After the price level doubles, a higher proportion of nominal income, namely $20,000, is paid in taxes. That is because the income tax is progressive. That means that the real value of after-tax income falls with the price level and that the real value of taxes paid to the government rises with the price level—taxes increase from $7,000 to $20,000 in Table 16-9. In terms of the initial price level, taxes increase in real value by $3,000. Thus, with tax rates unchanged and a progressive tax system, inflation tends to raise real taxes.

To alleviate this problem, the federal government introduced in the budget of February 1973 a system for *indexing* the personal income tax. Since then the basic exemptions and tax brackets have been adjusted each year in proportion to the price level so that changes in the price level do not affect real taxes.[14] For the taxpayer in Table 16-9, the nominal taxes would only double from $7,000 to $14,000 with doubling of the price level.

The major economic argument against indexation of the tax system is that a progressive tax system in nominal terms provides an automatic stabilizer for the economy in response to changes in the price level. We recall the role of automatic stabilizers from Chapter 3. The argument there was that a proportional income tax would reduce the marginal propensity to spend out of income and therefore would reduce the size of the multiplier. The argument here is that with progressive taxation of nominal income, that is, taxes that increase as a proportion of income as nominal income rises, we would have further stabilizing effects. With progressive taxation of nominal income, an increase in the price level such as would arise from an aggregate demand disturbance would be dampened because tax rates rise with the increase in nominal income and thus reduce multipliers. While a simple proportional tax system provides for a built-in stabilizer, the further benefits of progressive taxation for built-in stabilizer purposes are small. Thus the economic argument against indexation of the tax system is weak.

16-6   ALTERNATIVE STRATEGIES TO REDUCE INFLATION

Suppose the inflation rate in the economy is 10 percent, and concerned policy makers decide to fight inflation and bring the rate down to the range of 2 to 3 percent. How fast should they aim to reduce inflation?

Gradualism

Figure 16-5 shows the choices. A policy of *gradualism* (in the left panel) attempts a slow steady return to low inflation. The policy begins with a small reduction in the money growth rate that shifts the economy a little way along the short-run Phillips curve *PC*, from *E* to *E'*. The increased unemployment at *E'* causes the short-run Phillips curve to move from *PC* to *PC'*. Policy makers then make a further small cut in the growth rate of money, moving to *E'''*. In response to the slightly higher unemployment, and because the expected inflation rate is falling, the short-run Phillips curve again shifts down (not shown in the figure). The policy continues, with policy makers gradually cutting the growth rate of money as the short-run Phillips curve slowly moves down in response to both unemployment and the falling inflation rate that reduce the expected rate of inflation.

Eventually the economy returns to low inflation with full employment at point *E''*. There has not been any massive unemployment during the adjustment process, although unemployment has remained above normal.

Cold Turkey

The right panel of Figure 16-5 shows the alternative. The *cold turkey strategy* tries to cut the inflation rate fast. The strategy starts with an immediate sharp cutback in money growth, creating a large recession as the economy moves from *E* to *E'*. Even so, the reduction in inflation is small to begin with, because the short-run Phillips curve is flat.

By creating massive unemployment immediately, though, the cold turkey strategy causes the short-run Phillips curve to shift down rapidly. The *PC'* curve in the right panel of Figure 16-5 is lower than *PC'* under gradualism. That is because the much bigger recession of the cold turkey strategy drives down the rate of wage increase more quickly than happens under gradualism. The cold turkey strategy keeps up the pressure, by holding the rate of money growth low. Eventually the rate of inflation falls sufficiently that output and employment begin to recover. The economy returns to point *E''* with full employment and a lower rate of inflation.[15]

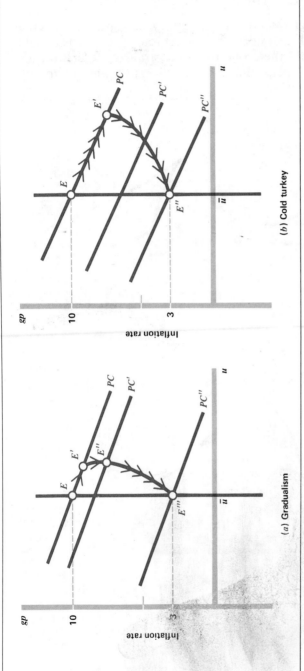

(a) Gradualism

(b) Cold turkey

FIGURE 16-5. STRATEGIES TO REDUCE INFLATION. Under the gradualist strategy, the growth rate of money is reduced slowly, so that the unemployment rate does not increase much. The economy gradually moves from E to E'', with the growth rate of money being cut all the way down, and the short-run Phillips curve slowly moving down from PC to PC''. The cold turkey strategy, by contrast, starts with a large cut in the growth rate of money. The economy moves initially from E to E' on PC. There is a lot of unemployment and not much reduction in the inflation rate. But then the short-run Phillips curve moves down faster than it does under the gradualist strategy. The economy reaches E'' more rapidly than it would under gradualism, but with higher unemployment on the way.

Gradualism versus Cold Turkey

Figure 16-6 presents the gradualist and cold turkey strategies in an alternative form. In the gradualist strategy the growth rate of money is initially reduced only slightly, and the economy never strays very far from the natural rate of unemployment. But the inflation rate comes down only

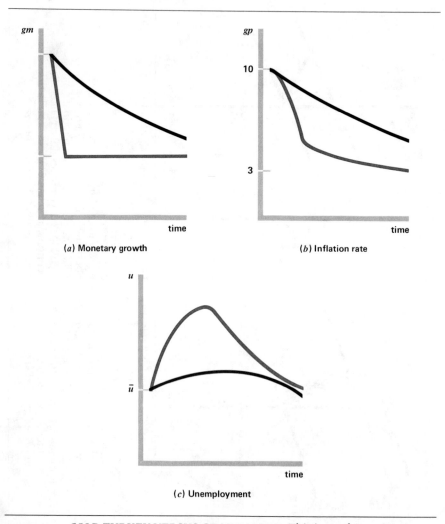

(a) Monetary growth

(b) Inflation rate

(c) Unemployment

FIGURE 16-6   COLD TURKEY VERSUS GRADUALISM. This is an alternative way of comparing the two strategies. Cold turkey (coloured curves) cuts the growth rate of money immediately to its new steady-state level, producing a massive recession and relatively rapid reduction in the inflation rate. The gradualist strategy (black curves) produces less unemployment, but also a much less rapid reduction in the inflation rate.

slowly. The cold turkey strategy, by contrast, starts with a massive cut in the growth rate of money and a large recession. The unemployment rate is much higher than it ever is in the gradualist strategy, but the reduction in inflation is more rapid.

Credibility

The cold turkey strategy has one major point in its favour, though. It is clear in the case of cold turkey that a decisive policy change has been made, and that policy has the firm aim of driving down the inflation rate. The gradualist strategy, which takes a long time to be implemented, is more likely to be abandoned if it seems to be producing more unemployment than expected, or if the policy-making team changes.

Thus people forming their expectations rationally will be more likely to believe policy has changed under the cold turkey strategy than under gradualism. A belief that policy has changed will by itself drive down the expected rate of inflation, and for that reason cause the short-run Phillips curve to shift down. A credible policy is one that the public believes will be kept up and succeed. The cold turkey policy gets a *credibility bonus* that gradualism does not.

Contracts and Disinflation

However credible a policy is, it will not lead to instant disinflation in an economy that has long-term wage contracts, that is, contracts that run for a year or more. On the other hand disinflation is somewhat easier if contracts include indexation of wages.

When contracts are indexed, disinflation is more rapid, because any success at reducing inflation translates automatically into reduced rates of wage and cost increases. To see this, compare two contracts. One is nominal, with the wage scheduled to rise automatically by 10 percent at the beginning of each of the next 2 years. The other is indexed, and the wage is scheduled to grow by 2 percent plus the rate of inflation that actually occurred during the past year. If the inflation rate were 8 percent, the two contracts would imply the same wage increases. On the other hand, if a disinflation program succeeds in reducing the rate of inflation to 5 percent, wages in the indexed contracts will rise by only 7 percent in the following year, while in the other contract the increase is unaffected. In the latter case firms would suffer severe losses, and that would tend to reduce the willingness and ability of the authorities to implement rapid disinflation. By contrast, with indexation, reduced wage inflation allows still further rounds of inflation reduction in rapid succession.

It is easiest to change the inflation rate when there are no long-term contracts in the economy. There will be few contracts of that kind if inflation is high and variable. Under such conditions no one will want to sign agreements in nominal terms because they will be gambling too much on the future behaviour of the price level. Since there are delays in producing the price index, even indexed contracts become risky. At high and variable rates of inflation, long-term contracts disappear, and wages and prices are frequently reset. A credible policy will have rapid effects, but such rapid success cannot be expected in an economy where the structure of contracts has not yet been destroyed by extreme inflation.

Is There a Better Way?

The treatments for the inflation disease summarized in Figure 16-6 are painful, and have led to a search for better ways. In this section we briefly describe two other anti-inflationary policies, incomes policy and tax incentive plans.

Incomes Policy

Inflation stabilization takes time and involves unemployment because that is what is needed to get the rate of wage change down. Incomes policies try to short-circuit that slow process by getting the rate of wage change down fast, either by law (wage-price controls) or by persuasion. *Incomes policies* are policies that attempt to reduce the rate of wage and price increases by direct action. Either wages and prices are controlled, or the government tries to persuade labour leaders and business to raise wages and prices more slowly than they otherwise would. Incomes policies, if successful, shift the short-run Phillips curve down.

A wage-price freeze certainly brings the inflation rate down. So why not get rid of inflation that way? The reason is that wages and prices have to change if resources are to be allocated efficiently in the economy. Anti-inflationary policy has to try to reduce the average rate of price increase without interfering with the role of prices in allocating resources. Over a short period, misallocations of resources from frozen wages and prices will be small and not costly. But if wages and prices are kept fixed for a long time, shortages of labour and particular goods will develop. The problem then is to find a way out of controls that does not reignite inflation.

Less formal income policies, for instance, trying to persuade labour union leaders that they should moderate their wage claims, should work in the same way as wage-price controls. But such policies have rarely been successful in bringing down the inflation rate over any prolonged period.

One reason incomes policies have rarely if ever succeeded is that they have not been combined with appropriate aggregate demand policies. The long-run inflation rate cannot be reduced if the short-run Phillips curve is shifted down while the rate of money growth stays high. That will reduce the inflation rate in the short run, but will also reduce unemployment. Then wages will again start increasing more rapidly, and eventually the incomes policy will break down and the economy move right back to where it started.

For incomes policies to have a chance of reducing the inflation rate in a lasting way, they have to be accompanied by restrictive aggregate demand policies. That rarely happens. Indeed, many observers argue that governments turn to incomes policies when they are not serious about reducing the inflation rate. They hope to get the inflation rate down in the short run without doing anything about the long-run rate of inflation.

It is entirely possible that incomes policy could help reduce the unemployment costs of an anti-inflationary program, so long as the incomes policy is indeed combined with restrictive aggregate demand policies.

TIP

Tax incentive plans (TIP) to reduce the inflation rate encourage workers and firms to keep wage and price increases low by providing tax incentives to do so.

For instance, TIP might set a baseline rate of wage increase of 5 percent. Any firm that pays a higher rate of wage increase to its employees has its taxes increased. Any firm paying a lower rate of wage increase receives a tax break. Or the penalties and rewards might be placed directly on the workers. Any worker receiving an increase in excess of 5 percent would have his or her tax rate increased, and so forth.

The major problem with TIP is that it would be very difficult to administer. The aim is to discourage wage or price increases that are being made only to compensate for inflation. We would not, for instance, want to penalize a worker who has a large wage increase because he or she has worked hard and has been promoted. But how can the law discriminate between these two cases? If the law says anyone who is promoted is not penalized for receiving a rate of wage increase above the baseline rate, firms and workers who find it in their joint interest to raise the wage will do so by promoting people.

Both incomes policies and TIP run into the same difficulty. The difficulty is that relative wages and prices in the economy do have to change if the price mechanism is to work. Policies that operate directly on wages and prices have to try to prevent the overall price level from rising while relative prices are permitted to change. This is either impossible or extremely difficult over any extended period.

In the following chapter, we look at the policy choices that have been made by the policy authorities in Canada and consider the consequences for the Canadian economy.

16-7 SUMMARY

1   The anatomy of unemployment for Canada reveals frequent and short spells of unemployment. Nonetheless, a substantial fraction of unemployment is accounted for by those who are unemployed for quite a long time.

2   There is considerable variation of unemployment rates across different regions and groups in the labour force.

3   The concept of the natural rate of unemployment singles out that part of unemployment which would exist even at full employment. The unemployment arises in part because of a high frequency of job changes. The natural rate of unemployment is hard to conceptualize and even harder to measure. It has recently been estimated to be about 6 percent compared with 4.5 percent in the fifties.

4   The cost of unemployment is the psychic and financial distress of the unemployed as well as the loss of output. The loss of output is not compensated by the unemployed's enjoying leisure. For one thing, a large part of unemployment is involuntary. For another, the social product of labour exceeds the wage rate because of income taxes.

5   The economy can adjust to perfectly anticipated inflation by moving to a system of indexed taxes and to nominal interest rates that reflect the expected rate of inflation. Thus there are no important costs to perfectly anticipated inflation. The only costs are those of changing price tags periodically and the cost of suboptimal holdings of currency.

6   Imperfectly anticipated inflation has important redistributive effects among sectors. Unanticipated inflation benefits monetary debtors and hurts monetary creditors. The government gains real tax revenue, and the real value of government debt declines.

7   If the real interest rate is constant, the Fisher equation implies that an increase in the rate of inflation will lead to an equal increase in the nominal interest rate once the expected rate of inflation has adjusted to the actual rate.

8   Wage indexation links increases in money wages to increases in the price level. It prevents changes in real wages that would otherwise come about if the actual inflation rate differs from what was anticipated.

9   Under a progressive income tax, inflation raises real taxes. This problem can be alleviated by indexing exemptions and tax brackets.

10   There are alternative approaches to reducing the inflation rate. A gradualist policy tries to keep unemployment low by reducing the inflation rate slowly. A cold turkey policy attempts to get the inflation rate down rapidly by creating a big recession to begin with. The cold turkey policy has the advantage that it is more credible.

11   Alternative policies to reduce inflation include incomes policies (wage-price controls and less formal approaches) and tax incentive plans. They have not been implemented successfully.

KEY TERMS

Unemployment pool
Duration of unemployment
Natural rate of unemployment
Structural unemployment
Perfectly anticipated inflation
Fisher equation

Wage indexation
Gradualism
Cold turkey
Incomes policy
Tax incentive plans (TIP)

PROBLEMS

1 Discuss strategies whereby the government could reduce unemployment in or among:
   (a) Depressed industries
   (b) Unskilled workers
   (c) Depressed geographical regions
   (d) Teenagers
   Include comments on the *type* of unemployment you would expect in these various groups (that is, relative durations of unemployment spells).

2 Discuss how the following changes would affect the natural or structural rate of unemployment. Comment also on the side effects of these changes.
   (a) Elimination of unions
   (b) Increased participation of women in the labour market
   (c) Larger fluctuations in the *level* of aggregate demand
   (d) An increase in unemployment benefits
   (e) Elimination of minimum wages
   (f) Larger fluctuations in the *composition* of aggregate demand

3 Discuss the differences in unemployment between adults and youths. What does this imply about the types of jobs (on average) the different groups are getting?

4 Some people say that inflation can be reduced in the long run without an increase in unemployment, and so we should reduce inflation to zero. Others say a steady rate of inflation at, say, 6 percent is not so bad, and that should be our goal. Evaluate these two arguments and describe what, in your opinion, are good long-run goals for inflation and unemployment. How would these be achieved?

5 The following information is to be used for calculations of the unemployment rate. There are two major groups, adults and youths. Youths account for 25 percent of the labour force and adults for 75 percent. Adults are divided into men and women. Women account for 40

percent of the adult labour force. The following table shows the unemployment rates for the groups.

Group	Unemployment rate, u
Youths	15%
Adults:	
Men	7%
Women	8.5%

(a) How do the numbers in this table compare (roughly) with the numbers for the Canadian economy?
(b) Calculate the aggregate unemployment rate.
(c) Assume the unemployment rate for youths rises from 15 to 20 percent. What is the effect on female unemployment? (Assume 50 percent of the youths are men.) What is the effect on the aggregate unemployment rate?
(d) Assume the share of women in the adult labour force increases to 45 percent. What is the effect on the unemployment rate? What is the effect on the aggregate unemployment rate?
(e) Relate your answers to methods of estimating the natural rate of unemployment.

6 Use the data in Table 16-6 to calculate what 1975 and 1980 unemployment would have been if each group in 1975 and 1980 had the unemployment rate of the group in 1966. What does the answer tell you?

7 (a) What are the economic costs of inflation? Distinguish between anticipated and unanticipated inflation.
(b) Do you think anything is missing from the list of costs of inflation that economists present? If so, what?

8 (a) Explain the Fisher equation that describes the relationship between the nominal interest rate and expected inflation.
(b) Use figure 16-4 to show that the real interest rate was very high in 1981.

CHAPTER 16: FOOTNOTES

[1]For a detailed description of the definitions used and the data collection procedures, see notes at the end of Statistics Canada, 71-001.

[2]We should recognize that when the labour force is growing and the unemployment rate is constant, the pool of unemployed grows over time. For example, with a labour force of 8 million and 5 percent unemployment, total unemployment is 400 thousand people. With a labour force of 10 million and 4.5 percent unemployment, there are 450 thousand unemployed, and the unemployment pool has grown by 50 thousand people.

[3]See E. Phelps, "Economic Policy and Unemployment in the Sixties," *Public Interest*, Winter 1974.

[4]See P. Fortin and L. Phaneuf, "Why is the Unemployment Rate So High in Canada?" Paper presented at the meetings of the Canadian Economics Association, May 1979. The estimates for 1979 and 1980 are from F. Reid and D. A. Smith, "The Impact of Demographic Changes on Unemployment," *Canadian Public Policy*, 1981.

[5]See Robert J. Gordon, "The Welfare Cost of Higher Unemployment," *Brookings Papers on Economic Activity*, 1973:1 (Washington, D.C.: The Brookings Institution, 1973); and Edmund S. Phelps, *Inflation Policy and Unemployment Theory* (New York: Norton, 1972).

[6]See Harry Maurer, *Not Working* (New York: Holt, Rinehart and Winston, 1979), and Kay L. Schlozman and Sidney Verba, *Injury to Insult* (Cambridge: Harvard University Press, 1979).

[7]The relationship between nominal interest rates and the rate of inflation is called the Fisher effect and is discussed in more detail in the next section.

[8]See William J. Fellner, introductory essay in William J. Fellner (ed.), *Contemporary Economic Problems* (Washington, D.C.: American Enterprise Institute, 1973).

[9]Arthur M. Okun, "The Mirage of Steady Inflation," *Brookings Papers on Economic Activity*, 1971:2 (Washington, D.C.: The Brookings Institution, 1971).

[10]See Charles R. Nelson, "Inflation and Rates of Return on Common Stocks," *Journal of Finance*, May 1976. See also Franco Modigliani and Richard Cohn, "Inflation, Rational Valuation and the Market," *Financial Analysts Journal*, March-April 1979, for a controversial view of the reasons why inflation affects the stock market.

[11]Fisher (1867–1947) taught at Yale, and was an effective and sophisticated developer of the quantity theory of money. (See Box 13-1.) He had other interests too; he was the inventor of the card index file still used for keeping addresses, and was a health food enthusiast who wrote several books on the subject. Fisher was an early, if long forgotten, discoverer of the Phillips curve. See the reprinted version of his 1926 article "A Statistical Relation between Unemployment and Price Changes," under the heading "Lost and Found," *Journal of Political Economy*, March/April 1973, pp. 496–502.

[12]Irving Fisher, *The Theory of Interest* (New York: A. M. Kelly Publishers, 1965, reprint of 1930 edition), p. 427.

[13]The initial argument is due to Eugene Fama, "Short-Term Interest Rates as Predictors of Inflation," *American Economic Review*, 1975. For subsequent discussion see David Begg, *The Rational Expectations Revolution in Macroeconomics* (Baltimore: Johns Hopkins University Press, 1982), and Frederic Mishkin, *A Rational Expectations Approach to Macroeconomics* (Chicago: University of Chicago Press, 1983).

[14]This scheme does not make the personal income tax fully neutral. For example, full indexing would require the taxation of interest to be on the *real* (after-inflation) return on assets. A rough allowance for this was made in the budget of November 1974 by permitting $1,000 of interest income tax free.

[15]It is possible that the economy does not return directly to equilibrium but rather overshoots the new equilibrium, with the inflation rate falling below the new equilibrium rate and perhaps fluctuating before settling down. For simplicity we concentrate on the paths shown in Figure 16-5.

Current Issues in Macroeconomic Policy

In this chapter we focus on both current policy issues and the theories of economic policy that help explain the policy choices that have been made and their failure or success. The use of active discretionary policy has been increasingly questioned in recent years. The view that active use of stabilization policy might be destabilizing was discussed in Chapter 12 and had long been argued by adherents of *monetarism*. Monetarist views were influential in the formulation of policy by the early 1970s. In the latter part of the decade, a more sophisticated critique of discretionary policy, developed by the *rational expectations* school, gained influence. In the 1980s there has been a major debate about the effects of large government deficits.

Any student may wonder about a field where opinions and policy prescriptions change so often, and he or she may worry too about the difference of views among macroeconomists at a given time. For instance, what should you conclude when one economist says that the budget deficit is the biggest problem facing the economy in the 1980s, and another says that it is better to maintain the current level of government spending and taxes by borrowing to finance the deficit?

This chapter describes the interaction of policy and ideas in the 1970s and early 1980s. It takes up the historical evolution from where we left it in Chapter 12. In that chapter we considered the 1930s which gave birth to the Keynesian revolution. Keynesian economics remained the mainstream of macroeconomic theory until inflation began to get out of hand in the late 1960s. Since then, macroeconomic theory has struggled with the problem of inflation, analysing the roles of the money stock, expectations, and the supply side in determining the levels of output and prices.

Because policy and ideas are so intertwined, we shall, in discussing the main macroeconomic currents, refer also to economic events of the time. We show how theories influence policies, and how the results of policies influence views about theory. It is entirely appropriate that we change our views of the way the economy works on the basis of experience. There is never certainty about the way the world works, and any worthwhile field of study develops over time as new evidence comes in.

It is also true that the disagreements among economists, and the distinguishing features of different points of view, are systematically exaggerated by the media. Macroeconomic controversies are always in the newspapers because macroeconomics concerns some of the most important issues of daily life — whether jobs are hard or easy to find, whether prices are rising slowly or fast, whether living standards will rise fast or hardly at all. The disagreements are systematically exaggerated because disagreements are news.

Behind the rapidly changing macroeconomic fashions of the media is a more balanced macroeconomic analysis that addresses current economic problems while at the same time weighing carefully evidence that leads to changes — mostly small, but sometimes large — in macroeconomic theories.

17-1 MONETARISM

Milton Friedman and monetarism are almost synonymous. Monetarism appears, however, in many shades and covers quite a spectrum from a hard monetarism, beyond the Friedman variety, to eclectic Keynesianism. In that spectrum one would include Karl Brunner of the University of Rochester, Allan Meltzer of Carnegie-Mellon, Thomas Mayer of the University of California at Davis, Phillip Cagan of Columbia University, David Laidler and Michael Parkin of the University of Western Ontario, and William Poole of Brown University, to name only some of the most prominent. Monetarism is not confined to academic economists. Indeed, the Federal Reserve Bank of St. Louis has long been a haven for the monetarist perspective on macroeconomics. If monetarism admits of some diversity, it nevertheless comes down to the proposition that money is extremely important for macroeconomics, that money is more important than other things such as fiscal policy, and, in some variants, that money is virtually all that matters.

We define monetarism by describing Friedman's views, but we should warn you that in so doing we overemphasize Friedman's role in developing and sustaining monetarism. Friedman's views on macroeconomics have been laid out in a series of scholarly articles, books, and popular writing.[1] Outstanding among his publications is *A Monetary History of the United States, 1867–1960*, a book written jointly with Anna J. Schwartz of the National Bureau of Economic Research. Despite its length, the *Monetary History* is an absorbing book that skilfully relates the behaviour of the economy to the behaviour of the stock of money. The book generally attributes changes in the level of prices and in economic activity, including the Great Depression, to movements in the stock of money.

What are the main features of monetarism?

Emphasis on the Stock of Money

Monetarism emphasizes the importance of the behaviour of the money stock in determining (1) the rate of inflation in the long run and (2) the behaviour of real GNP in the short run. Friedman has said:[2]

> I regard the description of our position as "money is all that matters for changes in *nominal* income and for *short-run* changes in real income" as an exaggeration but one that gives the right flavor of our conclusions.

The view that the behaviour of the money stock is crucial for determining the rate of inflation in the long run is consistent with the analysis of Chapter 15, as we noted there. The view that the behaviour of the money stock, by which Friedman usually means the *growth rate* of the money stock, is of primary importance in determining the behaviour of nominal and real GNP in the short run is not one we have accepted. Our treatment so far has given emphasis to *both* monetary and fiscal variables in determining the short-run behaviour of nominal and real GNP. But there is no doubt that monetary variables play an important role in determining nominal and real GNP in the short run.

An important part of monetarism is the insistence that changes in the growth rate of money — accelerations and decelerations — account for changes in real activity. Instability in monetary growth is mirrored in variability in economic activity. Thus Friedman argues:[3]

> Why should we be concerned about these gyrations in monetary growth? Because they exert an important influence on the future course of the economy. Erratic monetary growth almost always produces erratic economic growth.

Friedman's view of the primary importance of money is based in part on his careful historical studies, in which he was able to relate the booms and recessions of United States economic history to the behaviour of the money stock. In general, it appeared that increases of the growth rate of money produced booms and inflations, and decreases in the money stock produced recessions and sometimes deflations.

Long and Variable Lags

Monetarism has emphasized that although the growth rate of money is of prime importance in determining the behaviour of GNP, the effects of changes in the growth rate of money on the subsequent behaviour of GNP occur with long and variable lags. On average, it takes a long time for a change in the growth rate of money to affect GNP, so the lag is long. In addition, the time it takes for this change to affect GNP varies from one historical episode to another — the lags are variable. These arguments are based on empirical and not theoretical evidence. Friedman estimates the lags may be as short as six months and as long as two years.

The Monetary Rule

Combining the preceding arguments, Friedman argues against the use of active monetary policy. He suggests that because the behaviour of the money stock is of critical importance for the behaviour of real and nominal GNP, and because money operates with a long and variable lag, monetary policy should not attempt to "fine-tune" the economy. The active use of monetary policy might actually destabilize the economy, because an action taken in 1984, say, might affect the economy at any of various future dates, such as in 1985 or 1986. By 1986, the action taken in 1984 might be inappropriate for the stabilization of GNP. Besides, there is no certainty that the policy will take effect in 1986 rather than 1985. For example, suppose that the economy is currently in a recession, and that the money supply is increased rapidly today to increase the growth rate of real GNP. Today's increase in the growth rate of money might affect GNP within 6 months, and achieve its purpose. However, it might work only in 2 years, by which time GNP might well already have increased without the aid of the monetary policy action. And if the expansionary monetary policy affects an economy by then close to full employment, inflation will result.

Thus monetarists argue that although monetary policy has powerful effects on GNP, it should not be actively used lest it destabilize the economy. Accordingly, their view is that the money supply should be kept growing at a constant rate, to minimize the potential damage that inappropriate policy can cause.[4]

The Unimportance of Interest Rates

In the *IS-LM* model changes in the money stock affect the economy primarily by affecting interest rates, which, in turn, affect aggregate demand and thus GNP. When interest rates are low, monetary policy seems to be expansionary, encouraging investment and thus producing a high level of aggregate demand. Similarly, high interest rates seem to indicate contractionary policy. Since the central bank can control the level of interest rates, and since interest rates provide a guide to the effects of monetary policy on the economy, it seems perfectly sensible for it to carry out monetary policy by controlling interest rates. Through the 1950s and most of the 1960s, central banks did carry out monetary policy by attempting to set the level of interest rates.

Friedman and monetarism brought two serious criticisms of the procedure of attempting to set interest rates as the basis for the conduct of monetary policy. The first is that the behaviour of nominal interest rates is not a good guide to the direction, whether expansionary or contractionary, of monetary policy. The *real* interest rate, the nominal interest rate minus the expected rate of inflation, is the rate relevant to determining the level of investment, as we saw in Chapter 8. A high nominal interest rate, together with a high expected rate of inflation, means a low real rate of interest. Thus monetary policy might be quite expansionary in its effects on investment spending even when nominal interest rates are high. Consequently, Friedman and other monetarists argued, the central bank should not concentrate on the behaviour of nominal interest rates in the conduct of monetary policy.

The second criticism is that attempts to control nominal interest rates might be destabilizing. Suppose that the central bank desired that monetary policy should be expansionary and that the interest rate should be lowered. To achieve these goals it buys bonds in the open market, increasing the money supply. The expansionary monetary policy itself tends to raise the inflation rate. It thus tends to raise the nominal interest rate as investors adjust their expectation of inflation in response to the behaviour of the actual inflation rate. However, then the central bank would have to engage in a further open market purchase in an attempt to keep the nominal interest rate low, and that would lead to further inflation, further increases in nominal interest rates, and further open market purchases. The end result is that an attempt to keep nominal interest rates low may lead to increasing inflation. Therefore, Friedman argues, the central bank should not pay attention to the behaviour of nominal interest rates in the conduct of monetary policy,[5] and should, rather, keep the money supply growing at a constant rate.

Each of these arguments on the dangers of conducting monetary policy by reference to nominal interest rates is important. It is indeed correct that real, and not nominal, interest rates provide the appropriate measure of the effects of monetary policy on aggregate demand. It is also true that the central bank could, by attempting to keep nominal interest rates low forever, destabilize the economy. However, once the latter danger has been pointed out, the probability that it will destabilize the economy by operating with reference to interest rates is reduced. The use of interest rates as a guide to the direction of monetary policy does not mean that the central bank has to attempt to keep the interest rate fixed forever at some level. Instead, it may aim each month or quarter for an interest rate target that it regards as appropriate for the current and predicted economic situation.

The monetarist case for concentrating on the behaviour of the money stock in the conduct of monetary policy is a strong, but not conclusive, one. The major weakness in the argument is that the demand for real balances may change over time and indeed has done so. A simple numerical example should help make the point. Suppose that real income is constant, and that the nominal interest rate is constant. Suppose also that the demand for real balances is constant. Then if the money supply grows at, say, the rate of 5 percent, the price level, too, will grow at 5 percent, so that the stock of real balances remains constant. Now suppose, instead, that the demand for real balances is falling by 2 percent per year. Then if the nominal money supply increases at 5 percent per year, the price level has to increase at 7 percent per year to keep the supply of real balances equal to the demand. Thus, shifts in the demand for money affect the rate of inflation, given the growth rate of money. In this example, if the demand for real balances grew at 5 percent per year, 5 percent money growth would not be inflationary at all. These shifts in demand raise the possibility that concentration on the behaviour of the nominal stock may be seriously misleading and inappropriate for the conduct of monetary policy.

The possibility is not purely hypothetical. For instance, in the fourth quarter of 1976, the rate of growth of the money supply fell below the Bank of Canada's target range at a time when real income was rising and interest rates were falling. Under these circumstances, the demand for real balances should, according to the demand for money function of Chapter 9, have been increasing. However, real balances were actually falling at the time, despite the rising real income. This suggests that the demand for money was shifting — that people were reducing their demand for real balances at given levels of interest rates and income. It was appropriate then for the Bank of Canada to allow the supply of real balances to fall. Concentration on the behaviour of the money stock as a guide to monetary policy would have been inappropriate and inflationary.

Given the possibility, and the actual experience of shifts in the demand for money, we see that the behaviour of the money stock is not a perfect guide to the conduct of monetary policy. Neither is the behaviour of nominal interest rates. However, the behaviour of the nominal money stock and the behaviour of nominal interest rates both provide some information about the direction in which monetary policy is pushing the economy, imperfect as each measure is. Accordingly, the central bank should pay attention to the behaviour of both interest rates and the supply of money in the conduct of its monetary policy.[6]

The Importance of Fiscal Policy

Friedman has frequently, if tongue in cheek, said that fiscal policy is very important. Although we noted earlier that he argues fiscal policy itself is not important for the behaviour of GNP, he does contend that it is of vital importance in setting the size of government and the role of government in the economy. Friedman is an opponent of big government. He has made the interesting argument that government spending increases to match the revenues available. The government will spend the full tax collection — and some more. Accordingly, he is in favour of tax cuts as a way of reducing government spending.

Friedman stands out in arguing that fiscal policy does not have strong effects on the economy except to the extent that it affects the behaviour of money. Thus he has remarked:[7]

> To have a significant impact on the economy, a tax increase must somehow affect monetary policy — the quantity of money and its rate of growth. . . .
>
> The level of taxes is important — because it affects how much of our resources we use through the government and how much we use as individuals. It is not important as a sensitive and powerful device to control the short-run course of income and prices.

The Inherent Stability of the Private Sector

The final aspect of monetarism we consider here is the monetarist view that the economy, left to itself, is more stable than when the government manages it with discretionary policy, and that the major cause of economic fluctuations lies in inappropriate government actions. This view is quite fundamental in that it underlies many other monetarist positions, and it may be the litmus test for distinguishing monetarists from other macroeconomists. It is because this point is so fundamental that a major stage in the acceptance of monetarism occurred when Friedman and Schwartz published their *Monetary History of the United States*. In it they provided evidence for the view that the Great Depression was the result of bad monetary policy rather than private sector instability, arising, say, from autonomous shifts in consumption or investment demand.

Summary: We Are All Monetarists

From the viewpoint of the conduct of economic policy, the major monetarist themes are (1) an emphasis on the growth rate of the money stock, (2) arguments against fine tuning and in favour of a monetary rule, and (3) a greater weight that monetarists, as compared for example with Keynesians, place on the costs of inflation relative to those of unemployment.

Although we describe these as the major monetarist propositions relating to policy,[8] it is not true that macroeconomists can be neatly divided into two groups, some subscribing to the monetarist religion and others to a less fundamentalist faith called neo-Keynesianism. Most of the arguments advanced by Friedman and his associates are technical and susceptible to economic analysis and the application of empirical evidence. Many of those propositions are now widely accepted and are no longer particularly associated with monetarism. As Franco Modigliani has remarked, "We are all monetarists now." He adds that we are monetarists in the sense that all (or most) macroeconomists believe in the importance of money.

Much of the analysis of this book would, a few years ago, have been considered monetarist. For example, we have assumed that the Phillips curve is vertical, a proposition that was originally associated with monetarism. We have laid considerable stress on the behaviour of the money stock and less stress on the behaviour of interest rates. We have emphasized that fiscal policy affects long-run inflation to the extent that it affects the long-run growth rate of money. Older readers will doubtless detect other places at which we appear monetarist to their eyes. That is all to the good. If economists did not modify their analyses in the light of new theories and evidence, the field would be barren.

Friedman and his associates have indeed changed macroeconomics. The forceful and persuasive way in which he has emphasized the role of money has changed the views of most economists on the importance of monetary policy. It is always possible that those views would have changed anyway, in the light of the increasing inflation of the sixties. The fact remains, however, that it was Friedman, and not someone else, who hammered away at the importance of money.

17-2   MONETARISM AND THE BANK OF CANADA

As we saw in Chapter 11, in the early 1970s the Bank of Canada moved toward greater emphasis on the control of the money supply in implementing monetary policy. In 1975 it began the practice of announcing target ranges for the rate of growth of the money supply.

In his *Annual Report* for 1975, the governor stressed the importance of bringing down the rate of inflation and addressed the question of how this should be accomplished:[9]

> One answer sometimes given to this question is that the Bank of Canada should do the job through a sharp and immediate reduction of the growth rate of the money supply to a rate approximately in line with the sustainable real growth of the economy. If that were to happen, it is asserted, inflation would readily come to an end.
>
> The trouble with this prescription is not with the medicine but with the dosage, which would be so great that the patient would suffer excessively while it was working. It would sharply curtail the growth of spending on goods and services in the face of continuing large increases in production costs already built into the economy, and this would almost certainly result in extremely weak markets, widespread bankruptcies and soaring unemployment. It must be recognized that the annual rate of increase in average Canadian money incomes that is consistent with price stability is no higher than the trend rate of increase in national productivity, which is usually put at around 2 per cent per year, and we are a long way from that situation. All sorts of existing arrangements, including virtually all wage contracts, are based on the assumption of some continuing inflation. The attempt to force

as rapid a transition to price and cost stability as this prescription involves would be too disruptive in economic and social terms to be sensible or tolerable.

Thus the Bank of Canada clearly rejected a cold-turkey policy and opted for gradualism. This strategy was subsequently implemented by successive reductions in the target to the range of 4 to 8 percent established in February 1981. As can be seen in Figure 17-1, the Bank generally kept monetary growth within the target range until the second half of 1981.[10] As discussed in the next section, the Bank abandoned gradualism at that time in response to a severe tightening of monetary policy in the U.S.

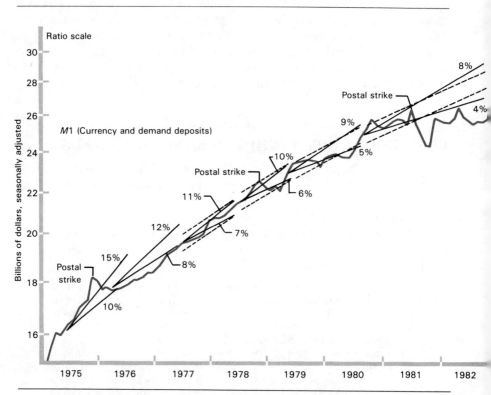

FIGURE 17-1   TARGET GROWTH RANGE FOR M_1
(Source: Bank of Canada, *Annual Report*, 1982)

Since the adoption by the Bank of Canada of a monetarist strategy, the governor has annunciated the philosophy and principles underlying it on a number of occasions. In a statement before the House of Commons

Standing Committee on Finance, Trade and Economic Affairs, the governor put forward three basic propositions.[11] The first reaffirmed the overriding importance of bringing down the rate of inflation:

> For quite a few years now the nature of the major threat to the future economic welfare of the country has been unusually clear. That threat is inflation. The idea that some inflation is on balance helpful to the performance of an economy, that inflation is benign — an idea that was never more than superficially plausible but was nevertheless quite popular — is now thoroughly discredited. What has discredited it so effectively is not economic theory but economic experience. The experience of the world economy and the widely varying experience of its national members have shown beyond reasonable question that inflation is malignant. The matter is no longer seriously debated.

As to the role of monetary policy in fighting inflation, the governor stated:

> there is one proposition that must never be forgotten, and that is that in a free society no strategy for dealing with inflation will succeed unless it is well supported by firm and continuing control of the rate of monetary expansion in the society. That proposition is, I assure you, as reliable as any general proposition in the whole field of economics. Every central banker in the world knows it to be true, and I doubt that any serious and experienced student of financial affairs would question it. It is a very firm proposition indeed, and anyone who wants to participate responsibly in the debate on how to deal with inflation would be well advised to keep it uppermost in his mind.

In his third proposition, the governor put forward the distinction between real and nominal interest rates:

> The basic reason why interest rates are so high is because current and expected rates of inflation are so high. If you make allowance for the current rate of inflation, interest rates are not in fact unusually high. They are not so high as to provide savers with a large real return before taxes or in many cases with a real return at all after taxes. They are not so high as to discourage borrowers who expect continued high rates of inflation.

Thus the Bank of Canada has made a clear commitment to an anti-inflation policy based on monetary gradualism. In doing so, it recognized the consequences not only for the levels of output and employment, but also for the behaviour of nominal interest rates. In his *Annual Report* for 1978, the governor stated:[12]

> Whatever their object, however, central bank actions that have the effect of speeding up or slowing down the trend over time in the rate of growth of the money supply have longer run effects on the level of interest rates that can be quite the opposite of the effects produced in the short run. A stepped-up rate of monetary expansion that temporarily lowers interest rates will, if it is sustained, lead eventually to a higher rate of price increase than would otherwise have occurred. With money losing its value more rapidly, borrowers will be less reluctant to incur

debt since they can repay in dollars of lesser value, while savers and lenders will for the same reason be more reluctant to provide loans. The consequence of rising inflation will thus be a growing excess demand for credit in relation to the supply which will put increasing upward pressure on interest rates. Thus the eventual result of letting the money supply grow too rapidly is not low interest rates but high interest rates.

If a country wants to have and maintain low interest rates, there is no secret about how to achieve that. Monetary growth must be reduced until it is only just sufficient to finance the expansion in production that the economy is capable of achieving over the longer run without putting pressure on the over-all level of prices, and it must be kept there. The immediate effect of this policy will be to raise interest rates but the longer term effect will be to lower them. The low interest rate countries of the world are the ones that have had the greatest success over the years in resisting the temptation to allow inflationary pressures to be underwritten by excessive monetary expansion. The countries that have experienced less success in controlling the process of domestic monetary expansion have higher rates of inflation and higher interest rates.

17-3   THE FIGHT AGAINST INFLATION, 1975–1983

As discussed in the previous section, the Bank of Canada instituted a policy in late 1975 of gradually reducing the rate of growth of the money supply. At the same time, the government announced a program of wage and price controls to be administered by an Anti-Inflation Board (AIB). The board was given statutory power to control wages and profit margins of private firms with 500 or more employees. Provincial and municipal government wage setting was brought into the program through agreements with the provinces to apply the guidelines established by the federal board. The controls remained in effect until they were phased out beginning in April 1978. Let us examine the performance of the Canadian economy in response to these two policy initiatives.

Wage Settlements and the AIB

The first panel of Figure 17-2 shows the average annual percentage increased in base rates of pay negotiated in wage contracts over the period 1974 to 1980. Prior to the information of the AIB, wage settlements had risen to nearly 19 percent per year, but during 1976 and 1977 there was a substantial moderation in the rate of increase. However, as shown in the fourth panel of Figure 17-2, during the same period the seasonally adjusted unemployment rate rose from 6.8 percent to 8.4 percent. To measure the effect of the controls it is necessary to estimate on the basis of historical experience what wage increases would have occurred in the absence of controls given the actual economic conditions experienced.

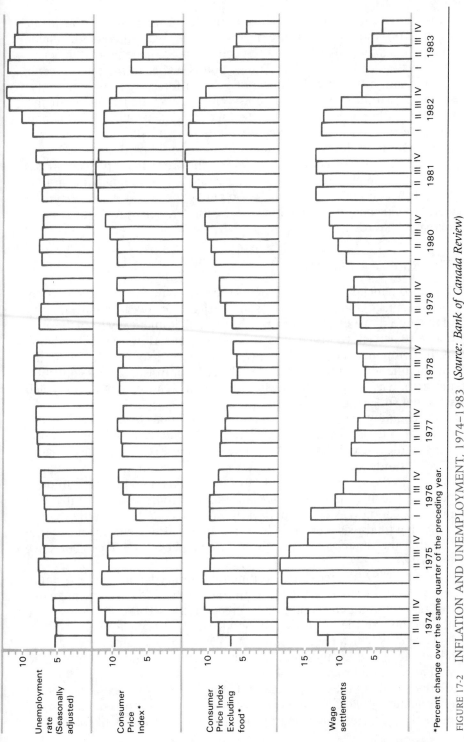

*Percent change over the same quarter of the preceding year.

FIGURE 17-2   INFLATION AND UNEMPLOYMENT, 1974–1983   (*Source: Bank of Canada Review*)

In a study undertaken for the Economic Council of Canada, Cousineau and Lacroix estimated that the average annual wage increase in major collective agreements would have been 1.7 percentage points higher in the private sector and 4.3 percentage points higher in the public sector had the anti-inflation guidelines not been in force.[13] In another study, Auld, Christofides, Swidinsky and Wilton concluded that:[14] "in the period of AIB wage controls, union wage settlements in the private and public sectors have been between 2½ and 3½ percentage points per annum lower than the pre-AIB wage structure would predict; by 1977 the cumulative wage affect of the AIB was on the order of 3.2 per cent in the private and 4.6 per cent in the public sectors." Thus it would appear that controls had an impact particularly on public sector wages, but that they were responsible for a limited part of the moderation in negotiated wage increases that occurred.

The Rate of Inflation

The third panel of Figure 17-2 shows the rate of inflation as measured by the percentage change in the Consumer Price Index over the same quarter of the preceding year. During 1976 the rate fell dramatically from the level above 10 percent recorded in 1975 to 5.9 percent. However, a closer look at the components of the CPI shows that very little of this decline in the rate of inflation can be attributed to the AIB controls. A major contributing factor was the sharp decline in the rate of increase of food prices which were not subject to controls.

Since food prices typically exhibit wide variations from year to year, it is common to use the CPI excluding food as a measure of the underlying trend in the rate of inflation. As can be seen in the second panel of Figure 17-2, this index shows a slow but steady decline from the fourth quarter of 1975 to the second quarter of 1978 when it fell to 6 percent. Unfortunately in the third quarter of 1978, the downward trend in the underlying rate of inflation was reversed, and by the third quarter of 1981, the CPI excluding food was increasing at a rate above 13 percent, in spite of the fact that the unemployment rate had remained above 7 percent since mid-1976.

In June 1982, the federal government introduced a limited program of wage controls known as the 6 and 5 program that limited wage increases to 6 percent in the first year and 5 percent in the second. The restrictions applied only to the federal public service and Crown corporations. Federal agencies which regulate prices such as telephone rates were asked to adhere to the guidelines and most provincial governments introduced similar restraint programs.

Concern about the rising rate of inflation also led to a severe tightening of monetary policy. During the first half of 1981, the Federal Reserve pushed up interest rates sharply in the U.S. and the Bank of Canada followed suit. By the middle of the year short-term interest rates in Canada had risen above 20 percent. As can be seen in Figure 17-2, the rate of inflation subsequently declined sharply, but this was achieved by exploiting the short-run Phillips curve tradeoff and allowing a drastic increase in the unemployment rate.

Was Monetarism a Failure?

The performance of the Canadian economy over the period 1975 to 1983 led to considerable controversy over the monetarist strategy of the Bank of Canada.[15] The success of the Bank's policy was hindered by the impact of supply shocks, problems with the implementation of gradualism, and difficulties in using money supply measures as targets of policy.

Supply Shocks and Inflation

One can accept the monetarist view that control of the money supply is an essential part of any anti-inflationary policy while at the same time recognizing that other factors influence short-run movements in the price level. In particular, the sharp increases in world prices of oil and other commodities that occurred in 1973–74 and 1978–79 led to increases in both the rate of inflation and the unemployment rate.[16]

Gradualism

The Bank of Canada has argued on a number of occasions that the failure of its anti-inflation policy over the period 1975–1980 was in part caused by excessive gradualism. For example, in a statement before the House of Commons Standing Committee on Finance, Trade and Economic Affairs, Governor Bouey stated:[17]

> The experience of the past few years appears to have led some observers to conclude that the Bank's approach to reducing inflation has failed. If they mean that progress in reducing inflation is less than the Bank hoped, I agree with them. But if they mean, as I think some of them do, that the Bank's approach was misconceived, then they have misread the history of the period. What they should conclude is that given the economic and financial developments over that period, many of which were unpredictable, it would have been better if the slowing of monetary growth had been less gradual so that it would have had more impact on inflation. That is the moral that should be drawn. In this connection I would point out that the rate of monetary expansion today is very much lower than it was five years ago and although we have arrived at this position through a very gradual process, the impact on total spending can be expected to be much firmer from now on than it was when we started on this path.

This view was supported by the experience of the period 1981–1983 when the Bank of Canada abandoned gradualism. Following the lead of the Federal Reserve in the United States and Prime Minister Thatcher's government in Britain, the bank brought down the inflation rate by a severe tightening of monetary policy. Experience in all three countries showed that controlling monetary growth can indeed bring down the rate of inflation, but, because of the long lags, the process is very slow unless the economy is pushed into a very deep recession.

The Use of Monetary Targets

The Bank of Canada's Annual Reports for 1981 and 1982 both contained detailed discussions of the Bank's experience with the use of $M1$ as a target of monetary policy. It is argued that the usefulness of this measure of the money supply has been impaired by innovations in banking practice such as daily interest savings accounts and expanded cash management services for businesses. Initially the Bank attempted to adjust for these influences on the demand for money, but in November 1982 it announced that it would no longer establish $M1$ targets.

As we saw in Chapter 11, the use of money supply targets is appropriate when the demand for money is stable and the main source of disturbances is the goods market. The breakdown in the stability of the money demand thus forced the Bank to abandon money supply targets.

17-4   THE RATIONAL EXPECTATIONS APPROACH

The failure to reduce inflation in the 1970s and the apparent inability of macro policy to achieve its goals led to a reconsideration of the premises of modern macroeconomics. The reconsideration places great emphasis on expectations, on the credibility of policies, and on the limited scope for discretionary stabilization policies. The general emphasis on expectations and the credibility of policies is widely shared. Indeed, we have explained much of the behaviour of the inflation rate and wage increases by appealing to expectations of inflation and the belief that anti-inflationary policies would not be long-lived. This emphasis and its implications have been taken further by a group of economists who have developed the *rational expectations approach* to macroeconomics. Among the leading members of the school are Robert Lucas of the University of Chicago and Thomas Sargent and Neil Wallace of the University of Minnesota.[18] Most other macroeconomists have by the 1980s accepted some parts of the rational expectations approach.

We distinguish between two aspects of the rational expectations approach.

1   *Rational expectations as a theory of expectations.* As a theory of expectations, the notion of rational expectations assumes that individuals use information efficiently and do not make *systematic* mistakes in expectations. This

assumption is made on occasion by almost all macroeconomists, and its use does not automatically qualify the user as a member of the rational expectations school.

Rational expectations as a theory of expectations implies that policy cannot rely for its effectiveness on systematic misunderstandings by the public. For instance, if at first the public does not understand that counter-cyclical tax changes are transitory, those changes will have powerful effects on the economy. However as people begin to realize that tax changes are reversed as the economy reaches full employment, such a policy comes to have less powerful effects because the tax changes are understood to be transitory. The expectations part of rational expectations suggests that it is best, in formulating policy, to assume that the public will soon understand how a particular policy is working. It also implies that any policy which works for some time only because the public does not correctly anticipate its effects is doomed to eventual failure.

2   *The market clearing approach.* Economists belonging to the rational expectations school (as we define it here) assume that markets always are in equilibrium, or *clear*, and that economic agents set wages and prices, given the information they have, so as to achieve maximum profits and utility.

It is the market clearing assumption that distinguishes the rational expectations school. This strong assumption has three major implications. The first is that there is no involuntary unemployment. Why? Because anyone who expects to be unemployed, or who is currently unemployed and would prefer to work, can find work by asking for it at a wage below the existing wage. If, at the existing wage, the individual prefers not to work but rather to continue searching for a job, then the unemployment is voluntary. Of course, the theory recognizes that there is some normal level of unemployment corresponding to individuals who are between jobs or looking for their first job.

If there is no involuntary unemployment, why, then, does the level of output vary? Here the theory points to two factors. The first consists of changes in the level of potential output. The second, more important, involves mistakes in perceiving the current economic situation. Suppose that individuals do not know the aggregate price level in the current period. Of course, they do know the wage at which they can work. They have to form an estimate of the *real* wage on the basis of the price level they expect to hold during the period. Now, if the price level should turn out to be unexpectedly high, then individuals overestimate the real wage and work harder than they would if they knew the true situation. Thus, *unexpectedly* high prices lead to a higher level of output than at full employment. Individuals are working harder than they would at full employment.

This mechanism is very subtle,[19] and it is regarded by some as implausible. It clearly requires that individuals do not have complete information about the current state of the economy. Otherwise, with all markets clearing, the economy would be at the full-employment level of output. Indeed, one of the consequences of the development of the rational expectations school has been a growing emphasis on the information that individuals use and process in making their economic decisions.

The Ineffectiveness of Monetary Policy

The second implication follows closely from the first. It is that the level of output cannot be affected by changes in monetary policy unless those changes are not perceived by individuals in the economy. Suppose that it is believed and known that the money supply has changed. Then individuals know the price level should be higher and adjust their prices and wages accordingly so as to produce full employment immediately. If there is a lag in the publication of data on the money stock, individuals will adjust prices to the level of the money stock they expect. If the money stock turns out to be higher than expected, aggregate demand will be higher, and output will rise because of the mechanism, described earlier, in which individuals mistakenly work harder, believing the real wage is above the level at which it currently is. We thus arrive at the most famous proposition advanced by the rational expectations school, that *with regard to monetary policy, only unexpected changes in the stock of money affect the level of output*.

The lack of policy effectiveness that the rational expectations school advances as a central proposition is well summarized in the following quote:[20]

> Whatever the government does, individuals will catch on, and if not immediately, then quickly. . . .
>   That is what the rational expectations hypothesis says: individuals, anxious to do as well as they can, make the best possible forecasts. And it is an implication that the government cannot influence the unemployment rate, except maybe over a very short short run.
>   It may be a bit hard for you to swallow, my contention that the public is always pretty much aware of what the government's stabilization policy is — what its objectives are and what it will be doing to achieve those objectives. Each of us has at least one rather dim relative, an uncle perhaps, maybe even an aunt, who does not have the faintest notion what the phrase ''stabilization policy'' means, let alone know what the actual policy of the moment is. It is, however, not required that everyone know, only some, those who are strategically located. For example, where trade unions represent workers, it is enough that the leadership know. And it would seem right that the typical present-day union leadership is pretty well informed.

If only unanticipated changes in the stock of money affect the level of output, then monetary policy cannot affect the level of output except by producing *surprises*. This leads to the third implication: Under these circumstances, there appears to be no role for monetary policy systematically to affect output or unemployment. Any systematic policy, such as increased monetary expansion in a recession (remember that recessions are possible as a result of surprises), would be predicted by market participants, and wages and prices would be set accordingly. Unless the central bank had better information or shorter reaction lags than the market, it could not, according to this theory, have a systematic *real* effect.

The proposition that only monetary *surprises* affect output has been the subject of intense empirical research. Early work by Robert J. Barro[21] appeared to support the proposition. Later research by, among others, Frederic Mishkin and Robert Gordon cast substantial doubt on the early findings.[22] The later results suggest that both expected and unexpected changes in the money stock affect output. By this stage, the evidence does not support the strong implication of the market clearing approach that only unanticipated changes in the money stock affect output. Accordingly, the evidence also does not support the view that systematic monetary policy does not affect the behaviour of output.

BOX 17-1   DISEQUILIBRIUM ECONOMICS AND POST-KEYNESIAN
ECONOMICS

In the main text we have developed the history of ideas as running from Keynesian economics to monetarism and the rational expectations challenge. However, two other strands of macroeconomics are sufficiently distinct and fruitful to deserve attention.

The Disequilibrium Approach

As early as the 1950s economists recognized the implications of disequilibrium in one market for supply or demand in other markets. If workers cannot sell all the labour they wish at the going wage, and cannot borrow, how will this affect their consumption decision? If they cannot buy all the goods they wish at the going prices, how does this affect their supply of labour or their demands for money and other assets? If firms cannot sell at the going price all the output they would like to produce, how does this affect their demand for labour?

The disequilibrium approach answers these questions by constructing a model of the economy that explicitly takes into account the *quantity constraints* on the decisions which households and firms face. Quantity constraints are present when households or firms cannot at the going wages or prices buy or sell all the quantities they wish. Central to the approach is the assumption that wages and prices do not move rapidly, leaving markets in disequilibrium, which gives rise to quantity adjustments. These quantity adjustments in different markets are interdependent through the quantity constraints under which households and firms make their optimal decisions.*

The most interesting contribution of the disequilibrium approach so far has been to influence empirical work. For example, studies of consumption pay close attention to the role of income and wealth, reflecting the possibility that individuals cannot borrow against future income so that *liquidity constraints* affect spending behaviour. In studies of the labour market the approach suggests the important distinction between "high-wage" or classical unemployment on one side and Keynesian or "lack of demand" unemployment on the other. (See Box 15-1.)

Post-Keynesian Economics

Post-Keynesians are a diverse group of economists who share the belief that modern macroeconomics leaves aside or explicitly assumes away many of the very central elements of Keynes' *General Theory*.†

Five elements of this approach stand out distinctly. First, adjustment, just as in the disequilibrium approach, takes place primarily through quantity adjustment, not price changes. Indeed, price changes where they occur are often seen as disequilibrating. Second, the distribution of income between profits and wages plays a central role in affecting consumption and investment decisions. Third, expectations (Keynes' animal spirits), together with profits, are the chief determinant of investment plans. Fourth, institutional features — credit constraints on households and self-finance by firms, as well as the financial structure involving credit creation in a pyramid — interact in shaping the business cycle and on occasion financial crises. Finally, unlike in classical macroeconomics, the focus of post-Keynesian economics is to explain why the economy does not work well.

Post-Keynesian economics remains an eclectic collection of ideas, not a systematic challenge, as, for example, the rational expectations hypothesis. It has influenced economists in their research program, but the deliberate downplaying, indeed rejection, of individual rationality and maximization as a basis of behaviour by firms and households has kept the approach at odds with the mainstream of the profession that has been attempting to bring macroeconomics into closer touch with microeconomics.

---

*The early reference is D. Patinkin, *Money, Interest and Prices* (New York: Harper & Row, 1956). The complete working out of these ideas can be found in R. Barro and H. Grossman, *Money, Employment and Inflation* (London: Cambridge University Press, 1976); and E. Malinvaud, *The Theory of Unemployment Reconsidered* (Oxford: Basil Blackwell, 1977), and *Profitability and Unemployment* (Oxford: Basil Blackwell, 1981).
†For an introduction see A. Eichner (ed.), *A Guide to Post-Keynesian Economics* (White Plains, N.Y.: M. E. Sharpe, 1979), and the essays on post-Keynesian economics in the *American Economic Review*, May 1980.

Relative Wages, Wage Contracts, and Rational Expectations

The strongest form of the rational expectations theory just outlined, which assumes market clearing in every period and attributes fluctuations to imperfect information, has not been supported by the evidence and is not widely accepted. There are, however, models that use rational expectations as a theory of expectations but also recognize economic institutions such as long-term contracts and the importance of the relative wages of various groups in the labour market.[23] Relatively simple amendments have gone far in removing some of the least plausible implications of the strong market clearing form of rational expectations theory.

Suppose we have 2-year labour contracts and that half the contracts in the economy come up for renewal every year. Suppose further that we start from price stability and that an unanticipated decline in the money stock occurs. If all wages and prices were instantaneously flexible, they would immediately decline in proportion to the fall in money, and no real effects would arise. This does not occur, however, if we have long-term contracts that fix nominal wages. With a lowering in the money stock, there is potentially a decline in employment. Unemployed workers whose wages come up for renewal now have the choice of reducing their wages enough to become employed. If they do so, the price level will fall because the average wage has fallen. But when the price level falls, the real wage being paid to workers on existing contracts rises (the nominal wage they receive is fixed, and the price level has fallen), and some of them lose their jobs.

In addition, workers may be concerned that their *relative* wages not fall. If those whose contracts come up for renewal now accept cuts in wages large enough to keep them fully employed, their wages will have to fall relative to those whose wages were negotiated earlier. Workers may be willing to accept some unemployment if they can keep their wages in line with those of others. If so, current wages will be set somewhere in between the full-employment level and the level of wages contracts still running. That means wages do *not* adjust immediately to money changes; that is, wages are less than fully flexible. It takes some time until the whole wage structure adjusts. The fact that we have long-term, nonsynchronized wage setting, and that relative wages matter, directly implies the possibility of extended periods of wage stickiness and unemployment.

The model is thus able to explain simultaneous wage inflation and unemployment. Suppose there is a contraction in demand, as we have just discussed, and that labour knows that policy will be expansionary in the future. Then those whose wages are currently up for renegotiation recognize that if they set too low a wage, they will be out of line with the wages that will be set next year by a group that will then be facing strong demand. Accordingly, even with the possibility of current unemployment, the prospect of expansionary aggregate demand policies in the future will make current economic slack less effective in dampening wage and price inflation. Rational expectations enter here in that the groups currently setting their wages look ahead and ask themselves what will be the macroeconomic environment in which other groups set their wages next period. If the policy setting next period is expected to be expansionary, this fact will already be anticipated in this year's wages.[24]

The relative wage model, combined with rational expectations, thus has two important features: first, wages are sticky downward in the face of unemployment; and second, wage inflation may persist in the face of unemployment. The extent of persistence is determined by, among other things, the degree to which the policy setting is accommodating or not.

Rational Expectations, Credibility, and Disinflation

At the end of Chapter 16 we discussed the choice between gradualist and cold turkey approaches to inflation reduction. That choice was widely considered at the end of the 1970s as the inflation rate increased to the double-digit range and the costs in terms of unemployment of policies to reduce inflation were weighed against the costs of continued inflation.

Members of the rational expectations school took a more optimistic view of the costs of reducing the inflation rate than did other economists. In its most extreme form, the rational expectations (market clearing) approach would argue that it takes only the announcement of a permanently lower growth rate of the money stock to get the inflation rate down immediately, but there were few who took such a suggestion seriously. Almost all economists recognized that some unemployment would be necessary to reduce the inflation rate. Members of the rational expectations school were on the more optimistic side, though.

The more optimistic view of the rational expectations school was based on two factors. First, like others, the members emphasized the role of expectations of inflation in determining the response of wages and prices to changes in policy. Second, they argued that the effects of policy depend on the *credibility* (believability) of the policy. In particular, they argued that if the central bank implemented a new policy, and was understood to be serious about the change in policy (that is, if the policy was credible), expectations would adjust rapidly and the recession could be short-lived.

The idea that credibility plays a role in an anti-inflation strategy can be accepted without embracing the rational expectations view in total. Indeed, the Bank of Canada has frequently alluded to the importance of public confidence in the resolve of the policy authorities. For example, in March 1982, Governor Bouey commented on the lack of progress in bringing down the inflation rate as follows:[25]

> It does not seem to me that Canadians are yet convinced that public policies will be firm or persistent enough to bring about a substantial reduction in the rate of inflation in Canada. Such imbedded expectations make the return to a better economic performance in Canada much more difficult.

Policy Making under Rational Expectations

The rational expectations approach has led to a more sophisticated view of policy making than prevailed earlier. The rational expectations approach emphasizes that economic agents do not react mechanically to every policy change. Rather, they try to figure out what the policy change means for the behaviour of the economy, and for future changes in policy. And they behave accordingly. For instance, as we noted in Chapter 7, economic agents adjust their consumption more in response to a permanent income tax cut than to a transitory tax cut of the same size.

The approach leads also to an emphasis on institutional changes as ways of altering the behaviour of the economy. Members of the rational expectations school are less interested in what policy should be *now* than they are in ways of making it possible for policy to operate better in general. Members of the rational expectations school doubt that we know enough to predict how the public will respond in the short run to a particular policy change, because the response depends on how the policy measure affects expectations. However in the long run the public will catch on to the effects of any policy change, and it thus becomes possible to predict the long-run effects of long-run policy changes.

A rational expectations economist confronted with the inflationary experience of the seventies would argue that the best way to change the behaviour of the central banks is to change the institutional environment in which they work. Accordingly, such an economist is likely to support a monetary rule, for example, requiring the money supply to grow at 4 percent per year.[26]

Monetarists, too, support a monetary rule. Indeed, there is considerable overlap between the policy views of monetarists and those of members of the rational expectations school. The similarity extends to the usually conservative views of policy held by members of both groups. But there are important differences between the monetarist and rational expectations approaches to macroeconomics. Monetarists are willing to assume that expectations may be systematically wrong and that markets are very slow to clear, whereas a member of the rational expectations school would not make such assumptions. Monetarism can be viewed as operating within the same framework and model as Keynesianism, while disagreeing over the relative importance of monetary and fiscal policy. The rational expectations school believes that the standard framework is fundamentally flawed and thus has developed the market clearing approach, which argues that imperfect information is responsible for the business cycle. It is thus a more radical attack on standard macroeconomics than is monetarism.

Where will the rational expectations attack on conventional macroeconomics lead? It has already had a substantial influence on the way macroeconomists think. First, rational expectations is widely used as a theory of expectations. Second, the sophisticated view of policy, in which responses to policy depend on the public's analysis of what policy measures will do to current and future behaviour of the economy, is widely adopted. The market clearing approach, however, is more controversial than other components of the rational expectations view, and seems to be inconsistent with the slow reaction of the economy to policy measures.[27] A modified approach, such as that described above involving wage contracts and other institutional features of the economy, may emerge as a synthesis of the rational expectations approach and more traditional macroeconomics. Such a synthesis is fully consistent with the approach to macroeconomics developed in this book.

17-5   DEFICITS, INFLATION, AND INSTABILITY

This is the section where we finally discuss the consequences of deficits. The main question is, What, if anything, is wrong with running budget deficits? The common beliefs are that deficits are inflationary and that they crowd out investment. We will see that the inflationary impact of a deficit depends on how it is financed. The impact of deficits also depends on whether they are short-lived or permanent.

We draw on the discussion of money and inflation in Chapter 15 to make the first point. *Inflation, in the long run, is determined by the rate of money growth. If the budget deficit does not affect long-run money growth, then it will not affect long-run inflation. If the method of financing the deficit does lead to higher money growth in the long run, it also leads to higher inflation.*

In those cases where the method of financing the deficit does not affect the long-run rate of money growth, the deficit does not lead to higher *long-run* inflation. For instance, if the deficit is short-lived, it will not affect the long-run rate of growth of the money stock, and will not lead to long-term inflation. It will, though, lead to higher inflation in the short run through the normal channels of fiscal expansion.

In this section we concentrate on money-financed deficits. We ask to what extent deficits can be financed through the printing of money, and what happens when not enough money can be printed to cover a given deficit. We start with a temporary budget deficit.

Money-Financed Transitory Deficits

The first case we consider is that of a deficit, say, due to a temporary cut in taxes, that is transitory and financed by money creation. The central bank buys the debt that the government issues to cover its deficit. The deficit is known to be temporary.

In Figure 17-3 we show a short-run Phillips curve *PC* and the vertical long-run Phillips curve *LPC*. Suppose now that the government cuts taxes and that there is consequently a budget deficit. The immediate impact of the reduction in taxes is to increase aggregate demand, shifting the economy up along the short-run Phillips curve *PC* to point *E'* from *E*.

As long as the deficit lasts, the central bank is increasing the money stock by buying debt. The rising money stock keeps aggregate demand rising. While the money stock is rising, inflation expectations increase, and aggregate demand expands because the money creation lowers interest rates and raises investment spending relative to the level that would obtain if the money supply were kept constant. However in the long run, by assumption, the deficit disappears. There is no further need for increas-

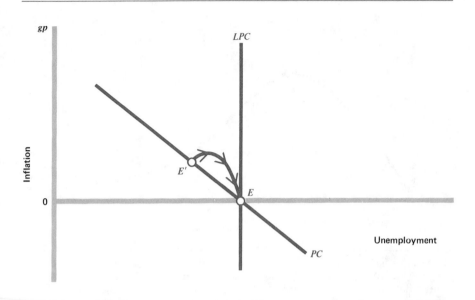

FIGURE 17-3 THE EFFECTS OF A TRANSITORY, MONEY-FINANCED DEFICIT. Initial equilibrium is at point E with zero inflation and unemployment at the natural rate. A transitory fiscal expansion raises aggregate demand, and this effect is reinforced by the money creation that finances the budget. The economy moves in the short run to E' with higher inflation and less unemployment. Once the government spending declines again, the economy returns to E. In the long run the only effect is the cumulative increase in the money stock and hence a cumulative increase in the level of prices.

ing the money stock, and inflation disappears along with the deficit. The economy therefore will follow a cycle as shown in Figure 17-3, with inflation above trend and unemployment below trend.

In the long run, inflation returns to its original level. The only effect of the transitory deficit is that it raises the money stock and the price *level*. Thus so long as a deficit is going to be transitory, it can be financed through the printing of money without any long-run effect on the inflation rate — though, of course, the increase in the money stock during the period of the deficit does result in a temporarily higher inflation rate.

Money-Financed Permanent Deficits

Permanent deficits financed by money creation necessarily affect the long-run inflation rate. We show now the relationship between the budget deficit and the inflation rate as the schedule AA in Figure 17-4.

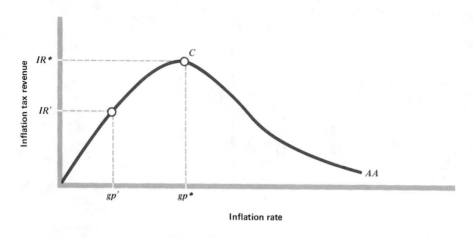

FIGURE 17-4 THE INFLATION TAX. At a zero inflation rate, the inflation tax revenue is zero. As the inflation rate rises, the government receives more revenue from inflation, up to point C, where the tax revenue reaches its maximum of IR^*. The corresponding inflation rate is gp^*. Beyond point C the demand for real balances is falling so much as the inflation rate increases that total tax revenues decline.

The Inflation Tax

When the government finances a deficit by creating money, it in effect keeps printing money, period after period, which it uses to pay for the goods and services it buys. This money is absorbed by the public. But why would the public choose to increase its holdings of nominal money balances period after period?

The only reason, real income growth aside, that the public would be adding to its holdings of nominal money balances is to offset the effects of inflation. Assuming there is no real income growth, in the long run the public will hold a constant level of *real* balances. But if prices are rising, the purchasing power of a given stock of *nominal balances* is falling. To maintain the real value of its money balances at a constant level, the public has to be adding to its stock of nominal balances, exactly at the rate that will offset the effects of inflation.

When the public is adding to its stock of nominal balances in order to offset the effects of inflation on holdings of real balances, it is using part of its income to increase holdings of nominal money. For instance, suppose someone has an income of $20,000 (nominal) this year. Over the course of the year, inflation reduces the value of his or her real balances. The person therefore has to add, say, $300, to his or her bank account just to maintain a constant level of real value of his or her money holdings. That $300 is not available for spending. The person seems to be saving $300 in the form of money holdings, but in fact in real terms he or she is not increasing wealth by adding $300 to nominal balances. All this person is doing is preventing wealth from falling as a result of inflation.

Inflation acts just like a tax because people are forced to spend less than their income and pay the difference to the government in exchange for extra money.[28] The government thus can spend more resources, and the public less, just as if the government had raised taxes to finance extra spending. When the government finances its deficit by issuing money, which the public adds to its holdings of nominal balances to maintain the real value of money balances at a constant level, we say the government is financing itself through the inflation tax.[29]

How much revenue can the government collect through the inflation tax? The amount of revenue produced by the inflation tax is the product of the tax rate (the inflation rate) and the object of the taxation (in this case the stock of real balances). When real output is constant, inflation tax revenue is given by

$$\text{Inflation tax revenue} = \text{inflation rate} \times \text{real balances} \qquad (1)$$

Now we can explain the shape of the curve *AA* in Figure 17-4. When the inflation rate is zero, the government gets no revenue from inflation. As the inflation rate rises, the amount of inflation tax received by the government increases. But, of course, as the inflation rate rises, people reduce their holdings of real balances, because it is becoming increasingly costly to hold money.[30] Eventually the quantity of real balances falls so much that the total amount of inflation tax revenue received by the government falls. Beyond point *C* the amount of inflation tax revenue actually falls as the inflation rate rises. This means that there is a maximum amount of revenue the government can raise through the inflation tax: it is shown as amount *IR** in Figure 17-4. There is a corresponding inflation rate, denoted *gp**, at which the inflation rate is at its maximum.

We can now turn to Figure 17-5 to study the long-run effects of money-financed deficits. We start at point *E* on the short-run Phillips curve *PC*. Now the government cuts taxes and finances the deficit by printing money. We assume the deficit is equal to amount *IR'* (in Figure 17-4), which is less than *IR** and thus can be financed entirely through the inflation tax. The tax cut moves us, in the short run, to point *E'*. But now money growth has been permanently increased, and inflation will in the long run move to the rate *gp'*, corresponding to the inflation tax revenue *IR'*.

The new steady-state inflation rate *gp'* is shown by the horizontal line in Figure 17-5. In the long run the economy reaches point *E''*. In that equilibrium expectations have fully adjusted to the inflation, and unemployment is back at the natural rate. Inflation equals the growth rate of money, and the inflation rate depends on the size of the deficit. The larger the deficit, the higher the inflation rate. Of course, it is even possible that the maximum amount that can be raised through the inflation tax is smaller than the budget deficit, and thus that long-run money financing of the deficit is impossible.

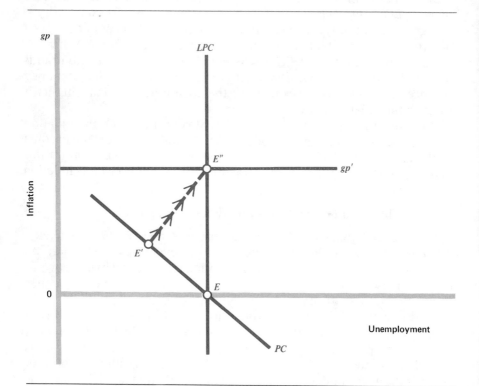

FIGURE 17-5   THE EFFECTS OF A PERMANENT MONEY-FINANCED DEFICIT. The long-run vertical Phillips curve is *LPC*. The schedule *gp'* shows the inflation rate required to finance the given real budget deficit. Starting from a zero deficit and long-run equilibrium at *E*, a permanent money-financed deficit first expands aggregate demand and leads the economy to *E'*. But over time, inflationary expectations adjust, and the economy returns to full employment at the permanently higher inflation rate *gp'*.

Hyperinflation

Money-financed deficits are inevitably part of the extreme inflations of 50 or 100 percent or more that we see on occasion in Latin America or Israel. They are also part of the even more extreme cases of *hyperinflation*. Hyperinflations are periods of very rapid inflation, in excess of 1,000 percent per year.

Suppose that the government is running a deficit larger than $IR*$ in Figure 17-4. This means it cannot raise enough revenue through inflation to cover the deficit. Suppose also that whenever it finds itself unable to pay for what it buys, it prints more high-powered money. In this case the inflation rate will keep on increasing. The public and the government will be competing for goods, with the government printing money, and the public trying to reduce its holdings of real balances and thereby driving up the inflation rate. Eventually the economy will experience a hyperinflation. For instance, in the German hyperinflation of 1922–1923, the average inflation rate was 322 percent *per month*. In October 1923, just before the end of the hyperinflation, prices rose by over 29,000 percent.[31] In dollars, that means that something that cost $1 at the beginning of the month would have cost $290 at the end of the month.

Keynes, in a masterful description of the hyperinflation process in Austria after World War I, tells of how people would order two beers at a time because they grew stale at a rate slower than their price was rising.[32] Other stories include those of a woman who carried her (almost worthless) currency in a basket and found that when she set down the basket for a moment, it was stolen, but the money was left.

To return now to the budget deficit, the basic point is that there are real deficits that simply cannot, in the long run, be financed by borrowing from the central bank, that is, by the issuing of high-powered money. Attempts to finance in that way would lead to hyperinflation. The fear that hyperinflation will result from large budget deficits may be one of the arguments in the minds of those most concerned over the budget deficit. However it is foolish to assume that any budget deficit, however small, will lead to a hyperinflation, even if it is financed by borrowing from the Bank of Canada.

The analysis of the inflation tax is not of great importance for Canada, with its well-functioning tax system and central bank. In other countries, with less well-developed tax systems, the printing of money may be one of the few ways the government has of obtaining resources. To put it differently, in some countries, large parts of government spending are financed by borrowing from the central bank and thus by inflation.

A Debt-Financed, Transitory Deficit

Figure 17-6 presents the aggregate demand and supply diagram of Chapter 14. We are once again considering the effects of a tax cut. The tax cut is temporary, and the budget deficit is financed by the selling of debt to the private sector. The initial effect of the cut in taxes is to shift the aggregate demand curve out from AD to AD_1. Because the private sector is buying bonds during the period of the deficit, it ends up holding a higher stock of government bonds. What effect does that higher stock of government debt held by the private sector have on aggregate demand?

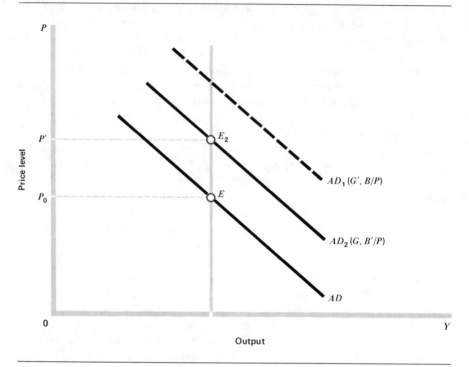

FIGURE 17-6   A TRANSITORY, DEBT-FINANCED DEFICIT. A cut in taxes shifts the aggregate demand curve from AD to AD_1. In the short run, aggregate demand expands. Because the deficit is transitory, the tax cut is later reversed. The rise in public debt that financed the transitory deficit raises the wealth of the debt holders. Once the deficit has returned to normal, the effect of increased debt outstanding implies higher aggregate demand. AD_1 shifts back only to AD_2 rather than to AD. There is a permanent increase in the price level and, given nominal money, a rise in interest rates.

Individuals holding government bonds regard those bonds as part of their wealth. Thus it would seem that given the level of income, aggregate demand should rise when the stock of government bonds rises, because individuals holding those bonds have higher wealth. The higher wealth increases consumption demand.[33] Accordingly, the aggregate demand curve would shift out to the right as a result of the increase in privately held wealth. Hence, we show the final aggregate demand curve, after government spending has returned to its original level, at AD_2 above the initial AD curve. The difference between the two aggregate demand schedules AD and AD_2 arises from the higher stock of government bonds B', compared with B on the initial aggregate demand curve. Since the effects of the higher wealth on consumption demand are likely to be small, we show the final aggregate demand curve AD_2 below the aggregate demand curve AD_1.

There are two complications to this analysis. The first is that the existence of the higher stock of debt raises the amount of interest payments in the federal budget. If the budget was originally balanced at point E, it may not be balanced at E_2. Of course, since the price level at E_2 is higher than at E, tax receipts may have risen at E_2 compared with E, and perhaps the budget would be balanced. But it need not be. If it were not, then further financing of the deficit would have to be undertaken, and that would have subsequent effects on the equilibrium.

Are Bonds Wealth?

The second complication is related to the first. It is possible that individuals in the economy calculate their wealth taking into account the tax payments they will have to make in the future. Suppose that everyone believed that the national debt would eventually be paid off. Then everyone would know that at some point in the future the federal government would have to run a surplus. Individuals might think the federal government would at some future date have to raise taxes in order to pay off the debt. In this case an increase in the debt would increase their wealth and at the same time suggest to them that their taxes would be higher in the future. The net effect on aggregate demand might then be zero. The issue raised by this argument is sometimes posed by the question, Are government bonds wealth?

There is another way of looking at this argument. Instead of concentrating on wealth, we concentrate on disposable income. An increase in the debt raises disposable income for the private sector because it raises the interest payments the private sector receives. The federal government has to finance those interest payments in some way. Suppose that it financed them by raising taxes or reducing other transfer payments. Then disposable income would be unaffected, despite the higher debt. Consumption demand in this case would be little affected by the increase in the national debt. With such a combined change in the debt and taxes that leave the budget balanced in the long run, the aggregate demand curve would return to its initial position at AD. There would be no (or little) long-run effect from the higher debt if the higher debt did not result in an unbalanced budget.

The theoretical and empirical issue of whether an increase in the national debt increases aggregate demand is not yet settled. It is difficult to isolate the effects of changes in the debt on consumption demand in empirical studies of consumption. The theoretical arguments we have are not conclusive. We are not certain whether individuals do take account of their future tax liabilities when they calculate their wealth. Thus we have to leave this question in an unresolved state.

Money and Debt Financing

There is one important difference between debt financing and money financing of a given short-run budget deficit. Money financing of the deficit tends to reduce the interest rate in the short run compared with debt financing. That is because money financing increases the nominal money stock (shifting up the *LM* curve in the *IS-LM* model), whereas debt financing does not. In the short run, then, debt financing reduces the level of investment compared with money financing. That is an issue connected with the crowding-out question.

We want also to compare the effects on the price level of money and debt financing of a temporary increase in government spending. The price level is higher with money financing than with debt financing. There are two reasons. First, money financing increases the money stock, and debt financing does not. The higher the money stock, the greater the aggregate demand at any given price level. Second, we attributed a price level rise in the case of debt financing to the wealth effect of a greater stock of debt on consumption. While there is some argument about whether bonds are wealth, there is no question that money is wealth. So the wealth effect on consumption is larger in the case of money financing than debt financing. That, too, means that aggregate demand at any given price level will be higher with money than with debt financing.

We now summarize the effects of a temporary budget deficit financed by debt creation. Such financing probably increases aggregate demand, but because of the possible effects of anticipated future tax liabilities on consumption, that is not certain. Debt financing, starting from a balanced budget and if not compensated for by higher taxes or reductions in other transfer payments, leads to a permanent deficit in the budget because interest has to be paid on the debt. Debt financing raises the interest rate and reduces investment in the short run as compared with the effects of money financing.

Interest Payments and the Government Deficit

Because of the rapid growth in the public debt in recent years, there has been a steep rise in interest payments. In 1974, interest payments on federal government debt amounted to $3 billion or 10 percent of federal expenditures. By 1983, interest payments had risen above $17 billion and accounted for nearly 20 percent of expenditures.

During the same period there was, of course, a substantial increase in the rate of inflation and nominal interest rates.[34] It can be argued that the government's deficit is overstated in a period of inflation because part of the government's interest payments on its outstanding debt is offset by the decline in the real value of the debt. The argument is thus that the interest payment component of expenditures should be calculated using the real interest rate rather than the nominal rate.

TABLE 17-1   ACTUAL AND INFLATION-ADJUSTED
FEDERAL BUDGET BALANCE (percent of GNP)

Year	Actual Balance	Inflation-Adjusted Balance
1970	.3	.8
1971	−.2	.1
1972	−.5	−.1
1973	.3	1.1
1974	.8	1.6
1975	−2.3	−1.8
1976	−1.8	−1.2
1977	−3.5	−3.0
1978	−4.6	−3.9
1979	−3.5	−1.9
1980	−3.3	−1.8
1981	−2.1	−.3
1982	−5.7	−4.2
1983	−6.2	−5.2

Source: Dept. of Finance, The Fiscal Plan, Feb. 1984.

Table 17-1 shows the actual and inflation-adjusted federal deficit as a percent of GNP. The difference is quite substantial particularly from 1979 onward when the debt was rising rapidly and there was a high inflation rate. In 1981, the adjusted deficit was comparatively small and when the calculation is made for all levels of government, the adjusted balance actually becomes a small surplus. The jump in the deficit in 1982 reflects the effect of the recession.

Viewed from this perspective, recent deficits do not appear nearly as large. Further, the impact of the deficit on aggregate demand may not be as large as the unadjusted figures suggest. To the extent that holders of government bonds treat the inflation component of interest as repayment of principal rather than current income, the deficit will be less stimulative.

Debt-Financed Permanent Deficits

We turn now to a permanent real deficit. Suppose, to begin with, that the economy is not growing. Then any attempt to run a permanent real deficit, financed by debt, will fail since, as the debt accumulates over time, interest payments on the debt increase. These rising interest payments can initially be handled by reducing other government expenditures, or by raising taxes, but eventually there are no other government expenditures to cut, and no more taxes to raise, and the ever-increasing interest payments cannot be paid by the government. Thus attempts to finance a given real deficit purely through debt financing cannot be viable in the long run in an economy that is not growing.[35]

Debt, Growth, and Instability

The impossibility of running a permanent debt-financed deficit in a non-growing economy is a dramatic conclusion, which certainly seems to justify concern over the massive deficits the Canadian economy faces for the next decade. It is therefore worth emphasizing what the problem is, and also showing why the problem is less serious in a growing economy.

Suppose the economy is not growing and the government is running a budget deficit. It can finance the deficit by issuing debt. But next period it has to pay interest on all the debt that existed in the past, *and also on the new debt that it issued to cover last period's deficit*. How can it pay this interest? One way is to borrow some more. But then next period the interest needed to service the debt is even larger, and hence even more debt needs to be issued, and so on.

The national debt in Canada has typically risen year after year for the past 30 years. Does that mean the government budget is bound to get out of hand, with interest payments rising so high that taxes have to keep rising, until eventually something terrible will happen? The answer is no, because the economy has been growing.

As we saw in Figure 12-5 in Chapter 12, until 1975 the ratio of debt to nominal GNP was falling even though the debt itself was rising as a result of budget deficits. This reflected the fact that GNP was increasing more rapidly than the debt.

Why is it useful to look at the ratio of debt to income rather than at the absolute value of the debt? The reason is that GNP is a measure of the size of the economy, and the debt-GNP ratio is thus a measure of the magnitude of the debt relative to the size of the economy. A national debt of $100 billion would have been overwhelming in 1950 when Canadian GNP was about $20 billion — even if the interest rate had been 2 percent, the government would have had to raise 10 percent of GNP in taxes to pay interest on the debt. However when GNP is nearly $400 billion, a $100 billion debt is not so overwhelming.

If the debt-GNP ratio starts out at a reasonably low level, government deficits that are small enough to ensure that the debt is not growing more rapidly than GNP are sustainable. But if the deficit is so large that the debt-GNP ratio is growing, with no obvious signs of the situation turning around, then there will be concern over the size of the deficit.

What would happen if the deficit were too large, so that debt grows relative to income seemingly without bounds? Such a process can really not go on forever. Ultimately the public debt totally overshadows and displaces other assets, and crowding out becomes so pervasive that the public comes to expect *some* action to balance the budget. This might involve either inflation or special taxes to balance the budget.[36]

How does inflation help solve the deficit problem? First, the inflation tax can make some small contribution to financing the deficit. But more importantly, a large *unanticipated* inflation will reduce the real value of the outstanding stock of government debt. The national debt in most countries is *nominal*, meaning that the government is obliged only to pay a certain number of dollars to the holders of the debt. A policy that raises the price level thus reduces the real value of the payments the government is obliged to make. The debt can therefore virtually be wiped out by a large enough unanticipated inflation, so long as the debt is a nominal debt.

The potential instability brought about by ever-growing debt means that ultimately some policies will be undertaken to handle the deficit problem. There may be tax increases, or reductions in government spending, or inflation, or all three.

It is important to have some perspective on the relevance of these extreme conditions to the world today. They are in no way relevant to the Canadian economy of the mid-1980s. There is no massive "debt problem," and there is no threat of instability even if deficits are large for some years. However, the debt to income ratio has been rising since 1975 and this cannot go on indefinitely.

SUMMARY

Table 17-2 summarizes the effects of alternative deficit scenarios. The table makes it clear that the really serious problems arise only when deficits are large and persistent. In that case inflation and possibly, in extreme cases, hyperinflation or instability are possible. Moderate deficits and especially small, temporary deficits do not pose a macroeconomic problem. In fact, over the business cycle it is entirely appropriate that there should be (larger) deficits during recessions offset by smaller deficits or surpluses during booms.

TABLE 17-2 EFFECT OF BUDGET DEFICITS ON LONG-RUN INFLATION AND PRICE LEVEL

	Permanent deficit	Transitory deficit
Money-financed	Higher inflation Huge deficits lead to hyperinflation	Higher price level
Debt-financed	Leads to instability, except for moderate deficits	Small long-run effects

The problems of the 1980s are budget deficits, but we could likewise talk about problems arising from budget surpluses. What would happen if the government embarked on a permanent tax increase leading to a surplus? Either debt would be retired until none was left, or the money stock would be declining without limit, causing prices to fall. At present the risk of persistent surpluses is not a realistic problem.

1   Monetarism lays heavy stress on the money stock as determining the level of output in the short run and the inflation rate in the long run.

2   Monetarists generally view the money supply as having powerful, but not easily predictable, effects on the economy. Money works with long and variable lags, and for that reason monetarists favour a monetary rule. They argue that interest rates are a poor guide to the direction of monetary policy, and they also believe that the private sector of the economy is inherently stable.

3   Monetarism's influence on monetary policy in Canada was reflected in the adoption of money supply targets in 1975. This practice was abandoned in 1982 because of instability in the demand for money.

4   The rational expectations approach to macroeconomics has two components. The first is a theory of expectations, arguing that people form expectations using all available information, and do not make systematic mistakes. The second is the market clearing approach. This assumes that markets are in equilibrium each period, and attributes deviations of output from full employment to imperfect information.

5   The market clearing approach implies that monetary policy can affect real output only by creating surprises. Early empirical evidence supported this view, but later evidence is less favourable.

6   A synthesis of rational expectations with more standard macroeconomics combines rational expectations assumptions with institutional features of the economy, such as long-term labour contracts. This can explain the slow adjustment of the economy to changes in monetary policy.

7   The rational expectations approach emphasizes the credibility of policies as an important factor determining their success or failure. The approach also views institutional reform as the main way to get better policy.

8   A temporary increase in government spending financed by an increase in the stock of high-powered money increases the price level permanently.

9   A permanent increase in government spending financed by money creation results in a permanent increase in the inflation rate.

10   Inflation can be regarded as a tax on real balances. The federal government collects the tax through the issue of high-powered money that it provides during inflation to meet the increased demand for

high-powered money. There is a maximum revenue that can be raised through the inflation tax.

11 A temporary increase in government spending financed by debt creation increases the price level permanently.

12 In a period of inflation, the government's deficit is overstated in the sense that part of the interest payments on outstanding debt is offset by a decline in the real value of the debt.

13 Debt financing of a permanent increase in government spending is not viable if the economy is not growing. The interest payments on the debt would continually increase, making for a rising deficit that has to be funded by ever-increasing borrowing. In a growing economy, small deficits can be run permanently without causing the debt-GNP ratio to rise.

KEY TERMS

Monetarism
Monetary rule
Anti-inflation Board (AIB)
Rational expectations
Market clearing
Credibility

Money-financed deficits
Inflation tax
Hyperinflation
Debt-financed deficits
Inflation-adjusted deficit

PROBLEMS

1 Outline the main tenets of monetarism.

2 Distinguish the two components of the rational expectations approach to macroeconomics.

3 Under what circumstances are fiscal and monetary policy related rather than existing as two completely independent instruments in the hands of the government?

4 In some countries there is virtually no capital market in which the government can borrow, and only a rudimentary tax system, so that taxes produce only very small revenues.
    (a) What is the relationship between monetary and fiscal policy in such countries?
    (b) What does the inflation tax analysis imply about the ability of the government in such a country to spend a large share of GNP permanently?

5 Analyse the difference in the impact on the interest rate, investment, and the price level of a temporary change in government spending, financed by money creation and borrowing, respectively.

6 What would be the effect of inflation on real income taxes if income taxation was:
(a) Regressive?
(b) Proportional?
(c) Indexed?

7 Analyse the effects on the economy of a permanent increase in the level of government spending financed by money creation.

8 Trace the path the economy follows when there is a permanent increase in government spending that is financed by borrowing from the public. Assume the economy is growing.

9 Evaluate the argument that the budget should be balanced every period.

*10 The elasticity of demand for real balances (M/P) with respect to the inflation rate (gp) is given by

$$\frac{\Delta(M/P)}{\Delta gp} \cdot \frac{gp}{(M/P)}$$

Prove that the elasticity is one at point C in Figure 17-4 where revenue is maximized.

CHAPTER 17: FOOTNOTES

[1] Some of Friedman's major articles are reprinted in *The Optimum Quantity of Money* (Chicago: Aldine, 1969). See also his book *A Program for Monetary Stability* (New York: Fordham University Press, 1959), and Milton Friedman and Anna J. Schwartz, *A Monetary History of the United States, 1867–1960* (Princeton, N.J.: Princeton University Press, 1963).

[2] "A Theoretical Framework for Monetary Analysis," *Journal of Political Economy*, March/April 1970, p. 217.

[3] "Irresponsible Monetary Policy," *Newsweek*, Jan. 10, 1972. Reprinted in Friedman's collection of public policy essays, *There's No Such Thing as a Free Lunch* (La Salle, Ill.: Open Court Publishing, 1975), p. 73.

[4] For a concise statement, see Milton Friedman, "The Case for a Monetary Rule," *Newsweek*, Feb. 7, 1972. Reprinted in Milton Friedman, *Bright Promises, Dismal Performance* (New York: Harcourt, Brace, Jovanovich, 1983), pp. 225–227. See too his article "The Role of Monetary Policy," *American Economic Review*, March 1968.

[5] The details of the argument are spelled out in Friedman's "The Role of Monetary Policy," *American Economic Review*, March 1968.

[6] The argument is worked out in Benjamin M. Friedman, "Targets, Instruments, and Indicators of Monetary Policy," *Journal of Monetary Economics*, October 1975.

[7] Milton Friedman, "Higher Taxes? No," *Newsweek*, Jan. 23, 1967. Reprinted in *There's No Such Thing as a Free Lunch, op. cit.*, p. 89.

[8] For a range of views on monetarism, see Franco Modigliani, "The Monetarist Controversy," *American Economic Review*, March 1977; Thomas Mayer, *The Structure of Monetarism* (New York: Norton, 1978); D. Batten and C. Stone, "Are Moneta-

rists an Endangered Species?'', Federal Reserve Bank of St. Louis, *Review*, May 1983; and J.H. McCulloch, *Money and Inflation* (New York: Academic Press, 1982).

[9]Bank of Canada, *Annual Report*, 1975, p. 10.

[10]The exceptions have been periods in which the payments system was disrupted by postal strikes as indicated in the chart.

[11]Reprinted in the *Bank of Canada Review*, November 1980, pp. 13–19. The earliest statement was given in an address to the Canadian Chamber of Commerce in Saskatoon in September 1975. This speech has been dubbed the ''Saskatoon monetary manifesto'' by Thomas Courchene. See T. J. Courchene, *Monetarism and Controls: The Inflation Fighters* (C.D. Howe Research Institute, 1976).

[12]Bank of Canada, *Annual Report*, 1973, p. 14.

[13]See Economic Council of Canada, Fourteenth Annual Review (1977), p. 20.

[14]D. Auld, L. Christofides, R. Swidinsky, and D. Wilton, ''The Impact of the Anti-Inflation Board on Negotiated Wage Settlements,'' *Canadian Journal of Economics*, May 1979, p. 209.

[15]See for example the following two studies sponsored by the Canadian Institute for Economic Policy: A. W. Donner and D. D. Peters, *The Monetarist Counter-Revolution, A Critique of Canadian Monetary Policy 1975–1979*; and C. L. Barber and J. C. P. McCallum, *Unemployment and Inflation, the Canadian Experience*.

[16]See the analysis of supply shocks in Section 15-5.

[17]See *Bank of Canada Review*, November 1978, p. 17.

[18]For an introduction, see Thomas Sargent and Neil Wallace, ''Rational Expectations and the Theory of Economic Policy,'' *Journal of Monetary Economics*, April 1976. See also the very useful paper by Bennett McCallum, ''Macroeconomics after a Decade of Rational Expectations: Some Critical Issues,'' in Federal Reserve Bank of Richmond, *Economic Review*, November/December 1982; and R. Lucas and T. Sargent, ''After Keynesian Macroeconomics,'' Federal Reserve Bank of Minneapolis, *Quarterly Review*, Spring 1979. (Also in Federal Reserve Bank of Boston, *After the Phillips Curve*, Conference Series No. 19, 1978.)

[19]The mechanism is discussed in more detail in Robert E. Lucas, Jr., ''Understanding Business Cycles,'' in Karl Bruner and Allan Meltzer (eds.), *Stabilization of the Domestic and International Economy*, Carnegie-Rochester Conference Series, vol. 5.

[20]J. Kareken, ''Inflation: An Extreme View,'' Federal Reserve Bank of Minneapolis, *Quarterly Review*, Winter 1978.

[21]Robert J. Barro, ''Unanticipated Money, Output, and the Price Level in the United States,'' *Journal of Political Economy*, August 1978.

[22]Frederic Mishkin, ''Does Anticipated Monetary Policy Matter? An Econometric Investigation,'' *Journal of Political Economy*, February 1982 (this is difficult reading); and Robert Gordon, ''Price Inertia and Policy Ineffectiveness in the United States, 1890–1980,'' *Journal of Political Economy*, December 1982.

[23]The discussion here follows a paper by John Taylor, ''Staggered Wage Setting in a Macro-Model,'' *American Economic Review*, May 1979. For a careful, advanced introduction see D. Begg, *The Rational Expectations Revolution in Macroeconomics* (Baltimore: Johns Hopkins University Press, 1983).

[24]Similar implications follow if workers are concerned about the real wages they will be receiving in future years, rather than relative wages.

[25]Remarks before the House of Commons Standing Committee on Finance, Trade and Economic Affairs; reprinted in *Bank of Canada Review*, April 1982. p. 15.

[26]You might wonder why members of the rational expectations school should care at all about monetary policy if they believe that (*a*) only unexpected changes in money affect real output, and (*b*) the public's expectations eventually catch up with reality. The two assumptions (*a*) and (*b*) seem to suggest that whatever the central bank is doing, it will eventually have no effect on real output. However, the strong form of rational expectations does not argue that monetary policy is irrelevant to the behaviour of *prices*. Thus members of the rational expectations school concerned about keeping inflation low can logically be in favour of a monetary rule that will prevent the average rate of growth of money from becoming high.

[27]See the discussion, especially by A. Okun, "Rational Expectations with Misperceptions as a Theory of the Business Cycle," in the special issue of the *Journal of Money, Credit and Banking*, November 1980.

[28]There is one complication in this analysis. The amount that is received by the government is the increase in the stock of *high-powered* money, because the central bank is buying debt with high-powered money. But the public is increasing its holdings of both bank deposits and currency, and thus part of the increase in the public's holdings of money does not go to the government to finance the deficit. This complication in no way changes the essence of the analysis.

[29]Inflation is often referred to as the "cruelest tax." This does not refer to the above analysis of the inflation tax, but rather to the redistributions of wealth and income associated with unanticipated inflation, discussed in Chap. 16.

[30]If bank deposits pay interest, then the interest rate on such deposits will rise with inflation, and the quantity of deposits demanded will not necessarily fall as the inflation rate increases. But no interest is paid on currency, and the quantity of currency demanded will fall as the inflation rate rises.

[31]Data based on C. L. Holtferich, *Die Deutsche Inflation, 1914–1923* (New York: Walter de Gruyter, 1980).

[32]See John Maynard Keynes, *A Tract on Monetary Reform* (New York: Macmillan, 1923), which remains one of the most readable accounts of inflation. See also Phillip Cagan, "The Monetary Dynamics of Hyperinflation," in Milton Friedman (ed.), *Studies in the Quantity Theory of Money* (Chicago: The University of Chicago Press, 1956). Cagan's article contains data on inflation rates in seven hyperinflations.

[33]Recall the discussion of wealth as a factor in consumption spending in Chap. 7.

[34]See Chap. 16 for a discussion of the Fisher effect and the relationship between nominal interest rates and inflation.

[35]The long-run effects of debt-financed changes in government spending are analysed in a well-known paper by Alan Blinder and Robert Solow, "Analytic Foundations of Fiscal Policy," in A. S. Blinder *et al.*, *The Economics of Public Finance* (Washington, D.C.: The Brookings Institution, 1974).

[36]See T. Sargent and N. Wallace, "Some Unpleasant Monetarist Arithmetic," Federal Reserve Bank of Minnesota, *Quarterly Review*, Fall 1981. As the title suggests, the treatment is technical. The main point the authors make is that debt problems ultimately become inflation problems.

Macroeconomic Policy and Inflation in an Open Economy

The analysis of income determination and the balance of payments in Chapters 5 and 6 was developed on the assumption that domestic prices were fixed and did not respond to changes in demand. In this chapter we consider a more realistic model incorporating the aggregate demand and supply analysis of Chapters 13 to 15.

In the first section we consider the determination of income, prices and the trade balance under fixed exchange rates, and describe the collapse of the fixed exchange rate system in the world economy during the early 1970s. The second section considers the flexible exchange rate case, and is followed by a review of Canadian experience under a flexible exchange rate since 1970. The chapter concludes with a discussion of some further issues concerning the functioning of a flexible exchange rate system.

18-1 TRADE BALANCE AND PRICES UNDER FIXED EXCHANGE RATES

We begin by considering the adjustment of income, prices and the trade balance under fixed exchange rates. In this section we ignore capital flows and treat the trade balance as the total balance of payments.

Aggregate Demand in an Open Economy

In the closed economy case considered in Chapter 13, the process by which the price level affects aggregate demand is as follows. A higher level of prices implies lower real balances, higher interest rates, and lower spending. In an open economy, the relation is slightly more complicated because now an increase in our prices reduces demand for our goods for two reasons. The first is the familiar higher interest rate channel summarized above. The second is that an increase in our prices leads to a loss of competitiveness. For a given exchange rate, an increase in domestic prices decreases the relative price of imports and raises the relative price of exports in foreign markets. Thus demand shifts from domestic goods to foreign goods.

The relative price that affects the trade balance and the demand for domestic goods can be represented in terms of the three determining variables as follows:

$$\frac{eP^*}{P} \tag{1}$$

P denotes the domestic price level, P^* denotes the price of foreign goods in terms of foreign currency (pounds per unit), and e is the domestic currency price of foreign exchange (Canadian dollars per pound). Thus the numerator of expression (1) is the price of foreign goods in terms of domestic currency. This relative price is often referred to as the *terms of trade*.

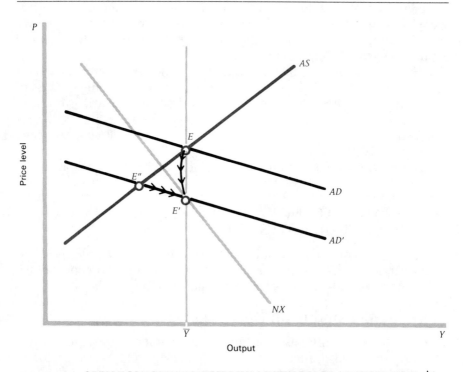

FIGURE 18-1   OPEN ECONOMY EQUILIBRIUM WITH PRICE ADJUSTMENT. At the point E, aggregate demand is equal to aggregate supply but the price level is too high so that we have a trade deficit. External balance can be achieved by contractionary policy that leads to a short-run equilibrium at E'' and an adjustment path among AD' to E'. Alternatively, under a fixed exchange rate with no sterilization, the money supply will decline and the economy will move from E to E' along the path shown.

In Figure 18-1, we show the downward-sloping demand curve for domestic goods, AD. It is drawn for a given level of the nominal money supply and given fiscal policy. In addition, the level of foreign prices (P^*) and the exchange rate (e) are given.

Internal and External Balance

The short-run aggregate supply curve, AS, and the full-employment level of output are also shown in Figure 18-1. The economy is shown in equilibrium at the point E where output is at full employment so that we have internal balance.

The external balance schedule NX is the set of combinations of income and the domestic price level along which we have a zero balance of trade for given levels of the exchange rate and foreign prices. An increase in domestic income raises imports and worsens the trade balance. To restore external balance domestic prices must fall so as to improve domestic competitiveness. Thus we show the external balance schedule as downward sloping.[1] We assume that it is steeper than the aggregate demand schedule.

The Adjustment Process

At the equilibrium point E in Figure 18-1, the domestic price level is too high in relation to the foreign price level so that we have a trade deficit. To achieve external balance, we have to use contractionary policies to shift the aggregate demand curve down to AD' so that it intersects the external balance schedule at E'. The short-run equilibrium will be at E" where we have unemployment. This puts downward pressure on wages and prices so that the aggregate supply curve shifts to the right and the economy moves along AD' to E'. Thus we are forced to push the economy into a recession to achieve external balance.

This process would occur automatically if the government did not pursue an active stabilization policy and pegged the exchange rate without engaging in sterilization operations. As we saw in Section 5-5, in the absence of offsetting open market operations there will be a link between the balance of payments and the domestic money supply. Indeed the central bank cannot offset a trade deficit indefinitely through sterilized exchange market intervention since it will use up its stock of foreign exchange reserves.

Since there is a deficit at point E, pegging the exchange rate without sterilization will lead to a decline in the stock of high-powered money (and hence the money supply) as the central bank sells foreign currency in exchange for domestic currency. This will cause the aggregate demand curve to shift down thereby creating excess supply. This will cause the aggregate supply curve to shift down as well so that the economy will follow the alternative adjustment path shown in Figure 18-1.

Price Level Versus Exchange Rate Adjustment

The adjustment process we have just described is called the *classical adjustment process*. It relies on price adjustments and an adjustment in the money supply based on the trade balance. This process "works" in the sense that it moves the economy to a long-run equilibrium with internal and external balance. However, the mechanism is far from attractive since it imposes a protracted recession simply to achieve a cut in prices.

An alternative solution is to recognize that external balance can be achieved in either of two ways. To restore competitiveness, domestic prices have to decline relative to foreign prices. As can be seen from the expression given in (1), this can occur either through a decline in domestic prices (P) as in the classical adjustment process, or by a devaluation of the currency (increase in e) with unchanged domestic prices. An appropriate devaluation will shift the NX schedule up so that it intersects the AS and AD schedules at the point E.

The devaluation strategy has the obvious advantage that it does not require a protracted recession to reduce domestic wages and prices. However it is important to recall the analysis of a devaluation given in Section 5-3. In order to achieve internal and external balance it is necessary to combine the devaluation with contractionary policies that reduce aggregate demand. If this is not done the aggregate demand curve will shift up and to the right as a result of the effect of the devaluation on demand for domestic goods. We will then have excess demand for domestic goods and a consequent increase in wages and prices. In the end the improvement in competitiveness achieved through the devaluation will be offset by an increase in domestic wages and prices.

An Increase in the Foreign Price Level

We conclude this section with an analysis of the domestic policy options in the face of an increase in the foreign price level. As discussed in Section 18-3 below, this was the situation faced by Canada in the second half of the 1960s when the inflation rate was rising in the U.S.

Figure 18-2 illustrates an initial equilibrium at point E with both internal and external balance. An increase in the foreign price level shifts the NX curve up to NX'. What will be the increase in the domestic price level represented by the vertical shift in this curve? In order to restore trade balance at the same level of income, the domestic price level must increase *in proportion* to the foreign price level so as to restore the initial relative price of foreign and domestic goods.

The improvement in competitiveness also shifts the AD curve up to AD'. The short-run equilibrium is thus at E' where we have excess demand for domestic goods and a trade surplus.

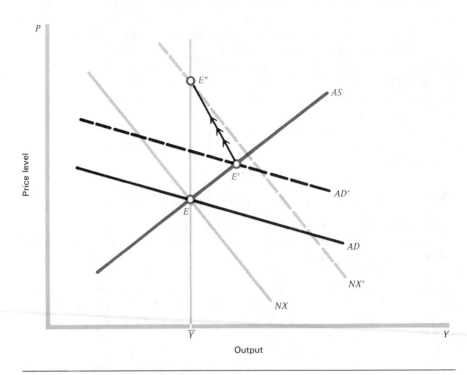

Output

FIGURE 18-2   AN INCREASE IN THE FOREIGN PRICE LEVEL. An increase in foreign prices shifts both the *AD* and the *NX* curves upward and to the right. The short-run equilibrium is at *E'* where we have excess demand for goods and a trade surplus. In the absence of sterilization, the money supply will increase and the *AS* curve will shift up so that the economy moves along an adjustment path to *E"*. At this point internal and external balance are restored with an increase in the domestic price level proportional to that of the foreign price level. Alternatively, if the domestic currency is devalued in proportion to the foreign price increase, the economy will remain in equilibrium at the point *E*.

Policy Options

One option to restore internal–external balance is to allow the automatic adjustment process to operate. Since there is a trade surplus at *E'*, pegging the exchange rate will cause the money supply to rise and the aggregate demand curve will shift up. Since we also have excess demand for goods, the aggregate supply curve will also shift up and the economy will move along an adjustment path like the one shown in Figure 18-2.

The final equilibrium will be at the point *E"* where internal and external balance are restored. The relative price of foreign and domestic goods will be unchanged from its initial value since the domestic price level will have risen in proportion to the foreign price level.

In this case, revaluation is again a more attractive option. If the domestic currency is revalued in proportion to the increase in the foreign price level, the relative price of foreign and domestic goods will remain unchanged and the economy will stay at point E. Thus a revaluation enables the domestic economy to maintain a stable price level and avoid importing foreign inflation.

The important implication of this analysis is that a country on a fixed exchange rate ties its price level to that of its trading partners and is forced to import foreign inflation.

The Collapse of the Fixed Exchange Rate System

From 1946 to 1973 most countries had exchange rates that were fixed in terms of the U.S. dollar. This was the *Bretton Woods system* that at the end of World War II replaced the unstable exchange rates and restrictive trade policies of the 1930s. Under the Bretton Woods system countries fixed the exchange rates among currencies. This was achieved by specifying the rate at which the central bank would buy and sell dollars in the foreign exchange market, for example, DM4/$. These exchange rates were to remain fixed over time, or at least change only infrequently.

As we have seen, a system of fixed exchange rates requires that countries pursue very similar policies so that prices of goods in different countries do not get out of line. This was not the case in the late 1960s when the inflation rate in the United States increased significantly without a similar increase in other countries. The discrepancy was particularly significant in Germany. The United States was losing competitiveness (its goods were becoming increasingly expensive for foreigners to buy), and Germany was gaining. The difference in inflation rates led to the belief that the Deutsche mark would be revalued (for example, from DM4/$ to DM3/$). That way the prices of German goods would rise relative to the prices of American goods, and trade between the countries would come closer to being balanced.

Investors expecting a revaluation of the DM favoured holding DM assets rather than dollar assets. That way they would benefit if there was a change in the exchange rate. For instance, anyone using $1 million to buy DM4 million worth of German bonds before the revaluation could sell them after a revaluation for $1.333 million, a nice profit. The speculation in favour of the mark and against the dollar meant that capital was flowing from the United States toward Germany. Germany's balance of payments showed a large surplus, and the central bank was forced to buy large amounts of dollars as it kept the exchange rate fixed. Germany's continued purchases of dollars grew into increasingly large holdings, as

Figure 18-3 shows. At the same time the German inflation rate began to increase as aggregate demand in all countries shifted toward the relatively low-priced German goods. This was called "imported inflation."

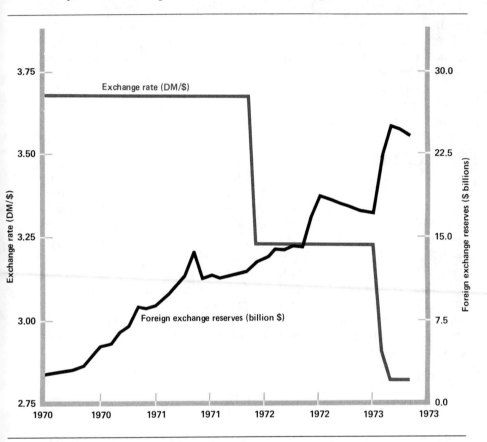

FIGURE 18-3   THE DEUTSCHE MARK/U.S. DOLLAR EXCHANGE RATE AND GERMAN FOREIGN EXCHANGE RESERVES, 1970–1973.

To German policy makers, forced to buy dollars and facing imported inflation, the fixed rate system became more and more difficult to accept and, because of *speculation*, increasingly difficult to maintain. Speculation involves buying an asset cheaply in the expectation that it can be resold dearly. Speculators bear the risk that they will lose their money if their predictions turn out to be wrong.[2]

But there was little risk of loss in the case of the dollar-DM exchange rate. Speculators forced a one-way bet. The Deutsche mark could only be *revalued* against the dollar. There was no risk that it could be *devalued*. No one could be certain when revaluation would take place, but anybody who was willing to be patient could be almost certain to win if he or she placed his or her bets on a Deutsche mark revaluation. Capital therefore flowed into Germany, and in defending the overvalued dollar and the undervalued DM, the Bundesbank (German central bank) bought up huge amounts of dollars.

Figure 18-3 shows the stock of U.S. dollars accumulated by the Bundesbank. From less than $3 billion at the beginning of 1970 it grew to more than $25 billion in 1973. But the problems of the fixed rate system were not limited to rapid increases in foreign exchange reserves. In buying U.S. dollars in the foreign exchange market, countries increased their own money supplies — because they bought the dollars with their own currencies.

The monetary expansion increased aggregate demand and inflationary pressures outside the U.S. At the same time in the United States the outflow of dollars forced the Federal Reserve to pursue a tighter monetary policy than it would otherwise have chosen. The system could not last. On three occasions the dollar-DM rate was changed. A first revaluation of the DM or devaluation of the dollar occurred in 1969, a second occurred in 1971, and a third in 1973. Every time, the adjustment lasted only a short period before investors again saw an undervalued DM or an overvalued dollar and once again speculated against the dollar. In May 1973, after a last unsuccessful attempt to keep exchange rates fixed, the fixed rate system broke down, and the world economy moved to *flexible exchange rates* between the dollar and other important currencies such as the yen or the DM.[3]

18-2 MONEY AND PRICES UNDER FLEXIBLE EXCHANGE RATES

In this section we consider the effects of price level and exchange rate changes on income and the interest rate under flexible exchange rates. As in Chapter 6, we make the simplifying assumption of perfect capital mobility so that the domestic interest rate is always equal to the foreign rate. An incipient decline in interest rates, say, because of an increase in the money supply, leads to an *immediate* depreciation and income expansion that counteracts the tendency for the interest rate to fall.

For purposes of graphical illustration, we return to the *IS-LM* framework of Chapters 4–6. However we relax the assumption of fixed prices that was maintained in those chapters and assume that prices rise when output is above full employment and fall when output is below full employment.

Figure 18-4 summarizes the adjustment process. At points to the right of full employment, prices are rising and at points to the left prices are

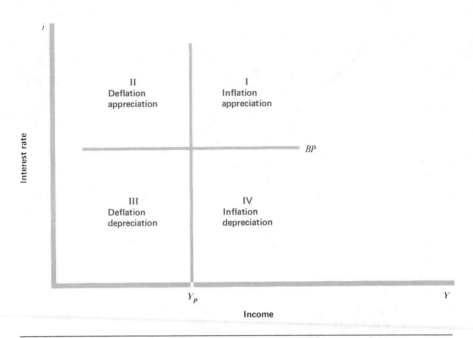

FIGURE 18-4   ADJUSTMENT OF EXCHANGE RATES AND PRICES. Prices move in response to the deviation of the economy from full employment. When output is above potential, prices are rising (regions I and IV), and they are falling at output levels below potential (regions II and III). With perfect capital mobility the balance of payments is highly sensitive to interest rates. If our interest rate falls below the foreign level, capital tends to flow out, and that leads to a deficit and depreciation of the currency (regions III and IV). Conversely, a rise in interest rates leads to capital inflows, a surplus, and appreciation (regions I and II).

falling. The *BP* schedule is horizontal at the foreign interest rate and at points above it the currency is appreciating while at points below it the currency is depreciating.

Short- and Long-Run Effects of a Monetary Expansion

We saw in Chapter 6 that with fixed prices and flexible exchange rates, an increase in the money supply leads to a depreciation and an increase in income. We now ask how that result is modified once we take adjustments in prices into account. We will show that the output adjustment is now only transitory. In the long run a monetary expansion leads to exchange depreciation and to higher prices with no change in competitiveness. Figure 18-5 helps make these points.

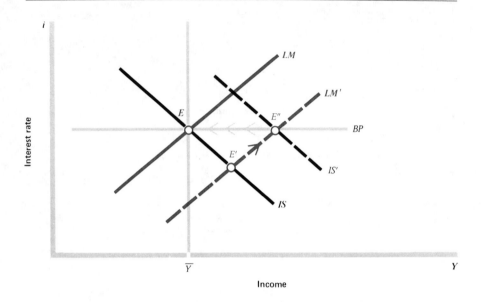

FIGURE 18-5   THE SHORT-AND LONG-RUN EFFECTS OF A MONETARY EXPAN-
SION. The economy is in initial equilibrium at *E* when a monetary expansion
shifts the *LM* schedule to *LM'*. The goods and money market equilibrium at *E'*
involve an interest rate below the foreign level. Capital outflows now lead to
immediate depreciation, and therefore the *IS* schedule shifts to *IS'*. The economy
thus moves rapidly from *E* to *E"*. But at *E"* there is overemployment, and hence
prices are rising. Rising prices reduce real balances and shift the *LM* schedule
back toward *E*. As real balances decline, interest rates tend to rise, drawing in
capital and leading to appreciation, which shifts the *IS'* schedule back toward *E*.
In the long run, output returns to normal, and money, prices, and the exchange
rate all rise in the same proportion.

In Figure 18-5 we start at an initial equilibrium with full employment,
payments balance, monetary equilibrium, and equilibrium in the domestic
goods market. All this occurs at point *E*. Now a monetary expansion takes
place and shifts the *LM* schedule to *LM'*. The new goods and money market
equilibrium at *E'* involves an interest rate below the world level, and
therefore the currency immediately depreciates, raising home competitiveness and thus shifting the *IS* schedule to *IS'*. The economy moves
rapidly from *E* via *E'* to *E"*. Output has risen, the currency has depreciated,
and the economy has thereby gained in external competitiveness, but that
is not the end of the story.

At *E"* output is above the full-employment level. Prices are therefore
rising, and that implies real balances are falling. As the real money stock
M/P declines because of rising prices, the *LM* schedule starts shifting to the

left. Interest rates tend to rise, capital tends to flow in, and the resulting appreciation leads now to a decline in competitiveness that also shifts the IS schedule back toward the initial equilibrium. Both the IS and LM schedules thus move back toward point E. The process continues until point E is reached again.

What adjustments have taken place once the economy is back to point E? At point E interest rates have returned to their initial level and so have relative prices eP^*/P. In moving from E to E' the exchange rate depreciated immediately, ahead of the rise in prices, but when prices increased and real balances fell, some of that depreciation was reversed. Over the whole adjustment process, prices and exchange rates rose in the same proportion, leaving relative prices eP^*/P and therefore aggregate demand unchanged. In the long run money was therefore *entirely neutral*. Table 18-1 summarizes these results. Neutrality of money means, in terms of the second row of the table, that nominal money, prices, and the exchange rate all increase in the same proportion so that real money and relative prices are unchanged.

TABLE 18-1   THE SHORT- AND LONG-RUN EFFECTS OF A MONETARY EXPANSION

	M/P	e	P	eP^*/P	Y
Short run	+	+	0	+	+
Long run	0	+	+	0	0

Purchasing Power Parity

The long-run neutrality of money discussed above illustrates the potential role of exchange rates in offsetting the effects of changes in the price level at home and abroad on the terms of trade. In the preceding analysis, the exchange rate rose by precisely the right amount to offset the effects of domestic inflation on the terms of trade. That is, the exchange depreciation maintained the *purchasing power* of our goods in terms of foreign goods between the initial and the final equilibrium positions.

An important view of the determinants of the exchange rate is the theory that exchange rates move primarily as a result of differences in price level behaviour between the two countries in such a way as to maintain constant terms of trade. This is the *purchasing power parity* (PPP) theory. The theory argues that exchange rate movements primarily reflect divergent rates of inflation. Examining the terms of trade, eP^*/P, the theory maintains the following: When P^* and/or P change, e changes in such a way as to maintain eP^*/P constant.

PPP is a plausible description of the trend behaviour of exchange rates, especially when inflation differentials between countries are large. In particular, we have seen that the PPP relationship does hold in the face of an increase in the money stock. If price level movements are caused by monetary changes, as they are likely to be if the inflation rate is high, then we should expect PPP relationships to hold in the long term.

Figure 18-6 shows the exchange rate (Canadian dollar price of one U.S. dollar) and the terms of trade in relation to the U.S. The terms of trade is calculated using the U.S. and Canadian GNE deflators to measure P^* and P.

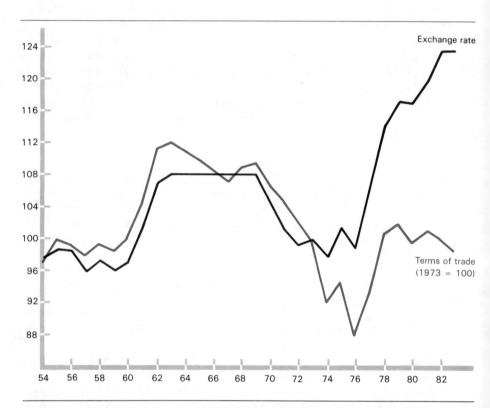

FIGURE 18-6   EXCHANGE RATE AND TERMS OF TRADE RELATIVE TO THE U.S.
(*Source*: Department of Finance, *Economic Review*; U.S. Department of Commerce, *Survey of Current Business*)

From 1954 to 1967 similar inflation rates were experienced in the two countries so the two indexes moved together. The U.S. rate of inflation was above the Canadian rate during the period 1968 to 1971, and this is reflected in an improvement in the competitive position (or worsening of the terms of trade) in 1968 and 1969. Following the floating of the Canadian dollar in 1970, there was a sharp appreciation which dominated the

movement of the terms of trade. From 1972 to 1976, the Canadian inflation rate was substantially above the U.S. rate, and the terms of trade
improved until late 1976 when the Canadian dollar began to depreciate.
By 1978 Canada's competitive position had been restored to the level of
the early 1970s, and from 1979 to 1983 the terms of trade fluctuated
within a narrow range.

Figure 18-6 suggests some tendency for the terms of trade to maintain
a constant level in the long run, but there is considerable short-run variation.
This reflects two important qualifications to the PPP theory. First, even a
monetary disturbance affects the terms of trade in the short run. Exchange
rates tend to move quite rapidly relative to prices, and thus we observe
substantial deviations from PPP.

The second important qualification concerns the role of nonmonetary
disturbances in affecting exchange rates. For example, we saw in Chapter 6 that an increase in exports improves our terms of trade or leads to
currency appreciation at unchanged domestic prices. If we look at an
increase in potential output as another example, we will find that the
equilibrium terms of trade worsen. To absorb the increased output, demand must rise, implying a decline in the relative price of our goods.
Thus, it is apparent that, over time, adjustments to *real* disturbances will
affect the *equilibrium* terms of trade. In the longer run, exchange rates and
prices do *not* necessarily move together, as they do in a world where all
disturbances are monetary. On the contrary, we may have important
changes in relative prices. Such changes run counter to the purchasing
power parity view of exchange rates.

Exchange Rate Expectations and Inflation

In Section 6-3 of Chapter 6, we modified our model, in the case of flexible
exchange rates and perfect capital mobility, by introducing the interest
parity condition. We replaced the condition that the domestic interest rate
(i) is equal to the foreign rate (i^*) with

$$i = i^* + x \tag{2}$$

where x is the expected rate of depreciation of the domestic currency.

As we indicated in our discussion in Chapter 6, exchange rate expectations can be a source of short-run instability. In the longer run, we would
expect differences in inflation rates between countries to be the major
factor in the trend movements in exchange rates. Thus in long-run
equilibrium, a country with a relatively high inflation rate would have a
relatively high nominal interest rate (because of the Fisher equation discussed in Chapter 16), and a depreciating currency. The rate of depreciation would match the inflation differential so as to maintain the terms of
trade at a constant equilibrium level.

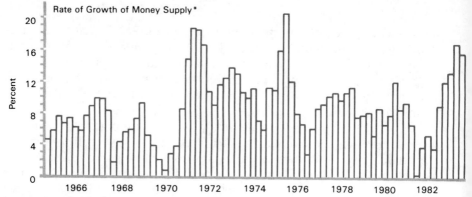

Rate of Growth of Money Supply*

*Percent change over same quarter of preceding year
(1965–68: *M*1; 1969–83: *M*1A)

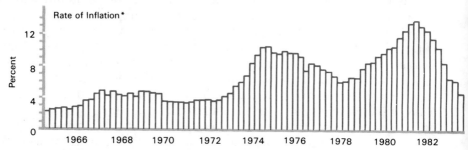

Rate of Inflation*

*Percent change in CPI (excluding food) over same quarter of preceding year.

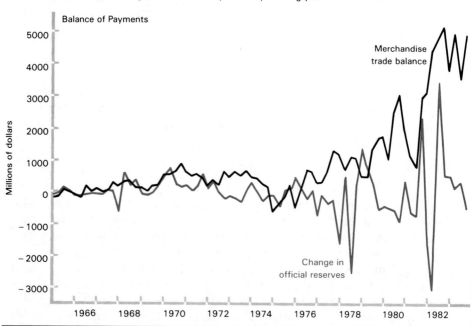

Balance of Payments

Merchandise
trade balance

Change in
official reserves

FIGURE 18-7   MONETARY POLICY, INFLATION AND THE BALANCE OF PAY-
MENTS, 1965–1983 (*Source: Bank of Canada Review*)

Denoting the domestic and foreign inflation rates by gp and gp^* respectively, and substituting the differential for x in Equation (2), we obtain

$$i = i^* + gp - gp^*$$

or $\qquad i - gp = i^* - gp^* \qquad\qquad (3)$

Thus, in long-run equilibrium the interest parity condition states that *real* interest rates are equalized across countries. Nominal rates will differ according to the differences in inflation rates.

18-3 THE EXCHANGE RATE AND MONETARY POLICY IN CANADA SINCE 1970

In Chapter 6, we reviewed the Canadian experience under flexible exchange rates in the 1950s when inflation was not a serious problem for policy makers. In this section, we consider the operation of a flexible rate since 1970 when inflation became a major preoccupation.

The Buildup of Inflation in the 1970s

The inflation problem of the 1970s had its origins in the second half of the 1960s when the U.S. economy was experiencing boom conditions to a considerable extent as a result of expenditures related to the Vietnam War. Demand pressure in the United States spilled over into Canada in the form of demand for our exports, and this resulted in a large surplus on merchandise trade as shown in Figure 18-7. This process was intensified by the favourable competitive position that Canada enjoyed at the time. The longer term trends in the Canada-U.S. terms of trade shown in Figure 18-6 suggest that the choice of 92.5 U.S. cents when the Canadian dollar was pegged in 1962 involved a substantial undervaluation of our currency. This proposition is confirmed by the fact that maintenance of this rate required substantial intervention in the foreign exchange market. As can be seen in Figure 18-7, official reserves rose in every year of the fixed rate period, with the exception of 1966, as the Bank of Canada held down the exchange rate by supplying Canadian dollars to the market in exchange for foreign currency.

As pressure on the Canadian dollar built up, the Bank of Canada was unwilling or unable to sterilize the effects of exchange market intervention on the money supply. Thus the classical adjustment process discussed in Section 18-1 was brought into play and the rate of growth of the money supply increased (see Figure 18-7). In 1967, the rate of growth of $M1$ was nearly 10 percent as compared with an average of about 5 percent between 1960 and 1964. In 1968, the inflationary pressure was intensified by an acceleration of inflation in the United States. As pointed out in the previous section, the U.S. inflation rate was above the Canadian rate from 1968 to 1972.

The freeing of the Canadian dollar in 1970 provided the Bank of Canada with an opportunity to stem the inflationary pressures. The rate of growth of the money supply was sharply curtailed and the inflation rate eased thereafter. As would be expected, there was a substantial appreciation of the Canadian dollar. However, shortly after the Bank of Canada had freed itself from the restrictions imposed by a fixed exchange rate and made substantial progress in bringing inflation under control, it appears to have become reluctant to exploit the benefits of a flexible rate.

To begin with, the Bank of Canada attempted to resist the appreciation of the Canadian dollar in 1970 and 1971 by intervening heavily in the foreign exchange market. This is reflected in the large increase in official reserves shown in Figure 18-7. A substantial appreciation was required to restore the terms of trade to the equilibrium level, and intervention to prevent this from taking place intensified inflationary pressure in Canada.

The second error in policy was the sharp turnaround in monetary policy that occurred in 1971. Subsequent events indicated that the Bank of Canada overreacted to the slowdown in economic activity and rising unemployment experienced in 1970. As can be seen in Figure 18-7, the rate of growth of $M1$ shot up to a level close to 13 percent in 1971 and rose to 14 percent in 1972. In 1973, there was a sharp increase in the inflation rate, and by 1975 the consumer price index was rising at a rate in excess of 10 percent. There was an increase in the rate of inflation in the United States as well but the acceleration was more rapid in Canada. As shown in Figure 18-6, the exchange rate was held close to 100 U.S. cents over the period 1972 to 1976 while the difference in inflation rates lead to a substantial deterioration in our competitive position.

In retrospect, it appears that Canada missed an opportunity to avoid at least some of the inflation that plagued the world economy in the 1970s. Monetary policy was immobilized in the late sixties by a commitment to a fixed exchange rate at a time when inflation rates began to rise in other countries. In the early 1970s the full benefits of a flexible rate were not realized, since the Bank of Canada resisted the appreciation of the Canadian dollar. It appears to have been influenced by a misguided concern for the effect of an appreciation on the competitive position of Canada's export industries. This led the Bank to hold down the appreciation by direct intervention in 1970 and 1971, and to stabilize the rate near 100 U.S. cents in 1972 and 1973 by permitting a rapid rate of growth in the money supply. As indicated by the discussion of a money supply increase in the previous section, the short-run effect of an expansionary monetary policy is to hold down the exchange rate. However, the longer-run consequence is an increase in prices which restores the competitive position of domestic industries to the equilibrium level. In this case, the monetary expansion induced an overshooting of the price level and a temporary improvement in our competitive position that was reversed by the depreciation that began in late 1976.

A second reason for the mismanagement of monetary policy in the early 1970s was the delayed recognition of the importance of controlling the rate of growth of the money supply. As indicated in Chapter 10, it was not until 1973, when inflationary forces were already entrenched, that the Bank of Canada began to move towards greater emphasis on control of the money supply and explicit target rates of growth were not adopted until late 1975.

Monetary Policy and the 1981–1982 Recession

As we saw in Chapter 17, the Bank of Canada's gradualist strategy of bringing down the rate of growth of the money supply in successive stages achieved limited success in bringing down the rate of inflation. The abandonment of gradualism came in the first half of 1981 when the Federal Reserve pushed up interest rates sharply in the U.S. and brought on a severe recession that finally produced a substantial easing of the inflation rate.

What options did the Bank of Canada have in the face of this sharp rise in interest rates in the U.S.? The effects of an increase in the foreign interest rate are illustrated in Figure 18-8. The initial equilibrium is at E and the increase in the foreign interest rate is represented by an upward shift in the BP schedule. In the absence of a parallel reduction of the money supply in Canada, the Canadian dollar undergoes an immediate depreciation, causing the IS curve to shift up and to the right so that the short-run equilibrium is at E'. At this point there is excess demand so that the price level rises and the Canadian dollar appreciates as we move along the adjustment path to E''.

We thus conclude that: If the Bank of Canada does not respond by reducing the growth rate of the Canadian money supply, a tightening of monetary policy in the U.S. will cause the Canadian dollar to depreciate and create inflationary pressure in Canada. For this reason, the Bank of Canada was reluctant to maintain an independent policy strategy and followed the American lead. The result was a sharp decline in the Canadian inflation rate, but as we have noted this was achieved by exploiting the short-run Phillips curve tradeoff and allowing a drastic increase in the unemployment rate.

The spillover effects of U.S. tight money in this period created problems for other industrialized countries as well. Policy makers were forced to accept higher inflation caused by American policy or to change their own policy. Since most countries did not want to import inflation, they reacted by tightening money. This reduced the effects on exchange rates but it also meant that American tight money and recession became the world's tight money and a world recession.

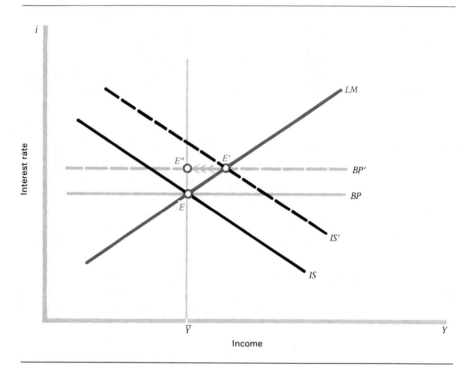

FIGURE 18-8   AN INCREASE IN THE FOREIGN INTEREST RATE. An increase in the foreign interest rate shifts the *BP* curve up and leads to a depreciation of the domestic currency. The depreciation causes the *IS* curve to shift up and to the right so that we have a short-run equilibrium at *E'*. At this point there is excess demand so that the domestic price level rises and the currency appreciates as we move along the adjustment path to *E'*.

18-4   EXCHANGE RATE CHANGES AND TRADE ADJUSTMENT: TWO EMPIRICAL ISSUES

In this section we take up two important empirical issues related to the possibilities for adjusting current account imbalances by changes in the exchange rate. In our theoretical model of Chapter 6, we assumed that prices here and abroad were fixed, so that exchange rate changes affected relative prices one for one. In this chapter, by contrast, we explore a world where prices (and wages) are flexible and full employment is maintained in the long run. In this section, we consider the alternative possibility, that wages and prices are flexible, but that they may respond to movements in the exchange rate in a way that makes it impossible or at least difficult to change relative prices through changes in the exchange rate. This issue is particularly important if formal wage indexation arrangements link wage behaviour to import prices and thus to the exchange rate.

The second issue we consider is whether changes in relative prices, assuming that they are possible, will affect the current account in the direction we have so far assumed. The assumption, so far, has been that a decline in the relative price of our goods improves the current account, but the possibility arises that at least in the short run there might be a perverse reaction. With import prices rising, for example, import demand may not decline sufficiently to compensate for higher prices, and thus total import spending (price times quantity) may actually increase. We turn now to these two issues.

Exchange Rates and Relative Price Adjustment

In studying the flexible wage-price model, we assumed that wages and prices adjust to achieve full employment. Now we consider as an alternative the possibility that prices are based on labour cost or wages and that wages are inflexible in real terms. Suppose that labour wants to maintain the purchasing power of wages or to keep real wages constant. In such a world, changes in the cost of living would lead to changes in money wages, in labour cost, and therefore in prices, which in turn feed back into wages. Two points emerge from this description. The first is that in such a world, we may not be able to get to full employment. Labour may set the real wage too high, and at least in the intermediate run, the full-employment level of output cannot be sustained. The second point is that a process in which changes in prices feed back into wages and from there into prices is one of a *wage-price spiral* that may produce considerable volatility in the price level. Small disturbances can set off quite large changes in the price level.

Suppose, first, that the real wage is fixed in terms of the consumer price index that includes both domestic goods and imports. Let us assume, second, that changes in the consumer price index are fully passed on into wages, and third, that changes in wages are fully passed on into increased domestic prices. Now assume that starting from an initial equilibrium, there is an exchange depreciation brought about by some short-term, reversible disturbance. The depreciation raises import prices and thereby has a direct effect on consumer prices and wages. To maintain the purchasing power of their wages, workers increase money wages and firms pass on the wage increase into higher prices. Where are we after the process ends? Real wages are constant, which means wages and the price level (a weighted average of the prices of domestic and imported goods) have risen in the same proportion; wage increases have been fully passed on, which means that real wages *in terms of domestic output* are also unchanged. The two results imply that relative prices are unchanged, or that the exchange depreciation is fully matched by domestic inflation.

Of course, this is not really the end because we have to ask how the higher price level affects the macroeconomic equilibrium. To the extent that lower real balances lower aggregate demand, we would have a reduction in employment. To round out our story, we can imagine that the central bank steps in to prevent unemployment by raising the money stock. If nominal money rises in proportion to the price increase, then the full-employment equilibrium, at the same terms of trade, is reestablished but, of course, at a higher level of wages and prices. This is an economy where there is very little stability in the price level because the slightest change in exchange rate expectations leads to actual exchange rate movements that are fully *validated* by domestic wage, price, and monetary developments.

A second context in which the idea of *sticky real wages* is important is that of real disturbances. Suppose our export demand declines permanently because of, say, the introduction of superior technology abroad. To return to full employment, the relative price of our goods must fall so as to encourage foreign demand, but how can the relative price fall? In Chapter 6, we argued that the exchange rate will depreciate, thereby raising import prices relative to domestic prices and restoring our competitiveness. In the present context we have to recognize that import price increases would be immediately matched by wage increases and that these wage increases would be fully passed on into price increases. Relative prices cannot change. The consequence would, of course, be protracted unemployment. Unemployment would continue until the *real* wage declines.

The empirical question, then, is, How flexible are real wages? This is, to an important extent, a question of institutional arrangements. In small open economies with substantial cost-of-living indexation in wage agreements, it may indeed be very difficult to change real wages and relative prices through exchange rate changes. The governor of the Bank of Canada has argued that this problem is of some importance in Canada. For example, in a speech given in November, 1980, Governor Bouey stated:[4]

> In certain circumstances, for example, a significant decline in the exchange value of the Canadian dollar brought about by unusual interest rate relationships between Canada and the United States would not only add almost immediately to the upward pressure on prices and spending but would also, before long, threaten to put increased upward pressure as well on negotiated wage settlements and thus on our on-going costs of production.

Relative Prices and the Trade Balance: The J Curve

We come now to the second issue, the effect of changes in relative prices on the trade balance and the possibility that a depreciation *worsens* the trade balance. To make this point, we write out the trade balance, mea-sured in terms of domestic goods, as

$$NX = X - \left(\frac{eP^*}{P} \cdot Q \right) \tag{4}$$

where X denotes the foreign demand for our goods or exports and Q denotes our own import quantity. The term $(eP^*/P)Q$ thus measures the *value* of our imports in terms of domestic goods.

Suppose that we now have an exchange depreciation and that in the first instance, domestic and foreign prices, P and P^*, are unchanged. Then the relative price of imports, eP^*/P, rises. This leads to two effects. First, if the physical *volume* of imports does not change, their *value* measured in domestic currency unambiguously increases because of the higher price. With unchanged physical import volume, Q, higher prices mean increased import spending and thus a worsening of the trade balance. This is the source for the potentially perverse response of the trade balance to ex-change depreciation. However, there is an adjustment that runs in the opposite direction. The increased relative price of imports makes us more competitive and shifts demand in volume terms toward domestic goods. This *volume effect* of substitution in response to changed relative prices shows up in Equation (4) in the form of increased export volume, X, and reduced import volume, Q. The volume effects thus unambiguously im-prove the trade balance.

The question, then, is whether the volume effects on imports and ex-ports are sufficiently strong to outweigh the price effect, that is, whether depreciation raises or lowers net exports. The empirical evidence on this question is quite strong and shows the following result: *The short-term volume effects, say, within a year, are quite small and thus do not outweigh the price effect.*[5] *The long-term volume effects, by contrast, are quite substantial, and certainly enough to make the trade balance respond in the normal fashion to a relative price change.*

Where does this asymmetry come from, and what does it imply about trade adjustment to relative prices? First, the low short-term and high longer-term volume effects result from the time consumers and producers take to adjust to changes in relative prices. Some of these adjustments may be instantaneous, but it is clear that tourism patterns, for example, may take six months to a year to adjust and that relocation of production internationally, in response to changes in relative costs and prices, may take years. A case in point is increased foreign direct investment in Can-ada — say, Volvo moving assembly operations from Sweden to Nova Scotia. In the long term, such direct investment leads to reduced Volvo imports by Canada, and thus to an improved trade balance, but such an adjustment takes years, not weeks or months.

The lag in the adjustment of trade flows to changes in relative prices is thus quite plausible. The next question is, What do these lags imply about the impact of relative price changes on the trade balance? Suppose that at a particular time, starting with a deficit, we have a depreciation that raises the relative price of imports. The short-term effects result primarily from increased import prices with very little offsetting volume effects. Therefore, the trade balance initially worsens. Over time, as trade volume adjusts to the changed relative prices, exports rise and import volume progressively declines. The volume effects come to dominate, and in the long run, the trade balance shows an improvement. This pattern of adjustment is referred to as the *J-curve effect*, because diagrammatically the response of the trade balance looks like a *J*.

The medium-term problem of sticky real wages and the J-curve effect are important qualifications to the macroeconomics of flexible rates as spelled out in Sections 18-1 and 18-2. They imply that flexible exchange rates do not provide for instant, costless flexibility of relative prices and trade flows. At the same time, these considerations provide important clues for the interpretation of macroeconomic experiences across countries, particularly in showing why depreciations typically do not lead to improvements in the current account in the short term.

18-5   EXCHANGE RATE FLUCTUATIONS AND INTERDEPENDENCE

In the 1960s there was growing dissatisfaction with fixed exchange rates. The Bretton Woods system was called a crisis system because from time to time exchange rates would get out of line and expectations of exchange rate changes would mobilize massive capital flows that often precipitated the exchange rate changes that speculators expected. Is the flexible rate system of the 1970s and early 1980s better? Is it less crisis-prone, and does it provide a better framework for macroeconomic stability? Before providing an answer, we look briefly at how flexibly the system has, in fact, operated.

Dirty Floating and Intervention

Under *fully* flexible exchange rates the government takes no action in the foreign exchange market. Far from buying or selling foreign exchange at a fixed price, the government does not conduct *any* foreign exchange transactions. It stays out of the foreign exchange market, whatever happens to the exchange rate. Such a system is almost unheard of, although the United States did behave that way in 1981–1982. More commonly, governments intervene in the foreign exchange market to a lesser or greater extent. Foreign exchange market *intervention* occurs when a government buys or sells foreign exchange in an attempt to influence the exchange rate. The extent to which governments intervene varies substantially.

They may only try to offset short-term fluctuations and buy or sell foreign exchange to maintain "orderly markets." But they also may try to keep an overvalued exchange rate from depreciating or an undervalued exchange rate from appreciating. *Dirty floating* (as opposed to clean) is the practice of using substantial intervention to try to maintain an exchange rate against the pressure of market forces.

During the 1973–1983 period, exchange market intervention has been of the decidedly dirty variety. Governments have intervened on a very large scale. This leads naturally to the question of why a government should try to resist market forces, to prevent an appreciation or a depreciation of the currency.

Why Governments Intervene

Central banks intervene to affect exchange rates for several reasons. Probably the main reason is the belief that many capital flows merely represent unstable expectations, and that the induced movements in exchange rates move production in the economy in an unnecessarily erratic fashion. The second reason for the intervention is a central bank's attempt to move the terms of trade in order to affect trade flows. The third reason arises from the effects of the exchange rate on domestic inflation. Central banks sometimes intervene in the exchange market to prevent the exchange rate from depreciating, with the aim of preventing a depreciation-induced increase in the inflation rate.

Should central banks intervene in the exchange market? The basic argument for such intervention is that it is possible for intervention to smooth out fluctuations in exchange rates. At one extreme, the argument would assert that any movements in exchange rates produce unnecessary fluctuations in the domestic economy and that exchange rates therefore ought to be fixed. This is the basic argument for dirty floating. The only, and overwhelming, objection to the argument that the central bank should smooth out fluctuations is that there is no simple way of telling an erratic movement from a trend movement. How can we tell whether a current appreciation in the exchange rate is merely the result of a disturbance which will soon reverse itself, rather than the beginning of a trend movement in the exchange rate? There is no way of telling at the time a change occurs, although with the benefit of hindsight, one can see which exchange rate movements were later reversed.

There is one circumstance under which central bank intervention might be desirable. It is clear from our earlier analysis that one of the key determinants of exchange rate behaviour consists of expectations of economic policy. It may sometimes be possible to make it clear that there has been a change in policy only by intervening in the foreign exchange market. This is a case of putting your money where your mouth is.

Should Governments Intervene?

There is disagreement on whether governments should intervene in the foreign exchange market. The United States, for example, in 1981–1982 strongly refused consideration of any kind of intervention. The reason was that policy makers in the United States, unlike those in Europe, felt the market knows better than policy makers what level the exchange rate should be. But there is another and more interesting disagreement: it concerns the effectiveness of intervention. Does it make any difference to the exchange rate if the Bundesbank sells $1 billion from its reserves?

To judge the effectiveness of intervention we must make a distinction between *sterilized* and *nonsterilized intervention*. In the case of sterilized intervention a central bank, say, buys foreign exchange, issuing domestic money. But then the increase in home money is reversed by an open market sale of securities. In the sterilized intervention case, therefore, the home money supply is kept unchanged. By contrast in the case of nonsterilization, there is a change in the money stock equal to the amount of intervention.

Thus nonsterilized intervention results in a change in the money stock. It is widely agreed that nonsterilized intervention, because it changes the money supply, will affect exchange rates. There is widespread skepticism, however, about the effectiveness of sterilized intervention. In 1978–1979 the U.S. dollar was depreciating in currency markets even though there was intervention on a massive scale, but that intervention was carefully sterilized. Only in late 1979, when the dollar depreciation had come to alarm the Federal Reserve did a change in policy take place. Monetary policy was tightened, and immediately the dollar depreciation was stopped and soon massively reversed.

The episode strongly suggests the effectiveness of nonsterilized intervention and of intervention that is backed by credible policies. It also suggests that without such policies intervention accomplishes little.[6]

Interdependence and Policy Synchronization

It used to be argued that under flexible exchange rates countries can pursue their own national economic policies and determine their own inflation rates without having to worry about the balance of payments. That is certainly correct, but it is also misleading. There are important linkages between countries whatever the exchange rate regime.

These *spillover* or *interdependence* effects have been at the centre of the discussion about flexible exchange rates. As we have seen, the effects of U.S. tight monetary policy in 1981–1982 created problems for the other industrialized countries. In addition, if policies are not synchronized between countries, the resulting large changes in exchange rates pose a major threat to a world of free trade.

When import prices fall by 20 or 30 percent because of a currency appreciation, large shifts in demand will occur. Domestic workers become unemployed, and they have no trouble seeing that it is foreigners who gain the jobs they just lost. Accordingly, there will be pressure for protection — tariffs or quotas — to keep out imports that are "artificially cheap" due to the currency appreciation. In the United States repeated calls for protection in the automobile industry, in steel, and in many other industries reflect in large part the side effects of a U.S. dollar that appreciated sharply in response to tight money.

On the question of independence or interdependence under flexible exchange rates, the experience of the last 10 years offers a quite unambiguous answer. Under flexible exchange rates there is as much or more interdependence as there is under fixed rates. Moreover, because exchange rates are so flexible and so ready to respond to (bad) policies, macroeconomic management does not become easier. Further, to the extent that exchange rate movements cause sharp changes in competitiveness, they lead to protectionist sentiment.

On all counts then, flexible rates are far from being a perfect system, but there is no better system. Therefore we can ask only whether through international coordination of interests and policies, we can make the system work better than it has in the recent past.

18-6   SUMMARY

1   In an open economy, aggregate demand is reduced by an increase in the price level through a reduction in domestic competitiveness as well as through a reduction in real balances as in the closed economy case.

2   If there is a trade deficit at full employment, contractionary policy is required to reduce the price level so as to achieve external balance. This adjustment occurs automatically via a decline in the money supply if the central bank pegs the exchange rate without sterilization. Devaluation can also be used to achieve external balance.

3   A country on a fixed exchange rate ties its price level to that of its trading partners. Canada was on a fixed rate in the second half of the 1960s and was forced to import U.S. inflation.

4   From 1946 to 1973, most countries had fixed exchange rates. This system collapsed because of divergent policies followed in the major industrial countries.

5   In the short run, an increase in the money supply leads to a depreciation and an increase in income. In the long run the initial levels of income and the terms of trade are restored by proportional increases

in the price level and exchange rate. This neutrality result leads to the purchasing power parity theory of exchange rates. It does not always hold because the terms of trade varies in response to nonmonetary disturbances and is affected even by monetary factors in the short run.

6   In the long run, high inflation countries have high nominal interest rates and depreciating currencies. The interest parity condition implies that real interest is equalized across countries in the long run.

7   The floating of the Canadian dollar in 1970 did not stem inflationary pressure because the Bank of Canada failed to control the rate of growth of the money supply until it adopted money supply targets in 1975.

8   The 1981–1982 recession was brought on by tight monetary policy in the U.S. which forced other industrial countries to follow a similar policy to avoid an increase in inflation rates. This was an example of the interdependence among countries that exists even with flexible exchange rates.

9   A currency depreciation can, in the short run, lead to a worsening of the trade balance. This occurs when the effect of changes in relative prices on the volume of trade is small because adjustments take time. Over time, trade adjusts and the depreciation improves the trade balance. This is called the J-curve effect.

10   Because it raises import prices, depreciation of the exchange rate raises the cost of living and may spill over into increased wage demands. If such spillovers are substantial, then a flexible rate system will have large movements in nominal prices, and exchange rate movements may perform poorly in bringing about relative price changes.

11   Since the beginning of the flexible rate system in 1973, there have been substantial fluctuations in exchange rates. These movements are hard to explain. They affect the allocation of resources. A central bank which wants to intervene to smooth out the fluctuations has to know when an exchange rate change is going to be reversed and when it is permanent. For this reason, foreign exchange intervention to smooth out exchange rate fluctuations is extremely difficult.

KEY TERMS

Terms of trade
Classical adjustment process
Bretton Woods system

Purchasing power parity
The J curve

PROBLEMS

1 Consider the model depicted in Figure 18-1. Illustrate the short-run equilibrium of an economy with unemployment and a zero balance of trade. Show the adjustment process assuming (a) sterilization, and (b) no sterilization.

2 Consider an economy with a fixed exchange rate and perfect capital mobility. Use LM, IS and BP curves to analyse the effects on domestic income and prices of a change in government spending. What are the short-run and long-run effects on the exchange rate? (You may need to review the analysis of Chapter 5 to do this question.)

3 Suppose in year 1 we have price levels $P = 100$ and $P^* = 100$. Suppose next that in year 2 the respective price levels are $P_2 = 180$ and $P_2^* = 130$. Let the exchange rate initially be $2/£.
   (a) If there were no real disturbances between year 1 and year 2, what would be the equilibrium exchange rate in year 2?
   (b) If the terms of trade eP^*/P had deteriorated between year 1 and year 2 by 50 percent, what would the exchange rate be in year 2?

4 How would the adjustment path in response to an increase in the money supply (see Figure 18-5) change if we take account of the interest parity condition discussed in Section 6-3 of Chapter 6?

5 Explain the purchasing power parity theory of the long-run behaviour of the exchange rate. Indicate circumstances under which you would not expect the theory to hold.

6 Discuss the extent to which the Bank of Canada can set interest rates in Canada independently of rates in the United States. Does the Bank have more control over nominal rates or real rates?

CHAPTER 18: FOOTNOTES

[1] We assume that a decline in prices improves the trade balance. This requires that exports and imports are sufficiently responsive to prices. It is possible that a reduction in our price level (which reduces the prices of our exports) lowers our revenue from exports because the increased sales are not sufficient to compensate for the lower prices. We shall assume that this possibility does not occur.

[2] In speculation, for every winner there must be a loser, either another speculator or the central bank. That means speculation is risky. Keynes is said to have lost two fortunes and made three, speculating on German currency during the hyper-inflation of the 1920s. Irving Fisher is said to have speculated on the stock market in the 1930s, making two fortunes and losing three. For a good but technical text on finance, see K. Garbade, *Securities Markets* (New York: McGraw Hill, 1982).

[3] In Europe exchange rates have remained fixed (with occasional adjustments) among currencies such as the DM and the Dutch guilder, the Italian lira, and the

French franc. The arrangement today is called the *European monetary system*, or EMS for short.

[4]See *Bank of Canada Review*, November, 1980, p. 10.

[5]See Michael C. Deppler and Duncan M. Ripley, "The World Trade Model: Merchandise Trade," *IMF Staff Papers*, March 1978; and Duncan M. Ripley, "The World Model of Merchandise Trade: Simulation Applications," *IMF Staff Papers*, June 1980.

[6]In 1982–1983 the main industrialized countries including Canada conducted a study of intervention to try to reconcile their different views. The result is contained in the *Report of the Working Party on Foreign Exchange Market Intervention*, U.S. Treasury, Washington, D.C., 1983.

Long-Term Growth and Productivity

From 1870 to 1983 per capita GNP in Canada grew at an average annual rate of 2.2 percent. This trend rate is shown in Figure 19-1 along with actual GNP. With this growth rate, per capita GNP doubles every 32 years.

Table 19-1 shows that growth in Canada in the period from 1973 to 1983 was below the historical average. During that decade per capita GNP grew at only 1 percent. At that rate it would take 70 years to double.

In this chapter we turn our attention away from the short-run problems of the business cycle, and look at where the economy has been and may be heading in the long term. To analyse the long-run behaviour of the economy we focus on *trend* or *potential output*. The major question we pose is, What determines the *growth rate* of potential output? Given today's level of potential output, and the growth rate of potential output, we then know also what determines the *level* of potential output in the future. In terms of Figure 19-1, we are asking what is behind the trend output line.

In discussing the growth rate of potential output, we are discussing the important question of what future levels of real GNP will be. Table 19-1 shows that small differences in the growth rate of output cumulate over time to large differences in levels of GNP. To see this, compare the number of years it takes for GNP per capita to double when the growth rate is 2.1 percent with the number of years it takes when the growth rate is 0.9 percent. Despite the difficulties of using GNP as a welfare measure, we can be quite sure that people with a 60 percent higher level of per capita GNP would be materially much better off.

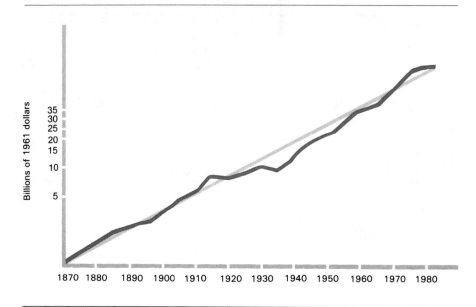

FIGURE 19-1   REAL GNP, 1870–1983
(*Source*: M.C. Urquhart, "New Estimates of Gross National Product, Canada, 1870 to 1926," NBER (forthcoming); Statistics Canada, 11–505, 13–201))

Because future per capita GNP levels are so sensitive to the growth rate of potential output, it is worth worrying about changes of even $\frac{1}{10}$ of 1 percent in the long-run growth rate of output. Certainly the large change between 1953–1973 and the following decade has been the cause of such concern. Is the change a lasting one, resulting from the beginning of an "age of limits," as many argued after the oil shock of 1973? Or is the sharp decline seen in Table 19-1 merely a temporary setback, soon to be reversed?

To answer questions about the growth rate of potential output, we go back to fundamentals. With output at the full-employment level, and hence the available factor supplies fully utilized, there are only two possible sources of growth. *Factor supplies may grow, or the productivity of factors of production may increase.* This, in turn, raises the questions of what determines the growth of factor supplies, including the role of supply-side fiscal policies, and what is the quantitative link between growth in factor supplies and output growth.

There are two complementary approaches to these questions. One is *growth theory*, which models the interactions among factor supplies, out-

TABLE 19-1   AVERAGE ANNUAL GROWTH RATES,
1870–1983

	1870–1953		1953–1973		1973–1983	
	GNP, real	Per capita real GNP	GNP, real	Per capita real GNP	GNP, real	Per capita real GNP
GNP growth, % per year	4.0	2.2	5.0	2.9	2.2	1.0
Time for per capita GNP to double, years		32		24		70

Source: See Figure 19-1.

put growth, saving, and investment in the process of growth. The other is *growth accounting*, which attempts to quantify the contribution of different determinants of output growth. The two approaches draw on a common analytical framework which we now outline.

BOX 19-1   THE LIMITS OF GROWTH

The record of growth since 1870 reviewed in Table 19-1 is impressive indeed. Per capita GNP in Canada has been doubling every 32 years over a period of more than a century. The question of the limits to growth is whether limited resources and the pressure of population on scarce land and food will ultimately bring the growth process to a dramatic halt. Are growing economies headed toward stagnation or even disaster?

The disaster scenario is a simple one. First, only so much oil, coal, copper, and other raw materials are in the earth. One day they will all be used up. Then what do we do? The "one day" seemed to come very close in the early seventies when many experts were predicting we would run out of oil by the year 2020. Second, there is the problem of an ever-growing population. The world, being of finite size, cannot accommodate an ever-growing population. Unless we can colonize other planets, population growth has to decline. In particular, there is the problem of food. Can we grow enough food to feed the nearly 6 billion people (compared with a current 4.5 billion) expected to be alive at the turn of the century? If not, will world population be forced down through starvation, as Malthus long ago predicted?*

The standard retort of the growth-oriented economist is to point out that all the concerns we have today about the limits to growth were equally valid a century ago. Indeed, in 1865 the famous English economist W. S. Jevons wrote a book about the impending exhaustion of Britain's coal resources—coal that is still being mined today.† The experience after the oil price shock in 1973 was that price changes can cause massive conservation of resources, and thus there is reason to hope that most *exhaustible* resources—resources present on earth in limited quantities—will be around for a long time, albeit with rising relative prices.

A more important challenge to the limits set by exhaustible resources is technical progress. Much technical progress takes the form of inventions and processes that save on scarce resources used up in production. The expectation or hope is that the same technical progress that has proved an important source of real growth in the last century will help overcome the effects of the reduced availability of raw materials.

Of course there is no assurance that the right technical progress will come along to bail us out when coal or oil run short in supply. Perhaps one should not bank on technical progress, innovation, and ingenuity to help us out. At the same time, it would surely be irresponsible to dismiss entirely the extraordinary record of technical progress that has contributed around one-half the average growth in real income. Public policy directed at encouraging research and development could help ensure continued technical progress.

---

*Thomas Malthus, *The Principle of Population*, 1798 (Homewood, Ill.: reprint by Richard D. Irwin, 1963).

†W.S. Jevons, *The Coal Question*, 1865 (New York: reprint by Augustus M. Kelley, 1865).

19-1   SOURCES OF GROWTH IN REAL INCOME

In this section we use the production function to study the *sources of growth*. We show that growth in labour, growth in capital, and improved technical efficiency are the three sources of growth.

The Production Function

In earlier chapters we introduced the concept of a production function. The *production function* links the amount of output produced in an economy to the inputs of factors of production and to the state of technical knowledge. Equation (1) represents the production function in symbols:

$$Y = AF(K,N) \tag{1}$$

where K and N denote the input of capital and labour and A denotes the state of technology. The production function $AF(K,N)$ in (1) states that the output produced depends on factor inputs K and N and on the state of technology. Increases in factor inputs and improved technology lead to an increase in output supply.

The next step is to make these links more precise by looking at an expression for the growth rate of output. In Equation (2) (which is derived in the Appendix) we show the determinants of output growth:[1]

$$\Delta Y/Y = (1 - \theta) \times \Delta N/N + \theta \times \Delta K/K + \Delta A/A$$

$$\underset{growth}{Output} = \underset{share}{labour} \times \underset{growth}{labour} + \underset{share}{capital} \times \underset{growth}{capital} + \underset{progress}{technical} \tag{2}$$

where $(1 - \theta)$ and θ are weights equal to the income shares of labour and of capital in production.

Equation (2) summarizes the contributions of growth of inputs and of improved productivity to growth of output:

1 The contribution of the growth of factor inputs is seen in the first two terms. Labour and capital each contribute an amount equal to their individual growth rate *multiplied by the share of that input in income.*

2 The rate of improvement of technology, called *technical progress* or the *growth of total factor productivity*, is the third term in Equation (2). The growth rate of total factor productivity is the amount by which output would be increasing as a result of improvements in methods of production, with all inputs unchanged. In other words, there is growth in total factor productivity when we get more output from the same factors of production.[2]

Example

Suppose the income share of capital is 0.3 and that of labour is 0.7. These values correspond approximately to the actual values for the Canadian economy. Furthermore, let labour force growth be 1.8 percent and growth of the capital stock be 4 percent, and suppose technical progress proceeds at the rate of 1.5 percent. What is the growth rate of full-employment output? Applying Equation (2) we obtain a growth rate of 4.0 percent (= 0.7 × 1.8 percent + .3 × 4 percent + 1.5 percent).

An important point to note in Equation (2) is that the growth rates of capital and labour are weighted by the respective income shares. The reason for these weights is that the importance of a 1 percent change in capital or labour to production differs, and that difference in importance is measured by their relative income shares. Specifically, if labour has a larger share than capital, output rises more when labour increases by, say, 10 percent than if capital increases by 10 percent.

Returning to our example, if labour alone grows by 1 percent, output will grow by 0.7 percent, using the 0.7 income share for labour. If capital alone grows by 1 percent, output will only grow by 0.3 percent, reflecting the smaller importance of capital in production. But if each grows by 1 percent, so does output.

This point — that growth in inputs is weighted by factor shares — turns out to be quite critical when we ask how much extra growth we get by raising the rate of growth of the capital stock, say by supply-side policies. Suppose in the example above, with everything else the same, capital growth had been 7 percent instead of 4 percent. Doing the calculations with the help of Equation (2) we find that output growth would increase to 4.9 percent, rising by less than a percentage point even though capital growth rises by three percentage points.

Empirical Estimates of the Sources of Growth

The previous section prepared us for an analysis of empirical studies that deal with sources of growth. Equation (2) suggests that the growth in output can be explained by growth in factor inputs, weighted by their shares in income, and by technical progress. An early and famous study by Robert Solow of MIT dealt with the period 1909–1949 in the United States.[3] Solow's surprising conclusion was that over 80 percent of the growth in output per labour hour over that period was due to technical progress, that is, to factors other than growth in the input of capital per labour hour. Specifically, Solow estimated for the United States an equation similar to Equation (2) that identifies capital and labour growth along with technical progress as the sources of output growth. Of the average annual growth of total GNP of 2.9 percent per year over that period, he concluded that 0.32 percent was attributable to capital accumulation, 1.09 percent per annum was due to the increases in the input of labour, and the remaining 1.49 percent was due to technical progress. Per capita output grew at 1.81 percent, with 1.49 percent of that increase resulting from technical progress.

The very large part of the growth contribution that is taken up by "technical progress" makes that term really a catchall for omitted factors and poor measurement of the capital and labour inputs. Further work therefore turned quite naturally to explore this residual, that is, growth not explained by capital accumulation or increased labour input.

Perhaps the most comprehensive of the subsequent studies is that by Edward Denison.[4] Using data for the period 1929–1969, Denison attributed 1.8 percent of the 3.4 percent annual rate of increase in real output to increased factor inputs. Output per labour hour grew at the rate of 2.09 percent, of which 1.59 percent was due to technical progress. Denison's findings thus support Solow's estimate that most of the growth in output per labour hour is due to technical progress.

The methods used by Denison have been applied to Canadian data for the period 1946 to 1967 in a study done for the Economic Council of Canada. Table 19-2 shows a breakdown of the contributions to growth of real output over this period. Out of an average rate of growth of 4.61 percent, 2.25 percent was estimated to be attributable to growth in factor productivity as a result of technical progress.

Technical progress explains almost half the growth in output, with growth in total factor inputs accounting for the other half of growth. Consider now the breakdown between labour and capital. Here increases in the labour force get a very large credit for their contribution to growth. Why? Because labour grows very fast? The answer is provided by Equation (4), which suggests that labour's growth rate has a relatively large weight because labour's share of income is relatively large. The counterpart is obviously the relatively low share of capital. Thus, even if capital and labour grew at the same rate, the fact that they have different shares in income — labour having a share of about 70 percent and capital having a share of about 30 percent — implies that labour would be credited with a larger contribution toward growth.

TABLE 19-2   SOURCES OF GROWTH OF REAL OUTPUT, 1946-67

Source of growth		Growth rate (percent per annum)
Total factor input		2.36
Labour:	1.24	
Capital:	1.12	
Output per unit of input		2.25
Total output		4.61

Source: Economic Council of Canada, Seventh Annual Review, 1970, p. 93.

In these measurements, the contribution of technical progress includes the effects of improved resource allocation. Here we can think of people leaving low-pay jobs or low-income areas and moving to better jobs or locations, thus contributing to increased output or income growth. An important element is relocation from farms to cities. Also included are the effects of *economies of scale*. This is a bit troublesome because we assumed away economies of scale in deriving Equation (4). Nevertheless as the scale of operation of the economy expands, fewer inputs were required per unit output presumably because we can avail ourselves of techniques that are economically inefficient at a small-scale level but yield factor savings at a larger scale of production.

The major significance of Denison's work, and the work in this area of others, including Simon Kuznets and J. W. Kendrick, is to point out that there is no single critical source of real income growth. The early suggestion by Solow that growth in the capital stock makes a minor, though not negligible, contribution to growth stands up well to the test of new research. Capital investment is certainly necessary, particularly because some technological improvements require the use of new types of machines, but it is clear that there are other sources of growth that can make an important contribution. Furthermore, since for most purposes we are interested in output per head, we have to recognize that we are left with only technical progress and growth in capital to achieve increased output per head. Here we have to ask, What are the components of technical progress? Advances in knowledge stand out as a major source and point to the roles of research, education, and training as important sources of growth.[5]

19-2   POTENTIAL OUTPUT AND PRODUCTIVITY

When policy makers decide to use monetary or fiscal policy to bring the economy closer to full employment, they need to know where to aim. If the full-employment unemployment rate were 6 percent, it would not make much sense to use expansionary fiscal policies at a 5.5 percent unemployment rate. Thus we need measures of the full-employment unemployment rate and the corresponding level of *potential output* or *full-employment output*. The concept draws on the ideas of growth accounting to construct a GNP series that can serve as a benchmark for policy planning.

There are two steps in estimating potential output. The first is to estimate the production function, Equation (1), and the second is to estimate the full-employment levels of capital and labour and any other inputs that might be taken into account. For example, in the production function of the "MACE" model of the Canadian economy, constructed by John Helliwell at the University of British Columbia, three factors of production are taken into account. In order to estimate the impact of the energy crisis, the production function determines output of the energy-using sectors of the economy as a function of labour, capital and energy inputs. This approach makes it possible to estimate the impact of the sharp increase in the price of energy in the 1970s.

Productivity Growth

Table 19-3 shows a breakdown of the contributions to productivity growth in Canadian manufacturing as estimated by the Economic Council of Canada. The estimates for the subperiods reveal a striking decline in the contribution of factor productivity in the 1970s. This is confirmed in Figure 19-2, which shows a slowdown in the growth of real GNE per person employed after 1973.

TABLE 19-3   CONTRIBUTIONS TO PRODUCTIVITY
GROWTH IN MANUFACTURING, 1958–76

Period	Growth rate of output per person-hour	Inputs per person-hour			Total factor productivity
		Capital	Energy	Materials	
1958–76	3.43	.30	.07	2.33	.74
1958–66	3.48	.19	.08	2.32	.89
1967–73	4.26	.35	.07	2.91	.94
1974–76	1.35	.48	.03	1.03	−.18

Source: Economic Council of Canada, *A Climate of Uncertainty*, Seventeenth Annual Review, 1980, Table C-1.

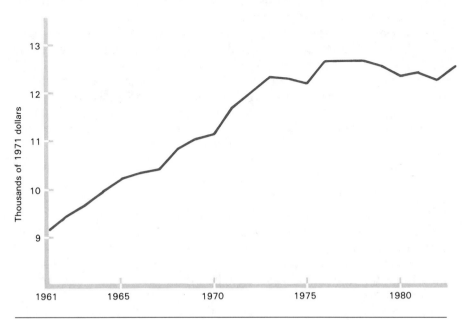

FIGURE 19-2   REAL GNE PER PERSON EMPLOYED, 1961–1983
(*Source*: Department of Finance, *Economic Review*)

This marked decline in productivity growth has been the subject of considerable interest and investigation. In a study undertaken by the Department of Finance, two factors were identified as being significant.[6] About one-quarter of the decline in overall productivity growth was attributed to a fall in productivity in the oil and gas industry. Output per person in this sector declined on average by nearly 10 percent per year over the period 1962 to 1973. Over the remainder of the 1970s, employment, particularly in the areas of exploration and drilling, grew rapidly, while output of oil declined and output of natural gas remained close to the 1973 level.

Another 25 percent of the post-1973 decline in productivity growth was attributed to a decline in the growth of the capital-labour ratio. Four other factors were examined but were found not to have had a significant impact. These were: (1) changes in the demographic composition of the labour force, (2) shifts in the share of employment from goods producing to services-producing industries, (3) governmental pollution-abatement regulations, and (4) changes in average hours worked per employee.

Analysis of the productivity slowdown based on the MACE model referred to above provides a quite different perspective.[7] As indicated, this model focusses on the energy using sectors and Helliwell estimates that 30 percent of the decline in labour productivity between 1973 and 1982, relative to a steady growth case, is attributable to substitution of labour for energy. This represents, of course, a desirable response of producers to the sharp increase in the relative cost of energy.

According to Helliwell's analysis, the other major factor in the productivity slowdown was the low level of capacity utilization. This conclusion is particularly important for projecting into the future. It implies that if we are able to return to more normal utilization rates then we can expect the longer term trend growth of productivity to resume.

19-3   OUTPUT GROWTH AND SUPPLY-SIDE ECONOMICS

In the early 1980s, partly as a result of disappointment with slow growth and generally poor macroeconomic performance, *supply-side economics* attracted much attention. The solid part of this view argues that the level and/or growth rate of output could be significantly increased through policies designed to promote greater efficiency, reduced regulation, greater willingness to work, and greater willingness to save and invest.

In discussing full-employment output in earlier chapters we took the labour supply to be given and independent of the real wage, and similarly, we assumed a given stock of capital. But the basic premise of supply-side economics is that capital and labour supplies are not given, independent of incentives to work, save, and invest. On the contrary, it is argued that the labour-leisure choice is strongly affected by the *after-tax* real wage and that the willingness to save and invest is likewise affected by the *after-tax* rates of return on assets. This perspective directs attention to fiscal policy as influencing factor supplies and hence the level and rate of increase of output.

Labour Supply

Households have to choose how much labour to supply. In practice that means choosing how many members of the family work and for how may hours per week or month. At first sight there appears to be little choice since the typical job comes with a given number of working hours per week. But that is not quite the case once we take into account the possibility that more than one family member might work, or the possibilities of working overtime hours or holding part-time jobs. Households' labour supply can thus vary in response to incentives.

The main determinant of labour supply is the after-tax real wage. Suppose the after-tax real wage increases. There are two effects on labour supply. First a given number of working hours now gives a higher income than before. Thus the worker can maintain the same income as before, while working fewer hours and enjoying more leisure. This is the *income effect*, tending to reduce the quantity of labour supplied when the real wage rises. But, second, every hour spent in leisure is more expensive in terms of real income foregone, tending to make the worker substitute work for leisure. This is the *substitution effect* of the higher real wage. The net effect of these two forces is, in general, uncertain, and we must therefore turn to empirical studies of the labour supply to find which effect dominates and whether the labour supply response is large.

Empirical Evidence

Jerry Hausman of MIT has shown in a number of studies that the household labour supply in the U.S. increases *significantly* in response to increased after-tax real wages.[8] This implies that changes in the tax structure that increase the after-tax real wage would increase labour supply and output. Hausman finds that the progressivity of income taxes reduces labour supply. The magnitude of the effect can be judged from the following experiment. Suppose the progressive income tax structure were eliminated and replaced by a flat 15 percent income tax which would lead to the same amount of revenue. What would happen to labour supply? Hausman estimates that total labour supply would rise by 5 percent. With an income share in the U.S. of 0.75, a 5 percent growth in labour supply would increase the level of full-employment output by 3.75 percent. This is certainly a nonnegligible gain, although the policy experiment — the move to a flat income tax — would be a major and controversial change in the structure of taxation.

Supply of Capital

The supply of capital represents the cumulation of past investment. The capital stock grows if additions to the stock more than offset the depreciation due to wear and tear and to obsolescence.

A supply-side point of view emphasizes the links between saving and investment. Recall that when the goods market clears and when net exports are zero, investment minus saving equals the budget surplus, or

$$I = S + (T - G) \tag{3}$$

Equation (3) shows that to raise investment and thus growth of the capital stock, we require increased saving or reduced government budget deficits. Supply-side economics has focussed on the incentives to save and invest. Supply-side economists argue that regulation has reduced the productivity of investment and that corporate and personal income taxes further reduce the rate of return eventually received by the savers who provide the funds needed to finance investment. If savers receive a lower rate of return as a result of taxation, say the supply-siders, they reduce saving, and therefore capital accumulation is reduced.

For instance, consider an investment that yields 12 percent per year in real terms. That is, someone who undertakes the investment, costing $100 in year 1, earns $12 per year in real terms forever after (net of labour and material costs). If the income tax rate is 40 percent, the saver can at most earn, after tax, 60 percent of 12 percent, or 7.2 percent. As a result of taxation, the return to saving is substantially reduced. Accordingly, claim supply-siders, the higher the tax rate, the less saving there will be.[9]

What supply-side policies increase the yield on saving? There are a variety of means of exempting the return on saving from taxation. For instance, the Canadian income tax exempts from taxable income contributions up to specified limits to a Registered Retirement Savings Plan. Some argue for the complete exemption of savings from tax by replacing the income tax with a *consumption tax*. A consumption tax levies taxes only on consumption spending, not on income. Since the difference between income and consumption is saving, a consumption tax effectively exempts any amount that is saved from being taxed in the year it is earned, and thereby encourages saving.

There is considerable disagreement on the issue of the response of saving to changes in its return. The contention that increased after-tax rates of return to saving will *strongly* raise saving does not have much support. Once again we have two opposing effects: With increased interest rates, less saving is needed to ensure a given future income, say, for retirement. This effect (actually an income effect) reduces saving. At the same time a dollar saved today yields increased future wealth and consumption and would therefore lead households to postpone consumption and increase saving (this is the substitution effect). The balance of effects is theoretically uncertain.

The empirical evidence does not settle the issue of whether changes in the after-tax rate of return affect the rate of saving.[10] Therefore policies that reduce taxes on saving as a means of generating more saving, capital formation, and growth have an uncertain effect on the economy.

Another line of argument questions the quantitative importance of policies to promote saving. We have noted that growth in capital receives a very small weight in determining output growth. Even if policies led to a 10 percent rise in the capital-labour ratio, output per head would only increase by 3 percent.

Regulation

Government regulation involves a tradeoff. Government regulations serve some social purpose (the environment, safety, conservation), but they also involve costs to firms that have to abide by them. Regulation therefore reduces business profitability. Policy makers are keenly aware that the trade-off exists and therefore, rightly, focus on inefficient regulation and particularly costly (nonmarket) regulation as requiring review, but it would be a mistake to expect major growth in output from reduced regulation.

Budget Deficits and Growth

In Equation (3) we showed that private investment and capital formation will be higher when saving is higher and the government budget deficit is smaller.[11] Government budget deficits thus imply, other things being equal, a reduction in full-employment output growth. Government budget deficits absorb private saving — households buy government securities rather than the stocks or bonds that firms issue to finance their investment. Therefore funds are diverted from growth toward other purposes. It is clear that if the only objective is to promote growth, the government should balance the budget or even run a surplus to free resources for investment. However, there is a tradeoff between growth and the social objectives that may lie behind a budget deficit.

Evaluating Supply-Side Economics and Growth Incentives

The emphasis on increasing incentives to work, save, and invest is the valid core of supply-side economics. There are two questions here. The first is, Will the proposed policies work, that is, increase future potential output? The second question is, If the policies do work, how far should we go in creating incentives to increase future potential output?

Policies to increase the labour supply by reducing taxes and policies to increase investment by reducing government budget deficits and through investment subsidies would be effective in increasing potential output today and in the future. Thus supply-side policies are available, but we can also go overboard on such policies. If we are reducing government budget deficits while reducing other taxes, we are also reducing government spending. We could reduce government spending by getting rid of the post office, but most people would think it better to have higher taxes and a post office than lower taxes and no post office. Similarly, the government provides many useful services through its welfare programs — services that most people prefer to have — rather than aiming purely to maximize the level of investment.

Further, given government spending, and at full employment, increases in saving imply reductions in consumption. Thus in supply-side economics we are trading off current consumption for future consumption. We are trading off the consumption of those now alive for the consumption of their children, and children who come later yet. This process also can go too far. In the extreme, we (society) would not want to force the current generation to consume at a bare survival level just so their grandchildren can sit around their pools doing very little work while automated factories made possible by a huge volume of past investment produce a high level of output. Somewhere between not saving now and saving almost all of output, there is an optimal amount of saving to be done.

It is no easy task for society to decide what that optimal amount of saving is. Those who will be consuming in the future are not here to vote, because they have not yet been born. And those who are around now will have different views. Some may ask, as reportedly has Joan Robinson, the famous English economist, ''What did posterity ever do for us?'' Others may feel it is the duty of the parents to sacrifice for their children's sake. Ultimately the policy decisions that affect growth are settled politically.

19-4 GROWTH THEORY

We turn now from empirical issues and the historical record to the theory of economic growth. The theory of economic growth asks what factors determine the full-employment growth rate of output over time. Growth theory is important because it both helps explain growth rates and helps explain why per capita income levels differ among countries. One of the central results of growth theory, for example, is the proposition that between two countries with the same technology and saving rates the one that has the higher rate of population growth will eventually have lower per capita income.

We have already examined the sources of growth in Equation (2), where we showed that full-employment output growth depends on the growth in factor inputs and on technical progress. In this section we pursue the issue further to ask what determines the growth of factor supplies and what is the link to long-run per capita incomes or standards of living.

We take a rather simple formulation here by assuming a given and constant rate of labour force growth, $\Delta N/N \equiv n$, and also that there is no technical progress, $\Delta A/A = 0$.[12] With these assumptions the only variable element left in Equation (2) is the growth rate of capital.

Capital growth is determined by saving, which, in turn, depends on income. Income or output, in turn, depends on capital. We are thus set with an interdependent system in which capital growth depends, via saving and income, on the capital stock. We now study the short-run behaviour, the adjustment process, and the long-run equilibrium of that interdependent system.

Steady State

We start by discussing the steady state of the economy. Here we ask whether in an economy with population growth and saving, and therefore growth in the capital stock, we reach a point where output per head and capital per head become constant. In such a steady state, current saving and additions to the capital stock would be just enough to equip new entrants into the labour force with the same amount of capital as the average worker uses.

The idea of a steady state is simply this: If capital per head is unchanging, given technology, so is output per head. But for capital *per head* to remain unchanging even though population is growing, capital must grow at just the right rate, namely, at the same rate as population. More formally, if output per head is to remain constant, output and population must grow at the same rates, or $\Delta Y/Y = \Delta N/N = n$. Therefore, from Equation (2), setting productivity growth equal to zero, we have $0 = (\Delta K/K - n)$, or

$$\Delta K/K = n \qquad (6)$$

Equation (6) states that in the steady state the growth rate of the capital stock is equal to the growth rate of population. Equivalently, in the steady state the amount of capital per head is constant.

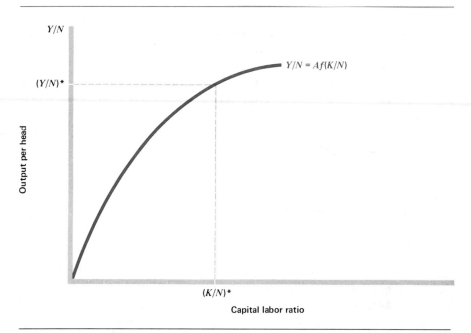

Y/N

$(Y/N)^*$

Output per head

$Y/N = Af(K/N)$

$(K/N)^*$

Capital labor ratio

FIGURE 19-3 OUTPUT PER HEAD AND THE CAPITAL-LABOUR RATIO. The production function shows output per head as a function of the amount of capital per head, or the capital-labour ratio. The higher the capital-labour ratio is, the higher output per head is, but the increment to output from raising the capital-labour ratio grows progressively smaller as the capital-labour ratio rises.

We now show the steady state graphically in Figure 19-3. We put output per head on the vertical axis and capital per head on the horizontal axis. The production function, which is central to understanding growth, exhibits diminishing returns. As capital per head increases, so that workers use increasing amounts of machinery, output per head increases, but at a diminishing rate. Thus an increase in the capital-labour ratio is productive, but there are diminishing returns. In steady state, the economy settles down to a fixed capital-labour ratio, $(K/N)^*$. The production function shows the corresponding amount of output per head, $(Y/N)^*$.

Saving and Growth

We gain insight by examining the link between saving and the growth in capital. We are assuming there is no government. Accordingly, investment, or the gross increase in capital, is equal to saving. To obtain the increase in the capital stock, however, we have to deduct depreciation. Therefore the net addition to the capital stock is equal to saving less depreciation.

$$\Delta K = \text{saving} - \text{depreciation} \tag{7}$$

Two assumptions take us from (6) and (7) to a complete description of the steady state. In (7) we need to specify saving behaviour and to make an assumption about depreciation. We assume first that saving is a constant fraction s of income (Y). Second, depreciation is at a constant rate of d percent of the capital stock. Concretely, we might assume that people save $s = 15$ percent of their income and that depreciation is at a rate of 10 percent per year so that every year 10 percent of the capital stock needs to be replaced to offset wear and tear.

Substituting these assumptions in Equation (7) yields

$$\Delta K = sY - dK \tag{7a}$$

or placing the right-hand side in Equation (6), we arrive at the following result that describes the steady state:[13]

$$sY = (n + d)K \tag{6a}$$

Equation (6a) states that in the steady state, saving (sY) is just sufficient to provide for enough investment to offset depreciation (dK) *and* to equip new members of the labour force with capital (nK). If saving were larger than this amount, net investment would be sufficiently large to make capital per head grow, leading to rising income per head. Conversely, if not enough were saved, capital per head would be falling and with it income per head.

The Growth Process

We next study the adjustment process that leads the economy from some initial capital-labour ratio over time to the steady state. The critical element in this transition process is the rate of saving and investment compared with the ratio of depreciation, and population growth.

Notation

The argument is made easier by a bit of new notation. We define the amount of output per head as $x = Y/N$ and the amount of capital per head, or the capital-labour ratio, as $k = K/N$. This is simply notation and in no way changes our model.

$$k = \text{capital-labour ratio} = \frac{K}{N} \qquad x = \text{output per head} = \frac{Y}{N} \qquad (8)$$

Thus in terms of Figure 19-3 the vertical axis will be labeled x and the horizontal axis k.

Capital Accumulation

We now turn to the transition to the steady state. Note from Equation (2) that output per head will grow if capital per head grows and that capital per head will grow if saving is *more than sufficient* to cover depreciation of the capital stock and also to equip new members of the population with capital. This can be formalized by writing the change in the capital-labour ratio as follows:[14]

$$\Delta k = sx - (n + d)k \qquad (9)$$

The growth process can now be studied with the help of Equation (6a) and Figure 19-4. Here we reproduce the production function from Figure 19-3, writing output per capita as a function of the capital-labour ratio.

We have added the savings function, which, for each capital-labour ratio, is simply the fraction s of output. Thus, for any capital-labour ratio, say, k_0, the corresponding point of the saving schedule tells us the amount of saving per head, $sx(k_0)$, that will be forthcoming at that capital-labour ratio.

We know that all saving is invested, so that gross investment or gross additions to the capital stock, in per capita terms, are equal to sx, given a capital-labour ratio of k_0. We know, too, from Equation (9) that the increase in the capital-labour ratio falls short of that gross addition for two reasons:

- Depreciation reduces the capital-labour ratio, and part of gross investment must be devoted to offsetting depreciation. In particular, if the depreciation rate is d, an amount dk is required as a depreciation allowance. For example, if the depreciation rate is 10 percent and the capital-labour ratio is 10 machines per person, each year the equivalent of 1 machine would depreciate and would have to be replaced; that is, 10 percent times 10 machines equals 1 machine that has to be replaced.

- Growth in the labour force implies that with a given stock of capital, the capital-labour ratio would be declining. To maintain the amount of capital per head constant, we have to add enough machines to the stock of capital to make up for the growth in population; that is, we need to invest at the rate nk.

It follows that we can write the investment required to maintain constant the capital-labour ratio in the face of depreciation and labour force growth as $(n + d)k$. When saving and hence gross investment are larger than $(n + d)k$, the stock of capital per head is increasing. If saving and gross investment are less, then we are not making up for depreciation and population growth, and, accordingly, capital per head is falling. We can therefore think of the term $(n + d)k$ as the investment requirement that will maintain constant capital per head and therefore, from Figure 19-3, output per head.

In Figure 19-4 we show this investment requirement as a positively sloped schedule. It tells us how much investment we would require at each capital-labour ratio just in order to keep that ratio constant. It is

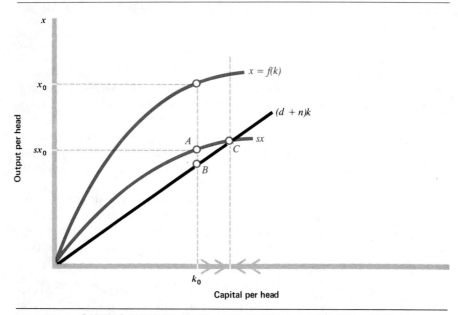

FIGURE 19-4   SAVING, INVESTMENT, AND CAPITAL ACCUMULATION. The saving function shows at each capital-labour ratio the part of income that is saved, sx. The straight line $(d + n)k$ shows the investment requirement. At low capital-labour ratios, saving exceeds the investment requirement, and hence output per head grows. Conversely at high capital-labour ratios, saving is less than the investment requirement, and capital per head is falling. The steady-state capital-labour ratio is k^*, where saving is just sufficient to maintain the capital-labour ratio constant.

positively sloped because the higher the capital-labour ratio, the larger the amount of investment that is required to maintain that capital-labour ratio. Thus, with the depreciation rate of 10 percent and a growth rate of population of 1 percent, we would require an investment of 1.1 machines per head per year at a capital-labour ratio of 10 machines per head to maintain the capital-labour ratio constant. If the capital-labour ratio were 100 machines per head, the required investment would be 11 machines (= 100 machines per head times 11 percent).

We have seen that the saving schedule tells us the amount of saving and gross investment associated with each capital-labour ratio. Thus, at a capital-labour ratio of k_0 in Figure 19-4, saving is sx_0 at point A. The investment requirement to maintain constant the capital-labour ratio at k_0 is equal to $(n + d)k_0$ at point B. Clearly, saving exceeds the investment requirement. More is added to the capital stock than is required to maintain constant the capital-labour ratio. Accordingly, the capital-labour ratio grows. Not surprisingly, the increase in the capital-labour ratio is equal to actual saving or investment less the investment requirement and is thus given by the vertical distance AB.

In the next period, capital per head will be higher. Thus on the horizontal axis we draw an arrow showing k increasing. You recognize the line of argument we are taking. From Figure 19-4 it is clear that with a somewhat higher capital-labour ratio, the discrepancy between saving and the investment requirement becomes smaller. Therefore the increase in the capital-labour ratio becomes smaller. However, the capital-labour ratio still increases, as indicated by the arrows.

The adjustment process comes to a halt at point C. Here we have reached a capital-labour ratio $k*$ for which saving and investment associated with that capital-labour ratio exactly match the investment requirement. Given the exact matching of actual and required investment, the capital-labour ratio neither rises nor falls. We have reached the steady state.

We can make the same argument by starting with an initial capital-labour ratio in excess of $k*$. From Figure 19-4 we note that for high capital-labour ratios, the investment requirement is in excess of saving and investment. Accordingly, not enough is added to the capital stock to maintain the capital-labour ratio constant in the face of population growth and depreciation. Thus, the capital-labour ratio falls until we get to $k*$, the steady-state capital-labour ratio.

To review our progress so far:

- To maintain the capital-labour ratio constant, saving and investment have to be sufficient to make up for the reduction in capital per head that arises from population growth and depreciation.

- With saving a constant fraction s of output, we established that the capital-labour ratio moves to a steady-state level $k*$ at which output and therefore saving (investment) are just sufficient to maintain constant the capital-labour ratio.

• The convergence to a steady-state capital-labour ratio $k*$ is ensured by the fact that at low levels of the capital-labour ratio, saving (investment) exceeds the investment required to maintain capital per head and therefore causes the capital-labour ratio to rise. Conversely, at high capital-labour ratios, saving (investment) falls short of the investment requirement, and thus the ratio declines.

Now we turn to a more detailed study of the steady-state equilibrium and the adjustment process. We note that the steady-state level of capital per head is constant, and thus the steady-state level of output per head is also constant. The steady-state is reached when all variables, in per capita terms, are constant. This means that in the steady state, output, capital, and labour all grow at the same rate. They all grow at a rate equal to the rate of population growth. Note particularly that the steady-state growth rate is equal to the rate of population growth and therefore is *not* influenced by the saving rate. (Recall that we are assuming no technical progress.) To explore this property of the steady state in more detail, we investigate the effects of a change in the saving rate.

A Change in the Saving Rate

Why should the long-run growth rate be independent of the saving rate? If people save 10 percent of their income as opposed to 5 percent, should we not expect this to make a difference to the growth rate of output? Is it not true that an economy in which 10 percent of income is set aside for additions to the capital stock is one in which capital and therefore output grow faster than in an economy in which only 5 percent of income is saved?

We show here that an increase in the saving rate does the following: In the short run, it raises the growth rate of output. It does not affect the *long-run growth rate* of output, but it raises the long-run level of capital and output per head.

Consider Figure 19-5 with an initial steady-state equilibrium at point C, where saving precisely matches the investment requirement. At point C, exactly enough output is saved to maintain the stock of capital per head constant in the face of depreciation and labour force growth. Next consider an increase in the saving rate. For some reason, people want to save a larger fraction of income. The increased saving rate is reflected in an upward shift of the saving schedule. At each level of the capital-labour ratio, and hence at each level of output, saving is larger.

At point C, where we initially had a steady-state equilibrium, saving has now risen relative to the investment requirement, and as a consequence,

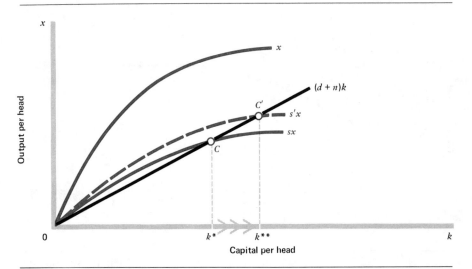

FIGURE 19-5   AN INCREASE IN THE SAVING RATE. An increase in the saving rate
implies that at each capital-labour ratio a larger fraction of output is saved. The
saving schedule shifts upward to $s'x$. At the initial steady state, saving now
exceeds the investment requirement, and hence the capital-labour ratio rises
until point C' is reached. An increase in the saving rate raises steady-state per
capita income. The growth rate rises only in the transition from C to C'.

more is saved than is required to maintain capital per head constant.
Enough is saved to allow the capital stock per head to increase.

It is apparent from Figure 19-5 that the capital stock per head will keep
rising until we reach point C'. At C', the higher amount of saving is just
enough to maintain the higher stock of capital. At point C', both capital
per head and output per head have risen. Saving has increased as has the
investment requirement. We have seen, therefore, that an increase in the
saving rate will in the long run raise only the level of output and capital
per head, but not the growth rate of output per head.

The transition process, however, involves an effect of the saving rate on
the growth rate of output and the growth rate of output per head. In the
transition from k^* to k^{**}, the increase in the saving rate raises the growth
rate of output. This follows simply from the fact that the capital-labour
ratio rises from k^* at the initial steady state to k^{**} in the new steady state.
The only way to achieve an increase in the capital-labour ratio is for the
capital stock to grow faster than the labour force (and depreciation). This
is precisely what happens in the transition process where increased saving per head, due to the higher saving rate, raises investment and capital
growth over and above the investment requirement and thus allows the
capital-labour ratio to rise.

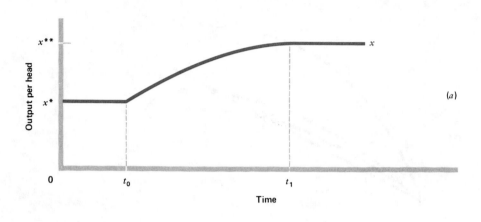

FIGURE 19-6a   THE TIME PATH OF PER CAPITA INCOME. A rise in the saving rate leads to a rising capital-labour ratio and therefore to increasing output per head until a new steady state is reached.

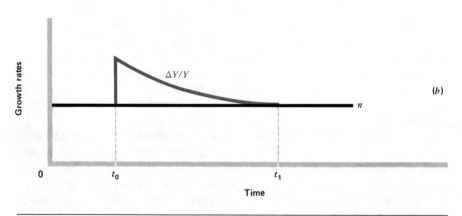

FIGURE 19-6b   THE TIME PATH OF THE GROWTH RATE OF OUTPUT. An increase in the saving rate raises investment above the investment requirement and thus leads to capital accumulation. Output growth transitorily rises and then falls back to the growth rate of population.

In summary, the long-run effect of an increase in the saving rate is to raise the level of output and capital per head but to leave the growth rate of output and capital unaffected. In the transition period, the rates of growth of output and capital increase relative to the steady state. In the short run, therefore, an increase in the saving rate means faster growth, as we would expect.

Figure 19-6 summarizes these two results. Figure 19-6a shows the level of per capita output. Starting from an initial long-run equilibrium at time t_0, the increase in the saving rate causes saving and investment to increase, the stock of capital per head grows, and so does output per head. The process will continue at a diminishing rate. In Figure 19-6b we focus on the growth rate of output and capital. The growth rate of output is equal to the growth rate of population in the initial steady state. The increase in the saving rate immediately raises the growth rate of output because it implies a faster growth in capital and therefore in output. As capital accumulates, the growth rate decreases, falling back toward the level of population growth.

Population Growth

The preceding discussion of saving and the influence of the saving rate on steady-state capital and output makes it easy to discuss the effects of increased population growth. The question we ask is, What happens when the population growth rate increases from n to n' and remains at that higher level indefinitely? We will show that such an increase in the rate of population growth will *raise* the growth rate of output and *lower* the level of output per head.

The argument can be conveniently followed in Figure 19-7. Here we show the initial steady-state equilibrium at point C. The increase in the growth rate of population means that at each level of the capital-labour ratio, it takes a larger amount of investment just to maintain the capital-labour ratio constant. Suppose we had 10 machines per head. Initially, the growth rate of population is 1 percent and depreciation is 10 percent, so that we require per year 11 percent times 10 machines, or 1.1 machine, just to offset population growth and depreciation and thus maintain capital per head constant. To maintain the capital-labour ratio constant in the face of a higher growth rate of population, say, 2 percent, requires a higher level of investment, namely, 12 percent as opposed to 11 percent. This is reflected in Figure 19-7 by an upward rotation of the investment requirement schedule.

It is clear from the preceding argument that we are no longer in steady-state equilibrium at point C. The investment that was initially just sufficient to keep the capital-labour ratio constant will no longer be sufficient in the face of higher population growth. At the initial equilibrium, the higher population growth with unchanged saving and investment means that capital does not grow fast enough to keep up with labour force growth and depreciation. Capital per head declines. In fact, capital per head will keep declining until we reach the new steady-state equilibrium at point C'. Here the capital-labour ratio has declined sufficiently for saving to match the investment requirement. It is true, too, that, corresponding to the lower capital-labour ratio, we have a decline in output per head. Output per head declines from x^* to x^{**}.

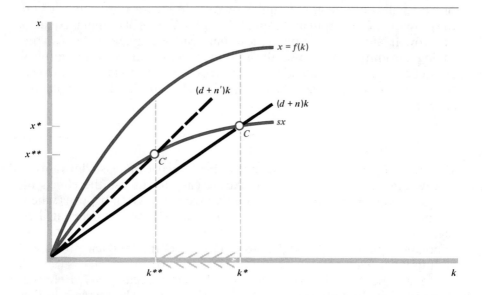

FIGURE 19-7   AN INCREASE IN THE POPULATION GROWTH RATE REDUCES PER CAPITA INCOME. Increased population growth raises the investment requirement, rotating the schedule upward to $(d + n')k$. At point C saving is insufficient to maintain capital per head constant in face of the more rapidly growing population. Capital and output per head decline until a new steady state at C' is reached.

The decline in output per head as a consequence of increased population growth points to the problem faced by many developing countries. Fast growth in population, given the saving rate, means low levels of income per head. Indeed, in poor countries one can trace poverty, or low income per head, to the very high rate of population growth. With high population growth, saving will typically be too small to allow capital to rise relative to labour and thus to build up the capital-labour ratio to achieve a satisfactory level of income per head. In those circumstances, and barring other considerations, a reduction in the rate of population growth appears to be a way of achieving higher levels of steady-state per capita income and thus an escape from poverty.

19-4   SUMMARY

1   A production function links factor inputs and technology to the level of output. Growth of output, changes in technology aside, is a weighted average of input growth with the weights equal to income shares. The production function directs attention to factor inputs and technological change as sources of output growth.

2   Growth theory studies the determinants of intermediate-run and long-run growth in output.

3   In Canada over the 1946–1967 period, growth in factor inputs and technical progress each accounted for roughly one-half the average growth rate of 4.6 percent of output.

4   Per capita output grows faster the more rapidly the capital stock increases and the faster is technical progress. In Canadian history since 1870, output per head has grown at an average rate of 2.2 percent.

5   From 1953 to 1973, per capita real GNP grew at an average rate of 2.9 percent, but over the following ten years, the growth rate dropped to 1 percent.

6   Supply-side economics argues that the level and rate of growth of potential output can be increased by creating improved incentives for work, saving and investment.

7   The concept of steady-state equilibrium points (in the absence of technical change) to the conditions required for output per head to be constant. With a growing population, saving must be just sufficient to provide new members of the population with the economywide amount of capital per head.

8   The steady-state level of income is determined by the saving rate and by population growth. In the absence of technical change, the steady-state growth rate of output is equal to the rate of population growth. An increase in the growth rate of population raises the steady-state growth rate of total output and lowers the level of steady-state output per head.

9   An increase in the saving rate transitorily raises the growth rate of output. In the new steady state, the growth rate remains unchanged, but the level of output per head is increased.

10   With technical change, per capita output in the steady state grows at the rate of technical progress. Total output grows at the sum of the rates of technical progress and population growth.

KEY TERMS

Potential output
Production function
Growth accounting
Sources of growth

Technical progress
Growth of total factor productivity
Supply-side economics
Steady state

---

*APPENDIX: PROPERTIES OF THE PRODUCTION FUNCTION

In this Appendix we briefly show how the fundamental growth equation (2a) is obtained. The material is presented for completeness; it is not essential to an understanding of the text.

We start with a production function that exhibits constant returns: increasing *all* inputs in the same proportion raises output in that same proportion. Thus if we double all inputs, output will double. With that property the change in output due to technical progress and to changes in inputs can be written as

$$\Delta Y = F(K,N)\,\Delta A + MPK\,\Delta K + MPN\Delta N \qquad (A1)$$

where MPK and MPN are the marginal products of capital and labour, respectively. We remember that the marginal product of a factor tells us the contribution to output made by employing one extra unit of the factor. Dividing both sides of the equation by $Y = AF(K,N)$ yields the expression

$$\Delta Y/Y = \Delta A/A + (MPK/Y)\,\Delta K + (MPN/Y)\,\Delta N \qquad (A2)$$

Equation (A2) further simplifies by multiplying and dividing the second term on the right-hand side by K and the third term by N.

$$\Delta Y/Y = \Delta A/A + (K{\cdot}MPK/Y)\,\Delta K/K + (N{\cdot}MPN/Y)\,\Delta N/N \qquad (A3)$$

We now argue that the terms in parentheses are the income shares of capital and labour. In a competitive market factors are paid their marginal product. Thus the term $N\cdot MPN/Y = wN/Y$, where w is the real wage. The right-hand side is recognized as the ratio of labour income to total income or the share of labour in income. Similarly, the term $K\cdot MPK/Y$ is the share of capital in income. With constant returns and competition, factor payments exhaust the total product. Therefore the shares of capital and labour sum to unity. Denoting the share of capital in income by θ and the labour share by $1 - \theta$, we arrive at Equation (2) in the text.

We note a further property of the constant returns production function. When returns to scale are constant, we can write the production function as follows:

$$Y = AF(K,N) = NAf(K/N) \tag{A4}$$

or using the notation $x = Y/N$ and $k = K/N$,

$$x = Af(k) \tag{A5}$$

This is the form used in the growth theory section of the text, where output per head is a function of the capital-labour ratio.

PROBLEMS

1 Which of the following government activities have effects on the long-term growth rate? Explain how they can do so.
   (a) Monetary policy
   (b) Labour market policies
   (c) Educational and research programs
   (d) Fiscal policy
   (e) Population control programs

2 Discuss the role of government policy in raising (a) the supply of labour and (b) the supply of capital. How successful can such policies be?

3 Since 1973, the growth rate of productivity has sharply declined in most industrialized countries. List several of the factors that are responsible for this decline and discuss why the decline in productivity growth is an important issue.

4 Suppose the share of capital in income is 0.4 and the share of labour is 0.6. Capital grows by 6 percent, and labour supply declines by 2 percent. What happens to output?

5 An earthquake destroys one-quarter of the capital stock. Discuss in the context of the growth model the adjustment process of the economy, and show, using Figure 19-4, what happens to growth.

6 (a) In the absence of technical progress, what happens to output per head and total output over time? Why?
   (b) What is the long-run effect of the saving rate on the *level* of output per capita? On *growth* of output per capita?

7 Evaluate this statement: "The saving rate cannot affect the growth of output in the economy. That is determined by the growth of labour input and by technical progress."

*8 Suppose we assume a production function of the form

$$Y = AF(K,N,Z)$$

where Z is a measure of the natural resources going into production. Assume this production function obeys constant returns to scale and diminishing returns to each factor [like Equation (1)].
   (a) What will happen to output per head if capital and labour grow together but resources are fixed?
   (b) What if Z is fixed but there is technical progress?
   (c) Interpret these results in terms of the limits to growth.

*9 Use the model of long-run growth to incorporate the government. Assume that an income tax at the rate t is levied and that, accordingly, saving per head is equal to $s(1 - t)x$. The government spends the tax revenue on public consumption.
   (a) Use Figure 19-4 to explore the impact of an increase in the tax rate on the steady-state output level and capital per head.
   (b) Draw a chart of the time path of capital per head, output per head, and the growth rate of output.
  *(c) Discuss the statement: "To raise the growth rate of output, the public sector has to run a budget surplus to free resources for investment."

10 Use Figure 19-4 to explore the impact of a *once-and-for-all* improvement in technology.
   (a) How does technical progress affect the level of output per head as of a given capital-labour ratio?
   (b) Show the new steady-state equilibrium. Has saving changed? Is income per head higher? Has the capital stock per head increased?
   (c) Show the time path of the adjustment to the new steady state. Does technical progress transitorily raise the ratio of investment to capital?

11 Discuss the statement: "The lower the level of income, the higher the growth rate of output."

CHAPTER 19: FOOTNOTES

[1] Equation (2) applies when there are *constant returns to scale* in production; that is, increases in both inputs, in the same proportion, increase output in that proportion.

[2] There is a distinction between *labour productivity* and total factor productivity. Labour productivity is just the ratio of output to labour input, Y/N. Labour productivity certainly grows as a result of technical progress, but it also grows because of the accumulation of capital per worker.

[3]"Technical Change and the Aggregate Production Function," *Review of Economics and Statistics*, August 1957.

[4]*Accounting for United States Economic Growth 1929–1969* (Washington, D.C.: The Brookings Institution, 1974). See also E. Denison's *Accounting for Slower Economic Growth: The United States in the 1970s* (*ibid.*, 1980).

[5]A collection of useful papers on the sources of growth are contained in Edmund Phelps (ed.), *The Goal of Economics Growth* (New York: Norton, 1969), and Dennis C. Mueller (ed.), *The Political Economy of Growth* (New Haven, Conn.: Yale University Press, 1983).

[6]Department of Finance, *Recent Changes in Patterns of Productivity Growth in Canada*, April 1980.

[7]See J.F. Helliwell, "Stagflation and Productivity Decline in Canada, 1974–1982," *Canadian Journal of Economics*, May 1984, pp. 191–216.

[8]J. Hausman, "Labor Supply and the Natural Unemployment Rate," in L. Meyer (ed.), *The Supply-Side Effects of Economic Policy* (St. Louis: Center for the Study of American Business, 1981), and "Labor Supply," in H. Aaron and J. Pechman (eds.), *How Taxes Affect Behavior* (Washington, D.C.: The Brookings Institution, 1981).

[9]See M. Boskin, "Economic Growth and Productivity," in M. Boskin (ed.), *The Economy in the 1980s: A Program for Growth and Stability* (San Francisco: Institute for Contemporary Studies, 1980); the *Economic Report of the President*, 1982 and 1983; and especially, Michael K. Evans, *The Truth about Supply-Side Economics* (New York: Basic Books, 1983).

[10]Gerald A. Carlino, in "Interest Rate Effects and Intertemporal Consumption," *Journal of Monetary Economics*, March 1982, reviews and extends the (ambiguous) evidence.

[11]To the extent that deficits are used to finance government investment, they, of course, do not reduce total investment.

[12]For further simplicity we also assume that the entire population works, so that the labour force and the population are the same.

[13]Placing Eq. (7a) in Eq. (6) yields $(sY - dK)/K = n$. By multiplying both sides by K and collecting terms, we obtain $sY = (n + d)K$.

[14]The percentage growth rate of the capital-labour ratio is equal to the difference between the growth rate of capital and the growth rate of labour, or $\Delta k/k = \Delta K/K - n$.

Now using Eq. (7a) to replace ΔK, we have $\Delta k/k = sY/K - d - n = \dfrac{s(Y/N)}{K/N} -$

$(d + n) = \dfrac{sx}{k} - (d + n)$. Multiplying both sides by k yields Eq. (9) in the text.

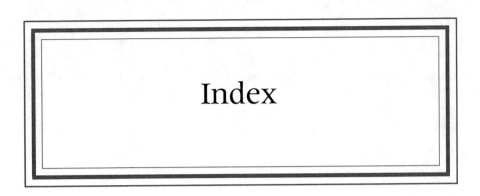

Index